The
Knights Templars
& the
Complete History
of
Masonic
Knighthood

From the Origin of the
Orders to the Present Time

(1874)

C.G. Addison & Robert Macoy

ISBN 0-7661-0019-7

THE

KNIGHTS TEMPLARS.

BY C. G. ADDISON.

ENLARGED FROM THE RESEARCHES OF NUMEROUS AUTHORS,

DE VERTOT, MICHAUD, DE VOGÜÉ, TAAFFE, PROCTOR, MACKEY,
SCOTT, BURKE, BURNES, MILLS, PIKE, JAMES, MORRIS,
BOUTELL, CREIGH, WOOF, GOURDIN, GARDNER,

AND

OTHERS IN THE DEPARTMENTS OF CHIVALRY, HERALDRY, AND THE
CRUSADES, THE WHOLE AFFORDING A

COMPLETE HISTORY OF MASONIC KNIGHTHOOD,

FROM

THE ORIGIN OF THE ORDERS TO THE PRESENT TIME,

ADAPTED TO

THE AMERICAN SYSTEM.

BY

ROBERT MACOY, 33°.

GRAND RECORDER OF THE GRAND COMMANDERY OF NEW YORK; REPRESENTATIVE OF THE
GRAND COMMANDERIES OF TENNESSEE, CALIFORNIA AND TEXAS; AUTHOR
OF CYCLOPEDIA OF FREEMASONRY, ETC., ETC., ETC.

NEW YORK:
MASONIC PUBLISHING COMPANY,
No. 626 BROADWAY.
1874.

ADMISSION OF A NOVICE TO THE VOWS OF THE ORDER OF THE TEMPLE.

GODFREY DE BOUILLON, FIRST KING OF JERUSALEM.

TO

ALL CHRISTIAN MASONS,

STRIVING IN THE

Numerous Commanderies of the United States,

TO HONOR THE PROFESSION OF JESUS

BY AN UPRIGHT WALK, CHARITABLE DEEDS, AND THE CULTIVATION OF THE
SOCIAL GRACES,

This Enlarged Edition

OF

ADDISON'S KNIGHTS TEMPLARS

IS

Courteously Dedicated.

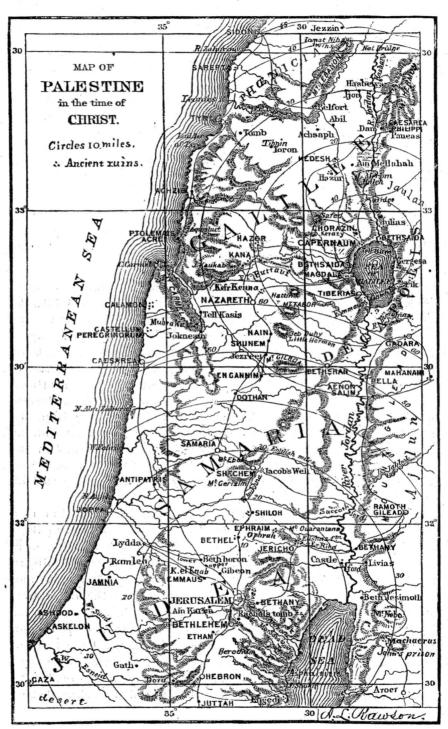

MAP OF JERUSALEM.

·PREFACE

TO THE AMERICAN EDITION.

IN the first edition of Addison's KNIGHTS TEMPLARS, 1846, the author informs us that having been favored with the (then) rare opportunity of visiting the Mosk el-Aksa—the ancient Temple of the Knights Templars, still existing on Mount Moriah, Jerusalem, as a Moslem Mosk in a good state of preservation—and having inspected many of the ruined fortresses and castles of the ancient ORDER OF THE TEMPLE, whose shattered walls are still seen at intervals in Palestine and Syria, from Gaza to Antioch, and from Kerak to Belfort, and transversely from the mountains of the Dead Sea to the shores of the Mediterranean, he became greatly interested in the History of this ORDER, and in the numerous remains and monuments of the KNIGHTS TEMPLARS still to be met with, in various stages of decay, in almost every part of Europe.

But the circumstance which set him upon the preparation of a book was the restoration of the Temple Church at London in 1828, which occurred under his personal observation. This is the most beautiful and best preserved of all the ancient ecclesiastical edifices of the western provinces of the Order of KNIGHTS TEMPLARS, and the curious discoveries that came to light during the restoration aforesaid, first suggested to Mr. Addison to write out, in popular form, an account of the varied fortunes of that great religious and military fraternity of knights and monks by whom it was erected, and of their dark and terrible end. The *impulse* was happy: the *result* one of the most readable and entertaining works yielded by the English press for many years. It supplied an acknowledged want. A second and greatly enlarged edition was soon demanded, and in 1852 a third. Addison's KNIGHTS TEMPLARS has been accepted by all English-reading people as the best presentation of Templary matters available to the ordinary student. As was handsomely said by one of the most erudite critics of the day, "It is a very valuable historical record, and should be in every well-ordered library. It is a production of great research, written with much spirit and animation, filled with curious and interesting details, and presents splendid and lively pictures of scenes, customs, and events passed away forever." Another reviewer expatiates thus: "What a mournful and yet inspiring history is that of the KNIGHTS TEMPLARS! What zeal for the service of Christendom! What heroic achievements! What wonderful success bought by what innumerable martyrdoms! What discipline! What piety! What self-devotion! What services! What an earthly reward!"

The compiler of the present volume long hesitated between republishing Addison's book and preparing one upon the same subject. On the one hand, the accumulations of valuable matter during twenty-five years' researches, prompted him to *an original publication.* To this we add the fact that Mr. Addison makes no allusion to Freemasonry in his volume, while the great body of American students in Knight Templary are Freemasons. On the other hand, the credit justly due to the English author for his patient study and splendid ability calls for so many quotations from his invaluable history as to deter an author from attempting a work entirely new. Counsel being taken with intelligent members in the ranks of the Knightly Brotherhood, a *middle plan* has been adopted, as the present work evinces. The History of Mr. Addison is followed with considerable accuracy, while large additions are made from other authors. Maps of great value are inserted. Engravings in numbers are added, until the present volume, by measure, is considerably more than twice as large as Mr. Addison's.

The American compiler most heartily endorses these sentiments of the English author:

"The memory of these holy warriors, the KNIGHTS TEMPLARS, is embalmed in all our recollections of the wars of the CROSS. They were the bulwarks of the Latin kingdom of Jerusalem during the short period of its existence, and the last band of Europe's host that contended for the possession of Palestine. To the vows of the monk, and the austere life of the covenant, they added the discipline of the camp, and the stern duties of the military life, thus blending the fine vocation of the sword and lance with the holy zeal and body-bending toil of a poor brotherhood. The vulgar notion that they were wicked as they were fearless and brave, has not yet been entirely exploded ; but it is hoped that the copious accounts of the proceedings against the Order in England, given in the ensuing volume, will dispel many unfounded prejudices, still entertained against the Fraternity, and excite emotions of admiration for their constancy and courage, and of pity for their unmerited and cruel fate." This is the spirit in which American Masons have been taught to consider the Order of KNIGHTS TEMPLARS.

Nor must we overlook in this connection the fascination that romance and fable have thrown around the whole subject, and we may endorse the glowing words of Montaigne:

"The age of chivalry indeed is gone. We have piled away its helmets and its spears : but its blazonry is invested with a more poetic charm. Still we love the past. We love the heroic in man's history, we hate to divest it even of its fictions. The independent spirit of chivalry, bent on the accomplishment of lofty ends, without calculation of chances, or fear of failure, so generous in action, so munificent in courtesy, so frank in friendship, and so gallant in danger, must ever have rare attractions to the enthusiastic and the aspiring. There is something peculiarly delightful and exciting in those stories which represent the hero of the Middle Ages, loyal and brave, superbly mounted, cased in glittering steel, surrounded by his men-at-arms, and issuing forth from his lordly castle, in quest of adventures, or on an errand of love. Wwho does not love to read of the fair and haughty dames encouraging their champions at the tilt, and rewarding their valor with sacred banners, and embroidered scarfs, worked with their own hands ?

"Who does not dwell with delight on the gorgeous description of the tournament, where the place enclosed for combat is surrounded with sovereigns and bishops and barons, and all that rank and beauty had ennobled among the fair ; when the combatants, covered with shining armor, and only known by a device or emblazoned shield, issued forth, not without danger, to win the prize of valor, bestowed by the Queen of beauty, amid the animating music of minstrels, and the shouts of the assembled multitude ! "

To comprehend all the changes made from the original volume comparisons must be made, viz. :

FIRST. The foot-notes referring to Arabic and other Oriental authorities in Mr. Addison's work are omitted. The class of readers to whom ours is directed will not so much care for them, and the space is better filled. So, quotations are translated from the French and Latin into English, and passages in the old English modernized.

SECOND. An important purpose of the present volume is to exhibit the connection between Freemasonry and the Land of Solomon, Zerubbabel, and Godfrey, that land which alone has felt the footsteps of Incarnate DEITY: also between Freemasonry and the Military Orders of Knighthood. Therefore our *opening* portion, strictly original, reviews the History of the Church of Christ to the period of the Crusades, A.D. 1095; our closing portion the History of the Military Orders from the extinction of Knight Templary as a Papal Order, A.D. 1313, to the transfer of its forms and spirit to the Masonic Fraternity, and so down to the present era, when 30,000 swords, emblazoned with the Templars' Cross, are stored up in the armories of five hundred American Commanderies. The compiler has also inserted numerous Masonic allusions in different parts of this volume, following the theory of Preston and Laurie, that the Monks of the three great Military Orders, viz: Templars, Hospitalers, and the Teutonic Knights, were FREEMASONS.

THIRD. We have amended the orthography of proper names under the authority of the American lexicographer, Webster. Mahomet is *Mohammed ;* Panias, *Banias ;* Saphet, *Safed ;* Naplous, *Nablous ;* Gabala, *Gebal ;* D'Jeneen, *Jenin ;* Beisan, *Bethshean,* etc. These changes in spelling bring the Oriental words to the standard of modern biography and geography. We, however, accept the phrase *Knights Templars* from Mr. Addison, in the face of some adverse criticism, even from the Grand Encampment of the United States.

FOURTH. The title-page of the present volume will indicate the line we have pursued in combining the history of the St. Johns and the Teutonic Knights with that of the Templars. To American readers the glory of the three shines with undivided light ; and it is not possible for us to share in that jealousy which causes even an Addison to disparage the Order of St. John, and drives a De Vertot, a Taaffe, and other advocates of the Hospital, to disparage the Templars. We have, therefore, stricken out some of Mr. Addison's Templary matter and supplied its place with history of the rival Orders.

FIFTH. The large number of illustrations in the present volume cannot fail, we think, to commend it to every reader. By the help of our maps we can trace with accuracy the relative spread of Christianity, the routes of the Crusaders, and all the military movements and battles in Palestine. It is upon the proper understanding of these that the interest of our History depends, and their want has proved a positive defect in previous works upon the Crusades. The views of battle-fields, sketches of ancient ruins, and of arms, armor, and armorial bearings, will afford additional interest to the student and speak their own praise.

SIXTH. It will, perhaps, seem odd to some, but we have felt it necessary in the preparation of this work, to soften the *English bias* of Mr. Addison. Sharing in no local prejudice, having no particular regard for monarchical institutions, and feeling but little interest in the English, Scotch, and Irish branches of Knight Templary above those of Continental jurisdictions, the American reader would not justify us in devoting *one-third* of the volume, as Mr. Addison has done, to glorifying the labors and sufferings, however remarkable, of the English Knights. In this connection, we introduce Federal money and American measures when practicable. And we yield more credit to French, German, and Spanish authorities upon Chivalry, the Crusades, and the History of the Military Orders than Mr. Addison has done.

SEVENTH. The compiler has given much time and pains to perfecting the Chronology of the periods embraced in this volume. The perverse contradictions of historians of the Middle Ages are nowhere more evident than in this branch of history, and it is not often that a writer can entirely satisfy himself as to a date. To compile the tables of Grand Masters, the List of Crusades, and the Catalogue of the leaders of the First Crusades has cost more labor than the reader will credit us with.

EIGHTH. The researches in the field of chivalry and knighthood, of the authors named upon our title page, are so blended with the labors of Mr. Addison, as to enlarge and enrich the work without changing its general drift. The invaluable monograph by Baron De Vogüeé, *Churches of the Holy Land* (*Les Églises de la Terre Sainte*); *Freemasonry in Holy Land*, by Brother Dr. Morris; *Biblical Researches in Palestine*, by Dr. Edward Robinson; Brother Prof. Tristam's *Land of Israel;* Brother Captain Warren's *Recovery of Jerusalem;* and the copious and most original MS. notes of Robert Morris, LL.D., Secretary of the *American Holy Land Exploration*, enlarged by Brother Rolla Floyd, Esq., long a resident of Joppa, and President of the same society, and Rev. John Sheville, one of the most recent explorers in that field—these, with scores of other authorities of more or less value, in the same department, have been made available in every manner that could conduce to the interest of the subject. The meed of *honest industry* and *good intention*, in a department of study which has been our delight for a quarter of a century, is not more than, upon a perusal of this volume, the Christian Mason will yield to us, and it is all we crave.

The Holy Land! What manifold associations cluster around that little spot of earth on which break the blue waves of the Mediterranean when they reach its easternmost limit! Memories the most sacred, the most tender and the most thrilling, cause the very name to call up before us a vista of the past such as no other land possesses. How many feet have sought that land! The pathways to it, from every part of earth, have been worn by the staves and the footsteps of pilgrims. In the front, we see the venerable form of him who, when he was called to go out, into a place which he should after receive for an inheritance, obeyed, and "he went out, not knowing whither he went." Thence, down to these busier times, stretches the long procession of those that have traveled far, to kneel and to dwell on sacred soil. And as it has been in the past, it will be in the future. Older shrines may be deserted, superstitions may pass away, but the *sense of reverence*, and the *power of association*, will never so far perish, that they who have the Bible will no longer care to visit the Holy Land. Poets may tell us of romance, but there is no romance like that of this consecrated Palestine, consecrated by the lives that have illumined it, by the love that has been lavished on it, by the blood that has been shed for it, by the VOICE that has been heard in it! What land is like that ancient Canaan, which, so fair and so cherished, has given us all a name for Heaven!

NEW YORK. *January*, 1874.

CARAVAN AND VIEW AMONG THE PYRAMIDS

CONTENTS.

16 CONTENTS.

PART THIRD.

PART FOURTH.

PART FIFTH.

ILLUSTRATIONS.

Part First.

FROM THE DEATH OF JESUS CHRIST, A.D. 33, TO THE ORIGIN OF THE
FIRST CRUSADE, A.D. 1095.

SWIFT fly the years, and rise the expected morn!
Oh, spring to light, auspicious BABE, be born!
See nature hastes her earliest wreaths to bring,
With all the incense of a breathing spring!
See lofty Lebanon his head advance!
See nodding forests on the mountains dance!
See spicy clouds from lowly Saren rise,
And Carmel's flowery top perfume the skies!
Hark! a glad voice the lonely desert cheers,
"Prepare the way! a GOD, a GOD appears!"
"A GOD, a GOD!" the vocal hills reply,
The rocks proclaim th' approaching Deity!

ZION, my chosen hill of old,
　My rest, my dwelling, my delight,
With loving-kindness I uphold,
　Her walls are ever in my sight.

BEYROUT (ST. GEORGE'S BAY), WITH THE MOUNTAINS OF LEBANON IN THE DISTANCE.

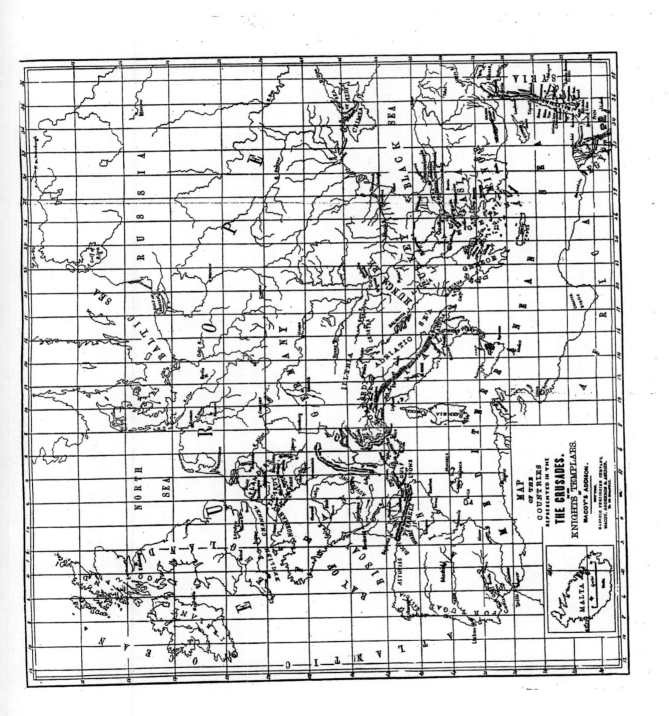

MAP
OF THE
COUNTRIES
REPRESENTED IN THE

THE CRUSADES.

KNIGHTS TEMPLARS.

MACOY'S ADDISON.

MASONIC PUBLISHING COMPANY,
MACOY, ANDERSON & ARCHEL.

CHAPTER I.

FROM THE CRUCIFIXION OF JESUS TO THE DAY OF PENTECOST.

The preaching of the Cross is to them that perish, foolishness; but unto us which are saved, it is the power of God.—1 Cor. i. 18.

THE death of Jesus, as a malefactor, was attended with every circumstance that could serve to discredit his divine claims, and give to his memory that cloud of contempt that smothers whatever of great and noble the friends of a deceased man may presume to attribute to him. When we see how, in modern society, families impoverish themselves to preserve one of their number from the deserved *gallows*, we can conjecture the mortification with which John, and James, and Peter would recall their Master's disgraceful end upon the *Cross*. That fatal Friday, when there was "darkness over the land," "and the sun was darkened," and "the earth did quake, and the rocks were rent," would naturally recur to their memories, and be thrown into their teeth by their fellow-fishermen as they resumed their vocation at Bethsaida, poorer by the lapse of three years than when they "left their nets and followed him." What a life-long shame to the women who, "when he was in Galilee, followed him and ministered unto him," that the man whom they had *known* as a worker of miracles, and had *believed* "the Son of God with power," should be subjected to that disgraceful, indecent and most barbarous death, over which the bitter reproach of the law of Moses ever impended: "he that is hanged is *accursed of God!*"

And this man, Jesus, had claimed so much of his followers and his hearers! He had persistently gone down to the lower strata of society in selecting his agents and ministers, claiming by this that his own communicable wisdom was amply sufficient for them all. He had openly cast himself and his followers upon the charity of the world, claiming by this that the world owed them a living in exchange for the priceless benefits the new Dispensation was about to bestow. He had, with astonishing want of prudence, predicted his own miserable end, the scattering of his followers, the darkness that should enwrap the world for a season, and the strange events that should follow. Mingling metaphor with matter of fact; embodying in parable and fable the most abstruse doctrines; claiming and exercising powers superior to those of the mightiest of his precursors, yet submitting tamely to rebuffs that stirred the indignation of the humblest of his followers, he had made himself an enigma to which the only solution was THE CROSS. The kindest epitaph to the tomb furnished by Joseph of Arimathæa would have been "honorable, well-meaning, but mistaken." This, indeed, is the judgment to-day of the French infidel, Renan.

This train of thought, in the opening of a work like this, is obvious. To project one's self, in imagination, to that Saturday following the crucifixion of Jesus, and to question the affrighted and astounded group who had "all forsaken him and fled," at his seizure in *Gethsemane*, and had "stood afar off," viewing him at his death upon Golgotha, are duties that the historian of the nineteen centuries following, cannot avoid. In the dramatic spirit in which the Holy Scriptures are written, this is *the first Scene* in *the first Act* in the splendid drama of Christian history, nor can the play be comprehended without a vivid appreciation of the opening part.

We will not, however, enlarge upon it further. It is enough to remember that THE CROSS was not the earthly end of THE CRUCIFIED. Golgotha and the tomb of Joseph were but accessories to the scene. The drama goes on. The grave does not hold its dead. The "new tomb" of Joseph is rent open like the tomb of King Godfrey at the present day. The lacerated figure, central in that group of three, before which "they that passed by had wagged their heads" in cruel contempt and utter scorn. That man with pierced hands and feet and side, "burst the bars of death and triumphed over the grave." He rose. "Very early in the morning, on the first day of the week," the greatest of all his miracles was accomplished. If, of his shameless and unjust punishment he could say *It is finished*—of his long and splendid reign, ever increasing in glory and destined in time to embrace all the powers of heaven and earth, it might with equal justness have been said by the angel that descended from heaven and rolled back the stone from the door of his sepulchre, and sat upon it, *It is begun*. Shall we now pursue, in a rapid summary, the progress of Christianity after the crucified malefactor had been transformed into the risen Saviour?

After meeting his disciples in an upper chamber in Jerusalem, and bestowing upon them the SALAAM ALEIKAM (" peace be with you"), still exchanged by friendly travelers throughout the East, conferences were held between them on the shore of the Sea of Galilee, and upon a mountain near by. Then all returned to Jerusalem, and forty days after the Resurrection, Jesus led them out to the neighborhood of Bethany, a mile or more east of the Holy City, and there " he blessed them and was parted from them," ascending to Heaven. He went up in their sight. He passed into a cloud. The rapt disciples stood gazing into that part of the heavens where they had last beheld their Lord. Suddenly two men in white apparel stood beside the silent group, one of whom said, " Ye men of Galilee, why do you stand gazing up into heaven? this same Jesus which is taken from you into heaven, shall so come in like manner as you have seen him taken into heaven."* And thus ended the closing scene in the First Act of this marvelous drama, in which all who prize their immortal nature above the present life are chiefly concerned.

The curtain rises upon another of the marvels, not second in mysteriousness to any yet narrated in this " strange, eventful history." The birth of Jesus, His baptism, temptation, lowliness of life and mind, His sufferings, death, burial, resurrection, and ascension—all bear witness to the reasonableness of the Centurion's ejaculation at Golgotha, " Truly, *this* is the Son of God;"

* We have preferred here to use the words of our eloquent Christian brother, Rev. Charles F. Deems, D.D., of "The Church of the Strangers," New York, whose "JESUS" ranks among the best of those valuable biographies of our Lord for which the present age is remarkable.

Fulfillment of the Law.   The Promise, Guide and Spirit of Truth.

but the descent of the Holy Ghost upon His disciples on the day of Pentecost, was in no respect inferior, as a matter of testimony, to the former.   They were anxiously waiting for it, in fulfillment of his command.   They were all " with one accord in one place." Two days had elapsed since their return from Bethany.   It was the day of Pentecost, the fiftieth after the Passover, which, for fifteen centuries, had been kept as a solemn festival by the Jews, in commemoration of the gift of the Law, after the departure from Egypt, and as the day on which they were to offer to the God of the Harvest *the first fruits* of the harvest.   It was the 26th of May (admitting the chronologer's conclusion that Jesus was crucified April 6), and the sacred record is as follows : " Suddenly there came a sound from heaven, as of a rushing mighty wind, and it filled all the house where they were sitting.   And there appeared unto them cloven tongues, like as of fire, and it sat upon each of them.   And they were all filled with the Holy Ghost, and began to speak with other tongues, as the Spirit gave them utterance." Thus was fulfilled the promise of Jesus, that the Holy Ghost should come THE COMFORTER, to guide them into all truth—to teach them all things, and to bring all things to their remembrance which He had said unto them ; the SPIRIT OF TRUTH, that should testify of Him, and should reprove the world of sin, of righteousness, and of judgment.   It was in all respects a practical demonstration, and on that very day the doubting Thomas surrendered forever his doubts ; on that day the vacillating Peter stood up manfully before the multitude, lifted up his voice and preached the first Christian discourse with such power that *three thousand converts* were gathered into the infant church before the sun went down.   On that day the gentle and amiable John became literally one of the " sons of thunder " (*Boanerges*), and each of the Apostles, in his own way, began a career which, pursued through much earthly tribulation, and subjected to the test of martyrdom, terminated, let us believe, in a crown of glory that fadeth not away.*

---

* It is one of the most cherished traditions of the ancient church, that each of the Apostles, except John, suffered martyrdom.

CHAPTER II.

LOOK up my soul, pant towards th' eternal hills,
  Those heavens are fairer than they seem;
There pleasures all sincere glide on in crystal rills;
There not a dreg of guilt defiles,
  No grief disturbs the stream.
That Canaan knows no noxious thing,
No cursed soil, no tainted spring;
No roses grow on thorns, nor honey wears a sting.

Draw near, ye weary, bowed, and broken-hearted;
  Ye onward travelers to a peaceful bourne;
Ye, from whose path the light hath all departed;
  And ye who're left in solitude to mourn:
Though o'er your spirits hath the storm-cloud swept,
Sacred are sorrow's tears since " Jesus wept."

God hath chosen the foolish things of the world to confound the wise. And God hath chosen the weak things of the world to confound the things which are mighty.—1 Cor. i. 27.

TO condense into a few pages the history of the Church of God for *three centuries*, demands a choice of theme and power of concentration that fall to the lot of but few. We must acknowledge our indebtedness to those patient laborers in ecclesiastical history, whose useful lives have been given to the study of " the rise and progress of that Society of which God is the *head*, souls bought and washed with the most precious blood of Christ, the *members*, and eternity the *end* and *aim*."

The founder of the Christian faith himself compares it (*Mark*

iv. 30–32) to " a grain of mustard-seed which, when it is sown in the earth, is less than all the seed that be in the earth. But when it is sown, it groweth up and becometh greater than all herbs, and shooteth out great branches, so that the fowls of the air may lodge under the shadow of it." Surely the similitude is most apt. At first a man of humble birth and life is baptized of John in the waters of Jordan. Less than four years afterwards, his earthly career closes, and his work is intrusted to eleven Apostles, none of them men of learning or parts. The world, save a single nationality, is entirely Pagan, and the task allotted to these men is to *Christianize it.* Verily that grain of mustard-seed *was* " less than all the seeds that be in the earth." But that which had been predicted, should come to pass. A *sound* had gone out into all the earth, and *words* unto the ends of the world. Their *Founder,* in his last charge to them, had claimed and commanded: " All power is given unto me: go ye therefore and *teach all nations* to observe all things that I have commanded you—and they went and preached everywhere, the Lord working with them, and confirming the word, with signs following."

Shortly after the pentecostal marvel described above, we find the number of men professing Christianity, five thousand. A little later and " the word of the Lord had increased, and the number of the disciples had multiplied in Jerusalem greatly ; and a great company of *the priests* was obedient to the word." Considering the incredulity and bigotry of the Jewish priests in the presence of Jesus, and under the sight of his own miracles, this fact gives strong evidence of the power of Christian doctrine, and the influence of the Holy Spirit that had been granted to his laborers. But this was only in *Jerusalem,* only in one city, one remote and obscure province of the Roman Empire. How was the new faith to reach the philosophies, idolatries and superstitions of the world, so that all should be prostrated before it ?

The death of Stephen, deacon and proto-martyr, A.D. 37, followed by a severe persecution of the Church in Jerusalem, scattered the Christian teachers, heretofore congregated in that city, throughout Syria and the adjacent countries, only the Apostles remaining in the Holy City. Seven years later, A.D. 44, the

The constant Advancement of Christianity.   Power of the Christian Teachers.

conversion of Saul, afterwards Paul, of Tarsus, afforded to the still-growing band the powerful aid of one whose learning was only paralleled by his zeal, and through whose industry the faith was planted first throughout the southern provinces of Asia Minor, then through the centre of the same wealthy and distinguished region, next through Macedonia and Greece, finally through the western provinces of Asia Minor. During this period of fifteen years (A.D. 44 to 59), other missionaries were sowing the seed of Christian life in various parts of Italy, so that when Paul was carried a prisoner to Rome, A.D. 59, he was able to extend the influence of the Church which he found there with great rapidity. Released from his first imprisonment, it is thought that for nine years longer Paul "labored abundantly," visiting Crete, Spain, and other quarters, and that, returned to Rome, A.D. 68, he "suffered for Christ" in martyrdom there.

By this almost all the civilized parts of the earth had "heard the glad sound." The northern provinces of Asia Minor, Chaldæa, Mesopotamia, Egypt, Persia, Arabia and Ethiopia had received the gospel, and thus, in about thirty years, scarcely a generation even in the short life of the human race, amidst the movements of armies, battles, earthquakes, revolts of the Jews, ending in the destruction of their country and dispersion of their race; the uneasy reigns of Tiberius, Caligula, Claudius and Nero, each ending in a violent death, that "little grain of mustard-seed" had expanded into a mighty tree, whose roots had struck deep in all parts of the civilized world, having already extended from the river Euphrates to the ends of the earth.

Eight years later, as the pagan historian, Tacitus, acknowledges, "a vast multitude of Christians," at Rome, suffered martyrdom. Pliny, another writer of the same class (both entirely reliable as historians, and the more trustworthy witnesses to us, because enemies to Christianity), declares, A.D. 107, that in the northern part of Asia Minor the new faith had nearly caused the heathen-worship in those parts to be deserted. His letter to the Emperor Trajan declares with singular earnestness, and an air of unquestionable candor, that many of all ages, of every rank, of both sexes, likewise, were accused of being Christians, and that "the contagion of

28   KNIGHTS TEMPLARS.

Persecution of the Early Christians.   The Spread of Christianity.

this superstition had not only seized cities, but the lesser towns also, and the open country." This proves that in about one-half century the new religion, without any political power, or extraneous influences, had almost subverted idolatry in some of the wealthiest provinces of the Roman Empire.

The first Christian historian, after the death of St. John, A.D. 100, was Justin Martyr, who wrote about A.D. 150. He describes the spread of Christianity, that "there was no race of men, whether barbarian or Greek, by whatever other name they might be designated, whether wandering in wagons or dwelling in tents, amongst whom prayers and thanksgivings were not offered to the Father and Creator of all in the name of the crucified Jesus." This was the work of the first century from the tragedy of Golgotha, a work done, it will be seen, without the aid of locomotive or telegraph, printing-press or theological school, treasure or governmental influence—a work accomplished only by men who went about the world "forsaking all, denying themselves, taking up their cross daily, providing neither gold nor silver, nor brass in their purses, nor scrip, neither two coats, neither shoes, nor yet staves," but telling to plain people the story of a crucified, risen and glorified Saviour, in whom there was welcome for the poorest and the worst. Under such preaching the most obdurate repented, were converted, their sins were blotted out, and they were "refreshed for the presence of the Lord."

Twenty-eight years later (about A.D. 178) we have the testimony of *Irenæus*, Bishop of Lyons, that the new faith had been disseminated through Germany, France, Spain, and Libya. Twenty years later Tertullian announces (A.D. 198) that Parthia, Media, Armenia, the Getuli, and Moors in Africa, parts of Britain, the Sarmatians, Dacians, Scythians, and other nations and islands innumerable, had become subject to the spiritual dominion of Christ. The language of Turtullian is exceedingly fervent: "We are but of yesterday, yet we have filled your empire, your cities, your islands, your castles, your corporate towns, your assemblies, your very camps, your tribes, your companies, your palace, your Senate, your forum. Your temples alone are left to you. We constitute almost the majority in every town!"

Persecution of the Early Christians. The Spread of Christianity.

Sixteen years later (A.D. 214) and new nations have been gathered under this now widely-spread "mustard-tree." The labors of Origen had converted the Arabs to Christianity; the Goths of Mysia and Thrace had owned the meek sway of the Son of God. And all this, it will be remembered, amidst the struggles of nine Roman Emperors and pretenders innumerable to the throne of empire. These successive reigns are thus summed up: Vespasian (A.D. 69 to 79); Titus (A.D. 79 to 81); Domitian (A.D. 81 to 96); Nerva (A.D. 96 to 98); Trajan (A.D. 98 to 117); Hadrian (A.D. 117 to 138); Antoninus Pius (A.D. 138 to 161); Marcus Aurelius (A.D. 161 to 180); and Commodus (A.D. 180 to 218).

The marvelous drama, whose progress we are reviewing, will be poorly understood, stripped of its accessories. Government opposition of every character, bigoted prejudices, political jealousies, persecutions, accompanied by every description of cruelty that could be devised by the most fiendish malignity, even to martyrdom,—these were the rebuffs clearly pointed out by the Immortal Founder, and he who went into pagan lands to preach this new faith, literally "took his life in his hand." Not to enumerate all the fiery trials recorded of the period, the first great persecutor of the Church was Nero, a tyrant whose name became proverbial, even with the heathen, for all that was abominable in impurity and fearful in cruelty. To conciliate the populace who had accused him of setting fire to the city of Rome, out of sheer love of mischief, he condemned the Christians to death, and contrived their fate so as to expose them to derision and contempt. Some were covered over with the skins of wild beasts, that they might be torn to pieces by dogs. Some were subjected to the fate of their Crucified Master. Some were daubed over with inflammable materials, set up in the night time in the public gardens, and so burned to death. This was the commencement of persecution, and, continuing from A.D. 64 to 68, was accompanied by so many incidents of horror, that the Christians began at last to be commiserated as a people whose death was designed merely to gratify the cruelty of one man.

Twenty-five years later, A.D. 93, the second general persecution began under Domitian, a monster only second in baseness to Nero.

The meek spirit in which this was met by the Christians was regarded as nothing better than obstinacy and insanity, and the more patiently it was submitted to, by the one, the more inflamed was the wrath of the other.   For two centuries, from Domitian to Diocletian, A.D. 81 to A.D. 285, the fire of persecution rarely slackened, and never went out.   Millions upon millions of the new faith were destroyed.   The combat between Rome and Christ was *à l'outrance et à la mort* (unto extremity and unto death).   No method of torture was neglected, and new trials of human endurance were continually invented.   A diabolical ingenuity possessed the minds of pagans whose religious faith had not the least effect upon their *own* morals, but who were resolved that the profession of Christianity should be, as the Emperor Diocletian himself threatened, *stamped out.*

We are in no danger of enlarging too much, under this head, in the opening chapters of a work written for Christian believers of the nineteenth century.   Had not the doctrines of Jesus Christ been reasonable ones, and the faith in His death and resurrection an intelligent faith, how could this unequal strife have been so long maintained!   The lives of those early Christians during the first three centuries exhibited in the face of the world the power of faith.   Their morality and virtue were patent to every beholder.   The writers publicly appealed to this, without the fear of contradiction.   " We formerly rejoiced in licentiousness," says one, "but *now* we embrace discretion and chastity.   We formerly set our affections upon wealth ; *now* we share our means with the poor.   We formerly were so bigoted that we would not dwell with those of a different race ; *now* we live together and pray for our enemies."

The question, how far the institutions of Freemasonry existed and were made use of in those early days to extend and strengthen the ties of Christian brotherhood, is one that has been ably discussed in an anonymous work entitled *The Secret Discipline*, published some forty years since.   That all the great associations of antiquity, the objects of which were to civilize and improve the condition of mankind, were *secret societies*, is admitted by many historians.   The mysteries of India, Egypt, Greece, and Rome, were *secret orders*, educational institutions established for the advancement of mankind in wisdom and virtue. Secret societies have their origin in the deepest and most pressing wants of humanity. And if, at the present day, and in a land of freedom, we find this craving for esoteric brotherhood covering the United States with its secret philanthropies, how rational to conclude that in the periods of which we are treating, when government was oppressive and all its energies devoted to "stamping out" the new faith, that the great principle of *Esotery* was brought to bear. As we have already seen, there was nothing novel in this. Did the teachers of the new faith convert a Jew? He was already familiar with the mysterious band of brotherhood in the Essenian, and perhaps other fraternities. An Egyptian? but Egypt had been the seat of esotoric fraternities for thousands of years. A Syrian? he was already familiar with the secret rites of Adonis, and other orders of that class. A Greek? his ancient country was the abode of some of the most renowned secret societies ever inaugurated. A Roman? the Imperial City swarmed with secret fraternities, both male and female.

We are frank to confess, that while acknowledging due faith in the *inspiration* of Scripture, and the animating spirit that upheld a Paul, a Justin Martyr, a Polycarp, and other founders of the Christian Church, we cannot conceive the spreading abroad this new evangel without the assistance of secret Brotherhood, such as Freemasonry. We feel confident, after a full review of Church History from Golgotha to Byzantium, that the key to its success, viewed in its human aspects alone, is the "Secret Discipline" of which our anonymous author wrote. The author of this faith admonished his converts to be as "wise as serpents." Paul, the great expounder and exemplar of the new faith, never disdained to use human wit and wisdom to circumvent the cunning of his adversaries; and it is no more derogatory to the Divine spirit in which these men labored, to suppose that they traveled, preached, forwarded epistles, held conferences, and performed other acts of their ministry under *masonic assistance*, a thing with which every public man of their day was familiar, than that they ate the common food to sustain life, and put on the common clothing to shield

Influence of Secret Institutions throughout the Ancient World.

their bodies from the inclemencies of the season. The principle of *secrecy* furnishes a mysterious bond of unity and strength found in nothing else; and unless we suppose these early Christians worked miracles for their daily preservation, a thing to which they made no claim, we can do no better than to give credit to that.

And so the drama went on for three centuries, and the world was becoming educated slowly but surely, and at infinite expense of human life and suffering, to accept the "Story of the Cross," as no longer an *esoteric* but an *exoteric* fact,—a thing no longer to be taught in whispers and "upon the square," and at the peril of all that was dear to common humanity, but *openly*, without reserve or disguise, before a sinful and dying world.

SOLOMON'S SEALED FOUNTAIN, NEAR BETHLEHEM.

CHAPTER III.

FROM THE CONVERSION OF CONSTANTINE THE GREAT, A.D. 312, TO HIS DEATH, A.D. 337.

AWAKE, awake !
Put on thy strength, O Zion !
Put on the garments of thy beauty,
O Jerusalem, the holy city !

Shake thyself from the dust,
Arise, sit down, O Jerusalem.
Loose thyself from the bands of thy dead,
O captive daughter of Zion !

Lead, kindly Light, amid the encircling gloom
Lead thou me on :
The night is dark, and I am far from home,
Lead thou me on !
Keep thou my feet, I do not ask to see
The distant scene ; one step's enough for me !

We are troubled on every side, yet not distressed ; we are perplexed, but not in despair ; persecuted, but not forsaken ; cast down, but not destroyed ; always bearing about in the body the dying of the Lord Jesus, that the life also of Jesus might be made manifest in our body.—2 Cor. iv. 8-10.

THERE are few incidents in history that have aroused so much debate, and elicited such conflicting opinions as the conversion of Constantine the Great. Ecclesiastical writers have inclined to view the fact as parallel to that of the conversion of St. Paul, as detailed in Acts ix., which was a strictly miraculous intervention. Modern historians, on the other hand, incline to view the circumstance as merely a poitical change of base on the part of Constantine. The truth, perhaps, lies between the two extremes. So great had been the progress of the Christian faith, notwithstanding the violent and cruel persecutions to which from the beginning it had been subjected, that it was clearly the interest of a Roman Emperor, contemplating the inauguration of a new era in politics, and the establishment of a new seat of government, to act as the defender of the Christian faith and relieve the Church from persecution, even though he went no further. At the same time, as a conscientious man, he must have given the preference to Christianity over the paganism that had been so thoroughly weighed in the balance and found wanting.

The history of the great change that made Christianity, from being "a sect everywhere spoken against," the State Religion of the Roman Empire can be but briefly sketched here. Diocletian (crowned Emperor A.D. 284, deceased 313) had signalized himself as the most inveterate persecutor of all the imperial line since Nero, two centuries before. In February, A.D. 303, he had issued an edict against Christianity designed literally "to stamp out" the faith of the Cross. All Christian churches were ordered to be *pulled down ;* all copies of the Holy Scriptures and sacred books to be burned ; all Christians of every grade to be dismissed from offices, civil and military. The barbarities that followed this edict are utterly indescribable. Malicious ingenuity was racked to its utmost to devise tortures for the denounced followers of Jesus. For the space of ten years, and to the death of Diocletian, in 313, this persecution raged with unmitigated horrors. Such multitudes were massacred in all parts of the Empire, and so thoroughly did this edict drive the new faith into secret places, that at last the imperial murderer ventured to erect a triumphal Column, bearing the boastful inscription that " the Christian name and superstition were extinguished, and the worship of the gods restored to its former purity and splendor." This was the last *general persecution* in the Roman empire. The following is a literal copy of this inscription, still extant in the city of Rome :

KNIGHTS TEMPLARS. 35

Conversion of Constantine. Continued Persecution of the Christians.

DIOCLETIANO CAES AVG
GALERIO IN ORIENTE ADOPT
SVPERSTITIONE CHRISTI
VBIQVE DELETA
ET CVLTV DEORVM PROPAGATO.

Freely translated, this great lie reads: " By Diocletian, Cæsar Augustus, and Galerius adopted in the East. The superstition of Christ having been everywhere effaced (wiped out, stamped out), and the worship of the gods propagated!"

Constantine, styled Maximus, sometimes *Magnus* (the Great), born A.D. 274, was made Cæsar (or Lieutenant-Emperor) upon the death of his father, A.D. 306. He administered the government of Gaul until A.D. 312, when he became a competitor for the Imperial throne, against Maxentius, Maximian, and Licinius. Upon his march to Rome, at the head of his army, and upon the eve of the tremendous battle that was to decide his fate and that of the Emperor, he made an open and public declaration in favor of Christianity. This, however, was not the first evidence of his favorable consideration of the subject. Had it been so, a different complexion might be given to the whole circumstances. But during the worst of the Diocletian persecution, his father, Constantius, had labored to mitigate the edict to which we have referred, and Constantine himself was popularly known to have shown marks of *positive favor* to the Christians, in consequence of which considerable numbers of that faith had joined his standard, and thus swelled the ranks of his army. Their peaceful, orderly, and faithful conduct, contrasting so forcibly with the turbulent and dissolute behavior of those who formed the mass of the common armies had won his entire confidence, until, as we have seen, he was, A.D. 312, openly ranked himself with those of whom it had been affirmed, " He which persecuted us in times past now preacheth the faith which once he destroyed (*Galatians* i. 23).

The history of the conversion of Constantine, composed by a cotemporary, Cæcilius, declares that " in the night which preceded the final struggle with Maxentius, Constantine was admonished *in a dream* to inscribe the shields of his soldiers with ' the celestial

36   KNIGHTS TEMPLARS.

The Vision of Constantine.   The Labarum, or Sacred Standard.

sign of God, the Sacred Monogram of the name of Christ;' that he executed the commands of heaven, and that his valor and obedience were rewarded by the decisive victory that followed." And this reminds us of a similar vision connected with a victory gained by Achaius, a Scottish prince, about A.D. 930, over Athelstan, King of England, during which there appeared in the heavens a *white Cross* in the pattern of what is now termed St. Andrew's Cross. This event is commemorated in "The Most Ancient and Noble Order of the Thistle," a highly distinguished Scottish fraternity.

The Christian writer Eusebius gives, however, a different account from that of Cæcilius. According to his statement Constantine saw with *his own eyes* the luminous trophy of the Divine Monogram placed above the meridian sun and inscribed *in Greek*, with the following words: *En touto Nika* ("By this conquer"). The appearance in the sky astonished the whole army as well as its commander, who was yet undetermined as to the choice of a religion. But his astonishment was converted into faith during the following night, for THE CRUCIFIED ONE appeared before his eyes and, displaying the same Celestial Sign, directed Constantine to make a similar standard, and to march under it, with an assurance of victory against all his enemies. The Sacred Banner or Standard, which unquestionably took its origin at that period, was called the *Labarum*. It was a long pike, intersected by a transverse beam. A silken veil of a purple color, hanging down from the beam, was adorned with precious stones, and curiously inwrought with the images of the reigning monarch and his children. The summit of the pike supported a crown of gold which enclosed the mysterious Monogram, combining the two initial letters (X and P) of the Greek name of Christ. The safety of the *Labarum* was intrusted to a Color-Guard of fifty men of approved valor and fidelity, whose station was marked with honors and emoluments, and such superstitious reverence surrounded it that the sight of the *Labarum* in battle scattered terror and dismay through the opposing forces. The name *Labarum* is derived from *lavar*, "a command," in allusion to the command "Conquer, through the power of this Sign!"

The reader is referred to the numerous authorities cited by

DECISIVE BATTLE BETWEEN CONSTANTINE AND MAXENTIUS, AT THE MILVIAN BRIDGE, NEAR ROME.

The decisive Battle at Milvian Bridge.   Constantine received with great Joy.

Gibbon (*Decline and Fall of the Roman Empire*) for the various accounts of this event.   That Constantine made public profession of this long-despised faith upon the eve of his decisive battle of the Milvian Bridge, and that the Roman standard and coins were for that period purged of their pagan symbols and signalized by Christian emblems are facts that no skepticism can weaken.   The opposing legions joined in battle-array near the little stream Cremena, about nine miles from Rome.   The Emperor Maxentius, after a bloody conflict, lost the day, and endeavoring to enter the city by the Milvian Bridge was precipitated into the Tiber and drowned.   Constantine was received by the Romans with acclamations.   All Italy hastened joyfully to accept his rule.   Africa followed without delay.   Then an edict of religious toleration in favor of the Christians startled the whole Empire.   With the greatest exertions and perseverance the new ruler put down all opposition, conquered the enemies of Rome around the entire borders of the empire, crushed his rivals, one by one, and on July 3, A.D. 323, removed the last competitor for the crown, Licinius, at Adrianople, and was henceforth recognized sole master of the Roman world.   In A.D. 328 he removed the capital of the Empire to Byzantium, named, in his honor, *Constantinople*, and the same year issued a decree which, in a sense, was retaliatory of that fulminated by Diocletian, twenty-five years before.   In this edict idolatry was *suppressed by law;* heathen temples were ordered to be destroyed, and the churches and property of which the Christians had been deprived during the last general persecution, were, as far as possible, restored to them.   The Roman Empire was reconstructed upon a plan entirely new, and this renovated empire was pervaded by the worship and institutions of Christianity. Constantine died at Nicomedia May 22, A.D. 337, after a reign of thirty-one years from the death of his father, and fourteen from the final conquest of the Roman Empire.

In connection with the symbolisms of modern Knight Templary, this subject of the CELESTIAL SIGN OF CONSTANTINE demands a more particular attention.   Ward, in his "History of the Cross," has done a special service to the Masonic historian in his exposition of the idolatries of the Cross foisted upon the Christian

Church at an early day. "This *error of form*," says Mr. Ward, "pervades the symbolisms of all the American Commanderies, and the flags of the Knights Templars." We give in juxtaposition the two best-known forms of Crosses in the Catholic Church.

THE LATIN CROSS, also the Cross of Calvary. It differs only from the Passion Cross in being *raised on three steps*.

THE MALTESE CROSS, called also "The Eight-pointed Cross." This formed the distinctive badge of the Knights of Malta.

But these in no sense resemble the CELESTIAL VISION of Constantine. Eusebius, to whom we have already referred, and who received the account of the affair from the lips of Constantine himself, says: "The Sign had the first two letters of the Saviour's name, 'Chi' (X) and 'Rho' (P), which plainly signifies the whole name *Christ*. These letters the Emperor always afterwards wore in his helmet."

The existing medals and coins of Constantine furnish us with the very best evidence possible on this subject. We copy from Mr. Ward's book already cited.

MEDALS AND COINS OF CONSTANTINE.

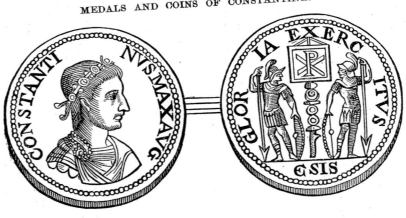

Coins and Medals used during the Reign of Constantine.

The coins and medals of Constantinus Augustus show the monogram on his helmet, on his shield, and on his person; and in one instance wreathed with a motto, " Gloria Exercitus," *the Glory of the Army.*

The following is a medal of the Emperor Jovian, A.D. 367. This figure, universally called " the Cross," is the monogram found in the catacombs, until the Pontificate of Damascus.

The monogram of Christ held its place upon coins and standards until after the dissolution of the Western Empire of Rome, when the Passion Cross supplanted it. Still, in Papal and Protestant Episcopal churches, we see the original " Chi-Rho" or Celestial Emblem, upon painted windows and in obscure places; but the other reigns supreme on spire, pulpit, book, and priest.

42 KNIGHTS TEMPLARS.

The Cross and Monogram of Christ. History of St. Helena.

And the spirit of quasi-idolatry which surrounds it is well expressed in these lines by a fanatic of the Papal Church:—

> Oh faithful Cross, thou peerless tree,
> No forest yields the like of thee,
>   Leaf, flower, and bud;
> Sweet is the wood and sweet the weight,
> And sweet the nails that penetrate
>   Thee, thou sweet wood!

So many references are made in Christian history to Helena, mother of Constantine, and the part she played in the restoration of Palestine is of so much interest in the history of Knight Templary, that the reader will welcome a reference to this celebrated lady here. The natural reverence for those countries sanctified and elevated by so many miracles, and rendered sublimely dear to the heart of every Christian as the land in which his salvation was brightly but terribly worked out, had even before that day rendered Palestine an object of pilgrimage; but the visit of Helena made it far more so.

Helena, commonly styled in Church history Saint *Helena*, was born in Drepanum, in Bithynia, then an insignificant village—afterward raised, by her son Constantine, to the rank of a city, under the name Helenopolis, "the City of Helena." Her husband Constantius, on being made *Cæsar* (Lieutenant-Emperor), A.D. 292, divorced her, for State reasons, and married Theodora, daughter of the Emperor Maximian. Helena then withdrew into retirement until her son became Emperor, when she was called to court, with the rank of Augusta ("Empress-Mother"). Besides the city of Helenopolis, one in Syria was named Helenopontus, in her honor; and other tokens of respect were paid to her. The interest which Constantine took in the spread of Christianity, which has been made the subject of so much discussion, may be in a measure estimated by his liberality to his mother. Enormous sums of money were committed to her to build and endow Christian churches. About the year A.D. 325, she visited Palestine in person, at an advanced age, and explored the site of Jerusalem. Here the singular event, styled "The Invention of the Cross" occurred; and a Basilica named The Church of the

Holy Sepulchre was erected under her orders upon the spot of the "Invention." At Bethlehem she commemorated the place of Our Saviour's Nativity in the same manner. Many other sacred edifices, which will be referred to in their proper places, were built by her authority previous to A.D. 327, when she returned to the West; and died at Nicomedia, in the arms of her son.

The celebrated church that marks the spot of our Saviour's Nativity, is of such extraordinary interest to all lovers of Christian history, that we, with pleasure, refer the reader to De Vogüé's *Les Eglises de la Terre Sainte*—(" Churches of the Holy Land "), the account given by that master-writer of this edifice, as it now appears, our space not permitting us to give at length. Of all the churches on earth, this is the most interesting to Holy Land students. Upon its floor walked the Imperial Saint Helena. Millions of pilgrims trod its hallowed precincts, through all the perils of the Pagan and Moslem occupation.

The second king of Jerusalem, Baldwin I., was crowned there, December 25, 1101—as the valor of Tancred had saved it from destruction two years before. The Crusaders worshipped there for nearly a century. Saladin and his officers inspected, with reverence and admiration, its noble proportion, as they halted there a day on their way, October, 1187, to the capture of Jerusalem. And every reader of the present volume, who may enjoy the privilege of visiting Holy Land will covet above most other things, a day in the Basilica of St. Mary or Church of the Nativity, at Bethlehem.

The biography of Constantine and his family is forcibly illustrated by coins extant in the museums and numismatic collections of Europe and America. In fact the customs and religions of all historical nations are often best learned from a critical examination of their coins. These disks of unwasted metal show, in their greater or less degree of legibility, the faith of the rulers under whose government they were minted. In this respect, as in many others, coins are what old Patin declares them to be, " the breviaries of antiquity; the torchlight of history; the supplement of our ancient faith, that is wasting away (priscæ fidei vacillantes); the food of private reading." In studying suits of Roman coins, we

COINS OF CONSTANTINE THE GREAT AND HIS FAMILY.

are struck with the persistency with which the rulers of the mint fastened their theological symbols upon the national money in all metals, and so kept before the eyes of all the people the legends in which all their religion was embodied. It might be ludicrous, were it not deemed a master-stroke of policy, to see the endless forms under which the theft of Mercury, the sensuousness of Venus, and the omnipotence of Jupiter, were thus presented to the understanding of the people. In the absence of books these coins were their *horn-books*. For the want of the knowledge of letters, the stamps from coin dies made up their *catechism*. The whole heathen mythology can be gathered from the hundreds of thousands of ancient coins yet extant.

We have before us, as we write, a package of some seven thousand coins, bronze, brass and copper, collected in the lands of which our history treats. About nineteen-twentieths of these illustrate in emblems and inscriptions the theological system of the Romans, and their conquered provinces. About one-twentieth bear the emblems of the Christian successors of Constantine. The peculiarities of the latter, which have puzzled so many amateurs in numismatics, are best explained by an examination of the former.

For a thousand years, the moneyers of the Greek, Roman, Syrian and Egyptian mints had exhausted divine epithets upon the most contemptible wretches ever raised by accident, murder or skill, in arms to the imperial power. Thus they had inscribed the brutal *Tiberius* upon their money as the Divine Augustus; *Elagabalus* as "the Pious Augustus," etc.; nor ever scrupled to obey the decrees of the Roman Senate in placing the vilest monarchs, their wives, children and concubines among the gods and goddesses of Rome. In this blasphemy Antiochus IV. of Syria set them the example, as Alexander the Great had set the example before him, of assuming the name "Illustrious God" (Theos Epiphanes).

So, when all-conquering Rome herself became subject to "the true God, and Jesus Christ whom he had sent," there was no medium of conveying this radical change to the people like that of the *circulating medium*, the money of the day. This was copi-

Coins of Rome during the Reign of Constantine and other Emperors.

ously used, both by Constantine himself, the first Christian Emperor, and by his successors.

In their ideal portraiture of saintly personages upon coins and paintings, the artists of the Middle Ages were accustomed to encircle the heads of their figures with a luminous halo, which they called a nimbus. It was also their practice to distinguish the different individuals whom they represented in sculpture, painting, or engraving, by some device or emblem. The nimbus is represented by a circular figure placed immediately above and partly behind the head. In representations of the person of Our Lord, the nimbus is cruciform, that is, it has a cross upon its under-surface. Of this cross three of the limbs only are visible, the fourth being concealed by the back of the head. The head of the Dove, which is the emblem of the Holy Spirit, is encircled with a cruciform nimbus. The radiated nimbus does not appear until late in the fifteenth century. When an entire figure is represented, encompassed by a glory, the radiant figure is styled an aureole. The aureole is generally in the form of a pointed oval. This pointed oval represents the outline of a fish, which was a primitive Christian symbol, the letters which compose the Greek word $I\chi\vartheta\upsilon\varsigma$ (a fish), forming the initials of the words $IH\Sigma OT\Sigma$. $XPI\Sigma TO\Sigma$. ΘEOT. $TIO\Sigma$. $\Sigma\Omega THP$. (Jesus Christ, the Son of God, the Saviour).

CASTLE AND KNIGHTS OF THE MIDDLE AGES.

CHAPTER IV.

FROM THE DEATH OF CONSTANTINE THE GREAT, A.D. 337, TO THE
FIRST CRUSADE, A.D. 1095.

But turn thee now to Salem-ward, and see
   Yon monument of thy Lord's power and love;
That hill is Sion, and that pool where He
   Doth wet his foot is Siloam; above
Its bottom lies; for in the mountain's breast
Its springs of *living* water make their nest.

   Rejoice, O Christendom, rejoice!
   Dry every tear, and lift thy voice
      In songs of praise alone.
   Forget the past, and look on high,
   There leads the road from Calvary,
      And Christ has reached the throne.

There is among you envying and strife and divisions.—1 Cor. iii. 3.

THE history of Christianity from its adoption as the State religion of Rome to the Crusades, belongs but indirectly to our subject. It may reasonably be doubted whether the change made in its favor from a *proscribed* to a *prescribed* faith was not upon the whole an injury to the Church. The time of persecution for the name of Christ had indeed passed away, but the watchful enemy of man seized the moment when prosperity began to lull the Church into security, to introduce errors destructive of all true faith and which led to divisions and innumerable calamities unknown before. Teachers arose whose doctrines shook the new Church to its centre. Arius, Presbyter of Alexandria in Egypt, opened a controversy, A.D. 315, which kept

48   KNIGHTS TEMPLARS.

History of the Christian Church—Its Expansion.   Œcumenical Councils.

the Church in turmoil for fifty years.   Eusebius of Nicomedia, A.D. 341, Photinus, Apollinaris, Pelagius, A.D. 412, and others founded new sects, it is not our part to say upon what bases of truth, but the consequences were " envying, strife, and divisions."   Of these the historian Gibbon has made the best use, and the reader is referred to his pages for full accounts.   Yet the Church continued to expand among the heathen.   Ethiopia was converted by Frumentius, who was consecrated first bishop of the Ethiopians by Athanasius.   Iberia, Thrace, Mœsia, and Dacia received the light of the Gospel.   Martin, bishop of Tours, completed the conversion of the Gauls, and all this before the close of the Fourth Century.   Thus did " the grain of mustard-seed," sown by Christ, continue to extend into a great tree.   In the Fifth Century, Arabia and Ireland acknowledged the Christian faith.   Clovis, the founder of the French monarchy, was baptized A.D. 496.   In the Sixth Century, St. Augustine and others preached the Gospel with great power and founded several Christian churches in Britain, and at the beginning of the period of which our volume mainly treats, that of Knight Templary, " the Story of the Cross " had been effectually promulgated in every part of the civilized world.

To set the doctrines of Christ and his Apostles in forcible contrast with the errors that were being disseminated on every hand, eight General (Œcumenical) Councils were held, prior to the period of the Crusades, of which we insert the list.   Omitting the conference of elders, etc., described in Acts xv., held at Jerusalem A.D. 50, the following gives times and places with sufficient detail :—

I. At Nice (Nicæ) in Bithynia, Asia Minor, A.D. 325.   Over this council Constantine the Great presided.   It condemned the Arian theory, composed the Nicene Creed, and decreed that " Jesus was very God and very man."

The same year a Lesser Council was held at Tyre.   Various others of this class were held at different times and places.

II. At Constantinople, May to July, A.D. 381.   Summoned by the Emperor Theodosius.   Pope Damasus presided.   350 bishops in attendance.

III. At Ephesus, in Asia Minor. June 22 to July 31, A.D. 431. Pope Celestine presided. The Pelagian theory was condemned. 200 bishops in attendance.

IV. At Chalcedon, opposite Constantinople, October 8, A.D. 451. The Emperor Marcian and his Empress in attendance. The doctrines of Dioscorus and Eutychus censured. 630 bishops in attendance.

V. At Constantinople, May 4 to June 2, A.D. 553. Summoned by the Emperor Justinian. Pope Vigilius presided. Pronounced judgment against Origen.

VI. At Constantinople, November 7, A.D. 680, to September 16, 681. Pope Agatho presided. Gave judgment against the Monothelites.

VII. At Nice, September 24 to October 23, A.D. 787. 350 bishops in attendance. Decided against Iconoclasts.

VIII. At Constantinople, October 5, A.D. 869 to February 28, A.D. 870. Emperor Basil in attendance. Decided against Iconoclasts and others.

A Special Council was convened at Clermont, France, by Pope Urban II., A.D. 1095, at which the First Crusade was decided upon. 310 bishops in attendance.

It is important to bear in mind here that the decision of these Œcumenical Councils was not so much *the right or wrong* of a doctrine *per se* as *a testimony* whether the Holy Scriptures approved or disapproved it. The theory of a Grand Lodge is much the same; its *Decisions* are (or ought to be) references to ancient landmarks, written or unwritten, and in point of fact they are obligatory only so far as they are so referred. A bishop in any of those ancient churches was, in spirit, obligated as a Masonic Past Master "that no man or body of men should make innovations" in the body of Christ.

The rise of Mohammedanism belongs to the present chapter. As the argument of Knight Templary was "Jesus *vs.* Mohammed," one grand merit of the Great Military Order of the Middle Ages is that they presented a bulwark against the Moslem. There was a day, October 10, A.D. 732, says Creasy, in his "Fifteen Decisive Battles," when "the arm of Charles Martel saved

Mohammed the Founder of the Islam Religion.   His History.

and delivered the Christian nations of the West from the deadly grasp of all-destroying Islam;" and the historian Arnold ranks that victory "among those signal deliverances which have affected for centuries the happiness of mankind." Gibbon acknowledges the danger from which the world then escaped, in his sneering observation that "had not the Saracen conquests then been checked perhaps the interpretation of the Koran would now be taught in the schools of Oxford, and her pulpits might demonstrate to a circumcised people the morality and truth of the revelation of Mohammed." The Moslems, in such multitudes that no man could reckon them, met the nations of the North upon the battle-field of Tours. This foe stood "firm as a wall and impenetrable as a zone of ice, and the Arabs were slain with the edge of the sword." The defeat was thorough, and Christendom, though disunited, was safe.

Mohammed, the founder of the Islam or Mohammedan religion, was born at Mecca, a city of Arabia, A.D. 569. His lineage was honorable and illustrious, being derived from the powerful tribe of Koreish. His father's name was Abdallah, his mother's Anima. In the division of his father's estate, the youthful Mohammed received but five camels and a slave. At the age of thirteen he accompanied a travelling caravan into Syria, where, it is thought, he gained his first knowledge of the Jewish Scriptures. A few years after, he served as a soldier in the civil wars then agitating Arabia. Having made a second visit to Damascus, and other parts of Syria, as factor for the widow Kodijah, she rewarded his fidelity with the gift of her hand and fortune. This was A.D. 597, when he was twenty-eight years of age. Eight children crowned this union.

The next twelve years of his life were passed at Mecca in affluence and ease. He now meditated and matured the bold design of palming a new religion upon the world. The paganism of his native people on the one hand, and the corruptions that had crept into the Christian faith on the other, encouraged him to hope that a Form of Faith whose grand article should be *The Unity of God*, might liberate his countrymen from error and establish himself as the prophet of a new Faith. He began to issue from time to time

Progress of the Mohammedan Religion. The Hegira.

scraps of pretended revelation under the name of the KORAN (from *Kara*, to read, or "the Book that ought to be read "), and to give out his claim as a divine messenger. After years of deliberation he ripened his plans, and proceeded in a gradual and cautious manner to put them into execution. He retired daily to a cave near Mecca for fasting, prayer, and holy meditation. He broke first to his wife the solemn intelligence of his call, and she became a convert. Her cousin, Waraka, followed her example. His servant was the third. Abu Beker, a man of powerful influence at Mecca, now professed the religion of Islam ("Consecration to God "). In four years he won *nine* converts. He was then forty-four years of age. In A.D. 611, he made the first public announcement of his call.

Ten years elapsed, when such an opposition arose that he fled northward some seventy miles to Medina, where his doctrines had been favorably received. This flight, called the *Hegira*, took place July 16, A.D. 622, in the fifty-third year of Mohammed's age. It was adopted as the Era of the New Dispensation, and the Arabian chronology of the Crusades is always referred to it. At Medina, the fugitive became a king. An army devoted to his person and obedient to his will, was soon formed. He now assumed the temporal and religious power, and began that career of conquest which makes his history a counterpart, in this respect, of King David's. He became leader of the army, judge of the people, and pastor of the flock. He died of poison, June 7, A.D. 632, aged sixty-three years, having conquered in person or by deputies, all Western Asia and much of Africa. Abu Beker took up the sword of conquest with the title of Caliph ("Successor "). He was followed, A.D. 634, by Omar I.; he by Othman, A.D. 644; by Ali, A.D. 655; by Hassan, A.D. 661. Persia was conquered in a single battle. During the reign of Omar, the Moslem destroyed 36,000 cities, towns, and castles, and 4,000 temples of Christian, Magian, and Pagan faiths; and erected 1,400 works, including, A.D. 637, the celebrated *Kubbet es-Sakhrah*, or "Dome of the Rock," upon the ancient site of the Temple of Solomon.

Under the rule of Othman, the Mohammedan sway extended to the borders of India on the east, to Northern Africa on the

52 KNIGHTS TEMPLARS.

Progress of the New Faith.   Its vast Numbers.

KUBBET ES-SAKHRAH, OR DOME OF THE ROCK.

west, and to the island of Cyprus.   And from this time forward, for several centuries, the progress of the new faith was steady, often rapid.   In the Eighth Century the Moslem invaded Europe, conquered Spain; and had so nearly overrun France that nothing but the victory of Tours saved that kingdom.   In the Fifteenth Century, Constantinople surrendered to the Sultan, Mohammed II., who made it his capital and the chief seat of his religion.   At the present day it is calculated that two hundred millions of souls are under the sway of the doctrines of Mohammed.

CHAPTER V.

HISTORY OF THE HOLY LAND FROM THE ENTRANCE OF ABRAM, B. C. 1921, TO THE PERIOD OF THE CRUSADES, A. D., 1095.

ONLY a tomb, no more!
A rock—hence sepulchre,
And this, and this is all that's thine,
Fair Canaan's mighty heir

Only a tomb, no more!
A future resting-place,
Where God shall lay thee down and bid
All thy long wanderings cease

Where is the beauty of that ancient land,
Where patriarchs fed their flocks by living streams?
Still tower to heaven its mountain summits grand,
Still o'er them flings the sun his glorious beams.
But bowed on Lebanon the cedar's pride,
Nor vine nor olive waves on Carmel's rugged side.

AMONG the early travellers to the Holy Land, whose narratives have been preserved in whole or in a mutilated state, we have extant, at the present day, the following: A.D., 333, a Christian traveller of Bordeaux, France, whose account is preserved under the title of "Itinerary from Bordeaux to Jerusalem." He was at Jerusalem two years before the Holy Sepulchre was completed and dedicated. But, previous to this time, pilgrimages had become very common. About A.D. 380, Porphyry, a Greek monk, visited the Holy Land and became bishop of Goga. June 385, Paulina and her daughter left Rome for Palestine, and settled at Bethlehem till her death. About A.D. 610, Antoninus made a visit to the Holy Land. But the nine following travellers left most instructive accounts:—Arculf about A.D. 700; Willibald, 721–27; Bernard the Wise, 867; Saewulf, 1102–3; Sigurd the Crusader, 1107–11; Rabbi Benjamin, 1160–73; John Maundeville, 1322–56; Bertrandon, 1432; Henry Maundrell, 1697. The uniformity of their descriptions is remarkable. There is of course a marked difference in their powers of observation, but what each one sees agrees with the testimony of the rest.

The small and mountainous country that, under the name of Palestine, has occupied such a space, as the theatre of the most momentous events in the world's history, is a strip of territory, if we accept the ancient *termini* of *Dan* and *Beersheba*, one hundred and thirty-one American miles in length, with an average width of forty. The area, therefore, 5,560 square miles, approximates it to the State of Connecticut, which has 4,730. The "Great Sea" (Mediterranean) on the west, and the enormous trench of the Jordan valley on the east, enclose the Holy Land as natural barriers on the sides. The deserts of Arabia on the south, through which the forty years' migration of the Israelites occurred, make a defence equally formidable upon that end, so that the only approach to invading armies in the early history of the East, was from the north. Our map of Palestine, page 19, may be referred to here.

This is "that chosen possession," "that goodly land," which Moses so longed to visit. This is that portion of the earth which Jehovah "sware unto the fathers," that region that "floweth with milk and honey," (*Deut.* xxxi. 20). It was this that was promised by God to *El Khalil* (the Arabic name of Abraham, signifying "the Faithful Man"); and as a father, dividing his possessions, gives the favorite child a goodly inheritance, so the FATHER OF MANKIND chose for His well-beloved, one of the most fertile and productive portions of the earth; a country impregnable by nature as a natural mountain-fastness against an enemy, yet possessing such extraordinary variety of level as to produce almost every fruit and grain coveted by man. The commendation of Moses was not overcharged when he described it to his people as " a good land, a land of brooks of water, of fountains and depths that spring out of valleys and hills; a land of wheat and barley, and vines and fig-trees and pomegranates; a land of oil olive, and honey; *a land wherein thou shalt eat bread without scarceness, thou shalt not lack anything in it*,"—(*Deut.* viii. 7–9.)

Into this romantic and fertile tract, small, compact, easily remembered, easily defended, possessing everything to intensify those sentiments of patriotism common to mountaineers—into the land of CANAAN, then but sparsely inhabited, came the Oriental *Emeer* (Prince), Abram, nearly forty centuries ago. Down southwest and by the caravan-road he came, for roads in the East are *landmarks*, and never changed. At the gates of Damascus he halted, for Damascus is a landmark in Syria from the remotest ages, a *necessity* of the country. Around the back of Mount Hermon, snow-crowned then as now, fording the Jordan, cool and noisy then as now, at the place so famous seven hundred years ago under the name of "Jacob's Bridge," winding across by the Horns of Hattin, which should witness such calamities (A.D. 1187) three thousand years later, and the Sea of Galilee, then, as now, teeming with food, the patriarch made his first halt in the beautiful valley of Shechem, between Ebal and Gerizim, to which his descendants should return in such array 470 years afterwards.—(*Joshua* viii. 30–35.) "There builded Abram an altar unto the Lord which appeared unto him.—(*Genesis* xii. 7.) To follow him further to Bethel, to Egypt, to Hebron and to Beersheba, needs but the aid of our map, as seen on page 19.

The peaceful life of Isaac is distinctly read upon that map. So is that of Jacob, whether we study his life as a petted son, a fugitive, a wealthy Sheikh, an unhappy parent, or finally, an emigrant to Egypt. The wanderings of the tribes under Moses, (B.C. 1490–1450), and their conquest of Canaan under Joshua the following year, need no further reference here. The partition of the land of Canaan at Shiloh (B.C. 1444) distributed those cities, afterwards most famous in the history of the Crusades, among the following tribes, viz: Bethlehem to Judah; Ascalon and Gaza to Simeon; Joppa, Ramleh and Lydda to Dan; Jerusalem jointly to Judah and Benjamin; Bethel to Benjamin; Shechem (afterwards Nablous), to Ephraim ; Tiberius and Hattin to Zebulun ; Acre and Nazareth to Asher, and Safed to Naphtali.   The cities of Tyre, Sidon, Beyrout and Tripoli remained in possession of the Canaanites, afterwards distinctively termed *Phœnicians*, from whom the Jews were never able to wrest the sea coast.   Damascus only accepted the Jewish dominion for a short period during the reign of David.

Under all the vicissitudes incident to the history of nations, the CHOSEN RACE held their mountain-land for sixteen centuries.   A division occurred under Rehoboam, B.C. 975.   The first general deportation of the Jews by Nebuchadnezzar, King of Babylon, B.C. 588, was compensated by the permission granted them fifty-three years later, to return from Babylon and reoccupy the land.   In the time of Christ, although deprived of their political liberty by the Romans, yet the Jews were never more numerous or prosperous, and the fact that, for several years, that mere strip of territory defied the legions of Rome, led by their best generals, is an evidence of the number and courage of the people not to be gainsayed.   The conquest and destruction of Jerusalem, A.D. 70, by the Romans led to a second general deportation of the Jewish nation.   Yet they were soon allowed to return again, for we see, only seventy years later, A.D. 132 to 135, a revolt under Barkobas, only second in interest to that which demanded the best generalship of Vespasian and Titus to overcome it.   580,000 Jews perished during the three years of this last insurrection, and the country was at last *converted into a desert*, the inhabitants either remorselessly slain or driven into exile, and the divine threats, pronounced at the mouth of Moses 1600 years before, fully accomplished.

It was not, however, the policy of the Romans to remain stern and intolerant.   Under the milder sway of the Emperor Antoninus Pius, A.D. 137 to 161, the Jews were restored to some of their ancient privileges and to the freedom of worship, although not permitted to rebuild their temple, or to dwell in the precincts of Jerusalem.   When Constantine ascended the throne, A.D. 312, the Jews had their seat of religious rule at Tiberias, on the Sea of Galilee.   (See Map, page 19)   Under his powerful patronage, as we have shown in the preceding Chapter, splendid structures were

Stately Edifices built in behalf of the Christian Faith.

raised by Queen Helena throughout the Holy Land, in honor of the Christian faith. The country began to be overspread with memorials of Christianity. Chapels, altars, and houses of prayer marked every spot memorable for the sayings and doings of Jesus. Jerusalem was filled with the emblems of the new faith, and crowds of pilgrims were attracted from the most distant countries by an eager desire of contemplating the place of our Redeemer's Passion, and of all the previous events of His holy life.

Upon the death of Constantius II., A.D. 361, the last of the Constantine family, Julian, the Apostate, endeavored during his brief reign of three years, to restore the Pagan faith. He encouraged the Jews to re-establish an order of priests who might revive the observance of the Mosaic rites. He even went so far as to collect a colony of Jews at Jerusalem. Upon the site of the Temple, then many years in ruins, he laid the foundation of a new structure that should eclipse the splendor of Helena's Holy Sepulchre, that stood on the brow of the hill a quarter of a mile west. The Jews gratefully accepted his proposals, and crowded to the Holy City in large numbers. They also sent liberal contributions there from all lands, and for a time this last expiring effort of Jewish zeal promised great success. But the early death of Julian, A.D. 363, and the Christian zeal of his successors, destroyed their hopes. The Roman policy, after this period, tended to depress the Jews in Palestine, and discourage their increase.

Under Khosroes, the Persians devastated Palestine, A.D. 614. In this invasion they were joined by 24,000 Jews, burning with the desire of revenge, and animated by the hope of recovering the "promised possession" of which they had so long been deprived. A new and happier era of freedom and independence had been preached to them, and it really seemed as if their "promised time" had come. In the sack of Jerusalem, they were satiated with a full measure of revenge: 90,000 Christians perished, and the magnificent monuments of the Christian faith were mostly consumed by fire. This invasion, however, was soon checked. The Greek Emperor Heraclius, A.D. 627, defeated the Jews and Persians, and rescued all the provinces that had been overrun, and restored the Sacred Edifices to their former glory. The Jews were terribly punished, and were then forbidden to approach *within three miles* of the Holy City.

The next great change was occasioned by the spread of the Mohammedan religion. The Moslem, as we have seen in a preceding Chapter, having extended their doctrines and dominions by fire and sword, rapidly subdued Syria, Palestine, and Egypt. In the year A.D. 637, the victorious Omar, having occupied the other portion of the country, sat down before Jerusalem; and after a siege of four months, during which his forces suffered much from the inclemency of the winter, took it by capitulation. Under his powerful sway, the so-called Mosk of Omar (*Kubbet es-Sakhrah,* or "Dome of the Rock") was erected upon the site of Solomon's Temple—an edifice which still stands, giving evidences of antiquity after a history of 1250 years. A.D. 868, Jerusalem was conquered by the Turks under Achmet. The Saracens retook it, A.D. 906. Again, the Turks under Mohammed Ikschid, A.D. 978, gained possession of the prize. It was captured by Ortok; and in A.D. 1076 by Meleschah, a Turk. Retaken by the Ortokides; finally by the Fatimes; it came again into Christian hands at the storming by the Crusaders, July, A.D. 1099.

From even this brief sketch it is easy to comprehend why of all countries in the world Palestine is pre-eminently *the Land of Pilgrimage.* To the *Jew* it is the home of all his prophets, priests, and kings; nor can he ever renew his system of rites and ceremonies, or ever again eat his Passover-Lamb until his altar is erected on MOUNT MORIAH. To the *Christian* it bears the same sacred relationship as to the Jew, with additions. For there lived and died Jesus his Saviour. Thence went forth the Word of His testimony. All places hallowed to a Christian's memory are in Palestine. To the *Mussulman* it bears the same relationship as to Jew and Christian, with the addition afforded by his sacred legends of Mohammed and his flight to Heaven from Jerusalem. To the historian, the student of Oriental manners, the student of religious cults, the tourist, to every class of travellers in fact except those given to commercial interests, Palestine is pre-eminently the LAND OF PILGRIMAGE.

Part Second.

FROM THE PREACHING OF THE FIRST CRUSADE, A.D. 1095, TO
THE CALAMITOUS BATTLE OF HATTIN, A.D. 1187.

JOPPA, THE PRINCIPAL LANDING-PLACE OF PILGRIMS TO JERUSALEM.

CHAPTER I.

THEORY OF ORIENTAL PILGRIMAGE.

SHE sits beneath her withering palm
　　In solitary state,
With not a hope to cheer or calm
　　The horrors of her fate:
And He who once illumed her path,
Hath now withdrawn his face in wrath.

THE history of the times of which we treat is sadly confused. In battles, retreats, and conflagrations, papers and parchments are soon lost or burned. So to make up for them, writers employed their imaginations, with a sort of foundation. William of Tyre, to whom we are largely indebted for the facts incorporated in this work, was no contemporary of what he relates prior to A.D. 1174, but was one of those fabulists, and either from not knowing, or not *wishing* to know the real state of the case, was himself misinformed and so misinformed others.* His prejudices, like those of too many more recent authors, run against certain persons, until we dare not accept his statements until they are put to the square of other and more reliable (if less diffuse) authorities. Mr. Addison says, he was averse to the Order on account of its vast powers and privileges, and carried his complaints to a General Council of the Church of

---

* The title of his book in Latin is, " Historia Rerum in partibus transmarinis, etc., seu Historia Belli Sacri." He was made Archbishop of Tyre, A.D. 1174, commenced his history 1184, and brought it down in twenty-two books, from the commencement of the Crusades to the raising of the Siege of Kerak by Saladin, 1187.

62   KNIGHTS TEMPLARS.

Writers on the Crusades.   Their Opinions and Reliability.

Rome. The Bishop of Acre, James of Vitry, a most learned and talented prelate who wrote subsequently to William of Tyre, and copies largely from the latter, opposed him in his statements against the Knights Templars, and declares "they were universally beloved by all men for their piety and humility."

The late William B. Hubbard, for many years Grand Master of Knights Templars in the United States, was the first to warn American writers of the unreliability of William, Archbishop of Tyre, as a historian.   In the present volume, we have endeavored to verify his statements before accepting them.   Yet, as a matter of justice, we quote Mr. James's opinion :—

"William of Tyre is beyond all doubt the most illustrious of the many historians who have written on the Crusades.   Born in Palestine, and though both educated for the Church and raised step by step to its highest dignities, yet mingling continually in the political changes of the Holy Land, the preceptor of one of its kings, frequently employed in embassies to Europe, and ultimately Archbishop of Tyre and Chancellor of the kingdom of Jerusalem, William possessed the most extensive means of gathering materials for the great work he has left to posterity.   He brought to his task, also, a powerful mind, as well as considerable discrimination ; and was infinitely superior in education and every intellectual quality to the general chroniclers of his age.   He was not born, however, at the time of the First Crusade; and consequently, where he speaks of the events of that enterprise, we may look upon him as an historian, clear, talented, elegant, and not extremely credulous; but we must not expect to find the vivid identity of contemporaneous writing.   In regard to the history of his own days he is invaluable; and in respect to that of the times which preceded them, his work is certainly superior, as a whole, to anything that has since been written on the subject."

And it is not pleasant to say that the American student of the Crusades learns to look with suspicion upon his English authorities generally.   It is not so much that Addison, Mills, James, Proctor, and others, deliberately *falsify* the subject of which they are so competent to treat,—we should be the last to charge them with that,—but that they give such unfounded prominence to the *English* branch of the history, and so little to the *French* and *German*, as to leave an essentially false impression upon the mind.

To quote Mr. James's words in his own *History of Chivalry :* " A favorite theory is too often like the bedstead of the ancient

Writers on the Crusades. Their Opinions and Reliability.

Greek; facts are either stretched or lopped away to agree with it." If he had added that facts are often severely *omitted*, he would have perhaps missed his Procrustean figure, but hit the brad more truly on the head, and afforded a positive criticism on his own work, which, professing to be based upon such European authorities as Albert of Aix, Fulcher of Chartres, etc., glorifies his own countrymen past all reason. The reader of almost every English authority that we have seen upon the Crusades and the Holy Land, clear down to Murray's "Hand-Book of Syria and Palestine," must concede that the Military Orders were *English* in their origin, that the first Crusades were largely under *English* impulses; and that, in point of fact, if the name of King Richard I. were taken from the history of Palestine in the Twelfth Century, there would be but little left worth reading. Walter Scott in his romances so thoroughly conveys this idea, that the generation who (like the writer of the present volume) grew up upon the pabulum of Scott's historical novels, acquired most unfounded notions under this head—the worst possible ideas in fact for historical study. We make an exception in these remarks to Mr. Taaffe's "History of the Holy, Military, Sovereign Order of St. John of Jerusalem;" for this gentleman has so far divested himself of British bias as to call the French "that noble and high-minded nation, who usually take the lead wherever there is anything of great or good to be undertaken;" which, for an Englishman, is certainly saying much, considering that even Mr. Robson, in his excellent translation of Michaud's "History of the Crusades," has thought it necessary to disfigure the work with numerous foot-notes.

In collecting the authorities at hand, we have given more credit to European than English authors; not because a Frenchman is less patriotic than an Englishman, or less prone to national exaggeration, but because the Crusades were so much more largely due to French than English impulses that the Chronicles of the times are, in the proportion of a hundred to one, *French*.

The spirit of Pilgrimages to the East, although not absolutely due to Helena, mother of Constantine, was made popular and intensified by the imperial state in which the Queen-Mother visited the lands of the Bible, A.D. 326–7, and the splendid structures everywhere reared, at incalculable cost, under her direction, upon every spot marked in the narrative of Jesus. She first made it *fashionable* to go to the Holy Land, as she first enabled the tourist to identify the sacred localities. With some positive mistakes of location, such as the place of the Ascension, which *could not* have been on the summit of Mount Olivet without positive contradiction of the Sacred Text, and some probable errors (such as the location of the Holy Sepulchre, which could scarcely have been in what is now the heart of the Holy City), her visits established with accuracy very many famous places, and set the Christian world on foot to identify others. And there are few incidents in history more curious than the indisputable fact that more has been done in this way during the forty years ending in 873 than in all the long interval from Queen Helena, A.D. 327, to Edward Robinson, A.D. 1843, although for an entire century the country was in the possession of the most civilized nations of Europe.

Jerusalem, whether in a state of glory or of abasement, was always held dear and sacred by the Christian. St. Jerome, A.D. 360, writes that people began to *pilgrimage* to Jerusalem, directly after the ascension of Christ. In the early ages of the Church a religious curiosity prompted people to visit those places which the Scriptures have sanctified ; and as perceptible objects awaken associated thoughts and feelings, the travellers found their sympathies stronger, and their devotions more fervent in beholding the scenes of the Ministry of their Divine Master than in simply reading the narrative of His life. It is so to this day. Every spring a band of many thousand pilgrims of the Greek Church, gathered from all parts of that widely extended denomination, visit the Holy Land to kneel at the sacred places, to be immersed in the swift waters of the Jordan, to feast their eyes upon scenes once hallowed by the presence of the Son of man, and to return home, this one romance of their hard and poverty-stricken lives gratified. Not that Deity can only be adored there, for He is Omnipresent ; but if we are devoted to any object, every circumstance relative to it interests us (Theodoretus).   What man is there not seized with admiration and astonishment, who beholds the Mount of Olives, the Sea of Tiberias, the Jordan, Jerusalem, and other places which

Jesus so frequently beheld! (Heland.) If the Roman Cicero, in contemplating the ruins of Greece, found that a noble sympathy for the woes of nations banished all personal sorrows, surely the view of Golgotha could not excite feeble emotions in the breast of a Christian! (Mills.)

Let us find a softer word than *superstition* for that sentiment which fancied that there was some peculiar sanctity in *the very dust* on which the Man of Sorrows had wept. It was as one stands above the grave of a beloved parent. True, the religious education of the times—never changed until Luther elevated faith above works—taught that repose to anxious, restless guilt might be had by him who underwent the pains of pilgrimage, and who made the sacrifice of prayer in a land which, above all other countries, seemed to have been favored by Deity. As expiation was then the purpose of the religious traveller, it devolved upon the directors of consciences to determine on what occasions the penance was necessary. The Bible acquainted the pious with the manners of the East. A scrip and a staff were in conformity with Asiatic customs, considered to be the accompaniments of every traveller. They were the only support of the poor, and were always carried by the rich. The village pastor delivered a staff into the hands of the pilgrim and put around him a scarf or girdle to which a leathern scrip was attached. Friends and neighbors walked with him to the next town, and benedictions and tears sanctified and embittered the moment of separation. On his return he placed the branch of the sacred palm-tree (which he had brought from Jerusalem) over the altar of his church, in proof of the accomplishment of his vow; religious thanksgivings were offered up; rustic festivity saluted and honored him, and he was ever after revered for his piety and successful labors. No wonder so many went to Holy Land.

"Hope," says Mr. Taaffe, "was in the East, and the world was desirous of hope. Many devout or repentant Germans, tired of life's turbulent scenes, set out to make what they, perhaps, did not know that St. Jerome and St. Austin had made several centuries earlier—a pilgrimage to the tomb of the Founder of their Divine Creed, and though some of those scalloped travellers had died on the road to or at Jerusalem, and some on their way back, yet some of them also returned home, and lived to enliven it with spirit-stirring stories of adventure, or holy unction."

Sometimes pilgrimage was attended with real danger and considerable cost. A service of risk and insult rather than certain death ; disguise often necessary, and contumely and privations always sure. Remarkable courage or very warm devotion cannot but be predicated of a lady who, under those circumstances, visited Jerusalem ; but what will not a new convert do? She had come from Sweden, then still in idolatry, into England, where she got converted, and thence set out for the Holy Sepulchre.

What follows in the present chapter we have chiefly condensed from Michaud's " History of the Crusades."

From the earliest ages of the Church, a custom had been practised of making pilgrimages to the Holy Land. Judea, full of religious remembrances, was still the promised land of the faithful ; the blessings of heaven appeared to be in store for those who visited Calvary, the tomb of Jesus Christ, and renewed their baptism in the waters of the Jordan. Under the reign of Constantine A.D. 312 to 337, the ardor for pilgrimages increased among the faithful ; they flocked from all the provinces of the empire to worship Jesus Christ upon His own tomb, and to trace the steps of their God in that city which had but just resumed its name from that which the Romans had given it, viz.: *Ælia Capitolina*, and which the piety of an emperor had caused to issue from its ruins.

The Holy Sepulchre presented itself to the eyes of the pilgrims, surrounded by a magnificence which redoubled their veneration.

An obscure cavern had become a marble temple paved with precious stones and decorated with splendid colonnades. To the east of the Holy Sepulchre appeared the Church of the Resurrection, in which they could admire the riches of Asia, mingled with the arts of Greece and Rome. Constantine celebrated the twenty-first year of his reign, A.D. 333, by the inauguration of this church, whose corner-stone had been planted under the auspices of his sainted mother, and thousands of Christians came, on occasion of this solemnity, to listen to the panegyric of Christ from the lips of the learned and holy Bishop Eusebius.   St. Jerome, who, towards the end of the Fourth Century, had retired to Bethlehem for literary labors and religious solitude, informs us, in one of his letters, that pilgrims arrived in crowds in Judea, and that around the holy tomb the praises of the Son of God were to be heard uttered in many languages.   From this period pilgrimages to the Holy Land were so numerous that several doctors and fathers of the Church thought it their duty to point out the *abuses* and *dangers* of the practice.   They told Christians that long voyages might turn them aside from the path of salvation ; that their God was not confined to one city ; that Jesus Christ was everywhere where faith and good works were to be found.   But such was the blind zeal which then drew Christians towards Jerusalem that the voice of the holy doctors was scarcely heard.   The counsels of enlightened piety were not able to abate the ardor of the pilgrims who believed they should be wanting in faith and zeal if they did not adore Jesus Christ in the very places where, according to the expression of St. Jerome, " the light of the Gospel first shone from the top of the Holy Cross."

As soon as the people of the West became converted to Christianity they turned their eyes to the East.   From the depths of France, from the forests of Germany, from all the countries of Europe, new Christians were to be seen hastening to visit the cradle of the faith they had embraced.   An itinerary for the use of pilgrims served them as a guide from the banks of the Rhone and the Dordogne to the shores of the Jordan, and conducted them on their return from Jerusalem to the principal cities of Italy.

When the world was ravaged by the Goths, the Huns, and the Vandals, pilgrimages to the Holy Land were not at all interrupted.   Pious travellers were protected by the hospitable virtues of the barbarians who began to respect the Cross of Christ, and sometimes even followed the pilgrims to Jerusalem.   In these times of trouble and desolation, a poor pilgrim who bore his scrip and staff often passed through fields of carnage and travelled without fear amidst armies which threatened the empires of the East and the West.

Illustrious families of Rome came to seek an asylum at Jerusalem and by the tomb of Christ. Christians then found, on the banks of the Jordan, that peace which seemed banished from the rest of the world. This peace, which lasted several centuries, was not troubled before the reign of Heraclius, A.D. 610–641. Under this reign the armies of Chosroës, King of Persia, invaded Syria, Palestine, and Egypt. The Holy City fell into the hands of the worshipers of fire. The conquerors bore away into captivity vast numbers of Christians and profaned the churches of Jesus Christ. All the faithful deplored the misfortunes of Jerusalem, and shed tears when they learned that the King of Persia had carried off, among the spoil of the vanquished, *the Cross of the Saviour*, which had been preserved in the Church of the Resurrection.

Heaven, at length, touched by the prayers and afflictions of the Christians, blessed the arms of Heraclius, who, after ten years of reverses, triumphed over the enemies of Christianity and the Empire, and brought back to Jerusalem the Christians whose chains he had broken. Then was to be seen an Emperor of the East walking barefooted in the streets of the Holy City, carrying on his shoulders to Calvary the wood of the True Cross, which he considered the most glorious trophy of his victories. This imposing ceremony was a festival for the people of Jerusalem and the Christian Church, which latter still every year celebrates the memory of it. When Heraclius re-entered Constantinople he was received as "the Liberator of the Christians," and the kings of the West sent embassadors to congratulate him.

All the persecutions of Moslemism could not stop the crowd of Christians who repaired to Jerusalem ; the sight of the Holy City sustained their courage as it heightened their devotions.

There were no evils, no outrages that they could not support with resignation when they remembered that Christ had been loaded with insults, and had died upon the Cross in the places they were about to visit. Among the faithful of the West who arrived in Asia in the midst of the early conquests of the Mussulmans, history has preserved the names of St. Arculphus and St. Antonius of Plaisance. The latter had borne arms with distinction, when he determined to follow the pilgrims who were setting

out for Jerusalem.   He traversed Syria, Palestine, and Egypt.
On his arrival on the banks of the Jordan, Judea had not yet
fallen into the hands of the infidels; but the fame of their victories already filled the East, and their armies were threatening the
Holy City.   Several years after the pilgrimage of St. Antonius,
Arculphus, accompanied by Peter, a French hermit, set out from
the coast of England bound for Syria.   He remained nine months
at Jerusalem, then under the dominion of the enemies of Christ.
On his return to Europe he related what he had seen in Palestine
and in all the sacred spots visited by the pilgrims of the West.
The account of his pilgrimage was drawn up by a holy monk of
the Hebrides for the information and edification of the faithful.

The Christians of Palestine, however, enjoyed some short intervals of security during the civil wars of the Mussulmans.   If
they were not freed from their bondage they could at least weep
in peace upon the tomb of Christ.   The dynasty of the Ommi-
ades which had established the seat of the Mussulman empire at
Damascus, A.D. 661 to 750, was always odious to the ever-formi
dable party of the Alides, and employed itself less in persecuting
the Christians than in preserving its own precarious power.   Mer-
wan II., the last Caliph of this house, was the most cruel towards
the disciples of Christ, and when he with all his family sunk under the power of his enemies, the Christians and the infidels united
in thanks to heaven for having delivered the East from his
tyranny.

To the desire of visiting the tomb at Jerusalem was joined the
earnest wish to *procure relics*, which were then sought for with
eagerness by the devotion of the faithful.   All who returned from
the East made it their glory to bring back to their country some
precious remains of Christian antiquity, and above all the bones
of holy martyrs, which constituted the ornaments and riches of
their churches, and upon which princes and kings swore to respect
truth and justice.

The Christians of the West, almost all unhappy in their own
countries, and who often lost the sense of their evils in long voyages, appeared to be only employed in seeking upon earth the
traces of a consoling and helpful divinity, or of some holy person-

age. There existed no province without its martyr, or its apostle, whose support they went to implore. There was no city or secluded spot which did not preserve the tradition of a miracle, or had not a chapel open to pilgrims. The most guilty of sinners, or the most fervent of the faithful, exposed themselves to the greatest perils, and repaired to the most distant places. Sometimes they directed their steps to Apulia and Calabria. They visited Mount Gargan, celebrated by the apparition of St. Michael, or Mount Cassia, rendered famous by the miracles of St. Benedict. Sometimes they traversed the Pyrenees, and in a country given up to the Saracens, esteemed themselves happy in praying before the relicts of St. Jago, the patron saint of Galicia. Some, like King Robert, went to Rome and prostrated themselves on the tombs of the Apostles St. Peter and St. Paul. Others traveled as far as Egypt where Christ had passed his infancy, and penetrated to the solitudes of Scete and Memphis, inhabited by the disciples of Anthony and Paul. A great number of pilgrims undertook the voyage to Palestine; they entered Jerusalem by the Northern or Damascus gate, where they paid a money-tribute to the Saracens. After having prepared themselves by fasting and prayer, they presented themselves in the Church of the Holy Sepulchre, covered with a funeral cloth or robe, which they preserved with care during the remainder of their lives, and in which they were buried after their death. They viewed with holy respect Mount Sion, the Mount of Olives, and the Valley of Jehoshaphat. They quitted Jerusalem to visit Bethlehem, where the Saviour of the world was born; Mount Tabor, supposed by them, though improperly, to have been the place of the Transfiguration; and all the places memorable for his miracles.

The pilgrims next bathed in the Jordan, and gathered in the territory of Jericho palm-branches which they bore back as evidences and relics to the West. Such were the devotion and spirit of the Tenth and Eleventh Centuries, that the greater part of Christians would have thought themselves wanting in the duties of religion if they had not performed *some pilgrimage.* He who had escaped from a danger, or triumphed over his enemies, assumed the pilgrim's staff and took the road to the holy places. He

KNIGHTS TEMPLARS.   71

Desire for Pilgrimage to Holy Places.   Protection to Pilgrims.

who had obtained by his prayers the preservation of a father or of a son, went to return his thanks to heaven, far from his domestic hearth, in places rendered holy by religious traditions.

A father often devoted his child in the cradle to a pilgrimage; and the first duty of an affectionate and obedient son, when past the age of childhood, was to accomplish the vow of his parents. More than once a dream, a vision in the midst of sleep, imposed upon a Christian the obligation of performing a pilgrimage. Thus, the idea of these pious journeys mixed itself up with *all the affections of the heart*, and with all the prejudices of the human mind.

Pilgrims were welcomed everywhere, and in return for the hospitality they received they were only asked for their prayers; often, indeed, the only treasure they carried with them. One of them, desirous to embark at Alexandria for Palestine, presented himself, with his scrip and his staff, on board a ship, and offered a book of the holy Evangelists in payment for his passage.

Pilgrims on their route had no other defense against the attacks of the wicked but the Cross of Christ, and no other guides but those angels whom God has told to watch over his children and to direct them in all their ways.

The greatest merit in the eyes of the faithful, next to that of pilgrimage, was to devote themselves to the service of the pilgrims. Hospitals were built upon the banks of rivers, upon the heights of mountains, in the midst of cities, and in desert places, for the reception of these travelers. In the Ninth Century the pilgrims who left Burgundy to repair to Italy were received in a monastery built upon Mount Cenis. In the following century two monasteries, in which were received travelers who strayed from their way, occupied the places of the temples of idolatry on Mount Jovis, and thence lost the name they had received from paganism, and took that of their pious founder, St. Bernard de Meuton. Christians who traveled to Judea found, on the frontiers of Hungary, and in the provinces of Asia Minor, a great number of asylums raised by charity. Christians established at Jerusalem went to meet the pilgrims, and often exposed themselves to a thousand dangers. Whilst conducting them on their

72   KNIGHTS TEMPLARS.

Enthusiasm and Devotion of Pilgrims. Love of Travel.

route. The Holy City contained hospitals for the reception of all travelers.

In one of the hospitals the women who performed the pilgrimage to Palestine were received by religious females devoted to the offices of charity. The merchants of Amalfi, Venice, and Genoa, the richest among the pilgrims, and several princes of the West, furnished by their benevolence the means of keeping these houses open for all poor travelers, even as we find at the present day free convents and hospices throughout Palestine. Every year monks from the East come into Europe to collect the self-imposed tribute of the piety of the Christians. A pilgrim was a privileged being among the faithful. When he had completed his journey he acquired the reputation of particular sanctity, and his departure and return were celebrated by religious ceremonies. When about to set out a priest presented to him his scrip and staff, together with a gown marked with a cross. He sprinkled holy water over his vestments, and accompanied him at the head of a procession as far as the boundaries of the next parish. On his return to his country the pilgrim gave thanks to God and presented to the priest a palm branch, to be deposited on the altar of the church as an evidence of his undertaking being happily terminated.

The poor in their pilgrimages found certain resources against misery ; when coming back to their country they received abundant alms. Vanity sometimes induced the rich, as in the present century, to undertake these long voyages, which made the Monk Glaber say that "many Christians went to Jerusalem to make themselves admired, and to be enabled, on their return, to relate the wonders they had seen." This is a good representation of the modern tourist. Many were influenced by the love of idleness and change, others by curiosity and an inclination to see various countries, and it was by no means rare to meet with Christians who had spent their lives in holy pilgrimages and had visited Jerusalem *several times*.

The Mohammedans respect pilgrims still more than the Christians do, and the natural consequence was tolerance in all things, even towards those of a different creed: pious makers of a hazardous pilgrimage from the distant West. The gates of the city of God were often opened to let in two parties nearly equal; one disciples of the Koran, directed to Omar's Mosk, the other Christians for the Holy Sepulchre !

The following List of Popes of Rome, A.D. 1088 to A.D. 1316, will be found useful for reference. The authority is Haydn's "Dictionary of Dates" :—

Urban II., . . . 1088.	Promoted the First Crusade from 1096–1099.
Pascal II., ... 1099.	
Gelasius II., . . . 1118.	
Calixtus II., . . . 1119.	
Honorius II., . . 1124.	
Innocent II., . . . 1130.	
Celestine II., . . 1143.	
Lucius II., ... 1144.	
Eugenius III., . . 1145.	Promoted the Second Crusade, 1146.
Anastasius IV., . . 1153.	
Adrian IV., . . . 1154.	
Alexander III., . . 1159.	
Lucius III., . . . 1181.	
Urban III., . . . 1185.	
Gregory VIII., . . 1187.	
Clement III., . . . 1187.	Promoted the Third Crusade, 1188.
Celestine III., . . 1191.	Promoted the Fourth Crusade, 1195–1197.
Innocent III., . . 1198.	Promoted the Fifth Crusade, 1198.
Honorius III., . . 1216.	
Gregory IX., . . . 1227.	Promoted the Sixth Crusade, 1228.
Celestine IV., . . . 1241.	
Innocent IV. . . . 1243.	Promoted the Seventh Crusade.
Alexander IV., . . 1254.	
Urban IV., . . . 1261.	
Clement IV., . . 1265.	The Eighth and Last Crusade.
Gregory X., . . . 1271.	

Innocent V., . . ⎫
Adrian V., . . ⎬ 1276.
Vicedominus, . . ⎪
John XX., . . . ⎭

Nicholas III., . . 1277.
Martin IV., . . . 1281.
Honorius IV., . . 1285.
Nicholas IV., . . 1288.
Celestine V., . . ⎰ 1294.
Boniface VIII., . ⎱

Benedict XI., . . . 1303.
Clement V., . . . 1305.
John XXII., . . . 1316.

CÆSAREA PHILIPPI PANEAS, SOURCE OF THE RIVER JORDAN

CHAPTER II.

"FORWARD let the people go,"
Israel's God will have it so;
Though the path be through the sea,
Israel, what is that to thee?
He who bids thee pass the waters,
Will be with his sons and daughters.

E append as a useful prefatory note a chronological list of the Eight Crusades undertaken by the Christian powers to drive the infidels from the Holy Land, as given in " Haydn's Dictionary of Dates."

CHRONOLOGICAL LIST OF THE EIGHT CRUSADES.

FIRST CRUSADE, A.D. 1095, promoted by Pope Urban II., and commanded by Godfrey de Bouillon, resulted in the capture of Jerusalem, July 15, 1099.

SECOND CRUSADE, A.D. 1142–1148, preached by Bernard, led by the Emperor Conrad II. of Germany, and Louis VII. of France. Both armies mainly perished passing through Asia Minor.

THIRD CRUSADE, A.D. 1188–1191, led by King Richard of England, Philip II., and the Emperor Frederick I. of France and of Germany. Resulted in the capture of Acre.

FOURTH CRUSADE, A.D. 1195–1198, led by Henry VI. of Germany. Gained some victories, but ruined by internal dissensions.

FIFTH CRUSADE, A.D. 1198–1204, led by Baldwin, Count of Flanders, was perverted to the conquest of Constantinople, 1202, and so brought to a close.

SIXTH CRUSADE, A.D. 1228, by the Emperor Frederick II. of Germany. Entered Jerusalem. This was accompanied by that strange episode entitled " The Children's Crusade."

SEVENTH CRUSADE, A.D. 1256, by King Louis IX. of France (called St. Louis), defeated and captured in Mansourah, Africa.

EIGHTH CRUSADE, A.D. 1270, by the same. Died at Carthage, Africa. Pope Clement IV. discouraged, but could not prevent, this Crusade. In 1291 the Turks took Acre and dispossessed the Christian powers of all their hold upon the Holy Land.

As a comment upon the chronological confusion of the times, we append from Dr. Barclay's " City of the Great King," a second Table of the Crusades:

Crusade I.,	. . 1096–1099.	Capture of Jerusalem.
" II.,	. . 1147.	
" III.,	. . 1189.	
" IV.,	. 1202.	
" V.,	. . 1217.	
" VI.,	. 1238.	
" VII.,	. . 1245.	
" VIII.,	. 1270.	

Dr. Barclay wisely adds : " The cessation of the Crusades was not produced by any abatement of the love of arms, or of the thirst of glory in the chivalry of Europe. But the union with these martial qualities, of that fanatical enthusiasm which inspired the Christian warriors of the eleventh century, had been slowly but almost thoroughly dissolved."

The immediate causes of that unparalleled outbreak, entitled " The First Crusade," may easily be traced out by a due consideration of the preceding matter. The spirit of Pilgrimage just described was intensified by the Moslem persecution that was becoming more and more oppressive, and threatened soon to close the gates of the Holy City upon all Christian pilgrims. As European nations became more Christian, they looked eastward " for more light." The cruel oppression under which the people labored at home, suggested improvement through change of any sort. " The humane spirit of Christianity, the religion of love and kindness, had indeed struggled long with the manners and

Plain and Simple Customs of the People of the Middle Ages.

PREACHING THE CRUSADES.

maxims of the world; and as far back as the thick night of the
Sixth Century, Gregory had told his hearers that nature had *made
all men free*, and that the yoke of servitude, introduced by what
was called 'the law of nations,' was utterly repugnant to the law
of Christ.   Rude indeed were the manners then; man and wife ate
off the same trencher.   A few wooden-handled knives, with blades
of rugged iron, were a luxury for the great.   Candles were unknown.   A servant-girl held a torch at supper.   One, or at most
two mugs of coarse brown earthenware formed all the drinking
apparatus in a house.   Rich gentlemen wore clothes of unlined
leather.   Ordinary persons scarcely ever touched flesh-meat.   Noble mansions drank little or no wine in summer.   A little corn
seemed wealth."—(TAAFFE.)

As often happens, in great events, a strange and mighty *pre-
sentiment* had invaded all the nations in Europe for nearly a
century; a growing disquietude that at last broke out at the same
instant everywhere—north, south, east, and west.   It was a moment, too, when adventurers, and idlers, and vagabonds, were un

usually numerous in consequence of the recent civil wars and dis-charged armies. Bands of robbers and famishing soldiery were roving everywhere at discretion. Then, all at once, as if at the wave of some conjurer's wand, crimes and illegal proceedings ceased, and merged into THE CRUSADE. Europe enjoyed, during some months, a peace she had not known for a long time. Almost everything virtuous and everything vicious took the same direc-tion. Not one plunderer, robber, murderer, was any more to be found within the precincts of all Europe. One only thought and deed pervaded every community.* Nothing else was worth alluding to. Great and little, poor and rich, literate and illiterate, folly and wisdom, males and females, parents and children, sove-reign and subjects, priests and people — all had no other grave concern. Soon was there nothing but mutual encouragement; and who at first had blamed it as madness, became at last fully as mad as the rest. Impatient all to sell their property, and none to purchase but what was portable.

The opinion of most Christians then was, that the end of the world was at hand. All people were expecting *some great event;* no one knew what, yet something surpassing human vicissitudes. To popular imagination it seemed that all nature was busy an nouncing, by prodigies of every sort, and every day, what was the will of Heaven, and proclaiming it too clearly and loudly for any to misunderstand. Human laws were as nothing to those who conceived themselves called on *by the voice of God.* Moderation

---

* There is nothing connected with this whole subject that demonstrates the religious earnestness of the Crusades so much as the slight interest they gave to the geographical and archæological questions connected with the Bible and the Holy Land. The student, from the huge tomes of that period, the *Gesta Dei,* and a hundred others crowded with historical details, will learn absolutely nothing of the botany, the geology, the natural history of that most remarkable country. He will find no description of those extraordinary ruins of Baalbec and Palmyra. Although the Crusaders twice made campaigns into Egypt and up the Nile, no allusion to the Pyramids, so far as we have seen, appear in their Chronicles. In Palestine, we have no practical account by their writers of the Sea of Galilee and the Jordan, or that marvelous phenomenon, the Dead Sea. The Assyrian Inscriptions, near Beyrout, seem never to have attracted the atten-tion of the Warriors of the Cross. All this is a phase of the human mind worthy of special consideration.

Peter the Hermit—His Preaching and Character.

was cowardice, indifference, treason; opposition, sacrilege. Subjects scarcely recognized their sovereigns, and slave and master were all one to Christians. Domestic feelings, love of country, family, and every tender affection of the heart, were to be sacrificed to the ideas and reasonings that carried away all Europe. The whole West resounded with these holy words: "Whosoever bears not His Cross, nor follows me, is unworthy of me." So, when Peter the Hermit began riding on his mule from town to town, from province to province—a crucifix in his hand—his feet naked, his cowl thrown back, leaving his head quite bare, his lank body girt with a piece of coarse rope over his long, rugged cassock, with a pilgrim's mantle of the commonest stuff, the singularity of his attire, austerity of his manners, and his charity, had a great effect upon the people; and caused his being everywhere revered as a saint, and followed with enthusiasm by a great crowd, showing him a reverence not dissimilar to what Mohammedans of our own day have shown a Hadji just returned from Mecca, or beyond, where their prophet sleeps in Medina.

The Pope, Victor III., A.D. 1088, died without realizing his promise of attacking the infidels in Asia. The glory of delivering Jerusalem belonged to a simple pilgrim, possessed of no other power than the influence of his character and his genius. Some assign an obscure origin to Peter the Hermit; others say he was descended from a noble family of Picardy; but all agree that he had an ignoble and vulgar exterior. Born with a restless, active spirit, he sought in all conditions of life, for an object which he could meet with in none. The study of letters, bearing arms, celibacy, marriage, the ecclesiastical state, offered nothing to him that could fill his heart or satisfy his ardent mind. Disgusted with the world and mankind, he retired amongst the most austere Cenobites. Fasting, prayer, meditation, the silence of solitude, exalted his imagination. In his visions he kept up an habitual commerce with heaven, and believed himself the instrument of its designs and the depository of its will. He possessed the fervor of an apostle, with the courage of a *martyr*, and in the spirit of Oriental symbolism, it may be said that "he poured forth a shower of wisdom from his heart." His zeal gave way to no obstacle, and all

Peter the Great—His Preaching and Character.

that he desired seemed easy of attainment. When he spoke, the passions with which he was agitated animated his gestures and his words, and communicated themselves to his auditors.

Such was the extraordinary man who gave the signal to the Crusaders; and who without fortune and without name, by the ascendancy of his tears and prayers alone, succeeded in moving the West to precipitate itself in a mass upon Asia. As we explained in the preceding chapter, the fame of the pilgrimages to the East drew Peter from his retreat, and he followed into Palestine the crowd of Christians who went to visit the holy places. The sight of Jerusalem excited him much more than any of the other pilgrims; for it created, in his ardent mind, a thousand conflicting sentiments. In the city, which exhibited everywhere marks of the mercy and the anger of God, all objects inflamed his piety, irritated his devotion and his zeal, and filled him by turns with respect, terror, and indignation. After having followed his brethren to Calvary and the tomb of Christ, he repaired to the Patriarch of Jerusalem.

The white hairs of Simeon, his venerable figure, and, above all, the persecutions which he had undergone, bespoke the full confidence of Peter; and they wept together over the ills of the Christians.

With his heart torn, his face bathed in tears, Peter asked if there was no termination to be looked for, no remedy to be devised for so many calamities? "Oh, most faithful of Christians!" replied the Patriarch, "is it not plain that our iniquities have shut us out from all access to the mercy of the Lord? All Asia is in the power of the Mussulmans; all the East is sunk into a state of slavery; no power on earth can assist us." At these words Peter interrupted Simeon, and pointed out to him the hope that the warriors of the West might at no distant day be the liberators of Jerusalem.

"Yes, without doubt," replied the Patriarch; "when the measure of our afflictions shall be full, when God will be moved by our miseries, He will soften the hearts of the princes of the West, and will send them to the succor of the Holy City."

At these words Peter and Simeon felt their hearts expand with

Influence of the Hermit's Enthusiasm.

hope, and embraced each other, shedding tears of joy. The Patriarch resolved to implore, by his letters, the help of the Pope and the princes of Europe, and the Hermit swore to be the interpreter of the Christians of the East, and to rouse the West to take arms for their deliverance.

After this interview the enthusiasm of Peter knew no bounds; he was persuaded that heaven itself called upon him to avenge its cause. One day, while prostrated before the Holy Sepulchre, he believed that he heard the voice of Christ saying to him—" Peter, arise! hasten to proclaim the tribulations of my people; it is time my servants should receive help and that the Holy Places should be delivered." Full of the spirit of these words, which sounded unceasingly in his ears, and charged with letters from the Patriarch, he quitted Palestine, crossed the sea, landed on the coast of Italy, and hastened to cast himself at the feet of the Pope.

The chair of St. Peter was then occupied, A.D. 1088, by Urban II., who had been the disciple and confidant of both Gregory and Victor. Urban embraced with ardor a project which had been entertained by his predecessors; he received Peter as a prophet, applauded his design, and bade him go forth and announce the approaching deliverance of Jerusalem.

Then Peter traversed Italy, crossed the Alps, visited all parts of France and the greatest portion of Europe, inflaming all hearts with the same zeal that consumed his own. He went from city to city, from province to province, working upon the *courage* of some and upon the *piety* of others; sometimes haranguing from the pulpits of the churches, sometimes preaching in the high roads or public places. His eloquence was animated and impressive, and filled with those vehement apostrophes which produce such effects upon an uncultivated multitude.

He described the profanation of the Holy Places and the blood of Christians shed in torrents in the streets of Jerusalem. He invoked by turns Heaven, the Saints, the Angels, whom he called upon to bear witness to the truth of what he told them. He apostrophized Mount Sion, the Rock of Calvary, and the Mount of Olives, which he made to resound with sobs and groans. When he had exhausted speech in painting the miseries of the faithful,

Living Evidences of the Barbarity of the Infidels.

he showed the spectators the CRUCIFIX which he carried with him, sometimes striking his breast and wounding his flesh, sometimes shedding torrents of tears.

The people followed the steps of Peter in crowds. The preacher of the Holy War was received everywhere as a messenger from God. They who could touch his vestments esteemed themselves happy, and a portion of hair pulled from the mule he rode upon was preserved as a holy relic. At the sound of his voice differences in families were reconciled, the poor were comforted, the debauched blushed at their errors. Nothing was talked of but the virtues of the eloquent Cenobite. His austerities and his miracles were described, and his discourses were repeated to those who had not heard him and been edified by his presence. He often met in his journeys with Christians from the East who had been banished from their country, and wandered over Europe, subsisting on charity. Peter the Hermit presented them to the people as *living evidences* of the barbarity of the infidels; and pointing to the rags with which they were clothed, he burst into torrents of invectives against their oppressors and persecutors. At the sight of these miserable wretches the faithful felt by turns the most lively emotions of pity and the fury of vengeance; all deploring, in their hearts, the misery and the disgrace of Jerusalem. The people raised their voices toward heaven to entreat God to deign to cast a look of pity upon His beloved city; some offering their riches, others their prayers, but all promising to lay down their lives for the deliverance of the Holy Places. After this sketch, mostly from Michaud's "History of the Crusades," we have only room for two eloquent paragraphs from English and American writers:

" Nor did that poorly-dressed envoy of Christianity, preaching alike in churches, fields, and market-places, mid a scanty or unwilling auditory, when he descanted on the dangers, insults, afflictions, he had undergone, and far worse, those he had been a tearful eye-witness of, where so many of their fellow-Christians were doomed to suffer all kinds of ill-treatment and bitter scoffs, and horrid tortures for their religion. And he called upon them, by all they held dear, or deserving tenderness or veneration, and in the name of Him whom they feared and worshiped, and His divine, immaculate, and, far above all the rest of creation, most blessed Mother, and the

The Captivity of Jerusalem. The Standard of the Cross.

Godhead of her uncreated Son, that thrice-sacred Redeemer, that dearest Lord Jesus, when in His sempiternal, unearthly cause, He summoned every professor of this heavenly creed, to join hand in hand, without any distinction of country, sex, condition, rank, as the best preparation for that mighty day of Judgment that was surely very near, in one immense CRUSADE to expel those infidel dogs from where He left His mortal remains for our prayers and consolation, and to which no Christian but has undoubtedly a full right to go, for that worthiest of purposes, and far greater right than any person can have to any earthly inheritance from any mortal parent, or any lands from a worldly father, or houses, or money, or chattels" (TAAFFE).

"All the emotions of piety that had lain dormant were roused into lively action by a recital of the wrongs inflicted by the barbarians who held dominion over Palestine. The wild enthusiasm of the Hermit, Peter, sent a clarion blast ringing through Alpine passes and Switzer vales, from the vine-clad hills of France to the snow-carpeted plains of Scandinavia. He had a glowing, thrilling theme with which to play upon the heart-strings of the people. The Turk's proud foot spurned the dust once pressed by the meek footsteps of Christ. Jerusalem was captive. Through her courts and palaces a Moslem strode in defiance and reigned without rebuke. The Saracen's insulting heel was upon the Sepulchre of their Lord. Broken-hearted pilgrims, who came from afar, with faith and humility, to gaze upon those hallowed scenes, were buffeted, scourged, and pierced, brained, beheaded, and crucified. Their religion was profaned, their temples polluted. With these facts firing his own heart with indignation, and with his lips touched with a live coal from off the altar of eloquence, the zealous Anchorite hurried from place to place, from hamlet to city, from court to court, with the touching story of the suffering pilgrims, until every Christian prince and potentate was electrified, and all Europe was vocal with the battle-cry of the Crusaders. The Moslem war-drum, the taunting clash of the Turkish cymbals, and the shout of the haughty Saracen gave an answering echo from Lebanon's cedar heights, and Palestine's sacred mounts, baptized in the glory and blood of incarnate DEITY. The impetuous valor of Europe's chivalry, doubly armed and animated as they were with religious enthusiasm, could not long be resisted. The victory was won ; Jerusalem delivered ; the polluting infidels driven from the Holy Tomb, and the Moslem crescent made to trail beneath the floating standard of the Cross. Then came the pilgrims in increased numbers, of both sexes, all ages and conditions in life."

The prudent Pope Urban avoided trying to arouse the ardor of the Italians; he did not think their example at all likely to lead on other nations. In order to take a decided part in the civil war then raging, and to interest all Europe in its success, he resolved to assemble a second synod in the bosom of that warlike nation,

France, which, from the most distant times, had been accustomed to give impulsion to Europe. The new Council assembled at Clermont, in Auvergne, in November, A.D. 1095, was neither less numerous nor respectable than that of Plaisance; the most renowned holy men and learned doctors came to honor it with their presence and enlighten it with their counsels. The city of Clermont was scarcely able to contain within its walls all the princes, ambassadors, and prelates who had repaired to the council, so that towards the middle of the month of November the cities and villages of the neighborhood were so filled with people that they were compelled to erect tents and pavilions in the fields and meadows, although the season and the country were extremely cold. The council held its tenth sitting in the great square or place of Clermont, which was soon filled by an immense crowd. Followed by his cardinals, the Pope ascended a species of throne which had been prepared for him. At his side was Peter the Hermit, clad in that whimsical and uncouth garb which had everywhere drawn upon him attention and the respect of the multitude. The apostle of the Holy War spoke first of the outrages committed against the religion of Christ. He reverted to the profanations and sacrileges of which he had been a witness. He pictured the torments and persecutions which a people, enemies to God and man, had caused those to suffer who had been led by religion to visit the Holy Places. "He had seen," he said, "Christians loaded with irons, dragged into slavery, or harnessed to the yoke like the vilest animals. He had seen the oppressors of Jerusalem sell to the children of Christ permission to salute the temple of their God, tear from them even the bread of their misery, and torment their poverty itself to obtain their tribute. He had seen the ministers of God dragged from their sanctuaries, beaten with rods, and condemned to an ignominious death."

Whilst describing the misfortunes and degradation of the Christians, the countenance of Peter was cast down, and exhibited feelings of consternation and horror; his voice was choked with sobs; his lively emotion penetrated every heart. Pope Urban, who spoke after Peter, represented as he had done the Holy Places as profaned by the domination of the infidels. That land, consecrated by the presence of the Saviour, that place whereon He expiated our sins by His sufferings, that tomb in which He deigned to be enclosed as a victim to death, had all become the heritage of the impious. The altars of false prophets were raised within those walls which had contained the august assembly of the apostles. God had no longer a sanctuary in His own city. The East, the cradle of the Christian religion, now witnessed nothing but sacrilegious pomps. Impiety had spread its darkness over all the richest countries of Asia. Antioch, Ephesus, Nicea, had become Moslem cities. The Turks had carried their ravages and their odious dominion even to the Straits of the Hellespont, to the very gates of Constantinople, and from thence they threatened the West.

The Pope now addressed himself to all the nations represented at the council, and particularly to the French, who formed the majority: "Nation beloved by God," said he, " it is in your courage that the Christian Church has placed its hope. It is because I am well acquainted with your piety and your bravery that I have crossed the Alps and am come to preach the word of God in these countries. You have not forgotten that the land which you inhabit has been invaded by the Saracens, and but for the exploits of Charles Martel (A.D. 732) and Charlemagne (A.D. 768–800) France would have received the laws of Mohammed. Recall without ceasing to your minds the dangers and glory of your fathers. Led by heroes, whose names shall never die, they delivered your country, they saved the West from shameful slavery. More noble triumphs await you, under the guidance of the God of armies. You will deliver Europe and Asia; you will save the city of Jesus Christ—that Jerusalem which was chosen by the Lord, and from whence the law is to come to us."

As Urban proceeded, the sentiments by which he was animated penetrated to the very souls of his auditors. When he spoke of the captivity and misfortunes of Jerusalem the whole assembly was dissolved in tears; when he described the tyranny and the perfidy of the infidels the warriors who listened to him clutched their swords and swore in their hearts to avenge the cause of the Christians.

6

Urban redoubled their enthusiasm by announcing that God had chosen them to accomplish his designs, and exhorted them to turn those arms against the Mussulmans which they now bore in conflict against their brothers. They were not now called upon to revenge the injuries of *men*, but injuries offered to *Divinity*. It was now not the conquest of a town or a castle that was offered to them as the reward of their valor, but the riches of Asia, the possession of a land in which, according to the promises of the Scriptures, flowed "streams of milk and honey." The Pontiff sought to awaken in their minds by turns, ambition, the love of glory, religious enthusiasm, and pity for their Christian brethren. "There scarcely exists," said he, "a Christian family into which the Mussulmans have not brought mourning and despair. How many Christians every year leave the West to find in Asia nothing but slavery or death? Bishops have been delivered over to the executioner; the virgins of the Lord have been outraged; holy places have been despoiled of their ornaments; the offerings of piety have become the booty of the enemies of God; the children of the faithful have forgotten in bondage the faith of their fathers, and bear upon their bodies the impression of their opprobrium. Witnesses of so many calamities, the Christians of Jerusalem would long since have left the Holy City, if they had not imposed upon themselves the obligation of succoring and consoling pilgrims; if they had not feared to leave without priests, without altars, without worshipers, a land where still smokes the blood of Jesus Christ. I will not seek to dry the tears which images so painful for a Christian, for a minister of religion, for the common father of the faithful, must draw from you. Let us weep, my brethren, let us weep over the errors which have armed the anger of God against us, let us weep over the captivity of the Holy City! but evil be to us if, in our sterile pity, we longer leave the heritage of the Lord in the hands of the impious. Why should we taste here a moment's repose whilst the children of Jesus Christ live in the midst of torments, and the queen of cities groans in chains? Christian warriors, who seek without end for *vain pretexts* for war, rejoice, for you have to-day found *true ones*. You, who have been so often the terror of your fellow-citizens, go and fight against the barbarians, go and fight for the deliverance of the Holy Places; you, who sell for vile pay the strength of your arms to the fury of others, armed with the sword of the Maccabees, go and merit an eternal reward! If you triumph over your enemies, the kingdoms of the East will be your heritage; if you are conquered, you will have the glory of dying in the very same place as Jesus Christ, and God will not forget that he shall have found you in his holy ranks. This is the moment to prove that you are animated by a true courage; this is the moment in which you may expiate so many violences committed in the bosom of peace, so many victories purchased at the expense of justice and humanity. If you must have blood, bathe your hands in the blood of the infidels. I speak to you with harshness, because my ministry obliges me to do so. Soldiers of Hell, become soldiers of the Living God! When Jesus Christ summons you to his defence, let no base affections detain you in your homes. See nothing but the shame and the evils of the Christians; listen to nothing but the groans of Jerusalem, and remember well what the Lord has said to you: He who loves his father or his mother more than Me is not worthy of Me; whoever will abandon his house, or his father, or his mother, or his wife, or his children, or his inheritance, for the sake of My name shall be recompensed a hundred-fold, and possess life eternal."

At these words, the auditors of Urban displayed an enthusiasm that human eloquence had rarely before inspired. The assembly arose in one mass as one man and answered him with the unanimous cry, "*Dieu le vent! Dieu le vent!* (It is the will of God! It is the will of God!" "Yes, without doubt, it *is* the will of God," continued the eloquent Urban; "you to-day see the accomplishment of the word of our Saviour, who promised to be in the midst of the faithful when assembled in His name. It is He who has dictated to you the words that I have heard. Let them be your war-cry, and let them announce everywhere the presence of the God of Armies." On finishing these words, the Pontiff exhibited to the assembled Christians the sign of their redemption. "It is Christ Himself," said he to them, "who issues from His tomb, and presents to you His Cross. It will be the sign raised among the nations, which is to gather together again the dispersed children of Israel.   Wear it upon your shoulders and upon your breasts.   Let it shine upon your arms and upon your standards. It will be to you the surety of victory or the palm of martyrdom. It will unceasingly remind you that Christ died for you, and that it is your duty to die for him."

When Urban had ceased to speak, loud acclamations burst from the multitude.   Pity, indignation, despair at the same time agitated the tumultuous assembly of the faithful.   Some shed tears over Jerusalem and the fate of the Christians.   Others swore to exterminate the race of the Mussulmans.   But all at once, at a signal from the Sovereign Pontiff, the most profound silence prevailed.   Cardinal Gregory, afterwards St. Innocent II., pronouncing in a loud voice a form of General Confession, the assembly all fell upon their kness, beat their breasts, and received absolution for their sins.

WAILING PLACE, JERUSALEM.

POPE URBAN II. PREACHING THE FIRST CRUSADE.

CHAPTER III.

FROM EUROPE TO ANTIOCH.

BLEST land of Judea! thrice hallow'd of song,
Where the holiest of memories pilgrim-like throng;
In the shade of thy palms, by the shores of thy sea,
On the hills of thy beauty, my heart is with thee.

With the eye of a spirit I look on that shore,
Where pilgrim and prophet have lingered before;
With the glide of a spirit I traverse the sod
Made bright by the steps of the angels of God.

EARLY in the spring, A.D. 1096, it had become quite out of all possibility to restrain the impatience of the people. Further, penitence the most austere and sincere, and piety the most fervent, were henceforth to associate with the grossest impurity and every kind of low gaiety, worldly, and disfigured with vice. From the Tiber to the Northern Ocean, from the Danube to Portugal, all were hurrying to the Crusade. "The Welshman left his hunting; the Scotch abandoned his field sports; the Dane his drinking party; the Norwegian his raw fish." These all *in tears* who were to remain in Europe; those marching towards Asia showed nothing but *smiles* of hope and joy. They declared themselves the volunteers of heaven, and would not hear of any mixture of what is human. At every village the children asked, "Is that Jerusalem?" Happy in their ignorance, not a word of reason came from old or young, clerk or layman, nor did any one express astonishment at what now surprises *us*. All were actors; there

Heterogeneous and undisciplined Crowd of Crusaders.

was no audience,—posterity were to be that. To every class of the community the Crusade became the great business of life—the only real business—all things else were playthings for children. This was the mighty, universal law, absorbing or comprehending all other laws, civil, criminal, ecclesiastical, military, political, international. Those all were mere gewgaws or primers in comparison. Nor was there any exception even for the clergy; since they were men too! as pious and learned as you will, but still men like ourselves in substance, mere mortal men, and bound to worship Christ and prepare for doomsday, make their souls square and get in order for salvation. Yet swearers, cursers, pickpockets, highwaymen, robbers of every description, murderers, whole parties of the most scandalous of ruffians, and the vilest Delilahs and Jezebels, and such like, who embraced the adventure as a glorious speculation, resolved on the very reverse of any amendment of manners.

Immense armies, many of them, might have been formed out of that multitude; enough and far more than enough. But the chief captains agreed among themselves to set about making the preparations absolutely necessary, and then to take different roads, and meet again at Constantinople. But first of all it was requisite to skim off the dross and rid themselves of that heterogeneous and most unmilitary crowd. All the various gangs of that description proceeded in three divisions, with Sansavior leading the vanguard. The zealous Peter the Hermit, as fit for the mad hospital as any of them, convinced that a good hot will is enough to insure success in war, and that the undisciplined mob would obey his voice, figured at the head of that oddest of columns, in his woolen gown and with cowl and sandals, riding jovially that same she-mule which had carried him over all Europe, England included. But he had outriders, with his penniless lieutenant, Walter, who had been followed close by two of the horsemen; so there were only eight horses to be scattered through the main body. Altogether this division comprised at least a hundred thousand men, followed by a long train of rude vehicles, women, children, and the aged sick, decrepit, or valetudinarians: all relying on the miraculous promises of their more than Moses, for their holy Peter needed but to tread where he had trod already. They expected that the rivers would open to let them pass, manna to fall from Heaven to feed them.

The commanders were as miserable as their soldiers, "To the East asking alms;" and as long as they were in France or Germany they were not wrong in their expectations, for they *were* fed by the charitable.

Not so in Hungary; although its king had been known to the Hermit on his way home from Jerusalem, when that new convert had heard with sympathy of the poor palmers' sufferings. But his majesty was now dead; nor did his successor, though a recent Christian also, and in correspondence with the Pope, look with a kindly eye on these lawless crusaders. Neither would the Bulgarians, though Christians likewise, recognize the desperate fellows as their brethren, but treated them worse than they had ever treated former pilgrims. Cold charity was quickly over. So the crusaders, not contented with stealing, or with the strong hand seizing the cattle and driving them off openly, or sacking cottages, set them on fire, insulted, beat, even murdered the peasantry, and acted in like manner in the outskirts of some towns; whereupon the terrified and irritated Bulgarians rushed to arms and cut many of them to pieces, to say nothing of sixty whom they *burned in a church*, to which they had fled for protection, but perhaps deserved to find none; on which Sansavior struck off into the forests and wildernesses. Nevertheless, a considerable portion of the wretched forerunners got to Constantinople, and remained two months under its walls, the Emperor wisely refusing to let them inside the gates, but permitting them to wait there for the Hermit; where they sorrily could keep soul and body together on the coarsest food, doled out to them with the unkindest parsimony.

At length the Hermit reached Semlin—a city called by him *Maleville*, from the bad reception it offered them, namely sixteen, not indeed corpses, but arms and garments of so many of their own vanguard, by way of a scarecrow to deter them from following the example of those culprits. At which Peter in a rage gave the signal for war, and at the blast of a trumpet the desperate assailants slew forty thousand of the peaceable inhabitants; which horrid atrocity made the King of Hungary advance with a large army. But before his arrival Hermit and congregation had all run away and contrived to cross the Save, where they found villages and towns abandoned, even Belgrade, without a creature. Every one had sought refuge in the hills and woods.

Thence onward did our famishing crowd labor sadly, and at last approached, with expectations that were to be frustrated, the fortified town of Nyssa. Here, alas! they could not enter, and were only given some little food beneath its walls, on their promise of forthwith proceeding without perpetrating any misdemeanor. But a party of them, certain children of Belial, recklessly firing some windmills in the vicinity belonging to the citizens, these, vexed beyond all longer endurance, rushed out against the rear and put multitudes to death, likewise took numbers of prisoners, mothers and infants, many of whom were found living there in bondage several years afterwards. The miserable remnant crept forward without either food or arms, and so reduced in numbers found themselves in a far worse condition than ever.

But this extreme misery produced pity, which answered better than force, and the Greek Emperor charitably sent what enabled them to reach the walls of Constantinople. Yet the Greeks, not liking the Latins—and pardonably enough, if to judge by this sample—interiorly applauded the courageous Bulgarians, though the Emperor himself, not fearing the garrulous Peter nor his corps now unarmed and in the rags of indigence, advised them, with as much condescension as sincerity, to wait for the Princes of the Crusade.

But the second division had yet to come. This resembled the Hermit's, but rather worse. They were for the most part from the north of the Rhine and towards the Elbe, and led by a priest of the Palatinate, of the name of Gotschalk. Wholly occupied with robbing and all kinds of pillage, rapes, quarrels, murders, these worthies soon forgot Constantinople, Jerusalem, Jesus Christ himself. If any of them had ever had any religion they certainly lost the last traces of it. Not a law, human or divine, did they consider sacred. They were quite hurried away with their passions. The slenderest temptation was irresistible to them. Their ferocity was accompanied by imbecility, and would have worn itself out, probably, but that they fell victims to perfect barbarity, nor could expect to be saved by the laws of humanity which they had broken themselves.

Yet was there a third division of such frightful eminence in iniquity, anarchy, sedition, that no one had the hardihood to be its captain. These desperadoes scorned every obedience—civil, military, ecclesiastical; all to them a grievous yoke. And they would have none, but would live and die as free as born. What property does a baby carry into the world? or a corpse out of it? What lawgivers have they? Choosing to believe that the Crusade washed away all sins, they committed the most heinous crimes with the utmost indifference and a safe conscience. With a fanatical pride—or they feigned it—they despised and assaulted every one who did not join in their march. Not all the riches on earth were sufficient to recompense *their* self-devotedness; let God and the Church know that, in whose services they are, the only service they acknowledge. They declared themselves "the volunteers of Heaven," and would not hear of any mixture of what is *human.* All that should fall into their hands was rightfully their own, and but a small part of what was due them, an anticipated quota of the arrears of their pay, so much taken from the heathen. Of the lands they were traversing they were themselves the true owners; the proprietors should thank them if they left anything, and were in reality their debtors.

From such principles imagine what followed. This troop moved disorderly, and obeyed but the fits of their own insanity. They observed peremptorily that it was an enormous wrong to go against those who profaned the tomb of Christ without first slaying those who had crucified Him. Miraculous or pretended visions so inflamed their hate and horror, and all their diabolical appetites, that *they massacred all the Jews* on their line of march with the most abominable and unnatural tortures. So the contents of each miserable Jewry craved for *death* as other men for *life.* But the boon, without the preamble of being tortured, was rarely or never granted. Since they could find no captain they took *a goose* and made it march at their head, strutting pompously with a wave of

96   KNIGHTS TEMPLARS.

Massacre of the Jews.   Flight of the Hermit.

its body; or *a goat*, with a coquilico ribbon round its neck, and ascribed something of divine to it, and assured astonished beholders that it was equal to any priest or bishop. For which impudent jeer they are condemned by the chronicles more than for their deeds of tremendous guilt.

This carnage of the unresisting Jews inebriated such felons, and made them as proud as if they had vanquished the Saracens. But the Hungarians exercised their implacable swords on this division *to a man.* At least a very few individuals of it lived to join the Hermit under the Constantinopolitan bastions.

With this offal and what remained of all three of the divisions re-enforced by Normans, Venetians, Pisans, Genoese, and others that he had picked up, Peter the Hermit formed a new army of a hundred thousand, quite as undisciplined and simple, and wicked as his first, and at the head of this collection he set out along with his aide-de-camp Sansavior to try a fresh campaign. Many who left home pious, their piety went out on the road. Bold men got the upper hand, and bad example gives the law. Thus their robberies roused Constantinople and even various churches in its suburbs. Suffering from their neighborhood, the Emperor engaged to give them ships to transport them into Asia without any further delay. Advancing with the same temerity as before, a Turkish army cut them to pieces; poor Sansavior was run through the body *ten several times*, and the Hermit escaped by flight, so that in one single day that whole vast gathering disappeared, and left only a great heap of bones in a valley near Nice.

Europe was horror-struck at learning that of four hundred thousand Crusaders she had sent out all were totally butchered! Yet the extermination of their less worldly parts only increased the spirit-stirring glow of heroic and religious chivalry. The princes of the Crusade had not yet been ready. With Godfrey de Bouillon at their head, gathered nearly all the most illustrious captains of the time, and in a mass the nobility of France and of both banks of the Rhine and many of the English, and, indeed, of all Europe. No wonder then that the price of a war-horse rose to an excessive height, the funds of a good estate hardly sufficing to arm and mount a single knight. Germans and Hungarians

Advancement of the Crusaders.

were shown quite a different sight from the Hermit's army, which was only a villainous mob, and thus re-established the honor of the Crusaders in every land they went through. Hungary and Bulgaria wished Godfrey success, as he deplored the bad conduct and severe chastisement of those who had preceded him, but he did not once attempt to avenge their cause.

Nor is his conduct or that of any of the Crusade to be ascribed to deep political views, for such matters were utterly unknown to them. But what was purely accidental in those remote times, became to posterity, who judged of it by their own wisdom, the product of long foresight. The brother of the King of France and the King of England's eldest son were there mingled with their equals or superiors, many of them of the noblest birth and qualities and as unambitious as themselves. Several of the others nourished views of earthly ambition, no doubt, yet was it ambition of a very lofty kind. Monarchies, empires, diadems, and the summit of military reputation might enter for some share and mix with their religious feelings, even without their knowing it; still Hugh of Vermandois and Robert of Normandy had no projects whatever but *heaven* and *glory*.

Going round by Rome one division of the Crusaders were so scandalized to see the soldiery of a Pope and of an Anti-pope fighting for the Lateran, the capital of Christianity serving as a theatre of a civil war, that some of them refused to go any further and returned home. Profounder thinkers, reflecting that, in this life, a portion of the human must ever unite with the best of the divine, and that inasmuch as it *is* human it must be subject to imperfections, whence it is written, "the just man falls seven times a day," endeavored to shut their eyes and, after saying their prayers and visiting the curiosities, hurried away, and all the divisions of that mighty army soon met at Constantinople.

And most sumptuously were they treated in that celebrated metropolis, and entered it with all honors and every demonstration of joy and public welcome. Only it was expected that they would do homage to the Emperor; which Raymond, Count of Toulouse, refused, declaring he had not come so far to look for a master. Yet by surprise or cunning something that could be explained into

Capture of Nice. Bravery of the Crusaders.

homage was worked out of him, though an idle show. Tancred was the single exception, and he hastened his departure as the only way to avoid taking what at present was termed nothing, but might afterwards be construed into an oath of allegiance to Alexis. Amidst such amplitude of luxury and a constant variety of splendid amusements, few of the Crusaders but seemed to have forgotten the Turks; nearly all but Godfrey, who at last asked for boats. And the Latins crossed the Bosphorus and had advanced but a few leagues in Asia Minor when they accosted some slaves who had left Europe with the Hermit; and further on, towards Nice, a quantity of human bones told of that slaughter. That unfortunate Christian multitude had never been buried. Wolves and vultures had well-nigh consumed their flesh. So in sad silence the heroes of the Cross continued their march. It was a sight to end all discord and put a curb on every worldly ambition, at least for a time, but only warmed their zeal for the Holy War. So they took Nice June 20, 1097, and won the glorious battle of "Dorylæum," on the fourth of July.

This Crusade was equipped as hardy warriors ought to be, and in this sense it may be doubted if the world ever possessed a fairer army than that led by Godfrey, the victors of Nice and Dorylæum.

When they took the Turkish camp at this latter place, they found camels, animals till then unknown in Europe. This was July 4th, 1097. The Franks praised the Turks highly, and vaunted of their common origin. And chroniclers avowed that were the Turks but Christians, they would be equal to the Crusaders; that is, the bravest, wisest, ablest soldiers in the world. What the Turks thought is evident from their attributing the victory to a miracle. "And what wonder, since St. George and St. Demetrius were with our enemy?" "One sees you do not know the Franks," said Kilzig Arslan to the Arabs, who blamed his retreat; "you have never experienced their astonishing bravery! Such power is not human, but comes either from God or the devil."

On the 6th July, 1097, the Crusaders renewed their march eastward; nor found any more resistance throughout all Asia Minor, so completely had it been terrified by the day of Dorylæum; to

GATES AT NICÆA (now ISNIK) in BITHYNIA.

Capture of Antioch. Great Loss among the Crusaders.

which was now to be added the approach of the main body of the Frank army, to both of which was it owing that Tancred, with two or three hundred cavalry, galloping rapidly about, took town after town, the whole of Celicia and up to the south of Iskanderoon (Alexandretta), killing every Turk without repose or mercy.

The Crusading hosts reached the vicinity of Antioch, October 18, A.D. 1097, and undertook the siege. The city, four miles in circumference, contained a population of more than 200,000 souls. It was surrounded by a ditch deep and wide, and massive walls of

ANTIOCH.

defense. Its garrison of 30,000 was commanded by Baghasian, a most accomplished general; and so well did he use the means of defense that, assisted by famine, disease, discord among the assailants, and weariness of service, seven long months intervened before the city was taken. In the meantime, the greater part of the Crusaders were destroyed either in battle or by the unparalleled sufferings they endured. A number of the leaders returned to Europe. Baldwin, the brother of Godfrey, leaving the main army, marched to Edessa, a city 100 miles east of Antioch, where he was adopted by the King of that city, who dying shortly afterwards, Baldwin was crowned in his place.

This far-celebrated city of Antioch, was founded B.C. 300, by Seleucus Nicator, King of Syria, in memory of his father Antiochus. By the Christian period, it had attained to a great extent, and was extremely beautiful; it was reckoned as the third city in the world for beauty, greatness, and population. A vast street, with colonnades like "the straight street" in Damascus, was a marked feature in Antioch. Pompey enlarged the city; Herod the Great adorned it. Here the Christians had become so numerous about A.D. 41, that "the disciples were called Christians first in Antioch;" *Acts* xi. 26. It was a highly important situation in a military point of view; and the leaders of the Crusades felt the absolute necessity of reducing it before passing on 300 miles further to Jerusalem. The result vindicated their judgment; for its capture, A.D. 1098, and its possession until A.D. 1268—a period of 170 years—gave the Christian powers a strong center of operations, while its loss in A.D. 1268 was felt to be the irrevocable loss of Oriental dominion. Antioch was half-way between Constantinople and Alexandria in Egypt, being 700 miles from each. The place for a long time past has been known as Antakia. It was desolated by an earthquake as late as 1872, and now lies in almost indiscriminate ruins.

When the capture of Antioch was effected, May 3, A.D. 1098, and the Crusaders were preparing for repose, they were suddenly assailed by an incalculable host of Mohammedans from every portion of the surrounding country. Twenty-eight powerful princes (Emirs) led as many divisions of their forces to rescue this important city from the Christians. The whole, numbering more than half a million, was led by Kerboga, Prince of Mosul, as Lieutenant of the Sultan of Persia. The unexpected attack by such numbers, drove the Crusaders within the walls, where for a considerable period they, in their turn, were compelled to submit to a siege. A series of desperate battles followed; and at last, by the display of the same personal valor on the part of the leaders that had kept up the spirit of the enterprise from the beginning,

Armor of the Saracens.   Knights of the West.

these new forces of the enemy were defeated, and nothing further in the way of battles was experienced until after the capture of Jerusalem the succeeding year.

It seems proper here, to offer a brief account of the arms and armor of the period—to which this part of our book refers.

The Saracen chiefs wore armor of ring or chain mail, admirably wrought, strong, and capable of resistance; yet light and flexible, and in every respect *very greatly, superior* to the more massive and cumbersome personal equipment which the Crusaders carried with them to the first Crusade. This Oriental mail also was richly and delicately adorned with gilding, but had no additional defenses of plates attached to it. The head-piece, in like manner, was light, and afforded a remarkable contrast to the Western *heaume*. It was gilt and damaskeened with gold, with a far higher art than was then known amongst the armorers of the West. This casque, which was made of iron, was globular in form, or somewhat pointed at the crown. It was provided with a *nasal*, which was prolonged until it rose above the crown of the head-piece, where it expanded to receive a plume. The shield was small in size, round, boldly convex, and with an *umbo*, or boss, which projected and ended in a point. The offensive weapons were the dart, the scimitar, the dagger, the bow and arrows; and after the first Crusade, the lance was added. The inferior soldiers of the Saracens were, for the most part, archers.

The Knights of the West, well padded as they were, armed in mail and plate, and fastened to their saddles by the weight of their helms and of their double and triple armor, armed with long and strong lances, and mounted on immense Norman and Flemish horses, when formed in their long, well-dressed, and serried line, brought to bear upon their opponents a weight and a pressure that at first proved to be irresistible. Thus in the earliest engagements the Saracens were almost invariably broken and discomfited. But when they had acquired some experience of their invaders, the Saracens were not long in recovering all the advantages which for a while had been in abeyance. It was not possible for them to be unconscious of the fact that in their climate theirs was the superior equipment, and the more advantageous system of warfare. So they returned undismayed to a conflict which, for the moment, had appeared to be almost hopeless. Lighter and more alert than the Crusaders, they rushed, now on one flank of their massive battalions and now on the other. As their opponents were firm, yet almost powerless, they would sweep round them like a whirlwind; or if at any point they met with even a severe repulse, they returned speedily to the attack, with fresh vigor and in increased numbers. And they were brave warriors, those dexterous and indefatigable horsemen. They would beat down the leveled lances with their scimitars; and while the Knights, compelled to use their swords, were with difficulty bringing those weapons into play, the quick-eyed Saracens sought and found weak points where they might drive home their finely-tempered blades.

And again comparatively trifling obstacles, such as might naturally arise from the nature of the ground whereon they fought, would check, and perhaps completely paralyze, the otherwise resistless charge of the heavy cavalry (it was the old story of the phalanx repeating itself), and would expose them to be sifted by the Saracens with showers of arrows and with the tremendous Greek fire, which, above all, was the terror of the Crusaders. As a comment upon the ancient mode of warfare, we add a curious conclusion of a celebrated writer: "For myself, in my estimation the little modern *foot-soldier*, in the cloth tunic of his simple uniform, who stands firm and steady in the face of both rifled cannon and rifles, approaches nearer to the realization of the military ideal, and a more truthful impersonation of the chivalrous than the great Baron of the olden time, covered from head to foot with an iron sheathing of mail and plate. They certainly had the name chivalry in these days; but whether they possessed the thing itself—*the chivalrous*—is questionable."

The bows of the Moslem, whom the Crusaders encountered in Syria, were made of horn. Godfrey himself excelled in the use the bow, and more than one legend is preserved of his matchless skill in its use.

Concerning the sling but little can be said. It was made of woolen stuff. The slingers formed the lowest rank in the army

Armor of the Fourteenth Century.

Their position was in the rear of the men-at-arms, from whence they discharged stones from their slings; and in order to avoid the heads of their comrades in their front, they must necessarily have been high.

The infantry, in the Fourteenth Century, began to arise from out of its nothingness, and to assume on the field of battle that importance which, from thenceforth, was destined continually to increase. The power of this arm was first shown by the foot-soldiers and the archers of England, and this was done by them in a manner that was felt very severely by the French. At Crecy (August 26, 1346) the first lesson was given, and it was a very harsh one. On that day, however, the French army had in its ranks an infantry force which ought to have been able to have decided the victory. This was the corps of Genoese cross-bowmen, in the pay of France, which, in the first instance, was opposed to the English archers. Unhappily, the cross-bowmen had to open the discharge of their bolts while their bow-strings were still wet from a heavy shower, and so the missiles would not fly with their proper force. On the other hand, the archers of England had succeeded in keeping their bow-strings dry. When the Genoese desired to retire (and they had good reason for such a desire), King Philip, who, with his knights and men-at-arms, was in the rear of the Genoese, would not suffer them to fall back, and in his violent indignation, as a warrior of the knightly class, he exclaimed, "Forward, and strike down this useless rabble who thus are blocking up the way in our front!" And with his squadrons of cavaliers the king charged the army of England, *trampling under foot* the dead bodies of his own Genoese cross-bowmen.

A first rate archer, who in a single minute was unable to draw and discharge his bow *twelve times* with a range of 240 yards, and who, in these twelve shots, once missed his man, was very lightly esteemed. It is doubtful whether, at so great a distance, an arrow could have struck its mark with sufficient force to penetrate a knight's surcoat and hauberk of mail; but it would *kill his horse*, which was not yet provided with defensive armor, and this was the very circumstance which caused that change in tactics which has been mentioned. At all periods in history of warfare it always has been a matter of great difficulty for infantry to resist and repel the shock of a cavalry charge. In some ages, as for example in the Twelfth Century, this was a military problem for which it was held to be hopeless to seek for any solution; while at other periods, as in antiquity, this same problem was considered to be difficult, though by no means impossible to be solved.

IMPLEMENTS OF WAR.

In the ancient sacred Scriptures there is no evidence to show of what metal the swords of the warriors of Israel was made. In the Old Testament, however, iron and brass (or bronze) are mentioned together on several occasions, as in *Genesis* iv. 22; *Deuteronomy* xxxiii. 25; 1 *Samuel* xviii. 5–7; and 2 *Chronicles* xxiv. 12. The spear-head of Goliath of Gath (B.C. 1063) was of iron, while his defensive armor—helmet, target, greaves—was of brass: 2 *Samuel* xxii. 4–7. But the spear of that son of the giant who, in after days, when girded with a new sword, thought to have slain David, " was of brass; " 2 *Samuel* xxi. 16.

The earliest engines for discharging projectiles—in all probability the projectiles themselves were stones of great weight—were invented early in the world's history. Eight hundred years before the Christian era it is recorded of Uzziah, King of Judah (2 *Chron.* xxvi., 15) that " he made in Jerusalem engines, invented by cunning men, to be on the towers and upon the bulwarks, to shoot arrows and great stones withal." These engines were the *ballista*, originally designed to throw stones, and the *catapulta*, arrows; the *espringal, trebucket, mangonel*, etc., all having one purpose, but each one distinguished by some peculiarity either in its construction or operation. Then came names of animals, so-called; thus, the *scorpion* discharged small envenomed darts; and *the onager*, a machine for hurling stones. This had its name from the wild ass of the desert, which, on being hunted, was said to fling up stones with its heels at its pursuers. As the Middle Ages advanced efforts were made to improve the various military engines, but without any great success, until at length gunpowder was universally admitted to be the one supreme propellant. The use of gunpowder in Europe, however, did not prove so decisive for those

Gunpowder.   Use of Artillery.

who first availed themselves of it as to mark distinctly in history the precise time when its practice first took place.   The first mention of cannon in England is in June, 1338.   The first allusion to cannon by Froissart occurs in 1340, and then he appears to take it for granted that they were well known.   Edward III. of England certainly had cannon in 1346 ; and it may be assumed as certain that he used them at Crecy in that same year.   In 1378, Richard II. had four hundred pieces of artillery at St. Malo.   From the commencement of the Fifteenth to the middle of the Sixteenth Century the use of artillery is mentioned in various bombards of both large and small caliber, the later being designed to sustain an uninterrupted fire during the intervals required for reloading and discharging the former.   From the middle of the Sixteenth Century for a considerable time, the improvements in artillery chiefly consisted in rendering the guns more easily and expeditiously movable.   In 1500 Louis XII. of France was able to move his artillery from Pisa to Rome, two hundred and forty miles, in five days ; and his light pieces were taken rapidly from one point to another in a battle.   Francis I. of France had seventy-four pieces of ordnance in Italy in 1515.   And in 1556 the Emperor Ferdinand marched against the Turks with twelve heavy and one hundred and twenty-seven light pieces of artillery.   Such is a glance at the early progress of this powerful arm which, in the early part of the Seventeenth Century became of greatly increased importance under Henry IV. of France, Maurice of Nassau, and Gustavus Adolphus.   Although retaining too many calibers, the artillery of Gustavus Adolphus was admirably organized, embracing as it did limbers, carrying canister shot and other kinds of ammunition ready for action ; and what was no less important, having the allotment of a proportion of reserve artillery, in addition to that destined to accompany the troops during their movement in action. Moreover this distinguished commander was the first who fully appreciated the importance of causing the artillery to act in concentrated masses, and who well understood the saving of life consequent on taking into the field a due proportion of this arm.

To return to the subject of gunpowder; it may be traced up to a very early period, certainly to the Seventeenth Century before

Christ in China; and it is probable that the knowledge of it was brought to Europe from the Chinese through the Arabs, or, perhaps, direct by the Venetians. Or brought by the same means, it might have come to our quarter of the world from India, where a noisy propellant powder was known as early as the time of Alexander the Great, B.C. 330—this is recorded by Philostratus. Other writers speak of Indian combustibles; but a distinction must always be observed between the ancient inflammable compounds (such as might be used in peace for fire-works, or for causing conflagration in war) and those which have a propellant and explosive powder. In China, jingals, or small cannon, were in use three centuries before Christ; and probably much earlier. In some of the northern parts of China very ancient breech-loading jingals, with movable chambers for the charge and projectile, may still be seen. There is an authentic record of the use of cannon in China A.D. 757; and again A.D. 1232. In the year A.D. 1200, cannon balls were employed in warfare in India, and cannon were certainly known and used in the peninsula of Hindostan in great numbers long before they were known in Europe. Sulphur and niter are found in great abundance in both China and India; in the Sanscrit, gunpowder is *aigmaster*—" weapon of fire; " but, though the true propellant compound was certainly known in very ancient times in Hindostan, there exists in that country no positive historical record of the invention of it.

FLAGS.

The display of flags, always necessary in battle, was a marked incident in the combats of this period. In the Middle Ages three distinct classes of military heraldic flags were in general use, each class having a distinct and well-defined signification.

The PENNON, the ensign of knightly rank, small pointed, or swallow-tailed, and charged with a badge or other armorial device, was displayed by a Knight upon his own lance as his personal ensign.

The BANNER, square or oblong in form, larger than a pennon, and charged with a complete coat of arms, was the ensign of the sovereign, prince, noble, or Knight-Banneret, and also of the entire force attached to his person, and under his immediate command.

STANDARDS, BEAUSEANT, PENNON, FLAGS.

Battle Flags. War-Cries.

The STANDARD, introduced about the middle of the Fourteenth Century, large, of great length (its size varying with the owner's rank), appears to have been adapted for military display rather than for any specific significance and use in war. Except in Royal standards the English standard had the Cross of St. George next to the staff, and the rest of the field displayed various badges, sometimes accompanied with a motto.

WAR-CRIES.

" The blyssyd and holy martyr Saynt George is patron of this realme of Englande, and the crye of men of warre."—*Golden Legend*, 1500.

" To every erle and knyghte the word is gyven,
  And *cries a guerre* and slughones shake the vaulted heaven."—CHATTERTON.

The war-cry, *cri de guerre* of the French, is of the remotest antiquity. "The sword of the Lord and of Gideon"—the battle-cry of the Israelites when engaging the hosts of Midian in the valley of Jezreel. "To your tents, O Israel," is, perhaps, the earliest record of the use of the war-cry, which is now little used among civilized nations.

Each nation usually invoked its patron saint; but in war each party had its separate cry. The "*droit de bannière et le cri de guerre*," were conjointly the attributes of nobility.

The usual war-cry of the kings of England was "*Montjoie*," * "*Notre Dame*," " St. George."

At the siege of Jaffa the watchword of Richard I. was, "*Guyenne au Roi d'Angleterre*," and the war-cry " St. George, Guyenne."

"*Dieu et mon droit*," was probably a war-cry long before it was adopted as a royal motto, for Richard I. is recorded to have said, " Not I but God and our right have vanquished France at Gisors."

---

* This is the Mountjoye of the pilgrims to the Holy Land. A hill near Jerusalem, whence pilgrims first caught a glimpse of the Holy City, was called Mountjoy, or Montegioia; it was surrounded by a tower for their protection, and an Order of Knights instituted for their defense. Hence the term was applied to wayside marks showing the road to holy places. A heap of stones surmounted by a cross or by plaited branches of plants; and sometimes towers of refuge on the high road were so called. Pilgrims called these road-signs " monte gaudii "—mountjoyes—because, when they saw them they began to rejoice at having arrived at the end of their journey.

The war-cries of the Templars in battle were such passages in Latin, and Norman French, as were of Scriptural origin, such as military monks could use:—"*Dieu le veut*," or "*Deus id vult ;*" "*Non nobis, Domine;*" "St. Jacques for the Holy Cross;" "Ho for the Sepulchre;" and similar texts were used we know upon their guidons and in their documents. It is most probable, however, that those grim warriors went silently into mortal strife, and died as they lived in the taciturn spirit so much insisted upon in the Statutes instituted for them by St. Bernard.

It will serve to connect in a lucid chain the complicated events in this and the following chapters, if we present here: *First*, a list of the Chiefs and Patrons of the First Crusade, alphabetically arranged; *second*, the composition of the four Great Divisions engaged therein; and *third*, the march of each through Europe. Having these tables in view, and aided by the map, the reader can follow with understanding the routes from Europe to Antioch:

TABLE FIRST.

LEADERS AND PATRONS OF THE FIRST CRUSADE.

Adhemar, *Bishop of Puy* (France), Papal Legate and Spiritual Chief of the Crusades, accompanied the Fourth Division—wore the armor of a knight, and fought with undaunted valor. Died of pestilence at Antioch, A.D. 1099. He is reckoned " one of the mighty five " who deserve the most honorable record of the First Crusade.

Alexis I. (often written Alexius), *Emperor of Constantinople*. Played fast and loose with the Crusaders from the first. He reigned from A.D. 1081 to 1118, and was succeeded by his son John Comnenus.

Baldwin, Count of Hainault, brother of Godfrey. Made second King of Jerusalem, A.D. 1100. Died, at El-Arish, A.D. 1118. Held only the rank of Knight in the Crusade. Marched with the First Division. Quarreled with Tancred, and left the Crusade to be made King of Edessa in 1097; which place he resigned in A.D. 1100, to be made King of Jerusalem.

Baldwin du Bourg, cousin of Godfrey. Made third King of

Jerusalem A.D. 1118, under the title Baldwin II. Died 1131. Held only the rank of Knight in the Crusade. Marched with the First Division. His brother Almeric succeeded him as King of Jerusalem, 1162.

Bohemond, Prince of Tarentum (Italy), bastard son of Prince Robert Guiscard (the Sly), Commander of the Third Division. Of immense physical proportions, an eloquent orator, a dauntless warrior. Antioch was placed in his government when the column set out in the spring of 1099 for Jerusalem. He is reckoned among the five indomitables of the Crusade. Returned a few years later to Italy, and died.

Eustace, Earl of Boulogne (France), brother of Duke Godfrey. Marched with the Second Division.

Godfrey de Bouillon, Duke of Lorraine (France), leader of the First Division. In chapter vi., part 2, we give an account of this extraordinary man. Made first King of Jerusalem in 1099. Died, 1100. His two brothers, Baldwin and Eustace, and his cousins Baldwin and Almeric, were in the Crusade.

Henry IV., King of Germany, deposed 1106 by his son, Henry V.

Hugh, Earl and Count of Vermandois (France), known as " the Great Earl." Joint Commander of the Second Division. Brother of Philip I., King of France. Went back to Europe in some disgrace, but returned with valuable aid a few years later, and was killed, gloriously fighting, at Tarsus, in Cilicia.

Odo, Earl of Kent (England), *Bishop of Bayeaux* (France). Died 1096, in Italy, on his way to Palestine. Was attached to Duke Robert.

Peter the Hermit. Died 1115.

Philip I., King of France. Died August 3, 1108. A monster of sensuality and sluggishness, as his nickname, *L'Amoreux* (the Amorous), shows. He was excommunicated by the Pope, Urban II., in 1094.

Raymond, Count of Toulouse and St. Gilles, Duke of Narbonne (France). Clermont was in his dominions. An aged man, but hasty and impetuous; haughty and inflexible. He was the first temporal Prince who assumed the Cross. Had fought the

Leaders and Patrons of the First Crusades.

Saracens in Spain from his youth. Commanded the Fourth Division. Was accompanied by Bishop Adhemar and the nobility and bishops of Southern France. He was one of the noble five whose constancy and courage throughout the Crusade were unshaken.

Richard, Prince of Salerno (Italy), marched with the Fourth Division.

Robert Court-heuse, Duke of Normandy (France). Joint Commander of the Second Division; eldest son of William I., King of England. To his hand was entrusted, by Pope Urban II., the Great Standard of St. Peter. His grandfather, Robert I., a great sinner, had made the pilgrimage to Jerusalem, A.D. 1035, but died at Nice on his return, 1036. Performed deeds of great strength and valor, both in the capture of Antioch and Jerusalem.

Robert, Count of Flanders. So gallant a knight as to enjoy the title, "The Christian Lance and Sword." Joint Commander of the Second Division.

Robert, Count of Paris. Marched with the Second Division. Killed, July 4, at Dorylæum. Reckless as well of his own life as others'. Ventured to insult the Emperor Alexis in his own capital.

Stephen, Count of Blois and Chartres (France). Joint Commander of the Second Division. The wealthiest nobleman in Europe. His military skill was great, his contingent large. Went home in some disgrace, but returned to Holy Land a few years later with needed re-enforcements. Was taken prisoner at Ramleh by the Turks and murdered.

Stephen, Earl of Albemarle. Marched with the Second Division.

Tancred, cousin of Bohemond, and Lieutenant-General of the Third Division. Renowned in history and romance as the brightest exemplar of chivalry that the Crusades present. One of the first at the storming of Jerusalem. Died A.D. 1112. He was one of the five indomitables in the First Crusade. "A man sublimer than chiefs of Homer or Virgil; above even the love of praise," says one writer. King Godfrey used to say, "It will, by Heaven, be a very vile generation when the high name of Tancred ceases to be in honor." To boast of one's own bravery was in the purest spirit of Paganism; but only Christianity could inspire the heroic magnanimity of Tancred, when he bade his squire swear never to relate his feats to any one. Sublimer than chiefs of Homer or Virgil is he; above even the love of praise. It surpasses the heroic age. Yet is this reference to another world quite in unison with our religion.

Dr. Robinson (in "Biblical Researches") says that "after the Crusaders had got possession of Jerusalem, the country of Galilee, extending from Tiberia to Caifa, was given by Godfrey of Bouillon as a fief to the noble leader, Tancred. He immediately subdued Tiberias, administered the province with justice and equity, erected churches at Nazareth, Tiberias, and on Mount Tabor, and richly endowed them; so that his memory was long cherished in this region."

Urban II., Pope of Rome. Died A.D. 1099, the same year of the capture of Jerusalem. Declined to lead the Crusade on account of his general duties as Pope, but sent Bishop Adhemar as his legate. Succeeded by Pascal II., in 1099.

William II., King of England. Called also Rufus. Accidentally killed August 2, 1100, by Sir Walter Tyrrell.

TABLE SECOND.

COMPOSITION OF THE FOUR DIVISIONS OF THE FIRST CRUSADE, 1096–1099.

I. The *First Division* consisted of about 10,000 cavalry (Knights) and 80,000 foot. It was enlisted in the Rhenish provinces of France and the northern parts of Germany. It was under the command of Godfrey de Bouillon, who was accompanied by his brother Baldwin and his cousins Baldwin du Bourg and Almeric.

II. The *Second Division* has not given its numbers to history. It was enlisted in central and northern France, Normandy, Flanders, and the British Islands. It was under the joint command of Hugh, Earl and Count of Vermandois; Stephen, Count of Blois and Chartres; Robert (Court-heuse), Duke of Normandy; and Robert, Count of Flanders.

III. The *Third Division* consisted of about 10,000 cavalry (Knights) and 20,000 foot. It was enlisted chiefly among the Italians. It was under command of Bohemond, Prince of Tarentum, Italy, aided by his cousin Tancred.

IV. The *Fourth Division* was reckoned at about 100,000. It was enlisted in the south of France, the north of Italy, Spain and Portugal. It was under the command of Raymond, Count of Toulouse, and St. Gilles, accompanied by Adhemar, Bishop of Puy, who was the Papal Legate; the Archbishop of Toledo, and the Bishop of Orange.

TABLE THIRD.

THE MARCH OF THE RESPECTIVE DIVISIONS.

The *First Division*, under Godfrey, about 90,000 strong, left the River Moselle, August, 1096, and proceeded with perfect discipline to northern Hungary (see large Map). After a conference with the Sovereign Coloman (crowned 1095, died 1114), Godfrey continued to the south of Hungary, leaving his brother Baldwin and family as an hostage for the good behavior of his troops. At Malleville where they entered Greece, the hostages were released. Past Belgrade and Philippopoli, hearing of the imprisonment of Earl Hugh, by Alexis, Godfrey declared war in Thrace and pillaged the country for eight days. Informed of the release of his fellow-crusaders he continued the march, and the First Division reached Constantinople December 23, 1096. Then, after various contests with the Greeks, they crossed the Hellespont and encamped around Chalcedon.

The *Second Division*, under Hugh, Stephen of Blois, Robert of Normandy, and Robert of Flanders, set out early in the autumn of 1096, crossed the Alps into Italy, intending to make the journey to Palestine by sea. Receiving the consecrated banner from the Pope, they waited considerable time in the dissipations of Italy. Earl Hugh, impatient at the delay, engaged vessels for the East, but was shipwrecked and taken prisoner to Alexis, who released him and made him a friend. The rest of the Second Division left Apulia in November, and were the last at the rendezvous in the plains of Nice.

The *Third Division*, under the command of Prince Bohemond, assisted by the matchless Tancred, sailed for the shores of Apulia the last of November, and landed at Durazzo. Passing through Epirus, their crossing of the Vandar was disputed by the soldiers of Alexis, but they succeeded with some loss. Leaving the army at Rossa under command of Tancred, Bohemond went to Constantinople and held a conference with Alexis in the presence of Godfrey. Then Tancred led the army to Constantinople, where they arrived late in 1096.

CANA OF GALILEE.

The *Fourth Division,* under the command of Raymond, Count of Toulouse, etc., left Southern France in 1096, and occupied forty days in their march through Lombardy into Dalmatia to the confines of Epirus. The Greeks contested every step of the way, after their country was reached, and the Fourth Division reached Rossa after considerable loss. Here the army was left under command of Adhemar, and Count Raymond met his fellow-crusaders in Constantinople. His army was attacked by night and much cut up, but in time reached the Imperial City, and crossing the Hellespont joined the other three Divisions early in the spring of 1097, on the plains of Nice.

CHAPTER IV.

THE CAPTURE OF JERUSALEM.

WARRIORS and chiefs! Should the shaft or the sword
Pierce me in leading the host of the Lord,
Heed not the corpse, though a king's, in your path,
Bury your steel in the bosoms of Gath!

Thou who art bearing my buckler and bow,
Should the soldiers of Saul look away from the foe,
Stretch me that moment in blood at thy feet;
Thine be the doom which they dared not to meet!

Farewell to others, but never we part,
Heir to my royalty, son of my heart!
Bright is the diadem, boundless the sway,
Or kingly the dead which awaits us to-day.

THE city of Antioch, captured in the spring of 1098, had been for more than a year under Christian rule before the final march to Jerusalem was decided upon. As Mr. Taaffe elegantly says: "All this while was Godfrey stopped by Antioch, hard both to take and to maintain; and for a year and a half before it or within it, besieging or besieged, equally had the Franks to endure much and to suffer immense losses. This capital of Syria, with its massive fortifications of huge blocks of stone, and the iron bridge over the Orontes and both its banks were in quiet possession of the Latins, and the Turkish forces driven far away eastward of the Euphrates, but consequent on— ah! what tremendous sacrifices of life! Of all who left Europe only about fifty thousand now remained to set out for Jerusalem."

The distance, nearly three hundred miles, was over country one of the worst, for military aggression, in the world.   Along the great WAR PATH of Sesostris (B.C. 1400), Sennacherib (B.C. 700), and Cambyses (B.C. 500),—a path so hemmed in between the Lebanon mountains and the sea that rarely is there room for the narrowest column to deploy—along that military route whose every expansion has been battle-field, and where flanking parties can destroy the mightiest forces in detail, the Army of the Cross was to march to its objective point, Jerusalem.

It was March, A.D. 1099, when the "Armies of the Lord" were in full march down the coast.   Prince Bohemond, of the Red Flag, remained at Antioch as sovereign.   By a friendly agreement the cities of Tripoli, Beyrout, Sidon, Tyre, Acre, Cæsarea, and Joppa supplied them with provisions as they passed.   The harvests of the country had just been gathered, and there was no lack of supplies.   Their fleets sailed along the coasts, keeping usually in full view.   Setting out with fifty thousand fighting men from Antioch, they preserved their strength and numbers, with moderate losses, until in June they took possession of Lydda and Ramleh, eighteen miles west of Jerusalem.   The chiefs had bound themselves by the most solemn vows not to abandon each other or the cause they had undertaken; and Tancred, always the first where chivalrous enthusiasm was concerned, pledged himself by oath not to turn back from the road to Jerusalem so long as *forty knights* would follow his banner!   As they approached the Holy City all dissensions and pride seemed forgotten.   In their impatience to see it neither mountains nor defiles appeared difficult to them.   The soldiers scarcely allowed themselves time for repose, and often, against the commands of their leaders, marched swiftly forward.

In truth, this march from Antioch to Jerusalem demands a volume by itself, and if, in details, we observe a discrepancy among authors, this is not to be wondered at when we remember the illiteracy of the times and the proneness to exaggeration which characterizes chroniclers of all ages.   Mr. Taaffe, whose brain was a treasure-house of legendary lore, thus describes the march: " The memory of their exploits heightened their own constancy and confidence in themselves and valor; and the terror they had spread through the East made them be still held an innumerable army.

If they had yet somewhat of a train, all armies have camp-followers; but in their case that idle appendage kept every day decreasing. So the Emir of Tripoli paid them a contribution for peace, and without entering his town, they continued on. It was the end of May. Admirable was the order in the army—wonder of all beholders, say the chronicles. Every movement was by sound of trumpet; the least error in discipline punished severely; a regular school for all the details of a soldier's day, on or off guard, and nightly guards and videttes. The chaplains, too, were active in instructing; brave, patient, sober, charitable as ever they could, were those gallant warriors. Nor did the Moslem ever dare to stop them, such respect preceded their advance; not even in those defiles of which we read. A hundred Saracen warriors would have been sufficient to stop the entire of the human race. Beyrout's rich territory, and Sidon's and Tyre's they traversed, and reposed in the laughing gardens of those ancient cities and beside their delightful waters; the Moslem shut up peacefully within their walls, and sending plenteous provisions to the passing pilgrims, conjuring them not to damage their flowers and orchards, decoration, and wealth of their lands."

In a cool valley on the banks of the Sweet River they encamped three days. No more dreams of ambition, no attempt at getting rich. To be able to pay their troops, the chiefs, who for the most part had become poor, took service under the Count of Toulouse, though it must have galled their fierce spirits. But the nearer they drew to Jerusalem the more they seemed to lose something of their worldly loftiness and indomitable pride, and to have forgotten their pretensions, disputes, and pique. They passed Acre (accepting tribute from its Emir), Joppa, and the plain of that St. George who had so often aided them in battle, and thence off to Ramleh, within eighteen miles of the object of all their toils and wishes. On arriving they had not one single loiterer or superfluous creature. It was a selection of the very best warriors of all Christendom, such as it is not to be expected shall ever meet again. Most assuredly nothing similar is to be found in the history of past eras. Heroes whose like the world never saw, and will hardly see again; and therefore is unwilling to admit they ever existed, but rather insists

upon their being imaginary, and inventions of story-tellers and
poets.   But in truth they were of the same flesh and blood as
ourselves, but with sublimer minds and more energy of purpose.
We would not wrong our own period either.   Perhaps if we could
concentrate the choicest of every nation in Christendom, and
extract the quintessence of five or six millions, we might get
together such a band of heroes even now.   But it is very improbable that circumstances will ever occur again to call out such
multitudes of willing victims.   With time and fashion, weapons
and systems change.

EMMAUS—NEAR JERUSALEM.

At Emmaus, a few miles nearer Jerusalem, they were met by
a deputation of Christians from Bethlehem, who solicited a guard
of Crusaders to protect the venerable Church of the Nativity.
Whereupon the gallant Tancred was sent forward at midnight
with a choice detachment of warriors, and took possession of Bethlehem at daylight.   An eclipse of the moon occurred on that
same night, June 9, which served as an auspicious sign to the pilgrim warriors and has proved of eminent service to chronologers
ever since.

By day-break, June 10, 1099, the Army of the Lord ascended
the mountains of Benjamin 2,600 feet above the sea, and enjoyed

FIRST VIEW OF JERUSALEM BY THE CRUSADERS.

their FIRST VIEW of the Holy City. The whole assemblage was thrown into frenzy at the sight. It seemed too good to be true. Knights dismounted from their horses and bared their feet, as Moses at the Acacia Bush at Horeb. God had at last commanded the light into them out of darkness. Alternately they laughed and wept. They renewed the oath so frequently taken, " that they would deliver the city from the sacrilegious yoke of the Mohammedans." The afflictions they had suffered seemed to them but for a moment, and about to work for them a far more exceeding and eternal weight of glory.

The remembrance of all that that mighty city had beheld ; the enthusiasm of faith ; the memory of dangers, and ills, and fatigues, and privations endured and conquered ; the fulfillment of hope ; the gratification of long desire ; the end of fear and doubt, combined in every bosom to call up the sublime of joy. The name was echoed by a thousand tongues—*Jerusalem ! Jerusalem !* Some shouted to the sky ; some knelt and prayed ; some wept in silence ; some cast themselves down and kissed the blessed earth. " All had much ado," says Fuller, with emphatic plainness, " to manage so great a gladness."

The Moslem defender of Jerusalem at that period, Iftikhar Eddaulah, a brave and decided ruler, had ravaged the suburbs of the city, destroyed the fruit-trees, broken the tanks and cisterns, poisoned the living springs, and, in brief, surrounded himself with a desert of barrenness. He had caused provisions for a long siege to be collected within the defenses of the city, and employed his prisoners and large numbers of his people to raise the walls, repair the bulwarks, deepen the ditches, and construct machines of war. As every dwelling in Jerusalem then, as now, had its private cisterns and the large public tanks, such as Hezekiah's Pool and others, were very capacious, there was water for a protracted siege. The army of defense was reckoned at 70,000. The assailants by this time less than 50,000. The spirit of Saracenic war, in which this defense was made, had its exemplar in the day long afterwards, when the black banner of Tamerlane was hung out—the first day's *white,* meaning *surrender ;* the second's *red,* meaning the blood of *a few ;* the third's *black,* meaning *universal destruction !*

To the Moslem, Jerusalem was precious as the apple of the eye. The recorded loss of the cities of Mecca and Medina during the Nineteenth Century, and the conflagration of Mohammed's Tomb and other sacred edifices by the Wahabees, seem not to have excited the wrath and indignation of those fierce religionists so much as the loss of Jerusalem, July 15, A.D. 1099. It was then, according to their legends, that Mohammed ascended to paradise. Then the lightning flashed, the night of mystery shone forth, and that truth beamed, which according to their sages, has illuminated every part of the world.

The situation of this celebrated city may be studied to best advantage from the map. Its latitude is 31° 46′ 35″ North, its longitude East from Greenwich 35° 18′ 30″. It is thirty-two miles in a direct line from the sea; eighteen from the Jordan; twenty from Hebron; forty from Nablous; seventy-five from Nazareth; eighty from Acre; one hundred from Tyre; three hundred from Antioch. Its elevation above the sea-level, as already said, is remarkable. The northwest corner of the city, the site of Godfrey's tent, stands 2,610 feet above the sea; Mount Sion at David's Tomb is 2,537 feet; Mount Moriah at the Mosk of Omar 2,429 feet; while the Mount of Olives, at the apocryphal *Church of Ascension* is 2,724 feet. The circuit of the wall as it now stands is a little over two and a half miles. It is somewhat patched and piebald in appearance but substantial in build, and of strong materials, averaging about forty feet in height, including its symmetrical embrasures. An Arabic inscription over the Joppa Gate attributes the erection of the present wall to the Sultan Suliman I., A.D. 1542. The population of Jerusalem in 1873 was not far from 25,000, of whom some 10,000 were Jews.

Although writers upon the Crusades give the circuit of the city in 1099 at *four miles*, yet there is better reason to believe that the present wall is nearly identical in extent with that erected by the Romans under Hadrian about A.D. 125. Often partially destroyed and rebuilt, there were good topographical and mechanical reasons for using the *same foundations*, and to a considerable extent the same material. As to the latter, we find wrought into the wall beveled blocks—dating back to the very earliest periods—granite columns, and whatever of "the hard and heavy" comes first to the hand of contractors.

To the wall of Jerusalem at the present day there are seven entrances as the map will show, two of them, however, being permanently closed. The five gates now open, from sunrise to sunset, are :—

I. The DAMASCUS GATE—The North. This by the natives is styled *Bab es-Sham* or "Gate of Syria," because it opens in that direction, and *Bab el-Amud*, "Gate of the Column." Here Godfrey took his station in the assault.

II. The ST. STEPHEN'S GATE on the East. By the natives this is called *Bab Sitté Miriam*, or "Gate of the Lady Mary," because it opens towards the traditional tomb of the Mother of Jesus. Here the two Roberts and Tancred exerted their mighty valor.

III. The MUGRABIN GATE, on the southeast, often called "The Dung Gate." This is used chiefly by bearers of water from the Pool of Siloam and the Well of Jacob (Beer Ayub), both of which lie down the valley opening from that gate.

IV. The SION GATE, on the southwest. Called by the natives *Bab en-Neby Daoud*, or "Gate of the Prophet David," because it opens towards the edifice popularly termed David's Tomb.

V. The JOPPA GATE, on the west, called by the natives *Bab el-Khalil*, or "Gate of the Friend (of God)," because it affords passage to those visiting the Tomb of Abraham the friend of God at Hebron. Here fought that indomitable warrior Raymond of Toulouse.

Of the two gates permanently closed one is termed HEROD'S GATE, a little way east of the Damascus Gate. This is popularly termed *Bab es-Zahari*, or "Gate of Flavus." The other is styled THE GOLDEN GATE, about 800 feet south of St. Stephen's Gate. This is popularly named *Bab ed-Dahariah*, "The Eternal Gate." Besides these three are several closed doorways in the south wall of "The Noble Enclosure," or Mount Moriah.

The military situation of Jerusalem as against darts, bolts, stones, and battering-rams, to which it yielded July 15, 1099, seemed almost impregnable. If horrid ravines upon three sides, and immense walls guarded by deep moats can give confidence to a besieged city, they were there. If an army of defense nearly one-half stronger than their assailants could give confidence they were there. Truly there was not that " fair wind and equal partition of sun and wind " in this forty days' contest which the laws of European chivalry prescribe, nor did the Saracens display that furious "contempt of stone walls" with which their historians have accredited them. But this is only what Gibbon says of their founder, Mohammed, " when *weak* he recommended *patience*, when *stronger, defense*, when *strong, aggression !* "

On the 15th June, 1099, the fifth day after their arrival, the chiefs of the Crusade, having divided amongst themselves the work of assault, made the first attack upon Jerusalem. From the Joppa Gate to the Damascus Gate (2,868 feet as the wall runs) Godfrey de Bouillon, assisted by his relative, Baldwin de Bourg, and his brother, Eustace de Boulogne, undertook the assault. Here, as at the present day, the wall was the highest, the towers the strongest. Here, the battering rams of Titus had been set, 1,000 years before. Here, the generals of Nebuchadnezzar's army had made a breach and entered the city, 700 years still earlier. Every conqueror of Jerusalem since the time of David, who had effected an entrance by violence, had entered here. The tent of Godfrey de Bouillon, which was large, and distinguished by a silver cross on its summit, was pitched on the ground now occupied by the great Russian Convent. A ruined tower yet standing by that place is called by the natives " Tancred's Tower;" and it was near the Damascus Gate that Captain Warren found, in August, 1867, a stone with a Templar's Cross, which had formed a portion of an old wall, whose foundations he was exploring. He thinks the wall was built by the Crusaders 1099–1187, and was destroyed when the city was taken from them in 1187.

At the northeast corner of the city the work was parceled out to Robert, Duke of Normandy; Robert, Count of Flanders, and the irrepressible Tancred, who, having established his garrison at Bethlehem, five miles south, as recorded on a previous page, had ridden round by way of Mount Olivet to bear his part in the last act of this tremendous drama. This division reached from Herod's

Gate (2,262 feet as the wall stands) to St. Stephen's Gate, near the corner of The Noble Enclosure in which the Temple of Solomon once stood. South of that point the wall rose so high and was composed of stones so large that no assault by any numbers the Crusaders could command could possibly succeed.

Between this last division and that of Godfrey a space of about 1,200 feet was entrusted to Duke Alain Fergent, commanding the Bretons, an English party under Edgar Atheling, the Sire de Chateau-Giron, and Viscount de Dinan. To the south of Godfrey the western wall was given to Raymond, Count of Toulouse, aided by Rambaud of Orange, William of Montpellier, and Garston of Bearn. It will be seen that only about one-half the circuit of the walls could be subjected to assault, the deep ravines of Gihon and Hinnom on the west and south, and that of Jehoshaphat on the east, acting as natural defenses, not to be overcome by ten times the forces then assailing the city. Yet a modern traveler, viewing Jerusalem from the top of Mount Olivet, cannot avoid seeing that a single twelve-pounder from that eminence, under the modern appliances of war, would have shattered the defenses of the city in one day.

APPROACH OF THE ARMY TO JERUSALEM.

The assault of June 15, though undertaken without sufficient preparation, was keen and well-nigh successful. A chosen band

Assault on the City.   Immense Efforts.

of the bravest warriors, forming a close battalion, locked their shields together, and under this impenetrable canopy labored with pickaxes and sledges to demolish the walls. A party of their companions, ranged behind, kept the enemy at bay with arrows and slings. Although boiling oil, melted pitch, enormous wooden beams, and huge stones were showered down incessantly from above, these heroic men maintained their ground, and by their united exertions the outer wall was shattered in many places; but to their surprise and disappointment the inner one offered an insurmountable obstacle, owing to the steep and precipitous nature of the ground; neither had there been provided *more than one ladder* sufficiently high to reach the summit of the ramparts. But a few brave spirits, mounting this, fought hand to hand with the enemy, and it is probable the Crusaders would have entered Jerusalem that day had they been prepared with proper war-engines. The enemy they had to encounter, however, was brave and resolute, and as no miracle came to their aid they were obliged to sound a retreat.

All the energies of the host were now employed in constructing implements of war. Timber was procured from the Valley of Shechem, now Nablous, thirty miles north of Jerusalem. Some Genoese seamen having arrived at Joppa were pressed by the Crusaders into the service of the Cross, and by their mechanical skill greatly facilitated the construction of the engines required. Water in abundance existed at "Solomon's Pools," seven miles south, and in smaller quantities much nearer. Catapults, mangonels, and large movable towers were prepared, as in the siege of Nice, A.D. 1097; and to these were added a machine called the Sow, formed of wood, and covered with raw hides to protect it from fire, under cover of which soldiers were employed in undermining the walls, as a sow is seen to make excavations in search of food.

The engines being completed, the attack once more began. The towers were rolled on to the walls; the battering-rams were plied incessantly; the sow was pushed up to the foundations; and while the Saracens poured forth fire and arrows upon the besiegers, the Crusaders waged warfare with equal courage from their machines.

Thus passed the entire day (July 14) in one of the most tremendous fights that the hosts of the Cross had ever sustained.   Night fell, and the city still was not taken.   The wall of the town was much injured, but so were the engines used by the assailants.

Friday, July 15, 1099, was now appointed for a general assault, and it is safe after a thorough review of the situation, to affirm that a failure upon this day would have been the death of the Crusade.   As after Bonaparte's eighth assault upon Acre in 1799, the French army returned to Egypt and all his bright visions of an Eastern Empire were dissolved like a day-dream, so it must have been with the chiefs of the Crusades.   Their return to Joppa, to Antioch, and to Europe, would probably have quenched the Crusading spirit forever.   But this was not to be.   Godfrey, who was in command of the general assault, changed his plan of attack, and transported his great tower from the northwest to that part of the northeastern side of the wall between the Gate of Herod and the corner.   Here the fortification was lower, and the surrounding ditch being so deep, the enemy had placed fewer soldiers to defend it.   Three days had been spent by the Christians in filling up this trench; a stimulus having been given by the offer of a piece of gold to every man who would throw three stones in it!

The aid of religious enthusiasm had been called into requisition.   The soldiers had made a circuit of the doomed city, fully armed, in imitation of their predecessors in the armies of Joshua, twenty-five centuries earlier, when they besieged the city of Jericho, twelve miles east of Jerusalem, and "on the seventh day, rising early, about the dawning of the day, they compassed the city seven times" and the priests blew with the trumpets and the people shouted and "the wall fell down flat" (*Joshua* vi.).   The clergy with naked feet, bearing images of the Cross, had led the Crusaders in the sacred way.   Cries of *Dieu le vent, Dieu le vult* ("it is the will of God") had echoed in the pure mountain air, from Olivet, and from Scopus, and the voices of the little garrison of 100 lances in Bethlehem had responded *Dieu le vent*.   The melody of hymns and psalms took the place of trumpets in that circumambulation, and it is doubtful whether, in all the strange incidents connected

with the Holy City, anything more romantic had ever occurred
than that morning circumambulation.   It seemed then that every
man was resolved to die for Christ or to restore His own city to
Christian freedom.

And now the Saracens had repaired their wall and the Christians their engines, the assault recommenced, and was renewed
with equal ardor.   The leaders of the Christian army occupied the
higher stages of their movable towers and Godfrey de Bouillon
himself, armed with a bow, was seen directing his shafts against
all who appeared upon the walls.   The soldiers whom the machines could not contain were ranged opposite the walls, urging
the battering-rams, plying the mangonels, and, by flights of arrows, covering the attack from the towers.   The enthusiasm was
great and general; the old, the sick, and the feeble lent what weak
aid they could, in bringing forward the missiles and other implements of war, while the women encouraged the warriors to daring, both by words and their example; and hurried through the
ranks, bearing water to assuage the thirst of toil and excitement.
Still the Saracens resisted with desperate valor.   For their homes
and for their hearths they fought; and so courageously, that when
more than half the day was spent, the host of the Crusade was
still repulsed in all quarters.

At that moment a soldier was suddenly seen on Mount Olivet,
waving on the Crusaders to follow.   How he arrived there or who
or what this apparition was does not appear, or whether he was
not the mere creature of fancy.   But the idea instantly raised the
fainting hopes of the Christians.   Immense and almost supernat-
ural efforts were made in every quarter.   The tower of Godfrey
de Bouillon was rolled up till it touched the wall.   The movable
bridge was let down, and a Knight named Letoldus of Tournay
sprang upon the battlements—his brother Engelbert followed—
Godfrey himself came as the third in the noble contest—another
and another came to their support.   Baldwin de Bourg, and Eustace de Bouillon, who had stood by his brother as a lion by the
side of a lion, rushed in, and the glorious Ensign of the Cross announced to the anxious eyes of the army that Christians *stood
upon the battlements of Jerusalem.*   Tancred and the two Rob-

Flight of the Saracens. Terrible Slaughter.

erts, viz: Robert of Normandy and Robert of Flanders, burst open St. Stephen's Gate on the east, while Raymond of Toulouse, at the head of his Provençals, almost at the same instant, forced his way into the opposite part of the city by escalade, and in an inconceivably short space of time Jerusalem had changed hands.

We confess that we are not able to share in the feeling of horror and disgust evinced by almost every historian at the slaughter which followed. Surely they have overlooked the military rule that " a garrison resisting a general assault forfeit their lives." In the accounts of every war, in ancient and modern times, the usage has prevailed to put a garrison captured under such circumstances *to the sword*. The reproaches heaped with unsparing severity upon the brave men who captured Jerusalem after forty days' incessant assault apply equally to every great commander in every age. Yet Mr. Mills attributes the destruction of the Saracens, whose cry from the first had been " No quarter," to remorseless fanaticism. Mr. James, who as a romancer of history should have known better, says : " It is dreadful to read of the doings of the Crusaders that day." Major Proctor, of the British army, forgetting the horrors of the Peninsular War, and of the Sikh insurrection, styles the Army of the Lord " savage destroyers." Mons. Michaud's imagination " turns with disgust from the horrible picture." It will be well for mankind when all war and bloodshed meet the reproaches thus heaped upon the conquerors of Jerusalem. In the meantime let the circumstances be duly weighed and a more generous sentence yielded to them.

At the hour when the Saviour of the world had perished upon the Cross, 3 P.M., and upon that same day, Friday, forever infamous for his death, the feet of Letoldus touched the wall of Jerusalem. In this long summer day, July 15, there were yet five hours of daylight. The Moslem fought for a little while, then fled to their Mosks ; and notably to the Mosk of Omar, upon Mount Moriah, where, without further struggle, they submitted their necks to the slaughter. The Holy City, half a mile square, flowed with the blood of its defenders. Its streets—only lanes in width as compared with those of modern cities, for such is the Oriental manner—were piled with their bodies. Godfrey himself setting the example, the cry of *No quarter!* drowned every appeal for mercy; and all ages, both sexes, and all conditions shared alike in the horrors of the sack. Ten thousand people were killed in *The Noble Enclosure* alone (such is the name given to the level space on Mount Moriah); and it was exultingly reported to the Pope that in the Porch and Temple of Solomon, the Crusaders rode in the blood of Mohammedans "up to the knees of their horses"—a fanciful appreciation of *Revelation* xiv. 20. A few prisoners only were made, and then sold for slaves. Even the Jews were driven into their synagogues, and burned alive. Then the city was cleared of its carcasses, and its blood-stains washed away. Armor was reverently laid aside by the Knights, who, clothed themselves in linen mantles, led by Duke Godfrey, and with bare head and feet, walked in the habiliments of repentance, over all those places which the Saviour had consecrated by his presence, and in contrition of heart, with tears and groans, confessed their sins. Then the whole city was animated as by one spirit, "and the clamor of thanksgiving was loud enough to have reached the stars." And so Jerusalem was taken.

Mr. Taaffe sums up the siege, the assault, and the slaughter in these terse sentences:—

"One of the strongest fortresses in Asia, with a large valiant garrison, commanded by a noted Mohammedan, chosen on purpose for that arduous station, and well furnished with every necessary ammunition, and they themselves but a handful. Who ever heard, before or since, in the usual routine of war, of the besieged army being as numerous as the besieging? Here they are far more so. But none of the least worthy of these Franks but would have been a fit sergeant in our armies, or subaltern, or even captain, hundreds generals, and certainly several qualified to be commanders-in-chief to any army at present in Europe. Their discipline must much have struck the Arabs, for they continually talk of their coming on 'like a man.' In passing the narrow, rugged defiles of the hills of Judea, where the smallest resistance from an enemy would have delayed them, it is easy to believe that they interpreted their meeting none into a proof that He was delivering His Holy City up into their hands. And under the Moslem, who now held it, its circuit measured about three miles, in form an oblong square. The regular troops garrisoning it were forty thousand, the militia twenty thousand, and the body of Turks and other Mohammedans of every description that had come to join in the defence were at least ten thousand—in all seventy thousand

Consternation of the Saracens. March of the Army of Godfrey.

men, under the Fatimite lieutenant, an esteemed soldier, and his second in command, an Osmanli, of still greater military reputation. Its garrison, always numerous and brave, had been vastly increased for the occasion, and in every respect excellently provided to stand a siege. So when, during various attempts after forty days, they took it by assault at last, without any of the aids of modern warfare and little of the engineership then practised, not from want of talent and information, but want of timber; without even ladders, but only a few machines made on the spot; far from the sea, and with scarcity of wood and iron, there is something very like a miracle in their having taken it at all. Bloody was the struggle, indeed a giant fight, and too bloody necessarily the first unsparing blast of victory."

The consternation of the Moslem at the loss of Jerusalem is forcibly portrayed in a poem written by the Saracen bard, Modhaffer Abyverdy, upon this theme :—

"Our blood is mingled with our tears, and no part of our being remains to us that can be the object of the blows of our enemies.

"O misfortune! tears take the place of true arms when the fires of war break forth!

"How can the eye close its lids when catastrophes such as ours would awaken even those who slept in the most profound repose? 'Your brethren have no other resting-places in Syria but the backs of their camels and *the entrails of vultures!* '

"The Franks treat them like vile slaves, whilst you allow yourselves to be drawn carelessly along by the skirt of the robe of effeminacy, as people would do in perfect security!

"What blood has not flowed? how many women have been forced by modesty to conceal their beauty with their bracelets?

"Will the chiefs of the Arabs, the heroes of the Persians, submit to such degradation?

"Ah! at least, if they do not defend themselves, from attachment to their religion, let them be animated on account of their own honor, and by the love of all that is dear to them."

It was observed by the reader, that the army of Godfrey, in coming down from Antioch to Jerusalem in 1099, passed all the cities without attack. They were afterwards subdued, though with difficulty. Acre surrendered under Baldwin I., in 1104. Ascalon, August 12, 1099; Cæsarea and Joppa, shortly after. Beyrout and Sarepta were taken in 1104; Sidon, 1115; Tortose and Tripoli, about 1109.

A summary of the sieges, captures, and destructions to which the *City of the Great King* has been subject since the earliest period in which it appears on the page of history, will afford an appropriate termination of this chapter.

Upon the crown of Mount Zion stood "the City of Jesus" as early as the day of Abraham's return from the destruction of the kings, B.C. 1913; and Melchizedek went down from thence to "the king's dale" and gave him bread, wine, and a blessing (*Genesis* xiv).

Joshua fought against Jerusalem, took it and smote it with the edge of the sword, and set it on fire (*Judges* i. 8). This was B.C. 1451.

David, at the head of the choice warriors of Israel, 280,000 in number, headed by the indomitable Joab, took it by storm (1 *Chron.* xii). This was about B.C. 1046.

Shishak, King of Egypt, took the city from the feeble hands of Rehoboam and plundered it, B.C. 970.

The Philistines and Arabians captured Jerusalem about B.C. 885, and despoiled it of its treasures. This was its fourth siege.

Joash, King of Israel, captured the city about B.C. 835, and the walls were thrown down through a distance of 600 feet.

The Assyrians under Sennacherib, invested Jerusalem B.C. 711, under the rule of Hezekiah, but failed to take the city.

During the reign of Manasseh, and about B.C. 694, Jerusalem was captured by the Assyrians.

Under King Jehoahaz, B.C. 608, Jerusalem was taken by the Egyptians.

Under the reign of Jehoiakim and B.C. 606, the great Nebuchadnezzar possessed himself of Jerusalem.

The same fate befel the city under Jehoiachin B.C. 597, when a large number of the people were deported to Babylon.

Under King Zedekiah, B.C. 588, the Chaldeans again took Jerusalem; and now totally destroyed it, carrying into exile the few of the people who were spared. For more than fifty years the city was left uninhabited.

Under Zerubbabel, B.C. 543, a large company of Jews came from Chaldea, and began at once to rebuild the city.

Under Ezra, B.C. 457, a second contingent arrived.

Sieges, Captures, and Destructions of Jerusalem.

Under Nehemiah, B. C. 445, a third contingent arrived.

Then, for 280 years, Jerusalem was the shuttle-cock between Egypt on the west and the nations beyond the river Euphrates in the east. In this cruel game the Syrians took part, after B. C. 280.

Under the Maccabees, commencing B. C. 165, the city was again possessed by the Jews.

The Roman General Pompey captured it by assault, B. C. 65.

In A. D. 70, after a tremendous insurrection, the Romans imitated Nebuchadnezzar in his devastations 650 years before, and again Jerusalem was left a howling waste. For fifty years it disappeared from history.

The Emperor Hadrian, about A. D. 125, rebuilt the city. It was taken in an insurrection of the Jews under Bar-Kobas, about A. D. 132, and held for three years. Again the plough was passed over the ruins, salt was sown there, and "perpetual desolation" pronounced upon the site. A new city was erected under the name of *Ælia Capitolina*, as a compliment to Hadrian, whose surname was Ælia; and colonized by Roman soldiers. This was A. D. 136.

Under Constantine the Great, A. D. 312 to 337, Jerusalem recovered its ancient name, and was adorned with costly and magnificent Christian edifices. These were increased by the Emperor Justinian, A. D. 527 to 550.

In June, A. D. 614, the Persians under Chosroes captured the city by assault.

In 628, Jerusalem was recaptured by the Christians under the Emperor Heraclius.

Omar, the Moslem Caliph, took the city, A. D. 637; and from that period to 1099, it was held by one or the other nationalities professing the religion of Mohammed. Then it took its present name—El Khads.

July 15, 1099, the Holy City was taken by assault by the Army of the Crusade, under Godfrey, as we have shown in the present chapter.

October 18, 1187, the city capitulated to Saladin.

In 1219, it was ceded by the Saracens to the Emperor Fred-

Sieges, Captures, and Destructions of Jerusalem.

erick II.; and in 1243, it again came nominally into the hands of the Christians, but was soon abandoned as incapable of defense against the Khansmians. In 1277, it was nominally annexed to the Kingdom of Sicily. In 1517, it passed under the energetic sway of the Ottoman Sultan, Selim I.

Reckoning up the vicissitudes to which this most notable city has been subjected, we find that between Joshua (B.C. 1451) and Titus (A.D. 70), it was besieged *seventeen* times and twice *levelled to the ground!*

MOUNT CARMEL AND CAIFFA.

CHAPTER V.

ORGANIZATION OF THE KNIGHTS TEMPLARS.

I HAVE seen the flow of my bosom's blood,
  And gazed with undaunted eye;
I have borne the RED CROSS through fire and flood,
  And think'st thou I fear to die?

I have been where a crown of thorns was twined
  Round the dying Saviour's brow;
He spurned that life that lures mankind,
  And I reject it now?

I have been where thousands, by Salem's towers,
  Have bled for that NAME DIVINE;
And the Faith that cheered their closing hours
  Shall be the light of mine.

E begin this chapter with a List of the Grand Masters of Knights Templars from their organization, as a distinct military fraternity, A.D. 1113, to the martyrdom of James de Molay, A.D. 1313.

[Names are from Addison, corrected in orthography from Taaffe, Woof, Yarker, Mills, Mackey, and other authors. For dates we rely upon Addison, who differs much from others.]

1. HUGH DE PAYENS (Hugo de Payence; Hugh of the Temple). Installed February 15, 1113; died 1136.

2. ROBERT OF BURGUNDY (Lord Robert de Crayon). Installed 1136.

3. EVERARD DES BARRES (De Barri). Installed 1146; abdicated 1151, and devoted his life to penance and mortification.

4. BERNARD DE TREMELAY (Trenellape). Installed 1151; killed, in the battle of Ascalon, 1153. An illustrious Sir Knight, a valiant and experienced soldier.

Grand Masters of Templars.

5. BERTRAND DE BLANQUEFORT (Blanchefort) ([1]). Installed 1154; died June 19, 1156. A pious and God-fearing man.

6. PHILIP DE NAPLOUS (Philip of Nablous). Installed 1167; Abdicated in 1170. He was the first Grand Master born in Palestine. He resigned great possessions, and became a Templar after the death of his wife.

7. ODO DE ST. AMAND. Installed 1170; died, in captivity, 1179. A proud and fiery warrior, of undaunted courage and resolution.

8. ARNOLD DE TORROGE (Torrage, or Troye) ([2]). Installed 1180; died, on a visit to Europe, 1184. Had filled some of the chief situations of the Order.

9. GERARD DE RIDERFORT (Riderford or Ridefort). Installed 1185; killed, in the battle of Acre, October 4, 1189.

10. WALTER. ([3]) Installed 1189.

11. ROBERT DE SABLE (Sabloil, or Sabboil, or Sablæus). Installed 1191.

12. GILBERT HORAL (Erail, or Gralius). Installed 1194.

13. PHILIP DUPLESSIES (De Plesseis, or Du Plessis) ([4]). Installed 1201; died 1217.

14. WILLIAM DE CHARTRES (Carnota). Installed 1217; died, in Egypt, 1217.

15. PETER DE MONTAIGU (Thomas de Montagu). Installed 1218.

16. HERMANN DE PERIGORD (Herman Petragorius). Installed 1233; killed, in the battle of Gaza, 1244.

17. WILLIAM DE SONNAC ([5]). Installed 1247; killed, in the battle of Damietta, 1249.

18. REGINALD DE VICHIER (Vicherius). Installed 1251; died 1257.

19. THOMAS BERARD (Beraud) ([6]). Installed 1257; died, at Acre, 1273.

20. WILLIAM DE BEAUJEN. Installed 1273; killed in battle, at Acre, 1291.

21. THEOBALD GAUDIN (De Gaudini, or Gaudinius). Installed 1291; died 1295.

---

[1] Here Mackey inserts as No. 6 "Andrew de Montbar, 1165."
[2] Here Mackey inserts as No. 10 "John Terricus, 1185."
[3] Walter is omitted in Mackey's list.
[4] Yarker here inserts as his No. 13 "Terricus, or Thierry, 1198."
[5] Here Mackey inserts as his No. 17 "Armaud de Petragrossa, 1229."
[6] Here Mackey inserts as his No. 19 "William de Rupefort, 1244."

22. James de Molay (Jacques de Molai).   Installed 1295; burned at the stake, at Paris, 1313.

[For the list of successors of James de Molay, under the French system of Templary, see page 541.]

"Go forth to battle and employ your substance and your persons for the advancement of God's religion.   Verily, God loveth those who fight for his religion in battle array."—Koran, *Chapter* 56, *entitled* "Battle Array."

"Oh Prophet, stir up the faithful to war ! If twenty of you persevere with constancy they shall overcome two hundred, and if there be one hundred of you they shall overcome one thousand of those who believe not."— *Chapter* 8, *entitled* The Spoils.

"Verily, if God pleased, he could take vengeance on the unbelievers without your assistance, but he commandeth you to fight his battles that he may prove the one of you by the other ; and as to those who fight in defence of God's true religion, God will not suffer their works to perish."—Koran, *Chapter* 47, *entitled* War.

TO propagate religion by the sword was the life-work of the early Mohammedan.   War against infidels for the establishment and extension of the faith was commanded by the Prophet, and the solemn injunction became hallowed and perpetuated by success.

(732.)   Within a century after the death of Mohammed, which occurred June 7, A.D. 632, the Moslems had extended their religion and their arms from India to the Atlantic Ocean.   They had subdued and converted, by the power of the sword, Persia and Egypt, and all the north of Africa, from the mouth of the Nile to the extreme western boundary of that vast continent.   They had overrun Spain, invaded France, and, turning their footsteps towards Italy, entered the kingdoms of Naples and Genoa, threatened Rome, and subjected the island of Sicily to their laws and religion. But at the period when they were about to plant the Koran in the very heart of Europe, and were advancing with rapid strides to universal dominion, intestine dissensions broke out amongst them which undermined their power, and Europe for the time was released from the dread and danger of Saracen dominion.

In the Tenth Century of the Christian era, however, the ferocious and barbarous Turcomans appeared as the patrons of Mohammedanism, and the propagators of the Koran. These were wild pastoral tribes of shepherds and hunters, who descended from the frozen plains to the north of the Caspian, conquered Persia, embraced the religion and the law of Mohammed, and became united under the standard of the Prophet into one great and powerful nation. They overran the greater part of the Asiatic continent, destroyed alike the churches of the Christians and the tem-(1084.) ples of the Pagans, and appeared in warlike array on the Asiatic shore of the Hellespont in front of Constantinople. The terrified Emperor, Alexis I., sent urgent letters to the Pope and the Christian princes of Europe, exhorting them to assist him and their common Christianity in the perilous crisis. The preachings of Peter the Hermit, as we have seen, and the exhortations of the Pope Urban forthwith aroused Christendom. Europe was, as described in previous chapters, armed and precipitated upon Asia. The Turkish power was broken. The Christian provinces of the Greek empire of Constantinople were recovered from the grasp of the infidels; and the Latin Kingdom of Jerusalem was reared upon the ruins of the Turkish Empire of Sultan Soliman. The monastic and military Order of the Temple was then called into existence for the purpose of checking the power of the infidels, and fighting the battles of Christendom in the plains of Asia. Suggested by fanaticism, as Gibbon observes, but guided by an intelligent and far-reaching policy, this Order became the firmest bulwark of Christianity in the East, and mainly contributed to preserve Europe from Turkish desolation, and probably from Turkish conquest.

Many grave and improbable charges have been brought against the Templars by monks and priests who wrote in Europe concerning events in the Holy Land, and who regarded the vast privileges of the Order with indignation and aversion. Matthew Paris tells us that they were leagued with the infidels and fought pitched battles against the rival Order of Saint John. An American historian of high repute (Dr. A. G. Mackey) has also spoken of "the bitter feuds that always existed between the two Orders." But as cotemporary historians of Palestine, who describe the exploits of

Increase of the Christian Church.

the Templars, and were eye-witnesses of their career, make no mention of such occurrences ; and as no allusion is made to them in the letters of the Pope addressed to the Grand Master of the Order of St. John shortly after the date of these pretended battles, we omit all mention of them, feeling convinced, after a careful examination of the best authorities, that they *never did take place.**

At this distant day, when the times and scenes in which the Templars acted are changed, and the deep religious fervor and warm fresh feelings of bygone ages have given way to a cold and calculating philosophy, we may doubt the sincerity of the military friars, exclaim against their credulity, and deride their zeal. But when we call to mind the hardships and fatigues, the dangers, sufferings, and death, to which they voluntarily devoted themselves in a far distant land, the sacrifice of personal comforts, of the ties of kindred, and of all the endearments of domestic life, which they made without any prospect of worldly gain or temporal advantage, for objects which they believed to be just, and noble, and righteous, we must ever rank the generous impulses by which they were actuated among the sublime emotions which can influence the human character in those periods when men *feel* rather than *calculate*, before knowledge has chilled the sensibility, or selfish indifference hardened the heart. How can any one be indifferent to their nobleness, whose soul has been touched by this recorded lament over a deceased Knight. "Thou wert never matched of none earthly Knight's hand. And thou wert the courteousest Knight that ever bare shield. And thou wert the truest friend to thy lover that ever bestrode horse. And thou wert the truest lover of a sinful man that ever loved woman. And thou wert the kindest man that ever struck with sword. And thou wert the goodliest person that ever came among press of Knights. And thou wert the meekest man and the gentlest that ever ate in hall among ladies. And thou wert the sternest Knight to try mortal foe that ever put spear in the rest."

* It will be well, too, to keep in mind the foul imputations and slanders which any one sect of Papal Monks is in the habit of heaping upon another. The church books of the Middle Ages are filled with this. In this spirit the Knights Templars could not expect to escape slander.

That there should have been some small dissensions between the two Orders is a natural consequence of human defects, in which both parties may have erred from the strict rule. In the second and more diffuse edition of Addison's *Knights Templars*, that careful historian quotes De Molay himself as saying "there had been *no dissensions* between the Orders of the Temple and the Hospital prejudicial to the Christian cause; there was nothing more than a spirit of rivalry and emulation which should do best against the infidels, and a member of one Order had never been known to raise his hand against a member of the other!" This is a fine commentary upon an often-quoted passage of the Masonic lecture. What reader cannot recal the moment when, a neophyte in the Master's lodge, he was struck with admiration at this passage: "THE TROWEL is an instrument made use of by operative masons to spread the cement which unites a building into one common mass; but we, as Free and Accepted Masons, are taught to make use of it for the more noble and glorious purpose of spreading the cement of Brotherly Love and Affection—that cement which unites us into one sacred Band, or Society of Friends and Brothers, among whom no contention should ever exist but that noble contention, or rather emulation, of who *best can work* and *best agree!*"

(1099.) When intelligence of the CAPTURE OF JERUSALEM by the CRUSADERS had been conveyed to Europe, the zeal of pilgrimage blazed forth with increased fierceness. It had gathered intensity from the interval of its suppression by the wild Turcomans fifty years before, and promiscuous crowds of both sexes, old men and children, virgins and matrons, thinking the road then open and the journey practicable, successively pressed forward towards the Holy City. The infidels had indeed been driven out of *Jerusalem*, but not out of *Palestine*. The lofty mountains bordering the sea-coast were infested by warlike bands of fugitive Mussulmans, who maintained themselves in various impregnable castles and strong-holds, from whence they issued forth upon the high-roads, cut off the communication between Jerusalem and the seaports, and revenged themselves for the loss of their habitations and property by the indiscriminate pillage of all travelers. The Bedouin horsemen, moreover, making rapid incursions from beyond the Jordan, frequently kept up a desultory and irregular warfare in the plains; and the pilgrims, consequently, whether they approached the Holy City by land or by sea, were alike exposed to almost daily hostility, to plunder, and to death.

To alleviate the dangers and distresses to which they were exposed, to guard the honor of the saintly virgins and matrons, and to protect the gray hairs of the venerable palmer, nine noble knights, led by the stalwart Hugh de Payens, who had greatly distinguished themselves at the siege and capture of Jerusalem, formed a holy Brotherhood in arms, and entered into a solemn compact to aid one another in clearing the highways, and in protecting the pilgrims through the passes and defiles of the mountains to the Holy City. Their names are thus given by some authorities: 1. Hugh de Payens (that is, Sir Hugh of the Temple); 2. Godfrey de St. Aldemar (often written St. Omer); 3. Rolal; 4. Gondemar; 5. Godfrey Bisol; 6. Payens de Montidier; 7. Archibald de St. Amon; 8. Andrew de Montbar; 9. The Count de Provence.—WOOF. Warmed with the religious and military fervor of the day, and animated by the sacredness of the cause to which they had devoted their swords, they called themselves the *Poor Fellow-soldiers of Jesus Christ*. They selected as their Patroness *La douce Mère de Dieu*, " Mary, the Sweet Mother of God." At that period Knights were called Brothers (*Fratres*), and their guests *Christ's Poor*, or *The Poor*, without any consideration of their poverty or wealth, for it was the name given to the most opulent, and even royal or imperial personages.

These nine Knights renounced the world and its pleasures, and in the Holy Church of the Resurrection, in the year 1113, in the presence of Arnulph, Patriarch of Jerusalem, they embraced vows of perpetual chastity, obedience, and póverty, after the manner of monks. They elected as their first Master that true knight, Sir Hugh de Payens. Uniting in themselves the two most popular qualities of the age, *Devotion* and *Valor*, and exercising them in the most popular of all enterprises, they speedily acquired a famous reputation.

At first, we are told, they had no church, and no particular place

144   KNIGHTS TEMPLARS.

Mosk of Omar.   Knighthood of the Temple of Solomon.

of abode, but in the year of our Lord, 1118, nineteen years after
the conquest of Jerusalem by the Crusaders, they had rendered
such good and acceptable service to the Christians, that Baldwin
II., King of Jerusalem, the cousin of King Godfrey, granted them
a place of habitation within the sacred inclosure of the Temple on
Mount Moriah, amid those holy and magnificent structures, party
erected by the Christian Emperor Justinian, A.D. 540, and partly

MOSK OF OMAR—EL AKSA.

built by the Caliph Omar, about A.D. 640, which were then
exhibited as the Temple of Solomon, whence the Poor Fellow-
Soldiers of Jesus Christ came thenceforth to be known by the name
of THE KNIGHTHOOD OF THE TEMPLE OF SOLOMON.

By Mussulmans, the site of the great Jewish temple on Mount
Moriah has always been regarded with peculiar veneration. Mohammed, in the first year of the publication of the Koran, A.D. 610,
directed his followers when at prayer *to turn their faces towards
it*, and pilgrimages have constantly been made to the holy spot by

devout Moslems.   On the conquest of Jerusalem (637) by the Arabians, it was the first care of the Caliph Omar to rebuild " the Temple of the Lord." * Assisted by the principal chieftains of his army, this Commander of the Faithful undertook the pious office of clearing the ground with his own hands, and of tracing out the foundations of the magnificent Mosk which now crowns with its dark and swelling dome the elevated summit of Mount Moriah.

This great House of Prayer, the most holy Mussulman Temple in the world after that of Mecca, is erected over the spot where " Solomon began to build the House of the Lord at Jerusalem in Mount Moriah, where the LORD appeared unto David his father, in the place that David had prepared in the threshing-floor of Ornan the Jebusite" (2 *Cor.* iii. 1).   It remains to this day in a fair state of preservation, considering its great age of 1,200 years and up-wards, and is one of the finest specimens of Saracenic architecture in existence.   It is entered by four spacious doorways, each door facing one of the cardinal points: the *Bab el D'jannat,* or Gate of the Garden, on the north—(*Bab* signifies *Gate*); the *Bab el Kiblah,* or Gate of Prayer, on the south; the *Bab ibn el Daoud,* or the Gate of the Son of David, on the east; and the *Bab el Garbi,* on the west.   By the Arabian geographers it is called *Beit Allah* (the House of God); also *Beit Almokaddas,* or *Beit Almacdes* (the Holy House).   From it Jerusalem derives its Arabic name, *El Khuds* (the Holy), *Es Schereef* (the Noble), and *El Mobarek* (the Blessed).

The Crescent was torn down by the Crusaders from the summit of this great Mussulman Temple, and replaced by an immense golden Cross, and the edifice was consecrated to the services of the Christian religion, retaining its simple appellation, the Temple of the Lord.   William, Archbishop of Tyre and Chancellor of the Kingdom of Jerusalem, about A.D. 1185, gives an interesting account of the building as it existed in his time during the Latin dominion.   He speaks (Book I., Chapter 2) of the splendid mosaic

---

* This is the opinion of Mr. Addison and the most of authorities.   But that erudite historian, Baron de Vogüe, as we shall see further on, affirms that Omar merely erected *one of the smaller edifices,* but that the great Mosk was built some years later.

work on the walls; the Arabic characters setting forth the name
of the founder and the cost of the undertaking; and the famous
rock under the center of the dome, which is to this day shown by
the Moslem as the spot whereon the destroying angel stood, "having
a drawn sword in his hand stretched out over Jerusalem" (1 *Chron.*
xxi. 16). This rock, he informs us, was left exposed and uncovered
for the space of fifteen years after the conquest of the Holy City
by the Crusaders, but was, after that period, cased with a handsome
altar of white marble, upon which the priests said mass daily.

To the south of this Mussulman temple, and on the extreme
edge of the summit of Mount Moriah, resting against the modern
walls of the city of Jerusalem, stands the venerable Christian
Church of the Virgin, erected about A.D. 540 by the Emperor Justinian. Its stupendous foundations, remaining to this day, fully
justify the astonishing description given of the building by Procopius in his work concerning the edifices erected by Justinian.
That writer informs us that in order to get a level surface for the
erection of the edifice, it was necessary, on the east and south sides
of the hill, to raise up a wall of masonry from the valley below,
and to construct a vast foundation, partly composed of solid stone
and partly of arches and pillars. The stones were of such magnitude, that each block required to be transported in a truck drawn
by forty of the Emperor's strongest oxen; and to admit of the
passage of these trucks, it was necessary to widen the roads leading to Jerusalem. The forests of Lebanon yielded their choicest
cedars for the timbers of the roof, and a quarry of variegated marble, in the adjoining mountains, furnished the edifice with superb
marble columns.*

On the conquest of Jerusalem by the Moslems, A.D. 637, this
venerable church was converted into a mosk, and was called *Mosk
el-Aksa.* It was enclosed, together with the great Mussulman
Temple of the Lord, within a large area by a high stone wall,
which runs around the edge of the summit of Mount Moriah, and
guards from the profane tread of the unbeliever the whole of that

---

* We have inserted this sentence entire, but must correct the statement relative to the "quarry of variegated marble." There is no marble, properly so-
called, in any part of Mount Lebanon; neither in the vicinity of Jerusalem.

Mosk el-Aksa.   The Palace.   Temple of Solomon.

sacred ground whereon once stood the gorgeous temple of Solomon, wisest of kings.   When the Holy City was taken by the Crusaders, the *Mosk el-Aksa*, with the various buildings constructed around it, became the property of the kings of Jerusalem. It is denominated by William of Tyre "the Palace," or "Royal House to the south of the Temple of the Lord, vulgarly called

INTERIOR VIEW OF THE MOSK.

the TEMPLE OF SOLOMON."   It was this edifice or temple on Mount Moriah which was appropriated to "the poor Fellow-Soldiers of Jesus Christ," as they had no *church* and no particular place of abode, and from it they derived their name of KNIGHTS TEMPLARS. The Rules made concerning the Temple of the Lord also conceded to them the large court extending between that building and the

148 KNIGHTS TEMPLARS.

Revenues of the Order.   Churches of the Holy Land.

Temple of Solomon, a distance of about 500 feet.   The king, Baldwin, the patriarch, and the prelates of Jerusalem, and the barons of the Latin kingdom, assigned them various gifts and revenues for their maintenance and support ; and the Order being now settled in a regular place of abode, the knights soon began to entertain more extended views, and to seek a larger theater for the exercise of their holy profession.

Following this brief sketch of the ancient edifices by Mr. Addison, we would respectfully refer all students seeking correct information on the subject of important and distinguished religious edifices in the Holy Land, to the more elaborate and scientific account of De Vogüé, in his justly celebrated work on the " Churches of the Holy Land " (*Les Eglises de la Terre Sainte*).   It was unfortunate for this thorough and scholarly traveler that at the period of his visit, 1854, no Christian was allowed, at the peril of life, to enter the *Noble Enclosure,* in which these buildings stand.   At the present day, however, any foreigner (unless he be a Jew) may do so on payment of a small *backsheesh.*   Yet the Baron De Vogüe made such good use of his opportunities, and so availed himself of the observations of those who had gone before him, that but little is wanting in his descriptions to place these two edifices, so interesting to Freemasons and Knights Templars, before the eye of the reader.

The first aim and object of the Knights Templars had been, as before mentioned, to protect the poor pilgrims on their journey backwards and forwards from the sea-coast to Jerusalem.   But as the hostile tribes of Mussulmans, which everywhere surrounded the Latin kingdom, were gradually recovering from the terror into which they had been plunged by the successful and exterminating warfare of the first Crusaders, and were assuming an aggressive and threatening attitude, it was determined that the Holy Warriors of the Temple should, in addition to the protection of pilgrims, make the defense of the Christian kingdom of Jerusalem, of the Eastern Church, and of all the holy places, a part of their particular profession.   The two most distinguished members of the fraternity were Hugh de Payens and Geoffrey de St. Aldemar, or St. Omer, two valiant soldiers of the Cross, who had fought with great credit

KNIGHTS TEMPLARS. 149

Master of the Temple.   Rules of the Order.

and renown at the siege of Jerusalem in 1099.   Hugh de Payens was chosen, in 1113, by the knights to be the Superior of the new religious and military Society, by the title of "The Master of the Temple," afterwards "Grand Master;" and he has, consequently, generally been called the Founder of the Order.

1127.   Baldwin I., King of Jerusalem, foreseeing that great advantages would accrue to the Latin Kingdom by the increase of the power and numbers of these holy warriors, despatched (A.D. 1127) two Knights Templars to Bernard, Abbot of Clairvaux, with a letter, telling him that the Templars whom the Lord had deigned to raise up, and whom in a wonderful manner he had preserved for the defense of Palestine, desired to obtain from the Holy See the confirmation of their institution, and a rule for their particular guidance, and beseeching him "to procure from the Pope the approbation of their Order, and to induce his holiness to send succor and subsidies against the enemies of the faith."   Shortly afterwards Hugh de Payens himself proceeded to Rome, accompanied by Geoffrey de St. Aldemar, and four other brothers of the Order.   They were received with great honor and distinction by Pope Honorius (A.D. 1124–1138).   A great ecclesiastical Council **1128.**   was assembled at Troyes, in France, which Hugh de Payens and his brethren were invited to attend, and the Rules to which the Templars had subjected themselves being there described, Bernard undertook the task of *revising and correcting them*, and of forming a Code of Statutes fit and proper for the governance of the great religious and military fraternity of the Temple.

ABSTRACT OF THE RULES OF THE POOR FELLOW-SOLDIERS OF CHRIST AND OF THE TEMPLE OF SOLOMON.

1128.   This form of government is principally of a religious character, and of an austere and gloomy cast.   It is divided into seventy-two heads or chapters, and is preceded by a short prologue, addressed to all who disdain to follow after their own wills, and desire with purity of mind to fight for the most High and True King, exhorting them to put on the armor of obedience, and to associate themselves together with piety and humility for the defense of the holy Catholic Church; and to employ a pure diligence, and a steady perseverance in the exercise of their sacred profession, so that they might share in the happy destiny reserved for the holy warriors who had given up their lives for Christ.

Rules of the Order of the Temple.

The Rules enjoin severe devotional exercises, self-mortification, fasting, and prayer, and a constant attendance at matins, vespers, and on all the services of the Church, that being refreshed and satisfied with heavenly food, instructed and established with heavenly precepts, after the consummation of the divine mysteries, none might be afraid of the *Fight*, but be prepared for the *Crown*. The following are extracts from these Rules:

"VIII. In one common hall, or refectory, we will that you take meat together, where, if your wants cannot be made known *by signs*, ye are softly and privately to ask for what you want. If at any time the thing you require is not to be found, you must seek it with all gentleness, and with submission and reverence to the board, in remembrance of the words of the apostle, *Eat thy bread in silence*, and in emulation of the Psalmist, *I have set a watch upon my mouth;* that is, I have communed with myself that I may not offend, that is, with my tongue; that is, I have guarded my mouth, that I may not speak evil.

"XI. Two and two ought in general to eat together, that one may have an eye upon another. . . . .

"XVII. After the brothers have once departed from the hall to bed, it must not be permitted any one to speak in public, except it be upon urgent necessity. But whatever is spoken must be said in an undertone by the knight to his esquire. Perchance, however, in the interval between prayers and sleep, it may behove you, from urgent necessity, no opportunity having occurred during the day, to speak on some military matter, or concerning the state of your house, with some portion of the brethren, or with the Master, or with him to whom the government of the house has been confided. This, then, we order to be done in conformity with that which hath been written: *In many words thou shalt not avoid sin;* and in another place, *Life and death are in the hands of the tongue.* In that discourse, therefore, we utterly prohibit scurrility and idle words moving unto laughter, and on going to bed, if any one among you hath uttered a foolish saying, we enjoin him, in all humility, and with purity of devotion, to repeat the Lord's Prayer.

"XX. . . . . To all the professed knights, both in winter and summer, we give, if they can be procured, WHITE GARMENTS, that those who have cast behind them a dark life may know that they are to commend themselves to their Creator *by a pure and white life.* For what is whiteness but perfect chastity, and chastity is the security of the soul and the health of the body. And unless every knight shall continue chaste, he shall not come to perpetual rest, nor see God, as the apostle Paul witnesseth: *Follow after peace with all men, and chastity, without which no man shall see God.* Heb. xii. 14.* . . . .

---

* The reader must not look for exact quotations in papal writings: the true text is, " Follow peace with all men, and *holiness,* without which no man shall see the Lord."

Rules of the Order of the Temple.

"XXI. . . . . Let all the esquires and retainers be clothed in *black* garments; but if such cannot be found, let them have what can be procured in the province where they live, so that they be of one color, and such as is of a meaner character, viz., brown.

"XXII. It is granted to none to wear WHITE habits, or to have WHITE mantles, excepting the above-named knights of Christ.

"XXXVII. We will not that gold or silver, which is the mark of private wealth, should ever be seen on your bridles, breastplates, or spurs, nor should it be permitted to any brother to buy such. If, indeed, such like furniture shall have been charitably bestowed upon you, the gold and silver must be so colored, that its splendor and beauty may not impart to the wearer an appearance of arrogance beyond his fellows.

"XLI. It is in no wise lawful for any of the brothers to receive letters from his parents, or from any man, or to send letters, without the license of the Master, or of the procurator. After the brother shall have had leave, they must be read in the presence of the Master, if it so pleaseth him. If, indeed, anything whatever shall have been directed to him from his parents, let him not presume to receive it until information has been first given to the Master. But in this regulation the Master and the procurators of the houses are not included.

"XLII. We forbid, and we resolutely condemn, all tales related by any brother, of the follies and irregularities of which he hath been guilty in the world, or in military matters, either with his brother or with any other man. It shall not be permitted him to speak with his brother of the irregularities of other men, nor of the delights of the flesh with miserable women; and if by chance he should hear another discoursing of such things, he shall make him silent, or with the swift foot of obedience he shall depart from him as soon as he is able, and shall lend not the ear of the heart to the vender of idle tales.

"XLIII. If any gift shall be made to a brother, let it be taken to the Master or the treasurer. If, indeed, his friend or his parent will consent to make the gift only on condition that he useth it himself, he must not receive it until permission hath been obtained from the Master. And whosoever shall have received a present, let it not grieve him if it be given to another. Yea, let him know assuredly, that if he be angry at it, he striveth against God.

"XLVI. We are all of opinion that none of you should dare to follow the sport of catching one bird with another: for it is not agreeable unto religion for you to be addicted unto worldly delights, but rather willingly to hear the precepts of the Lord, constantly to kneel down to prayer, and daily to confess your sins before God with sighs and tears. Let no brother, for the above especial reason, presume to go forth with a man following such diversions with a hawk, or with any other bird.

"XLVII. Forasmuch as it becometh all religion to behave decently and

Rules of the Order of the Temple.

humbly without laughter, and to speak sparingly but sensibly, and not in a loud tone, we specially command and direct every professed brother that he venture not to shoot in the woods either with a long-bow or a cross-bow; and for the same reason, that he venture not to accompany another who shall do the like, except it be for the purpose of protecting him from the perfidious infidel: neither shall he dare to halloo, or to talk to a dog, nor shall he spur his horse with a desire of securing the game.

"LI. Under Divine Providence, as we do believe, this new kind of religion was introduced by you in the holy places, that is to say, the union of WARFARE with RELIGION, so that religion, being armed, maketh her way by the sword, and smiteth the enemy without sin. Therefore we do rightly adjudge, since ye are called KNIGHTS OF THE TEMPLE, that for your renowned merit, and especial gift of godliness, ye ought to have lands and men, and possess husbandmen and justly govern them, and the customary services ought to be specially rendered unto you.

"LV. We permit you to have married brothers in this manner, if such should seek to participate in the benefit of your fraternity; let both the man and his wife grant, from and after their death, their respective portions of property, and whatever more they acquire in after life, to the unity of the common chapter; and, in the interim, let them exercise an honest life, and labor to do good to the brethren: but they are not permitted to appear in the white habit and white mantle. If the husband dies first, he must leave his portion of the patrimony to the brethren, and the wife shall have her maintenance out of the residue, and let her depart therewith; for we consider it most improper that such women should remain in one and the same house with the brethren who have promised chastity unto God.

"LVI. It is moreover exceedingly dangerous to join sisters with you in your holy profession, for the ancient enemy hath drawn many away from the right path to paradise through the society of women: therefore, dear brothers, that the flower of righteousness may always flourish amongst you, let this custom from henceforth be utterly done away with.

"LXIV. The brothers who are journeying through different provinces should observe the rule, so far as they are able, in their meat and drink, and let them attend to it in other matters, and live irreproachably, that they may get a good name out of doors. Let them not tarnish their religious purpose either by word or deed; let them afford to all with whom they may be associated, an example of wisdom, and a perseverance in all good works. Let him with whom they lodge be a man of the best repute, and, if it be possible, let not the house of the host on that night be without a light, lest the dark enemy (from whom God preserve us) should find some opportunity.*

---

* This, by the way, is an Oriental custom of great antiquity. If the "lamp in the dwelling" has expired, the passer-by may be confident that the *house is empty* of its human inhabitants.

Rules of Bernard.   Hugh de Paynes.   Armor of a Knight.

"LXVIII. Care must be taken that no brother, powerful or weak, strong or feeble, desirous of exalting himself, becoming proud by degrees, or defending his own fault, remain unchastened.   If he showeth a disposition to amend, let a stricter system of correction be added: but if by godly admonition and earnest reasoning he will not be amended, but will go on more and more lifting himself up with pride, then let him be cast out of the holy flock in obedience to the apostle, *Take away evil from among you.*   It is necessary that from the society of the Faithful Brothers the dying sheep be removed.   But let the Master, who *ought to hold the staff and the rod in his hand*, that is to say, *the staff* that he may support the infirmities of the weak, and *the rod*, that he may with the zeal of rectitude strike down the vices of delinquents: let him study, with the counsel of the patriarch and with spiritual circumspection, to act so that, as blessed Maximus saith, The sinner be not encouraged by easy lenity, nor hardened in his iniquity by immoderate severity.   LASTLY.   We hold it dangerous to all religion to gaze too much on the countenance of women; and therefore no brother shall presume to kiss neither widow, nor virgin, nor mother, nor sister, nor aunt, nor any other woman.   Let the knighthood of Christ shun *feminine kisses*, through which men have very often been drawn into danger, so that each, with a pure conscience and secure life, may be able to walk everlastingly in the sight of God.*

1128. After the confirmation by a Papal bull of the Rules and Statutes of the Order, Hugh de Payens proceeded to France, and from thence he came to England, and the following account is given of his arrival.   "This same year, Hugh of the Temple came from Jerusalem to King Louis VI., in Normandy, and the king received him with much honor, and gave him much treasure in gold and silver, and afterwards he sent him into England, and there he was well received by all good men, and all gave him

---

* It has always been a subject of curious inquiry to moderns how an ancient Warrior Knight *put on* his complicated and heavy harness.   The method adopted by a Miles (Knight) was this.   Aided by his armiger or armor-bearer (esquire) he first inducted himself in his sleeves and shirt of mail.   Then the long-pointed *sollerets* or overlapping pieces of steel for the defence of the feet with the formidable spurs screwed into them.   Then the greaves for the legs and *cuisses* for the thighs.   Next came the breastplates adjusted to the body, to which were attached the *twilletes* or overlapping pieces which hang from the waist over the hips, and were fastened by thin straps.   Then the *van-braces* or defences of the forepart of the arm up to the shoulder.   Now only the neck, head, and hands were unguarded.   The *camail* was hung on the neck, the *sallet* was placed upon the head and the *guilles* on the hands and wrists.   **And so the Knight was in his steel armor closed full knightly**

treasure, and in Scotland also, and they sent in all a great sum in gold and silver by him to Jerusalem, and there went with him and (1096.) after him so great a number as never before since the days of Pope Urban," viz: Urban II., when the Crusades began. Grants of lands, as well as of money, were at the same time made to Hugh de Payens and his brethren, some of which were confirmed by King Stephen on his accession to the throne in 1135.

Hugh de Payens, before his departure, placed a Knight Templar at the head of the Order in England, who was called the Prior of the Temple. The Procurator and Vicegerent of the Master, whose duty it was to manage the estates granted to the fraternity, and to transmit the revenues to Jerusalem. He was also delegated with the power of admitting members into the Order, subject to the control and direction of the Master, and was to provide means of transport for such newly-admitted brethren to the far East, to enable them to fulfill the duties of their profession. As the houses of the Temple increased in number in England, sub-priors came to be appointed, and the superior of the Order in that country was then called the Grand Prior, and afterwards Master of the Temple.

An astonishing enthusiasm was excited throughout Christendom in behalf of the Templars; princes and nobles, sovereigns and their subjects, vied with each other in heaping gifts and benefits upon them, and scarce a will of importance was made without an article in it in their favor. Many illustrious persons on their death-beds took the vows, that they might be buried in the habit of the Order. Sovereign princes, quitting the government of their kingdoms, enrolled themselves amongst the Holy Fraternity, and bequeathed even their dominions to the Master and the brethren of the Temple. Bernard, at the request of Hugh de Payens, 1146. again took up his powerful pen in their behalf. In a famous discourse, "In praise of the New Chivalry," the Abbot sets forth, in eloquent and enthusiastic terms, the spiritual advantages and blessings enjoyed by the military Friars of the Temple over all other warriors. He draws a curious picture of the relative situations and circumstances of the *secular* soldiery and the soldiery of CHRIST, and shows how different in the sight of God are the bloodshed and slaughter perpetrated by the one, from that committed by the other. Addressing himself to the *secular* soldiers he says: "Ye cover your horses with silken trappings, and I know not how much fine cloth hangs pendent from your coats of mail. Ye paint your spears, shields, and saddles; your bridles and spurs are adorned on all sides with gold, and silver, and gems, and with all this pomp, with a shameful fury and a reckless insensibility, ye rush on to death. Are these military ensigns, or are they not rather the garnishments of women? Can it happen that the sharp-pointed sword of the enemy will respect gold, will it spare gems, will it be unable to penetrate the silken garment? Lastly, as ye yourselves have often experienced, three things are indispensably necessary to the success of the soldier; he must be bold, active, and circumspect; quick in running, prompt in striking; ye, however, to the disgust of the eye, nourish your hair after the manner of women, ye gather around your footsteps long and flowing vestures, ye bury up your delicate and tender hands in ample and wide-spreading sleeves. Among you, indeed, nought provoketh war or awakeneth strife, but either an irrational impulse of anger, or an insane lust of glory, or the covetous desire of possessing another man's lands and possessions. In such causes it is neither safe to slay nor to be slain. But now I will briefly display the mode of life of the KNIGHTS OF CHRIST, such as it is in the field and in the convent, by which means it will be made plainly manifest to what extent the soldiery of GOD and the soldiery of the WORLD differ from one another.* The soldiers of Christ live together in common in an agreeable but frugal manner, without wives, and without children. And that nothing may be wanting to evangelical perfection, they dwell together without separate property of any kind, in one house, under one rule, careful to pre-

---

* The Beauseant, at this time assumed by the Templars as a standard, formed of black and white cloth, was, for the first time, to be flown under the sky of Judea, where, for nearly two hundred years, its presence carried dismay into the ranks of the infidel, who fled like sparrows from a hawk on its approach. 'Tis strange the power this flag had over the minds of both friend and foe. By the one it was looked upon as the talisman of victory, by the other as the thunderbolt of destruction; and when we remember that, as long so the Beauseant flew, so long was the battle maintained by the Templars, we cease to marvel at superstitious awe with which it was regarded by the enemy.

serve the unity of the spirit in the bond of peace.   You may say,
that to the whole multitude there is but one heart and one soul, as
each one in no respect followeth after his own will or desire, but is
diligent to do the will of the Master.   They are never idle nor

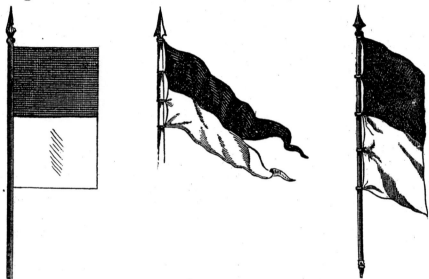

BEAUSEANT, OR BATTLE FLAGS OF THE TEMPLARS.

rambling abroad, but when they are not in the field, that they
may not eat their bread in idleness, they are fitting and repairing
their armor and their clothing, or employing themselves in such
occupations as the will of the Master requireth, or their common
necessities render expedient.   Among them there is no distinction
of persons; respect is paid to the best and most virtuous, not the
most noble.   They participate in each other's honor, they bear one
another's burdens, that they may fulfill the law of Christ.   An in-
solent expression, a useless undertaking, immoderate laughter, the
least murmur or whispering, if found out, passeth not without severe rebuke.   They detest cards and dice, they shun the sports of
the field, and take no delight in that ludicrous catching of birds,
which men are wont to indulge in.   Jesters, and soothsayers, and
story-tellers, scurrilous songs, shows, and games, they contemptu-
ously despise and abominate as vanities and mad follies.   They cut
their hair, knowing that, according to the Apostle, it is not seemly

in a man to have long hair. They are never combed, seldom washed, but appear rather with rough neglected hair, foul with dust, and with skins browned by the sun and their coats of mail. Moreover, on the approach of battle they fortify themselves with *faith within,* and with *steel without,* and not with gold, so that armed and not adorned, they may strike terror into the enemy, rather than awaken his lust of plunder. They strive earnestly to possess strong and swift horses, but not garnished with ornaments or decked with trappings, thinking of battle and of victory, and not of pomp and show, and studying to inspire fear rather than admiration.

"There is a Temple at Jerusalem in which they dwell together, unequal, it is true, as a building, to that ancient and most famous one of Solomon, but not inferior in glory. For truly, the entire magnificence of that consisted in corrupt things, in gold and silver, in carved stone, and in a variety of woods; but the whole beauty of this resteth in the adornment of an agreeable conversation, in the godly devotion of its inmates, and their beautifully-ordered mode of life. That was admired for its various external beauties, this is venerated for its different virtues and sacred actions, as becomes the sanctity of the house of God, who delighteth not so much in polished marbles as in well-ordered behavior, and regardeth pure minds more than gilded walls. The face likewise of this Temple is adorned with arms, not with gems, and the wall, instead of the ancient golden chapiters, is covered around with pendent shields. Instead of the ancient candelabra, censers, and lavers, the house is on all sides furnished with bridles, saddles, and lances, all which plainly demonstrate that the soldiers burn with the same zeal for the house of God, as that which formerly animated their great leader, when, vehemently enraged, he entered into the Temple, and with that most sacred hand, armed not with steel, but with a scourge which he had made of small cords, drove out the merchants, poured out the changers' money, and overthrew the tables of them that sold doves; most indignantly condemning the pollution of the house of prayer, by the making of it a place of merchandise."

Bernard then congratulates Jerusalem on the advent of the

Soldiers of Christ. "Be joyful, O Jerusalem," says he, in the words of the Prophet Isaiah, "and know that the time of thy visitation hath arrived.   Arise now, shake thyself from the dust," etc., etc. "Hail, O holy city, hallowed by the tabernacle of the Most High!   Hail, city of the great King, wherein so many wonderful and welcome miracles have been perpetually displayed!   Hail, mistress of the nations, princess of provinces, possession of patriarchs, mother of the prophets and apostles, initiatress of the faith, glory of the Christian people, whom God hath on that account always from the beginning permitted to be visited with affliction, that thou mightest thus be the occasion of virtue as well as of salvation to brave men!   Hail, land of promise, which formerly flowing only with milk and honey for thy possessors, now stretchest forth the food of life and the means of salvation to the entire world! Most excellent and happy land, I say, which, receiving the celestial grain from the recess of the paternal heart in that most fruitful bosom of thine, has produced such rich harvests of martyrs from the heavenly seed, and whose fertile soil has no less manifoldly engendered fruit a thirtieth, sixtieth, and a hundredfold in the remaining race of all the faithful throughout the entire world. Whence most agreeably satiated, and made most abundantly to overflow with the great store of thy pleasantness, those who have seen thee diffuse around them in every place the remembrance of thy abundant sweetness, and tell of the magnificence of thy glory to the very end of the earth to those who have not seen thee, and relate the wonderful things that are done in thee.   Glorious things are spoken concerning thee, City of God!"   This great and good man, to whom Knight Templary is so much indebted, died April 20, A.D. 1153, in the sixty-third year of his age.*

---

* This celebrated Churchman was born at Fontaine, near Dijon, in Burgundy, in 1091.   From his earliest days his aspirations had been towards the Church, and in 1113 he became Monk of Citeaux.   In 1115 he founded a new branch of the Cistercian Order at Clairvaux, in Champagne, and was elected its first Abbot. He died on 20th August, 1153, and was canonized by Alexander III. in 1174. His austerity, fastings, solitary studies, and burning eloquence made him, during his lifetime, the oracle of Christendom.   Crowds followed wherever he went, and listened with rapture and awe to his stirring language.   Dry, cold, scholastic argument characterized the Churchmen of his day; they never got beyond

Dress and Emblems of the Knights Templars.

The following illustrations of the dress and emblems of the Knights Templars, will be read with interest in this connection :

The Dress of the Pilgrim was an under-vest with an outer robe, having half open sleeves, showing the under sleeves, which continued to the wrists. On his head a broad-brimmed hat, with a shell in front; on his feet sandals, or short laced boots; in his hand a staff, and by his side a scrip.

An Escallop Shell was the Pilgrim's ensign in their pilgrimages to holy places. They were worn on their hoods and hats, and were of such a distinguishing character that Pope Alexander IV., by a bull, forbade the use of them but to pilgrims who were truly noble.*

A Calvary Cross represents the cross on which our Saviour suffered on Mount Calvary, and is always set upon three steps, term-

---

quibbles and rule, so that the vivid pictures flashing from the mind of Bernard, in the most eloquent language, relieved the darkness that had fallen upon the preachers of the Church. He was styled the "Mellifluous Doctor," and his writings "a river of Paradise." By his personal exertions he repressed the persecution of the Jews in Germany. Luther pays him the high, but justly-merited compliment, that " if there ever lived on earth a God-fearing and holy monk, it was St. Bernard of Clairvaux." A character of so much benevolence and devoutness, such as that of St. Bernard, could not but be enchanted with the Order of the Temple, as in it he recognized the offspring of his feelings that promoted to deeds of charity and acts in honor of God. He had already been prepossessed in favor of the Order, and three years before the arrival of the envoys, had written to the Count of Champagne, upon the occasion of that nobleman joining the ranks of the Templars, approving highly of the step, as one pleasing in the eyes of God. He had never recovered from the mortification he felt at the disastrous termination of the Second Crusade. According to Gibbon, he had been stigmatized as a false prophet, as the cause of public and private mourning; and while his friends were covered with confusion, his enemies exulted in his defeat. His justification was slow and unsatisfactory, and his principal defense was that he had obeyed the commands of the Pope. It preyed, however, so much on his mind that he gradually sank under mental agony and died.

* The sea-beach at Joppa presents a windrow of these shells, white, brown, purple, and red. Many species are collected there, the most common of which is the *Pilgrim's Scallop*, with its five ridges, representing the birth, life, death, resurrection and ascension of Jesus. By the labors of the *American Holy Land Exploration* many thousands of these historical objects have been distributed among Christian believers in this country.

ed grices.   The three steps are said to signify the three qualities whereby we mount up to Christ—Hope, Faith, and Charity.

A Patriarchial Cross is so called from its being appropriated to patriarchs.   It is said the Patriarchal Cross is crossed twice, to denote that the work of redemption which was wrought on the Cross extended to both Jews and Gentiles.

The Crozier (according to Polydore Virgil) was given to bishops to chastise the vices of the people.   It is called Bascules Pastoralis.   It is given to them in respect to their pastoral charge and superintendence over their flocks, as well for feeding them with wholesome doctrine as for defending them from the incursions of the wolf, wherein they imitate the good and watchful shepherd, to whose crook this Crozier has a resemblance.

The Cock is a bird of noble courage; he is always prepared for battle, having his comb for a helmet, his beak for a cutlass to wound the enemy, and is a complete warrior, armed cap-a-pie.   He hath legs armed with spurs, giving example to the valiant soldier to resist dangers by fight and not by flight.

Eminent Sir Knight F. Webber, A.M., of Louisville, Kentucky, an erudite writer upon this theme, says, in a late article: "To accomplish a pilgrimage to the Holy Land was a meritorious achievement, and at once commanded the respect, esteem, and admiration of all men, more particularly Christians; hence those who thus distinguished themselves chose an appropriate device for their shield or coat arms.   The escallop shell was generally chosen by pilgrims from two reasons: First, because they decorated their dress with these shells; and, secondly, because they allude to those of the apostles who were fishermen, and therefore invoked their protection for their arduous journey. So highly were these escallop shells prized by the Christians that Pope Alexander IV., by a bull, prohibited the assumption of escallop shells as armorial devices by all but 'pilgrims who were truly noble.' "

CHAPTER VI.

ORGANIZATION OF THE KNIGHTS OF ST. JOHN, OR KNIGHTS
HOSPITALERS.

A STEED! a steed! of matchless speed;
A sword, of metal keen;
All else to noble minds is dross,
All else on earth is mean.

E commence this chapter with a list of the sixty-nine Grand Masters of the Order of St. John, taken from Taaffe's History of the Order. The dates and spelling of names, however, do not agree with those assigned by Mr. Addison.

GRAND MASTERS OF THE ORDER OF ST. JOHN, RHODES AND
MALTA, A.D. 1099 TO 1799.

1. Gerard Tunc	Installed 1099	died 1118
2. Raymond du Puys	1118	" 1160
3. Otteger Balben	Jan. 1160	
4. Arnaud de Comps	1162	
5. Gilbert d'Ossaly (De Sailly)	1163	drowned 1170
6. Castus	1170	
7. Joubert (De Osbert)	1173	died 1177
8. Du Moulin (Roger de Moulin)	1177	killed May 1, 1187
9. N. Gardiner	1187	died at Askalon 1187
10. Godfrey de Duison	1192	died 1201
11. Alphonso	1202	abdicated ....
12. Godfrey Lo Rath	1205	died 1208
13. Gawen de Montacute	1208	" 1231
14. Bernard de Texis	1231	
15. Girino	1232	died 1236

Grand Masters of the Order of St. John.

16. Bertrand de Comps..Installed 1236 ....slain in battle 1241
17. Peter de Villebride.......... 1241 .... " " 1243
18. William de Chateau-neuf .... 1243 .... died 1259
19. Hugh de Revel .... 1259 .... " 1278
20. Nicholas de Lorgne .... 1278 ..died broken hearted 1289
21. John de Villiers .... 1289 .... died 1297
22. Otho de Pins.............. 1298
23. William Villaret............ 1300 .... died 1306
24. Fulk de Villaret .... 1307 ....deposed 1319
25. Helion de Villannova .... 1319 .... died 1346
26. Deodate de Gozon........... 1346 ......died December, 1353
27. Peter de Cornillan .... 1354 .... died 1355
28. Roger de Pins 1355
29. Raymond de Berenger....... 1365 .... died 1374
30. Robert de Julliac .... 1374 .... " 1377
31. Heredia Castellan d'Emposta 1377
32. Richard Caracciolo.......... 1383 .... died 1395
33. Phillip de Naillac........... 1396 ....died June, 1421
34. Antony Fluvian .... 1421 .....died October 26, 1437
35. John de Lastic .... 1437 ....died May 19, 1454
36. James de Milly............. 1454 .....died August 17, 1461
37. Peter Raymond Zacosta ..... 1461 ... died February 14, 1467
38. John Orsini................. 1467 .... died 1476
39. Peter D'Aubusson .... 1476 .... died June 30, 1503
40. Almeric Amboise .... 1503 ...died November 8, 1512
41. Guido de Blanchefort .... 1512 .... died 1512
42. Fabricius Carretto .... 1512 .... died January, 1521
43. Phillip Villers de l'Isle Adam 1521 .....died August 22, 1534
44. A. del Ponte .... 1534 ..... died November, 1535
45. Desiderio di S. Jalla......... 1536 .. died September 26, 1536
46. Homedez .... 1536 ... died September 6, 1553
47. Claudius de La Sengle....... 1553 ....died August, 1557
48. John de Valetta .... 1557 .....died August 21, 1568
49. Peter del Moate .... 1568 .... died January 20, 1572
50. Cassiere 1572
51. Verdale .... died 1595
52. Garzes .... 1595 ...... died February, 1601
53. Wignacourt................ 1601 .... died 1622
54. Vasconcellos............... 1622

Grand Masters of the Order of St. John.

55. De Paul...........Installed 1622 .... died 1636
56. Paul de Lascaris Castellar.... 1636 ..... died August 14, 1657
57. Redin .... 1657 .... died February 6, 1660
58. Clermont de Chattes Gessan.. 1660 .... died June 2, 1660
59. Raphael Cotoner......... ... 1660 .... died 1663
60. Nicholas Cotoner .... 1663 ....died April 29, 1680
61. Caraffa 1680
62. Wignacourt .... 1690 ... died September 4, 1697
63. Perrellas .... 1697 ..... died February, 1720
64. Zondadari .... 1720 .... died 1722
65. Anthony Manoel de Vilhena. 1722 .... " 1642
66. Pinto de Fonseca 1742
67. Ximenes.................. 1773 ..... died November, 1776
68. Rohan .... 1776 .... died 1797
69. Hompesch 1797

In consequence of the resort of pilgrims and traders from the West to Jerusalem, it had been found necessary to build there, with the consent of the Saracens, as early as the Eighth Century, *Hospitia*, or places of entertainment for them during their abode in the Holy City. For they could not consistently, with the religious animosity which prevailed between them and the Moslems, seek the hospitality of these last, and the Christians of the Greek Church, who dwelt in the Holy City; besides that they had no very friendly feeling towards their Catholic brethren; were loath to admit them into their houses, on account of the imprudent language and indecorous acts in which they were too frequently in the habit of indulging, and which were so likely to compromise their hosts with their Saracen lords.

Accordingly, the monk Bernard, surnamed Le Sage, who visited Jerusalem in the year A.D. 870, found there, in the valley of Jehoshaphat, near the Church of the Holy Virgin, a Hospital consisting of twelve mansions, for Western pilgrims, which was in the possession of some gardens, vineyards, and corn-fields. It had also a good collection-of books, the gift of Charlemagne (reigned A.D. 768 to 800). There was a weekly market held in front of it, which was much resorted to, a custom still maintained in the vil-

INSTITUTION OF THE ORDER OF ST. JOHN.

lages in the north of Galilee, and every dealer paid two pieces of gold to the overseer for permission to have a stand there. In the Eleventh Century, when the ardor of pilgrimage was inflamed anew, there was a Hospital within the walls of Jerusalem for the use of the Latin pilgrims, which had been erected by Italian traders, chiefly of Amalfi, about A.D. 1050. Near this Hospital, and within a stone's cast of the church of the Holy Sepulchre, they erected, with the permission of the Egyptian Caliph, a Church dedicated to the Holy Virgin, which was usually called *Saint Maria de Latina* ("St. Mary of the Latins"). In this Hospital abode an Abbot and a good number of monks, who were of the Latin Church, and followed the rule of St. Benedict. They devoted themselves to the reception and entertainment of pilgrims, and gave alms to those who were poor, or had been rifled by robbers, to enable them to pay the tax required by the Moslems for permission to visit the Holy Places.

Founding of the Fraternity of St. John the Almoner.

When the number of the pilgrims became so great that the Hospital was incapable of receiving them all, the monks raised another *hospitium* close to their church, with a chapel dedicated to a canonized Patriarch of Alexandria, named *St. John Eleemon* (the Almoner, or the Compassionate), who was the son of the King of Cyprus, and flourished in the Sixth Century. He was elected Patriarch of Alexandria, and afterwards founded a fraternity at Jerusalem, whose main object was to attend to the sick and wounded among the Christian pilgrims who visited the Sacred Land which had been consecrated by the footsteps of the Redeemer. Both the Greek and Roman Churches have canonized this arch-prelate under the name of St. John, of Jerusalem.

This new Hospital had no income of its own; the monks and the pilgrims whom they received derived their support from the bounty of the Abbot of the Convent of the Holy Virgin, or from the alms of pious Christians generally.

At the time when the Army of the Crusaders appeared before the walls of Jerusalem, the Hospital of St. John was presided over by Gerard, a native of Provence, a man of great uprightness and of exemplary piety. His benevolence was of a truly Christian character, and far transcended that of his age in general; for during the six weeks of the siege he relieved all who applied to him for succor, and not merely did the schismatic Greek share his bounty, even the unbelieving Moslem was not repelled when he implored his aid. So when the city was taken (July 15, 1099) numbers of the wounded pilgrims were received, and their wounds tended in this Hospital of St. John, and the pious Duke Godfrey, on visiting them, some days afterwards, heard nothing but the praises of the good Gerard and his monks. One writer forcibly says: " The new monarch immediately visited the House of St. John, which was then filled with wounded soldiers, to whom he personally administered aid and consolation, and, to mark his sense of the humane services rendered by the brethren, Godfrey endowed the Hospital with his own Lordship of Montboire, in Brabant, and all its dependencies."

Emboldened by the universal favor which they enjoyed, Gerard and his companions expressed their wish to separate themselves

11

The Brotherhood of the Fraternity of St. John.

from the monastery of Saint Mary *de Latina*, and pursue their works of charity alone and independently. Their desire met no opposition. They drew up a Rule for themselves, to which they made a vow of obedience in presence of the Patriarch, and assumed, as their dress, a black mantle with a white cross on the breast. The humility of these Hospitalers was extreme. They styled the poor and the sick their Lords and themselves their Servants; *to them* they were liberal and compassionate, to *themselves* rigid and austere. The finest flour went to compose the food which they gave the sick and poor; what remained after the poor were satisfied, *mingled with clay*, was the repast of the monks! As long as this brotherhood were poor they continued in obedience to the Abbot of St. Mary *de Latina*, and also paid tithes to the Patriarch. But a tide of wealth soon began to flow in upon them. King Godfrey, as we have said, enamored of their virtue, bestowed on them his Lordship of Montboire, in Brabant, with all its appurtenances; and his brother and successor, Baldwin I., gave them a share of all the booty which he had taken from the infidels. These examples were followed by other Christian princes; so that within the space of a very few years the Hospital of St. John was in possession of numerous manors, both in the East and in Europe, which were placed under the management of the members of their society.

The Hospitalers now coveted a total remission of all the burdens to which they were subject, and found no difficulty in obtaining all that they desired. Pope Pascal II., who succeeded Pope Urban II., A.D. 1099, confirmed their Rule in 1113 and gave them permission on the death of Gerard to elect their own Grand Master without the interference of any temporal or spiritual power whatever. He also freed them from the obligation of paying tithes to the Patriarch, and confirmed all the donations made or to be made to them. The Brotherhood of the Hospital was now greatly advanced in consideration, and reckoned among its members many gallant Knights, who laid aside their arms, and devoted themselves to the humble office of ministering to the sick and needy. In a short time, so great was the influx of new members, the Order was subdivided into eight languages or nations—

viz. : First, Provence ; second, Auvergne ; third, France ; fourth, Italy ; fifth, Aragon ; sixth, England, comprising Wales, Scotland, and Ireland ; seventh, Germany ; and eighth, Castile, which included Portugal and Leon.

The worthy Gerard died in the same year with King Baldwin I., viz., A.D. 1118, and Raymond Dupuy, a Knight of Dauphine, France, who had become a Brother of the Order, was unanimously elected to succeed him in his office.   Raymond Dupuy, who was a man of great vigor and capacity, drew up a series of Rules for the direction of the society, adapted to its present state of consequence and extent.   From these rules it appears that the Order of St. John admitted both clergy and laity among its members, and that both were alike bound to yield the most implicit obedience to the commands of their superior.   Whether Raymond had any ulterior views is uncertain, but in the regulations which he made we cannot discern any traces of the military spirit which afterwards animated the Order of St. John.

The modern costume of the Knights of the first class consists of a frock-coat of scarlet cloth, with white lining, facings, collar, hat and plume.   That of the second class is a similar coat, but with a black velvet lining, facings, and collar, and a black hat and plume.   Both classes have white hat flaps, epaulettes with thick golden tassels, buttons, spurs, and hat string equally of gold, pantaloons of white cassimere with golden trimmings.

Mr. Addison, in his History of the Knights Templars, also gives a brief account of the origin of this Society, agreeing in the main with the above.   We quote him entire.   We must now pause to take a glance at the rise of another great religio-military institution which, from henceforth, takes a leading part in the defense of the Latin kingdom.   In the Eleventh Century, when pilgrimages to Jerusalem had greatly increased, some Italian merchants of Amalfi, who carried on a lucrative trade with Palestine, purchased of the Caliph *Monstasserbillah*, a piece of ground in the Christian quarter of the Holy City, near the Church of the Resurrection, whereon two hospitals were constructed, the one being appropriated for the reception of male pilgrims, and the other for females. Several pious and charitable Christians, chiefly from Europe, devoted themselves in these hospitals to constant attendance upon the sick and destitute. Two chapels were erected, the one annexed to the female establishment being dedicated to St. Mary Magdalene, and the other to St. John the Eleemosynary, a canonized Patriarch of Alexandria, remarkable for his exceeding charity. The pious and kind-hearted people who here attended upon the sick pilgrims, clothed the naked and fed the hungry, were called The Hospitalers of St. John. On the conquest of Jerusalem by the Crusaders, these charitable persons were naturally regarded with the greatest esteem and reverence by their fellow-Christians from the West; many of the Soldiers of the Cross, smitten with their piety and zeal, desired to participate in their good offices, and the Hospitalers, animated by the religious enthusiasm of the day, determined to renounce the world, and devote the remainder of their lives to pious duties and constant attendance upon the sick. They took the customary monastic vows of obedience, chastity, and poverty, and assumed as their distinguishing habit a *black* mantle with a *white* cross on the breast. Various lands and possessions were granted them by the lords and princes of the Crusade, both in Palestine and in Europe, and the Order of the Hospital of St. John speedily became a great and powerful institution.

Gerard, a native of Provence, was at this period at the head of the Hospitalers, with the title of " Guardian of the Poor." He **1118.** was succeeded by Raymond Dupuy, a Knight of Dauphiny, who drew up a series of rules for the direction and government of his brethren. In these rules no traces are discoverable of the military spirit which afterwards animated the Order of the Hospital of St. John.* The first authentic notice of an intention on the part of the Hospitalers to occupy themselves with *military matters*, occurs in the bull of Pope Innocent the Second, dated A.D. 1130. This bull is addressed to the archbishops, bishops, and clergy of the Church universal, and informs them that the Hospitalers then retained, at their own expense, a body of horsemen

---

* The guardian of the Holy Sepulchre, at Jerusalem, has always preserved the privilege of creating Knights of the Order, and two or three English Roman Catholic gentlemen have recently (1870) obtained the time-honored cross of the illustrious Fraternity.

and foot soldiers, to defend the pilgrims in going to and returning from the holy places.   The Pope observes that the funds of the hospital were insufficient to enable them effectually to fulfill that pious and holy task, and exhorts the archbishops, bishops, and clergy, to minister to the necessities of the Order out of their abundant property.   The Hospitalers consequently at this period had resolved to add the task of *protecting* to that of *tending* and *relieving* pilgrims.

1168. After the accession of Gilbert d'Assalit to the Guardianship of the Hospital—a man described by De Vertot as "bold and enterprising, and of an extravagant genius"—a military spirit was infused into the Hospitalers, which speedily predominated over their pious and charitable zeal in attending upon the poor and the sick.   Gilbert d'Assalit was the friend and confidant of Amalric, King of Jerusalem, and planned with that monarch an invasion of Egypt in defiance of treaties.   The Grand Master of the Temple being consulted concerning the expedition, flatly refused to have anything to do with it, or to allow a single brother of the Order of the Temple to accompany the king in arms.   "For it appeared a hard matter to the Templars," says William of Tyre, "to wage war without cause, in defiance of treaties and against all honor and conscience, upon a friendly nation, preserving faith with us, and relying on our own faith."   Gilbert d'Assalit consequently determined to obtain for the king from his own brethren that aid which the Templars denied.   To tempt the Hospitalers to arm themselves generally as a great military society, in imitation of the Templars, and join the expedition to Egypt, he was authorized to promise them, in the name of the king, the possession of the wealthy and important city of Belbeis, the ancient Pelusium, in perpetual sovereignty.

According to De Vertot, the senior Hospitalers were greatly averse to the military projects of their chief. " They urged," says he, " that they were a religious order, and that the Church had not put arms into their hands to make conquests."   But the younger and more ardent of the brethren, burning to exchange the monotonous life of the cloister for the enterprise and activity of the camp, received the proposals of their superior with enthusiasm, and a majority of the chapter decided in favor of the plans and projects of their Guardian. They authorized him to borrow money of the Florentine and Genoese merchants, to take hired soldiers into the pay of the Order, and to organize the Hospitalers as a great military society.

1168. It was in the first year of the government of Philip of Nablous, Grand Master of Templars, that the King of Jerusalem and the Knights Hospitalers marched forth upon their memorable and unfortunate expedition. The Egyptians were taken completely by surprise; the city of Belbeis was carried by assault, and the defenseless inhabitants were barbarously massacred. The cruelty and the injustice of the Christians, however, speedily met with condign punishment. The King of Jerusalem was driven back into Palestine; Belbeis was abandoned with precipitation; and the Hospitalers fled before the infidels in sorrow and disappointment to Jerusalem. There they vented their indignation and chagrin upon the unfortunate Gilbert d'Assalit, their superior, who had got the Order into debt to the extent of 100,000 pieces of gold. They compelled him to resign his authority, and the unfortunate Guardian of the Hospital fled from Palestine to England, and was drowned in the Channel. From this period, however, the character of the Order of the Hospital of St. John was entirely changed. The Hospitalers appear henceforth as a great military body. Their superior styled himself Grand Master, and led in person the brethren into the field of battle. Attendance upon the poor and the sick still continued, indeed, one of the duties of the fraternity, but it must have been feebly exercised amid the clash of arms and the excitement of war.

Among the numerous works devoted to this glorious Order, St. John Hospitaler, we borrow from Mr. Taaffe the following vigorous sketch:

To create a corps of volunteers of the bravest warriors for the defense of the Holy Sepulchre and this kingdom a permanent Crusade, and exercise hospitality on its widest scale towards the pilgrims of all ranks and nations, were the measures proposed. To maintain with a few, what it has required a Crusade of all Europe to conquer; and day and night, in sanguinary regions and at such a distance, lodge as they are accustomed, and feed all classes, from the emperor to the peasant; and likewise attend to them when sick, and provide them with all necessaries of physic and physicians and sur geons, and all gratis, is no small undertaking. · If the duties of hospitality are three—to defend the guest going and coming—to feed and lodge him when well—to try to cure him if sick; to traverse so many disturbed lands, and to receive them all so that each shall be treated as far as possible according to his rank—with no vain attempt at equality, but each pretty nearly as used to require armies and treasures—although the third alone, an Infirmary, might perhaps cost little. The rule then determined on was this: First. Hospitality for all pilgrims and crusaders including defense of this new kingdom. Second. A military organization in three classes, clergy, knights, servants at arms. Third. Knights to have all the proofs required of a *Miles*, "none may be a knight unless the son of a knight." Fourth. The not regularly professed in the order may be *aggregated* to it. Fifth. Females also. Sixth. None professed can have any property of their own, but can only expect to be clothed and fed plainly and frugally; and freely dedicate their lives. Seventh. Therefore three vows—celibacy, obedience and individual poverty. Eighth. *Celibacy* cuts off from most of those domestic ties which are impediments to self-devotedness. *Obedience* the most implicit, particularly in battle, where, without an express command, they on no pretext whatever can retire; but death must be expected with heroic fortitude. Their being individually poor means that they renounce the right of property, so that the all of each belongs to the common treasury. Ninth. Their dress the white cross, their founder being a Norman. Tenth. Their future head to be selected by the Order from amongst themselves; and he is to have a council to which he must submit; and on important matters he must convene a general assembly of the Order where he may have a double vote, and then the majority *decide* beyond appeal.

The gift of King Godfrey was in these (translated) words:

"In the name of the Holy and Undivided Trinity, I, Godfrey de Bouillon, by the grace of God Duke of Lorraine, make it known to all present and future, that for the remission of my sins, having adorned my heart and shoulders with the sign of the cross of the Saviour crucified for us, I at length reached the spot where our most high Lord, Jesus Christ, trod for the last time, and, after I had visited the Holy Sepulchre and all those holy places, with the devotion of a full heart, finally I came where once stood a church of the Holy Hospital, founded in honor of God and his blessed mother, and St. John the Baptist; and seeing so many operations suggested by the grace of the Holy Ghost that it is impossible to count them, and more charity toward the sick and indigent of the faithful than human tongue can express, I promised to offer something to God also, and so now, to acquit my promise to the Omnipotent with whole effusion of spirit, give to the said house of the Hospital, and all the brethren within it, an habitation built on the Monab, called Wood Mount, in the Cold Mountain (in Sicily), and of the Castle of S. Abraham (near Bethlehem), and I make this, my donation,

172 KNIGHTS TEMPLARS.

Fraternity of Hospitalers.   Churches of the Holy Land.

in the year 1100, less than a year from the taking of Jerusalem; and I have done this for the benefit of the souls of my father and mother, and relations, and all the Christians, living and dead. And affix my seal to the same, in presence of these trusty witnesses, Arnold of Vismala, and many others."

The traveler to Jerusalem at the present day will find but few remains of antiquity so interesting as the ruins of the Hospital of St. John. (See map of Jerusalem.)

BETHANY.

CHAPTER VII.

HISTORY OF THE LATIN KINGDOM OF PALESTINE TO A.D. 1187.

Not where the Saviour bore
  Thorns on his brow;
Not where my king upon
  Cross-tree did bow;
Not where the Prince of Life
  Sorrowed and groaned;
Godfrey shall never be
  Homaged and crowned.

Mine be the humbler name,
  Fitter by far,
Warder of Tomb Divine,
  Christ's Sepulchre!
Mine at its portal
  In armor to lie!
Mine in death's ministry,
  When I shall die.

Knight of Christ's Sepulchre,
  Christ's Chevalier,
Good Sword of Jesus,
  Oh, lie grandly here!
Ashes of Godfrey, there's
  No place like this;
Crowned in Christ's glory,
  And reigning in bliss!

Rules of Jerusalem.   Godfrey first King.

HE following is the list of rulers of the Latin Kingdom of Palestine; A.D. 1099–1205:

   I. Godfrey de Bouillon.   Crowned A.D. 1099. Died July 11, 1100
   II. Baldwin I.   . .   "   1101. "   1118
  III. Baldwin II.   . .   "   1118. "   1131
  IV. Foulques (Fulk) Count Anjou. Crowned 1131. "   1144
   V. Baldwin III. . .   "   1144. "   1162
  VI. Almeric.   . .   Crowned Feb. 18, 1162. "   1174
 VII. Baldwin IV. . .   "   Abdicated, 1184
VIII. Baldwin V. . .   "   1184. Died,   1186
  IX. Sibylla and her husband, } 1186.
        Guy de Lusignan,   }
     Sibylla died, 1191.
     Guy abdicated, 1192.
   X. Henry Count of Champagne, 1192.   Killed by accident, 1194.
  XI. Amauri King of Cyprus, 1194.   Died, 1205.

The first care of the Crusaders, only eight days having elapsed since the surrender of Jerusalem, was to *choose a King*. This, the sternest republican must admit was an indispensable act considering the training and the present necessities of those warriors. Nothing less than a military dictatorship could hold together a band composed of so many nationalities and among whom so many rivalries existed, and whose hold upon the Orient was so precarious. Had they but avoided then and thenceforth the principle of *primogeniture* in the succession of their kings and trusted to the circumstances surrounding them, to rear up men worthy of the succession, the day of Hattin might have found the royal scepter in the hand of a Godfrey equal to the first, and the history of Palestine had been all the way through, a glorious one. That the Crusaders, the Templars, and Hospitalers should be condemned by this unhappy law of primogeniture to obey Baldwin the Leper and Guy de Lusignan, the Seceder and Coward, was enough in itself to insure the sequel of disasters in which the sun of the Crusades went down.

The choice of all fell upon Godfrey, Sixth lord of Bouillon,

Godfrey de Bouillon elected King of Jerusalem.

GODFREY DE BOUILLON ELECTED AND PROCLAIMED KING OF JERUSALEM.

France, Marquis of Anvers and Duke of Brabant, or *the Lower Lorraine,* which fifty years prior to this period had been made a province with a valiant peer named Godfrey at its head. Eustace II., Count of Boulogne, was the father of our hero; his mother was Ida daughter of Duke Godfrey just named. He was born about A.D. 1061. This first King of Jerusalem was qualified in his very nature to act a great part on the theater of the world. The Creator had bounteously bestowed upon him His choicest gifts. His understanding was enriched with the best knowledge and learning that the times afforded. His ready use of the Latin,

High Qualifications of Godfrey.

Teutonic, and Roman tongues qualified him to act as mediator among disputing nations. In him the gentlest manners were united to the firmest spirit. The amiableness of virtue was joined to its commanding gravity. He, more than others of his time, proved the pattern of chivalry so beautifully depictured by Burke: " The generous loyalty to rank and sex, the proud submission, the dignified obedience, and that subordination of the heart which kept alive, even in servitude itself, the spirit of an exalted freedom—that sensibility of principle, that chastity of honor which felt a stain like a wound, which inspired courage whilst it mitigated ferocity, which ennobled whatever it touched, and under which vice itself lost half its evil by losing all its grossness." Godfrey was the Washington of the enterprise of which he was made leader. He was distinguished alike for political courage and personal bravery. His lofty mind was capable of the grandest enterprises. His deportment was moral, his piety fervent. His servants even complained that he was so fond of remaining in church, pursuing his private devotions, after the close of the services, that the dinner near spoiled! He appeared to some better fitted for a cloister of reformed monks than the command of a furious and licentious soldiery. He often regretted the stern necessity which drove him from the immediate service of God, but when in arms he was a hero, and his martial spirit in the cause of heaven was always directed by prudence and tempered by philanthropy.

When the report of the intended crusade reached him, he was sick of a fever. But the blast of the holy trumpet and the sight of the new emblem roused his warlike and religious spirit, and he resolved, if God would restore his health, he *would go to the Holy Land*. Immediately the disease fell from his limbs! He rose with expanded breast as if from years of weakness, and shone with renovated youth. To raise money for the expedition, he cheerfully sold his castle and a lordship of Bouillon to the monks of Liege, receiving a sum equal to about $120,000. Godfrey had no children.

Under his banner marched his brother Baldwin (afterwards Count of Edessa, and then King Baldwin I.), and two cousins named Baldwin du Bourg, who became Baldwin II., and Almeric, who was also a king of Jerusalem, with many other knights of

KNIGHTS TEMPLARS. 177

A Struggle for Ruler.   Fierce Attack on Jerusalem.

eminence. The four "kings to be" set out August 15th, 1096, and in July, 1099, the assembly of princes and priests was held at Jerusalem, to make choice of the first king. The monks claimed that, as *spiritual* things had been more regarded in this holy war than *temporal*, a Patriarch should first be chosen. This suggestion, however, was spurned by the princes with contempt. A comparison of the rank, family and possessions, the warlike achievements, and finally, the personal virtues of the leaders of earth was then made, and Godfrey was conducted to the Holy Sepulcher, afterwards the place of his tomb, and there, at the age of 39 years, honored with the title of King of Jerusalem. He refused, however, to wear a crown where Jesus had worn thorns, and modestly avowed that "the honor of becoming the Defender of the Holy Sepulcher was the height of his aspirations."

Within a month after the election of Godfrey, Al Aphdal, former conqueror of Jerusalem, poured his Fatimite soldiers into the Holy Land, where they were joined by thousands of Turks and Arabians. Al Aphdal had taken a solemn oath before the Caliph to annihilate forever the power of the Crusaders in Asia, and to destroy Calvary, the tomb of Christ utterly, together with all the monuments revered by Christians. Godfrey, with Tancred, Raymond and the Duke of Normandy, met him near Ascalon at the head of 20,000 soldiers, and gave him a total defeat, slaying, it is said, 30,000 on the field, and 60,000 in the pursuit. The spoil of the camp was immense, and was all divided among the soldiers, save the sword and standard of the Sultan, which were hung over the altar of the Holy Sepulcher at Jerusalem. The form of the Christian camp was scientifically arranged, nine divisions making a sort of square battalion placed so as to be able, at need, to force the enemy at all points. In the great battle, the TRUE CROSS was borne among the ranks, as afterwards at Hattin, July, 1187. The Count of Toulouse commanded the right wing, Tancred and the two Roberts the left, and Godfrey the reserve. The enemy's forces were also in two lines, Al Aphdal occupying the center. At the moment of onset the Christians fell on their knees to implore the protection of heaven.

A quarrel which arose between King Godfrey and Count Raymond of Toulouse threatened for a time an intestine war, but was happily quieted when the city of Arzouf surrendered to their joint attack. This was the end of the First Crusade. The princes departed for Europe, leaving but three hundred knights, the wisdom of Godfrey and the sword of Tancred. Peter the Hermit, who had lived through all the events of these five years, retired to his native country, and secluded himself in a monastery at Huy for the rest of his life. He died 1115. Eustace, brother of Godfrey, and his cousin Baldwin also returned home, but the latter returned within a brief period.

A year, wanting five days, was the term of the short reign of Godfrey. He was buried amidst the tears alike of Christian and Moslem in the Church of the Holy Sepulcher, where, twelve months before, he had accepted the sovereignty but refused the crown. It was then decreed that that place should be the St. Denis and Westminster Abbey of the new kingdom. A tomb was reared above him, of which we give a representation from De Vogüé ("Churches of the Holy Land").

TOMB OF GODFREY, FIRST KING OF JERUSALEM.

The original epitaph was as follows :

"Hic jacet : inclitus : dux : Godefridus : De Bullon : qui totam istam : terram : Aquisivit : cultui christiano : cujus Anima : regnet cum Christo : Amen."

"Here lies the celebrated Duke Godfrey de Bouillon, who conquered all this country for the Christian religion. May his soul reign with Christ. Amen!"

Burial Place of Godfrey.   Order of the Holy Sepulchre.

Following his account of this tomb, the Baron de Vogüé adds: "It is known that this chevalier king, borne to the throne by his valor and his virtues, refused to put upon his head the crown which his companions in arms offered him. 'I will not,' he affirmed, 'bear a crown of gold where Jesus bore a crown of thorns!' His will was respected not only while living but after his death, as is shown by the inscription upon his tomb. His brother and successor, Baldwin, to remain faithful to the intention of Godfrey, took the title of 'First King of Jerusalem,' and began the notation followed by all his successors."

Here is the epitaph of Baldwin I., 1100–1118, who was buried by the side of Godfrey:

"Rex Baldewinus : Judas alter Machabeus Spes patriæ vigor Ecclesiæ virtus utriusque Quem formidabant cui dona tributa ferebant Cedar et Egyptus : Dan : ac homicida Damascus Proh dolor in modico clauditur hoc tumulo."

"King Baldwin, a second Judas Maccabee, the hope of his country, the strength of the Church, the power of both, whom Cedar and Egypt and murderous Damascus feared, and to whom they paid tribute: alas, inclosed in this narrow mound!"

De Vogüé finds in an ancient manuscript of the Twelfth Century an epitaph totally different, said to have been applied to Godfrey, but probably only proposed, with others, and refused. Doubtless numerous models were offered by learned priests. We give this form (omitting the Latin) as an elegant wreath laid upon so honored a tomb.

"Here rests the Duke Godfrey, a marvelous Star. He made the Egyptian tremble. He was the terror of the Arab. He trampled upon the Persian. Chosen King, he refused to bear the title and the crown, happy to serve Christ. He compelled himself ever to serve Zion with equity, to follow with strictness the sacred dogmas of the Catholic Church, to smother every schism against the law, and to practice justice. Thus he merited a celestial crown. Mirror of chivalry, the right arm of the people, the anchor of the clergy."

The Order of the Holy Sepulcher, indissolubly associated with the place of his burial, is thus mentioned in the *Almanac de Gotha*, 1873:

ORDER OF THE HOLY SEPULCHER.

"The Order of the Holy Sepulcher was cotemporaneous in origin with that of the Knights of St. John of Jerusalem, and originated in the same causes.   The custom of its officers during the Crusades was to give the *accolade* within the Holy Sepulcher. Pope Alexander VI. bestowed the exclusive control of this Order upon the Franciscan monks, which was confirmed by Pius X. as late as 1847.   In 1868 he divided the Order into three classes."

This learned writer, in his description of the Church of the Holy Sepulcher, says: "In front of the Chapel of Adam, in a little rectangular enclosure, surrounded by a low wall, the Crusaders placed the tombs of the two first kings of Jerusalem, Godfrey de Bouillon and Baldwin I."

The successor of Godfrey was his brother Baldwin, who had been King of Edessa, and to whom is the title Baldwin I.   He reigned until 1118.   He was succeeded by his cousin, Baldwin du Bourg, as Baldwin II., whose government extended to 1131.   During his reign a celebrated Council was held at Nablous, thirty miles north of Jerusalem, of whose doings we give an account.

COUNCIL OF NABLOUS, held by the authority of Garamond, Patriarch of Jerusalem, to reform the morals of the Christians of Palestine, in the presence of Baldwin II., King of Jerusalem, in the year of our Lord, 1120, in the Pontificate of Calixtus II.

This is the manner in which William of Tyre (book xii. of the Holy War, chap. xiii.) relates summarily the cause and the acts of the council : The same year (that is to say the year 1120) of the Incarnation of the Word, the kingdom of Jerusalem being tormented on account of its sins with many troubles, and in addition to the calamities inflicted by their enemies, a multitude of locusts and gnawing rats destroying the harvests to such a degree that it was feared *bread* would be wanting, the Seigneur Garamond, Patriarch of Jerusalem, a man religious and fearing God, the King, Baldwin II., the prelates of the churches, and the great men of the kingdom, repaired to Nablous, a small city of Samaria, and held a public assembly and a general court.   In a sermon addressed to the people it was said that as it appeared plain that it was the sins of the people which had provoked the LORD it was necessary to deliberate in common upon the means of correcting and repressing excesses, in order that, returning to a better life and worthily satisfying for their remitted sins, *the people* might render themselves acceptable to Him who desireth not the death of a sinner, but rather that he should turn from his wickedness and live.   Terrified, then, by the menacing signs of Heaven, by frequent earthquakes, by successive defeats, by the pangs of famine, by perfidious and daily attacks of their enemies, seeking to win back the Lord by works of piety, they have, to restore and preserve discipline in morals,

Articles established at the Council of Nablous.

decreed twenty-five acts, which shall have the force of Laws. If any one be desirous of reading them they will be easily found in the archives of many churches.

Present at this Council, Garamond, Patriarch of Jerusalem; the logician Baldwin, second king of the Latins; Ekmar, Archbishop of Cæsarea; Bernard, Bishop of Nazareth; the Bishop of Lydda; Gilden, Abbot elect of St. Mary of the Valley of Jehoshaphat; Peter, Abbot of Mount Tabor; Achard, Priest of Mount Sion; Payen, Chancellor of the king; Eustace Granier, William de Buret, Batisan, constable of Jaffa, and many others of the two Orders, of whom we forget the number and the names.

This synod, says Baronius, towards the end of 1120, succeeded in effecting such a reformation in morals that by the mercy of Heaven, in the following year, 1121, the leader of the Turks, coming against Antioch with considerable strength, was struck with apoplexy and died.

CHAP. I. As it is necessary that things which *commence* by God should *finish* in Him and by Him, with the intention of beginning this holy Council and terminating it by the Lord, I, Baldwin, second King of the Latins at Jerusalem, opening this Holy Assembly by God, I render and I grant, as I have ordered, to the Holy Church of Jerusalem and to the Patriarch here present, Garamond, as well as to his successors, *the tenths* of all my revenues, as far as concerns the extent of this Diocese; that is to say, the tenths of my revenues of Jerusalem, Nablous, and Ptolemais, which is further called Accon (Acre). They are the benefits of my royal munificence, in order that the patriarchs charged with the duty of praying the Lord for the welfare of the state may have wherewithal to subsist on. And if at any time, in consequence of the progress of the Christian religion, he, or one of his successors, should ordain a bishop in one of these cities he may dispose of the tenths as well for the King as for the Church.

CHAP. II. I, Bohemond, in the presence of the members of this Council, with the consent of the personages of the assembly and of my barons, who will do the same by their tenths, according to the extent of their ecclesiastical powers, I make restitution of the tenths, as I have said; and agreeing with them as to the injustice with which they and I have retained them, I ask pardon.

CHAP. III. I, Patriarch Garamond, on the part of the all-powerful God, by my power and that of all the bishops and brethren here present, I absolve you upon the said restitution of the tenths, and I accept charitably with them the tenths you acknowledge to owe to God, to me, and to your other bishops, according to the extent of the benefices of the brethren present or absent.

CHAP. IV. If any one fears being ill-treated by his wife let him go and find him whom he suspects, and let him forbid him, before legal witnesses, entrance to his house and all colloquy with his wife. If after this prohibition he or any one of his friends should find them in colloquy, in his house

Articles established at the Council of Nablous.

or elsewhere, let the man, without any cutting off of his members, be submitted to the justice of the Church; and if he purges himself by ardent fire let him be dismissed unpunished. But when he shall have undergone some disgrace for being surprised in colloquy, let him be dismissed unpunished and without vengeance for having violated the prohibition.

(The historian Michaud inserts the whole of these laws; but we omit the next twelve, as more likely to create disgust than to afford instruction or amusement.)

CHAP. XVI. The male or female Saracen who shall assume the dress of the Franks shall belong to the state.

CHAP. XVII. If any man already married has married another woman he has, to the first Sunday of Lent of our year, to confess himself to the priest and perform penance. Afterwards he has but to live according to the precepts of the Church. But if he conceals his crime longer his goods will be confiscated; he will be cut off from society and banished from this land.

CHAP. XVIII. If any man, without knowing it, marries the wife of another, or if a woman marries without knowing it a man already married, then let the one that is innocent turn out the guilty one, and be in possession of the right of marrying again.

CHAP. XIX. If any man wishing to get rid of his wife says he has another, or that he has taken her during the lifetime of the first, let him submit to the ordeal of red-hot iron, or let him bring before the Magistrates of the Church legal witnesses, who will affirm by oath that it is so. What is here said of men is applicable to women.

CHAP. XX. If a clerk take up arms in his own defense there is no harm in it; but if, from a love of war, or to sacrifice to worldly interests, he renounces his condition, let him return to the Church within the time granted; let him confess and conform afterwards with the instructions of the Patriarch.

CHAP. XXI. If a monk or regular canon apostatize let him return to his Order or go back to his country.

CHAP. XXII. Whoever shall accuse another without being able to prove the fact shall undergo the punishment due to the crime he has accused him of.

CHAP. XXIII. If any one be convicted of a robbery above the value of six sous let him be threatened with the loss of his hand, his foot, or his eyes. If the theft be below six sous let him be marked with a hot iron on the forehead, and be whipped through the city. If the thing stolen be found let it be restored to him to whom it belongs. If the thief has nothing let his body be given up to him he has injured. If he repeats the offense let him be deprived of all his members and of his life.

CHAP. XXIV. If any one under age commits a theft let him be kept until the King's Court decide what shall be done with him.

The Order of the Temple established. Death of Hugh de Payens.

CHAP. XXV. If any baron surprises a man of his own class in the act of theft the latter is not to be subject to the loss of his members, but let him be sent to be judged in the King's Court.

A perusal of this strange paper gives us an inner view to the customs and thoughts of that age and country.

1130. Hugh de Payens, having now laid in Europe the foundations of the great monastic and military institution of the Temple, which was destined shortly to spread its ramifications to the remotest quarters of Christendom, returned to Palestine at the head of a valiant band of newly-elected Templars, drawn principally from France and England. On their arrival at Jerusalem they were received with great distinction by the king, the clergy, and the barons of the Latin kingdom.

Then the days of Hugh de Payens drew to a close. After governing the Order for twenty-one years, and seeing it rise and hold the highest position among the warrior bands of Palestine under his care, and the continued patronage of St. Bernard, who never failed, while writing to the East, to mention it with honor, and to recommend it to the notice of kings and nobles, this gallant soldier of the Cross died in 1139. Everything that is estimable in man is to be discovered in the character of De Payens; no word of calumny has been breathed by the noble and the just upon this truly great man; and, though some later writers have attempted to blacken his fair fame, there can be little doubt that no dishonorable action sullied his life, and that he descended to the tomb, as he had lived, without reproach.

1136. Hugh de Payens was succeeded by Robert, the Burgundian, son-in-law of Anselm, Archbishop of Canterbury, who, after the death of his wife, had taken the vows and the habit of the Templars.

At this period the fierce religious and military enthusiasm of the Mussulmans had been again aroused by the warlike Zinghis, and his son Noureddin, two of the most famous chieftains of the age. The one was named *Emod-ed-deen* (the Pillar of Religion); and the other *Nour-ed-deen* (the Light of Religion), vulgarly, *Noureddin*. The Templars were worsted by overpowering numbers. The Latin kingdom of Jerusalem was shaken to its foundations, and the Oriental clergy in trepidation and alarm sent urgent letters to the Pope for assistance.

Robert, the Burgundian Grand Master of the Temple, had at this **1146.** period been succeeded by Everard des Barres, Prior of France, who convened a General Chapter of the Order at Paris. This was attended by Pope Eugenius III., Louis VII., King of France, and many prelates, princes, and nobles, from all parts of Christendom.   The Second Crusade was there arranged, and the Templars, with the sanction of the Pope, assumed the blood-red cross (the symbol of martyrdom), as the distinguishing Badge of the Order, which was appointed to be worn on their habits and mantles on the left side of the breast over the heart, whence they came afterwards to be known by the name of the *Red Friars* and the *Red Cross Knights*.   At this famous assembly various donations were made to the Templars, to enable them to provide more effectually for the defense of the Holy Land.   Bernard Baliol, through love of God and for the good of his soul, granted them his estate of Wedelee, in Hertfordshire, England, which afterwards formed part of the preceptory of Temple Dynnesley.   This grant is expressed to be made at the Chapter held at Easter, in Paris, in the presence of the Pope, the King of France, several archbishops, and one hundred and thirty Knights Templars clad in white mantles.

The Bull of Pope Eugenius III. published in 1145 to stimulate the Second Crusade will be of interest here.   It is vigorous and good reading.

"The servant of the servants of God, to his dear son Louis, illustrious and glorious King of the French, to his dear sons the princes and to all the faithful of the Kingdom of France, health and the apostolic benediction. We know by the history of times past, and by the traditions of our fathers, how many efforts our predecessors made for the deliverance of the Church of the East.   Our predecessor, Urban, of happy memory, sounded the evangelical trumpet and employed himself with unexampled zeal in summoning the Christian nations from all parts of the world to the defense of the Holy Land.   At his voice, the brave and intrepid warriors of the kingdom of the Franks and the Italians, inflamed with a holy ardor, took arms, and delivered at the cost of their blood THE CITY in which our Saviour deigned to suffer for us, and which contains the tomb, the monument of His passion. By the grace of God and by the zeal of our fathers, who defended Jerusalem,

Robert of Burgundy.   Second Crusade.   Bull of Pope Eugenius.

and endeavored to spread the Christian name in those distant countries, the conquered cities of Asia have been preserved up to our days, and many cities of the infidels have been attacked and their inhabitants have become Christians.   Now, for our sins and those of the Christian people (which we cannot repeat, without grief and lamentation), the city of Edessa (which in our own language is called Rohas, and which, if we can believe the history of it, when the East was subjected to the Pagan nations, alone remained faithful to Christianity)—the city of Edessa is fallen into the hands of the enemies of the Cross.

"Several other Christian cities have shared the same fate.   The archbishop of that city, with his clergy and many other Christians, have been killed.   Relics of saints have been given up to the insults of the infidels and dispersed.   The greatest danger threatens the Church of God and all Christendom.   We are persuaded that your prudence and your zeal will be conspicuous on this occasion.   You will show the nobleness of your sentiments and the purity of your faith.   If the conquests made by the valor of the fathers are preserved by the sons, I hope you will not allow it to be believed that the heroism of the French has degenerated.

"We warn you, we pray you, we *command* you, to take up the Cross and arms.   I warn you for the remission of your sins—you who are men of God— to clothe yourselves with power and courage, and stop the invasion of the infidels who are rejoicing at the victory gained over you; to defend the Church of the East delivered by our ancestors; to wrest from the hands of the Mussulmans many thousands of Christian prisoners who are now in chains. By this means the holiness of the Christian name will increase in the present generation, and your valor, the reputation of which is spread throughout the universe, will not only preserve itself without stain, but will acquire a new splendor.   Take as your example that virtuous Mattathias, father of the Maccabees, who, to preserve the laws of his ancestors, did not hesitate to expose himself to death with his sons and his family; did not hesitate to abandon all he held dear in the world, and who, with the help of Heaven, after a thousand labors, triumphed over his enemies.   We, who watch over the Church and over you, with a parental solicitude, we grant to those who will devote themselves to this glorious enterprise, the privileges which our predecessor Urban granted to the Soldiers of the Cross.

"We have likewise ordered that their wives and their children, their worldly goods and possessions shall be placed under the safeguard of the Church, of the Archbishops, the Bishops, and the other prelates.   We order by our apostolic authority that those who shall have taken the Cross shall be exempt from all kinds of pursuit on account of their property until their return, or until certain news be received of their death.   We order besides, that the soldiers of Jesus Christ shall abstain from wearing rich habits, from having great care in adorning their persons, and from taking with them dogs for the chase, falcons, or anything that may corrupt the manners of the warriors.   We warn them, in the name of the Most High, that they shall only concern themselves with their war-horses, their arms, and everything that may assist them in contending with the infidels.   The Holy War calls for all their efforts and for all the faculties they have in them; they who undertake the holy voyage with a right and pure heart, and who shall have contracted debts, shall *pay no interest*.   If they themselves, or others for them, are under obligations to pay usurious interest, we release them from that, by our apostolic authority.   If the lords of whom they hold, will not, or cannot lend them the money necessary, they shall be allowed to engage their lands or possessions to ecclesiastics or any other persons.   As our predecessor has done, by the authority of the all-powerful God, and by that of the blessed Saint Peter, prince of the apostles, we grant absolution and remission of sins, we promise Life Eternal to all those who shall undertake and terminate the said pilgrimage, or who shall die in the service of Jesus Christ, after having confessed their sins with a contrite and humble heart.

"Given at Viterbo in the Month of December, 1145."

1146.   Everard des Barres, the newly-elected Grand Master of the Temple, having collected together all the brethren from the western provinces, joined the Second Crusade to Palestine.   During the march through Asia Minor, the rear of the Christian army was protected by the Templars, who greatly signalized themselves on every occasion.   Odo of Deuil, or Diagolum, the chaplain of King Louis, and his constant attendant upon this expedition, informs us that the king loved to see the frugality and simplicity of the Templars, and to imitate it.   He praised their union and disinterestedness, admired above all things the attention they paid to their accoutrements, and their care in husbanding and preserving their equipage and munitions of war, and proposed them as a model to the rest of the army.

Conrad, Emperor of Germany, had preceded King Louis at the head of a powerful army, which was cut to pieces by the enemy in the north of Asia Minor.   He fled to Constantinople, embarked on board some merchant vessels, and arrived with only a few attendants at Jerusalem, where he was received and entertained by the Templars, and was lodged in their Temple in the Holy City. Shortly afterwards King Louis arrived, accompanied by the new Grand Master of the Temple, Everard des Barres; and the Templars now unfolded for the first time their Red Cross Banner upon

KNIGHTS RAISING RED-CROSS STANDARD.

the field of battle. This was a white standard made of woolen stuff, having in the center of it the blood-red cross granted by Pope Eugenius III. The reader will expect to see, at this place, the well-known

HYMN OF THE RED CROSS.

BLOW, warder, blow! thy sounding horn,
  And thy banner wave on high,
For the Christians have fought in the Holy Land,
  And have won the victory.
Loud the warder blew his horn,
And his banner waved on high.
    Let the mass be sung,
    And the bells be rung,
And the feast eat merrily.

The warder looked from his tower on high,
  As far as he could see;
"I see a bold knight, and by his Red Cross
  He comes from the east country."
Then loud the warder blew his horn,
And call'd till he was hoarse,
    "I see the bold knight,
    And on his shield bright,
He beareth a flaming Cross."

Then down the lord of the castle came,
  The Red Cross Knight to meet,
And when the Red Cross Knight he espied,
  Right loving he did him greet:
"Thou'rt welcome here, dear Red Cross Knight,
  For thy fame's well known to me;
    And the mass shall be sung,
    And the bells shall be rung,
And we'll feast right merrily."

" Oh! I am come from the Holy Land,
  Where Saints did live and die;

190   KNIGHTS TEMPLARS.

Siege of Damascus.   Valuable Services rendered by the Templars.

Behold the device I bear on my shield;
    A Red Cross Knight am I:
And we have fought in the Holy Land,
And we've won the victory;
        For with valiant might
        Did the Christians fight,
And made the proud Pagans fly."

" Thou'rt welcome here, dear Red Cross Knight;
    Come, lay thy armor by,
And for the good tidings thou dost bring,
    We'll feast us merrily;
For all in my castle shall rejoice
That we've won the victory;
        And the mass shall be sung,
        And the bells shall be rung,
And the feast eat merrily."

The two monarchs, Louis VII., King of France, and Conrad III., Emperor of Germany, took the field, supported by the Templars, and laid siege to the magnificent city of Damascus, "the Queen of Syria," which was defended by the great Noureddin, " Light of Religion," and his brother Saifeddin, " Sword of the Faith," but after immense losses they were compelled to retire in defeat.   The services rendered by the Templars are thus gratefully recorded in the following letter sent by King Louis, to his minister and vicegerent, the famous Suger, abbot of St. Denis; " I cannot imagine how we could have subsisted for even the smallest space of time in these parts, had it not been for the Templars' support and assistance, which have never failed me from the first day I set foot in these lands up to the time of my despatching this letter—a succor ably afforded and generously persevered in.   I therefore earnestly beseech you, that as these brothers of the Temple have hitherto been blessed with the love of God, so now they may be gladdened and sustained by our love and favor.   I have to inform you that they have lent me a considerable sum of money, which must be repaid to them quickly, that their house may not suffer, and that I may keep my word."

Among the English nobility who enlisted in the Second Crusade were the two renowned warriors, Roger de Mowbray and William de Warrenne. Roger de Mowbray was one of the most powerful

DAMASCUS.

and warlike of the barons of England, and was one of the victorious leaders at the famous Battle of the Standard. He marched with King Louis VII. to Palestine; fought under the banners of the Temple against the infidels, and, smitten with admiration of the piety and valor of the holy warriors of the order, he gave them, on his return to England, many valuable estates and possessions. So munificent were his donations, that the Templars conceded to him and to his heirs various special privileges. About the same period, Stephen, King of England, granted and confirmed "to God and the blessed Virgin Mary, and to the brethren of the Knighthood of the Temple of Solomon at Jerusalem, all the manor of Cressynge, with the advowson of the church of the same manor, and also the manors of Egle and Witham." Queen Matilda, likewise, granted them the manor of Covele or Cowley in Oxfordshire, two mills in the same county, common of pasture in Shotover forest, and the church of Stretton in Rutland. Ralph de Hastings and William de Hastings also gave to the Templars, in 1152, lands at Hurst and Wyxham in Yorkshire, afterwards formed into the preceptory of Temple Hurst. William Asheby granted them the estate whereon the house and church of Temple Bruere were afterwards erected; and the Order continued rapidly to increase in power and wealth in England, and in all parts of Europe, through the charitable donations of pious Christians.

The effect of the Second Crusade in beautiful France, was mournful, "Our castles and villages are deserted, widows and orphans are everywhere," says a historian of the period. After this miserable failure, Everard des Barres, Grand Master of the Temple, returned to Paris, with his friend and patron King Louis; and the Templars, deprived of their chief, were now left, alone and unaided, to withstand the victorious career of the fanatical Mussulmans. Their miserable situation is portrayed in a melancholy letter from the treasurer of the order, written to the Grand Master, Everard des Barres, during his sojourn at the court of the King of France, informing him of the slaughter of the Prince of Antioch and all his nobility. "We conjure you," says he, "to bring with you from beyond sea all our knights and serving brothers capable of bearing arms. Perchance, alas! with all your diligence, you may not find one of us alive. Use, therefore, all imaginable celerity; pray forget not the necessities of our house: they are such that no tongue can express them. It is also of the last importance to announce to the Pope, to the King of France, and to all the princes and prelates of Europe, the approaching desolation of the Holy Land, to the intent that they succor us in person, or send us subsidies."

The Grand Master, however, instead of proceeding to Palestine, abdicated his authority, and entered into the monastery of Clairvaux, where he devoted the remainder of his days to the most rigorous penance and mortification. He was succeeded by Bernard de **1151.** Tremelay, a nobleman of an illustrious family in Burgundy, in France, and a valiant and experienced soldier.

Shortly after the accession of De Tremelay, the Saracens crossed the Jordan, and advanced within sight of Jerusalem. Their banners waved on the summit of the Mount of Olives, half a mile

Defeat of the Saracens. Death of St. Bernard.

east of the city, where the warlike sound of their kettle-drums and trumpets was distinctly heard.   They encamped on the mount over against the Temple; and had the satisfaction of regarding from a distance the *Beit Allah*, or Temple of the Lord, their Holy House of Prayer.   But in a night attack they were defeated with terrible slaughter, and were pursued all the way, fifteen miles, to the Jordan, five thousand of their number being left dead on the plain.

On the 20th of April, the Templars lost their great patron Saint **1153.** Bernard, who died in the sixty-third year of his age.   On his deathbed he wrote three letters in behalf of the Order.   The first was addressed to the Patriarch of Antioch, exhorting him to protect and encourage the Templars, a thing which the abbot assures him will prove most acceptable to God and man.   The second was written to Melesinda, queen of Jerusalem, praising her majesty for the favor shown by her to the brethren of the Order; and the third, addressed to André de Montbard, a Knight Templar, conveys the affectionate salutations of St. Bernard to the Grand Master and brethren, to whose prayers he recommends himself.

The same year the Grand Master of the Temple, De Tremelay, perished at the head of his knights whilst attempting to carry the important city of Ascalon by storm.   Passing through a breach made in the walls, he penetrated into the center of the town, but was there surrounded and overpowered.   The dead bodies of the Grand Master and his ill-fated knights were exposed in triumph from the walls.   According to the testimony of an eye-witness, not a single Templar escaped.

De Tremelay was succeeded by Bertrand de Blanquefort, a **1154.** knight of a noble family of Guienne, called by William of Tyre, *a pious and God-fearing man.*   On Tuesday, June 19, 1156, the Templars were drawn into an ambuscade whilst marching with Baldwin III., king of Jerusalem, near Tiberias, three hundred of the brethren were slain on the field of battle, and eighty-seven fell into the hands of the enemy, among whom was the Grand Master, De Blanquefort, and Odo, marshal of the kingdom.   Shortly afterwards, a small band of the Knights Templars captured a large detachment of Saracens; and in a night attack on the camp of Noureddin, they compelled that famous chieftain to fly, without

Desperate Struggles between the Templars and the Saracens.

arms and half-naked, from the field of battle. In this last affair, the name of Robert Mansel, an Englishman, and Gilbert De Lacy, preceptor of the Temple of Tripoli, are honorably mentioned.

But the fiery zeal and warlike enthusiasm of the Templars were well matched by the stern fanaticism and religious ardor of the followers of Mohammed. Noureddin fought, says his Oriental biographer, like the meanest of his soldiers, saying, Alas! it is now a long time that I have been seeking martyrdom without being able to obtain it. The Imaum Koteb-ed-din, hearing him on one occasion utter these words, exclaimed, " In the name of God do not put your life in danger, do not thus expose Islam and the Moslem. Thou art their stay and support, and if (but God preserve us therefrom) thou shouldest be slain, we are all undone." " Ah! Koteb-ed-din," said he, " what hast thou said, who can save *Islam* and our country, but that great God who has no equal?" " What," said he, on another occasion, " do we not look to the security of our houses against robbers and plunderers, and shall we not defend RELIGION?" Like the Templars, Noureddin fought constantly with spiritual and with carnal weapons. He resisted the world and its temptations, by fasting and prayer, and by the daily exercise of the moral and religious duties and virtues inculcated in the Koran. He fought with the sword against the foes of Islam, and employed his whole energies, to the last hour of his life, in the enthusiastic struggle for the recovery of Jerusalem. In his camp, all profane and frivolous conversation was severely prohibited; the exercises of religion were assiduously practised, and the intervals of action were employed in prayer, meditation, and the study of the Koran. " The sword," says Mohammed, in that remarkable book, " is the key of heaven and of hell; a drop of blood shed in the cause of God, a night spent in arms, is of more avail than two months of fasting and of prayer. Whosoever falls in battle, his sins are forgiven him. At the Day of Judgment his wounds will be resplendent as vermilion, and odoriferous as musk, and the loss of limbs shall be supplied by the wings of angels and cherubim."

Among the many instances of the fanatical ardor of the Moslem warriors, are the following, extracted from the history of *Abu*

Abdollah Alwakidi, Cadi of Bagdad. "Methinks," said a valiant Saracen youth, in the heat of battle—"methinks I see the black-eyed girls looking upon me, one of whom, should she appear in this world, all mankind would die for love of her. And I see in the hand of one of them a handkerchief of green silk, and a cap made of precious stones, and she beckons me, and calls out, Come hither quickly, for I love thee." With these words, charging the Christian host, he made havoc wherever he went, until at last he was struck down by a javelin. "It is not," said another dying Arabian warrior, when he embraced for the last time his sister and mother—"it is not the fading pleasure of this world that has prompted me to devote my life in the cause of RELIGION. I seek the favor of GOD and his APOSTLE, and I have heard from one of the companions of the prophet, that the spirits of the martyrs will be lodged in the crops of green birds who taste the fruits and drink of the waters of Paradise. Farewell: we shall meet again among the groves and fountains which God has prepared for his elect."

The Master of the Temple, Bertrand de Blanquefort, captured at Tiberias A.D. 1156, was liberated from captivity at the instance of Manuel Comnenus, Emperor of Constantinople. After his release, he wrote several letters to Louis VII., King of France, describing the condition and prospects of the Holy Land; the increasing power and boldness of the infidels; and the ruin and desolation caused by a dreadful earthquake, which had overthrown numerous castles, prostrated the walls and defenses of several towns, and swallowed up the dwellings of the inhabitants. "The persecutors of the Church," says he, "hasten to avail themselves of our misfortunes. They gather themselves together from the ends of the earth, and come forth as one man against the sanctuary of God."

It was during his Grand Mastership that Geoffrey, the Knight Templar, and Hugh of Cæsarea, were sent on an embassy into Egypt, and had an interview with the Caliph. They were introduced into the palace of the Fatimites through a series of gloomy passages and glittering porticoes, amid the warbling of birds and the murmur of fountains. The scene was enriched by a display of costly furniture and rare animals; and the long order of unfolding doors was guarded by black soldiers and domestic eunuchs. The sanctuary of the presence-chamber was veiled with a curtain, and the Vizier who conducted the embassadors laid aside his scimitar, and prostrated himself three times on the ground; the veil was then removed, and they saw the Commander of the Faithful.

The Grand Master, in his letters, gives an account of the military operations undertaken by the order of the Temple in Egypt, and of the capture of the populous and important city of Belbeis, the ancient Pelusium. During the absence of the Grand Master with the greater part of the fraternity on that expedition, the Sultan Noureddin invaded Palestine. He defeated with terrible slaughter the serving brethren and Turcopoles, or light horse of the Order, who remained to defend the country, and sixty of the Knights who commanded them, were left dead on the plain. Amalric, King of Jerusalem, the successor of Baldwin III., in a letter "to his dear friend and father," Louis VII., King of France, beseeches the good offices of that monarch in behalf of all the devout Christians of the Holy Land. "But above all," says he, "we earnestly entreat your Majesty constantly to extend to the utmost your favor and regard to the Brothers of the Temple, who continually render up their lives for God and the faith, and through whom we do the little that we are able to effect, for in them, indeed, after God, is placed *the entire reliance* of all those in the eastern regions who tread in the right path." The Grand **1167.** Master, Bertrand de Blanquefort, was succeeded by Philip of Nablous, the first Grand Master of the Temple who had been born in Palestine. He had been lord of the fortresses of Kerak and Montreal in Arabia Petræa, and had taken the vows and the habit of the Order of the Temple after the death of his wife.

The Grand Master of the Temple, Philip of Nablous, resigned his authority after a short government of three years, and was **1170.** succeeded by Odo de St. Amand, a proud and fiery warrior, of undaunted courage and resolution; having, according to William, Archbishop of Tyre, the fear neither of God nor of man before his eyes. It was during his Grand Mastership that the Knight Templar Walter du Mesnil slew an envoy or minister of the

Order ot Assassins.   Death of Raimond.   Tribute of Assassins to Templars.

Assassins.   These were an odious religious sect, settled in the fastnesses of the Lebanon mountains, above Tripoli, and supposed to
be descended from the Ismaelians of Persia.   They devoted their
souls and bodies in blind obedience to a chief who is called by the
writers of the Crusaders the Old Man of the Mountain, and were
employed by him in the most extensive system of murder and
assassination known in the history of the world.   Both Christian
and Moslem writers enumerate with horror the many illustrious
victims that fell beneath their daggers.   They assumed all shapes
and disguises for the furtherance of their deadly designs, and carried,
in general, no arms except a small poniard, called in the Persian
tongue, *hassissin*, concealed in the folds of their dress, whence
these wretches were called *Assassins*, and their chief the Prince
of the Assassins.   So the word itself, in all its odious import, has
passed into most European languages.

Raimond, son of the Count of Tripoli, had been slain by these
fanatics whilst kneeling at the foot of the altar in the Church of
the Blessed Virgin at Carchusa, or Tortosa.   The Templars flew
to arms to avenge his death.   They penetrated into the fastnesses
and strongholds of the Mountain Chief, and at last compelled him
to purchase peace by the payment of an annual tribute of two
thousand crowns into the treasury of the Order.   In the ninth
1171. year of Almaric's reign, Sinan Ben Suleiman, imaum of the
Assassins, sent a trusty counselor to Jerusalem, offering, in the
name of himself and his people, to embrace the Christian religion,
provided the Templars would release them from the tribute money.
The proposition was favorably received.   The envoy was honorably
entertained for some days, and on his departure he was furnished
by the king with a guide and an escort to conduct him in safety to
the frontier.   The Ismaelite had reached the borders of the Latin
kingdom, and was almost in sight of the castles of his brethren,
when he was slain by the Knight Templar, Walter du Mesnil, who
attacked the escort with a body of armed followers.   The King of
Jerusalem assembled the barons of the kingdom at Sidon to determine on the best means of obtaining satisfaction for the injury;
and it was determined that two of their number should proceed to
the Grand Master, Odo de St. Amand, to demand the surrender

of the criminal. The haughty Grand Master of the Temple, how-ever, bade them inform his majesty the king that the members of the Order were not subject to his jurisdiction, nor to that of his officers; that the Templars acknowledged no earthly superior except the Pope; and that to the Pope alone belonged the cognizance of the offense. He declared, however, that the crime should meet with due punishment: that he had caused the criminal to be arrested and put in irons, and would forthwith send him to Rome. But till judgment was given in his case he forbade all persons, of whatsoever degree, to meddle with him.

The Templars were now destined to meet with a more formidable opponent than any they had hitherto encountered in the field—one who was again to cause the CRESCENT to triumph over the CROSS, and to plant the standard of Mohammed upon the walls of the holy city. When the Fatimite Caliph had received intelligence of King Almaric's invasion of Egypt he sent the hair of his women, one of the greatest tokens of distress known in the East, to Noureddin, who immediately despatched a body of troops to his assistance, headed by Sheerkoh, and his nephew, *Youseef-Ben-Acoub-Ben-Schadi*, afterwards the famous Saladin. Sheerkoh died immediately after his arrival, and Saladin succeeded to his command, and was appointed Vizier of the Caliph. He had passed his youth in pleasure and debauchery, sloth and indolence, but as soon as he grasped the power of the sword and obtained the command of armies he renounced the pleasures of the world, and assumed the character of a saint. His dress was a coarse woolen garment, water was his only drink. He carefully abstained from everything disapproved of by the Mussulman religion. Five times each day he prostrated himself in public prayer, surrounded by his friends and followers, and his demeanor became grave, serious, and thoughtful. His nights were often spent in watching and meditation. He was diligent in fasting and in the study of the Koran, and so his admiring brethren gave him the name of Salah-ed-deen (the Integrity of Religion).

Having aroused the religious enthusiasm of the Moslem, he proceeded to take vengeance upon the Christians for their perfidious invasion of Egypt. He assembled an army of forty thousand horse and foot, crossed the desert and besieged the fortified city of Gaza, which belonged to the Knights Templars, and was considered to be the key of Palestine towards Egypt.   The luxuriant gardens, the palm and olive groves of this city of the wilderness were de-

SALADIN IN COMPLETE EASTERN COSTUME.

stroyed by the wild cavalry of the desert, and the innumerable tents of the Arab host were thickly clustered on the neighboring sand-hills.   The warlike monks of the Temple in their turn fasted and prayed, and invoked the aid of the God of battles.   They made a desperate defense, and in an unexpected sally upon the enemy's camp they performed such prodigies of valor that Saladin, despairing of being able to take the place, abandoned the siege and returned to Egypt.

Saladin invades Palestine with a powerful Army.

1175. On the death of Noureddin, Sultan of Damascus, Saladin raised himself to the sovereignty both of Egypt and of Syria. He levied a second great army, crossed the desert, and again planted the standard of Mohammed upon the sacred territory of Palestine. His forces were composed of 26,000 light infantry, 8,000 horsemen, a host of archers and spearmen mounted on dromedaries, 18,000 common soldiers, and a body-guard of a 1,000 Mameluke

GAZA.

emirs (princes), clothed in yellow cloaks, worn over their shirts of **1177.** mail. In a great battle fought near Ascalon, Nov. 1, Odo de St. Amand, Grand Master of the Temple, at the head of eighty of his knights, broke through the guard of Mamelukes, slew their commander, and penetrated to the imperial tent, from whence Saladin escaped with great difficulty and almost naked upon a fleet **1178.** dromedary. The year following, the Templars, in order to

The Christian Army defeated.   Great Courage of the Templars.

protect and cover the road leading from Damascus to Jerusalem, commenced the erection of a strong fortress on the northern frontier of the Latin kingdom, close to Jacob's ford on the river Jordan, at the spot where now stands Jisr Benat Yacob, "the Bridge of the Sons of Jacob." Saladin advanced at the head of his forces to oppose the progress of this work, while Baldwin IV., King of Jerusalem, and all the chivalry of the Latin kingdom, gathered together in the plain to protect the Templars and their workmen. In a general action, June 1177, the entire army of the Cross was defeated with immense slaughter. The Templars and the Hospitalers, with the Count of Tripoli, stood firm on the summit of a small hillock, and for a long time presented a bold and undaunted front to the victorious enemy. The Count of Tripoli at last cut his way through the infidels and fled to Tyre,

TYRE, WITH THE ANCIENT AQUEDUCT.

twenty-five miles distant. The Grand Master of the Hospital, after seeing most of his brethren slain, swam across the Jordan, and fled, covered with wounds, to the castle of Beaufort. (See Map.) The Templars, after fighting with their accustomed zeal and fanaticism around the red-cross banner, which waved to the last over the field of blood, were all killed or taken prisoners, and the Grand Master, Odo de St. Amand, fell alive into the hands of the enemy. Saladin then laid siege to the newly-erected fortress, defended by thick walls, flanked with large towers furnished with military engines, and after a gallant resistance on the part of the garrison, set it on fire, and then stormed it. "The Templars," says Abulpharadge, an Arabian historian, "flung themselves, some into the fire, where they were burned, some into the Jordan. Some jumped down from the walls upon the rocks, and were dashed to pieces. Thus were slain the enemy." The fortress was reduced to a heap of ruins, and the enraged Sultan, it is said, ordered all the Templars taken in the place to be *sawn in two*, excepting the most distinguished of the knights, who were reserved for a ransom, and were sent in chains to Aleppo. Saladin offered the Grand Master his liberty in exchange for the freedom of his own nephew, who was a prisoner in the hands of the Templars. But Odo haughtily replied, that he would never, by his example, encourage any of his knights to be mean enough to surrender; that a Templar ought either to vanquish or die, and that he had nothing to give for his ransom but his girdle and his knife. The proud spirit of Odo de St. Amand, however, could but ill brook confinement. He languished **1180.** and died in the dungeons of Damascus, and was succeeded by Arnold de Torroge, who had filled some of the chief situations of the Order in Europe.

The following cut of the present appearance of this famous bridge and the remains of the ruined castle which once guarded it will be interesting in this connection. The bridge itself (*Jisr Benat Yacob*) is doubtless later than the time of the Crusades, and was probably constructed in connection with the great caravan road from Egypt to Damascus, with its numerous khans or houses of entertainment. According to a legendary supposition Jacob crossed here B.C. 1760 on his way to Padan-aram. The ruined khan which takes the place of the ancient castle, is at the eastern end of the bridge and the fifth upon this great public road after it enters the plain of Esdraelon at Leijun. The bridge is built of the basaltic rock of the vicinity. It has four pointed arches, is sixty paces long and forty wide. The corner-stone of a castle was laid by King Baldwin IV. in October, 1178, on the western side of the bridge.   The edifice, which was quadrangular and of great thickness and solidity, was completed in about six months and given to the keeping of the Knights Templars.   This is the edifice to which Mr. Addison refers above.

BRIDGE OVER JORDAN.

The affairs of the Latin Christians were at this period in a deplorable situation.   Saladin encamped near Tiberias, and extended his ravages into almost every part of Palestine.   His light cavalry swept the valley of the Jordan to within a day's march of Jerusalem, and the whole country as far as Banias on the one side, and Bethshean, Jenin and Sebaste, on the other, was destroyed by fire and the sword (see Map).   The houses of the Templars were pillaged and burnt.   Various castles belonging to the Order were taken by assault.   But the immediate destruction of the Latin power was arrested by some partial successes obtained by the Christian warriors, and by the skillful generalship of their leaders, so that Saladin was compelled to retreat to Damascus, after he had burnt Nablous, and depopulated the country around Tiberias, **1184.** the most fertile portion of Galilee.   A truce was proposed, and as the attention of the Sultan was then distracted by the intrigues of the Turcoman chieftains in the north of Syria, and he was again engaged in hostilities in Mesopotamia, he agreed to a suspension of the war for four years, in consideration of the payment by the Christians of a large sum of money.

Immediate advantage was taken of this truce to secure the safety of the Latin kingdom. A grand Council was called together at Jerusalem, and it was determined that Heraclius, the Patriarch of the Holy City, and the Grand Masters of the Temple De Torroge and of the Hospital Des Moulin should forthwith proceed to Europe, to obtain succor from the Western princes. The sovereign mostly depended upon for assistance was Henry II., King of England, grandson of Fulk, King of Jerusalem, 1131 to 1144, and cousin-german to Baldwin IV., the then reigning sovereign. Henry had received absolution for the murder of Thomas à Becket, on condition that he should proceed in person at the head of a powerful army to the succor of Palestine, and should, at his own expense, maintain two hundred Templars for the defense of the holy territory. The Patriarch and the two Grand Masters landed in Italy, and after furnishing themselves with letters of the Pope, threatening the English monarch with the judgments of heaven if he did not forthwith perform the penance prescribed him, they set out for England. At Verona, the Grand Master of the Temple, De Torroge, fell sick and died, but his com-
1185. panions proceeding on their journey, landed in safety in England at the commencement of the year. They were received by the King at Reading, and throwing themselves at the feet of the English monarch, they with much weeping and sobbing saluted him in behalf of the King, the princes, and the people of the Kingdom of Jerusalem. They explained the object of their visit, and presented him with the Pope's letters, with the keys of the Holy Sepulcher, the Tower of David, and the City of Jerusalem, together with the royal banner of the Latin kingdom. Their eloquent and pathetic narrative of the fierce inroads of Saladin, and of the miserable condition of Palestine, drew tears from King Henry and his courtiers. The English sovereign gave encouraging assurances to the Patriarch and his companions, and promised to bring the whole matter before the Parliament, which was to meet the first Sunday in Lent.

The Temple Church. Refusal of Assistance to the Christian Cause.

The Patriarch, in the mean time, proceeded to London, and was received by the Knights Templars at the Temple in that city, the chief house of the Order in Britain, where, in the month of February, he consecrated the beautiful Temple Church, dedicated to the blessed Virgin Mary, which had just then been erected. A detailed account of this ancient and beautiful edifice is given in a subsequent chapter.

The Grand Master, Arnold de Torroge, was succeeded by Gerard de Riderfort.

On the 10th of the calends of April, a month after the consecration by the Patriarch Heraclius of the Temple Church, the Grand Council or Parliament of England, composed of the bishops, earls, and barons, assembled in the house of the Hospitalers at Clerkenwell in London. It was attended by William, King of Scotland, and David his brother, and many of the counts and barons of that distant land. The august assembly was made acquainted, in the King's name, with the object of the solemn embassy just sent to him from Jerusalem, and with the desire of the royal penitent to fulfill his vow and perform his penance. But the barons were at the same time reminded of the old age of their sovereign, of the bad state of his health, and of the necessity for his presence in England. They accordingly represented to King Henry that the solemn oath taken by him on his coronation was an obligation antecedent to the penance imposed on him by the Pope; that by that oath he was bound to stay at home and govern his dominions, and that, in their opinion, it was more wholesome for the King's soul to defend his own country against the French, than to desert it for the purpose of protecting the distant kingdom of Jerusalem.

Fabian, in his chronicle, gives the following account of the King's answer to the Patriarch.

"Lastly, the King gave answer, and said that he might not leave his lands without keeping, nor yet leave it to the prey and robbery of Frenchmen. But he would give largely of his own to such as would take upon them that voyage. With this answer the Patriarch Heraclius was discontented, and said: We seek a *man* and not *money*. Nearly every Christian region sendeth unto us *money*, but no land sendeth unto us a *prince*. Therefore we ask a prince that needeth money, and not money that needeth a prince. But the king laid before him such excuses that the Patriarch departed from him discontented and comfortless.   Wherefore the King, being advised, intending somewhat to re-comfort him with pleasant words, followed him to the seaside.   But the more the King thought to satisfy him with his fair speech, the more the Patriarch was discontented, insomuch that at the last he said unto him: Hitherto thou hast reigned gloriously, but hereafter thou shalt be forsaken of Him whom thou, at this time, forsakest!   Think on Him, what he hath given thee, and what thou hast yielded to Him again!   How first thou wert false unto the King of France, and afterwards slew that holy man, Thomas of Canterbury, and now thou forsakest the protection of Christ's faith!   The King was moved with these words, and said unto the Patriarch: Though all the men of my lands were of one body, and spake with one mouth, they durst not speak to me such words.   No wonder, said the Patriarch, for they love *thine* and not *thee;* that is to say, they love thy goods temporal, and fear for the loss of promotion, but they love not thy soul. And when he had so said, he offered his head to the King, saying: Do by me right as thou didst to that blessed man, Thomas of Canterbury, for I had sooner be slain of thee than of the Saracens, for thou art worse than any Saracen.   But the king kept his patience and said: I may not go out of my land, for *my own sons* would rise against me were I absent.   No wonder, said the Patriarch, for of the devil they came, and to the devil they shall go! And so he departed from the King in great wrath."

1185. According to Roger de Hovenden, however, the Patriarch, on the 17th of the calends of May, accompanied King Henry into Normandy, where a conference was held between the sovereigns of France and England, concerning the proposed succor to the Holy Land.   Both monarchs were liberal in promises and fair speeches; but as nothing short of the presence of the King of England, or of one of his sons, in Palestine, would satisfy the Patriarch, that haughty ecclesiastic failed in his negotiations, and returned in disgust and disappointment to the Holy Land.   On his arrival at Jerusalem with intelligence of his ill success the greatest consternation prevailed amongst the Latin Christians; and it was generally observed that the True Cross, which had been recovered from the Persians by the Emperor Heraclius, was about to be lost under the pontificate, and by the fault of a patriarch of the same name.*

---

* The news of the immense gathering of the Saracens filled the hearts of the Christians with dismay, and nothing but desolation and destruction was prophesied to the Holy Land.   The heavens were filled with signs, that proved how plainly God held in abomination their wickedness.   Impetuous winds, tempests,

Weakness of the Latin Kingdom.   A Regency adopted.

1185.   Baldwin IV., who was the reigning sovereign of the Latin kingdom at the period of the departure of the Patriarch Heraclius and the Grand Master of the Temple for Europe, was afflicted with a frightful leprosy, which rendered it unlawful for him to marry, and he was consequently deprived of all hope of having an heir of his body to inherit the crown.   As early as 1184 he had lost his eyes, and his extremities had petrified and fallen off.   He had lost the faculties both of mind and body, and tormented by his sufferings, he every day drew nearer the tomb, presenting but too faithful an image of the weakness and decline of his kingdom. Sensible of the dangers and inconvenience of a female succession, he selected William V., Marquis of Montferrat, surnamed Long Sword, as a husband for his eldest sister, Sibylla, she who died so miserably with all her children, six years later, at Acre.   Shortly after his marriage the Marquis of Montferrat died, leaving by Sibylla an infant son named Baldwin.   Sibylla's second husband was Guy de Lusignan, a nobleman of a handsome person, and descended of an ancient family of Poitou, in France, who first seduced and then married her.   Her choice was at first approved of by the King, who received his new brother-in-law with favor, loaded him with honors, and made him regent of the kingdom.   Subsequently, through the intrigues of the Count of Tripoli, King Baldwin IV. was induced to deprive Guy de Lusignan of the regency, and to set aside the claims of Sibylla to the throne in favor of her son, the young Baldwin, who was then about five years of age.   He gave orders for the coronation of the young prince, and resigned his authority to the Count of Tripoli, who was appointed regent of the kingdom during the minority of the sovereign, whilst all the

---

and storms arose on all sides ; the light of the sun was obscured during several days, and hail-stones as large as the egg of a goose fell from heaven. The earth, equally agitated by frequent and horrible earthquakes, gave notice of coming ruin and destruction, with disasters and defeats in war, which were soon to visit the kingdom.   Neither could the sea confine itself within its bounds and limits, but announced to the Christians, by its horrible floods and its unusually impetuous waves, the anger of God ready to fall upon them.   Fire was seen blazing in the air like a house in flames.   All the elements and architecture of God were angry, as if they abhorred the excesses, wickedness, dissoluteness, and offenses of the human race.

fortresses and castles of the land were committed to the safe keeping of the Templars and Hospitalers.   The youthful Baldwin was
carried with vast pomp to the great Church of the Holy Sepulcher,

CHURCH OF THE HOLY SEPULCHER.

and was there anointed and crowned by the Patriarch Heraclius,
1186. in the presence of the Grand Masters of the Temple and the
Hospital.   According to ancient custom, he was taken, wearing his
crown, to the Temple of the Lord, to make certain offerings, after
which he went to the Temple of Solomon, where the Templars
resided, and was entertained at dinner, together with his barons,
by the Grand Master of the Temple and the military friars. Shortly after the coronation the ex-king, Baldwin IV., died at Jeru-

salem, and was buried in the Church of the Resurrection, by the side of Godfrey de Bouillon, and the six other Christian kings, viz.: Godfrey, died 1100; Baldwin I., died 1118; Baldwin II., died 1131; Fulk, died 1144; Baldwin III., died 1162; Almeric, died 1174. The death of Baldwin IV., March 15, 1185, was followed, in the short space of seven months, by that of the infant sovereign, Baldwin V., and Sibylla thus became the heiress to the throne, by the most unfortunate rule of succession. The Count of Tripoli, previously named, refused, however, to surrender the regency, accusing Sibylla of the horrible and improbable crime of poisoning her own child. But Gerard de Riderfort, Grand Master of the Temple, invited her to repair to Jerusalem, and gave orders for the coronation. He sent letters in the Queen's name to Raymond, Count of Tripoli and Galilee, and the rebellious barons who had assembled with their followers in arms at Nablous, requiring them to attend at the appointed time to do homage and take the oath of allegiance, but the barons sent back word that they intended to remain where they were; and they despatched two Cistercian abbots to the Grand Master of the Temple, and the Patriarch Heraclius, exhorting them, for the love of God and his Holy Apostles, to refrain from crowning Sibylla as long as she remained the wife of Guy de Lusignan. They represented that the latter had already manifested his utter incapacity for command, both in the field and in the cabinet; that the kingdom of Jerusalem required an able general for its sovereign; and they insisted that Sibylla should be immediately divorced from Guy de Lusignan, and should choose a husband better fitted to protect the country and undertake the conduct of the government.

As soon as this message had been received, the Grand Master of the Temple, de Riderfort, directed the Templars to take possession of all the gates of the city of Jerusalem, and issued strict orders that no person should be allowed to enter or withdraw from the Holy City without an express permission from himself. Sibylla and her husband, Guy de Lusignan, were then taken, guarded by the Templars, to the great Church of the Resurrection, where the Patriarch Heraclius and all his clergy were in readiness to receive them. The crowns of the Latin kingdom had been kept in a

large chest in the treasury, fastened with two locks.   The Grand
Master of the Temple kept the key of one of these locks, and the
Grand Master of the Hospital had the other.   On their arrival at
the church the key of the Grand Master of the Temple was produced, but the key of the Grand Master of the Hospital was not
forthcoming, nor could that illustrious chieftain himself anywhere
be found.   Gerard de Riderfort and Heraclius at last went in
person to the Hospital, and after much hunting about they found
the Grand Master, Du Moulin, and immediately demanded the
key in the Queen's name.

The following is a list of the Patriarchs of Jerusalem, A.D. 1099
to 1187, from De Vogüé.   The spelling is French:

Daimbert ⎫	
Arnulphe ⎬	1099 to 1107
Ebremard ⎭	
Gibelin	1107 to 1111
Arnulphe..........................	1111 to 1118
Gormond..........................	1118 to 1128
Etienne (Stephen)...................	1128 to 1130
Guillaume (William)	1130 to 1146
Foulcher	1146 to 1157
Amanry...........................	1157 to 1180
Eraclius (Heraclius)................	1180 to 1190

The Pope re-established this Patriarchate of Jerusalem in 1847,
in the person of Bishop Valerga, "the actual titulary."   He only
has the authority to confer the Order of Knights of the Holy
Sepulcher.   This is done in the apartment styled "The Chapel of
the Apparition," where Jesus is said to have appeared to Mary after
the resurrection.   The candidate, kneeling before the Patriarch,
answers the traditional questions, and is then girded with the sword
and spurs of King Godfrey.

This authoritative demand of the keys of the crown was at first
refused by the Grand Master of the Hospitalers, Du Moulin; but
being pressed by many arguments and entreaties, he at last took
out the key and flung it upon the ground, whereupon the Patriarch
Heraclius picked it up, and proceeding to the treasury, speedily
produced the two crowns, one of which he placed upon the high

KNIGHTS TEMPLARS. 211

Crowning of the Queen.   Revolt of the Count of Tripoli.

altar of the Church of the Resurrection, and the other by the side
of the chair upon which Sibylla, Countess of Joppa, was seated.
Heraclius then performed the solemn ceremony of the coronation,
and when he had placed the crown on the Queen's head he reminded
her that she was a frail and feeble woman, but ill-fitted to contend
with the toil and strife in which the beleaguered kingdom of
Palestine was continually involved, and he therefore exhorted her
to make choice of some person to govern the kingdom in conjunction with herself.   Whereupon, taking up the crown which had
been placed by her side, and calling for her husband, Guy de
Lusignan, she thus addressed him : " Those whom God hath joined
let no man put asunder.   Sire, receive this crown, for I know none
more worthy of it than yourself."   And immediately Guy de
Lusignan was crowned ninth king of Jerusalem, and received the
blessing of the Patriarch Heraclius.

1186.   Great was the indignation of the Count of Tripoli and the
barons when they received intelligence of these events.   They
raised the standard of revolt, and proclaimed the princess Isabella,
the younger sister of Sibylla (who had been married, at the early
period of eight years, to Humphrey de Thoron), Queen of Jerusalem.   As soon, however, as Humphrey de Thoron heard of the
proceedings of the Count of Tripoli and the barons, he hurried with
his wife, the princess, to Jerusalem, and the two, throwing themselves at the feet of the King and Queen, respectfully tendered to
them their allegiance.   This conduct struck terror and dismay into
the hearts of the conspirators, most of whom now proceeded to
Jerusalem to do homage ; whilst the Count of Tripoli, deserted by
his adherents, retired to the strong citadel of Tiberias, of which
place he was the feudal lord, and there remained, defying the royal
power.

The King at first sought to avail himself of the assistance of the
Templars against his vassal, and exhorted them to besiege Tiberias ;
but they refused, as it was contrary to their oaths and the spirit of
their institution for them to undertake an aggressive warfare against
any Christian prince.   The King then gave orders for the concentration of an army at Nazareth.   The Count of Tripoli prepared
to defend Tiberias, and it appears unquestionable that he sent to

Saladin for assistance, and entered into a defensive and independent alliance with that monarch.   The citadel of Tiberias was a place of great strength, the military power of the Count was very considerable, and the friends of the King, foreseeing that the infidels would not fail to take advantage of a civil war, earnestly besought his majesty to offer terms of reconciliation to his powerful vassal. It was accordingly agreed that the Grand Masters of the Temple

TIBERIAS, WITH OLD CASTLE OF THE TEMPLARS.

(De Riderfort) and the Hospital (Du Moulin) should proceed with the Archbishop of Tyre, the Lord Balian d'Ibelin of Nablous, and the Lord Reginald of Sidon, to Tiberias, and attempt to bring back **1187.** the Count to his allegiance.   These illustrious personages set out for Jerusalem, and slept the first night at Nablous, thirty miles north, of which town Balian d'Ibelin was the feudal lord, and the next day they journeyed on towards Nazareth, forty miles further.   As they drew near that place the Grand Master of the Temple proceeded to pass the night at a neighboring fortress of the Knights Templars, called "the Castle of La Feue," and was eating his supper with the brethren in the refectory of the convent,

KNIGHTS TEMPLARS. 213

Chronicle of the Holy Land. The Infidels' Attack upon the Christians.

when intelligence was brought to him that a strong corps of the Mussulman cavalry, under the command of Malek al Afdal, one of Saladin's sons, had crossed the Jordan at sunrise, and was marching through the territories of the Count of Tripoli.

The Chronicle of the Holy Land, written by Radolph, abbot of the Monastery of Coggleshale in Essex, forms the most important and trustworthy account now in existence of the conquest of Jerusalem by Saladin, for the writer was, as he tells us, an eye-witness of all the remarkable events he relates. It covers the period 1187 to 1191. Radolph was an English monk of the Cistercian Order, and a man of vast learning and erudition. He went on a pilgrimage to Palestine, and was there on the breaking out of the war which immediately preceded the loss of the Holy City. He was present at the siege of Jerusalem, and was wounded by an arrow, which, says the worthy abbot, pierced through the nose of the relator of these circumstances; the wood was withdrawn, but a part of the iron barb remains to this day. His chronicle was published in 1729, by the fathers Martene and Durand, in their valuable collection of ancient chronicles and manuscripts.

1187. As soon as the Grand Master of the Temple heard that the infidels had crossed the Jordan and were ravaging the Christian territories, he sent messengers to a castle of the Templars called "The Convent of Caco," situate four miles distant from La Feue, commanding all the Knights that could be spared from the garrison at that place to mount and come to him with speed. The Knights had retired to rest when the messengers arrived, but they arose from their beds, and at midnight they were encamped with their horses around the walls of the Castle of La Feue. The next morning, May 1, as soon as it was light, the Grand Master, at the head of ninety of his Knights, rode over to Nazareth and was joined at that place by the Grand Master of the Hospital, Du Moulin, and forty Knights of the garrison of Nazareth. The Templars and Hospitalers were accompanied by four hundred of their foot soldiers, and the whole force, under the command of the two Grand Masters, amounted to about six hundred men. With this small but valiant band, they set out in quest of the infidels, and had proceeded about seven miles from Nazareth in the direc-

Sudden Attack of Templars upon a Body of Mussulmans.

NAZARETH.

tion of the Jordan, at the south side of Mount Tabor, when they came suddenly upon a strong column of Mussulman cavalry amounting to several thousand men, who were watering their horses at the brook Kishon. Without waiting to count the number of their enemies, the Templars raised their war-cry, unfolded the Blood-red Banner, and dashed into the midst of the astonished and terrified Mussulmans, dealing around them, to use the words of Coggleshale, "death and damnation." The infidels, taken by surprise, were at first thrown into confusion, discomfited, and slaughtered. But when the smallness of the force opposed to them became apparent, they closed in upon the Templars, overwhelmed them with darts and missiles, and speedily thinned their ranks with a terrific slaughter. An eye-witness tells us that the Knights of the two Orders were to be seen bathed with blood and sweat; trembling with fatigue; with their horses killed under them, and with their swords and lances broken, closing with the Mussulman warriors, and rolling headlong with them in the dust. Some tore the darts with which they had been transfixed from their bodies, and hurled them back with a convulsive effort upon the enemy; and others, having lost all their weapons in the affray, clung around the necks of their opponents, dragged them from their horses, and endeavored to strangle them under the feet of the combatants. Jacqueline de Mailly, Marshal of the Temple,

performed on that day prodigies of valor.   He was mounted on a
white horse, and clothed in the white habit of his Order, with the
Blood-red Cross, the symbol of martyrdom, on his breast.   He became, through his gallant bearing and demeanor, an object of
admiration, even to the Moslem.   Radolph compares the fury and
the anger of this warlike monk, as he looked around him upon his
slaughtered brethren, to the *wrath of the lioness who has lost her
whelps ;* and his position and demeanor in the midst of the throng
of infidels, he likens to that of the wild boar when surrounded by
dogs whom he is tearing with his tusks.   Every blow of this furious man, says the worthy abbot, " despatched an infidel to hell."
But with all his valor Jacqueline de Mailly was slain.   The place
where this terrific fight occurred is the battle-field on which the
French under Napoleon discomfited the Turks in 1799.

MOUNT TABOR.

The beautiful Mount Tabor, which impends over the place made
sorrowful by such a calamity, is a landmark in Galilee, and at the
time of which we speak, was believed by all to be the place of our
Saviour's Transfiguration.   It was a saying of the Jewish Talmud

The Church on the Summit of Mount Tabor.

that "the Temple ought of right to have been on Tabor, but by revelation was placed on Moriah." It rises abruptly from the northeastern arm of the plain of Esdraelon and stands entirely insulated, except on the west, where a narrow ridge connects it with the hills of Nazareth. It is almost perfectly symmetrical in proportion, rounded off like a hemisphere. It is composed of the tertiary limestone of the country, and studded with a dense forest of oaks, pistachios, and other trees affording shelter for wolves, wild boars, lynxes, and various reptiles. Its height is about 1,000 feet. It lies six miles due east of Nazareth.

The church which in 1187 crowned the summit of Mount Tabor is now in ruins, scarcely presenting a trace of their ancient purpose. We give from De Vogüé's notes (1854) a brief account. We do this the more readily as the place once belonged to the illustrious Tancred.

Although the text of the New Testament has passed in silence the *name* of "the high mountain" upon which Jesus Christ was transfigured, the tradition which places this scene upon the summit of Tabor is sufficiently ancient to merit our respect. St. Cyril, and then St. Jerome, accepted it as being perfectly established in their time. This belief built, in a very good time, churches and monasteries in this place. One city was grouped about religious edifices; its ruins partly covered the summit of the mountain. They are surrounded by the *débris* of the rampart which was built by Josephus during the Jewish War, and which was restored, in the middle age, by the Sultan Malekadel. In the midst of piles of rubbish and of large-leaved oaks may be distinguished the remains of two churches, one appearing very ancient, the other which dates from the Crusades.

The first one offers the greatest interest. It is a little rectangle, four metres in length and whose width does not exceed five or six metres, terminated at the east by a demi-circular apside. The walls are constructed in mean display, very strictly Roman, and covered on the interior with a white stucco, upon which may be distinguished traces of foliage painted in red. The pavement is in mosaic, formed of large cubes, white and black, describing a large circle and lozenges. This little structure bears the character of the oratories of the Fourth and Fifth Centuries. For my part, I make no hesitation in considering it one of the most ancient religious edifices in the Holy Land.

The second ruin is composed of some little underground halls, vaulted *d'arête*, to which descent is made by a stone stairway. It is the ruined crypt of a Roman church, which ought to have three naves and three chapels, in memory of the three tabernacles that the Apostles wished to have built in

Church on Mount Tabor. Disastrous Battle of the Templars.

that place after the Transfiguration. It belongs to the convent founded in the first years of the Twelfth Century, under the name of The Holy Saviour.

The first travelers who mention the churches on Mount Tabor are Antonine de Plaisance and Arculph. They saw, the one and the other, three churches and a convent occupied by numerous priests. The travelers of the following centuries speak of them much in the same terms. During the Frank occupation, two convents received the pilgrims; the one *Latin*, occupying the culminating point of the mountain; the other *Greek*, situated a little further north. These two positions perfectly agree with the two ruins I have described.

The Latin monastery of the Holy Saviour was founded and richly endowed by Tancred, Count of Galilee, in favor of the priests of Cluny. This is found already cited in the acts of 1111 and 1112. It was destroyed in 1113 by the Mussulmans, and then rebuilt. In 1183 the Abbé concluded a convention with the Superior of the Monastery of St. Paul at Antioch, by which he engaged, in case of invasion, to collect together all his community into it. This clause was advantageous, for the position was very strong, the walls high and solid, the garrison valiant, already wearing the frock. In the same year, "owing to the thickness of the walls," says William of Tyre, "the number of the towers and the valor of the priests," run aground against Mount Tabor and could not take the place. Four years later he had his revenge, after the celebrated victory of Hattin, in razing the city and the monastery to the earth. From that time to our day no permanent religious establishment has existed on Mount Tabor."

In this bloody battle of May 1, 1187, perished the Grand Master of the Hospital, Du Moulin, and all the Templars excepting the Grand Master, De Riderfort, and two of his knights, who broke through the dense ranks of the Moslem, and made their escape to Nazareth, the Grand Master himself being severely wounded. The Mussulmans severed the heads of the slaughtered Templars from their bodies, and attaching them with cords to the points of their lances, they marched off in the direction of Tiberias. This disastrous engagement was fought on Friday, the 1st of May, A.D. 1187, the feast of St. James and St. Philip. "In that beautiful season of the year," says Abbot Coggleshale, "when the inhabitants of Nazareth were wont to seek the rose and the violet in the fields, they found only the sad traces of carnage, and the lifeless bodies of their slaughtered brethren. With mourning and great lamentation they carried them into the burial-ground of the Blessed Virgin Mary at Nazareth, crying aloud, 'Daughters of Galilee, put on your mourning clothes, and ye daughters of Zion, bewail the misfortunes that threaten the kings of Judah.' " *

1187.   Whilst this bloody battle was being fought, the Lord Balian d'Ibelin of Nablous was journeying with another party of Templars from his own city to join the Grand Master at Nazareth, and the following interesting account is given of their march towards that place.   " When they had traveled two miles, they came to the city of Sebaste (ancient Samaria), which is on the most traveled route.   It was a lovely morning, and they determined to march no further until they had heard mass.   They accordingly turned towards the house of the bishop and awoke him up, and informed him that the day was breaking.   In Oriental countries the best hours for travel are just before day.   The bishop accordingly ordered an old chaplain to put on his clothes and say mass, after which they hastened forwards.   Then they came to the castle of La Feue, close to Nazareth, and there they found, outside the castle, the tents of the convent of Caco pitched, and there was no one to explain what it meant.   A varlet was sent into the castle to inquire, but he found no one within but two sick people who were unable to speak.   Then they marched towards Nazareth, and after they had proceeded a short distance from the castle of La Feue, they met a brother of the Temple on horseback, who galloped up to them at a furious rate, calling out, ' Bad news, bad news.'   He informed them how that the Master of the Hospital had had his head cut off, and how of all the Brothers of the Temple there had perished but three, the Grand Master of the Temple and two others, and that the knights whom the King had

---

* Omens were not wanting to discourage them, for Venisauf relates a fearful vision which appeared to the King's chamberlain, who dreamed that an eagle flew past the Christian army, bearing seven missiles and a balista in his talons, and crying with a loud voice, " Woe to thee, Jerusalem !"   " To explain the mystery of this vision," says Venisauf, " we need, I think, only take the words of Scripture, ' The Lord hath bent his bow, and in it prepared the vessels of death.'   What are the seven missiles but a figure of the seven sins by which that unhappy army was soon to perish ?   By this number, seven, may also be understood the number of punishments that impended over the Christians, which was some time after fulfilled by the event, that too faithful and terrible interpreter of omens."

placed in garrison at Nazareth, were all taken and killed." " If Lord Balian d'Ibelin," says the chronicler, " had marched straight to Nazareth, with his knights, instead of halting to hear mass at Sebaste,

SEBASTE, ANCIENT SAMARIA.

he would have been in time to have saved his brethren from slaughter." As it was, he arrived just in time to hear the funeral service read over their dead bodies by William, Archbishop of Tyre. 1187. The Grand Master of the Temple, de Riderfort, who was at Nazareth, suffering severely from his wounds, hastened to collect together a small force at that place to open the communications with Tiberias, which being done, the Lord Balian d'Ibelin and the Archbishop William of Tyre proceeded to that place to have their interview with the Count of Tripoli. The Grand Master accompanied them as far as the hill above the citadel, but not liking to trust himself into the power of the Count, he then re-

220   KNIGHTS TEMPLARS.

Supposed Treachery of the Count of Tripoli.   Reconciliation.   Jacob's Well.

traced his steps to Nazareth. Both the Moslem and the Christian writers agree in asserting that the Count of Tripoli had at this period entered into an alliance with Saladin.   Nevertheless, either smitten with remorse for his past conduct, or moved by the generous overtures of the King, he consented to do homage and become reconciled to his sovereign, and for this purpose immediately set

JACOB'S WELL.

out from Tiberias for Jerusalem. The interview and reconciliation between the King and the Count took place at Jacob's well, near Nablous, in the presence of the Templars and Hospitalers, and the bishops and barons. The Count knelt upon one knee and did homage, whereupon the King raised him up and kissed him, and they then both returned together to Nablous to take measures for the protection of the country.

Saladin, on the other hand, was concentrating a large army and

Saladin preparing to invade Palestine with a large Army.

rapidly maturing his plans for the reconquest of the Holy City, the long-cherished enterprise of the Mussulmans. Whilst discord and dissensions had been gradually undermining the strength of the Christian empire, Saladin had been carefully extending and consolidating his power. He had reduced the various independent chieftains of the north of Syria to submission to his throne and government. He had conquered the cities of Mecca and Medina, and the whole of Arabia Felix; and his vast empire now extended from Tripoli, in Africa, to the Tigris, in Asia, and from the Indian Ocean to the mountains of Armenia. The Arabian writers enthusiastically recount his pious exhortations to the true believers to arm in defense of Islam, and describe with enthusiasm his glorious preparations for the holy war. Bohadin, son of Sjeddadi, his friend and secretary, and great biographer, before venturing upon the sublime task of describing his famous and sacred actions, makes a solemn confession of faith, and offers up praises to the one true God. "Praise be to GOD," says he, "who hath blessed us with Islam, and hath led us to the understanding of the true faith beautifully put together, and hath befriended us; and, through the intercession of our prophet, hath loaded us with every blessing. I bear witness that there is no God but that one GREAT GOD who hath *no partner* (a testimony that will deliver our souls from the smoky fire of hell); that MOHAMMED is his *servant* and *apostle*, who hath opened unto us the gates of the right road to salvation. These solemn duties being performed, I will begin to write concerning the victorious DEFENDER *of the* FAITH, the tamer of the followers of the Cross, the lifter up of the standard of justice and equity, the saviour of the world and of religion, Saladin Aboolmodaffer Joseph, the Son of Job, the son of Schadi, Sultan of the Moslem, aye, and of Islam itself; the deliverer of the holy house of God (the Temple) from the hands of the idolaters; the servant of two holy cities, whose tomb may the Lord moisten with the dew of his favor, affording to him the sweetness of the fruits of the faith."

In his circular Saladin was not ashamed to call all Moslems to join him, whether they acted from religion or love of plunder and prodigious wealth and untold hoards of money, and all kinds of luxury and delights; every morsel of land from Persia to the Nile, towns and villages for his bravest emirs, the spoils of every Christian family, and every farm and estate, to be divided among the descendants of those Mussulmans who had been driven from Palestine; all spiritual blessings from the Caliph of Bagdad, and his warmest orisons for those who marched to the conquest of Jerusalem. Thus was it written on his colors: " This is the banner for all who love Mohammedans or hate Christians, or desire unbounded wealth, or lands or palaces." The Orders of the Templars and Hospitalers he declared to be a swinish race, which he vowed to exterminate.

1187. Crowds of Mussulmans from all parts of Asia crowded round the standard of Saladin, and the Caliph of Bagdad and all the imaums put up daily prayers for the success of his arms. After protecting the return of the spring caravan from Mecca, Saladin marched to Ashtara, not far from Damascus. He was there met by his son, *Al Malek al Afdal*, "most excellent prince," and *Mohhafferoddin ibn Zinoddin*, with the army under their command. Being afterwards joined by the forces of *Al Mawsel*, commanded by *Màsûd al Zaf'arâni*, *Maredin*, and *Hamah*, he reviewed his army, first on the hill called Tel Taisel, and afterwards at Ashtara, the place of general rendezvous. Whilst completing his preparations at this place, Saladin received intelligence of the reconciliation of the Count of Tripoli with the King of Jerusalem, and he determined instantly to lay siege to Tiberias. For this purpose, on Friday, the 17th of the month *Rabi*, he advanced in three divisions upon Al Soheira, a village situate at the northern end of the Lake of Tiberias, where he encamped for the night. The next day he marched round to the western shore of the lake, and proceeded towards Tiberias in battle array. On the 21st *Rabi*, he took the town by storm, put all who resisted to the sword, and made slaves of the survivors. The place was then set on fire and reduced to ashes. The Countess of Tripoli retired with the garrison into the citadel, from whence she sent messengers to her husband and Guy, King of Jerusalem, earnestly imploring instant succor. The answer to this appeal cost the Christian world the land of Jesus and all the fruits of a century of strife.

CHAPTER VIII.

THE CALAMITOUS BATTLE OF HATTIN AND ITS RESULT.

How, on a summer day,
The warriors of the RISEN LORD went down
In blood, and left their bones to whiten on the plain
Of HATTIN; Christian Craftsmen, hear me tell!
Then sunk the Cross; it fell! mid'st press of knights,
And bursting hearts, and wild appeals to God,
The EMBLEM OF SALVATION sunk to rise
On that bright pasture land no more!

IN the last chapter we conducted our readers to the eve of the deplorable and fatal event of July 3–5, 1187. The system of primogeniture in the succession of the Latin kingdom had brought the country, in this greatest hour of its peril, under the government of a base woman and an imbecile man. The two great Military Orders, paralyzed for want of a leader, could only fight and slay and die. Too far from Europe to hope for succor, there was nothing for it but to go down before the foe, nobly contending. On the other hand, the Saracens were *as one man* under the command of Saladin, the bravest, most experienced, and most intelligent leader their race had ever produced. With ample forces, thoroughly acquainted with the country, thoroughly acquainted with the condition of his opponents, he had staked his all upon the hazard of the die, and was resolved to conquer Palestine or perish in the attempt.

The Christian forces had pitched their camps at the fountain of Sepphoris, five miles north of Nazareth, and on the high road to Acre. All the chivalry of the Latin kingdom had been summoned to join the standard of the King, and make a last effort in defense of the tottering kingdom of Jerusalem. The Templars and Hospitalers collected together a strong force from their different **1187.** castles and fortresses, and came into the camp with the Holy Cross which had been brought from the Church of the Resurrection at Jerusalem, to be borne in front of the Christian array. Raymond, Count of Tripoli, joined them with the men of Tripoli and Galilee. Prince Reginald, of Mount Royal, made his appearance at the head of a body of light cavalry. The Lord Balian, of Nablous, came in with all his armed retainers, and Reginald, Lord of Sidon, marched into the camp with the men from the sea-coast.

To examine that quite deserted spot at the present day suggests nothing of the tremendous doom that impended over that Christian array. The water of the abounding fountain, one and a half miles south of the village, flowed freely then as now. The royal eagle of Lebanon soared proudly over their heads. Baser birds were already gorged with the feast the Saracens had prepared for them. The Christian Church stood there intact, whose ruins, explored by that most learned *savant*, Baron de Vogüé, yield yet a few lucid testimonials:

Of the church built at Sepphoris, by the Crusaders, upon the traditional place of the house of St. Joachim and St. Anne, the greater part of those we have already described, the eastern extremity is the only one now preserved, but this suffices to characterize it. We recover the three demi-cylindrical *apsides*, contiguous, with the *colonettes engagés*, the arches of *ogivale* section, a little window in the center; in a word, a style proper to the Roman constructions in Palestine. The place ought not to differ sensibly from that of St. Anne of Jerusalem, and of many others in this country. It is composed of three naves, corresponding to the three apsides, with or without a cupola in the center of the transept. Quaresimus saw yet in 1620 a portion of the arches of the three naves. We remark, in passing, this new example of the uniformity of the churches constructed by the Crusaders, and the fidelity with which their architects followed the lessons of one only and the same school, when they were not obliged to adapt their structures to the more ancient buildings or to a particular form.

Sepphoris, the Dio-Cæsarea of the Romans, possessed a church celebrated in the Fourth Century. Divers objects were pointed out to pilgrims that belonged to the Virgin; among others, the seat upon which she sat when she was saluted by the angel.

Assistance for Defense.   The Saracens devastate the Country.

The Grand Master of the Temple, De Riderfort, had brought with him the treasure which had been sent to the Templars by the King of England, to be employed in the defense of the Holy Land, in expiation of the murder of St. Thomas à Becket, and this was found very acceptable in the exhausted condition of the Latin treasury. Whilst the Christian forces were assembling at Sepphoris, Saladin sent forward a strong corps of cavalry, which ravaged and laid waste all the country around the brook Kishon, from Tiberias to Bethoron, and from the Mountain of Gilboa to Nazareth. From all the eminences nought was to be seen but the smoking ruins of the villages, hamlets, and scattered dwellings of the Christian population. The whole country was enveloped in flame and smoke. The Christian camp was filled with fugitives who had fled with terror before the merciless swords of the Moslem, whose King had sworn that Reginald de Chatillon should die and the Holy Land should fall. To complete the misfortunes of the Latins, the King was irresolute and continually giving contradictory commands, so that the Christian chieftains, having lost all confidence in their leader, and despairing of being able to contend with success against the vast power of Saladin, seemed to be preparing for a retreat to the sea-coast, rather than for a desperate struggle with the infidels for the preservation of Jerusalem. Upon this ground only can be explained the long delay from May to July of the Christian army at Sepphoris. This place, the ancient capital of Galilee, is situated on the main road from Nazareth and Acre, and an army could at any time secure an easy and safe retreat from Nazareth to the port of the last-named city. Here, then, the Christians remained, quietly permitting Saladin to occupy a strong position from whence he could pour his vast masses of cavalry into the great plain of Esdraelon, and open for himself a direct road to the Holy City, either through the valley of the Jordan, or through the great plain along the bases of the mountains of Gilboa. To-day the traveler visiting Sepphoris finds the inhabitants raising quantities of bees, and obtaining great profit from the honey.

When the messengers from the Countess of Tripoli arrived in the Christian camp with intelligence that Saladin had stormed and

15

burned the town of Tiberias, and that the Countess had retired into the citadel, the King called a Council of War.   This council assembled in the Royal tent, on the evening of the second of July, A.D. 1187.   There were present Gerard de Riderfort, Grand Master of the Temple, the newly-elected Grand Master of the Hospital, N. Gardiner, William, the Archbishop of Tyre, the Count of Tripoli, Lord Balian d'Ibelin, of Nablous, and nearly all the bishops and barons of Palestine.   Raymond, Count of Tripoli, although his capital was in flames, his territories spoiled by the enemy, and his Countess closely besieged, advised the King to remain inactive where he was.   But the Grand Master of the Temple, hearing this advice, rose up in the midst of the assembly, and stigmatized the Count as a traitor, urging the King instantly to march to the relief of Tiberias.   The barons, however, sided with the Count of Tripoli, and it was determined that the army *should remain at Sepphoris.*

The council broke up; each man retired to his tent, and the King went to supper.   But the Grand Master of the Temple, agitated by a thousand conflicting emotions, could not rest.   At midnight he arose and sought the presence of the King.   He reproached him for remaining in a state of inaction at Sepphoris, whilst the enemy was ravaging and laying waste all the surrounding country, and reducing the Christian population to a state of hopeless bondage.   "It will be an everlasting reproach to you, sire," said he, "if you quietly permit the infidels to take before your face an important Christian citadel, which you ought to feel it your first duty to defend.   Know that the Templars will sooner tear the white mantle from their shoulders, and sell all that they possess, than remain any longer quiet spectators of the injury and disgrace that have been brought upon the Christian arms."

Moved by the discourse of Grand Master Riderfort, the King consented to march to the relief of Tiberias, and at morning's dawn, July 3, the tents of the Templars were struck, and the trumpets of the Order sounded the advance.   In vain did Raymond, Count of Tripoli, and the barons oppose this movement. The King and the Templars were resolute.   It was the first command of the licentious King that ever had been obeyed, and the

KNIGHTS TEMPLARS. 227

The Army on the March.   Numbers of the Christian Forces.

consequences were the loss of all for which they were contending. The host of the Cross soon covered, in full array, the winding road leading to Tiberias, about twenty miles from Sepphoris.   Count Raymond, of Tripoli and Galilee, insisted upon leading the van of the army, as the Christian forces were marching through his territories, and the Templars and Hospitalers consequently brought up the rear.   The debauchee Patriarch Heraclius, whose duty it was to bear the Holy Cross in front of the Christian array, *had remained at Jerusalem*, and had confided his sacred charge to the bishops of Acre and Lydda, a circumstance which gave rise to many gloomy forebodings amongst the superstitious soldiers of Christ. Heraclius afterwards died miserably at Acre in the great siege of 1191.

The number of the Christian forces is given so differently by the various authorities that we despair of a satisfactory computation.   Dr. Edward Robinson (in *Biblical Researches*. vol. ii., p. 372) makes the Christian strength " 2,000 Knights and 8,000 foot soldiers, besides large bodies of light-armed troops or archers." The usual estimate roughly made is 50,000 Christian troops against 80,000 Saracens.

An army so large as that of the Crusaders, 50,000, in a march of ten miles to the battle-ground, must needs have deployed through all the villages within several miles of the main route, especially as the demand for water in that thirsty season, was so great.   One detachment doubtless passed through Cana (Kefr Cana), then a place of considerable importance, now a village of two score low huts.   It is about four and a half miles northeast of Nazareth, and nearly due east of headquarters at Sepphoris.

Antonine de Plaisance, in the Sixth Century, says that he saw a church at Cana, in which were preserved two urns of stone that served for the first miracle of Jesus Christ.   St. Willibald mentioned the same building which then only contained one urn. During the Crusades there was in the same place a church named The House of Architriclinus, and there were shown at Jerusalem in the Church of St. John Baptist and in the Temple, the two urns of the miracle.   At the present time, at Kefer Kana are only shapeless ruins, and a little modern Greek church, in which are preserved two rude stone pots.   Although by their form, material, and simplicity, these two urns respond better to Jewish customs and to the narrative of the Evangelists, than to the vases of marble and porphyry preserved in many cities of Europe, I do not think they can be considered authentic, for they are not alluded to by any traveler prior to the last century.

1187.   As soon as Saladin heard of the advance of the Christian army, he turned the siege of the citadel of Tiberias into a blockade, called in his detachments of cavalry, and hastened to occupy all the passes and defiles of the mountains leading to Tiberias.   The march of the infidel host, which amounted to 80,000 horse and foot against 50,000 Christians, over the hilly country, is compared by an Arabian writer, an eye-witness, to mountains in movement, or to the vast waves of an agitated sea.   Saladin encamped on the hills west of Tiberias, resting his left wing upon the lake, and planting his cavalry in the valleys, six miles distant.   When the Latin forces had arrived within nine miles of Tiberias they came in sight of the Mussulman army, and were immediately assailed by the light cavalry of the Arabs.   During the afternoon of that day (July 3) a bloody battle was fought.   The Christians attempted, but in vain, to penetrate the defiles of the mountains; and when the evening came, they found that they had merely been able to hold their ground without advancing a single step.   Their destruction was now reduced to a certainty.   Instead of fighting his way at all hazards to the lake of Tiberias, or falling back upon some position where he could have procured a supply of water, the King, following the advice of the Count of Tripoli, committed the fatal mistake of ordering the tents to be pitched.   When the Saracens saw that the Christians had pitched their tents, says the Chronicler, they came and encamped so close to them that the soldiers of the two armies could converse together, and not even a cat could escape from the Christian lines without the knowledge of the Saracens. It was a sultry summer's night (the month of July in Galilee is of the hottest), the army of the Cross was hemmed in amongst dry and barren rocks, and both the men and horses, after their harassing and fatiguing march, threw themselves on the parched ground, sighing in vain for water.   During the livelong night not a drop

TERRIFIC ENCOUNTER OF THE CHRISTIAN ARMY AND THE SARACENS AT MOUNT HATTIN. JULY 4, 1187.

of that precious element touched their lips, and the soldiers arose exhausted and unrefreshed for the toil, and labor, and fierce warfare, and defeat of the ensuing day.

At sunrise, Friday, July 4, the Templars and Hospitalers formed in battle array in the van of the Christian army, having passed clear through the host for that purpose, and prepared to open a road through the dense ranks of the infidels to the lake of Tiberias. An Arabian writer, who witnessed the movement of their dense and compact columns at early dawn, speaks of them as "terrible in arms, having their whole bodies cased with triple mail." He compares the noise made by their advancing squadrons to the *loud humming of bees,* and describes them as animated with "a flaming desire of vengeance." Saladin had on his left flank the lake of Tiberias, his infantry was in the center, and the swift cavalry of the desert was stationed on either wing, under the command of Faki-ed-deen. The Templars rushed, we are told, like lions upon the Moslem infidels, and nothing could withstand their heavy and impetuous charge.

The ground was broken and narrow; the knights could not place their lances in rest, nor bring their chargers to the career, while the enemy rained down upon them from the heights clouds of darts and other missiles. Never, says an Arabian doctor of the law, have I seen bolder or more powerful soldiers; none more to be feared by the believers in the true faith. Saladin set fire to the dry grass and dwarf shrubs which lay between both armies, and the wind blew the smoke and the flames directly into the faces of the Knights and their horses. The fire, the noise, the gleaming weapons, and all the accompaniments of the horrid scene, have given full scope to the descriptive powers of the Oriental writers. They compare it to the last judgment; the dust and the smoke obscured the face of the sun, and the day was turned into night. Sometimes gleams of light darted like the rapid lightning amid the throng of combatants. Then you might see the dense columns of armed warriors, now immovable as mountains and now sweeping swiftly across the landscape, like the rainy clouds over the face of heaven. "The sons of paradise and the children of fire," say they, "then decided their terrible quarrel; the arrows rustled through the air like the

wings of innumerable sparrows; the sparks flew from the coats of
mail and the glancing sabres, and the blood spurting forth from the
bosom of the throng, deluged the earth like the rains of heaven."
"The avenging sword of the true believers was drawn forth
against the infidels; the faith of the UNITY was opposed to the faith
of the TRINITY, and speedy ruin, desolation, and destruction over-
took the miserable sons of baptism!"*

The lake of Tiberias was now only two miles distant from the
Templars, and ever and anon its blue and placid waters were to
be seen from the hill-tops calmly reposing in the bright sunbeams,
or winding gracefully amid the bosom of the distant mountains.
But every inch of the road was fiercely contested. The expert
archers of the Mussulman lined all the eminences, and the thirsty
soil was drenched with the blood of the best and bravest of the
Christian warriors. After almost superhuman exertions the Templars and Hospitalers halted, and sent to the King for succor. At
this critical juncture, Count Raymond of Tripoli, who had always
insisted on being in the van, and whose conduct from first to last
had been most suspicious, dashed with a few followers through a
party of Mussulmans, who opened their ranks to let him pass, and
retreated to Tyre. The flight of this distinguished nobleman gave
rise to a sudden panic, and the troops that were advancing to the
support of the Templars were driven in one confused mass upon

---

* Another writer, elevated by his theme, paints the scene thus: "The smoke
blinded the eyes of the Knights and their horses, while the flames surrounded
them, setting fire to the mantles of the Templars, and scorching their chargers'
hoofs. This caused some confusion, upon which Saladin ordered a large body of
troops to attack them. Undismayed, the gallant Templars continued the battle.
Swords gleamed through the flames, and the Knights, rushing from behind
masses of smoke and fire, precipitated themselves, lance in hand, upon the
enemy. The spectacle which this extraordinary sight presented appears to have
fired the imagination of the Arabian authors. The tongues of flame, the thick
smoke, the clang of battle, the glancing weapons, fill them with admiration, and
in vain seeking for an earthly parallel, they compare the fight to the Last Judgment. The thick smoke, through which might be dimly seen the rush of contending troops, the clouds of sparks swirling up into the air beneath the tread
of horses, the gleam of spears, and the flames of the cloaks of the Knights on
fire, the yells of the combatants, the groans and shrieks of the dying, and the
screams of wounded horses plunging madly in their death-throes, presented a
spectacle alike terrible as it was sublime."

MOUNT HATTIN, THE BATTLE-GROUND OF THE TEMPLARS, AS IT NOW APPEARS.

The Christian Army overpowered.   Terrible Slaughter.

the main body.   The Knights, who rarely turned their backs upon the enemy, maintained, alone and unaided, a short, sharp, and bloody conflict, which ended in the death or captivity of every one of them excepting the Grand Master of the Hospital (N. Gardiner), who clove his way from the field of battle, and reached Ascalon, 100 miles in the southwest, in safety, but died of his wounds the day after his arrival.*

The Christian soldiers now gave themselves up to despair.   The infantry, which was composed principally of the native population of Palestine, men taken from the plough and the pruning-hook, crowded together in disorder and confusion around the bishops and the holy cross.   They were so wedged together that they were unable to act against the enemy, and they refused to obey their leaders.   Sir Knight Terric, Grand Preceptor of the Temple, who had been attached to the person of the King, the Lord Reginald of Sidon, Lord Balian d'Ibelin of Nablous, and many of the lesser barons and knights, collected their followers together, rushed over the rocks, down the mountain sides, pierced through the enemies' squadrons, and leaving the infantry to their fate, made their escape to the sea-coast.   The Arab cavalry dashed on, and surrounding, with terrific cries, the trembling and unresisting foot soldiers, they mowed them down with a frightful carnage.

In vain did the bishops of Ptolemais and Lydda, who supported with difficulty the Holy Cross in the midst of the disordered throng, attempt to infuse into them some of that daring valor and fiery-religious enthusiasm which glowed so fiercely in the breasts of the Moslem.   The Christian fugitives were crowded together like a flock of sheep when attacked by dogs, and their bitter cries for mercy ever and anon rent the air, between the loud shouts of ALLAH her *akbar*—"GOD is greater."   The Moslem chieftains pressed into the heart of the throng, and cleft their way towards

* Amongst the rumors prevalent after such an event is the following, to which, however, we give no credence : " During the night Baldwin de Fortune, Raymond Buch, and Laodicious de Tiberias, with three companions—being all Knights of the King—instructed by the diabolic Count Raymond of Tripoli, deserted from the Christian standard, went over to Saladin, and became Mohammedans.   They informed him of every particular of the state, intentions, and resources of the Christians ; and Saladin thereupon determined to crush them on the morrow."

236 KNIGHTS TEMPLARS.

The Holy Cross in possession of the Infidels. Success of the Saracens.

the Holy Cross. The bishop of Ptolemais was slain. The bishop of Lydda was made captive. The Cross itself fell into the hands of the infidels. The King of Jerusalem, the Grand Master of the Temple, Gerard de Riderfort, the Marquis of Montferrat, the Lord Reginald de Chatillon, the immediate author of this terrible evil, and many other nobles and knights, were at the same time taken prisoners and led away into captivity. Alas, alas, says Abbot Coggleshale, that I should have lived to have seen in my time these awful and terrible calamities. When the sun had sunk to rest, and darkness had put an end to the slaughter, a crowd of Christian fugitives, who survived the long and frightful carnage, attempted to gain the summit of Mount Hattin, a mile northward, in the vain hope of escaping from the field of blood, under cover of the obscurity of the night. But all the passes and avenues were strictly watched, and when morning came they were found cowering on the elevated summit of the mountain. They were maddened with thirst and exhausted with watching, but despair gave them some energy. They availed themselves with success of the strength of their position, and in the first onslaught the Moslems were repulsed. The sloping sides of Mount Hattin were covered with dry grass and thistles, which had been scorched and killed by the hot sun of July, and the Moslem again resorted to the expedient of setting fire to the parched vegetation. The heat of the season, added to that of the raging flames, soon told with fearful effect upon the weakened frames of the poor Christian warriors, who were absolutely dying of thirst of three days' continuance. Some threw away their arms and cast themselves upon the ground. Some cried for mercy. Others calmly awaited the approach of death.

The Moslem appetite for blood had at this time been slaked. Feelings of compassion for the misfortunes of the fallen had arisen in their breasts, and as resistance had now ceased in every quarter of the field, the lives of the fugitives on Mount Hattin were mercifully spared. Thus ended the memorable battle of Tiberias, which commenced on the afternoon of the third of July, and ended on the morning of Saturday, the fifth. The multitude of captives taken by the Moslem was enormous. Cords could not be found to bind them, the tent ropes were all used for the purpose, but were insufficient, and the Arabian writers tell us, that on seeing the dead, one would have thought that there could have been *no prisoners*, and on seeing the prisoners, that there could be *no dead*. "I saw," says the secretary and companion of Saladin, who was present at this terrible fight, and is unable to restrain himself from pitying the disasters of the vanquished—"I saw the mountains and the plains, the hills and the valleys, covered with their dead. I saw their fallen and deserted banners sullied with dust and with blood. I saw their heads broken and battered, their limbs scattered abroad, and the blackened corses piled one upon another like the stones of the builders. I called to mind the words of the Koran, 'The infidel shall say, What am I but dust?' I saw thirty or forty tied together by one cord. I saw in one place, guarded by one Mussulman, two hundred of these famous warriors gifted with amazing strength, who had but just now walked forth amongst the mighty. Their proud bearing was gone. They stood naked with downcast eyes, wretched and miserable. The lying infidels were now in the power of the true believers. Their king and their cross were captured, that cross before which they bow the head and bend the knee; which they bear aloft and worship with their eyes; they say that it is the identical wood to which the God whom they adore was fastened. They had adorned it with fine gold and brilliant stones; they carried it before their armies; they all bowed towards it with respect. It was their first duty to defend it; and he who should desert it would never enjoy peace of mind. The capture of this cross was more grievous to them than the captivity of their king. Nothing can compensate them for the loss of it. It was their God; they prostrated themselves in the dust before it, and sang hymns when it was raised aloft!"

As soon as all fighting had ceased on the field of battle, Saladin proceeded to a tent whither, in obedience to his commands, Guy, King of Jerusalem, with Gerard de Riderfort, Grand Master of the Temple, and Reginald de Chatillon had been conducted. The latter was Lord of Kerak, now a village of 1,500 inhabitants, three-fourths Christian. The Crusaders' Castle, partly cut off and partly built upon the mountain top 3,000 feet above the Dead Sea, may be seen with a good glass from the towers of Jerusalem.   The remains exhibit both the pointed Gothic arch of the Crusades and the older Roman arch.   A steep glacis-wall skirts the whole.   The castle was built of heavy well-cut stones, and there were seven arched towers, one above the other.   The vast extent of the castle fills the mind with astonishment.   It has five gates and seven walls and cisterns, and the whole area is perforated with subterraneous passages.   Reginald de Chatillon had greatly distinguished

KERAK.—CASTLE OF THE CRUSADERS.

himself in various piratical expeditions against the caravans of pilgrims traveling to Mecca, and had become on that account particularly obnoxious to Saladin.   The Sultan, on entering the tent, ordered a bowl of sherbet, the sacred pledge amongst the Arabs of hospitality and security, to be presented to the fallen monarch of Jerusalem, and to the Grand Master of the Temple.   But when Reginald de Chatillon would have drunk thereof, Saladin prevented him, and reproaching the Christian nobleman with perfidy and impiety, he commanded him instantly to acknowledge the prophet whom he had blasphemed, or to be prepared to meet the death he had so often deserved.   On Reginald's refusal to recant Saladin struck him with his scimitar, and he was immediately despatched by the guards.   Bohadin, Saladin's friend and secretary, an eye-witness of the scene, gives the following account of it : Then Saladin told the interpreter to say thus to the King, " It is thou not I, who givest drink to this man ! "   Then the Sultan sat down at the entrance of the tent, and they brought Prince Reginald before him, and after refreshing the man's memory, Saladin said to him, Now then, I myself will act the part of the defender of Mohammed !   He then offered the man the Mohammedan faith, but he refused it.   Then the King struck him on the shoulder with a drawn scimitar, which was a hint to those that were present to do for him.   So they sent his soul to hell, and cast out his body before the tent door !

1187.   The next day (Sunday, July 6) Saladin proceeded in cold blood to enact the grand concluding tragedy.   The warlike monks of the Temple and of the Hospital, the bravest and most zealous defenders of the Christian faith, were, of all the warriors of the Cross, the most obnoxious to zealous Mussulmans, and it was determined that death or conversion to Mohammedanism should be the portion of every captive of either Order, excepting De Riderfort, the Grand Master of the Temple, for whom it was expected a heavy ransom would be given.   Accordingly, on the Christian Sabbath, at the hour of sunset, the appointed time of prayer, the Moslem were drawn up in battle array under their respective leaders.   The Mameluke Emirs stood in two ranks clothed in yellow, and at the sound of the holy trumpet, all the captive Knights of the Temple and of the Hospital were led on to the eminence above Tiberias, in full view of the beautiful lake of Gennesareth, whose bold and mountainous shores had been the scene of so many of their Saviour's miracles.   There, as the last rays of the sun were fading away from the mountain tops, they were called upon to deny Him who had been crucified, to choose God for their Lord, Islam for their faith, Mecca for their temple, the Moslem for their brethren, and Mohammed for their prophet.   *To* *a man they refused*, and were all decapitated in the presence of Saladin by the devout zealots of his army, and the doctors and expounders of the law.   An Oriental historian, who was present says that Saladin sat with a smiling countenance viewing the execution, and that some of the executioners cut off the heads with a degree of dexterity that excited great applause. Oh, says Omad'eddin Mohammed, how beautiful an ornament is the blood of the infidels sprinkled over the followers of the faith and the true religion! If the Mussulmans displayed a becoming zeal in the decapitation and annihilation of the infidel Templars and Hospitalers, these last manifested a no less praiseworthy eagerness for martyrdom by the swords of the unbelieving Moslems. The Knight Templar Nicholas strove vigorously, we are told, with his companions to be the first to suffer, and with great difficulty accomplished his purpose. It was believed by the Christians, in accordance with the superstitious ideas of those times, that Heaven testified its approbation by a visible sign, and that for three nights, during which the bodies of the Templars remained unburied on the field, celestial rays of light played around the corpses of those holy martyrs.   This same legend is applied to an event of like character at Safed a century later.

1187.   Immediately after this fatal battle, the citadel of Tiberias surrendered to Saladin, and the Countess of Tripoli was permitted to depart in safety in search of her fugitive husband.   There was now no force in the Latin kingdom capable of offering the least opposition to the victorious career of the infidels, and Saladin, in order that he might overrun and subjugate the whole country with the greatest possible rapidity, divided his army into several bodies, which were to proceed in different directions, and assemble at last under the walls of Jerusalem.   One strong column, under the command of Malek el Afdal, proceeded to attack La Feue or Faba, near Nazareth, the castle of the Knights Templars.   Nearly all the garrison had perished in the battle of Tiberias, and after a short conflict the infidels walked into the fortress, over the dead bodies of the last of its defenders.   From thence they crossed the great plain to Sebaste, and entered the magnificent church erected by the empress Helena, over the prison in which, according to a most erroneous tradition, St. John the Baptist was beheaded, and over the humble grave where still repose the remains of St. John and of Zacharias and Elizabeth his parents.   The terrified bishop and clergy had removed all the gold and silver vessels from the altars and the rich copes and vestments of the priests, to conceal them from the cupidity of the Moslems, whereupon these last caused the bishop to be stripped naked and beaten with rods, and led away all his clergy into captivity.

SAMARIA.

There are no ruins, outside of Jerusalem, so interesting as those of this church of Sebaste (Samaria), and we would gladly have enriched our pages with the best description now published, that from De Vogüé's "Churches of the Holy Land," did our space admit.

From Sebaste the wild Turcoman and Bedouin cavalry dashed up the beautiful valley of Succoth to Nablous, which they found deserted and desolate.   The inhabitants had abandoned their dwellings and fled to Jerusalem, and the Mussulmans planted their banners upon the gray battlements of the castle, and upon the lofty summits of Mounts Gerizim and Ebal.   They then pitched their tents around the interesting well where our Saviour spoke

Jacob's Well.   The Place of meeting of Christ and the Woman of Samaria.

with the woman of Samaria, and pastured their cavalry in the valley where Joseph's brethren were feeding their flocks when they sold him to the wandering Ishmaelites. (*Genesis* xxxvii.)

NABLOUS—ANCIENT SHECHEM.

The most interesting monument of ancient Shechem is, without contradiction, this Well of Jacob or of the Samaritan woman situated a mile east of the city upon the route to Jerusalem at the foot of Mount Gerizim. Its authenticity is not contested by any one. All agree, Catholics, Mohammedans, Jews, and Protestants, to consider it as the well dug in " the field bought by Jacob of the sons of Hemor," and by the side of which Jesus was seated when he made to the Samaritan woman the rapid and admirable exhibit of His doctrine. Its place, its depth, all agree with the details given in the Holy Writings; and the recital of the Evangelist enables us to follow, at this distance from Jesus Christ, the tradition which belongs to biblical epochs. I felicitate myself, says Baron De Vogüé, this time that I am in union of sentiment with Dr. Robinson, and I can do no more than to reiterate the not suspicious

KNIGHTS TEMPLARS. 243

The Church at Nablous.   Ravages and continued Slaughter of the Saracens.

pleading that he makes in favor of the authenticity of the Well of Jacob.

Despite the respect which has surrounded it in all ages, this venerable object is in the most complete state of abandon. A mass of ruins, among which are seen some columns of gray granite, evident remains of a church of the Fourth or Fifth Century, only indicates its place. There, in removing the great stones, is uncovered the entrance of a vaulted cave, into which one slips with difficulty, and, in the center of a small underground room, is seen the mouth of the well, which is dug in the living rock to a great depth. The cave, without doubt, belongs to a church built by the Crusaders, seen by Edrisi in 1154, and destroyed in 1187. In the Fourth Century, when the primitive church was built, the ground was not so high. The opening of the well was before the enclosure of the choir. The church had the form of a cross, whose four branches were directed towards the four cardinal points. The well was situated in the center, at the intersection of the two naves. Arculph has left a rough plan, which perfectly explains this disposition.

In the interior of the city of Nablous are seen the remains of a beautiful church of the time of the Crusades. The portal is perfectly preserved, and recalls that of the church of the Holy Sepulcher. It is formed of three *archivottes ogivales* in successive *retraites*, bearing on each side, upon three colonettes, *engagès* in the re-entering angles of the jambs. The extreme archivotte is covered with sculptures, stamped with Roman ornamentation. The church was built by the canons of the Holy Sepulcher, upon ground conceded to them by King Almeric (1162–1174). Finished in 1167, it bore the double name of *The Passion* and *The Resurrection* of the Saviour. Not far from this, I saw a mosk and minaret, which seemed to be a church and steeple of the Crusades. The fanaticism of the inhabitants rendered an examination difficult, and a drawing impossible. There existed in Nablous, in 1156, a Hospital served by the Knights of St. John.

I also observed, on the summit of Gerizim, without alluding to the Samaritan ruins discovered by Mr. de Sauley, the remains of ancient Byzantine churches, which are of interest to study and compare with the edifices attributed by Procopius to the Emperor Justinian.

At Nablous the Saracens remained to gather some tidings of the operations of their fellow-soldiers on the other side of the Jordan, and then proceeded to ravage and lay waste all the country between Nablous and Jerusalem, continuing, says Abbot Coggleshale, both by night and by day to slaughter every living thing they met.

1187. The column which was to proceed through the valley of the Jordan, entered the great plain of Esdraelon by Mount Tabor,

244 KNIGHTS TEMPLARS.

Rapid Marches of the Saracens.   Attack against the Templars in every Quarter.

and taking the direction of Nain and Endor to Jezreel, they crossed the mountains of Gilboa to Bethshean, and descended the valley of the Jordan, as far as Jericho. Thence they proceeded to lay siege to a solitary castle of the Templars, seated upon that celebrated mountain where, according to tradition, our Saviour was tempted by the Devil with the visionary scene of "all the kingdoms of the world, and the glory of them." (*Matt.* iv. 8.) In this castle the Templars had long maintained a garrison for the pro-

JERICHO.

tection of the pilgrims who came to bathe in the Jordan, and visit the holy places in the neighborhood of Jericho. From the toppling crag, whereon it was seated, the eye commanded an extensive view of the course of the Jordan, from the base of Mount Herman an hundred miles to the northward, until it falls into the Dead Sea, also of the eastern frontier of the Latin kingdom, and of the important passes communicating with Jerusalem. The place was culled *Maledoim*, or "the Red Mountain," on account of the blood that had been shed upon the spot. Fifty Tyrian dinars had been offered by Saladin for the head of every Knight Templar that was brought him, and the blood-thirsty infidels surrounded the doomed castle eager for the reward. The whole garrison was put to the sword, and the place was left a shapeless ruin. The infidels then marched westward in the direction of Jerusalem, ten miles further, and laid waste all the country between Jericho and the Holy City. They pitched their tents at Bethany, two miles from Jerusalem, upon the spot where stood the houses of Simon the leper, and of Mary and Martha, and destroyed the church built over the house and tomb of Lazarus. The wild Arab cavalry then swept over the Mount of Olives, took possession of the Church of the Ascension constructed upon the summit of that sacred edifice, and extended their ravages to the very gates of Jerusalem.

The present condition of these edifices destroyed by Saladin, at Bethany, is strikingly described by Baron de Vogüé in his complete work.

1187. In the meantime Saladin's brother, Saifeddin, had crossed the desert from Egypt to participate in the plunder and spoil of the Christian territories, and had laid waste all the country from Daron and Gerar to Jerusalem. In front of his fierce warriors were to be seen the long bands of mournful captives tied together by the wrists, and behind them was a dreary desert, soaked with Christian blood. Saifeddin had besieged the strong town of Mirabel, and placed his military engines in position, when the terrified inhabitants sent a suppliant deputation to implore his clemency. He agreed to spare their lives in return for the immediate surrender of the place, and gave them an escort of four hundred Mussulmans to conduct them in safety to Jerusalem. Accompanied by their wives and little ones, the miserable Christians cast a last look upon their once happy homes, and proceeded on their toilsome journey to the Holy City. On their arrival at an eminence two miles from Jerusalem, their Arabian escort left them, and immediately afterwards a party of Templars dashed through the ravine, charged the retiring Moslem, and put the greater part of them to the sword.

1187. Saladin, on the other hand, immediately after the battle of Tiberias, hastened with the main body of his forces to Acre. The terrified inhabitants threw open their gates at his approach. From

Continued Destruction of the Templars by Saladin.

thence he swept the whole sea-coast to Joppa, reducing all the maritime towns, excepting the city of Tyre, which manfully resisted him. The savage Turcomans from the north, the predatory Bedouins, the fanatical Arabians, and the swarthy Africans hurried across the frontiers to share in the spoil and plunder of the Latin kingdom. Radolph, Abbot of Coggleshale, one of those who fled before the ruthless swords of the infidels, gives a frightful picture of the aspect of the country. He tells us that the whole land was covered with dead bodies, rotting and putrefying in the scorching sunbeams. At *early morning* you might see the rich and stately church, with the bright and happy dwellings scattered around it, the blooming garden, the silvery olive grove, and the rich vineyard; but the fading rays of the *evening* sun would fall on smoking masses of shapeless ruins and on a dreary and solitary desert. The holy abbot mourned over the fall of Nazareth, and the desecration by the infidels of the magnificent church of the Holy Virgin at that place. Our readers will be instructed from the pen of the same enthusiastic writer, whose account of the ruins of Holy Land churches has already enriched our pages. (See APPENDIX VI.)

Sidon, Caifa, Sepphoris, Nazareth, Cæsarea, Joppa, Lydda, and Ramleh successively fell into the hands of the Moslem. The inhabitants were led away into captivity and the garrisons put to the sword. The infidels laid waste all the country about Mount Carmel and Caifa, and burnt the celebrated Church of Elias, on the mountain above the port of Acre, which had served as a beacon for navigators.

The government of the Order of the Temple, in consequence of the captivity of the Grand Master, Gerard de Riderfort, who was **1187.** detained in prison, with Guy, King of Jerusalem, at Damascus, devolved upon Sir Knight Terric, Grand Preceptor of Jerusalem, who immediately addressed letters from Gaza to all the brethren in the West, imploring aid and assistance. One of these letters was duly received by Geoffrey, Master of the Temple at London, as follows: "Brother Terric, Grand Preceptor of the poor house of the Temple, and every poor brother, and the whole convent, now, alas! almost annihilated, to all the preceptors and brothers of the Temple to whom these letters shall come, salvation through him to whom our fervent aspirations are addressed, through Him who causeth the sun and the moon to reign marvelous.   The many and great calamities wherewith the anger of God, excited by

MOUNT CARMEL.

our manifold sins, hath just now permitted us to be afflicted, we cannot for grief unfold to you, neither by letters nor by our sobbing speech.   The infidel chiefs having collected together a vast number of their people fiercely invaded our Christian territories, and we, assembling our battalions, hastened to Tiberias to arrest their march.   The enemy having hemmed us in among barren rocks fiercely attacked us.   The Holy Cross and the King himself fell into the hands of the infidels, the whole army was cut to pieces, 230 of our knights were beheaded, without reckoning the sixty who were killed on the 1st of May.   The Lord Reginald of Sidon, the Lord Ballovius, and we ourselves escaped with vast difficulty from that miserable field.   The Pagans, drunk with the blood of our Christians, then marched with their whole army against the city of Acre and took it by storm.   The city of Tyre is at present fiercely besieged, and neither by night nor by day do the infidels discontinue their furious assaults.   So great is the multitude of them that *they cover like ants* the whole face of the country from Tyre to

Jerusalem, and even unto Gaza.   The holy city of Jerusalem,
Ascalon, and Tyre, and Beyrout are yet left to us and to the Christian
cause, but, the garrisons and the chief inhabitants of these places
having perished in the battle of Tiberias, we have no hope of
retaining them without succor from heaven and instant assistance
from yourselves."

On the other hand, Saladin sent triumphant letters to the Caliph.
" GOD and his ANGELS," says he, " have mercifully succored ISLAM.
The infidels have been sent to feed the *fires of* HELL!   The Cross
is fallen into our hands, around which they fluttered like a moth
round a light; under whose shadow they assembled, in which they
boldly trusted as in a wall; the Cross, the center and leader of their
pride, their superstition and their tyranny."

1187.   Saladin pursued his rapid conquests along the sea-coast to
the north of Acre, and took by storm several castles of the Templars.   After a siege of six days the strong fortress of Tibnin, on
the road from Tiberias to Beyrout, was taken by assault, the garrison put to the sword, and the fortifications razed to the ground.
On the 22d of *Jomada* the important city of Beyrout, seventy
miles north of Acre, surrendered to Saladin, and shortly afterwards
the castles of Hobeil and Bolerum.   After the reduction of most
of the maritime towns between Acre and Tripoli, Saladin ordered
his different detachments to concentrate before Jerusalem, and
hastened in person to the south to complete the conquest of the
few places which still resisted the arms of the Mussulmans.   He sat
down before Ascalon, and whilst preparing his military engines for
battering the walls, sent messengers to the Templars at Gaza,
representing to them that the whole land was in his power, that all
further efforts at resistance were useless, and offering them their
lives and a safe retreat to Europe if they would give up to him the
important fortress committed to their charge.   But the military
friars sent back a haughty defiance to the victorious Sultan, and
recommended him to take Ascalon before he ventured to ask for
the surrender of Gaza.   The season was now advancing.   Vague
1187. rumors were flying about of stupendous preparations in
Europe for the recovery of Palestine, and Saladin was anxious to
besiege and take Jerusalem ere the winter's rains, which along that

maritime plain are extremely copious, commenced.   When, therefore, his military engines were planted under the walls of Ascalon
he once more, as the place was strong, summoned the inhabitants
to surrender, and they then agreed to capitulate on receiving a
solemn promise from Saladin that he would forthwith set at liberty

ASCALON.

the King of Jerusalem (Guy de Lusignan) and the Grand Master
of the Temple (De Riderfort), and would respect both the persons
and the property of the inhabitants.   These terms were acceded
to, and on the 4th of September the gates of Ascalon were thrown
open to the enemy.

1187.   The inhabitants of this interesting city appear to have
been attached to King Guy and his Queen Sibylla.   They had received them when they came from Jerusalem, as fugitives from

Gaza, the powerful Fortress of the Templars. Saladin overrunning the Country.

the wrath of Baldwin IV., and protected them against the power of that monarch. The Sultan imposed such conditions upon the prisoners as were necessary for his own security. They were to quit Palestine never more to return, and were in the mean time, until a fitting opportunity for their embarkation to Europe could be found, to take up their abode at Nablous, under the surveillance of the Moslem garrison. Immediately after the capture of Asca-

HEBRON.

lon, Saladin pitched his tents beneath the walls of Gaza, the great fortress of the Knights Templars. He had been repulsed by the military friars with great loss in a previous attack upon this important station, and he now surrounded it with his numerous battalions, thirsting for vengeance. The place surrendered after a short siege. The fortifications were demolished, but the fate of the garrison has not been recorded.

Bethlehem and its magnificent Church.

1187. Having subjugated so much of the country bordering upon the sea-coast, from Tripoli to Gaza (see Map), Saladin moved forward in great triumph towards the city of Jerusalem.

BETHLEHEM.

Passing round by Hebron he encamped the first night at Beersheba, by the well digged by Abraham, in the land of the Philistines, and on the spot where Abraham delivered the seven ewe lambs, and made a covenant with Abimelech, and planted a grove, and called "on the name of the LORD, the everlasting God" (*Genesis* xxi. 33, 34). The next day, early in October, Saladin marched towards Bethlehem, halting on the way before a castle of the Hospitalers, which he summoned to surrender, but in vain. Leaving a party of horse to watch the place, he pitched his tents the same evening around Bethlehem, and the next morning at sunrise, the Moslem soldiers might be seen pouring into the vast convent, where Baldwin I. had been crowned King eighty-seven years before, and the magnificent church erected by the Empress Helena and her son Constantine A.D. 327, over the sacred spot where the Saviour of the world was born. The present condition of this most ancient and beautiful Basilic is described in another chapter. They wandered with unbounded admiration amid the unrivaled Corinthian colonnade, formed by a quadruple row of forty ancient columns, which support a barn-roof constructed of the cedar of Lebanon. They paused to admire the beautiful mosaics which covered the lofty walls, the richly carved screen on either side of the high altar, and the twenty-five imperial eagles. Saladin was present in person, so that no serious disorders appear to have been committed. The inhabitants of the town had all fled to Jerusalem, with whatever property they could carry with them, and in the afternoon, after establishing a garrison in the place, the Sultan commenced his march towards the Holy City, five miles further north.

1187. At the hour of sunset, October 2d, when the bells of the churches of Jesusalem were tolling to vespers, the vast host of Saladin crowned in dark array the bleak and desolate eminences which surround the city of David. The air was rent with the loud Mussulman shouts El Khuds, El Khuds—"The Holy City, the Holy City!" The green and yellow banners of the Prophet, and the various colored emblems of the Arabian tribes, were to be seen standing out in bold relief upon the lofty ridges of the hills, and gleaming brightly in the last trembling rays of the setting sun. The Arabian writers descant with enthusiasm upon the feelings experienced by their countrymen on beholding the long-lost sister of Mecca and Medina, on gazing once more upon the swelling dome of the Mosk of Omar, and on that sacred eminence from whence, according to their traditions, Mohammed ascended from earth to heaven. It must have been, indeed, a strange and an awful scene. The Moslem host took up their stations around the Holy City at the very hour when the followers both of the Christian and Mohammedan religions were wont to assemble to offer up their prayers to the one Great God, the common Father of us all. On the one hand, you might hear the sound of the sweet vesper bells from the towers of the Christian churches wafted softly upon the evening breeze, the hoarse chant of the monks and priests, and the loud swelling hymn of praise; while on the other, over all the hills and eminences around Jerusalem, stole the long shrill cry of 'the muezzins,* loudly summoning the faithful to their evening devotions. Within the walls, for one night at least, the name of CHRIST was invoked with true piety and fervent devotion; while without the city the eternal truth and the Moslem fiction were loudly blended, "There is but one GOD and Mohammed is his prophet."

1187. That very night, when the Mussulmans had finished their prayers, and ere darkness spread its sable shroud over the land, the loud trumpets of Saladin summoned the Christians to surrender the House of God to the arms of the faithful. But the Christians returned for answer, that, please God, the Holy City should *not* be surrendered. The next morning at sunrise, the terrified inhabitants were awakened by the clangor of horns and drums, the loud clash of arms, and the fierce cries of the remorseless foe. The women and children rushed into the churches, and threw themselves on their knees before the altars, weeping and wailing, and lifting up their hands to heaven, whilst the men hastened to man the battlements. The Order of the Temple could no longer furnish its hundreds and thousands of brave warriors for the defense of the holy sanctuary of the Christians. A few Knights, with some serving brethren, alone remained in the now silent halls and deserted courts of their head-quarters. Yet for fifteen days did the Christians successfully resist the utmost efforts of the enemy. Monks and canons, bishops and priests, took arms in defense of the Holy Sepulcher, and lined in warlike array the dark gray battlements and towers of Jerusalem. But the Mussulman archers soon became so numerous and so expert, that the garrison durst not show themselves upon the walls. Their arrows fell, says Abbot Coggleshale, one of the defenders of the place, as thick as hail upon the battlements, so that no one could lift a finger above the walls without being maimed. So great, indeed, was the number of the wounded, that it was as much as all the doctors of the city and of the Hospital could do to extract the weapons from their bodies. The face of the narrator of these events was lacer-

---

* The Muezzin is the officer of the Mohammedan mosk who cries the hour of prayer. If the mosk has a minaret (steeple) the call is made from the top. The word is Arabic from *azzana* to inform. (The *ear* in Arabic is *uzn*.)

ated with an arrow which pierced right through his nose ; the wooden shaft was withdrawn, but a piece of the iron head, he says, remains there to this day.

Jerusalem was crowded with fugitives who had been driven into the Holy City from all the provinces. The houses could not contain them, and the streets were filled with women and children, who slept night after night upon the cold pavement. At the expiration of a fortnight, Saladin, finding his incessant attacks continually foiled, retired from the walls, and employed his troops in the construction of military engines, stationing ten thousand cavalry around the city to intercept fugitives and prevent the introduction of supplies. When his engines were completed, he directed all his efforts against the northern wall of the city, which extends between St. Stephen's gate and the gate of Joppa, the same from which the successful assaults had been made by the Crusaders eighty-eight years before. Ten thousand soldiers were attached to the military engines, and were employed day and night in battering the fortifications. Barefoot processions of women, monks, and priests were continually made to the Holy Sepulcher to implore the Son of God to save his tomb and his inheritance from impious violation. The females, as a mark of humility and distress, cut off their hair and cast it to the winds. The ladies of Jerusalem made their daughters do penance by standing up to their necks in tubs of cold water placed upon Calvary. But it availed nought, for our Lord Jesus Christ, says the chronicler, would not listen to any prayer that they made. For the filth, the luxury, and the adultery which prevailed in the city did not suffer prayer or supplication to ascend before God.

To prevent the garrison from attempting to break the force of the battering-rams, Saladin constructed vast mangonels (engines used for throwing stones), and other machines, which cast enormous stones and flaming beams of timber, covered with pitch and naptha, upon the ramparts and over the walls into the city. He moreover employed miners to sap the foundations of the towers, and on the 16th of October, 1187, the angle of the northern wall at the northwest, where it touches the valley of Hinnon, was thrown down with a tremendous crash. This appalling intelligence spread

Surrender of Jerusalem. Ransom and disgraceful Terms.

 rough the city and filled every heart with mourning. Friends
 mbraced one another as it were for the last time; mothers clung
) their nttle ones, anticipating with heart-rending agony the fear-
 il moment when they would be torn from them forever; the men
 azed around in gloomy silence, appalled and stupefied. Young
 iothers might be seen carrying their babes in their arms to Calvary
 nd placing them before the altars of the Church of the Resurrec-
 on, as if they thought that the sweet innocence of these helpless
 bjects would appease the wrath of heaven. The panic-stricken
 arrison deserted the fortifications, but the infidels fortunately
 eferred the assault until the succeeding morning. During the
 ight attempts were made, but in vain, to organize a strong guard
) watch the breach. With my own ears, says Abbot Coggleshale,
  heard it proclaimed, between the wall and the counterscarp, by
 he Patriarch and the chief men of the city, that if fifty strong
 nd valiant foot-soldiers would undertake to guard for one night
 nly the angle which had been overthrown they should receive fifty
 ;olden bezants (equal to $3,750); but none could be found to
 mdertake the duty.

In the morning a suppliant deputation proceeded to Saladin to
 mplore his mercy, but ere they reached the imperial tent the
 .ssault had commenced, and twelve Moslem banners waved in
 riumph upon the breach. The haughty Sultan accordingly refused
 o hear the messengers and dismissed them, declaring that he would
 ake Jerusalem from the Franks as they had taken it from the
 Vloslem, that is to say, *sword in hand*. But some spirit of resist-
 ince had at last been infused into the quailing garrison, the few
 Templars and Hospitalers in Jerusalem manned the breach, and in
 . desperate struggle the Moslem were repulsed and their standards
 orn down from the walls. The messengers then returned to
 Saladin, and declared that if he refused to treat for the surrender
)f Jerusalem, the Christians would set fire to the TEMPLE or Mosk
)f Omar, would destroy all the treasures they possessed in the city,
 ind massacre their Moslem prisoners. The announcement of this
 lesperate determination, which was accompanied with the offer of
 . very considerable ransom, induced Saladin to listen to terms, and
 . treaty was entered into with the Christians to the following

Poorer Classes reduced to Slavery.   Misery of the Christian Woman.

effect: The Moslem were immediately to be put into possession
all the gates of Jerusalem, and the liberty and security of the
habitants were to be purchased by every man paying to Saladin t
golden bezants ($750) as a ransom, every woman five, and eve
child under seven years one bezant.

When these terms, so disgraceful to the Christian negotiato
were known in the Holy City, nothing could exceed the grief a
indignation of the poorer classes of people, who had no mon
wherewith to pay this enormous ransom, and had consequent
been delivered up to perpetual bondage by their richer *Christi*
brethren.   All resistance on their part, however, to the treaty w
then hopeless.   The poor had been betrayed by the rich.   T
infidels were already (October 18) in possession of the Tower
David, and their spears were gleaming in the streets of the Ho
City.   It is recorded to the praise of the few Templars a
Hospitalers who were then in Jerusalem, that they spent all tl
money they possessed in ransoming their poor Christian brethre
whom they escorted in safety to Tripoli, 200 miles northwar
The number of those who, being unable to pay the ransom, we
reduced to a state of hopeless slavery is estimated at 14,000 me
women, and children.   They were sold in the common slav
markets, and distributed through all the Mussulman countries c
Asia.   The women became the concubines and handmaids
their masters; the children were educated in the Mohammeda
faith.

The Arabian writers express their astonishment at the numbe
of the Christian captives, and give a heart-rending account of the
sorrows and misfortunes.   One of them tells us that he saw in h
native village a fair European woman, bright as the morning sta
who had two beautiful children; she seldom spoke, but remaine
the live-long day absorbed in melancholy contemplation.   Thei
was, says he, such a sweetness and gentleness in her deportmer
that it made one's heart ache to see her.   "When I was at Aleppo,
says the historian Azz'eddin Ali Ibn-Al'atsyr, who fought i
Saladin's army, and was present at the battle of Tiberias, 1187, "
had for a slave one of the Christian women taken at Jaffa.   Sh
had with her a little child, about a year old, and many a bitter tea

id she shed over this tender infant.   I did my best to comfort her,
ut she exclaimed, 'Alas, sir, it is not for this child that I weep; I
ad a husband and two sisters, and I know not what has become of
iem.   I had also six brothers, all of whom have perished.'   This
; the case of one person only.   Another day I saw at Aleppo a
!hristian slave accompanying her master to the house of a neigh-
or.   The master knocked at the door, and another Frank woman
ame to open it.   The two females immediately gave a loud cry;
iey rush into each other's arms; they weep; they sit down on the
round and enter into conversation.   They were two sisters who
ad been sold as slaves to different masters, and had been brought
rithout knowing it to the same town."

Thus fell the holy city of Jerusalem, eighty-eight years after its
onquest by Godfrey de Bouillon and the Crusaders in July, 1099.
)ur chronicler, Radolph, Abbot of Coggleshale, who was redeemed
rom bondage by payment of the ten golden bezants ($750), throws
 pitying glance upon the misfortunes and miseries of the poor
aptives, but attributes the fall of Jerusalem, and all the calamities
onsequent thereon, to the sins and iniquities of the inhabitants.
'hey honor God, says he, with their lips, but their hearts were far
·om him.   He speaks of the beautiful women who thronged
erusalem, and of the general corruption of the city, and exclaims,
i the words of the prophet, " The Lord hath said unto the heathen,
o ye up against the walls and destroy, take away her battlements,
)r they are not the Lord's."

Immediately after the surrender of the city October 18, the
Ioslem rushed to the TEMPLE in thousands.   The imaums and
he doctors and expounders of the law first ascended to the Tem-
le of the Lord, called *Beit Allah* (the House of God), in which,
s a place of prayer and religion, they place their great hope of
alvation.   With horrible bellowings they proclaimed the law of
Iohammed, and vociferated, with polluted lips, ALLAH *hu achbar*
–ALLAH *hu achbar*.   They defiled all the places that are contain-
d within the Temple; *i. e.* the place of the Presentation, where
Iary delivered the Son of God into the hands of the just Simeon;
nd the place of the Confession, looking towards the porch of Sol-
mon, where the Lord judged the woman taken in adultery.   They

placed guards that no Christian might enter within the seven *atri*
(entrances) of the Temple. And as a disgrace to the Christian
with vast clamor, with laughter and with mockery, they hurle
down the golden Cross from the pinnacle of the building, an
dragged it with ropes throughout the city, amid the exultin
shouts of the infidels and the tears and lamentations of the follow
ers of Christ.

When every Christian had been removed from the precincts c
the Temple, Saladin proceeded with vast pomp to say his prayer
in the *Beit Allah*, the holy house of God, or " Temple of th
Lord," erected by the Caliph Omar. He was preceded by fiv
camels laden with rose-water, which he had procured from Damas
cus, where acres of sweet flowers had been exhausted to yield thei
perfume for this service; or his servants may have procured th
perfumed liquid in the Wady el Werd, or Valley of Roses, lyin;
but a mile northwest of Jerusalem, and still cultivated in rose
for the enjoyment of the hareems of the faithful of that city, an
he entered the sacred courts to the sound of martial music, an
with his banners streaming in the wind. The *Beit Allah*, th
Temple of the Lord, was then again consecrated to the service o
one God and his prophet Mohammed; the walls and pavement
were washed and purified with rose-water; and a pulpit, the labo
of Noureddin, was erected in the sanctuary.

The following account of these transactions was forwarded t
Henry II., King of England. " To the beloved Lord Henry, b
the grace of God, the illustrious King of the English, Duke o
Normandy and Guienne, and Count of Anjou, Brother Terric
formerly Grand Preceptor of the House of the Temple at JERU
SALEM, sendeth greeting,—salvation through him who saveth kings
Know that Jerusalem, with the Citadel of David, hath been sur
rendered to Saladin. The Syrian Christians, however, have the
custody of the Holy Sepulcher up to the fourth day after Michael
mas, and Saladin himself hath permitted ten of the brethren of
the Hospital to remain in the house of the Hospital for the space
of one year, to take care of the sick. Jerusalem, alas, hath fallen.
Saladin hath caused the Cross to be thrown down from the summit
of the Temple of the Lord, and for two days to be publicly kicked

and dragged in the dirt through the city. He then caused the Temple of the Lord to be washed within and without, upwards and downwards, with rose-water, and the law of Mohammed to be proclaimed throughout the four quarters of the Temple with wonderful clamor."

Bohadin, Saladin's secretary, mentions as a remarkable and happy circumstance, that the Holy City was surrendered to the Sultan of most pious memory, and that God restored to the faithful their sanctuary on the *twenty-seventh of the month Regeb*, on the night of which very day their most glorious prophet Mohammed performed his wonderful nocturnal journey from the Temple of the Lord, through the seven heavens, to the throne of God. He also describes the sacred congregation of the Mussulmans gathered together in the Temple and the solemn prayer offered up to God; the shouting and the sounds of applause, and the voices lifted up to heaven, causing the holy buildings to resound with thanks and praises to the most bountiful Lord God. He glories in the casting down of the golden cross, and exults in the very splendid triumph of Islam.

Saladin restored the sacred area of the Temple to its original condition under the first Mussulman conquerors of Jerusalem. The ancient Christian Church of the Virgin (the mosk *El Aksa*, and Temple of Solomon) was washed with rose-water, and was once again dedicated to the religious services of the Moslem. On the western side of this venerable edifice the Templars had erected, according to the Arabian writers, an immense building in which they lodged, together with granaries of corn and various offices, which enclosed and concealed a great portion of the edifice. Most of these were pulled down by the Sultan to make a clear and open area for the resort of the Mussulmans to prayer. Some new erections placed between the columns in the interior of the structure were taken away, and the floor was covered with the richest carpets. Lamps innumerable, says Ibn Alatsyr, were suspended from the ceiling. Verses of the Koran were again inscribed on the walls. The call to prayer was again heard. The bells were silenced. The exiled faith returned to its ancient sanctuary. The devout Mussulmans again bent the knee in adoration of the one only God, and the voice of the Imaum* was again heard from the pulpit, reminding the true believers of the resurrection and the last judgment.

The Friday after the surrender of the city, the army of Saladin, and crowds of true believers, who had flocked to Jerusalem from all parts of the East, assembled in the Temple of the Lord upon Mount Moriah to assist in the religious services of the Mussulman Sabbath.   Omad, Saladin's secretary, who was present, gives the following interesting account of the ceremony, and of the sermon that was preached.   On Friday morning at daybreak, says he, everybody was asking whom the Sultan had appointed to preach. The Temple was full; the congregation was impatient; all eyes were fixed on the pulpit; the ears were on the stretch; our hearts beat fast, and tears trickled down our faces.   On all sides were to be heard rapturous exclamations of What a glorious sight! What a congregation!   Happy are those who have lived to see the resurrection of ISLAM.   At length the Sultan ordered the judge (doctor of the law) *Mohieddin Aboulmehali-Mohammed* to fulfill the sacred function of imaum.   I immediately lent him the black vestment which I had received as a present from the Caliph.   He then mounted into the pulpit and spoke.   All were hushed.   His expressions were graceful and easy, and his discourse was eloquent and much admired.   He displayed the virtue and sanctity of Jerusalem; he spoke of the purification of the Temple; he alluded to the silence of the bells, and to the flight of the infidel priests. In his prayer he named the Caliph and the Sultan, and terminated his discourse with that chapter of the Koran in which God orders justice and good works.   He then descended from the pulpit, and prayed in the Mihrah.   Immediately afterwards a sermon was preached before the congregation.

This sermon was delivered by *Mohammed Ben Zeky:* "Praise be to God," said the preacher, "who by the power of his might

---

* An *Imaum* (spelt also *Imarm* and *Iman*) is a minister or priest who performs the regular service of the Mosk among the Mohammedans.   There is also a Mohammedan prince who unites in his person supreme spiritual and temporal power; as the Imaum of Muscat.   The word is Arabic, derived from *amma,* to walk before, to preside over.

KNIGHTS TEMPLARS. 261

Mohammedan Religious Services.   Sacred Rock of the Temple.

hath raised up Islamism on the ruins of polytheism; who governs all things according to his will; who overthroweth the devices of the infidels, and causeth the TRUTH to triumph! I praise God, who hath succored his elect, who hath rendered them victorious and crowned them with glory, who hath purified his holy house from the filthiness of idolatry. I bear witness that there is no God but that one great God who standeth *alone* and hath no PARTNER; sole, supreme, eternal; who begetteth not and is not begotten, and hath NO EQUAL. I bear witness that Mohammed is his servant, his envoy, and his prophet, who hath dissipated doubts, confounded polytheism, and put down LIES! O men, declare ye the blessings of God, who hath restored to you this Holy City, after it has been left in the power of the infidels for a hundred years! This HOLY HOUSE of the LORD hath been built, and its foundation hath been established for the glory of God. This sacred spot is the dwelling-place of the prophets, the Kiblah (place of prayer) towards which you turn at the commencement of your religious duties, the birth-place of the saints, the scene of the revelation. It is thrice holy, for the angels of God spread their wings over it. This is that blessed land of which God hath spoken in his sacred book. In this house of prayer Mohammed prayed with the angels who approach God. It is to this spot that all fingers are turned after the two holy places. This conquest, O men, hath opened unto you the gates of heaven; the angels rejoice, and the eyes of the prophets glisten with joy!" The preacher proceeds, in a high strain of enthusiasm, to enlarge upon the merits of the holy war. "The holy war, the holy war!" says he, "is better than religious worship; it is the noblest of your occupations. Aid God, and he will assist you; protect the Lord, and he will protect you; remember him, and he will have you in remembrance; do good to him, and he will do good to you. Cut off the branches of iniquity, purify the earth from unbelievers, and destroy the nations who have excited the wrath of God and his apostles."

Omad informs us that the marble altar and chapel which had been erected over the sacred rock in the Temple of the Lord, or Mosk of Omar, was removed by Saladin, together with the stalls for the priests, the marble statues, and all the abominations which

17

had been placed in the venerated building by the Christians.   The Mussulmans discovered with horror that some pieces of the holy stone or rock had been cut off by the Franks and sent to Europe. Saladin caused it to be immediately surrounded by a grate of iron. He washed it with rose-water, and Malek-Afdel covered it with magnificent carpets.   Saladin, in his famous letter to the Caliph, giving an account of the conquest of Jerusalem, exclaims, "God hath at length turned towards the supporters of the true faith ; he

MODERN HOSPICE ST. JOHN.

hath let loose his wrath against the infidels, and hath driven them from his sanctuary.   The infidels had erected churches in the holy city, and the great houses of the Templars and Hospitalers.   In these structures are rich marbles and many precious things.   Thy

Templars defending themselves in several parts of Palestine.

servant hath restored the Mosk Al-Aksa to its ancient destination. He hath appointed Imaums to celebrate divine service, and on the 14th Chaaban they preached the *khotbeh* (sermon). The heavens are rent with joy and the stars dance with delight. The word of God hath been exalted, and the tombs of the prophets which the infidel hath defiled have been purified." Saladin restored the fortifications of Jerusalem, founded several schools, and converted the great house of the Hospitalers into a college. He then quitted the Holy City to pursue his military operations in the field. **1187.** The Templars still maintained themselves in some of the strongest castles of Palestine, and the maritime city of Tyre continued to resist all the attacks of the Moslems. This important seaport was preserved to the Christians by the valor and military talents of the young Conrad, Marquis of Montferrat, who digged a ditch across the isthmus which connects Tyre with the main land, thus making it an island, as it was when Alexander sat down before it, B.C. 332, repaired the fortifications, and planted catapults and balistæ in boats, so as to command the only approach to the town. Saladin proceeded in person to Tyre to conduct the operations against this important place. He was on horseback from morn till night, and was assisted by his sons, his brother, and his nephew, all of whom commanded in the field under the eye of the Sultan, and animated the troops by their example. The following account of the state of affairs in Palestine is contained in a letter from Sir Knight Terric, Grand Preceptor of the Temple and Treasurer-General of the Order, to Henry the Second, King of England: "The brothers of the hospital of Belvoir as yet bravely resist the Saracens. They have captured two convoys, and have valiantly possessed themselves of the munitions of war and provisions which were being conveyed by the Saracens from the fortress of La Feue. As yet, also, Carach, in the neighborhood of Mount Royal, Mount Royal itself, the temple of Safed, the hospital of Carach, Margat, and Castellum Blancum, and the territory of Tripoli, and the territory of Antioch, resist Saladin. From the feast of Saint Martin up to that of the Circumcision of the Lord, Saladin had besieged Tyre incessantly, by night and by day, throwing into it immense stones from thirteen military engines. On the vigils of

The King of Jerusalem and the Grand Master set at liberty.

St. Sylvester, the Lord Conrad, the Marquis of Montferrat, distributed knights and foot-soldiers along the wall of the city, and having armed seventeen galleys and ten small vessels, with the assistance of the house of the Hospital and the brethren of the Temple, he engaged the galleys of Saladin, and, vanquishing them, he captured eleven, and took prisoners the great admiral of Alexandria and eight other admirals, a multitude of the infidels being slain. The rest of the Mussulman galleys escaping the hands of the Christians fled to the army of Saladin, and being run aground by his command were set on fire and burnt to ashes. Saladin himself, overwhelmed with grief, *having cut off the ears and the tail of his horse*, rode that same horse through his whole army in the sight of all. Farewell." Tyre continued to be valiantly defended until the winter had set in, and then the disappointed Sultan, despairing of taking the place, burnt his military engines and retired to Damascus.

Guy de Lusignan, King of Jerusalem, and De Riderfort, Grand Master of the Temple, who had, as before mentioned, been residing at Nablous, under the surveillance of Saladin's officers, were now set at liberty, pursuant to the treaty of Ascalon, on the understanding that they would immediately proceed to Tyre and embark for Europe. Queen Sibylla, who was in Jerusalem at the time of its surrender to Saladin, had been permitted to join her husband at Nablous, and the King, the Queen, and the Grand Master of the Temple, De Riderfort, consequently proceeded together to Tyre. But on their arrival at that place, they found the gates shut against them. The young Conrad declared, that as the city had been preserved solely by the swords of himself and his followers, it justly belonged to him, and that neither the King nor the Queen of Jerusalem any longer possessed authority within it. Repelled from Tyre, the King and Queen, with their infant children, the Grand Master of the Temple, and the patriarch Heraclius, went on 150 miles further north to Antioch.

Part Third.

FROM THE BATTLE OF HATTIN, A. D. 1187, TO THE LOSS OF ACRE
AND OF THE CHRISTIAN POSSESSION OF PALESTINE, A.D. 1291.

CHAPTER I.

THE CAPTURE OF ACRE BY THE CHRISTIANS A.D. 1191.

BUT the just, like palms, shall flourish,
Which the plains of Judah nourish,
Like tall cedars mounted on
Cloud-ascending Lebanon.
Plants set in thy courts below,
Spread their roots and upwards grow;
Fruit in their old age shall bring,
Ever fat and flourishing.
This God's justice celebrates;
He, my ROCK, injustice hates.

ALTHOUGH King Guy and Grand Master Riderfort of the Templars had sworn to Saladin in their captivity to renounce forever the Holy Land and return to Europe, yet such a promise, extorted by force, was not regarded as binding, in a war in which fanaticism set at naught the power of an oath on the one side or the other. In the surrender of Ascalon the Sultan had gained all he sought. It is not likely that he expected his captives to keep their promise. Or perhaps, as the weakness of Guy and the unmilitary order of De Riderfort had brought about his great victory of Hattin, he may have been willing to liberate them in hope that their presence *would bring discord* to the Christian powers.

In this he erred. The King and the Templar soon gathered round them the fragments of their forces, and in the siege of Acre gave a new impulse to Europe and a nucleus of operations to all who were willing to strike a blow at the Saracens. His extension of the Christian government in Palestine for one entire century was the result. We proceed, in the present chapter, to describe these four years' efforts.

1188. As soon as the winter rains had subsided, Saladin again took the field, and attempted to reduce various strong castles of the Templars and Hospitalers. The most formidable of these were the castles of Safed and Kaukab,* the one belonging to the Order of the Temple and the other to the Order of the Hospital of Saint John. Safed is one of the four holy cities of the Talmud, the other three being Jerusalem, Tiberias, and Hebron, but Safed is held in peculiar veneration by the Jews. The castle of the Templars crowned the summit of a lofty mountain, along the sides of which extended the houses and churches of the town. It was the strongest fortress possessed by the Order in Palestine. From the ramparts the eye ranged over a rich prospect of luxuriant vineyards and smiling villages, and embraced a grand panoramic view of lofty mountains. Through the valley below rolled the Jordan. To the southward extended the blue expanse of the little lake of Tiberias. In the northeast the snowy summits of Anti-Lebanon might be seen piercing the skies. This important fortress commanded the greater part of Galilee. It had always been a great check upon the incursions of the Saracens, and was considered one of the bulwarks of the Latin kingdom. Saladin's exertions, consequently,

---

* The word *Kaukab* denotes "a star," or more properly a meteor. The fortress of Kankab referred to above is the same as Belvoir ("The Beautiful View"), often named in the History of the Crusades. The Arabs called it Fuleh, the Europeans Faba, both words meaning "a bean." It is now known as Kankab el-Hawa ("Meteor of the Air"), situated between Bethshean and the Jordan. (See Map.) Dr. Robinson describes it ("Biblical Researches") as lying on the brow of the Jordan valley, near the extremity of the line of hills between the wadys of Osheh and El-Birch. It was equally termed Belvoir, and Belvedere, and Belliforth. It was erected by King Fulk about 1140. Professor Tristam ("Land of Israel"), viewing it from the northwest, says: "On a lofty green-clad hill to the southeast towers Kankab el-Hawa, the ruined Crusading castle of Belvoir, one of their most renowned fortresses, and commanding the most extensive panorama in Northern Palestine. It is not only one of the finest sites but one of the finest ruins in the country, with its deep, excavated fosse quite perfect, and resembling the castle of Belfort (Kulat es-Shukif), on the river Litany."

Siege of Safed by Saladin.   The Templars' noble Defense.

for the capture of the place were strenuous and incessant.   He planted a large body of troops around it, under the command of his talented brother Saifeddin; but the season was not far enough advanced for their operations to be carried on with any chance of success.   The tents of the besiegers were blown off the mountain by the furious whirlwinds, and the operation of the military engines was impeded by heavy rains.   The Templars made continued sallies upon the works, burnt the military engines, butchered the soldiers in their sleep, and harassed them with incessant alarms in the dead of night.

1188.   The siege was turned into a blockade, and Saladin drew off the greater part of his forces to attack the Christian possessions in the principality of Antioch.   He divided his army into several detachments, which were sent in different directions, with orders to

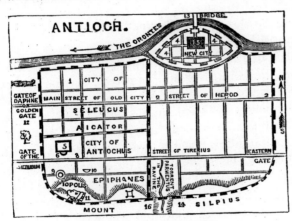

PLAN OF ANTIOCH, SYRIA.

ravage all the neighboring country, drive away the oxen, sheep, and cattle, and collect the booty together in the plain of the Orontes, along the banks of the lake of Kades.   He crossed the vast mountain ranges which extended between the Orontes and the sea-coast, and appeared in arms before the gates of Tripoli.   Strenuous preparations having been made to receive him, the Sultan contented himself with reconnoitering the place and examining its defenses; having done which he directed his march upon Tortosa.   De Riderfort, Grand Master of the Temple, who was anxiously watching Saladin's movements, immediately threw himself into the strong castle of the Templars at that place, and prepared to defend the town. But the fortifications were weak, the inhabitants were panic-stricken, and the Templars, after a short struggle, were compelled to abandon the city and retire behind their fortifications. There they maintained a fierce and bloody contest with the Moslem, and during the various assaults and sallies the town was set on fire and burnt to the ground. Bohadin gives a fearful account of the destruction by fire of the great cathedral church, and of the roaring and crackling of the flames as they burst through the huge cedar beams and timbers of the roof. He says that thousands of faithful Mussulmans gathered around the vast and venerable pile, and raised exulting shouts as they witnessed the progress of the fire, lifting up their voices to heaven, and returning thanks to the most bountiful Lord God!

Having failed in all his attempts to take the castle of the Templars there, Saladin drew off his forces, leaving the once populous and flourishing town of Tortosa a dreary desert. He then besieged and took the city of Gebal (now *Jebale*), and then approached in warlike array the far-famed Laodicea (now *Latakia*). The panic-stricken inhabitants refused to defend the town and abandoned the fortifications, but some Templars and other knights, throwing themselves into the citadel with their followers, boldly resisted the attacks of the infidels. After a desperate defense, a capitulation was signed, the garrison marched out with all the honors of war, and the banners of Islam were then planted upon the towers and battlements. Both Ibn Alatsyr and Bohadin give an enthusiastic description of the town and its environs. They speak of its noble harbor, its beautiful houses, elegant villas, rich marbles, luxuriant gardens, and shady groves. All these became the prey of the fierce Mussulman soldiery, who committed great excesses. They broke to pieces the choicest specimens of ancient sculpture, considering them hated evidences of idolatry; they stripped all the churches of their ornaments, and sold the sacred vestments of the priests. From Laodicea, Saladin marched to Sohioun, or Sekyun, a fortress of prodigious strength, situate amongst the mountains midway between Gebal and the Orontes. It was almost entirely surrounded

Assault and Success of Saladin. Siege of the Castle of the Templars.

by a deep precipitous ravine, the sides of which were in many places perpendicular. After a siege of five days a part of the Mussulman soldiers clambered over some rocks which were thought to be inaccessible, climbed the outer wall of the town, and opened the gates to their companions. The second and third walls were then carried by assault, and the citadel surrendered after a short siege. Many other important cities and castles speedily fell into the hands of the victorious Saladin. Amongst these were the city of Bakas, or Bacas, on the banks of the Orontes, and the castle of Al Shokhr, which was connected with the town by a bridge over the river; the castle of Al Jahmàhûnín, near Gebal; Blatanous, near Antioch; Sarminiah, or Sarmaniya, a fortress a day's journey northeast of Aleppo; and many other places of note. All the towns and castles between Sarminiah and Gebal surrendered to the Moslems. Glory be to God, says Ibn Alatsyr, who hath made easy that which appeared to be difficult.

1188. Saladin then recrossed the Orontes and laid siege to Berzyeh, or Borzya, a fortress which commanded the high road from Antioch to Emesa, or Hums, and was, therefore, a place of very great importance. During a very hot day, when the garrison had been fighting from sunrise till noon, Saladin suddenly called up his reserve, placed himself at their head, scaled the fortifications, and entered the town sword in hand. The houses were set on fire, the streets were drenched with blood, and all the inhabitants who escaped the general massacre were made slaves. From Berzyeh Saladin marched down the vast and fertile plain of the Orontes to the famous iron bridge over that river, about six or seven miles from Antioch (now *Antakia*), with a view of besieging the strong castle of the Knights Templars, called Derbazâc, or Darbêsak. On the 8th *Regeb*, having collected his forces together and procured a vast number of powerful military engines, he moved forward and invested the place. The walls were surrounded with wooden towers, filled with expert archers, who swept the battlements with their arrows. Under cover of these towers battering-rams were placed in position, and a vast breach was made in the walls. Saladin's body-guard moved forward to the assault, supported by crowds of archers on either flank, but the Templars filled up the

breach with their bodies, and after a bloody contest the Mussulmans were driven back, leaving the ground covered with their dead.
The Templars repaired the breach, and the Sultan shifted his
ground of attack.   Hurdles covered with raw hides were advanced
against the walls, and an expert party of miners were employed
under cover of these hurdles to undermine a huge tower, which
was considered to be the key of the fortifications.   The tower was
so well and strongly built that it resisted for a length of time all
the efforts of the miners.   They dug away a great part of the
foundations, and the tower appeared, says Ibn Alatsyr, to be suspended in the air.   At last, however, it fell with a tremendous
crash, carrying along with it into the ditch a vast portion of the
walls on either side, so that a large yawning gap was opened in the
fortifications.   Again the Mussulmans rushed to the assault with
loud shouts, and again they were hurled back by the stout arms of
the Templars, leaving the heaps of stones and the vast masses of
shattered walls around them crimsoned with the blood of their best
men.   Bohadin, who witnessed the assault, declares that he never
saw such an obstinate defense.   As soon as any one of the Templars
fell another, he tells us, would immediately take his place, and
thus they remained upon the breach, immovable as a rock.   At last
it was agreed that if the fortress was not succored by the Prince
of Antioch within a given period the Templars should surrender
it, and march out with their arms in their hands.   No succor
arriving by the appointed time, the place was consequently given
up to the Mussulmans.

Immediately after the surrender of Darbêsak, Saladin marched
upon Bagras, a town situate at the foot of Mount Al Locam, and
pushed on his advanced guard to the environs of the vast and populous city of Antioch, but he contented himself with the mere
sight of the place, and declined to undertake the siege of it.   He
remained for some time in observation before the city, and sent out
detachments in different directions to lay waste the surrounding
country, and collect spoil.   The population of Antioch was estimated at 150,000 souls.   Nearly all the surviving Templars of the
Principality were collected together within the walls, under the
command of their valiant Grand Master, De Riderfort, and the

Treaty between the Templars and Saladin.   Siege of the Fort at Safed.

Prince Bohemond was at the head of a numerous and well-organized force, fully prepared for a desperate struggle in defense of his rich and princely city.   Saladin consequently preferred entering into a truce to continuing the war, and concluded a treaty with Bohemond, whereby a suspension of arms was agreed upon for the term of eight months, to commence from the first of the approaching month of November, A.D. 1188, and it was stipulated that all the Moslem prisoners detained in Antioch should be set at liberty. Saladin then returned by the valley of the Orontes to Damascus. His troops becoming very impatient to be dismissed to their homes for the winter, he reminded them of the brevity and uncertainty of human life, told them that there was plenty of work before them, and that they ought not to leave for to-morrow that which could be done to-day.   He accordingly set out from Damascus at the head of a large body of forces, and proceeded to lay siege to Safed, the strong and important fort of the Knights Templars. This fortress, as repaired by the Turks, was totally destroyed in the memorable earthquake of January 1, 1837.   It was considered one of the most powerful military works in that country, having a deep moat and triple walls.   It crowned the rocky summit above the town of Safed, and formed a most conspicuous object at a great distance east, west, and south.   By many commentators it is thought to be " the city that is set upon a hill," referred to in the Sermon of the Mount.   It was one of four Crusading points for protecting the eastern borders of the land from the Saracens, viz., Montroyal or Montreal (now Shobek), and Kerak in the southeast, Belvoir (Kankub el-Hawa), in the east, and Safed in the northeast. In the campaign of Saladin to which we are now referring, his brother subdued the first two, and Saladin himself the others.

1188.   Bohadin accompanied the Sultan, and gives an interesting account of his incessant exertions for the capture of the place. During a windy and tempestuous night, he superintended the planting of five besieging engines.   To every soldier he allotted a specific task, and turning to his secretary he said, " Let us not go to bed to-night, until these five engines are completed."   Every now and then messengers came in to narrate the progress of the work, and Saladin spent the intermediate time in cheerful con verse with his friend. The night was dark and long, the weather miserably wet and cold, and the ground covered with mud. Bohadin ventured to address some observations to his royal master, upon the imprudence of exposing himself to the inclemency of the season, and to so much watching and fatigue, but the pious Sultan reminded him of the words of the prophet, " The fire of hell shall not prevail against the eye that wakes and watches in the service of God, and the eye that weeps through fear of God."

1188. The Templars manfully defended themselves, and their brethren in Tyre, twenty-five miles west, made an attempt to send them succor. Two hundred valiant and determined soldiers set out from that city, and marched through the country by night, sheltering themselves in the day-time in caverns and solitary places amongst the mountains. They reached Safed, and attempted to conceal themselves in the neighborhood of the castle, until they could find an opportunity of communicating with their beleaguered brethren. Unfortunately one of their number strayed from his place of concealment, and was seen by a Mussulman emir, who immediately called out a strong guard, searched the neighborhood, and took the whole party prisoners. They were brought into Saladin's presence and condemned to death; but before the sentence was carried into execution negotiations were entered into for the surrender of Safed. The Templars in the fortress were ill provided with provisions. They had now lost all hope of succor, and they agreed to surrender, on condition that they should be permitted to march out with their arms to Tyre, in company with the prisoners whom Saladin had just taken. These terms were acceded to, and the fortifications of the strong castle of Safed were speedily demolished.

In the meantime all Europe had been thrown into consternation by the dismal intelligence of the fall of Jerusalem. Public prayers were put up in the churches, and fasts were ordered, as in times of great national calamities. Pope Urban III. is said to have died of grief, A.D. 1187, and the Cardinals made a solemn resolution to renounce all kinds of diversions and pleasures, to receive no presents from any one who had causes depending in the court of Rome, and never to mount a horse as long as the Holy Land was

Renewed Efforts to regain Possession of Jerusalem. Templars again in the Field.

trodden under foot by the infidels. Pope Gregory VIII., successor to Urban III., addressed apostolical letters to the sovereigns, bishops, nobles, and people of all Christian countries, painting in pathetic terms the miserable disasters of the Latin Christians, the capture of the Holy Cross, the slaughter of the Templars and Hospitalers, and the fall of Jerusalem, and exhorting all faithful Christians immediately to assume the Cross, and march to the deliverance of the Holy City. Crowds of armed pilgrims again quitted the shores of Europe for Palestine, and the Templars, obedient to the pressing calls of their brethren, hurried from their preceptories to the seaports of the Mediterranean, and embarked in the ships of Genoa, Pisa, and Venice. The Grand Master of the Temple, De Riderfort, and De Lusignan, King of Jerusalem, placed themselves at the head of the newly arrived battalions, and established their head-quarters at Ras el Ain (or " Fountain Head," an abounding water-stream), at a small village on the main land two miles southeast of Tyre. Many valiant Templars from the Temple at London, and the different preceptories of England, Scotland, and Ireland, joined their chief, and brought with them arms, horses, clothing, and munitions of war, with a vast amount of treasure, which had been collected in the churches. They were the bearers likewise of a large sum of money which had been sent by King Henry II. of England for the defense of Tyre. This money was delivered to the Grand Master, but as the siege of Tyre had been raised before its arrival, and the young Conrad, Marquis of Montferrat, claimed the sovereignty of the city, and set up his authority in opposition to that of the King of Jerusalem, Grand Master De Riderfort very properly refused to deliver the money into his hands; whereupon Conrad wrote letters filled with bitter complaints to the Archbishop of Canterbury and to King Henry.

1189. At the commencement of the summer, 1189, the King and the Grand Master of Templars took the field at the head of an army of 9,000 men, and marched down the coast southward with the intention of laying siege to the important city of Acre. Saladin wrote to all the governors of the Moslem provinces, requiring them to join him without delay, and directed his army to concentrate at Sepphoris, five miles north of Nazareth. From thence he moved in order of battle to Tell Kaisan (*Tell*, signifies *a hill*), where the plain of Acre begins. The city of Acre had been regularly invested for some days previous to his arrival, and after reconnoitering the position of the Christian army, he encamped, extending his left wing to Al Nahr Al Halu, "the sweet river," and his right to Tel Al'Ayâdhiya, in such a manner, that the besiegers themselves became the besieged. He then made a sudden attack upon the weakest part of the Christian camp, broke through the lines, penetrated to the gate of Acre, called Karâkûsh, which he entered, and threw into the city a reinforcement of 5,000 warriors, laden with arms, provisions, clothing, and everything necessary for the defense of the place. Having accomplished this bold feat, Saladin made a masterly retreat to his camp at Tel Al'Ayâdhiya.

1189. On the 4th of October, the newly-arrived warriors from Europe, eager to signalize their prowess against the infidels, marched out of their intrenchments to attack Saladin's camp. The holy gospels, wrapped in silk, were borne by four knights on a cushion, before King Guy of Jerusalem, and the Patriarch Heraclius and the Western bishops appeared at the head of the Christian forces with crucifixes in their hands, exhorting them to obtain the crown of martyrdom in defense of the Christian faith. The Templars marched in the van, and led the assault. They broke through the right wing of the Mussulman army, which was commanded by Saladin's nephew, and struck such terror into the hearts of the Moslems, that some of them fled, without halting, as far as Tiberias, forty miles eastward. The undisciplined masses of the Christian army, however, thinking that the day was their own, rushed heedlessly on after the infidels, and penetrating to the tent of Saladin, abandoned themselves to pillage. The Grand Master of the Temple, foreseeing the result, collected his knights and the forces of the Order around him. The enemy rallied, led on by Saladin in person, and the Christian army would have been annihilated but for the Templars. Firm and immovable, they presented for the space of an hour an unbroken front to the advancing Moslem, and gave time for the discomfited and panic-stricken Crusaders to recover from their terror and confusion. But ere they had been

CITY OF ACRE.

KNIGHTS TEMPLARS. 279

Death of the Grand Master. Continued Succor to the Christians.

rallied, and had returned to the charge, the Grand Master, Gerard de Riderfort, was slain. He fell, pierced with arrows, at the head of his Knights; the Seneschal of the Order shared the same fate, and more than half the Templars present were numbered with the dead. So the brave De Riderfort, after escaping with only two others, from the slaughter at Tabor, May 1, 1187, and from the unparalleled defeat and captivity of July 3–5, 1187, fell at last, at the head of his forces, as a gallant Knight should.

1189. To Gerard de Riderfort succeeded Walter as Grand Master. Never did the flame of enthusiasm burn with fiercer or more destructive power than at the famous siege of Acre. Nine pitched battles were fought, with various fortune, in the neighborhood of Mount Carmel, and during the first year of the siege—1188–1189 —*three hundred thousand Christians* are computed to have perished, with as many Saracens. The tents of the dead, however, were replenished by new-comers from Europe. The fleets of Saladin succored the town. The Christian ships brought continual aid to the besiegers, and the contest seemed interminable. Saladin's exertions were incessant. The Arab authors compare him to a mother wandering with desperation in search of her lost child, and to a lioness who has lost its young. I saw him, says his secretary Bohadin, in the fields of Acre, afflicted with a most cruel disease, with boils from the middle of his body to his knees, so that he could not sit down, but only recline on his side, when he entered into his tent, yet he went about to the stations nearest to the enemy, arranged his troops for battle, and rode about from dawn till eve, now to the right wing, then to the left, and then to the center, patiently enduring the severity of his pain. Having received intelligence of the mighty preparations which were being made in Europe for the recovery of Jerusalem, and of the march of the Emperor, Frederick I., of Germany (Barbarossa) through Hungary and Greece to Constantinople, with a view of crossing the Hellespont into Asia, Saladin sent orders to the governors of Senjâr, Al Jazîra, Al Mawsel, and Arbel, ordering them to attend him with their troops, and directed his secretary Bohadin to proceed to the Caliph, Al Nâssr Deldin'illah, at Bagdad, humbly to request the Mussulman pontiff to use his spiritual authority and influence to

induce all the Moslem nations and tribes to heal their private
differences and animosities and combine together against the Franks
for the defense of Islam.   Bohadin was received with the greatest
distinction and respect by the Caliph and the whole divan at
Bagdad, and whilst the Pope, Clement III., was disseminating his
Apostolical letters throughout Christendom, calling upon the
Western nations to combine together for the triumph of the cross,
the Mussulman pontiff was addressing, from the distant city of
Bagdad, his pious exhortations to all Moslem to assemble under
the holy banners of the prophet, and shed their blood in defense
of *Islam*.

1190.   Shortly after the commencement of the new year, (586 of
the Hegira, which that year began Feb. 9th,) Saladin collected his
troops together and resolved at every cost to raise the siege of
Acre.   He moved from Al Kherûba to Tel Al Ajûl, where he
pitched his camp.   He was there joined by his son, Al Malek, Al
Daher Gayâtho'ddîn Gâzi, the governor of Aleppo, with a select
body of cavalry, and by Mohaffero'ddîn I'bn Zinoddin, with his
light horse.   The Templars and the Crusaders during the winter
had not been idle.   They had dug trenches around their camp,
thrown up ramparts, and fortified their position in such a way that
it would have been difficult, says the Arabian writer, for even a
bird to get in.   They had, moreover, filled up the ditch around
the town, and constructed three enormous towers, the largest of
which was much higher than the walls, was sixty cubits in length
(about ninety feet), and could contain from five to six hundred
warriors, with a proper quantity of arms and military engines.
These towers were covered with the raw hides of oxen, soaked in
vinegar and mud to render them incombustible by the Greek fire.
They were strengthened from top to bottom with bands of iron,
and were each divided into five platforms or galleries filled with
soldiers and military engines.   They were rolled on wheels to the
walls, and the Templars and the Crusaders were about to descend
from the platforms and galleries upon the battlements of the city,
when the towers, and all the warriors upon them, were consumed
by some inextinguishable inflammable composition, discharged out
of brass pots by a brazier from Damascus.   "We were watching,"

says Bohadin, who was standing in the Moslem camp by Saladin's side, "with intense anxiety the movements of the soldiers upon the towers, and thought that the city must inevitably be taken, when suddenly we saw one of them surrounded with a blaze of light, which shot up into the skies. The heavens were rent with one joyous burst of acclamation from the sons of Islam, and in another instant another tower was surrounded with raging flames and clouds of black smoke, and then the third. They were ignited one after the other in the most astonishing and surprising manner, with scarce an interval of a minute between them. The Sultan immediately mounted his horse and ordered the trumpets to sound to arms, exclaiming with a loud voice, in the words of the prophet, 'When the gate of good fortune is thrown open delay not to enter in.'"

1190. At the commencement of the summer Saladin detached a considerable portion of his forces to the north, to oppose the progress of the German Crusaders and Templars, who were advancing from Constantinople, under the command of the German Emperor, Frederick I. (Barbarossa). These advancing Templars were the especial favorites of Barbarossa, and after his melancholy death, June 10, 1190, either from drowning or from the effects of a cold bath in the river Calycadmus, in Cilicia, they formed part of the body-guard of his son, the Duke of Suabia, his successor in the war, who died a few months later.

The body of the great Emperor Frederick was brought to Tyre and interred in the cathedral of that city. Masonic travelers along that coast look with special interest upon the fragments of the splendid edifice honored with his remains, and marked on its Oriental exterior with a mason's mark. De Vogüé writes concerning it :

The cathedral of Tyre is one of the most beautiful churches constructed by the Crusaders. It measures seventy French meters long by twenty-two broad (a French meter is thirty-nine and thirty-six one-hundredths inches American measure), and offers this peculiarity, that its transepts are *saillic* by five meters upon each *bas-coté*. As to the rest, its general disposition is like that of the churches at Sebaste, Lyddo, and the other buildings of the same type. It has three naves, and the three contiguous apsides separated from the transept by a bay of joists (travée). The *piles* (piers of the arches) have entirely disappeared; and I can give no other indication upon their style, except that in their construction the spoils of the antique temples were utilized. We see, upon the ground, magnificent double columns of rose granite (Sienite) monoliths, which, by their dimensions, bélonged to edifices of the first order, and which, without doubt, decorated the central pillars of the cathedral.   Exteriorly, the windows have a singular ornamentation, composed of a *boudin* and a *frette*, rectangularly indented, which encircles all the bay.   Their *archivotte* is in *ogive*, and rests upon a plinth, whose profile is sufficiently complicated.

This edifice, I think, dates from the second half of the Twelfth Century. The only portion preserved is the eastern extremity.   The three apsides are enclosed within the rampart of the modern city.

LIST OF THE LATIN BISHOPS OF TYRE.

Odon, 1111–1124.	William 2d (the Historian), 1173–1184.
William 1st, 1124–1135.	Josse or Joseph, 1184–1206.
Foulcher Patr. of Jer. in 1147.	Simon, 1217–1227.
Raoul, 1147.	Pièrre 2d, 1227–1243.
Pièrre 1st, 1154–1163.	Pièrre 3d, 1251.
Frederick, 1163–1173.	Gilles, 1253–1266.

1190.   In the month of July, the Templars suffered severe loss in another attack upon Saladin's camp.   The Christian soldiery, deceived by the flight of the Mussulmans, were again lured to the pillage of their tents, and again defeated by the main body of Saladin's army, which had been posted in reserve.   The Templars were surrounded by an overpowering force, but they fought their way through the dense ranks of the infidels to their own camp, leaving the plain of Acre strewed with the lifeless bodies of the best and bravest of their warriors.   " The enemies of God," says Bohadin, " had the audacity to enter within the camp of the lions of Islamism, but they speedily experienced the terrible effects of the divine indignation.   They fell beneath the sabres of the Mussulmans as the leaves fall from the trees during the tempests of autumn. Their mangled corpses, scattered over the mountain side, covered the earth even as the branches and boughs cover the hills and valleys when the woodsman lops the forest timber."   " They fell," says another Arabian historian, " beneath the swords of the sons of Islam as the wicked will fall, at the last day, into the everlasting *fire* of HELL.   Nine rows of the dead covered the earth between the sea-shore and the mountains, and in each row might be counted the lifeless bodies of at least one thousand warriors."

SARACENS OVERPOWERING THE TEMPLARS.

The Moslem garrison continued perseveringly to defend the town. They kept up a constant communication with Saladin, partly by pigeons, partly by swimmers, and partly by men in small skiffs, who traversed the port in secrecy, by favor of the night, and stole into the city. At one period the besieged had consumed nearly all their provisions, and were on the point of dying with famine, when Saladin, it is said, hit upon the following stratagem, for the purpose of sending them a supply. He collected together a number of vessels at Beyrout, which was in his hands, laden with sacks of meal, cheese, onions, sheep, rice, and other provisions. He disguised the seamen in the Frank habit, put crosses on their pendants, and covered the decks of the vessels with hogs. In this way the little fleet sailed safely through the blockading squadron of the Christians, and entered the port of Acre. On another occasion Saladin sent 1,000 *dinars* to the garrison, by means of a famous diver named Isa. The man was drowned during his passage to the city, but the money, being deposited in three bladders, tied to his body, was a few days afterwards thrown ashore near the town, and reached the besieged in safety. At the commencement of the winter of 1190–91 the garrison was again reduced to great straits for want of food, and was on the point of surrendering, when three vessels from Egypt broke through the guard-ships of the Christians, and got safely into the harbor with a copious supply of provisions, munitions of war, and everything requisite to enable the city to hold out until the ensuing spring.

1190. To prevent the further introduction of succors by sea, the Crusaders endeavored to take possession of the tower of Flies, a strong castle, built upon a rock in the midst of the sea at the mouth of the harbor, which commanded the port. The Templars employed one of their galleys upon this service, and crowds of small boats, filled with armed men, military engines, and scaling-ladders, were brought against the little fortress, but without effect. The boats and vessels were set on fire by the besieged and reduced to ashes, and after losing all the men of the detachment the Christians gave over the attempt. On the land side, the combats and skirmishes continued to be incessant. Wooden towers, and vast military machines, and engines, were constantly erected by the besiegers, and as constantly destroyed by the sallies and skillful contrivances of the besieged. The Templars, on one occasion, con-

Investment of Tyre with fresh Troops. Dreadful Sufferings among the Christians.

structed two battering machines of a new invention, and most enormous size, and began therewith furiously to batter the walls of the town, but the garrison soon destroyed them with fire-darts, and beams of timber, pointed with red-hot iron.

1191. At the commencement of the next year (587, Hegira, which that year began Jan. 29th), a tremendous tempest scattered the fleet of the Crusaders, and compelled their ships to take refuge in Tyre. The sea being open, Saladin hastily collected some vessels at Caifas, threw a fresh body of troops into Acre, and withdrew the exhausted garrison, which had already sustained so many hardships and fatigues in defense of the town. This exchange of the garrison was most happily timed, for almost immediately after it had been effected, the walls of the city were breached, and preparations were made for an assault. The newly-arrived troops, however, repulsed the assailants, repaired the walls, and once more placed the city in a good posture of defense.

1191. Famine and disease continued to make frightful ravages amongst the Crusaders. The Duke of Suabia, son of the late German Emperor, Frederick I., Baldwin, Archbishop of Canterbury, the Patriarch Heraclius, four archbishops, twelve bishops, forty counts, and five hundred other nobles and knights, besides common soldiers, fell victims to the malady. From two to three hundred persons succumbed daily, and the survivors became unequal to the task of burying the dead. The trenches which the Christians had dug for their protection, now became their graves. Putrefying corpses were to be seen floating upon the sea and lining the sea-shore, and the air was infected with an appalling and intolerable effluvium. The bodies of the living became bloated and swollen, and the most trifling wounds were incurable. In addition to all this, numbers of the poorer class of people died daily from starvation. The rich supported themselves for a time upon horse-flesh, and Abbot Coggleshale tells us, that a dinner off the entrails of a horse cost twenty cents. Bones were ground to powder, mixed with water, and eagerly devoured, and all the shoes, bridles, and saddles, and old leather in the camp, were boiled to shreds, and greedily eaten.

1191. Queen Sibylla, who appears to have been sincerely attached to the unpopular husband, Guy, she had raised to the throne, was

Death of the Queen.   Conrad proclaimed King.   Guy claims his Rights.

present in the Christian camp with her four infant daughters. She had wandered with the King, Guy de Lusignan, from one place to another, ever since his liberation from captivity, and had been his constant companion through all the horrors, trials, and anxieties of the long siege of Acre. Her delicate frame, weakened by sorrow and misfortune, was unable to contend with the many hardships and privations of the Christian camp. She fell at last a victim to the frightful epidemic which raged amongst the soldiers, and her death was speedily followed by that of her four children. The enemies of the King now maintained that the crown of the Latin kingdom had descended upon Isabella, younger sister of Sibylla, and wife of Humphrey de Thoron, Lord of Montreal, or Mount Royal, south of Hebron; but the latter seemed to think otherwise, and took no steps either to have his wife made queen, or himself king. The enterprising and ambitious Conrad, Marquis of Montferrat, who played so gallant a part in the siege of Tyre two years before, accordingly determined to play a bold game for the advancement of his own fortunes. He paid his addresses to Isabella, and induced her to consent to be divorced from Humphrey de Thoron, and take him for her husband. He went to the Bishop of Beauvais, and persuaded that prelate to pronounce the divorce, and immediately after it had been done, carried off Isabella to Tyre and there married her. As soon as the nuptials had been performed, Conrad caused himself and his wife to be proclaimed King and Queen of Jerusalem, and forthwith entered upon the exercise of certain royal functions. He went to the Christian camp before Acre, where his presence caused serious divisions and dissensions amongst the Crusaders. The King, Guy de Lusignan, however, stood upon *his* rights. He maintained that, as he had been once a king, he *was always* a king, and that the death of his wife could not deprive him of the crown which he had solemnly received, according to the established usage of the Latin kingdom. A strong party in the camp declared themselves in his favor, and an equally strong party declared in favor of his rival, Conrad, who prepared to maintain his rights, sword in hand. The misfortunes of the Christians appeared now to have approached their climax. The sword, the famine, and the pestilence had successively invaded their camp, and now the demon of discord came to set them one against the other, and to paralyze all their exertions in the Christian cause.

1191. In the meantime the Third Crusade, glorious but fruitless in results, continued to be preached with great success in Europe. William, Archbishop of Tyre, 1173–1184, to whose history of these events all writers are chiefly indebted, had proceeded to the courts of France and England, and had represented in glowing colors the miserable condition of Palestine, and the horrors and abominations which had been committed by the infidels in the holy city of Jerusalem. The English King, Richard I., and the French King, Philip II., laid aside for the moment their private animosities, and agreed to fight under the same banner against the infidels. On the first of July, 1190, they had assembled their forces, one hundred thousand strong, on the plain of Vezelay, in France, and towards the close of the month of May, 1191, the royal fleets of Philip and Richard floated in triumph in the Bay of Acre. The Templars had again lost their Grand Master, and Robert de Sablè, or Sabloil,* a valiant Knight of the Order, who had commanded a division of the English fleet on the voyage out, had been placed at the head of the Fraternity. In all their proceedings the Templars had performed prodigies of valor; Their name and reputation, and the fame of their sanctity, says James of Vitry, Bishop of Acre, A.D. 1216–1228, like a chamber of perfume sending forth a sweet odor, were diffused throughout the entire world, and all the congregation of the Saints will recount their battles and glorious triumphs over the enemies of Christ. Knights, indeed, from all parts of the earth, dukes and princes, after their example, casting off the shackles of the world, and renouncing the pomps and vanities of this life, for Christ's sake, hastened to join them, and to participate in their holy profession and reli-

BEAUSEANT.

* See the list of Grand Masters on page 138 for the varieties in spelling these names. Every historian, French, English, Italian, German, or what not, exercised his fancy in orthography.

gion. They carried before them, at this time, to battle, a bipartite banner of black and white, which they called *Beauseant*, that is to say (in the Gallic tongue) *Bienseant*, because they are fair and favorable to the friends of Christ, but black and terrible to his enemies.

1191. Saladin had passed the winter of 1190–91 on the heights of Schaferan and Keruba, between Acre and Nazareth. His vast army had been thinned and weakened by incessant watching, by disease, and continual battles, and he himself was gradually sinking under the effects of a dreadful disease, which baffled all the skill of his medical attendants, and was gradually drawing him towards that grave which he entered March 13, 1193. But the proud soul of the great chieftain never quailed; nor were his fire and energy deadened. As soon as he heard of the arrival of the two powerful Christian monarchs, he sent envoys and messengers throughout all Mussulman countries, earnestly demanding succor, and on the Mussulman Sabbath, after prayers had been offered up to God for the triumph of his arms, and the deliverance of Islam, he caused to be read, in all the mosks letters to the following effect:—"In the name of GOD, the most MERCIFUL and COMPASSIONATE. To all devout Believers in the one only God, and his prophet Mohammed, our Master. The armies of the infidels, numerous as the stars of heaven, have come forth from the remote countries situate beyond Constantinople, to wrest from us those conquests which have gladdened the hearts of all who put their trust in the Koran, and to dispute with us the possession of that holy territory whereon the Caliph Omar, in bygone days, planted the sacred standard of the Prophet. O men, prepare ye to sacrifice your lives and fortunes in defense of *Islam*. Your marches against the infidels, the dangers you encounter, the wounds you receive, and every minute action, down to the fording of a river, are they not written in the book of God? Thirst, hunger, fatigue, and death, will they not obtain for you the everlasting treasures of heaven, and open to your gaze the delicious groves and gardens of Paradise? In whatsoever place ye remain, O men, death hath dominion over you, and neither your houses, your lands, your wives, your children, nor the strongest towers, can defend you from his darts. Some of you, doubtless, have said one to another, Let us not go up to fight during the heat of summer; and others have exclaimed, Let us remain at home until the snow hath melted away from the mountain tops; but is not the fire of hell more terrible than the heats of summer, and are not its torments more insupportable than the winter's cold? Fear GOD, and not the *infidels*. Hearken to the voice of your chief, for it is Saladin himself who calls you to rally around the standard of *Islam*. If you obey not, your families will be driven out of Syria, and God will put in their places a people better than you. JERUSALEM, the holy, the sister of Medina and Mecca, will again fall into the power of the idolaters, who assign to God a son, and raise up an equal to the Most High. Arm yourselves then, with the buckler and the lance. Scatter these children of fire, the wicked sons of hell, whom the sea hath vomited forth upon our shores, repeating to yourselves these words of the Koran, ' He who abandoneth his home and family to defend our holy religion, shall be rewarded with happiness, and with many friends.' "

1191. The siege of Acre was now pressed with great vigor. The combined fleets of France and England completely deprived the city of all supplies by sea, and the garrison was reduced to great straits. The Sultan despaired of being able to save the city, and was sick, Bohadin tells us, both in mind and body. He could neither eat nor drink. At night he would lie down upon the side of the hill Aladajia and indulge in some broken slumbers, but at morning's dawn he was on horseback, ordering his brazen drum to be sounded, and collecting his army together in battle array. At last letters were received, by means of pigeons, announcing that the garrison could hold out no longer. Saladin gazed, says Bohadin, long and earnestly at the city. His eyes were suffused with tears, and he sorrowfully exclaimed, "*Alas for Islam!* " On the morning of Thursday, the 12th of July, the Kings of France and England, the Christian chieftains, and the Turkish emirs with their green banners, assembled in the tent of the Grand Master of the Temple to treat for the surrender of Acre; and on the following day (Friday, July 13, 1191) *the gates were thrown open to the exulting warriors of the Cross*. The Templars took possession of their ancient quarters by the side of the sea, and mounted a large red-cross banner upon the tower of the Temple. They possessed themselves of three extensive localities along the seashore, and the Temple at Acre from thenceforth became the chief house of the Order, as the Church of Mary (Mosk el-Aksa), in the Noble Enclosure at Jerusalem, had been for seventy years. King Richard took up his abode with the Templars, whilst King Philip resided in the citadel.

Thus *July* retained its ancient reputation in the history of the Crusades. July 4, 1097, the terrible fight at Dorylæum had occurred. July 15, 1099, Jerusalem surrendered. July 3–5, 1187, the disaster of Hattin occurred. Other important events in this history happened in the same month.

The capture of the city of Acre cost the Christian powers not less than 300,000 men, including six archbishops, twelve bishops, forty earls, and five hundred barons.

We turn aside for a moment to give, from a most accurate observer of the present day, a scanty account of edifices that for nearly two centuries were the pride alternately of Christian and Mohammedan occupants. It will afford a certain relief to the perusal of the horrors that make up the early history of Acre. Baron de Vogüé, in his "Churches of Holy Land," says:

Of all the cities in the Holy Land, that of Acre ought to be the richest in churches of the middle age, for it rested even to 1291 in the hands of the Crusaders. But for all that, there is nothing in it. The wars, the sieges that this unhappy city has sustained at different epochs of history—the honor, fatal in Eastern lands, of being the residence of a Pasha—have contributed to the disappearance, almost entirely, of Christian monuments. We are, therefore, reduced to study them, not so much upon the earth, but in books and archives.

During the Twelfth Century, we find at Acre (Ptolemais) a church of the Holy Cross, belonging to the Holy Sepulcher at Jerusalem, an Episcopal Cathedral, and particular churches belonging to the Venetians, the Pisans, and the Genoese. After the capture of Jerusalem, in 1187, the city served as a refuge for all the religious Communities, and for all the military Orders, who established themselves there as formerly at Jerusalem, and built there convents and numerous churches. The city was then divided into nineteen quarters, or jurisdictions, each of which had a church or a chapel. Even Orders that we do not find in the Holy City, at the moment of its splendor,

The Christian Army in possession of important Points of the Holy Land.

had establishments at Acre during the Thirteenth Century; for example, the Order of St. Augustine, which had a convent of men and another of women, under the name of "Mary and all the Saints;" the *Order de Citeaux*, which had a house of Sisters, under the name of St. Mary Magdalene, with an Abbess in 1225 by the name of Mary; and the Order of St. Clare, whose sisters, hemmed in by the Mussulmans in 1291, mutilated their figures to save their virginity. Pococke still saw the church of this monastery, which, in his time, was entirely preserved. He also saw the cathedral, "a superb Gothic church," he says, "with a portico." This church, dedicated to St. Andrew, was sketched by Corneille Le Bruyn, and his very faithful engraving enables us to judge of the style of the construction. The general disposition of the building is that of the churches built by the Crusaders in the Twelfth Century; three naves, the central one being the highest, and lighted at its upper part by a series of windows; the roofs in flat terraces, with all the consequences that we have already explained; the walls smooth, without arcs-boutants. However, St. Andrew differs as much from St. Anne at Jerusalem, as St. Chappelle at Paris differs from St. Germain-de-Pres. It is apparent that French art, in the Thirteenth Century, stepped in to transform the methods of the first Crusaders. The building is lighter and more elegant, the ornamentation more graceful, the style of lighting more thorough and better understood. The façade is pierced for light, by three doors, on the ground floor, in face of the three naves; above, by three corresponding windows. That in the center is immensely large, formed of three bays embraced closely, surmounted by three roses in a triangle; it is elevated even to the upper entablement. The other windows are high and élancées, the bundles of colonettes garnishing all the embrasures. The appui reposes upon a running band, which makes the tower of the edifice, and appuis itself, upon an arcature ogivale, of better effect. The interior was not sketched by Le Bruyn, but I think it offers the same character. The arcs-ogives, which we have already seen employed at Sebaste, were doubtless applied to the arches, and ended in the modification of the forms of the pillars, and permitting to rebind the apsides with the rest of the building, in making a monument of the Thirteenth Century.

St. Andrew proves, even to the evidence, that the Crusader architects sought their general ideas, not among the Arabs, but in France, and that they permitted themselves to be guided by the instructions of the mother-country to the extent of following, at the distance of eight hundred leagues, the modifications of the school and taste, building their churches *Roman* in the Twelfth Century, *Gothic* in the Thirteenth. It is vexatious, under this point of view, that the original structure should not remain standing, as a permanent proof of the influence of French architecture in the Orient. In spite, however, of its destruction, and in spite of the ruin of the other churches of St. John Acre, there remain, nevertheless, in the city, fragments enough to verify what the engraving had apprised us of, and to confirm the consequences that we have drawn of its study. Among other things, I recall a panel of wall, bearing a chapiter and the fragments of an arch, which may be recognized at first view for Gothic, and which demonstrates, beyond dispute, that the traditions of Notre Dame at Paris, and of St. Chappelle, came to Ptolemais (Acre) in the suite of the armies of Philip Augustus and of St. Louis.

1191. By the terms of the surrender of Acre the inhabitants were to pay a ransom of 200,000 pieces of gold for their lives and liberties; 2,000 noble and 500 inferior Christian captives were to be set at liberty, and the True Cross, which had been taken at the battle of Tiberias, was to be restored to the Latin clergy. Two months were accorded for the performance of these conditions. I'bn Alatsyr, who was then in Saladin's camp, tells us that Saladin had collected together 100,000 pieces of gold, that he was ready to deliver up the 2,500 Christian captives, and restore the True Cross, but his Mameluke emirs advised him not to trust implicitly to the good faith of the Christian adventurers of Europe for the performance of their part of the treaty, but to obtain from the Templars, of whose *regard for their word and reverence for the sanctity of an oath* the Moslems had, he tells us, a high opinion, a solemn undertaking for the performance by the Christians of the stipulations they had entered into. Saladin accordingly sent to the Grand Master of the Temple, Robert de Sable, to know if the Templars would guarantee the surrender to him of all the Moslem prisoners if the money, the Christian captives, and the True Cross were sent to them; but the Grand Master declined giving any guarantee of the kind. The doubts about the agreement and the delay in the execution of it excited the fickle and ferocious mind of King Richard, who led out all his prisoners, 2,000 in number, into the plain of Acre and caused them to be beheaded in sight of the Sultan's camp! During his voyage from Messina to Acre this reckless potentate had revenged himself on Isaac Comnenus, the ruler of the island of Cyprus, for an insult offered Berengaria, Princess of Navarre, his betrothed bride, by disembarking his troops, storming the town of Limisso, and conquering the whole island, which, shortly after his arrival at Acre, he sold to the Templars for 300,000 *livres d'or*.

Institution of the Teutonic Order. An Asylum for German Pilgrims.

As the history of the Teutonic Order belongs to this period, we insert a brief sketch, from Sir B. Burke's "Book of Orders of Knighthood," as the best authority under this head : In the earlier part of the Twelfth Century, about the time when, in the East, the Knights of various countries began, after the model of the monks, to form themselves into different Orders for the purpose of vanquishing the infidels and protecting and supporting, with all the energy and enthusiasm inspired by vows of chastity, poverty, and obedience, the numerous pilgrims on their way to the Holy Sepulcher, a pious German, whose name is now lost, built at Jerusalem a hospital for the pilgrims of his native country, the then existing Orders of the Templars and of St. John having thought fit to devote their care exclusively to the comforts of the French and Italian pilgrims. This hospital soon counted for its patrons several wealthy merchants and knights, and being consecrated by the Patriarch, a chapel was joined to it, devoted to the Blessed Virgin. It soon became an important asylum for German warriors, especially in 1189, at the siege of Acre, when the founder, assisted by contributions from German merchants at Lubeck and Hamburg, took care of the sick and wounded soldiers, who lay in tents before that place.

In 1191 Frederick of Suabia, on his arrival before Acre with his army after the death of his father, Frederick I. (Barbarossa), Emperor of Germany, deemed it advisable to secure to the institution a more solid basis. He gave it a constitution, and prescribed to the Knights and merchants assembled regulations, the general outlines of which he formed after those of the Order of St. Augustine, while the rules and laws concerning the sick and poor he borrowed from the Knights of St. John, and those relative to war and peace from the Templars. He conceded to it all the rights and privileges peculiar to these corporations or colleges, and gave it, under sanction of Pope Celestin III., the name of " The Order of the German House of the Holy Virgin at Jerusalem," choosing for the insignia *a black cross* with white mountings, worn upon a white cloak.

By the provisions of the original statutes, only native Germans, of blameless character and nobility, were admissible. The members were, moreover, to be unmarried and to remain single the whole of their lives. They were also to give up to the Order all their private property, and to devote themselves exclusively to the service of God, the sick and the poor, and to the defense of the Holy Land. Their food was originally bread and water, and their couch only a sack of straw, all of which, together with their garment, were regularly distributed amongst them by their Grand Master.

After a long series of eventful vicissitudes the Order attained its culminating point, and assumed, at the same time, quite a different character under the Grand Master Herman of Salza, who well knew how to turn to account the disputes between Pope Honorius III. and the Emperor Frederick II., as also the warlike events in the provinces which now form a part of Eastern Prussia.

The Duke Conrad of Masovia and Cujavia having, in his religious zeal, attempted to force Christianity upon his pagan neighbors, the Prussians, was met with such an obstinate resistance from them that he was, in his turn, threatened with an invasion of his own dominions. In his dilemma he called to his assistance, in 1226, the *Teutonic* or *German Knights*, offering them in return for their service the concession of important rights and privileges; while the Pope and the Emperor granted them the possession of all the lands they might conquer from the heathens during the war. Herman had just returned from his third Crusade to Palestine and settled at Venice after the loss of Acre, in 1191, the headquarters of his Order. He so adroitly managed the opening Crusade against the heathen Prussians that thousands from all lands and countries rallied under his flag, by which the Order received an immense increase in numbers and property from Germany, Italy, Sicily, and Hungary. The war was successfully carried on under his General, Balk, who, within a few years, built the towers of Pulin, Thern, Marienwerder, Elbing, and others. The Order soon possessed large districts of land on the Baltic Sea, governed by a "Land Master," while the Grand Master fixed his residence at Merburg, in Hessia.

During these complicated, but fortunate events, the Order had assumed a new form and character. Instead of the original name

of BROTHERS and HOSPITALERS, the Knights were now called MAS-
TERS, and, indeed, acted as such in the strictest sense of the term.
They became imperious, tyrannical, despotic, and led a voluptuous
and luxurious life at the expense of their Prussian subjects, who
figured as the most wretched, oppressed, and miserable creatures in
Europe.   Nowhere in Europe was bondage carried to such a cruel
extent as under the rule of the German Knights, who were intox-
icated by war, and plunged in sensual enjoyments.   Hence the
continual insurrections, devastations of towns and lands, complaints, treaties and difficulties ; hence the despised decrees of the
Pope and the Emperor, the incessant disputes with the clergy and
bishops of rank, and the supervisions of the rules, statutes and
laws of the original Constitutions, which form the greatest portion
of the history of the Order, and which finally resulted in prostra-
tion and an exhaustion of its strength and power, especially after
the terrible battle near Tennenberg against the Poles and Lithua-
nians (15th July, 1410), in which the Grand Master, Ulrich of
Jungingen, and thirty thousand of his followers, lost their lives !
We add that the *Almanach de Gotha*, 1873, has this note :

Teutonic Knights, founded A. D., 1190 ; abolished 1809 ; restored 1840 and 1865 ; Austria.

CASTLE OF PANEAS.

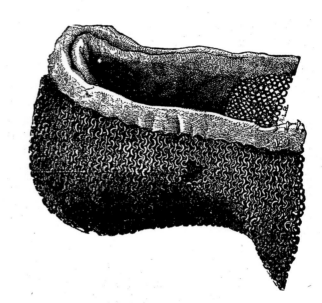

COIF OF MAIL—ABOUT A.D. 1180.

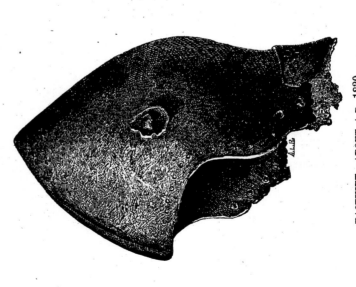

BASTINET—ABOUT A.D. 1330.

CHAPTER II.

RICHARD CŒUR DE LION AND HIS CAMPAIGN TO RESCUE JERUSALEM.

For here, though *Cœur de Lion*, like a storm
Pour on the Saracens, and do perform
Deeds past an angel, armed with wrath and fire;
Ploughed whole armies up, with zealous ire,
And walled cities, while he doth defend
That cause that should all wars begin and end;
Yet when with pride, and for humane respect,
The Austrian colors he doth here reject,
With too much scorn, behold at length how fate
Makes him a wretched prisoner to that state;
And leaves him, as a mark of fortune's spright,
When princes tempt their stars beyond their light.

Doggerel of the Thirteenth Century.

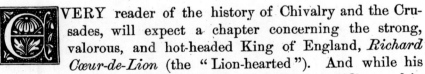VERY reader of the history of Chivalry and the Crusades, will expect a chapter concerning the strong, valorous, and hot-headed King of England, *Richard Cœur-de-Lion* (the " Lion-hearted "). And while his part in the history of the Crusades was in reality but trifling, and in the history of the two Military Orders he has no place at all, as a member of neither, yet romance has so usurped the place of sober history in this connection that to describe the period A.D. 1189–92 without an account of King Richard, would be like a performance of Hamlet *less* Hamlet. Sir Walter Scott, in his charming but most absurd perversion of history, has thrown a glamour over this part of our subject in the story of " The Talisman." We are loath to weaken the effect of such fascinating fables; but the narratives of Robinson Crusoe, Don Quixote, and Gulliver, and the accounts of

The Third Crusade.   Richard I.   His Traits of Character.

personages described in the Arabian Nights' Entertainments, are but little less reliable as matters of fact than the fictions of "The Talisman." The opinion of the cautious Michaud ("History of the Crusades") is, that Richard Cœur de Lion was more anxious to acquire the renown of a great captain, than the reputation of a great king. The glory of arms made him forget the cares of his kingdom. It may be remembered that before his departure he sold the charges, the prerogatives, and the domains of the crown, and he would have sold, as he himself said, the city of London, if he could have found a purchaser. His reverses and his captivity ruined his people, and his long absence kept up the spirit of faction among his nobles, and more especially in his own family.

We cannot go quite so far, however, in this direction as Mr. Anthony O'Neal Haye in his "History of the Knights Templars," who speaks of "the reckless and useless exploits of a Cœur de Lion and the ill-advised zeal of hot-headed holiday knights who looked upon a journey to the Holy Land as a prime bit of junketing." But we heartily indorse this sentiment of his: "The bright and shining stars in the history of the Chivalry of the Holy Land are not Richard of England, or St. Louis of France, but the Soldiers of the Temple, the Hospital, and the Teutonic Knights."

Taking whatever view we may of the valor and military skill of King Richard I., there is no question but that he was a bad son, a cold-hearted husband, and a foolish king. At the early age of sixteen he joined his two brothers in an unnatural rebellion against their own father, King Henry II. His education had been the best of his period, and in physical sports and military craft he was probably one of the foremost of his age. He was the favorite son of his father, but as we have said, he fled, at the early age named, to the Court of France with the avowed purpose of taking arms against his over-indulgent parent, in company with Henry, his elder, and Geoffrey, his younger brothers; and it was plainly charged at the time, by the venerable Bishops of Rouen and Lisieux, that Richard had threatened to add *murder* to rebellion. His unfilial conduct, however, was pardoned, and his return home made easy by immense gifts and honors on the part of his father (A.D. 1173).

Beginning his brief reign of ten years September 3, 1189, he joined the Crusade, as we have seen, in fellowship with Philip II., King of France, and Frederick I., King of Germany; and the final capture of Acre may doubtless be attributed to the timely arrival—May, 1191—of ships, men, and munitions of war, unreduced by the long land journey that had swallowed up so many of the contingents previously sent from Europe to the Holy Land. On his way to Palestine, Richard stopped to capture the island of Cyprus (a Christian country), and put its king (Comnenus) in chains.   There he married Berengaria, daughter of the King of Navarre, May 12, 1191.

As we have once or twice referred to Sir Walter Scott and his pleasing fables, which have invested the character of Richard with such a halo, we will treat our readers to an extract from "The Talisman," descriptive of the fountain at Jericho:

They had now arrived at the knot of palm-trees and the fountain which welled out from beneath their shade in sparkling profusion. We have spoken of a moment of truce in the midst of war; and this, a spot of beauty in the midst of a sterile desert, was scarce less dear to the imagination. It was a scene which, perhaps, would elsewhere have deserved little notice; but as the single speck, in a boundless horizon, which promised the refreshment of shade and living water, these blessings, held cheap where they are common, rendered the fountain and its neighborhood a little paradise. Some generous or charitable hand, ere yet the evil days of Palestine began, had walled in and arched over the fountain, to preserve it from being absorbed in the earth, or choked by the flitting clouds of dust with which the least breath of wind covered the desert. The arch was now broken and partly ruinous, but it so far projected over and covered in the fountain, that it excluded the sun in a great measure from its waters, which, hardly touched by a straggling beam, while all around was blazing, lay in a steady repose, alike delightful to the eye and imagination. Stealing from under the arch, they were first received in a marble basin, much defaced indeed, but still cheering the eye, by showing that the place was anciently considered as a station, that the hand of man had been there, and that man's accommodation had been in some measure attended to. The thirsty and weary traveler was reminded by these signs that others had suffered similar difficulties, reposed in the same spot, and, doubtless, found their way in safety to a more fertile country. Again, the scarce visible current which escaped from the basin served to nourish the few trees which surrounded the fountain, and where it sunk in the fount and disappeared, its refreshing presence was acknowledged by a carpet of velvet verdure. In this delightful spot the two warriors halted, and each, after his own fashion, proceeded to relieve his horse from saddle, bit, and rein, and permitted the animals to drink at the basin ere they refreshed themselves from the fountain-head, which arose under the vault. They then suffered the steeds to go loose, confident that their interest, as well as their domestic habits, would prevent their straying from the pure water and fresh grass.

These beautiful references are to the large spring-head called now Elisha's Fountain, and by the natives Ain es-Sultan (the Chief's Fountain) at the base of the mountain two miles back of Jericho. As a description it is totally unreliable.

1191. On Wednesday, the 21st of August, the Templars joined the standard of King Richard, and left Acre for the purpose of marching upon Jerusalem by way of the sea-coast. They crossed the River Belus, whose sands had made the first glass so many centuries before, and pitched their tents on its banks, where they remained for three days, to collect all the troops together. The most copious and authentic account of their famous march by the side of the King of England, through the hostile territories of the infidels, is contained in the history of King Richard's campaign, by Geoffrey de Vinisauf, who accompanied the Crusaders on their expedition, and was an actor in the stirring events he describes. On Sunday, 25th of August, the Templars, under the conduct of their Grand Master, and the Crusaders, under the command of King Richard, commenced their march southward towards Cæsarea. The army was separated into three divisions, the first of which was led by the Knights Templars, the last by the Knights Hospitalers, the former under their Grand Master, Robert de Sablè, the latter under their Grand Master, N. Gardiner. The extremely picturesque but unjust description given of Grand Master De Sablè by Scott ("The Talisman") will occur here to the mind of the reader. He says: "This celebrated Grand Master of the Templars, De Sablè, was a tall, thin, war-worn man with a slow yet penetrating eye, and a brow on which a thousand dark intrigues had stamped a portion of their obscurity. At the head of that singular body, to whom their Order was everything, and their individuality nothing—seeking the advancement of its power, even at the hazard of that very religion which the Fraternity were originally associated to protect—accused of heresy and witchcraft, although by their character Christian priests—suspected of secret league with the Soldan, though by oath devoted to the protection of the Holy Temple, or its recovery—the whole Order, and the whole personal character of its commander or Grand Master, was a riddle, at the exposition of which most men shuddered. The Grand Master was dressed in his white robes of solemnity, and he bore the Abacus, a mystic staff of office, the peculiar form of which has given rise to such singular conjectures and commentaries, leading to suspicions that this celebrated Fraternity of Christian Knights were embodied under the foulest symbols of Paganism."

The editor of Appleton's American Cyclopedia, under the head of *Abacus*, describes it as a mystic staff carried by the Grand Master of the Templars. Its head was of silver, marked with the peculiar Cross of the Order, but it bore another secret device, concealed or disguised and revealed only to the initiated, of portentous and obscure import, being no other than the orthophallic symbol of heathen antiquity, indicating the worship of the generative power as distinct from the creative attribute of God.

The baggage moved on the right of the army, between the line of march and the sea, and the fleet, loaded with provisions, kept **1191.** pace with the movements of the forces, and furnished them daily with the necessary supplies. Saladin, at the head of an immense force, exerted all his energies to oppose their progress, so that the march to Joppa formed one perpetual battle. Vast masses of cavalry hovered upon their flanks, cut off all stragglers, and put every prisoner that they took to death. The first night after leaving the Belus, the Templars and the Crusaders encamped along the banks of the brook Kishon, around some wells in the plain between Acre and Caifa. Monday, August 26, they forded the brook, fought their way to Caifa, and there halted for one day, in order that the reluctant Crusaders, who were lingering behind at Acre, might come on and join them. On Wednesday, August 28, at dawn of day, they prepared to force the difficult passes and defiles of Mount Carmel. All the heights were covered with dense masses of Mussulmans, who disputed the ground inch by inch. The Templars placed themselves in the van of the Christian army,

302   KNIGHTS TEMPLARS.

Continued March of the Christian Army.   Cæsarea, the Residence of St. Paul.

and headed the leading column, whilst the cavalry of the Hospitalers protected the rear. They ascended the cliffs through a dense vegetation of dry thistles, wild vines, and prickly shrubs, drove the infidels before them, crossed the summit of Mount Carmel, and descending into the opposite plain, encamped for the night at the pass by the sea-shore, called The Narrow Way, about eight miles from Caifa. Here they recovered possession of a solitary tower perched upon a rock overhanging the pass, which had been formerly built by the Templars, but had for some time past been in the hands of the Saracens. After lingering at this place an entire day, waiting the arrival of the fleet and the barges, laden with provisions, they recommenced their march (Friday, the 30th of August) to Tortura, the ancient Dor, about seven miles south. The Grand Master of the Temple, Robert de Sablè, and his valiant Knights, were, as usual, in the van, forcing a passage through the dense masses of the Moslem. The country in every direction around their line of march was laid waste, and every day the attacks became more daring. The military friars had thus far borne the brunt of the affray.

On Saturday, August 31, the Templars and the Crusaders approached the far-famed Cæsarea, now termed *Kaiseriyeh*, **1191.** where St. Paul so long resided, and where he uttered his eloquent oration before King Agrippa and Felix. But the town was no longer visible; the walls, the towers, the houses, and all the public buildings had been destroyed by command of Saladin, and the place was left deserted and desolate. The Templars pitched their tents on the banks of the Crocodile River (the *Flumen crocodilon* of Pliny), having been five days in performing the journey from the river Belus, a distance of only thirty-six miles. The army halted at Cæsarea during the whole of Sunday, 1st of September, and high mass was celebrated by the clergy with great pomp and solemnity, amid the ruins of the city. On Monday, the 2d of September, the tents of the Templars were struck at morning's dawn, and they commenced their march, with the leading division of the army, for the city of Joppa, about thirty miles south from Cæsarea. They forded the Crocodile River, and proceeded on their journey through a long and narrow valley, torn by torrents, and filled with vast masses of rock, which had been washed down from the heights by the winter rains. They had the sea on their right, and on their left a chain of craggy eminences. Every advantage was taken by the enemy of the irregularity of the ground. The Mussulman archers lined the heights, and vast masses of cavalry were brought into action, wherever the nature of the country admitted of their employment. The Christian warriors were encumbered with their heavy armor and military accoutrements, which were totally unfit for the burning climate, yet they enthusiastically toiled on, and perseveringly overcame all obstacles.

1191. It cannot but add to the interest of this narration to append an account of the ruins as they appeared in 1854, which mark the coast-road of this memorable campaign. The account is from our constant author upon these subjects, the Baron de Vogüé, " Churches of Holy Land."

ATHLIT.

The Arabs designate under the name of Athlit the ruins of a strong place founded by the Templars in 1218, upon the place of an ancient Phœnician city, to serve as a refuge for the pilgrims. It was built upon a scarped promontory, isolated from the side by a large ditch cut in the rock and defended by ramparts. These works of defense still, in part, exist, admirable for their grand character. The most interesting ruin is that of the church built upon a polygonal plan, in memory of the Temple at Jerusalem. It is a vast regular decagon in Gothic style. Three pentagonal contiguous apsides abut against the three faces that point northward, and form the choir of the church. Another church has three naves in ruins, built in the center of the city. The nervures of its arches are referable to the Thirteenth Century. There is remarked there a friese formed of animals sculptured in relief. There have been utilized, in these two erections, the walls of Roman masonry obtained from the ancient city. This establishment of Templars bore, all through the Middle Age, the name of "the Castle of the Pilgrims" (Castel Pelegrino), and "Pierre Incisé," or the *Cut Rock*, on account of the *fosse* cut in the rock; and "Districtum," because of the defiles whose entrances it protected.

The ruins of Cæsarea, that ancient city of Straton, of Herod,

CÆSAREA, AN IMPORTANT MILITARY STATION DURING THE CRUSADES.

and of St. Louis, occupy an immense space upon the sea-shore. There are two churches of the time of the Crusades—the one diminutive and without special interest, the other great, elongated, formed of three naves, and of three contiguous apsides, sustained

KNIGHTS TEMPLARS. 305

Bishops of Cæsarea.   March of the Christian Army.

by center-forts, built upon an ancient crypt, offering finally all the characters of the churches constructed by the Crusaders during the Twelfth Century.   Here is a list of the Latin bishops of Cæsarea:

Baldwin 1st . . . . .1107.
Ebremar . . . . .1123.
Gaudens . . . . .1136.
Baldwin 2d . . . . .1147–1156.
Ernest. . . . . .1157–1174.
Eracle (Heraclius), 1174.   Patriarch of Jerusalem in 1180.
Monachus. . . . . . . .1187.   "   "   1194.

1191.   The Arabic historian Bohadin speaks with admiration of the valiant and martial bearing of the warriors of the Cross, and of their fortitude and patient endurance during the long and trying march from Acre to Joppa.   " On the sixth day," says he, " the Sultan rose at dawn as usual, and heard from his brother that the enemy were in motion.   They had slept that night in suitable places about Cæsarea, and were now dressing and taking their food.   A second messenger announced that they had begun their march.   Our brazen drum was sounded, all were alert, the Sultan came out, and I accompanied him.   He surrounded them with chosen troops, and gave the signal for attack.   The archers were drawn out, and a heavy shower of arrows descended, still the enemy advanced.   Their foot-soldiers were covered with thick-strung pieces of cloth, fastened together with rings, so as to resemble coats of mail.   I saw with my own eyes several who had not one or two, but *ten darts sticking in their backs,** and yet marched on with a calm and cheerful step, without any trepidation.   They had a division of infantry in reserve, to protect those who were weary, and look after the baggage.   When any portion of their men became exhausted and gave way through fatigue or wounds, this division advanced and supported them.   Their cavalry in the meantime kept together in close column, and never moved away

---

* The Knights wore under their coats of mail a thick buff-coat which received and held the dart points as above.   Probably they were not even conscious of the presence of those darts.

from the infantry, except when they rushed to the charge. In vain did our troops attempt to lure them away from the foot-soldiers; they kept steadily together in close order, protecting one another and slowly forcing their way with wonderful perseverance.

After a short march of only eight miles from Cæsarea, the Templars pitched their tents on the banks of the Nahr al Kasab, a small river, called by Geoffrey de Vinisauf *"the Dead River."* Here they remained two nights, waiting for the fleet. On Wednesday, the 4th of September, they resumed their march through a desert country which had been laid waste in every direction by command of Saladin. Finding their progress along the shore impeded by the tangled thickets, they quitted the plain and traversed the hills which run parallel with the sea. Their march was harassed by incessant charges of cavalry. The Templars brought up the rear of the army, and lost so many horses during the day that they were almost driven to despair. At nightfall they descended again to the beach and encamped on the banks of a salt creek, close by the village of Um Khalid, near the ruins of the ancient Apollonias, having performed a march of five miles. This place, now called Mukhalid, is one of the principal villages of the plain of Sharon. The next morning, being Thursday, the 5th of September, the Templars set out at sunrise from Salt Creek in battle array, having received intelligence that Saladin had prepared an ambuscade in the neighboring forest of Arsoof, and intended to hazard a general engagement. Scouts were sent on into the forest, who reported that the road was clear; and the whole army, ascending a slight rising ground, penetrated through the wood and descended into the plain of Arsur, or Arsoof. Through the midst of this plain rolls a mountain torrent, which takes its rise in the mountains of Ephraim eastward. On the opposite side of this stream Saladin had drawn up his army in battle array. The Templars encamped for the night on the northern bank of the stream, having during the day marched nine miles.*

---

* Arsoof, so renowned in this history, is now a deserted village at the mouth of Nahr Arsoof, a small stream, two *hours* and a half north of the village of El-Haram, and six *hours* north of Joppa.

ARMY OF TEMPLARS CROSSING A RIVER.

1191. On Saturday, the 7th of September, King Richard, having completed all his arrangements for a general engagement, drew up his army at dawn. The Templars formed the first division, and were the first to cross the mountain torrent and drive in Saladin's advanced guard. They were followed by Guy, King of Jerusalem, at the head of the division of Poitou, and then by the main body of the army under the personal conduct of King Richard. Geoffrey de Vinisauf tells us that on all sides, far as the eye could reach, from the sea-shore to the mountains, nought was to be seen but a forest of spears, above which waved banners and standards innumerable. The wild Bedouins, the children of the desert, with skins blacker than soot, mounted on their fleet Arab steeds, coursed with the rapidity of lightning over the vast plain, and darkened the air with clouds of missiles. They advanced to the attack with horrible screams and bellowings, which, with the deafening noise of the trumpets, horns, cymbals, and brazen kettledrums, produced a clamor that resounded through the plain, and would have drowned even the thunder of heaven. King Richard received the onslaught in close and compact array, strict orders having previously been given that all the soldiers should remain on the defensive until two trumpets had been sounded in the front, two in the center, and two in the rear of the army, when they were in their turn to become the assailants.

The idea of these trumpet signals, so much referred to in the history of this fight, was borrowed from the signal system of the Israelites in the desert, where two silver trumpets were used "for the calling of the assembly and for the journeying of the camps." If *one trumpet* only was sounded the princes gathered together. When one alarm was blown the camps on the *east* side moved; a second alarm and the camps on the *south* side began their motion, etc.—(*Numbers* x.)

The ferocious Turks, the wild Bedouins, and the swarthy Æthiopians gathered around the advanced guard of the Templars and kept up a distant and harassing warfare with their bows and arrows, whilst the swift cavalry of the Arabs dashed down upon the foot-soldiers as if about to overwhelm them, then suddenly checking their horses they wheeled off to the side, raising clouds

GROUP OF SHAFTED WAR WEAPONS.

Military Flails; Marteaux; Axes; Fauchards; Corsesques; Military Forks;
Halberds; Partisans; Guisarmes.

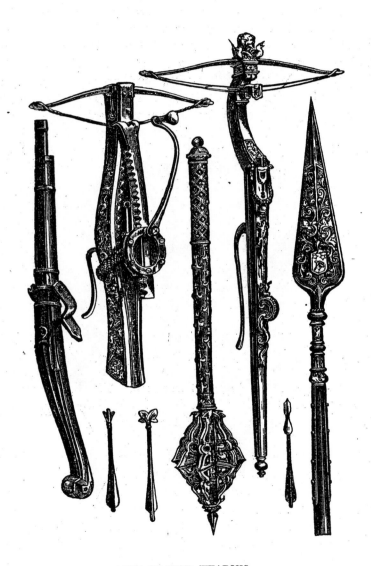

GROUP OF WAR WEAPONS.
Early Musket; Lever Cross-bow; Mace; Decorated Cross-bow; Decorated Pike; Cross-bow Bolts.

of smothering, suffocating dust, which oppressed and choked the toiling warriors.   The baggage moved on between the army and the sea, and the Christians thus continued slowly to advance under the scorching rays of an autumnal sun.   They moved, says Vinisauf, inch by inch; it could not be called walking, for they were pushing and hacking their way through an overpowering crowd of resisting foes.   Emboldened by their passive endurance, the Moslems approached nearer and began to ply their darts and lances. The Marshal of the Hospital then charged at the head of his Knights, without waiting for the signal, and in an instant the action became general.   The clash of swords, the ringing of armor, and the clattering of iron clubs and flails, as they descended upon the helmets and bucklers of the European warriors, became mingled with the groans of the dying, and with the fierce cries of the wild Bedouins.   Clouds of dust were driven up into the skies, and the plain became covered with banners, lances, and all kinds of arms, and with emblems of every color and device, torn and broken, and soiled with blood and dust.   King Richard was to be seen everywhere in the thickest of the fight, and after a long and obstinate engagement the infidels were defeated.   But amid the disorder of his troops Saladin remained on the plain without lowering his standard or suspending the sound of his brazen kettle-drums.   He rallied his forces, retired upon Ramleh, and prepared to defend the mountain passes leading to Jerusalem.   The Templars pushed on to Arsoof at the close of this "bloody Thursday," and pitched their tents before the gates of the town.

1191.   On Monday, September 9th, the Christian forces moved in battle array to Joppa, about eight miles from Arsoof.   Upon this occasion the Templars brought up *the rear* of the army.   After marching about five miles, they reached the banks of the Nahr el Arsoof, or river of Arsoof, which empties itself into the sea about three miles from Joppa, and pitched their tents in a beautiful olive grove on the sea-shore.   Saladin had laid waste all the country around them, driven away the inhabitants, and carried off all the cattle, corn, and provisions.   The towns of Cæsarea, Ramleh, Joppa, Ascalon, and all the villages for forty miles along this fertile plain of Sharon, had been set on fire and burnt to ashes, and all the castles and fortresses within reach of the Crusading army were dismantled and destroyed. Among these last were the castles of St. George, Galatia, Blancheward, Beaumont, Belvoir, Toron, Arnald, Mirabel, the Castle of the Plain, and many others. Every place, indeed, of strength or refuge was utterly destroyed by command of the inexorable Saladin. Bohadin tells us that the Sultan mourned grievously over the destruction of the fair and beautiful city of Ascalon, saying to those around him : By God, I would sooner lose my sons than touch a stone of this goodly city ; but what God wills, and the good of Islam requires, must be done.

The walls and fortifications of Ascalon were of great extent and stupendous strength, and an army of thirty thousand men was employed for fourteen days in the work of demolition. The weeping families were removed from their houses, amid the most heart-rending confusion and misery, says Bohadin, that I ever witnessed. Thousands of men were employed in dashing down the towers and the walls, and throwing the stones into the ditches and into the adjoining sea ; and thousands were occupied in carrying away property, and the contents of the public granaries and magazines. But ere half the effects had been removed, the impatient Sultan ordered the town to be set on fire ; and soon, says Bohadin, the raging flames were to be seen, tearing through the roofs, and curling around the minarets of the mosks. The great tower of the Hospitalers was the only edifice that resisted the flames and the exertions of the destroyers. It stood frowning in gloomy and solitary magnificence over the wide extended scene of ruin. We must not depart, said Saladin, until yon lofty tower has been brought low ; and he ordered it to be filled with combustibles and set on fire. It stood, says Bohadin, by the sea-side, and was of amazing size and strength. I went into it, and examined it. The walls and the foundations were so solid, and of such immense width, that no battering machines could have produced the slightest effect upon them. Every heart was filled with sorrow and mourning at the sight of the scorched and blackened ruins of the once fair and beautiful Ascalon. The city, says Bohadin, was very elegant, and in truth, exquisitely beautiful ; its stupendous, fortifications and lofty edifices possessed a majesty and grandeur which inspired one with awe. Ascalon, once the proudest of the five satrapies of the lords of the Philistines, is now uninhabited. The walls still lie scattered in huge fragments along the seashore, mixed with columns and broken pillars, which are wedged in among them; and amid the confused heaps of ruin which mark the site of the ancient city, not a single dwelling is now visible. " The king shall perish from Gaza," saith the prophet, "and Ascalon shall *not be inhabited*."—(*Zech.* ix. 5.)

1191. On the 16th of October, King Richard wrote a letter to Saladin, exhorting him to put an end to the Holy War; but he demanded, as the price of peace, the restitution of Jerusalem, of Palestine, and the True Cross. Jerusalem, says the King, we consider to be the seat of our religion, and every one of us will perish rather than abandon it. Do you restore to us the country on this side Jordan, together with the Holy Cross, which is of no value to you, being in your eyes a mere piece of wood, but which we Christians prize greatly; we will then make peace, and repose from our incessant toils. When the Sultan, says Bohadin, who was himself a participator in the negotiation, had read this letter, he took counsel with his Emirs, and sent a reply to the following effect:—The Holy City is held in as great reverence and estimation by the Moslem as it is by you, ay, and in much greater reverence. From thence did our prophet Mohammed undertake his nocturnal journey to heaven, and upon that holy spot have the angels and the prophets at different periods been gathered together. Think not that we will ever surrender it. Never would we be so unmindful of our duty, and of that which it behooves us to do, as good Mussulmans. As to the country you speak of, it hath belonged to us of old; and if you took it from the Moslem when they were weak, they have taken it from you now that they are strong, as they have a right to do. You may continue the war, but God will not give you a stone of the land as a possession; for he hath given the country to the Moslem, to be by them plentifully and bountifully enjoyed. As to the cross, the reverence you pay to that bit of wood is a scandalous idolatry, disrespectful to the Most High, and hateful in the sight of God. We will, therefore, not give it to you, unless by so doing we can secure some great and manifest advantage for Islam.

1191.   After a delay of more than seventy days since the glorious victory of Arsoof, on the 15th of November, the Templars marched out of Joppa with King Richard and his army, and proceeded through the plain towards Jerusalem.   As they advanced, Saladin slowly retired before them, laying waste the surrounding country, destroying all the towns and villages, and removing the inhabitants.   Between noon and evening prayers, the Sultan rode over to the city of Lydda, where St. Peter cured Æneas of the palsy, and employed his army, and a number of Christian slaves, in the destruction of the noble cathedral church and in the demolition of the town.   In examining the site of ancient Lydda as evidence of the terrible devastations of this period, the only definite remains are those of the ancient church of St. George, thus described by De Vogüé :

The same idea pervaded the construction of this church as that of Sebaste (Samaria).   But the only portion now remaining is the *eastern* extremity. And it is a fact that has often struck travelers, that in these ancient remains, whether of the early Christian edifices, or those of the Crusading period, the portion that remains longest and least impaired, and most easily recognized, is the eastern portion!   Either because more solidly built, or from some superstition that causes the natives to respect that part when they destroy the rest, you will rarely find the place in the Holy Land where an ancient church ought to be (according to history), but the foundation and some of the wall are found remaining at the *east* end.   It is so here.   We find, at the eastern extremity, three contiguous apsides, cylindrical *within*, prismatic *without*, following a *travée* (upper gallery), which served for the choir, in consequence of which comes the transept, then the naves, etc., now totally destroyed.   The central nave was higher than the two others, and was lighted by a range of upper windows.   This gave upon the *bas-cotês*, by the bays, whose archivotte was *en ogive*, like that of the windows, and the section of the vault of the apsides.   A crypt, situated under the choir, contained, according to tradition, the tomb of St. George.   The resemblance between this church and those at Jerusalem and Sebaste forbids us to separate it from the great family of monuments erected during the existence of the Latin kingdom.

Baron De Vogüé assigns it to the period 1150–87, and considers it the *same* church to which William of Tyre alludes (xxi., 21), when recounting the panic that affected the inhabitants of the plain of Sharon, after the invasion of the apostate Iverlin, A.D. 1177; he says the inhabitants of Lydda sought an asylum in the church of St. George. In 1186 it excited the admiration of Jean Phocas, who describes it as a church of grand dimensions, upon an elongated plan, with a crypt under the choir, containing the tomb of the Holy Martyr St. George. These details apply perfectly to the ruins now at Lydda. After the disaster of Hattin, 1187, Lydda followed the lot of the other cities of the Holy Land, and fell in the power of the infidels, as we have seen in the proper place. This church was respected, and remained untouched until September 5, 1191, when after the celebrated fight between Saladin and Richard, it was sacrificed to the system of defense adopted by the vanquished Mussulmans. All strong places, all constructions that could offer a point of resistance, should they fall into Christian hands, were destroyed without pity. Of this number was the church at Lydda. Bohadin, an ocular witness of the fact, affirms it in a positive manner, and says, expressly, that he saw the ruins. The church was never restored, although Lydda was occupied by the Christians during a part of the Thirteenth Century.

Baron de Vogüé, alluding to a local tradition, which assigns the erection of this church to King Richard, gives no importance to it. The legend first appeared in the Sixteenth Century, and was born in the consecration of the place (Lydda) to the patron of England. It is true, that by the treaty between Saladin and Richard in 1192, a part of the city of Lydda was ceded to Richard, and that twelve years later the whole city was given to the Christians; yet such was their condition, as stated by cotemporary historians, that it is impossible to suppose they had leisure or means for such a work. The edifice, so far as we can judge from the remains, was built at a single effort. It stood entire previous to A. D. 1191. It has no marks of the peculiar architecture of a later period.

The legend which assigns to Lydda (otherwise called Diospolis) the tomb of St. George is very respectable. It is found in the most ancient travels in Holy Land and has continued unbroken to the present time. It is probable that there was a Christian church here in the earliest times, although we have no record of it. William of Tyre pretends that Justinian built one here. The first pilgrim who found an edifice here was the Bernard, the Sage, in the Ninth Century. This building was destroyed by the Caliph Hakin, in 1010, at the same time as the church of the Holy Sepulcher at Jerusalem; but it was very shortly rebuilt. The new church was a grand Basilica, covered with splendid carpentry, so that at the approach of the Crusaders, June, 1099, the Mussulmans, fearing that the long timbers of this church might serve their assailants for making machines for the siege, destroyed it from base to cap-stone.

After the conquest of the country in 1099 the Crusaders established an Episcopal See at Lydda (or Diospolis) and built the new cathedral, which stood about ninety years. The list of Bishops is here given:

> Robert, of Normandy.................1099
> Roger,..... 1136
> Constantin,..................... 1140–1158
> Raynier,...........................1168
> Bernard,..................... 1169–1171

Having destroyed Lydda, etc., Saladin then fell back with his army to Beitnubah, a small village seated upon an eminence at the extremity of the plain of Ramleh, at the commencement of the hill country of Judea, and there encamped. This place still exists under the same name. It is but a small village. Jerome called it Nobe, and it is eight miles east of Lydda (Diospolis). Dr. Robinson ("Biblical Researches") describes it as celebrated in the Crusades, because the site of the *Castellum Arnaldi*, erected here by the patriarch and citizens of Jerusalem in order to protect the approaches from the sea-coast, and then as the place to which Richard led his army in June, 1192, on his way to besiege Jerusalem.

On Friday morning, at an early hour, says Bohadin, the Sultan mounted on horseback, and ordered me to accompany him. The rain fell in torrents. We marched towards Jerusalem. We dismounted at the monastery near the Church of the Resurrection, and Saladin remained there to pass the night. The next morning at

Great Preparations for the Defense of Jerusalem by Saladin.

dawn the Sultan again mounted on horseback, and rode round the walls of the Holy City. The whole population, together with two thousand Christian captives, had for weeks past been diligently employed in the reparation and reconstruction of the fortifications. Forty expert masons had arrived from Mossul, together with engineers and artificers from all the Mussulman countries of Asia. Two enormous towers were constructed, new walls were built, ditches were hollowed out of the rocks, and countless sums, says Bohadin, were spent upon the undertaking. Saladin's sons, his Emirs, and his brother Adel, were charged with the inspection of the works, and

RAMLEH, OR ARIMATHEA.

the Sultan himself was on horseback every morning from sunrise to sunset, stimulating the exertions of the workmen.

Whilst Saladin was making these vigorous preparations for the defense of Jerusalem, the Templars halted at Ramleh, the ancient Arimathea, situate in the middle of the plain, about nine miles from Joppa, and lingered with the Crusaders amid the ruins of the place for six weeks. In one of their midnight sallies they captured and brought into the camp more than two hundred oxen. On New Year's day, 1192, they marched to Beitnubah, described above, and encamped at the entrance of the gorges and defiles leading to the Holy City.   But these defiles were guarded by a powerful army under the personal command of Saladin, and the warriors of the Cross ventured not to penetrate them.   It was the rainy season, and in that month it rains almost every day.   The weather became frightful.   Tempests of rain and hail, thunder and lightning, succeeded one another without cessation ; the tents were torn to pieces by furious whirlwinds, and all the provisions of the army were destroyed by the wet.   Many of the camels, horses, and beasts of burthen perished from fatigue and the inclemency of the weather, and orders were given for a retrograde movement to Joppa, fifteen miles west.

1192.   The Templars faithfully adhered to the standard of King Richard, and marched with him from Joppa along the sea-coast to the ruins of Ascalon; but the other warriors, who owned no allegiance to the sovereign of England, abandoned him.   The Duke of Burgundy and the French remained in the city of Acre ; some of the Crusaders tarried at Joppa; others went to Tyre and joined the party of Conrad, Marquis of Montferrat.   During the march from Joppa to Ascalon, a distance of twenty-eight miles, the Templars suffered great hardships from hail-storms and terrific showers of rain and sleet ; and on their arrival amid the ruins of the once flourishing city they were nearly starved, by reason of the shipwreck of their vessels freighted with the necessary supplies. They, however, pitched their tents among the ruins on the 20th of January, A.D. 1192, and for eight days were compelled to subsist on the scanty supply of food they had brought with them from Joppa. During the winter they assisted King Richard in the reconstruction of the fortifications, and took an active part in the capture of several convoys and caravans which were traversing the adjoining desert from Egypt.   Among the places recaptured and repaired at that time was Beit Jibrin, built by King Fulk about A.D. 1134, described by William of Tyre as a fortress having impregnable walls, with a mound, bastion, and other advanced works.   Its defense was entrusted to the Knights Hospitalers, and it served to guard against the excursions of the Saracens from the southwest. A short distance north was another castle of great strength and importance on the site of ancient Gath.   The Arabs called it Tell es-Safieh, but the Crusaders *Collis Clarus*, the White Hill, or more commonly Blanche-garde. It is about eighteen miles from Ascalon. Other names for it were *Alba Specula*, and *Alba Custodia*, and *Candida Custodia*. It was built, with hewn stones, of four towers, to which the name Blanche-garde refers.

1192. Whilst the Templars and the Kings of England and Jerusalem thus remained under tents or in the open fields planning the overthrow and destruction of the infidels, Conrad, Marquis of Montferrat, an aspirant to the throne of the Latin kingdom, was intriguing with Saladin for the advancement of his own schemes of private ambition. He was supported by the Duke of Burgundy and the French, and was at the head of a strong party who hated King Richard, and envied him the fame of his military exploits. The Marquis of Montferrat went to Saladin's camp. He offered, according to the not unimpeachable testimony of Bohadin, to make war upon King Richard, to attack the city of Acre, and join his forces to those of the Sultan, provided the latter would cede to him the maritime towns of Tyre, Sidon, and Beyrout, and all the sea-coast between them. But before these traitorous designs could be carried into execution, Conrad, Marquis of Montferrat, was assassinated. Six days after his death the fickle Princess Isabella, his wife, the younger sister of the late Queen Sibylla, married Henry, Count of Champagne, nephew of King Richard. This nobleman possessed great influence in the councils of the Christian chieftains, and a general desire was manifested for his recognition as KING of JERUSALEM. The Templars accordingly induced Guy de Lusignan *to abdicate* in favor of Isabella and the Count of Champagne, offering him as a recompense the wealthy and important island of Cyprus, which had been ceded to them, as before mentioned, by King Richard.

1192. King Richard and the Templars remained for five months encamped amid the ruins of Ascalon, and employed themselves in intercepting the caravans and convoys which were crossing the neighboring desert from Egypt to Palestine. Thus they succeeded in setting at liberty many Christian captives. The second Sunday after Trinity the tents were struck, and they once more resumed their march, with the avowed intention of laying siege to the Holy

City.   They again proceeded by easy stages across the plain of Ramleh, and on the 11th of June, five days after they had left Ascalon, they again reached Beitnubah.   Here they halted for the space of *an entire month*, professedly waiting for Henry, the new King of Jerusalem, and the forces marching under his command from Tyre and Acre.   But the rugged mountains between Beitnubah and Jerusalem were the real cause of delay, and again presented a barrier to their further progress.

Saladin had fixed his station in the Holy City, leaving the main body of his army encamped among the mountains near Beitnubah. **1192.**   His Mamelukes appear to have been somewhat daunted by the long continuance of the war and the persevering obstinacy of the Christians.   They remembered the bloody fate of their brethren at Acre, and pressed the Sultan to reserve *his* person and *their* courage for the future defense of their religion and empire.   Bohadin gives a curious account of their misgivings and disinclination to stand a siege within the walls of Jerusalem.   He made an address to them at the request of the Sultan, and when he had ceased to speak Saladin himself arose.   A profound silence reigned throughout the assembly, " they were as still as if BIRDS *were sitting on their* HEADS."   "Praise be to God," said Saladin, " and may his blessing rest upon our master, Mohammed, his prophet.   Know ye not, O men, that ye are the only army of ISLAM and its only defense.   The lives and fortunes and children of the Moslems are committed to your protection.   If ye now quail from the fight (which God avert) the foe will roll up these countries as the angel of the Lord rolls up the book in which the actions of men are written down."   After an eloquent harangue from the Sultan, Saifeddin Meshtoob and the Mamelukes exclaimed with one voice, " My Lord, we are thy servants and slaves; we swear by God that none of us will quit thee so long as we shall live."   But the anxiety of Saladin and the Mamelukes was speedily calmed by the retreat of the Christian soldiers, who fell back upon the sea-coast and their shipping.   The health both of King Richard and of Saladin was in a declining state.   They were mutually weary of the war, and a treaty of peace was at last entered into between the Sultan, the King of England, Henry, King of Jerusalem, and the Templars and Hospitalers, whereby it was stipulated that the Christian pilgrims should enjoy the privilege of visiting the Holy City and the Holy Sepulcher without tribute or molestation; that the cities of Tyre, Acre, and Joppa, with all the sea-coast between them, should belong to the Latins, but that the fortifications recently erected at Ascalon should be demolished. Immediately after the conclusion of peace King Richard, being anxious to take the shortest and speediest route to his dominions, induced Robert de Sablè, the Grand Master of the Temple, to place a galley of the Order at his disposal, and it was determined that whilst the royal fleet pursued its course with Queen Berengaria through the Straits of Gibraltar to Britain, Richard himself, *disguised in the habit of a Knight Templar*, should secretly embark and make for one of the ports of the Adriatic. The plan was carried into effect on the night of the 25th of October, 1192, and King Richard set sail, accompanied by some attendants and four trusty Templars, his queen having embarked September 29. The habit he had assumed, however, protected him not from the vengeance of the Archduke of Austria, whom he had insulted during the siege in an unpardonable manner. After encountering a violent storm, which scattered his fleet and wrecked the greater number of his vessels, Richard, with a single ship, landed at Zara, on the coast of Hungary. From hence, in company with a few Knights Templars and two priests, he traveled through Germany by land. At a small town near Vienna he was recognized and captured by the Germans with a solitary attendant, the rest of his company having dispersed. By agreement between the King of France (Philip I.) and the Emperor of Germany (Henry VI.), Richard was closely imprisoned for a year or more. Brought before the Diet at Worms and indicted for grievous offenses, including the assassination of Conrad, Marquis of Montferrat, in 1192, he defended himself with such eloquence and power that he was finally put to ransom at 100,000 marks of silver (about $2,000,000), and so returned home to his impoverished people. He died April, A.D. 1199, of a wound received in battle, having reigned but ten years through a stormy and unhappy career.

FULL SUIT OF PLATE-ARMOR, A.D. 1422 TO 1461, VIZ.:

Helmet, covering the head and face; Cuirass, covering the whole figure, breast, and back; Epaulières, guards for the shoulders; Brassarts, or arm-guards; Coudières, elbow-guards, and coverings for the inside of the elbow joints; Avant-bras, guards for the lower arms; Faudes, or Taces, with the Tuilles, covering the hips and thighs; Haubergeon, or defense for the body, worn under the cuirass; Cuissarts, thigh-pieces; Genouillières, knee-guards; Grevières, leg-pieces; Sollerets, with the Spurs, laminated coverings for the feet; Gauntlets, leather gloves, with pieces of iron sewed on for the protection of the hands.

CHAPTER III.

TO THE CAPTURE OF DAMIETTA, A.D. 1217.

HEAVEN on their earthly hopes has frowned:
   Their dream of thrones has fled:
The table that His love hath crowned,
They ne'er again shall gather round,
   With Jesus at their head.

DURING the year Robert de Sablè, the Grand **1194.** Master of the Temple, was succeeded by Gilbert Horal or Erail,* who had previously filled the high office of Grand Preceptor of France. The Templars, to retain and strengthen their dominion in Palestine, again erected several strong fortresses, the stupendous ruins of many of which remain to this day. The most famous of these was the Pilgrim's Castle (*Castellum Perigrinorum*), which commanded the coast-road from Acre to Jerusalem. (See Map.) It is now called Athlit. It derived its name from a solitary tower erected by the early Templars to protect the passage of the pilgrims through a dangerous pass in the mountains bordering the sea-coast, and was commenced shortly after the removal of the chief house of the Order from Jerusalem to Acre. A small promontory which juts out into the sea a few miles below Mount Carmel, was converted into a fortified camp. Two gigantic towers, a hundred feet in height and seventy-four in width, were erected, together with enormous bastions connected together by strong walls fifteen feet thick, and

* See the Biographical Table of Grand Masters, p. 138, for the various orthography.

forty feet high, furnished with all kinds of military engines. The vast inclosure contained a palace for the use of the Grand Master and Knights, a magnificent church, houses and offices for the serving brethren and hired soldiers, together with pasturages, vineyards, gardens, orchards, and fishponds. On one side of the walls was the Mediterranean Sea, and on the other, within the camp, were delicious springs of fresh water. The garrison amounted to four thousand men in time of war.

Considerable remains of this famous fortress of Athlit are still visible on the coast, a few miles to the south of Mount Carmel, called in Italian, *Castel Pellegrino*. Pocock describes it as very magnificent, and so finely built, that it may be reckoned one of the things that are best worth seeing in these parts. It is encompassed, says he, with two walls fifteen feet thick, the inner wall on the east side cannot be less than forty feet high, and within it there appear to have been some very grand apartments. The offices of the fortress seem to have been at the west end, where I saw an oven fifteen feet in diameter. In the castle there are remains of a fine lofty church of ten sides, built in a light gothic taste: three chapels are built to the three eastern sides, each of which consists of five sides, excepting the opening to the church: in these it is probable the three chief altars stood. Irby and Mangles, referring at a subsequent period to the ruins of the church, describe it as a double hexagon, and state that the half then standing had six sides. Below the cornice are human heads and heads of animals in alto relievo, and the walls are adorned with a double line of arches in the Gothic style, the architecture light and elegant. All writers, indeed, agree in describing this edifice as one of singular wisdom, strength, and beauty.

The character of the Sultan Saladin, whose death we are now to chronicle, has been painted in the colors of fable so as to be wellnigh inexplicable at the present day. One thoughtful writer describes him as a monarch in whose character, though the good was not unmixed with evil, the great qualities so far preponderated that they overbalanced the effects of a barbarous epoch and a barbarous religion, and left in him a splendid exception to most of the vices of his age, his country, and his creed. (JAMES.) No Asiatic mon-

Death of Saladin.   Fourth Crusade.   Renewal of Hostilities.

arch has filled so large a space in the eyes of Europe as Saladin. He was a compound of the dignity and the baseness, the greatness and the littleness of man. A skillful general, a valiant soldier. Human sympathy mollified his rigor, and when his foes were suppliant he sometimes forgot the sternness of his creed. Fond of religious exercises and studies. He had gained the throne by blood, artifice, and treachery, yet he was simple in his manners and unostentatious in his deportment. Wars and rebellions had so filled his thoughts that he had established no principles of succession. (MILLS.)

1193. On the death of Saladin, 13th of March, A.D. 1193, aged fifty-seven years, the vast and powerful empire he had consolidated and ruled over for nineteen years, with more than despotic power, fell to pieces. The title to the thrones of Syria and Egypt was disputed between the brother, Saphadin, and three of the sons of the deceased Sultan. Then the Pope, thinking these dissensions presented a favorable opportunity for the recovery of the Holy **1196.** City, caused the Fourth Crusade to be preached. Two expeditions organized in Germany by Henry VI. proceeded to Palestine A.D. 1196 and 1197, and insisted on the immediate commencement of hostilities, in defiance of the truce. The Templars and Hospitalers, and the Latin Christians, who were in the enjoyment of profound peace under the faith of treaties, insisted upon the impolicy and dishonesty of such a proceeding, but were reproached with treachery and lukewarmness in the Christian cause; and the headstrong Germans sallying out of Acre, committed some frightful ravages and atrocities upon the Moslem territories. The infidels immediately rushed to arms. Their intestine dissensions were at once healed, their chiefs extended to one another the hand of friendship, and from the distant banks of the Nile, from the deserts of Arabia, and the remote confines of Syria, the followers of Mohammed rallied again around the same banner, and hastened once more to fight in defense of *Islam*. Al-Ma-lek, Al-a-del, Abou-bekr Mohammed, the renowned brother of Saladin, surnamed *Saif-ed-din* (Saphadin), "Sword of the Faith," took the command of the Moslem force, and speedily proved himself a worthy successor to the great "Conqueror of Jerusalem." He

21

326   KNIGHTS TEMPLARS.

German Crusaders occupying Joppa.   Death of King Henry.

concentrated a vast army, and by his rapid movements speedily compelled the Germans to quit all the open country, and throw themselves into the fortified city of Joppa. By a well-executed **1197.** manœuvre, November 11, on the Feast of St. Martin, he then induced them to make a rash sortie from the town, and falling suddenly upon the main body of their forces, he defeated them with terrific slaughter. He entered the city, pell-mell, with the fugitives, and annihilated the entire German force. The small garrison of the Templars maintained in the commanding of Joppa was massacred, the fortifications razed to the ground, and the city was left without a single Christian inhabitant. Such were the first results of the Fourth Crusade.

Fuller, writing of the destruction of the Germans at Joppa, quaintly says, in his Holy War : " At this time the spring-tide of their mirth so drowned their souls, that the Turks, coming in upon them, cut every one of their throats to the number of 20,000. And quickly they were stabbed with the sword that were cup shot before. The camp was their *shambles*, the Turks their *butchers*, and themselves the *beeves* from which the beastly drunkards differed but little."

1197.   The Templars on the receipt of this disastrous intelligence, assembled their forces and marched out of the city of Acre, in the cool of the evening, to encamp at Caiffa, ten miles distant. King Henry placed himself at the castle window to see them pass, and was leaning forward watching their progress across the neighboring plain, when he unfortunately overbalanced himself, and fell headlong into the moat. He was killed on the spot, and Queen Isabella was a second time a widow, her divorced husband, Humphrey de Thoron, being, however, still alive. She had three daughters by King Henry, Mary, who died young, Alix, and Philippine. Radolph, of Tiberias, became an aspirant for the hand of the widowed Queen, but the Templars rejected his suit because he was too poor, declaring that they would not give the Queen and the kingdom to a man who had nothing. They sent the Chancellor of the Emperor of Germany, who was staying at Acre, to Amauri, King of Cyprus, offering him the hand of Isabella and the crown of the Latin kingdom. Amauri had succeeded to the

KNIGHTS TEMPLARS.   327

The Templars again in the Field.   Defeat of the Turks.

sovereignty of the island on the death of his brother, Guy de Lusignan (A. D. 1194), and he eagerly embraced the offer. He immediately embarked in his galleys at Nicosia, landed at Acre, and was married to Queen Isabella and solemnly crowned a few weeks after the death of the late King.

1197. On the arrival of a second division of the Crusaders, under the command of the Dukes of Saxony and Brabant, the Templars again took the field and overthrew the Arab cavalry in a bloody battle, fought in the plain between Tyre and Sidon. The entire Mussulman army was defeated, and Saphadin, desperately wounded, fell back upon Damascus. Beyrout was then besieged and taken, and the fall of this important city was followed by the reduction of Gebal and Laodicea, and all the maritime towns between Tripoli and Jaffa. Intelligence now reached Palestine of the death of the Emperor Henry VI., of Germany, whereupon all the German chieftains hurried home, to pursue, upon another theater, their own schemes of private ambition. After having provoked a terrific and sanguinary war they retired from the contest, leaving their brethren in the East to fight it out as they best could. These last, on viewing their desolated lands, their defenseless cities, and their dwellings destroyed by fire, exclaimed with bitterness and truth, " Our fellow-Christians and self-styled allies found us at *peace*, they have left us at *war*. They are like those ominous birds of passage whose appearance portends the coming tempest." To add to the difficulties and misfortunes of the Latin Christians, a quarrel sprang up between the Templars and Hospitalers touching their respective rights to certain property in Palestine. The matter was referred to the Pope Innocent III., who gravely admonished them, representing that the Infidels would not fail to take advantage of their dissensions, to the great injury of the Holy Land, and to the prejudice of all Christendom. He exhorts them to maintain unity and peace with one another, and appoints certain arbitrators to decide the differences between them. The quarrel was of no great importance, nor of any long duration, for the same year Pope Innocent III. wrote to both Orders, praising them for their exertions in the cause of the Cross, and exhorting them strenuously and faithfully to support with all their might the new King of Jerusalem, Amauri. Yet certain writers upon this period, anxious to magnify every trifling breach between the two Brotherhoods, recur to it again and again. "These two Orders were then, as usual, contending with jealous rivalry," says one. "Ever at war with each other," whispers a second.

1201. In the year 1201 the Grand Master of the Temple, Gilbert Horal, was succeeded by brother Philip Duplessies, or De Plesseis, who found himself, shortly after his accession to power, engaged in active hostilities with Leon I., King of Armenia, who had taken possession of the castle of Gaston, which belonged to the Knights Templars. The Templars drove Leon I. out of Antioch, compelled him to give up the castle of Gaston and sue for peace. A suspension of arms was agreed upon; the matters in dispute between them were referred to the Pope Innocent III., and were eventually decided in favor of the Templars. The Templars appear at this period to have recovered possession of most of their castles and strongholds in the principalities of Tripoli and Antioch. Taking advantage of the dissensions between the neighboring Moslem chieftains, they gradually drove the Infidels across the Orontes, and restored the strong mountain districts to the Christian arms. Some European vessels having been plundered by Egyptian pirates, the Templars unfolded their war banner, and at midnight marched out of Acre, with the King of Jerusalem, to make reprisals on the Moslems. They extended their ravages to the banks of the Jordan, and collected together a vast booty, informing their brethren in Acre of their movements by letters tied to the necks of pigeons. Coradin, Sultan of Damascus, assembled a large body of forces at Sepphoris, near Nazareth, and then marched against the hill fort Doc, which belonged to the Templars. The place was only three miles distant from Acre, and the population of the town was thrown into the utmost consternation. But the military friars, assembling their forces from all quarters, soon repulsed the invaders, and restored tranquillity to the Latin kingdom.

1205. King Amauri died at Acre on the 1st of April. He had issue by Isabella one daughter; but before the close of the year both the mother and child died. The crowns of Jerusalem and Cyprus, which were united on the heads of Amauri and Isabella,

On the Death of the young Queen her Husband assumes the Government.

were now after their decease again divided. Mary, the eldest daughter of the Queen, by Conrad, Marquis of Montferrat, assassinated A. D. 1192, was acknowledged heiress to the crown of the Latin kingdom, and Hugh de Lusignan, the eldest son of Amauri by his first wife, succeeded to the sovereignty of the island of Cyprus. This young prince married the princess Alice, daughter of Isabella by King Henry, Count of Champagne, and half sister to the young Queen Mary by the mother's side. This princess who had just now succeeded to the throne of the Latin kingdom, was fourteen years of age, and the Templars and Hospitalers became her natural guardians and protectors. They directed the military force of the Latin empire in the field, and the government of the country in the cabinet; and defended the kingdom during her minority with zeal and success against all the attacks of the infidels. She soon arrived at marriageable years; they sent over the Bishop of Acre and Aimar, Lord of Cæsarea, to Philip I. (Augustus), King of France, requesting that monarch to select a suitable husband for her from among his princes and nobles. The King's choice fell upon the Count of Brienne, who left France with a large cortege of knights and foot-soldiers, and arrived in Palestine on the 13th of September, 1205. The day after his arrival he was married to the young Queen, who had just then attained her seventeenth year, and on the succeeding Michaelmas day he was crowned King of Jerusalem.

1205. At this period the truce with the infidels had expired, De Plesseis, the Grand Master of the Temple, having previously refused to renew it. Hostilities consequently recommenced, and the Templars again took the field with the new king of Jerusalem and his French knights. Some important successes were gained over the Moslems, when the death of the Queen occurred. She died at Acre, A.D. 1208, in the twentieth year of her age, leaving an infant daughter, named Violante. The Count de Brienne continued, after the example of Guy de Lusignan, to wear the crown, and exercise all the functions of royalty, notwithstanding the death of the Queen. Pope Innocent III. had long been endeavoring to throw an additional luster around his pontificate by achieving the reconquest of Jerusalem. By his bulls and apostolical letters he sought to awaken the ancient enthusiasm of Christendom in favor of the Holy War; and following the example of Pope Urban II., he at last called together a General Council of the Church to aid in the arming of Europe for the recovery of the Holy City. This council assembled at Rome in the summer of the year 1215, and decreed the immediate preaching of the Fifth Crusade. The Emperor Frederick II., of Germany; John, King of England; the King of Hungary, the Dukes of Austria and Bavaria, and many prelates, nobles, and knights, besides crowds of persons of inferior degree, assumed the Cross. Some prepared to fulfill their vow, and embark for the far East, but the far greater portion of them paid sums of money to the clergy to be exempt from the painful privations, dangers, and difficulties consequent upon the long voyage. The King of Hungary, and the Dukes of Austria and Bavaria, were the first to set out upon the pious enterprise. They placed themselves at the head of an army composed of many different nations, embarked from Venice, and **1217.** landed at Acre at the commencement of the year. The day after the Feast of All Saints they marched out of Acre, and pitched their tents upon the banks of the brook Kishon; and the next day the Patriarch of Jerusalem, and the Templars and Hospitalers, came with great pomp and solemnity into the camp, bearing with them " a piece of the true Cross!" It was said that this had been *cut off* before the battle of Tiberias, and carefully preserved by the Oriental clergy. It was sufficient that the Church indorsed it. The kings and princes went out barefoot and uncovered to receive the Holy Relic; they placed it at the head of their array, and immediately commenced a bold and spirited march to the Jordan.

1217. Under the guidance of the Templars they followed the course of the brook Kishon through the valley of Jezreel, and traversing the pass by way of Endor and Bethlehem through mountains of Gilboa, they descended into the valley of the Jordan by castle Bellevieu and pitched their tents on the banks of the sacred river. Thence they proceeded up the valley of the Jordan to Lake Tiberias, skirted its beautiful shores to Bethsaida, passing to the left of the strong citadel of Tiberias, then in the hands of the enemy, and so proceeded across the country to Acre without meeting an enemy to oppose their progress. The Templars then pressed the Christian chieftains to undertake, without further loss of time, the siege of the important fortress of Mount Tabor, and at the commencement of the autumn the place was regularly invested. But the height and steepness of the mountain rendered the transportation of heavy battering machines and military engines to the summit a tedious and laborious undertaking. The troops suffered from the want of water, their patience was exhausted, and the four kings and their followers, being anxious to return home, speedily found excuses for the abandonment of the siege. The customary scene of disorder and confusion then ensued. A large body of Arab horsemen, which had crossed the Jordan, infested the rear of the retiring Crusaders. The disordered pilgrims and foot-soldiers were panic-stricken, and fled to the hills; and the retreat would have been disastrous but for the gallant conduct of the Templars and Hospitalers, who covered the rear and sustained the repeated charges of the Arab cavalry. The two orders sustained immense loss in men and horses, and returned in sorrow and disgust to their quarters at Acre.

1217. The Grand Master, Philip Duplessies, had been unable to take part in the expedition; he was confined to the Temple at Acre by a dangerous illness, of which he died a few days after the return of the Templars from Mount Tabor. Immediately after his decease a general Chapter of Knights was assembled, and William de Chartres was elevated to the dignity of Grand Master. Shortly after his election, he was called upon to take the command of a large fleet fitted out by the order of the Temple against the Egyptians. He set sail from Acre in the month of May, 1217, cast anchor in the mouth of the Nile, and proceeded, in conjunction with the Crusaders, to lay siege to the wealthy and populous city of Damietta. The Templars pitched their tents in the plain on the left bank of the Nile, opposite the town, and surrounded their position with a ditch and a wall. They covered the river with their galleys and with floating rafts furnished with military engines, and directed their first attacks against a castle on an island in the midst of the stream, called the castle of Taphnis.

1217. Large towers were erected upon floating rafts to protect their operations, but they were constantly destroyed by the terrible Greek fire, which was blown out of long copper tubes, and could be extinguished with nothing but vinegar and sand. But at last a number of flat-bottomed boats were lashed together, and a tower, higher than the castle of the enemy, was erected upon them. It was ninety feet in height, twenty in length, and divided into platforms or stages, filled with archers. Numerous loop-holes were pierced in the walls, and the ponderous structure was thickly covered in every part with raw hides, to preserve it from the liquid fire of the enemy. Upon the top of the tower was a drawbridge, which could be raised and lowered with chains, and on each platform were grappling irons, to be made fast to the battlements and parapets of the castle. On the 24th of August, 1217, this vast floating tower was towed to the point of attack, and the left bank of the Nile was covered with a long procession of priests and monks, who traversed the winding shore, with naked feet and uplifted hands, praying to the God of battles for victory. Whilst the enemy were hurrying to the summit of the castle of Taphnis, to direct the Greek fire upon the wooden tower, and to pour boiling oil and red-hot sand upon the heads of the assailants, some Templars, who were stationed in the lowest platform of the structure near the water, threw out their grappling-irons, and made a lodgment upon the causeway in front of the castle. Without a moment's delay, they handed out a battering-ram, and with one blow knocked in the door of the fortress. Combustibles were immediately thrown into the interior of the building, the place was enveloped in smoke and flames, and the garrison surrendered at discretion. The vast chain between the castle and the river was then rent asunder, and the large ships of the Crusaders ascended the Nile, and took up a position in front of the town.

1217. Toward the close of autumn, when the inundation of the Nile was at its height, a strong north wind arose, and impeded the descent of the waters to the Mediterranean. The Christian camp was overflowed, the Templars losing all their provisions, arms, and baggage, and when the waters receded, fish were found in their tents. This catastrophe was followed by an epidemic fever, which carried off the Grand Master, William de Chartres, and many of the brethren. The Grand Master was succeeded, in 1218, by the veteran warrior Peter de Montaigu, Grand Preceptor of Spain. At this period the renowned Saif-ed-din, "Sword of the Faith," the brother and successor of Saladin, died, having appointed his *fifteen* sons to separate and independent commands in his vast dominions. After his decease they contended for the supremacy, and the Templars crossed the Nile to take advantage of the dispute. The infidels fiercely opposed their landing, and one of the Temple vessels being boarded by an overpowering force, the military friars cut a hole in the bottom of it with their hatchets, and all on board met with a watery grave in the deep bosom of the Nile. When the landing was effected, the Templars were the first to charge the enemy, the Moslems fled and abandoned their tents, provisions, and arms, and their camp was given up to plunder. A trench was then drawn around the city of Damietta, and the army took up a position which enabled them to deprive the town of all succor. Two bridges of boats were thrown across the Nile to communicate between the new camp of the Crusaders and the one they had just quitted; and one of these bridges was placed under the protection of the Templars. After many brilliant exploits and sanguinary encounters, Damietta was reduced to great straits; terms of surrender were offered and refused; and on the 5th of November, 1217, a wooden bridge was thrown over the ditch, scaling-ladders were reared against the battlements, and the town was taken by assault. But when the Templars entered the place, they found the plague in every house, and the streets strewed with the dead.

EAST GATE AT DAMASCUS.

CHAPTER IV.

TO THE GREAT DISASTER IN EGYPT A.D. 1251.

Those days are past; Bethsaida, where,
 Chorazin, where art thou?
His tent the wild Arab pitches there
 The babeer shades thy brow.

Tell me, ye moldering fragments, tell,
 Was the Templars' city hell?
Lifted to heaven, has it sunk to here
 With none to shed a tear.

IMMEDIATELY after the capture of Damietta, 1217. De Montaigu, Grand Master of the Temple, returned with the King of Jerusalem to Palestine, to oppose a fresh army of Moslems who, under the command of Coradinus, a famous chieftain, had invaded the country, blockaded the city of Acre, and laid siege to the Pilgrim's Castle at Athlit. In their intrenched camp at this castle, the Templars mustered a force of upwards of four thousand men, who valiantly and successfully defended the important position against the obstinate and persevering attacks of the infidels. During the different assaults upon the place, Coradinus lost six emirs, two hundred Mamelukes, and a number of archers; and on one day alone had a hundred and twenty valuable horses slain, one of which cost fourteen thousand marks. The Templars sent urgent letters to the Pope Honorius III. for succor. They exhorted him to compel the Emperor Frederick to perform his vow, and no longer to permit the Crusaders to compound with money for the non-fulfillment of their

engagements, declaring that such compositions had been most injurious to the cause of the Cross. The Grand Master also wrote to
the Pope, complaining to his holiness of the misapplication by the
clergy of the money collected from their flocks towards the expenses of the Holy War, declaring that not a twentieth part of it
ever reached the empty treasury of the Latin kingdom. In his
reply, the Pope protests that he has not himself fingered a farthing of the money. If you have not received it, says he, it is not
our fault, it is because we have not been obeyed.

In a mournful letter to the Bishop of Ely, Grand Master De
1220. Montaigu now gives a gloomy picture of the state of affairs.
" Brother Peter de Montaigu, Master of the Knights of the Temple, to the reverend brother in Christ, N, by the grace of God,
Bishop of Ely, salvation. We proceed by these our letters to inform your paternity how we have managed the affairs of our Lord
Jesus Christ since the capture of Damietta and the Castle of Taphnis. Be it known to you, that during the spring passage to Europe,
immediately subsequent to the capture of Damietta, so many of
the pilgrims returned home, that the residue of them scarce sufficed to garrison the town and the two intrenched camps. Our
lord the legate, and the clergy, earnestly desiring the advancement
of the army of Jesus Christ, constantly and diligently exhorted
our people forthwith to take the field against the infidels. But
the chieftains from these parts, and from beyond the sea, perceiving that the army was totally insufficient in point of numbers to
guard the city and the camps, and undertake further offensive operations for the advancement of the faith of Jesus Christ, would
on no account give their consent. The Sultan of Egypt, at the
head of a vast number of the perfidious infidels, lies encamped a
short distance from Damietta, and he has recently constructed
bridges across both branches of the Nile, to impede the further
progress of our Christian soldiers. He there remains, quietly
awaiting their approach ; and the forces under his command are so
numerous, that the faithful cannot quit their intrenchments around
Damietta, without incurring imminent risk. In the meantime, we
have surrounded the town, and the two camps, with deep trenches,
and have strongly fortified both banks of the river as far as the

Complaints of the Templars for Aid to carry on the Conquest of the Holy Land.

sea-coast, expecting that the Lord will console and comfort us with speedy succor. But the Saracens, perceiving our weakness, have already armed numerous galleys, and have inflicted vast injury upon us by intercepting all the succors from Europe ; and such has been our extreme want of money, that we have been unable for a considerable period to man and equip our galleys and send them to sea for our protection. Finding, however, that the losses go on increasing to the great detriment of the cause of the Cross, we have now managed to arm some galleys, galliots, and other craft, to oppose the ships of the infidels. Also be it known to you that Coradinus, Sultan of Damascus, having collected together a vast army of Saracens, hath attacked the cities of Tyre and Acre ; and as the garrisons of these places have been weakened to strengthen our forces in Egypt, they can with difficulty sustain themselves against his attacks. Coradinus hath also pitched his tents before our fortress, called the Pilgrim's Castle, and hath put us to immense expense in the defense of the place. He hath also besieged and subjugated the Castle of Cæsarea of Palestine. We have now for a long time been expecting the arrival of the Emperor, and the other noble personages who have assumed the Cross, by whose aid we hope to be relieved from our dangers and difficulties, and to bring all our exertions to a happy issue. But if we are disappointed of the succor we expect in the ensuing summer (which God forbid) all our newly-acquired conquests, as well as the places that we have held for ages past, will be left in a very doubtful condition. We ourselves, and others in these parts, are so impoverished by the heavy expenses we have incurred in prosecuting the affairs of Jesus Christ, that we shall be unable to contribute the necessary funds, unless we speedily receive succor and subsidies from the faithful. Given at Acre, xii. kal. Octob. A.D. 1220."

1220. The urgent solicitations of the Templars for money created loud murmurs in England, and excited the wrath of the great historian, Matthew Paris, the monk of St. Albans, who hated the Order on account of its vast privileges, and the sums it constantly drew away from the hands of other religious bodies. The clergy, who had probably misapplied the money collected by them for the relief of the Holy Land, joined eagerly in an outcry against the Templars, accusing them of squandering their funds upon magnificent churches and expensive buildings in Europe, or of spending them at home in luxurious ease at their different preceptories, instead of faithfully employing them in the prosecution of the Holy War. The Pope instituted an inquiry into the truth of the charges, and wrote to his legate at Damietta, to the Patriarch of Jerusalem, and the principal chieftains of the army of the Crusaders, for information. In their reply, the legate and the Patriarch state that the charges were untrue, and that the Templars had expended their money in the prosecution of the siege of Damietta, and had impoverished themselves by their heavy expenses in Egypt.

During the summer of the year 1221, considerable succors arrived in Palestine and Egypt from Europe. The troops of the Sultan of Damascus were repulsed and driven beyond the frontier of the Latin kingdom, and the Grand Master of the Temple returned to Damietta to superintend the military operations in Egypt. Cardinal Pelagius, the Papal legate, though altogether ignorant of the art of war, had unfortunately assumed the inconsistent character of commander-in-chief of the Army of the Cross. Contrary to the advice of the Templars, he urged the Crusaders during the autumnal season, when the waters of the Nile were rising, to march out of Damietta to undertake an expedition against Grand Cairo. The disastrous results of that memorable campaign are narrated in the following letter from Peter de Montaigu to the Master of the English province of the Order: "Brother Peter de Montaigu, humble Master of the soldiers of Christ, to our vicegerent and beloved brother in Christ, Alan Marcell, Preceptor of England. Hitherto we have had favorable information to communicate unto you touching our exertions in the cause of Christ; now, alas! such have been the reverses and disasters which our sins have brought upon us in the land of Egypt that we have nothing but ill news to announce. After the capture of Damietta our army remained for some time in a state of inaction, which brought upon us frequent complaints and reproaches from the Eastern and the Western Christians. At length, after the Feast of the Holy Apostles, the legate

Heavy Losses of the Christian Army by the Inundation of the Nile.

of the holy pontiff, and all our soldiers of the Cross, put themselves in march by land and by the Nile and arrived in good order at the spot where the Sultan was encamped, at the head of an immense number of the enemies of the Cross. The river Tapneos, an arm of the great Nile, flowed between the camp of the Sultan and our forces, and being unable to ford this river we pitched our tents on its banks and prepared bridges to enable us to force the passage. In the meantime the annual inundation rapidly increased, and the Sultan, passing his galleys and armed boats through an ancient canal, floated them into the Nile below our positions, and intercepted our communications with Damietta. Nothing now was to be done but to retrace our steps. The Sultans of Aleppo, Damascus, Hems, and Coilanbar, the two brothers of the Sultan, and many chieftains and kings of the pagans, with an immense multitude of infidels who had come to their assistance, attempted to cut off our retreat. At night we commenced our march, but the infidels cut through the embankments of the Nile, the water rushed along several unknown passages and ancient canals, and encompassed us on all sides. We lost all our provisions, many of our men were swept into the stream, and the further progress of our Christian warriors was forthwith arrested. The waters continued to increase upon us, and in this terrible inundation we lost all our horses and saddles, our carriages, baggage, furniture, and movables, and everything that we had. We ourselves could neither advance nor retreat, and knew not whither to turn. We could not attack the Egyptians on account of the great lake which extended itself between them and us. We were without food, and being caught and pent up like fish in a net, there was nothing left for us but to treat with the Sultan. We agreed to surrender Damietta, with all the prisoners which we had in Tyre and at Acre, on condition that the Sultan restored to us the wood of the True Cross and the prisoners that he detained at Cairo and Damascus. We, with some others, were deputed by the whole army to announce to the people of Damietta the terms that had been imposed upon us. These were very displeasing to the Bishop of Acre (James de Vitry, the historian), to the Chancellor, and some others, who wished to defend the town, a measure which we should indeed have greatly

340 KNIGHTS TEMPLARS.

The King of Palestine leaves the Holy Land.   Council of Clergy.

approved of, had there been any reasonable chance of success; for we would rather have been thrust into perpetual imprisonment than have surrendered, to the shame of Christendom, this conquest to the infidels.   But after having made a strict investigation into the means of defense, and finding neither men nor money wherewith to protect the place, we were obliged to submit to the conditions of the Sultan, who, after having extracted from us an oath and hostages, accorded to us a truce of eight years.   During the negotiations the Sultan faithfully kept his word, and for the space of fifteen days furnished our soldiers with the bread and corn necessary for their subsistence.   Do you, therefore, pitying our misfortunes, hasten to relieve them to the utmost of your ability. Farewell."

1223. Shortly after the disasters in Egypt, and the conclusion of the eight years' truce with the infidels, John de Brienne, the titular King of Jerusalem, prepared to bid adieu forever to Palestine. Since the death of the Queen he had regarded his kingdom as a place of exile, and was anxious to escape from the toil and turmoil and incessant warfare in which his feeble dominions were continually involved.   His daughter Violante, the Queen of Jerusalem, had just attained her thirteenth year, and the King was anxious to seek a suitable husband for her from among the European princes. Accompanied by Violante, he landed in Italy, and attended a council of the clergy and the laity assembled at Ferentino, in the Campagna di Roma, in the summer of the year 1223.   Pope Honorius III., the Emperor Frederick II., the Patriarch of the Holy City, the Bishop of Bethlehem, the Grand Master of the Hospital (De Montacute), and one of the Grand Preceptors of the Temple, were present at this council, and the Pope urged the Emperor to fulfill the vow which he had made eight years before, to lead an army to the succor of the Holy Land.   He offered him the hand of Violante, and with her the crown of the Latin kingdom.   This offer was accepted, the nuptials were shortly afterwards celebrated, and the Emperor solemnly took his oath upon the Holy Gospel to lead in person a great expedition for the recovery of Jerusalem.

1227. Violante had been accompanied from Palestine by a female

Improper Conduct of the German Emperor. He crowns himself at Jerusalem.

cousin, possessed of powerful charms and many graceful accomplishments. The Emperor became captivated with her beauty, dishonored her, and treated his young wife, a mere child in years, with coldness and neglect. He then, in the middle of August, set sail for Acre with a powerful army, and was at sea three days when he became sea-sick, and returned to land on a plea of ill-health. He was consequently publicly excommunicated by the Pope in the great church of Anagni. Without troubling himself to obtain a reconciliation with the holy see, he again embarked with his forces **1228.** and arrived in the port of Acre on the 8th of September. The Pope then sent letters to Palestine denouncing him as publicly excommunicated, and commanded the Templars not to join his standard. They accordingly refused to take the field, and as the forces under the command of the Emperor did not amount to ten thousand men, he was obliged to remain inactive during the winter. He, however, carried on friendly negotiations with the infidels, and a treaty was entered into whereby Jerusalem was nominally surrendered to him. It was stipulated that the Christian and Mussulman religion should meet with equal toleration in the Holy City; that the followers of Mohammed should possess the Mosk of Omar and the Christians the great Church of the Resurrection; that the Moslems should be governed by their own laws, and that the court of judicature in the forum of *Al Rostak* should be under the direction of a Moslem governor.

1229. At the conclusion of this curious treaty, the Emperor made a peaceful march to the Holy City with a few attendants, and performed the solemn farce of crowning himself in the Church of the Resurrection. After a stay of a few days in Jerusalem, he hurried back to Acre to prepare for his departure for Europe. No Christian garrison was established in the city, nor did the Templars and Hospitalers venture to return to their ancient abodes. His conduct, immediately preceding his departure, is thus described in a letter from the Patriarch of Jerusalem to the Pope: The Emperor placed archers at the gates of the city of Acre, to prevent the Templars from entering into or proceeding out of the town. He moreover placed soldiers in all the streets leading to our quarter and the Temple, keeping us in a state of siege; and it is evident

22

that he has never treated the Saracens half so badly as he has treated the Christians. For a long time he refused to permit any provisions to be brought to us, and instructed his soldiers to insult the priests and the Templars whenever they met them. He moreover got possession of the magazines, and removed all the military machines and arms, preserved for the defense of the city, with a view of rendering good service to his kind friend the Sultan of Egypt; and afterwards, without saying adieu to anybody, he embarked secretly on the 1st of May, leaving us worse off than he found us.

The Grand Master of the Temple, Peter de Montaigu, died at Acre at an advanced age, and was succeeded in 1233, by Hermann de Perigord, Grand Preceptor of Calabria and Sicily. Shortly after his accession to power, the truce with the Sultan of Aleppo expired, and William de Montferrat, Preceptor of Antioch, having besieged a fortress of the infidels, refused to retreat before a superior force, and was surrounded and overwhelmed, a hundred Knights of the Temple, and three hundred cross-bowmen being slain, together with many secular warriors, and a large number of foot-soldiers. The *Balcanifer*, or standard-bearer, on this occasion, named Reginald d'Argenton, performed prodigies of valor. He was disabled and covered with wounds, yet he unflinchingly bore the *Beauseant* aloft with his bleeding arms into the thickest of the fight, until he at last fell dead upon a heap of his slaughtered comrades. The Preceptor of Antioch, before he was slain, " sent sixteen infidels to hell." As soon as the Templars in England

1236. heard of this disaster, they sent, in conjunction with the Hospitalers, instant succor to their brethren. Having made their arrangements, says Matthew Paris, they started from the house of the Hospitalers at Clerkenwell in London, and passed through the city with spears held aloft, shields displayed, and banners advanced. They marched in splendid pomp to the bridge, and sought a blessing from all who crowded to see them pass. The Knights, uncovered, bowed their heads from side to side, and recommended themselves to the prayers of all.

1237. The Sixth Crusade was now preached in Europe by Pope Gregory IX., and the Templars, expecting the arrival of speedy

succor, and being desirous of taking advantage of the dissensions that had arisen amongst the Saracens, had recommenced hostilities with the Sultans of Egypt and Damascus.   Thibaut I., King of Navarre, and Count of Champagne; the Duke of Burgundy, and the Counts of Brittany and Bar, who had arrived in Palestine with several other nobles and knights, and a considerable force of armed pilgrims, marched with a party of Templars to attack the Sultan of Egypt, whilst the Grand Master, De Perigord, prepared to in-
1238. vade the territory of the Sultan of Damascus.   In a bloody battle fought with the Mamelukes, near Gaza, the Count de Bar and many Knights and persons of quality, and all the foot-soldiers, were slain.   The Count de Montfort was taken prisoner, and all the equipage and baggage of the army was lost.   The King of Navarre and the survivors then retreated to Joppa, and set sail from that port for Acre.   On their arrival at this place, they joined the Grand Master of the Temple, De Perigord, who was encamped at the palm-grove of Caifa.   Thence they marched towards Tiberias, and on their arrival at Sepphoris, met some messengers who were proceeding from Saleh Ismael, the Sultan of Damascus, to the Grand Master of the Temple, with overtures of peace, and offers to surrender Jerusalem upon the following terms :—The Moslem and Christian prisoners of war were immediately to be set at liberty; all Palestine, between the sea-coast and the Jordan, excepting the cities of St. Abraham (Hebron?), Nablous, and Bethshean, was to be surrendered to the Christians.   The Christians were to assist the Sultan of Damascus in a war which had broken out between him and Nojmoddin Ayoub, Sultan of Egypt.   They were to march with all their forces to the south to occupy Joppa and Ascalon, and prevent the latter potentate from marching through Palestine to attack the Sultan of Damascus.   And lastly, no truce was to be entered into with the Sultan of Egypt by the Christians, unless the Sultan of Damascus was included therein.   The Grand Master of the Temple, De Perigord, acceded to these terms, and induced the chiefs of the Crusaders to assent to the compact; but the Grand Master of the Hospital, Bertrand de Camps, refused to be a party to it.   It is said that he entered into a separate and independent treaty with Nojmoddin Ayoub, who had just mounted

the throne of Egypt, so that one of the great military orders re-mained at war with the Sultan of Damascus, and the other with the Sultan of Egypt.

1238. Immediately after the conclusion of this treaty, the Tem-plars assembled all their disposable forces and proceeded to Joppa with the Count de Nevers and a body of newly-arrived Crusaders, and co-operated with an army which the Sultan of Damascus had sent into that neighborhood to act against the Egyptians. In the meantime, Richard, Earl of Cornwall, the brother of Henry III., King of England, having assumed the Cross, arrived in Palestine, and proceeded with a small force of English pilgrims, knights, and foot-soldiers, to the camp of the Templars at Joppa. With this welcome re-enforcement the Grand Master of the Temple, De Peri-gord, marched at once upon Ascalon, reconstructed the castle and restored the fortifications to the state in which they were left by King Richard forty-five years before. The Templars then endeav-ored to obtain possession of their ancient fortress of Gaza, a place of very great importance. An invading army from the south could approach Jerusalem only by way of Gaza, or by taking a long and tedious route through the Desert of Arabia Petræa, to Kerak, and from thence to Hebron, by the southern extremity of the Dead Sea. The want of water and forage presented an insu-perable obstacle to the march of a large body of forces in any other direction. Towards the close of autumn, the Templars marched against Gaza in conjunction with Saleh Ismael, Sultan of Damascus, drove out the Egyptians, and obtained possession of the dismantled fortifications. Large sums of money were ex-pended in the reconstruction of the walls of the castle, a strong garrison was established in the important post, and the Templars then marched upon Jerusalem.

1240. The fortifications of the Holy City had been dismantled by Malek Kamel, at the period of the siege of Damietta, A.D. 1238, when alarmed at the military success of the Franks in Egypt, he was anxious to purchase the safety of the country by the cession of Jerusalem. The Templars, consequently, entered the Holy City without difficulty or resistance; the Mussulman population abandoned their dwellings on their approach, and the military friars once more entered the City of David, barefooted and bare-headed, singing loud hymns and songs of triumph. They rushed to the Church of the Resurrection, and fell prostrate on their knees before the shrine of the Holy Sepulcher. They ascended Calvary, and visited the reputed scene of the Crucifixion; and then hastened in martial array, and with sound of trumpet, through the forlorn and deserted streets of the City of Zion, to take possession of their ancient quarters on Mount Moriah, vacant for more than one hundred years.

1240. The golden Crescent was once more removed from the lofty pinnacle of the Temple of the Lord, or Mosk of Omar, and this holy Mussulman house of prayer was once again surmounted by the glittering Cross. The Temple of the Knights Templars (Mosk el Aksa) was again purified and re-consecrated; and its somber halls and spacious areas were once more graced with the white religious and military habit of the Knights of the Temple. The greater part of the old convent, adjoining the Temple, had been destroyed in 1187, by Saladin, and the military friars were consequently obliged to pitch numerous tents in the spacious area for the accommodation of the brethren. The sound of the bell once more superseded the voice of the muezzin, "the exiled faith returned to its ancient sanctuary," and the name of JESUS was again invoked in the high places and sanctuaries of *Mohammed*. The great court of the Mussulmans around the revered Mosk of Omar, called by them *Es Scham Schereef*, "the Noble," again rung with the tramp of the war-steed, and its solitudes were once more awakened with the voice of the trumpet.

1240. Nothing could exceed the joy with which the intelligence of the re-occupation of Jerusalem was received throughout Palestine, and through all Christendom. The Hospitalers, now that the policy of the Templars had been crowned with success, and that Jerusalem had been regained, no longer opposed the treaty with the Sultan of Damascus, but hastened to co-operate with them for the preservation of the Holy City, which had been so happily recovered. The Patriarch returned to Jerusalem, with all his clergy.

1241. The churches were re-consecrated, and the Templars and Hospitalers emptied their treasuries in rebuilding the walls. The following account of these gratifying events was transmitted by Grand Master Hermann de Perigord to the Master of the Temple at London: "Brother Hermann de Perigord, humble minister of the poor Knights of the Temple, to his beloved brother in Christ, Robert de Sandford, Preceptor in England, salvation through the Lord. Since it is our duty, whenever an opportunity offers, to make known to the brotherhood, by letters or by messengers, the state and prospects of the Holy Land, we hasten to inform you, that after our great successes against the Sultan of Egypt, and Nasser, his supporter and abettor, the great persecutor of the Christians, whom we have unceasingly endeavored with all our might to subdue, they were unwillingly compelled to treat with us concerning the establishment of a truce, promising us to restore to the followers of Jesus Christ all the territory on this side Jordan. We dispatched certain of our brethren, noble and discreet personages, to Cairo, to have an interview with the Sultan upon these matters. But the latter broke the promise which he had made to us, retaining in his own hands Gaza, St. Abraham, Nablous, Varan and other places; he detained our messengers in custody for more than half a year, and endeavored to amuse us with deceitful words and unmeaning propositions. But we, with the Divine assistance, were enabled to penetrate his craft and perfidy, and plainly saw that he had procured the truce with us that he might be enabled the more readily to subjugate to his cruel dominion the Sultan of Damascus, and Nasser, Lord of Kerak, and their territories; and then, when he had got possession of all the country surrounding our Christian provinces, we plainly foresaw that he would break faith with us, after the custom of his unbelieving generation, and attack our poor Christianity on this side the sea, which in its present weak and feeble state would have been unable effectually to resist him. Having therefore deliberated, long and earnestly, upon these matters, we determined, with the advice of the Bishops and some of the Barons of the land, to break off at once with the Sultan of Egypt, and enter into a treaty with the Sultan of Damascus, and with Nasser, Lord of Kerak, whereby all the country on this side Jordan, excepting St. Abraham, Nablous, and Bethshean, has been surrendered to the Christian worship; and, to the joy of

The Holy City again in possession of the Christians.

angels and of men, the holy city of Jerusalem is now inhabited by Christians alone, all the Saracens being driven out. The holy places have been re-consecrated and purified by the prelates of the churches, and in those spots where the name of the Lord has not been invoked for fifty-six years, now, blessed be God, the divine mysteries are daily celebrated. To all the sacred places there is again free access to the faithful in Christ, nor is it to be doubted but that in this happy and prosperous condition, we might long remain, if our Eastern Christians would from henceforth live in greater concord and unanimity. But, alas! opposition and contradiction, arising from envy and hatred, have impeded our efforts in the promotion of these and other advantages for the Holy Land. With the exception of the prelates of the churches, and a few of the Barons, who afford us all the assistance in their power, the entire burden of its defense rests upon our house alone. With the assistance of the Sultan of Damascus, and the Lord of Kerak, we have obtained possession of the city of Gaza, situate on the confines of the territory of Jerusalem and the territory of Egypt. And as this important place commands the entrance from the latter country into the Holy Land, we have, by vast exertions, and at an enormous expense, and after having incurred great risk and danger, put it into a state of defense. But we are afraid that God will take heavy vengeance for past ingratitude, by punishing those who have been careless, and indifferent, and rebellious in the prosecution of these matters. For the safeguard and preservation of the holy territory, we propose to erect a fortified castle near Jerusalem, which will enable us the more easily to retain possession of the country, and to protect it against all enemies. But indeed we can in no wise defend for any great length of time the places that we hold against the powerful and crafty Sultan of Egypt, unless Christ and his faithful followers extend to us an efficacious support."

We must now refer to a few events connected with the English province of the Order of the Temple. Geoffrey, Master of the Temple at London, at the period of the consecration of the Temple Church by Heraclius, Patriarch of Jerusalem, died shortly after the capture of the Holy City by Saladin, 1187, and was succeeded

by Amaric de St. Maur, who is an attesting witness to the deed
executed by King John (A. D. 1203), granting a dowry to his Queen,
Isabella.   King John frequently resided in the Temple for weeks
together, the writs to his lieutenants, sheriffs, and bailiffs, being
dated therefrom.   The orders for the concentration of the English
fleet at Portsmouth, to resist the formidable French invasion instigated by the Pope, are dated from the TEMPLE at London, and the
convention between the King and the Count of Holland, whereby
the latter agreed to assist King John with a body of knights and
men-at-arms, in case of the landing of the French, was published
at the same place.   In all the conferences and negotiations between
King John and the Roman Pontiff, the Knights Templars took an
active and distinguished part.   Two brethren of the order were
sent to him by Pandulph, the Papal legate, to arrange that famous
conference between them which ended in the complete submission
of the King to all the demands of the Holy See.   By the advice
and persuasion of the Templars, John repaired to the preceptory
of Temple Ewell, near Dover, where he was met by the Legate
Pandulph, who crossed over from France to confer with him, and
the King was there frightened into a resignation of his kingdoms
of England and Ireland, " to God, to the holy apostles, Peter and
Paul, to the holy Roman Church, his mother, and to his Lord,
Pope Innocent the Third, and his Catholic successors, for the remission of all his sins and the sins of all his people as well the living
as the dead."   The following year, the commands of King John for
the extirpation of the heretics in Gascony, addressed to the Seneschal of that province, were issued from the Temple at London, and
about the same period, the Templars were made the depositaries of
various private and confidential matters pending between King
John and his illustrious sister-in-law, " the royal, eloquent, and
beauteous " Berengaria of Navarre, the youthful widowed Queen
of Richard, *Cœur de Lion.*   The Templars in England managed
the money transactions of that fair princess.   She directed her
dower to be paid in the house of the New Temple at London,
together with the arrears due to her from the King, amounting to several thousand pounds.

1215.   John was resident at the Temple when he was compelled by the Barons of England to sign MAGNA CHARTA, June 15. Matthew Paris tells us that the Barons came to him whilst he was residing in the New Temple at London, "in a very resolute manner, clothed in their military dresses, and demanded the liberties and laws of King Edward, with others for themselves, the kingdom, and the Church of England."

Amaric de St. Maur, the Master of the English province of the Order, was succeeded by Alan Marcell, the friend and correspondent of Grand Master Peter de Montaigu. He was at the head of the Order in England for the space of sixteen years, and was employed by King Henry III. in various important negotiations. He was Master of the Temple at London, when Reginald, King of the Island of Man, by the advice and persuasion of the Legate Pandulph, made a solemn surrender at that place of his island to the Pope and his Catholic successors, and consented to hold the same from thenceforth as the feudatory of the Church of Rome.

1224. On the 28th of April, the Master, Alan Marcell, was employed by King Henry to negotiate a truce between himself and the King of France. The King of England appears at that time to have been resident at the Temple, the letters of credence being made out at that place, in the presence of the Archbishop of Canterbury, several bishops, and Hubert, the chief justiciary. The year after Alan Marcell was sent into Germany to negotiate a treaty of marriage between King Henry and the daughter of the Duke of Austria. Alan Marcell was succeeded by Amberaldus. The next Master of the English province was Robert Mounford, and he was followed by Robert Sanford.

1240. During the Mastership of Robert Sanford, on Ascension Day, the oblong portion of the Temple Church, which extended eastward from "THE ROUND," was consecrated in the presence of King Henry III. and all his court, and much of the nobility of the kingdom. "This portion of the sacred edifice was of a lighter and more florid style of architecture than the earlier Round Church consecrated by the Patriarch Heraclius. The walls were pierced with numerous triple lancet windows filled with stained glass, and the floor was covered with tesselated pavement. The roof was supported by dark gray Purbeck marble columns, and the vaulted

ceiling was decorated with the Star of Bethlehem, and with orna
ments of frosted silver placed on a blue ground. The extensive
area of the church was open and unencumbered by pews, and the
beauty of the columns and windows, the lively colors of the tiled
floor, and the elegant proportions of the fabric were seen at a
glance. After the consecration the King made provision for the
maintenance in the Temple of three chaplains, who were to say
three masses daily for ever, one for the King himself, another for
all Christian people, and the third for the faithful departed.

King Henry III.—1216–1272—was one of the greatest of the
benefactors of the Order. He granted to the Templars the manors
of Lilleston, Hechewayton, and Saunford, the wood of Carletone,
Kingswood, near Chippenham, a messuage and six bovates of land
with their appurtenances in Great Lymburgh; a fair at Walnesford, in the county of Essex, every three years for three days, to
commence on the anniversary of the beheading of St. John the
Baptist; also annual fairs and weekly markets at Newburgh,
Walnesford, Balsall, Kirkeby, and a variety of other places; he
granted them free warren in all their demesne lands; and by his
famous charter, dated 9th February, A.D. 1227, he confirmed to
them all the donations of his predecessors, and of their other benefactors, and conferred upon them vast privileges and immunities.

By the royal grant of *soc* and *sac*, *tol* and *theam*, etc., etc., the
Templars were clothed with the power of holding courts to impose
and levy fines and amerciaments upon their tenants, to judge and
punish their villeins and vassals, to take cognizance of quarrels
and controversies that arose amongst them, to try thieves and
malefactors belonging to their manors, and all foreign thieves taken
within the precincts thereof; to try and punish trespasses and
breaches of the peace, and all unlawful entries into the houses of
their tenants; to impose and levy amerciaments for cutting and
maiming, and for bloodshed; to judge and punish by fine or imprisonment the seducers of their bondwomen, and all persons who
committed adultery and fornication within their manors. They
had the power of trying criminals by ordeal, or the terrible test of
fire and water; and they had, lastly, the tremendous privilege of
pit or gallows, *i.e.*, the power of putting convicted thieves to death,

by hanging them if they were men, and drowning them if they were women! By the royal charter the Templars were, in the next place, freed from the fine of right payable to the king for the hanging of thieves without a formal trial and judgment according to law; they were exempt from the taxes on pasture lands, and plough lands, and horned cattle; from the Danish tribute, and from all military services, and from all the ordinary feudal burdens.

1242.   Shortly after the recovery of the Holy City (viz. A.D. 1240), Djemal'eddeen, the Mussulman, paid a visit to Jerusalem. " I saw," says he, " the monks and the priests masters of the Temple of the Lord. I saw the vials of wine prepared for the sacrifice. I entered into the Mosk el Aksa and saw a bell suspended from the dome. The rites and ceremonies of the Mussulmans were abolished, the call to prayer was no longer heard. The infidels publicly exercised their idolatrous practices in the sanctuaries of the Mussulmans." By the advice of Benedict, Bishop of Marseilles, who came to the Holy City on a pilgrimage, the Templars rebuilt their ancient and once formidable castle of Safed, the dilapidated ruins of which had been ceded to them by their recent treaty with Saleh Ismael. During a pilgrimage to the lake of Tiberias and the banks of the Jordan, the Bishop of Marseilles had halted at Safed, and spent a night amid the ruins of the ancient castle, where *he found a solitary Knight Templar keeping watch in a miserable hovel.* Struck with the position of the place, and its importance in a military point of view, he sought on his return to Acre an interview with the Grand Master of the Temple, De Perigord, and urged him to restore the castle of Safed to its pristine condition. The Bishop was invited to attend a general chapter of the Order of the Temple, when the matter was discussed, and it was unanimously determined that the mountain of Safed should immediately be refortified. The Bishop himself laid the first stone, and animated the workmen by a spirited oration. Eight hundred and fifty masons and artificers, and four hundred slaves, were employed in the task. During the first thirty months after the commencement of operations, the Templars expended $825,-000 upon the works, and in succeeding years they spent upwards

of $3,000,000.   The walls, when finished, were sixty French feet
in width, one hundred and seventy in height, and the circuit of
them was two thousand two hundred and fifty feet.   They were
flanked by seven large round towers, sixty feet in diameter, and
seventy-two feet higher than the walls.   The fosse surrounding
the fortress was thirty-six feet wide, and was pierced in the solid
rock to a depth of forty-three feet.   The garrison in time of peace
amounted to one thousand seven hundred men, and to two thousand two hundred in time of war.   Twelve thousand mule loads
of corn and barley were consumed annually within the walls of
the fortress; and in addition to all the ordinary expenses and requirements of the establishment, the Templars maintained a well-
furnished table and excellent accommodation for all way-worn pilgrims and travelers.   "The generous expenditure of the Templars
at this place," says a cotemporary historian, "renders them truly
worthy of the liberality and largesses of the faithful."

The ruins of this famous castle, crowning the summit of a lofty
mountain, torn and shattered by earthquakes, still present a stupendous appearance.   In Pocock's time "two particularly fine
large round towers" were entire : and Van Egmont and Heyman
give the following account of the condition of the fortress at the
period of their visit.   "The next place that engaged our attention
was the citadel, which is the greatest object of curiosity in Safed,
and is generally considered one of the most ancient structures remaining in the country.   In order to form some idea of this fortification in its present state, imagine a lofty mountain, and on its
summit a round castle, with walls of incredible thickness, and with
a *corridor* or covered passage extending round the walls, and ascended by a winding staircase.   The thickness of the walls and
corridor together was twenty paces.   The whole was of hewn
stone, and some of the stones are eight or nine spans in length.
This castle was anciently surrounded with stupendous works, as
appears from the remains of two moats lined with free-stone, several fragments of walls, bulwarks, towers, etc., all very solid and
strongly built; and below these moats other massive works, having corridors round them in the same manner as the castle ; so
that any person, on surveying these fortifications, may wonder

how so strong a fortress could ever be taken." Amongst the various interesting remains of this castle, these intelligent travelers describe " a large structure in the form of a cupola or dome. The stones, which are almost white, are of astonishing magnitude, some being twelve spans in length and five in thickness. The inside is full of niches for placing statues, and near each niche is a small cell. An open colonnade extends quite round the building, and, like the rest of the structure, is very massive and compact."

1240. When the Sultan of Egypt had been informed of the march of the Templars to Jerusalem, and the re-possession by the military friars of the Holy Places and Sanctuaries of the Mussulmans, he sent an army of several thousand men across the desert, to drive them out of the Holy City before they had time to repair the fortifications and reconstruct the walls. The Templars assembled all their forces and advanced to meet the Egyptians. They occupied the passes and defiles of the hill country leading to Jerusalem, and gained a glorious victory over the Moslems, driving the greater part of them into the desert. Ayoub, Sultan of Egypt, finding himself unable to resist the formidable alliance of the Templars with Saleh Ismael, called in to his assistance the fierce pastoral tribes of the Kharizmians. These were a warlike race of people, who had been driven from their abodes, in the neighborhood of the Caspian, by the successful arms of the Moguls, and had rushed headlong upon the weak and effeminate nations of the south. They had devastated and laid waste Armenia and the northwestern parts of Persia, cutting off by the sword, or dragging away into captivity, all who had ventured to oppose their progress. For years past they had been leading a migratory, wandering life, exhausting the resources of one district, and then passing onwards into another, without making any fixed settlement, or having any regular places of abode, and their destructive progress has been compared by the Arabian writers to the wasting tempest or the terrible inundation. The rude hardships of their roving life had endowed them with a passive endurance which enabled them to surmount all obstacles, and to overcome every difficulty. Their clothing consisted of a solitary sheep's skin, or a wolf's skin, tied around their loins. Boiled herbs and some water,

354   KNIGHTS TEMPLARS.

Migratory Character of the Kharizmians.   Jerusalem abandoned to the Infidels.

or a little milk, sufficed them for food and beverage; their arms
were the bow and the lance; and they shed the blood of their fellow-creatures with the same indifference as they would that of the
beasts of the field.   Their wives and their children accompanied
their march, braving all dangers and fatigues.   Their tents were
their homes, and the site of their encampment their only country.
Nothing could exceed the terror inspired in Armenia and Persia
by the military expeditions of these rude and ferocious shepherds
of the Caspian, who were the foes of all races and of all people,
and manifested a profound indifference for every religion.

1244.   The Kharizmians were encamped on the left bank of the
Euphrates, pasturing their cavalry in the neighboring plains, when
their chief, Barbeh Khan, received a deputation from the Sultan
of Egypt, inviting their co-operation and assistance in the reduction of Palestine.   Their cupidity was awakened by an exaggerated account of the fertility and the wealth of the land, and they
were offered a settlement in the country as soon as it was rescued
from the hands of the Franks.   The messengers displayed the
written letters of the Sultan of Egypt; they presented to the
Kharizmian chief some rich shawls and magnificent presents, and
returned to their master at Grand Cairo with promises of speedy
support.   The Kharizmians assembled together in a body; they
crossed the Euphrates (A.D. 1244) in small leathern boats, ravaged
the territories of the Sultan of Aleppo, and marched up the plain
of the Orontes to Hums, wasting all the country around them with
fire and the sword.   The intelligence of these events reached the
Grand Master of the Temple, De Perigord, when he was busily
engaged in rebuilding the vast and extensive fortifications of the
Holy City.   A council of war was called together, and it was determined that *Jerusalem was untenable,* and that the Holy City
must once again be abandoned to the infidels.   The Hospitalers
in their black mantles, and the Templars in their white habits,
were drawn up in martial array in the streets of Jerusalem, and
the weeping Christians were exhorted once again to leave their
homes and avail themselves of the escort and protection of the
military friars to Joppa.   Many gathered together their little
property and quitted the devoted city, and many lingered behind

Invasion and Barbarities of the Kharizmians.   The Holy City in their Possession.

amid the scenes they loved and cherished.   Soon, however, frightful reports reached Jerusalem of the horrors of the Kharizmian invasion, and the fugitives, who had fled with terror and astonishment from their destructive progress, spread alarm and consternation throughout the whole land.   Several thousand Christians, who had remained behind, then attempted to make their escape, with their wives and children, through the mountains to the plain of Ramleh and the seacoast, relying on the truce and treaty of alliance which had been established with Nasser Daoud, Lord of Kerak, and the mountaineers.   But the inhabitants of the mountain region, being a set of lawless robbers and plunderers, attacked and pillaged them.   Some were slain, and others were dragged away into captivity.   A few fled back to Jerusalem, and the residue, after having been hunted through the mountains, descended into the plain of Ramleh, where they were attacked by the Kharizmians, and only three hundred out of the whole number succeeded in reaching Joppa in safety.   All the women and children had been taken captive in the mountains, and amongst them were several holy nuns, who were sent to Egypt and sold in the common slave-markets.

1244. The Kharizmians had advanced into the plain of Ramleh by way of Baalbec, Tiberias, and Nablous, and they now directed their footsteps towards Jerusalem.   They entered the Holy City sword in hand, massacred the few remaining Christians in the Church of the Holy Sepulcher, pillaged the town, and rifled the tombs of the kings for treasure.   They then marched upon Gaza, stormed the city, and put the garrison to the sword, after which they sent messengers across the desert to the Sultan of Egypt to announce their arrival.   Ayoub immediately sent a robe of honor and sumptuous gifts to their chief, and despatched his army from Cairo in all haste, under the command of Rokmeddin Bibars, one of his principal Mamelukes, to join them before Gaza.   The Grand Masters of the Temple and the Hospital, on the other hand, collected their forces together, and made a junction with the troops of the Sultan of Damascus and the Lord of Kerak.   They marched upon Gaza, attacked the united armies of the Egyptians and Kharizmians, but were exterminated in a bloody battle of two days' continuance.   The Grand Master of the Temple, De Perigord, and the flower of his chivalry perished in that bloody encounter, and the Grand Master of the Hospital, De Chateauneuf, was taken prisoner, and led away into captivity.

1244. The government of the Order of the Temple, in consequence of the death of the Grand Master, temporarily devolved upon the Knight Templar William de Rochefort, who immediately despatched a melancholy letter addressed to the Pope and the Archbishop of Canterbury, detailing the horrors and atrocities of the Kharizmian invasion.   "These perfidious savages," says he, "having penetrated within the gates of the Holy City of Israel, the small remnant of the faithful left therein, consisting of children, women, and old men, took refuge in the Church of the Sepulcher of our Lord.   The Kharizmians rushed to that holy sanctuary; they butchered them all before the very sepulcher itself, and cutting off the heads of the priests who were kneeling with uplifted hands before the altars, they said one to another, ' Let us here shed the blood of the Christians *on the very place where they offer up wine to their* GOD, *who they say was hanged here.'*   Moreover, in sorrow be it spoken, and with sighs we inform you, that laying their sacrilegious hands on the very sepulcher itself, they sadly knocked it about, utterly battering to pieces the marble shrine which was built around that holy sanctuary.   They have defiled, with every abomination of which they are capable, Calvary, where Christ was crucified, and the whole Church of the Resurrection.   They have taken away, indeed, the sculptured columns which were placed as a decoration before the sepulcher of the Lord ; and, as a mark of victory and as a taunt to the Christians, they have sent them to the sepulcher of the wicked Mohammed.   They have violated the tombs of the happy kings of Jerusalem in the same church, and they have scattered, to the hurt of Christendom, the ashes of those holy men to the winds, irreverently profaning the revered Mount Sion.   The Temple of the Lord, the Church of the Valley of Jehoshaphat, where the Virgin lies buried, the Church of Bethlehem, and the place of the nativity of our Lord, they have polluted with enormities too horrible to be related, far exceeding the iniquity of all the Saracens, who, though they frequently occupied the land of the Christians, yet always reverenced and preserved the holy places." The subsequent military operations are then described: the march of the Templars and Hospitalers, on the 4th of October, A.D. 1244, from Acre to Cæsarea; the junction of their forces with those of the Moslem Sultans; the retreat of the Kharizmians to Gaza, where they received succor from the Sultan of Egypt; and the preparation of the Hospitalers and Templars for the attack before that place. "Those holy warriors," says he, "boldly rushed in upon the enemy, but the Saracens who had joined us, having lost many of their men, fled, and the warriors of the Cross were left alone to withstand the united attack of the Egyptians and Kharizmians. Like stout champions of the Lord and true defenders of Catholicity, whom the same faith and the same cross and passion make true brothers, they bravely resisted. But as they were few in number in comparison with the enemy they at last succumbed, so that of the convents of the house of the chivalry of the Temple, and of the house of the Hospital of St. John at Jerusalem, only thirty-three Templars and twenty-six Hospitalers escaped; the Archbishop of Tyre, the Bishop of St. George, the Abbot of St. Mary of Jehoshaphat, and the Master of the Temple, with many other clerks and holy men, being slain in that sanguinary fight. We ourselves, having by our sins provoked this dire calamity, fled half dead to Ascalon. From thence we proceeded by sea to Acre, and found that city and the adjoining province filled with sorrow and mourning, misery and death. There was not a house or a family that had not lost an inmate or a relation. The Kharizmians have now pitched their tents in the plain of Acre, about two miles from the city. They have spread themselves over the whole face of the country as far as Nazareth and Safed. They have slaughtered or driven away the householders, occupied their houses, and divided their property amongst them. They have appointed bailiffs and tax-gatherers in the towns and villages, and they compel the countrymen and the villeins of the soil to pay to themselves the rents and tribute which they have heretofore been wont to pay to the Christians, so that the Church of Jerusalem and the Christian kingdom have now no territory, except a few fortifications, which are defended with great difficulty and labor by the

23

Templars and Hospitalers.   To you, dear father, upon whom the burden of the defense of the cause of Christ justly resteth, we have caused these sad tidings to be communicated, earnestly beseeching you to address your prayers to the throne of grace, imploring mercy from the Most High, that He who consecrated the Holy Land with his own blood in redemption of all mankind may compassionately turn towards it and defend it, and send it succor.   But know assuredly that unless, through the interposition of the Most High or by the aid of the faithful, the Holy Land is succored in the next spring passage from Europe its doom is sealed and utter ruin is inevitable.   Given at Acre this 5th day of November, in the year of our Lord, 1244."

The above letter was read before a general council of the Church, which had been assembled at Lyons by Pope Innocent IV., and it was resolved that the Seventh Crusade should be preached.   It was provided that those who assumed the Cross should assemble at particular places to receive the Pope's blessing; that there should be a truce for four years between all Christian princes; that during all that time there should be no tournaments, feasts, nor public rejoicings; that all the faithful in Christ should be exhorted to contribute out of their fortunes and estates to the defense of the Holy Land; and that ecclesiastics should pay towards it the tenth, and cardinals the twentieth, of all their revenues, for the term of three years successively.   The ancient enthusiasm, however, in favor of distant expeditions to the East had died away; the addresses and exhortations of the clergy now fell on unwilling ears, and the Templars and Hospitalers for several years received only some small assistance in men and money.   The Emperor Frederick, who still bore the empty title of King of Jerusalem, made no attempt to save the wreck of his feeble kingdom.   His wife, Violante, had been dead several years, killed by his coldness and neglect; and the Emperor bestowed no thought upon his Eastern subjects and the Holy Land, except to abuse those by whom that land had been so gallantly defended.   In a letter to Richard, Earl of Cornwall, the brother of Henry III., King of England, Frederick accuses the Templars of making war upon the Sultan of Egypt, in defiance of a treaty entered into with that monarch, and of compelling him to

KNIGHTS TEMPLARS. 359

Chapter of Templars to choose a Grand Master. A Truce proposed by the Pope.

call in the Kharizmians to his assistance; and he compares the union of the Templars with the infidel Sultan, for purposes of defense, to an attempt to extinguish a fire by pouring upon it a quantity of oil. "The proud religion of the Temple," says he, in continuation, "nurtured amid the luxuries of the barons of the land, waxeth wanton. It hath been made manifest to us, by certain religious persons lately arrived from parts beyond sea, that the aforesaid Sultans and their trains were received with pompous alacrity within the gates of the houses of the Temple, and that the Templars suffered them to perform within them their superstitious rites and ceremonies, with invocation of Mohammed, and to indulge in secular delights." In the midst of all these terrible disasters a general chapter of Knights Templars was assembled in the Pilgrim's Castle at Athlit, and the veteran warrior, WILLIAM DE **1247.** SONNAC, was chosen Grand Master of the Order. Circular mandates were, at the same time, sent to the Western preceptories, summoning all the brethren to Palestine, and directing the immediate transmission of all the money in the different treasuries to the headquarters of the Order at Acre. These calls were promptly attended to, and the Pope praises both the Templars and Hospitalers for the zeal and energy displayed by them in sending out the newly-admitted Knights and novices, with armed bands and a large amount of treasure, to the succor of the holy territory.

1247. Whilst the proposed Crusade was slowly progressing, the Holy Pontiff wrote to the Sultan of Egypt, the ally of the Kharizmians, proposing a peace or a truce, and received the following grand and magnificent reply to his communication:—" To the Pope, the noble, the great, the spiritual, the affectionate, the holy, the thirteenth of the apostles, the leader of the sons of baptism, the High Priest of the Christians (may God strengthen him and establish him, and give him happiness!), from the most powerful Sultan ruling over the necks of nations; wielding the two great weapons, the sword and the pen; possessing two pre-eminent excellencies—that is to say, learning and judgment; King of two seas; ruler of the South and North; King of the region of Egypt and Syria, Mesopotamia, Media, Idumea, and Ophir; King Saloph Beelpheth, Jacob, son of Sultan Kamel, Hemevafar Mehameth,

Pacific Letter of the Sultan to the Pope.   The Kharizmians annihilated.

son of Sultan Hadel, Robethre, son of Jacob, whose kingdom may the Lord God make happy.* IN THE NAME OF GOD THE MOST MERCIFUL AND COMPASSIONATE. The letters of the Pope, the noble, the great, etc., etc., have been presented to us. May God favor him who earnestly seeketh after righteousness and doeth good, and wisheth peace, and walketh in the ways of the Lord. May God assist him who worshipeth him in truth. We have considered the aforesaid letters, and have understood the matters treated of therein, which have pleased and delighted us; and the messenger sent by the holy Pope came to us, and we caused him to be brought before us with honor, and love, and reverence; and we brought him to see us face to face, and inclining our ears towards him, we listened to his speech, and we have put faith in the words he hath spoken unto us concerning Christ, upon whom be salvation and praise. But we know more concerning that same Christ than ye know, and we magnify him more than ye magnify him. And as to what you say concerning your desire for peace, tranquillity, and quiet, and that you wish to put down war, so also do we; we desire and wish nothing to the contrary. But let the Pope know, that between ourselves and the Emperor (Frederick) there hath been mutual love, and alliance, and perfect concord, from the time of the Sultan my father (whom may God preserve and place in the glory of his brightness!), and between you and the Emperor there is as ye know, strife and warfare; whence it is not fit that we should enter into any treaty with the Christians until we have previously had his advice and assent. We have therefore written to our envoy at the imperial court upon the propositions made to us by the Pope's messenger, etc. . . . . . . This letter was written on the seventh of the month *Maharan*. Praise be to the one only GOD, and may his blessing rest upon our master, *Mohammed*."

In the course of a few years the Kharizmians were annihilated. The Sultan of Egypt, having no further need of their services, left them to perish in the lands they had wasted. They were attacked by the Sultans of Aleppo and Hums, and were pursued

---

* This is only the ordinary preface to an Oriental letter, as may be seen to-day by examining a Turkish *firman*. It is not much more absurd than the usual epistles of royalty even in the Nineteenth Century.

with equal fury by Moslem and by Christians. Several large bodies of them were cut up in detail by the Templars and Hospitalers, and they were at last slain to a man. Their very name perished from the face of the earth, but the traces of their existence were long preserved in the ruin and desolation they had spread around them. The Holy Land, although happily freed from the destructive presence of these barbarians, had yet everything to fear from the powerful Sultan of Egypt, with whom hostilities still continued ; and William de Sonnac, the Grand Master of the Temple, for the purpose of stimulating the languid energies of the English nation, and reviving their holy zeal and enthusiasm in the cause of the Cross, despatched a distinguished Knight Templar to England, charged with the duty of presenting to King Henry III. a magnificent crystal vase, containing, as it was alleged, a portion of the blood of Jesus Christ! Thus gross were the superstitions of that day inculcated by the Papal churches.

A solemn attestation of the genuineness of this precious relic, signed by the Patriarch of Jerusalem, and the Bishops, Abbots, and Barons of the Holy Land, was forwarded to London and was deposited, together with the vase and its contents, in the Cathedral Church of St. Paul. The King ordered the Bishops and clergy devoutly and reverently to assemble at St. Paul's, on the anniversary of the translation of St. Edward the Confessor, in full canonicals, with banners, crosses, and lighted wax-candles. On the eve of that day, according to the monk of St. Albans, who personally assisted at the ceremony, " our Lord the King, with a devout and contrite spirit, as became that most Christian Prince, fasting on bread and water, and watching all night with a great light, and performing many pious exercises, prudently prepared himself for the morrow's solemnity." On the morrow a procession of Bishops, Monks, and Priests, having been duly marshaled and arranged, King Henry made his appearance upon the steps at the south door of St. Paul's Cathedral, and receiving with " the greatest honor, and reverence, and fear, the little vase containing the memorable treasure, he bore it publicly through the streets of London, holding it aloft just above his face. Bareheaded, and clothed in a humble habit, he walked afoot without halting, to Westminster Abbey ; and although he passed over rough and uneven pavements, yet he invariably kept his eyes stead-fastly fixed, either on heaven or on that vase." He made a solemn procession round the Abbey, then round the palace at Westminster, and then round his own bed-chamber, all the while unweariedly bearing aloft the precious relic, after which he presented it to God, and the church of St. Peter, to his dear Edward, and the sacred convent at Westminster.*

1249. In the meantime the Comans, another fierce pastoral tribe of wandering Tartars, made their way through the Christian province of Armenia into the principality of Antioch, and ravaged both banks of the Orontes, carrying away the inhabitants into captivity. The King of Armenia and the Prince of Antioch despatched mes-sengers to the Templars and Hospitalers for succor, and the Grand Masters, collecting all their disposable forces, hurried to the relief of the distressed provinces. In a long and bloody battle, fought in the neighborhood of the iron bridge over the Orontes, the Co-mans were overthrown and slaughtered, and the vast and wealthy city of Antioch was saved from pillage. The Hospitalers suffered severe loss in this engagement, and Bertrand de Comps, their Grand Master, died of his wounds four days after the battle.

In the month of June, A. D. 1249, the galleys of the Templars left Acre with all their disposable forces on board, under the com-mand of the Grand Master William de Sonnac, and joined the great French expedition of Louis, King of France, which had been directed against the infidels in Egypt. After the capture of Da-mietta, the following letter was forwarded by Grand Master Wil-liam de Sonnac to the Master of the Temple at London:—
" Brother William de Sonnac, by the grace of God, Master of the poor chivalry of the Temple, to his beloved brother in Christ, Robert de Sanford, Preceptor of England, salvation through the Lord. We hasten to unfold to you by these presents, agreeable and happy intelligence. . . . . (He details the landing of the French, the defeat of the infidels with the loss of one Christian soldier, and the subsequent capture of the city.) Damietta, there-fore, has been taken, not by our deserts, nor by the might of our armed bands, but through the divine power and assistance. More-

---

* It would be a curious inquiry what has become of this farcical object.

over, be it known to you that King Louis, with God's favor, proposes to march upon Alexandria or Cairo for the purpose of delivering our brethren there detained in captivity, and of reducing, with God's help, the whole land to the Christian worship.   Farewell."

1249.   The Lord de Joinville, the friend of King Louis, and one of the bravest of the French captains, gives a lively and most interesting account of the campaign, and of the exploits of the Templars.   During the march towards Cairo, they led the van of the Christian army, and on one occasion, when the King of France had given strict orders that no attack should be made upon the infidels, and that an engagement should be avoided, a body of Turkish cavalry advanced against them.   " One of these Turks," says Joinville, " gave a Knight Templar in the first rank so heavy a blow with his battle-axe, that it felled him under the feet of the Lord Reginald de Vichier's horse, who was Marshal of the Temple. The Marshal, seeing his man fall, cried out to his brethren, ' At them in the name of God, for I cannot longer stand this.'   He instantly stuck spurs into his horse, followed by all his brethren, and as their horses were fresh, not a Saracen escaped."   After marching for some days, the Templars arrived on the banks of the Tanitic branch of the Nile (the ancient Pelusiac mouth of the river,) and found the Sultan encamped with his entire force on the opposite side, to prevent and oppose their passage.   King Louis attempted to construct a bridge to enable him to cross the stream, and long and earnestly did the Templars labor at the task, " but," says Joinville, " as fast as we advanced our bridge the Saracens destroyed it; they dug, on their side of the river, wide and deep holes in the earth, and as the water recoiled from our bridge it filled these holes with water, and tore away the bank, so that what we had been employed on for three weeks or a month they ruined in one or two days."   To protect the soldiers employed upon the construction of the bridge large wooden towers were erected, and *chas chateils* or covered galleries, and the infidels exerted all their energies to destroy them with the terrible Greek fire.   " At night," says Joinville, " they brought forward an engine called by them *La Perriere*, a dreadful engine to do mischief, and they flung from it such quantities of Greek fire that it was the most horrible sight ever witnessed. This Greek fire was like a large tun, and its tail was of the length of a long spear; the noise which it made was like to thunder, and it seemed a great dragon of fire flying through the air, giving so great a light with its flame, that we saw in our camp as clearly as in broad day."

The military engines and machines were all burnt, and the Christians were about to yield themselves up to despair, when a Bedouin Arab offered, for a bribe of $37,500 to show a safe ford. At dawn of day, on Shrove Tuesday, the French knights mounted on horseback to make trial of the ford of the Bedouin. "Before we set out," says Joinville, "the King had ordered that the Templars should form the van, and the Count d'Artois, his brother, should command the second division after the Templars; but the moment the Count d'Artois had passed the ford, he and all his people fell on the Saracens, and putting them to flight, galloped after them. The Templars sent to call the Count d'Artois back, and to tell him that it was his duty to march behind and not before them; but it happened that the Count d'Artois could not make any answer by reason of my Lord Foucquault du Melle, who held the bridle of his horse, and my Lord Foucquault, who was a right good knight, being deaf, heard nothing the Templars were saying to the Count d'Artois, but kept bawling out, '*Forward! forward!*' ('Or a eulz! or a eulz!') When the Templars perceived this, they thought they should be dishonored if they allowed the Count d'Artois thus to take the lead; so they spurred their horses more and more, and faster and faster, and chased the Turks, who fled before them, through the town of Mansourah, as far as the plains towards Babylon."

1249. The Arabian writers, in their account of the entry of the Templars into Mansourah, tell us that 2,000 horsemen galloped into the place, sword in hand, and surprised Fakho'ddin Othman, commonly called Ibn Saif, the Moslem general, and one of the principal Mameluke Emirs, in the bath, and barbarously cut him to pieces as he was painting his beard before a glass. But the impetuous courage of the Count d'Artois and the Templars had led them far away from the support of the main body of the army, and their horsemen became embarrassed in the narrow streets of Mansourah, where there was no room to charge or manœuvre with effect. The infidels rallied; they returned to the attack with vast re-enforcements; the inhabitants of the town mounted to their house-tops, and discharged stones and brickbats upon the heads of the Christian knights, and the Templars were defeated and driven out of the city with dreadful carnage. "The Count d'Artois and the Earl of Leicester were there slain, and as many as three hundred other knights. The Templars lost, as their chief informed me, full fourteen score men-at-arms, and all their horsemen." The Grand Master of the Temple, De Sonnac, also lost an eye, and cut his way through the infidels to the main body of the Christian army, accompanied only by two Knights Templars. There he again mixed in the affray, took the command of a vanguard, and is to be found fighting by the side of the Lord de Joinville at sunset.

At the close of the long and bloody day, the Christians regained their camp in safety. King Louis, Joinville, and the Grand Master of the Temple, De Sonnac, had been fighting side by side during a great part of the afternoon. Joinville had his horse killed under him, and performed prodigies of valor. He was severely wounded, and on retiring to his quarters he found that a magnificent tent had been sent to him by the Grand Master of the Temple, as a testimony of regard and esteem. On the first Friday in Lent, Bendocdar, the great Mameluke general and lieutenant of the Sultan of Egypt, advanced at the head of a vast army of horse and foot to attack the Crusaders in their intrenchments. King Louis drew out his army in battle array, and posted them in eight divisions in front of the camp. The Templars, under their venerable Grand Master, De Sonnac, formed the fourth division; and the fate of their gallant chieftain is thus described by the Lord de Joinville: "The next battalion was under the command of William de Sonnac, Master of the Temple, who had with him the small remnant of the brethren of his Order who survived the battle of Shrove Tuesday. The Master of the Temple made of the engines which he had taken from the Saracens a sort of rampart in his front; but when the Saracens marched up to the assault, they threw Greek fire upon it, and as the Templars had piled up many planks of fir-wood amongst these engines they caught fire immediately; and the Saracens perceiving that the brethren of the Temple were few in number, dashed through the burning timbers, and vigorously attacked them.   In the preceding battle of Shrove Tuesday, William, the Grand Master of the Temple, lost one of his eyes; and in this battle the said lord lost his other eye, and was slain.   God have mercy on his soul!   And know that immediately behind the place where the battalion of the Templars stood, there was a good acre of ground so covered with darts, arrows, and missiles, that you could not see the earth beneath them, such showers of these had been discharged against the Templars by the Saracens."

The command over the surviving brethren of the Order now devolved upon the Marshal, Reginald de Vichier, who, collecting together the small surviving remnant of the Templars, retreated to the camp to participate in the subsequent horrors and misfortunes of the campaign.   "At the end of eight or ten days," says Joinville, "the bodies of those who had been slain and thrown into the Nile rose to the top of the water.   These bodies floated down the river until they came to the small bridge that communicated with each part of our army; the arch was so low that it prevented the bodies from passing underneath, and the river was consequently covered with them from bank to bank, so that the water could not be seen.   God knows how great was the stench.   I never heard that any who were exposed to this infectious smell ever recovered their health.   The whole army was seized with a shocking disorder, which dried up the flesh on our legs to the bone; and our skins became tanned as the ground, or like an old boot that has long lain behind a coffer.   The barbers were forced to cut away very large pieces of flesh from the gums to enable their patients to eat; it was pitiful to hear the cries and groans, they were like the cries of women in labor."

1249.   The army attempted to retreat when retreat was almost impossible; the soldiers became dispersed and scattered.   Thousands died by the way-side, and thousands fell alive into the hands of the enemy, among which last were the King and Joinville.

They were both attacked by the disease; and King Louis laid himself down to die in an Arab hut, where he was found and kindly treated by the Saracens.   Reginald de Vichier, the Marshal of the Templars, and a few of his brethen, reached Damietta in safety, and took measures for the defense of the place.   All those of the prisoners who were unable to redeem their lives by services as slaves to the conquerors, or by ransom, were inhumanly massacred, and a grim circle of Christian heads decorated the walls and battlements of Cairo.   The Egyptians required as the price of the liberty of the French monarch, the surrender of all the fortresses of the Order of the Temple in Palestine; but the King told them that the Templars were not subject to his command, nor had he any means of compelling them to give effect to such an agreement. Louis and his friend Joinville at last obtained their deliverance from captivity by the surrender of Damietta, and by the payment of two hundred thousand pieces of gold ; and the liberation of the King's brother, and of the other captive nobles and knights was to be purchased by the payment of a similar sum.   The King immediately went on board the French fleet which was at anchor before Damietta, and exerted himself to raise the residue of the ransom ; and all Saturday and Sunday were employed in collecting it together.

"On Sunday evening," says Joinville, "the king's servants, who were occupied in counting out the money, sent to say that there was a deficiency of thirty thousand livres.   I observed to the King that we had better ask the Commander and Marshal of the Temple, since the Grand Marshal was dead, to give us the thirty thousand livres.   Brother Stephen d'Otricourt, Knight Commander of the Temple, hearing the advice I gave to the King, said to me, 'Lord de Joinville, the counsel you give the King is not right nor reasonable, for you know that we receive every farthing of our money on our oaths;' and Brother Reginald de Vichier, who was Marshal of the Temple, said to the King, 'Sire, it is as our Commander has said, we cannot dispose of any of the money intrusted to us but for the means intended, in accordance with the rules of our institution, without being perjured.   Know that the seneschal hath ill advised you to take our money by force, but in this you will act as you please ; should you, however, do so, *we will make ourselves amends out of the money you have in Acre.*'   I then told the King that if he wished I would go and get the money, and he commanded me so to do.   I instantly went on board one of the galleys of the Templars, and demanded of the treasurer the keys of a coffer which I saw before me.   They refused, and I was about to break it open with a wedge in the king's name, when the Marshal, observing I was in earnest, ordered the keys to be given to me.   I opened the coffer, took out the sum wanting, and carried it to the King, who was much rejoiced at my return."   King Louis returned with the Templars to Palestine ; and was received with great distinction by the Order at Acre, where he remained four years, until A.D. 1253.

HELM, WITH NASAL—12TH CENTURY.

CHAPTER V.

TO THE CLOSE OF THE CHRISTIAN OCCUPATION OF PALESTINE.

WHERE purer streams through happier valleys flow,
And sweeter flowers on holier mountains blow,
I love to walk,—where Gilead sheds her balm.
I love to walk on Jordan's banks of palm;
I love to wet my foot in Hermon's dews,
I love the promptings of Isaiah's muse;
In Carmel's holy grots I court repose,
And deck my mossy couch with Sharon's deathless rose.

  Fallen is thy throne, O Israel!
   Silence is o'er thy plains,
  Thy dwellings all lie desolate,
   Thy children weep in chains.
  Where are the dews that fed thee
   On Etham's barren shore?
  That fire from heaven that led thee,
   Now lights thy path no more.

IN the year 1251 a general chapter of Knights Templars being assembled in the Pilgrim's Castle, the Marshal, REGINALD DE VICHIER, who had commanded with great skill and prudence in Egypt after the death of Grand Master William de Sonnac, was chosen to fill the vacant dignity of Grand Master. Henry III., King of England, had assumed the Cross shortly after intelligence had been conveyed to England of the horrors and atrocities committed by the Kharizmians in the Holy City. Year after year he had promised to fulfill his vow, and the Pope issued numerous bulls, providing for the tranquillity and security of his dominions during his absence, and ordered prayers to be offered up to God for the success of his arms, in all the churches of Christendom. King Henry assembled a parliament to obtain the necessary supplies, and fixed the 24th day of **1255.** June as the period of his departure. His Knights and Barons, however, refused him the necessary funds, and the needy monarch addressed the military Orders of the Temple and the Hospital in the following very curious letter: "As you are said to possess a well-equipped fleet, we beseech you to set apart for our own use some of your strongest vessels, and have them furnished and equipped with provisions, sailors, and all things requisite for a twelvemonth's voyage, so that we may be able, ere the period for our own departure arrives, to freight them with the soldiers, arms, horses, and munitions of war that we intend to send to the succor of the Holy Land. You will also be pleased to provide secure habitations and suitable accommodation for the said soldiers and their equipage, until the period of our own arrival. You will then be good enough to send back the same vessels to England to conduct ourselves and suit to Palestine; and by your prompt obedience to these our commands, we shall judge of your devotion to the interests of the Holy Land, and of your attachment to our person."

1255. The French King, Louis IX., in the meantime assisted the Templars in repairing the fortifications of Joppa and Cæsarea. The Lord de Joinville, who was with him, tells us that the Sheik of the Assassins, who still continued to pay tribute to the Templars, sent embassadors to the King to obtain a remission of the tribute. He gave them an audience, and declared that he would consider of their proposal. "When they came again before the King," says Joinville, "it was about vespers, and they found the Grand Master of the Temple (De Vichier) on one side of him and the Grand Master of the Hospital (De Chateauneuf) on the other. The embassadors refused to repeat what they had said in the morning, but the Masters of the Temple and the Hospital commanded them so to do. Then the Grand Masters of the Temple and Hospital told them that their lord had very foolishly and impudently sent such a message to the King of France, and had they not been invested with the character of embassadors they would have thrown them into the filthy sea of Acre, and have drowned them in despite of their master. 'And we command you,' continued the Grand Masters, 'to return to your lord and to come back within fifteen days with such letters from your prince that the King shall be contented with him and with you.'" The embassadors accordingly did as they were bid, and brought back from their sheik a shirt, the symbol of friendship, and a great variety of rich presents—crystal elephants, pieces of amber, with borders of pure gold, etc., etc. "You must know that when the embassadors opened the case containing all these fine things the whole apartment was instantly embalmed with the odor of their sweet perfumes."

1254.   The treaty entered into in 1249, between King Louis and the infidels, having been violated by the murder of the sick at Damietta, and by the detention, in a state of slavery, of many knights and soldiers, as well as of a large body of Christian children, the Templars recommenced hostilities, and marched with Joinville and the French Knights against the strong castle of Banias, and after an obstinate resistance, carried the place sword in hand. The Sultan of Damascus immediately took the field; he stormed the Temple fort Dok, slaughtered the garrison, and razed the fortifications to the ground. The castle of Ricordane shared the same fate, and the city of Sidon was taken by assault whilst the workmen and artificers were diligently employed in rebuilding the walls; 800 men were put to the sword, and 400 masons and artificers were taken prisoners and carried off to Damascus. After residing nearly two years at Acre, and spending vast sums of money upon the defenses of the maritime towns of Palestine, King Louis IX. returned to France. He set sail from Acre on the 24th of April, with a fleet of fourteen sail, his ship being steered by Brother Rèmond, the pilot of the Grand Master of the Temple, De Vichier, who was charged to conduct the King across the wide water in safety to his own dominions. On his arrival in France, Louis manifested his esteem for the Templars by granting them the château and lordship of Bazèes, near Bauvez, in Aquitaine. The deed of gift is expressed to be made in consideration of the charitable works which the King had seen performed amongst the Templars, and in acknowledgment of the services they had rendered to him, and to the intent that he might be made a participator in the good works done by the fraternity, and be remembered in the prayers of the brethren. This deed was delivered on the Day of Pentecost to Brother Hugh, Grand Preceptor of Aquitaine, in the cathedral church of Angouleme, in the presence of numerous archbishops, bishops, counts, and barons.

1254. At the period of the return of the King of France to Europe, Henry III., King of England, was in Gascony, with Robert de Sanford, Master of the Temple at London, who had been previously sent by the English monarch into that province to appease the troubles which had there broken out. King Henry proceeded to the French capital, and was magnificently entertained by the Knights Templars at their Temple in Paris, which Matthew Paris tells us was of such immense extent that it could contain within its precincts a numerous army. The day after his arrival King Henry ordered an innumerable quantity of poor people to be regaled at the Temple with meat, fish, bread, and wine; and at a later hour the King of France and all his nobles came to dine with the English monarch. "Never," says Matthew Paris, "was there at any period in bygone times so noble and so celebrated an entertainment. They feasted in the great hall of the Temple, where hang the shields on every side, as many as they can place along the four walls, according to the custom of the Order beyond sea." The Knights Templars in this country likewise exercised a magnificent hospitality, and constantly entertained kings, princes, nobles, prelates, and foreign embassadors at the Temple. Immediately after the return of King Henry to England some illustrious embassadors from Castile came on a visit to the Temple at London; and as the King "greatly delighted to honor them," he commanded three pipes of wine to be placed in the cellars of the Temple for their use, and ten fat bucks to be brought them at the same place from the royal forest in Essex. He, moreover, commanded the Mayor and Sheriffs of London, and the commonalty of the same city, to take with them a respectable assemblage of the citizens and to go forth and meet the said embassadors without the city, and courteously receive them, and honor them, and conduct them to the Temple.

During the first and second years of the pontificate of Pope Alexander IV., A.D. 1254–'55, ten bulls were published in favor of the Templars, addressed to the bishops of the church universal, commanding them to respect and maintain the privileges conceded to them by the holy see; to judge and punish all persons who should dare to exact tithe from the fraternity; to institute to the ecclesiastical benefices of the Order all clerks presented to them by the preceptors, without previously requiring them to make a fixed maintenance for such clerks, and severely to punish all who appropriated to their own use the alms, gifts, and eleemosynary donations made to the brotherhood. By these bulls the Templars are declared to be exempt from the duty of contributing to the traveling expenses of all nuncios and legates of the holy see, under the dignity of a cardinal, when passing through their territories, unless express orders to the contrary are given by apostolic letters, and all the bishops are required earnestly and vigorously to protect and defend the right of sanctuary accorded to the houses of the Temple.

1257. In the year 1257, Reginald de Vichier, the Grand Master of the Temple, fell sick and died, at an advanced age. He was succeeded by the English Knight Templar, THOMAS BERARD. Shortly after his election the terrible Moguls and Tartars, those fierce vagrant tribes of shepherds and hunters whose victorious arms had spread terror and desolation over the greater part of Europe and Asia, invaded Palestine, under the command of the famous Holagou, and spread themselves like a cloud of devouring locusts over the whole country. The Templars, under the command of Etienne de Sisi, Grand Preceptor of Apulia, hastened to meet them and were cut to pieces in a sanguinary fight. The Tartars besieged and took the rich and populous cities of Aleppo, Hamah, Hums, Damascus, Tiberias, and Nablous, and at last entered in triumph the holy city of Jerusalem. The Grand Master, Thomas Berard, wrote a melancholy letter to King Henry III. for succor. "With continual letters and many prayers," says he, 'has our poor Christianity on this side the sea besought the assistance of the kings and princes of this world, and above all the aid and succor of your majesty, imploring your royal compassion with sighs and tears and a loud sounding voice, and crying out with a bitter cry in the hope that it would penetrate the royal ear, and reach the ends of the earth, and arouse the faithful from their slumbers, and draw them to the protection of the Holy Land." The King of England, however, was in pecuniary embarrassments, and unable to afford the necessary succor. He was reduced, indeed, to the cruel necessity of borrowing money in France upon the security of his regalia and crown jewels, which were deposited in the Temple at Paris, as appears from the letter of the Queen of France " to her very dear brother Henry, the illustrious King of England," giving a long list of golden wands, golden combs, diamond buckles, chaplets and circlets, golden crowns, imperial beavers, rich girdles, golden peacocks, and rings innumerable, adorned with sapphires, rubies, emeralds, topazes, and carbuncles, which she says she had inspected in the presence of the Treasurer of the Temple at Paris, and that the same were safely deposited in the coffers of the Templars.

1260. In the meantime the Mamelukes, " who had breathed in their infancy the keenness of a Scythian air," advanced from the banks of the Nile to contend with the Tartars for the dominion of Palestine. Under the command of Bendocdar, the Mameluke general, they gained a complete victory over them in the neighborhood of Tiberias, and drove back the stream of hostility to the eastward of the Euphrates. Bendocdar returned to Egypt the idol of his soldiers, and clothed with a popularity which rendered him too powerful for a subject. He aspired to the possession of the throne which he had so successfully defended, and slew with his own hand his sovereign and master Kothuz, the third Mameluke Sultan of Egypt. The Mamelukes hailed him with accla-**1260.** mations as their sovereign, and on the 24th day of October he was solemnly proclaimed Sultan of Egypt, in the town of Salahieh in the Delta. Bendocdar was one of the greatest men of the age, and soon proved the most formidable enemy that the Templars had encountered in the field since the days of Saladin. The first two years of his accession to power were employed in the extension and consolidation of his sway over the adjoining Mussulman countries. The holy cities of Mecca and Medina acknowledged him for their sovereign, as did Damascus, Aleppo, Hums, and Jerusalem. His sway extended over Egypt, Nubia, Arabia, and Syria; and his throne was defended by twenty-five thousand Mameluke cavalry. His power was further strengthened by an army of one hundred and seven thousand foot, and by the occasional aid of sixty-six thousand Arabians.

After receiving the homage and submission of the rulers and people of Aleppo, Bendocdar made a hostile demonstration against the vast and wealthy city of Antioch; but finding the place well defended, he retired with his army, by way of Hums, **1264.** Damascus, and Tiberias, to Egypt. The next year he crossed the desert at the head of thirty thousand cavalry, and overran all Palestine up to the very gates of Acre. He burned the great churches of Nazareth and Mount Tabor; and sought to awaken the zeal and enthusiasm of his soldiers in behalf of Islam by performing the pilgrimage to Jerusalem, and visiting with great devotion the Mosk of Omar. He then retired to Cairo with his troops, and the Templars and Hospitalers became the assailants. They surprised and stormed the Castle of Lilion, razed the walls and fortifications to the ground, and brought off three hundred prisoners of both sexes, together with a rich prize of sheep and oxen. On the 15th of June, 1264, they marched as far as Ascalon, surprised and slew two Mameluke emirs, and put twenty-eight of their followers to the sword. They then turned their footsteps towards the Jordan, and on the fifth of November they destroyed Bethshean, and laid waste with fire and sword all the valley of the Jordan, as far as the Lake of Tiberias.

1265. In the depth of winter, Bendocdar collected his forces together, and advanced by rapid marches, from Egypt. He concealed his real intentions, made a long march during the night, and at morning's dawn presented himself before the city of Cæsarea. His troops descended into the ditch by means of ropes and ladders, and climbed the walls with the aid of iron hooks and spikes. They burst open the gates, massacred the sentinels, and planted the standard of the prophet on the ramparts, ere the inhabitants had time to rouse themselves from their morning slumbers. The citadel, however, still remained to be taken, and the garrison being forewarned, made an obstinate defense. The Arabian writers tell us, that the citadel was a strong and handsome fortification, erected by King Louis IX., and adorned with pillars and columns. It stood on a small neck of land which jutted out into the sea, and the ditches around the fortress were filled with the blue waters of the Mediterranean. Bendocdar planted huge catapults and cross-bows upon the tower of the cathedral and shot arrows, darts, and stones, from them upon the battlements of the citadel. He encouraged the exertions of his soldiers by promises of reward, and gave robes of honor to his principal emirs. Weapons of war were distributed in the most lavish manner, every captain of a hundred horse receiving for the use of himself and his men *four thousand arrows !*

1265. During a dark winter's night the garrison succeeded in making their escape, and the next morning the Moslems poured into the citadel by thousands, and abandoned themselves to pillage. The fortifications were leveled with the dust, and Bendocdar assisted with his own hands in the work of demolition. He then detached some Mameluke emirs with a body of cavalry against Caifa, and proceeded himself to watch the movements of the Templars, and examine into the defenses of the Pilgrim's Castle at Athlit. Finding the place almost impregnable, and defended by a numerous garrison, he suddenly retraced his steps to the south, and stormed, after a brave and obstinate defense, the strongly fortified city of Arsoof, near Joppa, which belonged to the Knights Hospitalers of St. John. The greater part of the garrison was massacred, but one thousand captives were reserved to grace the triumph of the conqueror. They were compelled to march at the head of his triumphal procession, with their banners reversed, and with their crosses, broken into pieces, hung round their necks. Bendocdar had already despatched his bravest Mameluke generals, at the head of a considerable body of forces, to blockade Beaufort and Safed, two strong fortresses of the Order of the Temple, and he now advanced at the head of a vast army to conduct the siege of the latter place in person. On the 21st

Ramadan, the separate timbers of his military machines arrived from Damascus at Jacob's Bridge on the Jordan; the Sultan sent down his emirs and part of his army, with hundreds of oxen, to drag them up the mountains to Safed, and went with his principal officers to assist in the transport of them. "I worked by the Sultan's side, and aided him with all my might," says the Cadi Mohieddin; "being fatigued, I sat down. I began again, and was once more tired, and compelled to take rest, but the Sultan continued to work without intermission, aiding in the transport of beams, bolts, and huge frames of timber." The Grand Master of the Temple, Thomas Berard, ordered out twelve hundred cavalry from Acre to create a diversion in favor of the besieged, but a treacherous spy conveyed intelligence to Bendocdar, which enabled him to surprise and massacre the whole force, and return to Safed with their heads stuck on the lances of his soldiers. At last, after an obstinate defense, during which many Moslem, say the Arabian writers, obtained the crown of martyrdom, the huge walls were thrown down, and a breach was presented to the infidels; but that breach was so stoutly guarded that none could be found to mount to the assault. Bendocdar offered a reward of three hundred pieces of gold to the first man who entered the city. He distributed robes of honor and riches to all who were foremost in the fight, and the outer inclosure, or first line of the fortifications was, at last, taken.

1265. The Templars retired into the citadel, but their efforts at defense were embarrassed by the presence of a crowd of two thousand fugitives, who had fled to Safed for shelter, and they agreed to capitulate on condition that the lives and liberties of the Christians should be respected, and that they should be transported in safety to Acre. Bendocdar acceded to these terms, and solemnly promised to fulfill them; but as soon as he had got the citadel into his power, he offered to all the Templars the severe alternative of the Koran or death, and gave them until the following morning to make their election. The preceptor of Safed, a holy monk and veteran warrior, assisted by two Franciscan friars, passed the night in pious exhortations to his brethren, conjuring them to prefer the crown of martyrdom to a few short years of miserable existence in this sinful world, and not to disgrace themselves and their Order by a shameful apostasy. At sunrise, on the following morning, the Templars were led on to the brow of the hill, in front of the Castle of Safed, and when the first rays of the rising sun gilded the wooded summits of Mount Hermon, and the voice of the muezzin was heard calling the faithful to morning prayer, they were required to join in the Moslem chant, *La-i-la i-la Allah, Mahommed rou soul, Allah* ("There is no God but God, and Mohammed is his prophet"); the executioners drew near with their naked scimitars, but not a man of the noble company of knightly warriors, say the Christian writers, would renounce his faith, and one thousand five hundred heads speedily rolled at the feet of Bendocdar. "The blood," says Sanutus, "flowed down the declivities like a rivulet of water." The Preceptor of Safed, the priests of the Order, and Brother Jeremiah, were beaten with clubs, flayed alive, and then beheaded. The Arabian writers state that the lives of two of the garrison were spared, one being an Hospitaler whom the besieged had sent to Bendocdar to negotiate the treaty of surrender, and the other a Templar, named *Effreez Lyoub,* who embraced the Mohammedan faith, and was circumcised and entered into the service of the Sultan. Immediately after the fall of Safed, the infidels stormed the castles of Hounin and Tibnin, and took possession of the city of Ramleh, near Joppa.

1266. The Grand Master of the Hospital, Hugh de Revel, now sued for peace, and entered into a separate treaty with the infidels. He agreed to renounce the ancient tribute of one hundred pieces of gold paid to the Order by the district of Bouktyr; also the annual tribute of four thousand pieces of gold paid to them by the Sultans of Hums and Hamah; a tribute of twelve hundred pieces of gold, fifty thousand bushels of wheat, and fifty thousand bushels of barley annually rendered to them by the Assassins or Ismaelians of the mountains of Tripoli; and the several tributes paid by the cities or districts of Schayzar, Apamea, and Aintab, which consisted of five hundred crowns of Tyrian silver, two measures of wheat, and two pieces of silver for every two head of oxen pastured in the district. These terms being arranged, the

Emir Fakir-eddin, and the Cadi Schams-eddin were sent to receive the oath of the Grand Master of the Hospital to fulfill them, and a truce was then accorded him for ten years, ten days, and ten months.

1266. Bendocdar then concentrated his forces together at Aleppo, and marched against the Christian province of Armenia. The Prince of Hamah blockaded Darbesak, which was garrisoned by the Knights Templars, and forced the mountain passes leading into the ancient Cilicia. The Moslems then marched with incredible rapidity to Sis, the capital of the country, which fell into their hands after a short siege. Leon, King of Armenia, was led away into captivity, together with his uncle, his son and his nephew; many others of the royal family were killed, and some made their escape. All the castles of the Templars in Armenia were assaulted and taken, and the garrisons massacred. The most famous of these was the Castle of Amoud, which was stormed after an obstinate defense, and every soul found in it was put to the sword. The city of Sis was pillaged, and then delivered up to the flames; the inhabitants of all the towns were either massacred or reduced to slavery; their goods and possessions were divided amongst the soldiers, and the Moslems returned to Aleppo laden with booty and surrounded by captives fastened together with ropes. Great was the joy of Bendocdar. The musicians were ordered to play, and the dancing girls to beat the tambour and dance before him. He made a triumphant entry into Damascus, preceded by his royal captives and many thousand prisoners bound with chains. "Thus did the Sultan," says the Arabian historian, "cut the sugar-canes of the Franks!"

1267. On the 1st of May Bendocdar collected together a strong body of cavalry, divided them into two bodies, and caused them to mount the banners and emblems of the Hospital and Temple. By this ruse he attempted to penetrate the east gate of Acre, but the cheat was fortunately discovered, and the gates were closed ere the Arab cavalry reached them. The infidels then slaughtered five hundred people outside the walls, cut off their heads and put them into sacks. Amongst them were some poor old women who gained a livelihood by gathering herbs! The ferocious Mamelukes then pulled down all the houses and windmills, plucked up the vines, cut down all the fruit-trees and burnt them, and filled up the wells. Some deputies, sent to sue for peace, were introduced to Bendocdar through a grim and ghastly avenue of Christian heads planted on the points of lances, and their petition was rejected with scorn and contempt. "The neighing of our horses," said the ferocious Sultan, "shall soon strike you with deafness, and the dust raised by their feet shall penetrate to the inmost chambers of your dwellings."

1268. On the 7th of March, the Sultan stormed Joppa, put the garrison to the sword, set fire to the churches, and burnt the crucifixes and crosses and holy relics of the saints. "He took away the head of St. George and burnt the body of St. Christina," and then marched against the strongly fortified city of Beaufort, near Bethshean, which belonged to the Order of the Temple. Twenty-six enormous military engines were planted around the walls, and the doctors of the law and the *Fakirs*, or teachers of religion, were invited to repair to the Moslem camp, and wield the sword in behalf of Islam. The town was defended by two citadels, the ancient and the new one. The former was garrisoned by the Templars, and the latter by the native militia. These last, after sustaining a short siege, set fire to their post and fled during the night. "As for the other citadel," says the Cadi Mohieddin, "it made a long and vigorous defense," and Bendocdar, after losing the flower of his army before the place, was reluctantly compelled to permit the garrison to march out, sword in hand, with all the honors of war. The fortress was then razed to the ground so effectually that not a trace of it was left.

1268. The Sultan now separated his army into several divisions, which were all sent in different directions through the principality of Tripoli to waste and destroy. All the churches and houses were set on fire; the trees were cut down, and the inhabitants were led away into captivity. A tower of the Templars, in the environs of Tripoli, was taken by assault, and every soul found in it was put to death. The different divisions of the army were then concentrated at Hums, to collect together and to divide their spoil. They were then again separated into three corps, which

Concentrated Attack of the Turks upon the City of Antioch.

were sent by different routes against the vast and wealthy city of Antioch, the ancient " Queen of Syria." The first division was directed to take a circuitous route by way of Darbesak, and approach Antioch from the north; the second was to march upon Suadìa, and to secure the mouth of the Orontes, to prevent all succor from reaching the city by sea; and the third and last division, which was led by Bendocdar in person, proceeded to Apamea, and from thence marched down the left bank of the River Orontes along the base of the ancient Mons Casius, so as to approach and hem in Antioch from the south. On the 1st *Ramadan,* all these different divisions were concentrated together, and the city was immediately surrounded by a vast army of horse and foot, which cut off all communication between the town and the surrounding country, and exposed a population of 160,000 souls to all the horrors of famine. The famous stone bridge of nine arches, which spanned the Orontes, and communicated between the city and the right bank of the river, was immediately attacked; the iron doors which guarded the passage were burst open with battering-rams, and the standard of the prophet was planted beneath the great western gate. The Templars of the principality, under the command of their Grand Preceptor, made a vain effort to drive back the infidels and relieve the city. They sallied out of the town, with the constable of Antioch, but were defeated by the Mameluke cavalry, after a sharp encounter in the plain, and were compelled to take refuge behind the walls.

1268. For three days successively did the Sultan vainly summon the city to surrender, and for three days did he continue his furious assaults. On the fourth day, the Moslem scaled the walls where they touch the side of the mountain. They rushed across the ramparts, sword in hand, into the city, and a hundred thousand Christians are computed to have been slain. About eight thousand soldiers, accompanied by a dense throng of women and children, fled from the scene of carnage to the citadel, and there defended themselves with the energy of despair. Bendocdar granted them their lives, and they surrendered. They were bound with cords, and the long string of mournful captives passed in review before the Sultan, who caused the scribes and notaries to take down the names of each of them.   After several days of pillage, all the booty was brought together in the plain of Antioch, and equally divided amongst the Moslem.   The gold and silver were distributed by measure, and merchandise and property of all kinds, piled up in heaps, were drawn for by lot.   The captive women and girls were distributed amongst the soldiery, and they were so numerous that each of the slaves of the conquerors was permitted to have a captive at his disposal.   The Sultan halted for several weeks in the plain, and permitted his soldiers to hold a large market, or fair, for the sale of their booty.   This market was attended by Jews and peddlers from all parts of the East, who greedily bought up the rich property and costly valuables of the poor citizens of Antioch.

1268.   These last might have borne with fortitude the loss of their worldly possessions, and the luxuries of this life, but when they were themselves put up to auction—when the mother saw her infant child handed over to the avaricious Jew for the paltry sum of five pieces of silver, and sold into irredeemable bondage, the bitter cries that resounded through the plain, touched even the hearts of the Moslem.   " It was," says the Cadi Mohieddin, " a fearful and a heartrending sight.   Even the hard stones were softened with grief."   He tells us that the captives were so numerous, that a fine hearty boy might be purchased for *twelve* pieces of silver, and a little girl for *five!*   When the work of pillage had been completed, when all the ornaments and decorations had been carried away from the churches, and the lead torn from the roofs, Antioch was fired in different places, amid the loud thrilling shouts of ALLAH HU ACHBAR (" GOD *is* GREATER !")   The great churches of St. Paul and St. Peter burnt with terrific fury for many days, and the vast and venerable city was left without a habitation, and without an inhabitant !

1268.   Thus fell Antioch, one hundred and seventy years after its recovery, A.D. 1098, from the dominion of the infidels by the Crusaders, under the command of the valiant Godfrey, Bohemond, Tancred, and others.   Near six centuries of Moslem domination have now again rolled over the ancient Queen of the East, but the genius of destruction which accompanied the footsteps of the armies of the ferocious Bendocdar has ever since presided over the

Desolation of Antioch. The Christian Army completely destroyed.

spot. The once fair and flourishing capital of Syria, the ancient "throne of the successors of Alexander, the seat of Roman government in the East, which had been decorated by Cæsar with the titles of *free*, and *holy*, and *inviolate*," is, at this day, nothing more than a miserable mud village. The ancient and illustrious Church of Antioch, which, in the Fourth Century of the Christian era, numbered one hundred thousand persons, now consists only of a few Greek families, who still cling to the Christian faith amid the insults and persecutions of the infidels. Immediately after the destruction of the city, Bendocdar caused the following letter to be written to the Prince of Antioch, who was at Tripoli: "Since not a soul has escaped to tell you what has happened, we will undertake the pleasing task of informing you. We have slain all whom you appointed to defend Antioch. We have crushed your knights beneath the feet of our horses, and have given up your provinces to pillage. Your gold and silver have been divided amongst us by the quintal, and four of your women have been bought and sold for a crown. There is not a single Christian in the province that does not.now march bound before us, nor a single young girl that is not in our possession. Your churches have been made level with the dust, and our chariot-wheels have passed over the sites of your dwellings. If you had seen the temples of your God destroyed, the Crosses broken, and the leaves of the Gospel torn and scattered to the winds of heaven; if you had seen your Mussulman enemy marching into your tabernacles, and immolating upon your shrines and your altars, the priest, the deacon, and the bishop; if you had seen your palaces delivered to the flames, and the bodies of the dead consumed by the fire of this world, whilst their souls were burning in the everlasting *fire of* HELL; doubtless, you would have exclaimed, *Lord, I am become but as dust;* your soul would have been ready to start from its earthly tenement, and your eyes would have rained down tears sufficient to have extinguished the fires that we have kindled around you."

1268. On the fall of Antioch the Templars abandoned Bagras, a rich and flourishing town on the road to Armenia and Cilicia, which had belonged to the Order for more than a century. This town of the Templars, Mohieddin tells us, had long been a source of intense anxiety and annoyance to the Moslems. "Over and over again," says he, "it had been attacked, but the Templars foiled the utmost efforts of the faithful, until, at last, Providence gave it into our hands." The Templars also abandoned the castles of Gaston and Noche de Rusol, and the territory of Port Bounel, at the entrance of Armenia. The towns of Darbesak, Sabah, Al Hadid, and the sea-port of Gebar, successively fell into the hands of Bendocdar, and the whole country from Tripoli to Mount Taurus was made desolate, the houses were set on fire, the fruit-trees were cut down, and the churches were leveled with the dust. The wealthy and populous maritime towns of Laodicea, Tripoli, Tortosa, Beyrout, Tyre, and Sidon, however, still remained to the Christians; and as these cities were strongly fortified, and the Christian fleets kept the command of the sea, Bendocdar postponed their destruction for a brief period, and granted separate truces to them in consideration of the payment of large sums of money.

1269. In the year 1269, a terrible famine, consequent upon the ravages of the infidels, afflicted Syria and Palestine, and many of those whom the sword had spared, now died of hunger. Louis IX., King of France, being deeply affected by the intelligence of the misfortunes of the Latin Christians, attended an assembly of Preceptors of the Temple in France, to devise means of forwarding succor to the Holy Land, and caused a quantity of corn to be sent from Languedoc to Palestine. He moreover determined to embark in the Eighth Crusade, and induced prince Edward of England to assume the Cross, and prepare to join his standard. Bendocdar, on the other hand, returned from Egypt to Palestine. He surprised and cut to pieces several bands of Christians, and made his public entry into Damascus, preceded by many hundred ghastly heads stuck on the points of lances, and by a vast number of weeping captives of both sexes, and of every age. He then proceeded to Hamah and Kafarthab, and attempted to undertake the siege of the strong fortress of Merkab, but the winter rains and the snow on the mountain compelled him to abandon the enterprise. He then made an attack upon the castle of the Kurds, which belonged to the Hospitalers, but receiving intelligence of the sailing of the expedition of King Louis IX., who had left the ports of France with an army of sixty thousand men, and a fleet of eighteen hundred vessels, he hurried with all his forces to Egypt to protect that country against the French. Instead of proceeding direct to the Holy Land, King Louis was unfortunately **1270.** induced to steer to Tunis. There he fell a victim to the insalubrity of the climate, and his army, decimated by sickness, sailed back to France. Bendocdar immediately returned to Palestine. He halted at Ascalon, and completed the destruction of the fortifications of that place. He stormed Castel Blanc (*Blanchegarde*, the ancient Gath), a fortress of the Templars, and appeared with his Mameluke cavalry before the gates of Tripoli. He ravaged the surrounding country, and then retired into winter quarters, leading away many Christian prisoners of both sexes into captivity. The next year he stormed the fortified town of Safitza, and laid siege to Hassan el Akrad, or the castle of the Kurds. His vic- **1271.** torious career was checked by the arrival of Prince Edward of England, who joined Thomas Berard, Grand Master of the Temple at the head of a welcome reinforcement of knights and foot-soldiers. Various successes were then obtained over the infidels, and on the 21st *Ramadan* (April 23d, A. D. 1272), a truce was agreed upon for the space of ten years and ten months, as far as regarded the town and plain of Acre, and the road to Nazareth.

1272. On the 18th of June, Prince Edward was stabbed with a poisoned dagger by an assassin. Though dangerously wounded, he struck the assailant to the ground, and caused him to be immediately despatched by the guards. The same day the prince made his will, dated at Acre, Thomas Berard, Grand Master of the Temple, appearing as an attesting witness. The life of the prince, however, was preserved, the effects of the poison being obviated by an antidote administered by the Grand Master of the Temple. On the 14th of September, the same year, the prince returned to Europe, *and thus terminated the last expedition undertaken for the relief of Palestine.* Whilst Prince Edward was pursuing his voyage to England, his father, King Henry III., died, and the council of the realm, composed of the Archbishops of Canterbury and York, and the English bishops and barons, assembled in the Temple at London, and swore allegiance to the Prince.   They there caused him to be proclaimed King of England, as Edward I., and, with the consent of the queen-mother, they appointed Walter Giffard, Archbishop of York, and the Earls of Cornwall and Gloucester, guardians of the realm.   Letters were written from the Temple to acquaint the young sovereign with the death of his father, and many of the acts of the new government emanated from the same place.

1273.   The Grand Master of the Temple, Thomas Berard, died at Acre on the 8th of April, and on the 13th of May the General Chapter of the Templars, being assembled in the Pilgrim's Castle at Athlit, chose for his successor WILLIAM DE BEAUJEU, Grand Preceptor of Apulia.   The late Vice-Master, William de Poucon, was sent to Europe with Bertrand de Fox, to announce to him the tidings of his elevation to the chief dignity of the Order.   The following year, 1274, William de Beaujeu, accompanied by the Grand Master of the Hospital, Hugh de Revel, proceeded to Lyons, to attend a General Council which had been summoned by the Pope to provide succor for the Holy Land.   The two Grand Masters took precedence of all the embassadors and peers present at that famous assembly.   It was determined that a new crusade should be preached, that all ecclesiastical dignities and benefices should be taxed to support an armament, and that the sovereigns of Europe should be compelled by ecclesiastical censures to suspend their private quarrels, and afford succor to the desolate land of promise.   More than a thousand bishops, archbishops, and embassadors from the different princes and potentates of Europe, graced the assembly with their presence.   From Lyons, the Grand Master William de Beaujeu proceeded to England, and called together a General Chapter of the Order at London.   Whilst resident at the Temple in that city, he received payment of a large sum of money, which the young King Edward had borrowed of the Templars during his stay at Acre.

1275.   Pope Gregory X. died in the midst of his exertions for the creation of another crusade.   The enthusiasm which had been partially awakened subsided.   Those who had assumed the Cross

Death of Bendocdar. Templars regain Possession of a few Places.

forgot their engagements, and the Grand Master of the Temple at last returned, in sorrow and disappointment, to the far East. He reached Acre on St. Michael's day, A. D. 1275, attended by a band of Templars, drawn from the preceptories of England and France. Shortly after his arrival Bendocdar was poisoned, and was succeeded by his son, Malek Said. Malek Said only mounted the throne to descend from it. He was deposed by the rebellious Mamelukes, and the scepter was grasped by Malek-Mansour-Kelaoun, the bravest and most distinguished of the emirs. As there was now no hope of recovering the towns, castles, and territories taken by Bendocdar, the Grand Master directed all his energies to the preservation of the few remaining possessions of the Christians in the Holy Land. At the expiration of the ten years' truce, he entered into various treaties with the infidels. One of these, called "the peace of Tortosa," is expressed to be made between Sultan Malek-Mansour-Kelaoun, and his son Malek-Saleh-Ali, "honor of the world and of religion," of the one part, and Afryz Dybadjouk (William de Beaujeu), Grand Master of the Order of the Templars, of the other part. It relates to the territories and possessions of the Order of the Temple at Tortosa, and provides for their security and freedom from molestation by the infidels. The truce is prolonged for ten years and ten months **1282.** from the date of the execution of the treaty, and the contracting parties strictly bind themselves to make no irruptions into each other's territories during the period. To prevent mistakes, the lands and villages, towers, corn-mills, gardens, brooks, and plantations, belonging to the Templars are specified and defined, together with the contiguous possessions of the Moslems. By this treaty, the Templars engage not to rebuild any of their citadels, towers, or fortresses, nor to cut any new ditch or fosse in their province of Tortosa.

Another treaty entered into between Grand Master William de Beaujeu and the enemy, is called the peace of Acre. It accords to the Christians, Caifa, and seven villages; the province of Mount Carmel, the town and citadel of Alelyet, the farms of the Hospitalers in the province of Cæsarea, the half of Alexandretta, the village of Maron, etc., and confirms the Templars in the possessions of Sidon and its citadel, and its fifteen cantons. By this treaty, Sultan Malek Mansour conceded to the inhabitants of Acre a truce of ten years, ten months, and ten days; and he swore to observe its provisions and stipulations in the presence of the Grand Master of the Temple and the Vizir Fadhad. But all these treaties were mere delusions. Bendocdar had commenced the ruin of the Christians, and Sultan Kelaoun now proceeded to complete it.

1286. The separate truces and treaties of peace which Bendocdar had accorded to the maritime towns of Palestine, in return for payments of money, were encumbered with so many minute provisions and stipulations, that it was almost impossible for the Christians to avoid breaking them in some trifling and unimportant particular; and Sultan Kelaoun soon found a colorable pretense for recommencing hostilities. He first broke with the Hospitalers, and stormed their strong fortress of Merkab, which commanded the coast-road from Laodicea to Tripoli. He then sought out a pretext for putting an end to the truce which the Count of Tripoli had purchased of Bendocdar by the payment of eleven thousand pieces of gold. He maintained that a watch-tower had been erected on the coast between Merkab and Tortosa, in contravention of the stipulation which forbade the erection of new fortifications; and he accordingly marched with his army to lay siege to the rich and flourishing city of Laodicea. The Arabian writers tell us that Laodicea was one of the most commercial cities of the Levant, and was considered to be the rival of Alexandria. A terrible earthquake, which had thrown down the fortifications, and overturned the castle at the entrance of the port, unfortunately facilitated the conquest of the place, and Laodicea fell almost without a struggle. The town was pillaged and set on fire, and those of the inhabitants who were unable to escape by sea, were either slaughtered or reduced to slavery, or driven out homeless wanderers from their dwellings, to perish with hunger and grief in the surrounding wilderness. Shortly after the fall of Laodicea, the castle of Krak, which belonged to the Hospitalers, was besieged and stormed; the garrison was put to the sword, and some other small places on the sea-coast met with a similar fate.

1287. On the 13th Moharran (9th of February), the Sultan

Terrible and complete Destruction of Tripoli.   Captivity of its Inhabitants.

marched against Tripoli at the head of ten thousand horse, and thirty-three thousand foot.   The separate timbers of nineteen enormous military engines were transported in many hundred wagons drawn by oxen ; and fifteen hundred engineers and fire-work manufacturers were employed to throw the terrible Greek fire and combustible materials, contained in brass pots, into the city.   After thirty-four days of incessant labor, the walls were undermined and thrown into the ditch, and the engineers poured an incessant stream of Greek fire upon the breach, whilst the Moslems below prepared a path for the cavalry.   John de Breband, Preceptor of the Temple at Tripoli, fought upon the ramparts with a few Knights and serving brethren of the Order ; but they were speedily overthrown, and the Arab cavalry dashed through the breach into the town.   Upwards of one thousand Christians fell by the sword, and the number of captives was incalculable.   Twelve hundred trembling women and children were crowded together for safety in a single magazine of arms, and the conquerors were embarrassed with the quantity of spoil and booty.   More than four thousand bales of the richest silks were distributed amongst the soldiers, together with ornaments and articles of luxury and refinement, which astonished the rude simplicity of the Arabs.   When the city had been thoroughly ransacked, orders were issued for its destruction.   Then the Moslem soldiers were to be seen rushing with torches and pots of burning naphtha to set fire to the churches, and the shops, and the warehouses of the merchants ; and Tripoli was speedily enveloped in one vast, fearful, wide-spreading conflagration.   The command for the destruction of the fortifications was likewise issued, and thousands of soldiers, stonemasons, and laborers were employed in throwing down the walls and towers.   The Arabian writers tell us that the ramparts were so wide that three horsemen could ride abreast upon them round the town.   Many of the inhabitants had escaped by sea during the siege, and crowds of fugitives fled before the swords of the Moslem, to take refuge on the little island of Saint Nicholas at the entrance of the port.   They were there starved to death, and when Abulfeda visited the island a few days after the fall of Tripoli, he found it covered with the dead bodies of the unburied

Christians. Thus fell Tripoli, with its commerce, its silk manufactories, churches, and public and private buildings. Everything that could contribute to prosperity in peace, or defense in war, perished beneath the sword, the hammer, and the pick-axe of the Moslem. In the time of the Crusaders, the port was crowded with the fleets of the Italian republics, and carried on a lucrative trade with Marseilles, Amalfi, Genoa, Pisa, Venice, and the cities of the Grecian islands; but the rich stream of commerce has never since revisited the inhospitable shore.

1288. Shortly after the fall of Tripoli, Gebal, Beyrout, and all the maritime towns and villages between Sidon and Laodicea, fell into the hands of the infidels, and Sultan Kelaoun was preparing to attack the vast and populous city of Acre, when death terminated his victorious career. He was succeeded, 1291, by his eldest son, Aschraf Khalil, who hastened to execute the war-like projects of his father. He assembled the ulemas and cadis around his father's tomb, and occupied himself in reading the Koran, in prayer, and invocation of Mohammed. He then made abundant almsgiving, collected his troops together, and marched across the desert to Damascus, where he was joined by Hosameddin Ladjin, viceroy of Syria, Modaffer, prince of Hums, and Saifeddin, Lord of Baalbec, with the respective forces under their command. Ninety-two enormous military engines had been constructed at Damascus, which were transported across the country by means of oxen; and in the spring of the year, after the winter rains had subsided, Sultan Khalil marched against Acre at the head of sixty thousand horse, and a hundred and forty thousand foot.

1291. After the loss of Jerusalem, A.D. 1187, the city of Acre became the metropolis of the Latin Christians, and was adorned with a vast cathedral, with numerous stately churches, and elegant buidings, and with aqueducts, and an artificial port. The houses of the rich merchants were decorated with pictures and choice pieces of sculpture, and boasted of the rare advantage of glass windows. An astonishing, and probably an exaggerated account has been given of the wealth and luxury of the inhabitants. We read of silken canopies and curtains stretched on cords to protect the lounger from the scorching sunbeams, of variegated marble fountains, and of rich gardens and shady groves, scented with the delicious orange-blossom, and adorned with the delicate almond-flower; and we are told that the markets of the city could offer the produce of every clime, and the interpreters of every tongue. The vast and stupendous fortifications consisted of a double wall, strengthened at proper intervals with lofty towers, and defended by the castle called the King's Tower, and by the convent or fortress of the Temple. Between the ramparts extended a large space of ground, covered with the chateaus, villas, and gardens of the nobility of Galilee, the Counts of Tripoli and Joppa, the Lords of Tyre and Sidon, the Papal Legate, the Duke of Athens, and the Princes of Antioch. The most magnificent edifices within the town were the Cathedral Church of St. Andrew, the Churches of St. Saba, St. Thomas, St. Nicholas, and St. John, the tutelar saint of the city; the Abbey of St. Clare, the convents of the Knights Hospitalers and the Knights Templars, and various monasteries and religious houses.

1291. William de Beaujeu, Grand Master of the Temple, a veteran warrior of a hundred fights, took the command of the garrison of Acre, which amounted to about twelve thousand men, exclusive of the forces of the Temple and the Hospital, and a body of five hundred foot and two hundred horse, under the command of the King of Cyprus. These forces were distributed along the walls in four divisions. The siege lasted six weeks, viz., from about April 1st to May 20th, during the whole of which period the sallies and the attacks were incessant. Neither by night nor by day did the shouts of the assailants and the noise of the military engines cease. Huge stones and beams of timber, and pots of burning tar and naphtha, were continually hurled into the city. The walls were battered from without, and the foundations were sapped by miners who were incessantly laboring to advance their works. More than six hundred catapults, ballistæ, and other instruments of destruction, were directed against the fortifications; and the battering machines were of such immense size and weight that a hundred wagons were required to transport the separate timbers of one of them. Movable towers were erected by the Moslem, so as to overtop the walls. Their workmen and advanced

392 KNIGHTS TEMPLARS.

Gallant Defense of the City. Retreat of the King of Cyprus.

parties were protected by hurdles covered with raw hides, and all the military contrivances which the art and the skill of the age could produce were used to facilitate the assault. For a long time their utmost efforts were foiled by the valor of the besieged, who made constant sallies upon their works, burnt their towers and machines, and destroyed their miners. Day by day, however, the numbers of the garrison were thinned by the sword, whilst in the enemy's camp the places of the dead were constantly supplied by fresh warriors from the Desert of Arabia, animated with the same wild fanaticism in the cause of *their* religion as that which so eminently distinguished the military monks of the Temple.

On the 4th of May, after thirty-three days of constant fighting, the great tower considered the key of the fortifications, and called by the Moslems " The Cursed Tower," was thrown down by the military engines. To increase the terror and distraction of the besieged, Sultan Khalil mounted three hundred drummers, with their drums, upon as many dromedaries, and commanded them to make as much noise as possible whenever a general assault was ordered. From the 4th to the 14th of May the attacks were incessant. On the 15th, the double wall was forced, and the King of Cyprus, panic-stricken, fled in the night to his ships, and made sail for the island of Cyprus, with all his followers, and with near three thousand of the best men of the garrison. On the morrow the Saracens attacked the post he had deserted. They filled up the ditch with the bodies of dead men and horses, piles of wood, stones, and earth, and their trumpets then sounded to the assault. Ranged under the yellow banner of Mohammed, the Mamelukes forced the breach, and penetrated sword in hand to the very center of the city, but their victorious career and insulting shouts were there stopped by the mail-clad Knights of the Temple and the Hospital, who charged on horseback through the narrow streets, drove them back with immense carnage, and precipitated them headlong from the walls.

1291. At sunrise May 16 the air resounded with the deafening noise of drums and trumpets, and the breach was carried and recovered several times, the military friars at last closing up the passage with their bodies, and presenting a wall of steel to the advance of the enemy.   Loud appeals to God, and to Mohammed, to Jesus Christ, to the Virgin Mary, to heaven and the saints, were to be heard on all sides; and after an obstinate engagement from sunrise to sunset, darkness put an end to the slaughter.   The miners continued incessantly to advance their operations.   Another wide breach was opened in the walls, and on the third day (the 18th) the enemy made the final assault on the side next the gate of St. Anthony.   The army of the Mamelukes was accompanied by a troop of sectaries called *Chagis*, a set of religious fanatics, whose devotion consisted in suffering all sorts of privations, and in sacrificing themselves in behalf of Islam.   The advance of the Mameluke cavalry to the assault was impeded by the deep ditch, which had been imperfectly filled by the fallen ruins and by the efforts of the soldiers, and these religious madmen precipitated themselves headlong into the abyss and *formed a bridge with their bodies*, over which the Mamelukes passed to reach the foot of the wall.   Nothing could withstand the fierce onslaught of the Moslems.   In vain were the first ranks of their cavalry laid prostrate in the dust, and both horses and riders hurled headlong over the ruined walls and battlements into the moat below; their fall only facilitated the progress of those behind them, who pressed on sword in hand over the lifeless bodies of men and horses, to attack the faint and weary warriors guarding the breach.

1291.   The Grand Masters of the Temple, De Beaujeu, and of the Hospital, De Villiers, fought side by side at the head of their Knights, and for a time successfully resisted all the efforts of the enemy.   But as each Knight fell beneath the keen scimitars of the Moslem, there were none in reserve to supply his place, whilst the vast hordes of the infidels pressed on with untiring energy and perseverance.   Matthew de Clermont, Marshal of the Hospital, after performing prodigies of valor, fell covered with wounds, and Grand Master William de Beaujeu, as a last resort, requested the Grand Master of that Order to sally out of an adjoining gateway at the head of five hundred horse, and attack the enemy's rear. Immediately after the Grand Master of the Temple had given these orders, he was himself struck down by the darts and the arrows of the enemy; the panic-stricken garrison fled to the port.

and the infidels rushed on with tremendous shouts of *Allah hu
achbar!* "GOD is greater!" Thousands of panic-stricken Christians now rushed to the sea-side, and sought with frantic violence
to gain possession of the ships and boats that rode at anchor in the
port, but a frightful storm of wind, and rain, and lightning, hung
over the dark and agitated waters of the sea. The elements
themselves warred against the poor Christians, and the loud-peal-
ing thunder became mingled with the din and uproar of the assault and the clash of arms. The boats and vessels were swamped
by the surging waves ; and the bitter cries of the perishing fugitives ascended alike from the sea and shore. Thousands fled to
the churches for refuge, but found none. They prostrated themselves before the altars, and embraced the images of the saints, but
these evidences of idolatry only stimulated the merciless fanaticism of the Moslems, and the Christians and their temples, their
images and their saints, were all consumed in the raging flames
kindled by the inexorable sons of Islam. The churches were set
on fire, and the timid virgin and the hardened voluptuary, the nun
and the monk, the priest and the bishop, all perished miserably
before the altars and the shrines which they had approached in the
hour of need, but which many of them had neglected in days of
prosperity and peace. The holy nuns of St. Clare, following the
example and exhortations of their abbess, mangled and disfigured
their faces and persons in a most dreadful manner, to preserve
their chastity from violation by the barbarous conquerors, and
were gloriously rewarded with the crown of martyrdom by the
astonished and disgusted infidels, who slaughtered without mercy
the whole sisterhood !

Three hundred Templars, the sole survivors of their Order in
Acre, had kept together and successfully withstood the victorious
Mamelukes. In a close and compact column they fought their
way, accompanied by several hundred Christian fugitives, to the
Convent of the Temple at Acre, and shut the gates. They then
assembled together in solemn chapter, and appointed the Knight
Templar, GAUDINI, Grand Master. The Temple at Acre was surrounded by walls and towers, and was a place of great strength,
and of immense extent. It was divided into three quarters, the

Terms and Surrender of the Templars. Violation of the Terms by both Parties.

first and principal of which contained the palace of the Grand Master, the church, and the habitation of the Knights; the second, called the Bourg of the Temple, contained the cells of the serving brethren; and the third, called the Cattle Market, was devoted to the officers charged with the duty of procuring the necessary supplies for the Order and its forces. The following morning very favorable terms were offered to the Templars by the victorious Sultan, and they agreed to evacuate the Temple on condition that a galley should be placed at their disposal, and that they should be allowed to retire in safety with the Christian fugitives under their protection, and to carry away as much of their effects as each person could load himself with. The Mussulman conqueror pledged himself to the fulfillment of these conditions, and sent a standard to the Templars, which was mounted on one of the towers of the Temple. A guard of three hundred Moslem soldiers, charged to see the articles of capitulation properly carried into effect, was afterwards admitted within the walls of the convent. Some Christian ladies and women of Acre were amongst the fugitives, and the Moslem soldiers, attracted by their beauty, broke through all restraint, and violated the terms of the surrender. The enraged Templars closed and barricaded the gates of the Temple. Then they set upon the treacherous infidels, and put every one of them, "from the greatest to the smallest," to death. Immediately after this massacre, the Moslem trumpets sounded to the assault, but the Templars successfully defended themselves until the next day (the 20th). The Marshal of the Order and several of the brethren were then deputed by Grand Master Gaudini with a flag of truce to the Sultan, to explain the cause of the massacre of his guard. The enraged monarch, however, had no sooner got them into his power, than he ordered every one of them to be decapitated, and pressed the siege with renewed vigor.

1291. In the night, Grand Master Gaudini, with a chosen band of his companions, collected together the treasure of the Order and the ornaments of the church, and sallying out of a secret postern of the Temple which communicated with the harbor, they got on board a small vessel, and escaped in safety to the island of Cyprus. The residue of the Templars retired into the large tower of the

Temple, called " The Tower of the Master," which they defended with desperate energy. The bravest of the Mamelukes were driven back in repeated assaults, and the little fortress was everywhere surrounded with heaps of the slain. The Sultan, at last, despairing of taking the place by assault, ordered it to be undermined. As the workmen advanced, they propped the foundations with beams of wood, and when the excavation was completed, these wooden supports were consumed by fire ; the huge tower then fell with a tremendous crash, and buried the brave Templars in its ruins. The Sultan set fire to the town in four places. The walls, the towers, and the ramparts were demolished, and the last stronghold of the Christian power in Palestine was speedily reduced to a smoking solitude.

A few years back, the ruins of the Christian city of Acre were well worthy of the attention of the curious. You might still trace the remains of thirty churches ; and the quarter occupied by the Knights Templars continued to present many interesting memorials of that proud and powerful Order. " The carcass," says Sandys, " shows that the body hath been strong, doubly immured ; fortified with bulwarks and towers, to each wall a ditch lined with stone, and under those, divers secret posterns. You would think, by the ruins, that the city consisted of divers conjoining castles, which witness a notable defence, and an unequal assault ; and that the rage of the conquerors extended beyond conquest ; the huge walls and arches turned topsy-turvy, and lying like rocks upon the foundation." At the period of Dr. Clarke's visit to Acre, in 1802, the ruins, with the exception of the cathedral, the arsenal, the convent of the Knights, and the palace of the Grand Master, were so intermingled with modern buildings, and in such a state of utter subversion, that it was difficult to afford any satisfactory description of them. " Many superb remains were observed by us," says he, " in the palace of the Pasha, the infamous butcher, Djezzar, in the khan, the mosk, the public bath, the fountains, and other parts of the town, consisting of fragments of antique marble, the shafts and capitals of granite and marble pillars, masses of the verd antique breccia, of the ancient serpentine, and of the syenite and trap of Egypt. In the garden of Djezzar's palace, leading to his summer apartment, we saw some pillars of variegated marble of extraordinary beauty."

1291. After the fall of Acre, the headquarters of the Templars were established at Limisso in the island of Cyprus, and urgent letters were sent to Europe for succor.   The armies of Sultan Kelaoun in the meantime assaulted and carried Tyre, Sidon, Tortosa, Caiphas, and the Pilgrim's Castle at Athlit.   The last three places belonged to the Templars, and were stoutly defended, but they were attacked by the Egyptian fleet by sea, and by countless armies of infidels by land, and were at last involved in the common destruction.   The Grand Master, Gaudini, overwhelmed with sorrow and vexation at the loss of the Holy Land, and the miserable situation of his Order, stripped of all its possessions on the Asiatic continent, died at Limisso, after a short illness, and was succeeded **1295.** by Brother James de Molay, of the family of the lords of Longvic and Raon, in Burgundy, twenty-second and last Grand Master.   This illustrous nobleman was at the head of the English province of the Order at the period of his election to the dignity of Grand Master.   He was first appointed Visitor-General, then Grand Preceptor of England, and was afterwards placed at the head of the entire Fraternity.   During his residence in Britain he held several chapters or assemblies of the brethren at the Temple at London, and at the different preceptories, where he framed and enforced various rules and regulations for the government of the Fraternity in England.   Shortly after his election, he proceeded to Cyprus, carrying out with him a numerous body of English and French Knights Templars, and a considerable amount of treasure. Soon after his arrival he entered into an alliance with the famous Casan Cham, Emperor of the Mogul Tartars, King of Persia, and the descendant or successor of Genghis Khan, and landed in Syria with his knights and a body of forces, to join the standard of that powerful monarch.   Casan had married the daughter of Leon, King of Armenia, a Christian princess of extraordinary beauty, to whom he was greatly attached, and who was permitted the enjoyment and public exercise of the Christian worship.   The Tartar Emperor naturally became favorably disposed towards the Christians, and he invited the Grand Master of the Temple to join him in an expedition against the Sultan of Egypt.

1299. In the spring of the year the Templars landed at Suadia, and made a junction with the Tartar forces which were encamped amid the ruins of Antioch. An army of thirty thousand men was placed by the Mogul Emperor under the command of De Molay the Grand Master, and the combined forces moved up the valley of the Orontes towards Damascus. In a great battle fought at Hums, the troops of the Sultans of Damascus and Egypt were entirely defeated, and pursued with great slaughter until nightfall. Aleppo, Hums, Damascus, and all the principal cities, surrendered to the victorious arms of the Moguls, and the Templars once again entered Jerusalem in triumph, visited the Holy Sepulcher, and celebrated Easter on Mount Zion. Casan sent embassadors to the Pope, and to the sovereigns of Europe, announcing the victorious progress of his arms, soliciting their alliance, and offering them in return the possession of Palestine. But the Christian nations heeded not the call, and none thought seriously of an expedition to the East excepting the ladies of Genoa, who, frightened by an interdict which had been laid upon their town, assumed the Cross as the best means of averting the Divine indignation. De Molay, Grand Master of the Temple, advanced as far as Gaza, and drove the Saracens into the sandy deserts of Egypt; but a Saracen chief, who had been appointed by the Tartars governor of Damascus, instigated the Mussulman population of Syria to revolt, and the Grand Master was obliged to retreat to Jerusalem. He was there joined by the Tartar general, Cotulosse, who had been sent across the Euphrates by Casan to support him. The combined armies were once more preparing to march upon Damascus, when the sudden illness of Casan, who was given over by his physicians, disconcerted all their arrangements, and deprived the Grand Master of his Tartar forces. The Templars were then compelled to retreat to the sea-coast and embark their forces on board their galleys. The Grand Master sailed to Limisso, stationing a strong detachment of his soldiers on the island of Aradus, near Tortosa, which they fortified. But these were speedily attacked in that position by a fleet of twenty vessels, and an army of ten thousand men, and after a gallant defense they were compelled to abandon their fortifications, and were all killed or taken prisoners.

The last great Struggle between the Cross and the Crescent.

1299. Thus ended the dominion of the Templars in Palestine, and thus closed the long and furious struggle between the CRESCENT and the CROSS! The few remaining Christians in the Holy Land were chased from ruin to ruin, and exterminated. The churches, the houses, and the fortifications along the sea-coast were demolished, and everything that could afford shelter and security, or invite the approach of the Crusaders from the West, was carefully destroyed. The houses were all set on fire, the trees were cut down and burnt, the land was everywhere laid waste, and all the maritime country, from Laodicea to Ascalon, was made desert. "Every trace of the Franks," says the Arabian chronicler Ibn Ferat, "was removed, and thus it shall remain, please God, till the day of judgment!"

Near six centuries have swept over Palestine since the termination of the wars of the Cross, and the land still continues *desolate*. The proud memorials of past magnificence are painfully contrasted with present ruin and decay, and the remains of the rich and populous cities of antiquity are surrounded by uncultivated deserts. God hath said, " I will smite the land with a *curse*. I will bring the worst of the heathen and they shall possess it." " Thorns shall come up in her palaces, nettles and brambles in the fortresses thereof, and the defenced city shall be left desolate, and the habitation forsaken, and left like a wilderness." " The fig-tree shall not blossom, neither shall fruit be on the vine ; the labor of the olive shall fail, and the fields shall yield no meat ; the flock shall be cut off from the fold, and there shall be no herd in the stall." But brighter and happier times are yet to come, for the Lord God hath also said, " To the mountains of Israel, to the hills, and to the rivers, to the valleys, and the desolate wastes, and the cities that are forsaken, which became a prey and a derision to the heathen. Behold I am for you, I will turn unto you, and ye shall be tilled and sown, and I will multiply men upon you, and they shall build up the old waste cities, the desolation of many generations. In the land of Benjamin, and in the places about Jerusalem, and in the cities of Judah, shall the flocks pass again under the hand of him that telleth them, saith the LORD."

Part Fourth.

FROM THE END OF THE CHRISTIAN DOMINION IN PALESTINE, A. D. 1291,
TO THE MARTYRDOM OF JAMES DE MOLAY, AND THE DESTRUCTION
OF THE ORDER OF KNIGHTS TEMPLARS, A. D. 1313.

SIEGE OF CORINTH.

CHAPTER I.

THE PERSECUTIONS IN FRANCE.

Lo, the new *Pilate*, of whose cruelty
Such violence cannot fill the measure up;
With no decree to sanction, pushes on
Into the Temple his yet eager sails.

IT now only remains for us to relate the miserable and cruel fate of the surviving brethren of the Order of the Temple, and to tell of the ingratitude they encountered at the hands of their fellow-Christians in the West. After the loss of all the Christian territory in Palestine, and the destruction of every serious hope of recovering and retaining the Holy City, the services of the Templars ceased to be required, and men began to regard with an eye of covetousness their vast wealth and immense possessions. This was their true and only crime, their riches. The clergy regarded with jealousy and indignation their removal from the ordinary ecclesiastical jurisdiction, their exemption from tithe, and the privilege they possessed of celebrating divine service during interdict; and their hostility to the Order was manifested in repeated acts of injustice, which drew forth many severe bulls from the Roman pontiffs. The Templars, moreover, became unpopular with the European sovereigns and their nobles. The revenues of the former were diminished through the immunities conceded to the Order by their predecessors, and the paternal estates of the latter had been diminished by the grant of many thousand manors, lordships, and fair estates to the Fraternity by their pious and enthusiastic ancestors. Considerable dislike also began to be manifested to the annual transmission of large sums of money, the revenues of the Templars, from the European States, to be expended in a distant warfare in which Christendom now took but little interest.

1291. Shortly after the fall of Acre, and the total loss of Palestine, Edward I., King of England, seized and sequestered to his own use the moneys which had been accumulated by the Templars to forward to their brethren in Cyprus, alleging that the property of the Order had been granted to it by the Kings of England, his predecessors, and their subjects, for the defense of the Holy Land, and that since the loss thereof, no better use could be made of the money than by appropriating it to the maintenance of the poor. At the earnest request of Pope Nicholas IV., however, the King afterwards permitted their revenues to be transmitted to them in the island of Cyprus, in the usual manner. King Edward had previously manifested a thievish desire to lay hands on the property of the Templars. On his return from his victorious campaign in Wales, finding himself unable to disburse the arrears of pay due to his soldiers, he went with Sir Robert Waleran and some armed followers to the Temple, and calling for the treasurer, he pretended that he wanted to see his mother's jewels, which were there kept. Having been admitted to the house, he deliberately broke open the coffers of the Templars, and carried away $50,000 with him to Windsor Castle. His son, Edward II., on his accession to the throne, A. D. 1307, committed a similar act of knavery. He went with his favorite, Piers Gaveston, to the Temple, and took away with him fifty thousand pounds of silver, with a quantity of gold, jewels, and precious stones, belonging to the Bishop of Chester. The impunity with which these acts of robbery were committed, manifests that the Templars then no longer enjoyed the power and respect which they possessed in ancient times.

As the enthusiasm, too, in favor of the Holy War had died out, large numbers of the Fraternity remained at home in their Western Preceptories, and took an active part in the politics of Europe. Nor were their actions altogether excusable. They interfered in the quarrels of Christian Princes, and even drew their swords against their fellow-Christians. Thus we find the members of the Order taking part in the war between the houses of Anjou and Aragon, and aiding the King of England in his warfare against the King of Scotland. In the battle of Falkirk, fought on the **1298.** 22d of July, seven years after the fall of Acre, perished both the Master of the Temple at London, Brian de Jay, and his vicegerent, the Preceptor of Scotland. All these circumstances, together with the loss of the Holy Land, and the extinction of the enthusiasm of the Crusades, conspired to diminish the popularity of the Templars. The rolls of the English Parliament about this time begin to teem with complaints and petitions from the Fraternity, of the infringement of their charters, franchises, liberties, and privileges, in all parts of the realm.

1291. At the period of the fall of Acre, Philip IV., nick-named Le Bel (the Handsome), the son of King Louis IX., the Crusader, occupied the throne of France. He was a needy and avaricious monarch, and had at different periods resorted to the most violent expedients to replenish his exhausted exchequer. On the death of Pope Benedict XI., 1304, he succeeded, through the intrigues of the French Cardinal Dupré, in raising the Archbishop of Bordeaux, a creature of his own, to the pontifical chair. The new Pope removed the Holy See from Rome to France. He summoned all the Cardinals to Lyons, and was there consecrated **1305.** by the name of Clement V., in the presence of King Philip IV. and his nobles. Of the ten new Cardinals then created, *nine* were Frenchmen, and in all his acts the new Pope manifested himself the obedient slave of the French monarch. The character of this man has been painted by the Romish ecclesiastical historians themselves in the darkest colors; a knave, a murderer, and a vile extortioner.

1306. On the 6th of June, a few months after his coronation, he addressed letters from Bordeaux to the Grand Masters of the Temple and Hospital at Limisso, in the island of Cyprus; also, as reported by some writers, to the Teutonic Knights, expressing his earnest desire *to consult them* with regard to the measures necessary to be taken for the recovery of the Holy Land. The Grand Master of Templars was James de Molay (*Jacques de Molai,* as

26

often written), of an ancient family in Besançon, French Comptè, who had entered the Order of Knights Templars A. D. 1265, nearly fifty years before. He had been installed Grand Master of the Temple upon the death of Theobald Gaudini, A. D. 1297. He was then sixty years old, and at the time of his martyrdom, A. D. 1313, seventy-six years of age. De Molay was the second Grand Master since the expulsion of the Christian powers from Acre, in 1291. His name is a favorite one at the present day, in the nomenclature of American Commanderies. To this treacherous call of King Philip IV., the Hospitalers and Teutonics declined to accede, although he assured them that they were the persons best qualified to give advice upon the subject proposed, and to conduct and manage the enterprise in hand, both from their great military experience, and the interest they had in the success of the expedition. We order you, says he, to come hither without delay, *with as much secrecy as possible, and with a very little retinue*, since you will find on this side the sea a sufficient number of your Knights to attend upon you. The Grand Master of the Temple, De Molay, forthwith accepted the summons, and unhesitatingly placed himself and his treasury in the power of the Pope and the King of France. He landed in France, attended by sixty of his Knights, at the com-
1307. mencement of the year, and deposited the treasure of the Order, which he had brought with him from Cyprus, in the Temple at Paris. Unhesitatingly, he walked into his death-trap. He was received with distinction by the King, and then took his departure for Poictiers to have an interview with Pope Clement V.

1307. The secret agents of the French King immediately began to circulate various dark rumors and odious reports concerning the Templars. According to some writers, Squin de Florian, a citizen of Bezieres, who had been condemned to death or pepetual imprisonment in one of the royal castles for his iniquities, was brought before King Philip, and received a free pardon, and was well rewarded, in return for an accusation on oath, charging the Templars with heresy, and with the commission of the most horrible crimes. According to others, Nosso de Florentin, an apostate Templar, who had been condemned by the Grand Preceptor and Chapter of France to perpetual imprisonment for impiety and crime, made in his dungeon a voluntary confession of the sins and abominations charged against the Order. Be this as it may, upon the strength of an information sworn to by a condemned criminal, King Philip, on the 14th of September, 1307, despatched secret letters to all the baillies of the different provinces in France, accusing the Templars of infidelity; of mocking the sacred image of the Saviour; of sacrificing to idols; and of abandoning themselves to impure practices and unnatural crimes. "We being charged," says he, "with the maintenance of the faith; after having conferred with the Pope, the Prelates, and the Barons of the kingdom, at the instance of the Inquisitor, from the informations already laid, from violent suspicions, from probable conjectures, from legitimate presumptions, conceived against the enemies of heaven and earth, and because the matter is important, and it is expedient to prove the just like gold in the furnace, by a rigorous examination, have decreed that the members of the Order who are our subjects shall be arrested and detained to be judged by the Church, and that all their real and personal property shall be seized into our hands!" etc. The baillies and seneschals were required accurately to inform themselves, with great secrecy, and without exciting suspicion, of the number of the houses of the Temple within their respective jurisdictions; to provide an armed force sufficient to overcome all resistance, and on the 13th of October, 1307, to surprise the Templars in their preceptories, and simultaneously make them all prisoners. The Inquisition is then directed to assemble to examine the guilty, and to employ *torture* if it be necessary. "Before proceeding with the inquiry," says Philip, "you are to inform them (the Templars) that the Pope and ourselves have been convinced, by irreproachable testimony, of the errors and abominations which accompany their vows and profession; you are to promise them *pardon* and *favor* if they *confess* the truth, but if not, you are to acquaint them that they will be condemned to death."

As soon as Philip had issued these orders, he wrote to the principal sovereigns of Europe, urging them to follow his example, and sent a confidential agent, named Bernard Peletin, with a letter to King Edward II., who had just then (July 8, 1307) ascended the throne of England, representing in frightful colors the pretended sins of the Templars. On the 22d of September of the same year King Edward replied to this latter, observing that he had considered of the matters mentioned therein, and had listened to the statements of that discreet man, Master Bernard Peletin. That he had caused the latter to unfold the charges before himself, and many prelates, earls, and barons of his kingdom, and others of his council ; but that they appeared so astonishing as to be beyond belief. That such abominable and execrable deeds had never before been heard of by the king, and the aforesaid prelates, earls, and barons, and it was therefore hardly to be expected that an easy credence could be given to them. The English monarch, however, informs King Philip, that by the advice of his council he had ordered the seneschal of Agen, from whose lips the rumors were said to have proceeded, to be summoned to his presence, that through him he might be further informed concerning the premises ; and he states that, at the fitting time, after due inquiry, he will take such steps as will redound to the praise of God, and the honor and preservation of the Catholic faith.

1307. On the night of the 13th of October, all the Knights Templars in the French dominions were simultaneously arrested. Monk sand priests were appointed to preach against them in the public places and churches of Paris, and in the gardens of the Palais Royal ; and advantage was taken of the folly, the superstition, and the credulity of the age, to propagate the most horrible and extravagant charges against them. They were accused of worshiping an idol covered with an old skin, embalmed, having the appearance of a piece of polished oil-cloth. "In this idol," we are assured, " there were two carbuncles for eyes, bright as the brightness of heaven, and it is certain that all the hope of the Templars was placed in it ; it was their sovereign god, and they trusted in it with all their heart." They are accused of burning the bodies of the deceased brethren, and making the ashes into a powder, which they administered to the younger brethren in their food and drink, to make them hold fast their faith and idolatry ; of *cooking and roasting infants*, and anointing their idols with the fat ; of celebrating hidden rites and mysteries, to which young and tender virgins were introduced, and of a variety of abominations too absurd and horrible to be named. Guillaume Paradin, in his "History of Savoy," seriously repeats these monstrous accusations, and declares that the Templars had " a hollow place or cave in the earth, very dark, in which they had an image in the form of a man, which they had invested with the skin of a human body, and in which were inserted two bright and glittering carbuncles in lieu of eyes. At this horrible statue, they who craved to enter their damnable religion, were compelled to sacrifice, whom, before all ceremonies, they obliged to deny Jesus Christ, and to foul the Cross with their feet. After they had profaned the holy object, in which girls and boys seduced to be of their sect assisted, they put out the lamps and lights which they had in the cave. And if it happened that a *Templar* and a girl had a child, they ranged themselves in a circle and threw the babe from hand to hand until it died by violence. Being dead they roasted it (horrible act!) and of its fat anointed their grand statue!"

The character of the charges preferred against the Templars proves that their enemies had no serious crimes to allege against the Order. Their very virtues, indeed, were turned against them, for we are told that, " to conceal the iniquity of their lives, they made much almsgiving, constantly frequented church, comported themselves with edification, frequently partook of the holy sacrament, and manifested always much modesty and gentleness of deportment in the house, as well as in public."

During twelve days of severe imprisonment, the Templars remained constant in the denial of the horrible crimes imputed to the Fraternity. The King's promises of pardon extracted from them no confession of guilt, and they were therefore handed over to the tender mercies of the brethren of St. Dominic, who were the most refined and expert torturers of the day. On the 19th of October, 1307, the Grand Inquisitor proceeded with his myrmidons to the Temple at Paris, and a hundred and forty Templars were one after another put to the torture. Days and weeks were consumed in the examination, and thirty-six Templars perished in the hands of their tormentors, maintaining, with unshaken constancy to the very last, the entire innocence of their Order. Many of them lost the use of their feet from the application of the torture of fire, which was inflicted in the following manner: their legs were fastened in an iron frame, and the soles of their feet were greased over with fat or butter; they were then placed before the fire, and a screen was drawn backwards and forwards, so as to moderate and regulate the heat. Such was the agony produced by this roasting operation, that the victim often went raving mad. Sir Knight Bernarde de Vado, on subsequently revoking a confession of guilt, wrung from him by this description of torment, says to the commissary of police, before whom he was brought to be examined, " They held me so long before a fierce fire that the flesh was burnt off my heels, two pieces of bone came away, which I present to you." Another Templar, on publicly revoking his confession, declared that four of his teeth were drawn out, and that he confessed himself guilty to save the remainder. Others of the Fraternity deposed to the infliction on them of the most revolting and indecent torments, such as can only be made public in a dead language; and, in addition to all this, it appears that forged letters from the Grand Master De Molay were shown to the prisoners, exhorting them to confess themselves guilty. Many of the Templars were accordingly compelled to acknowledge whatever was required of them, and to plead guilty to the commission of crimes which, in the previous interrogatories, they had positively denied.

On the 28th of March, 1310, the proceedings assumed even a more sanguinary character. Five hundred and forty-six Templars, who had persisted in maintaining the innocence of their Order, were assembled in the garden of the Bishop's Palace at Paris, to hear the articles of accusation read over to them, and a committee of their number was authorized to draw up a written defense. They asked to have an interview with the Grand Master De Molay, and the other heads of the Order, but this was refused. The total number of Templars, immured in the prisons of Paris, was nine hundred. In the course of the examination before the Papal Commissioners, Sir Knight Laurent de Beaume produced a letter which had been sent to him and his fellow-prisoners at Sens, warning them against a retractation of their confessions in the following terms:

Confessions. Defense. Frightful Tortures. Maintaining their Innocence.

"Take notice that the Pope has given command that they who have made confessions before his Legates, and who do not persevere in those confessions, shall be committed to damnation and destruction by fire." This threat was carried into execution, and Laurent de Beaume was one of the first victims. The defense drawn up by the brethren and presented to the Commissioners by Sir Knight Peter de Bologna, begins by stating the origin and objects of their Institution, the vows to which they subjected themselves, and the mode in which persons were received into the Fraternity. They give a frightful account of the tortures that had been inflicted upon them, and declare that those who had escaped with life from the hands of the tormentors, were either ruined in health or injured in intellect; and that as pardon and forgiveness had been freely offered to those Knights who would confess, it was not wonderful that false confessions had been made. They observed that a vast number of Knights had died in prison, and they exhorted the Commissioners to interrogate the guards, jailers, and executioners, and those who saw them in their last moments, concerning the declarations and confessions they had made at the peril of their souls when dying. They maintained that it was a most extraordinary thing that so many Knights of distinguished birth and noble blood, members of the most illustrious families in Europe, should have remained from an early age up to the day of their death members of the Order, and should never, in days of sickness or at the hour of death, have revealed any of the horrid iniquities and abominations charged against it. All the Templars, indeed, who had made confessions were rapidly following one another's example in retracting them, and maintaining their innocence, and the King hastened to arrest the unfavorable march of events.

1310. The Archbishop of Sens, whose ecclesiastical authority extended over the Diocese of Paris, having died, the King obtained the vacant See for Philip de Martigny, a creature of his own, who was installed therein in the month of April. In a letter to Pope Clement V., urging this appointment, Philip reminds him that the new Archbishop would have to preside over a Provincial Council wherein would be transacted many things which immediately concerned the glory of God, the stability of the faith, and of the Holy Church.   Immediately after the enthronement of this new Archbishop, the Provincial Council of Sens was convoked at Paris, and on the 10th of May, A. D. 1310, all the Templars who had revoked their confessions, and had come forward to maintain the innocence of their Order, were dragged before it, and sentence of death was passed upon them by the Archbishop in the following terms : " You have avowed," said he, " that the Brethren who are received into the Order of the Temple are compelled to renounce Christ and spit upon the Cross, and that you yourselves have participated in that crime ; you have thus acknowledged that you have fallen into the sin of *heresy.*   By your confession and repentance you had merited absolution, and had once more become reconciled to the Church.   As you have revoked your confession, the Church no longer regards you as reconciled, but as having fallen back to your first errors.   You are, therefore, *relapsed heretics,* and as such, we condemn you to the fire ! "   As soon as the Commissioners had received intelligence of this extraordinary decree, they despatched messengers to the Archbishop and his suffragans, praying them to delay the execution of their sentence, as very many persons affirmed that the Templars who died in prison had proclaimed with their last breath the innocence of their Order.   But these representations were of no avail.   The Archbishop, who was paying the price of his elevation to a hard creditor, proceeded to make short work of the business.

1310.   *The very next morning* (Tuesday, May 12th), fifty-four Templars were handed over to the secular arm, and were led out to execution by the King's officers.   They were conducted, at daybreak, into the open country, in the environs of the Porte St. Antoine des Champs at Paris, and were there fastened to stakes driven into the ground, and surrounded by fagots and charcoal. In this situation, they saw the torches lighted, and the executioners approaching to accomplish their task, and they were once more offered pardon and favor if they would confess the *guilt* of their Order.   They persisted in the maintenance of its *innocence,* and were burnt to death in a most cruel manner before slow fires. All historians speak with admiration of the heroism and intrepidity with which they met their fate. Many hundred other Templars were dragged from the dungeons of Paris before the Archbishop of Sens and his council. Those whom neither the agony of torture nor the fear of death could overcome, but who remained steadfast in all their trials in the maintenance of their innocence, were condemned to perpetual imprisonment as *unreconciled heretics;* whilst those who, having made the required confessions of guilt, continued to persevere in them, received absolution, were declared reconciled to the Church, and were set at liberty.

1310. On the 18th of August, four other Templars were condemned as relapsed heretics by the council of Sens, and were likewise burnt by the Porte St. Antoine; and it is stated that a hundred and thirteen Templars were, from first to last, burnt at the stake in Paris. Many others were burnt in Lorraine; in Normandy; at Carcassone; and nine, or, according to some writers, twenty-nine, were burnt by the Archbishop of Rheims at Senlis. King Philip's officers, indeed, not content with their inhuman cruelty towards the living, *invaded the sanctity of the tomb,* by dragging a dead Templar, who had been treasurer of the Temple at Paris, from his grave, and burning the mouldering corpse as a heretic.

In the midst of all these sanguinary atrocities, the examinations continued before the ecclesiastical tribunal. Many aged and illustrious warriors, who merited a better fate, appeared before their judges pale and trembling. At first they revoked their confessions, declared their innocence, and were remanded to prison; and then, panic-stricken, they demanded to be led back before the papal commissioners, when they abandoned their retractations, persisted in their previous avowal of *guilt,* humbly expressed their sorrow and repentance, and were then pardoned, absolved, and reconciled to the Church. The torture still continued to be applied, and out of thirty-three Templars confined in the chateau d'Alaix, four died in prison, and the remaining twenty confessed, amongst other things, the following absurdities:—that in the provincial chapter of the Order held at Montpellier, the Templars set up *a head* and worshiped it; that the devil often appeared there in the shape of *a cat*, and conversed with the assembled brethren, and promised them a good harvest, with the possession of riches, and all kinds of temporal property.   Some asserted that the head worshiped by the Fraternity possessed a long beard.   Others that it was a woman's head; and one of the prisoners even declared that as often as this wonderful head was adored, a great number of devils made their appearance in the shape of beautiful women.

1311.   Similar measures had, in the meantime, been prosecuted against the Templars in all parts of Europe.   On the 18th of March, the Pope wrote to the Kings of Castile, Leon, Aragon, and Portugal, complaining of the omission to torture the Templars in their dominions.   " The bishops and delegates," says the Holy Pontiff, " have imprudently neglected these means of obtaining the truth; we therefore expressly order them to employ TORTURE against the Knights, that the truth may be more readily and completely obtained! "   The order for TORTURING the Templars was transmitted to the Patriarch of Constantinople, the Bishop of Negropont, and the Duke of Achaia; and it crossed the seas to the King of Cyprus, and the Bishops of Famagousta and Nicosia. The councils of Tarragona and Aragon, *after applying the torture,* pronounced the Order free from heresy.   In Portugal and in Germany the Templars were declared innocent: and in no place situate beyond the sphere of the influence of the King of France and his creature the Pope, was a single Templar condemned to death.

1311.   On the 16th of October the General Council of the Church which had been convened by the Pope to pronounce the abolition of the Order, assembled at Vienne, near Lyons in France.   It was opened by the Holy Pontiff in person, who caused the different confessions and avowals of the Templars to be read over before the assembled nobles and prelates.   Although the Order was now broken up, and the best and bravest of its members had either perished in the flames or were languishing in dungeons, yet nine fugitive Templars had the courage to present themselves before the Council, and demand to be heard in defense of their Order, declaring that they were the representatives of from 1,500 to 2,000 Templars, who were wandering about as fugitives and outlaws in the neighborhood of Lyons. The historian Raynouard has fortunately brought to light a letter from the Pope to King Philip, which states this fact, and also informs us how the Holy Pontiff acted when he heard that these defenders of the Order had presented themselves. Clement V. caused them to be thrown into prison, where *they languished and died.* He affected to believe that his life was in danger from the number of the Templars at large, and he immediately took measures to provide for the security of his person.

1311.   The assembled fathers, to their honor, expressed their disapprobation of this flagrant act of injustice, and the entire Council, with the exception of an Italian prelate, nephew of the Pope, and the three French bishops of Rheims, Sens, and Rouen, all creatures of Philip, who had severally condemned large bodies of Templars to be burnt at the stake in their respective dioceses, were unanimously of opinion, that before the suppression of so celebrated and illustrious an Order, which had rendered such great and signal services to the Christian faith, the members belonging to it ought to be heard in their own defense. Such a proceeding, however, did not suit the views of the Pope and King Philip, and the assembly was abruptly dismissed by the Pope, who declared that since they were unwilling to adopt the necessary measures, he himself, out of the plenitude of the papal authority, would supply every defect. Accordingly at the commencement of the following year, the Pope summoned a private consistory; and several cardinals and French bishops having been gained over, he abolished the Order by an apostolic ordinance, perpetually prohibiting every one from thenceforth entering into it, or accepting or wearing the habit thereof, or representing themselves to be Templars, on pain of excommunication.

1311.   On the 3d of April, the second session of the Council was opened by the Pope at Vienne. King Philip and his three sons were present, accompanied by a large body of troops, and the Papal decree abolishing the Order was published before the assembly. The members of the Council appear to have been called together merely to hear the decree read. History does not inform us of any discussion with reference to it, nor of any suffrages having been taken.

1313. James de Molay, the Grand Master of the Temple, Guy, the Grand Preceptor, a nobleman of illustrious birth, brother to the Prince of Dauphiny, together with Hugh de Peralt, the Visitor-general of the Order, and the Grand Preceptor of Aquitaine, had now languished in the prisons of France for the space of five years and a half. The secrets of their dark dungeons have never been brought to light, but on the 18th of March, A.D. 1313, a public scaffold was erected before the Cathedral Church of Notre Dame, at Paris, and the citizens were summoned to hear the Order of the Temple convicted by the mouths of its chief officers, of the sins and iniquities charged against it. The four Knights, loaded with chains and surrounded by guards, were then brought upon the scaffold by the provost, and the Bishop of Alba read their confessions aloud in the presence of the assembled populace. The Papal Legate then, turning towards the Grand Master and his companions, called upon them to renew, in the hearing of the people, the avowals which they had previously made of the guilt of their Order.

Hugh de Peralt, the Visitor-general, and the Preceptor of the Temple of Aquitaine, signified their assent to whatever was demanded of them, but the Grand Master, raising his arms bound with chains towards heaven, and advancing to the edge of the scaffold, declared in a loud voice, that to say that which was untrue was a crime, both in the sight of God and man. " I do," said he, " confess my guilt, which consists in having, to my shame and dishonor, suffered myself, through the pain of torture and the fear of death, to give utterance to falsehoods, imputing scandalous sins and iniquities to an illustrious Order, which hath nobly served the cause of Christianity. I disdain to seek a wretched and disgraceful existence by engrafting another lie upon the original falsehood." He was here interrupted by the provost and his officers, and, Guy, the Grand Preceptor, having commenced with strong asseverations of *his* innocence, they were both hurried back to prison.

King Philip was no sooner informed of the result, than, upon

De Molay burned to Death. His ample Acknowledgment of Innocence.

the first impulse of his indignation, without consulting either Pope, or Bishop, or Ecclesiastical Council, he commanded the instant execution of both these gallant noblemen. The same day at dusk they were led out of their dungeons, and were *burned to death* in a slow and lingering manner upon small fires of charcoal which were kindled on the little island in the Seine, between the King's garden and the Convent of Saint Augustine, close to the spot where now stands the equestrian statue of Henri IV. Thus perished the last Grand Master of the Temple of the antique series. His dying words are rendered as follows: "It is but just that in this terrible day, and in the last moments of my life, I lay open the iniquity of falsehood, and make truth to triumph. I declare, then, in the face of heaven and earth, and I confess to my eternal shame and confusion, that I have committed the greatest of crimes, but it has been only in acknowledging those that have been charged with so much virulence upon an Order, which truth obliges me to pronounce innocent. I made the first declaration they required of me only to suspend the excessive tortures of the rack, and mollify those that made me endure them. I am sensible what torments they prepare for those that have courage to revoke such a confession, but the horrible sight which they present to my eyes is not capable of making me confirm one lie by another. On a condition so infamous as that I freely renounce life, which is already but too odious to me, for what would it avail me to prolong a few miserable days when I must owe them only to the blackest of calumnies?"

In so important a matter as this, it is well to accumulate testimony. Thus speaks another writer: "The Cardinal Alba read the eighty-eight articles of accusation, followed by the so-called confessions of the prisoners, and then turning to them, called upon them to renew, in the hearing of the people, the avowals of guilt which, he said, they had admitted the Order to have incurred. Two, who seemed somewhat overcome and too languid to avow or deny, simply assented to whatever was required of them; but Jacques de Molai, the Grand Master, stepping to the front of the scaffold and raising his hands bound with chains towards heaven, first repeated the Lord's Prayer in a loud voice, and then exclaimed : ' To say that which is untrue is a crime both in the sight of God and man.   Not one of us has betrayed his God or his country.   I do confess my guilt, which consists in having, to my shame and dishonor, suffered myself, through the pain of torture and the fear of death, to give utterance to falsehoods imputing scandalous sins and iniquities to an illustrious Order which hath nobly served the cause of Christianity.   I disdain to seek a wretched and disgraceful existence by engrafting another lie upon the original falsehood.'   Guy, brother of the Prince of Dauphiny, echoed these assertions ; but before he could proceed very far the Cardinal and commissioners, astounded at this exhibition of firmness and courage, hurried the Knights back to prison and immediately waited on the King to acquaint him with the occurrence.   Enraged beyond measure at this unexpected declaration, King Philip the Fair, without consulting the puppet Pope Clement V., or any other spiritual person, summoned his councilors and decreed the two noble Knights should be burned to death.   A pile was erected on the island in the Seine where the statue now stands—or lately stood—of Henri Quatre, and here on the same evening they were led forth to execution before a crowd greatly outnumbering that of earlier assemblages, and the Grand Master addressed the citizens thus: ' France remembers our last moments.   We die innocent.   The decree which condemns us is an unjust decree, but in heaven there is an august tribunal to which the weak never appeal in vain.   To that tribunal within forty days I summon the Roman Pontiff.'   A violent shudder ran through the crowd, but the Grand Master continued, ' Oh, Philip, my master, my King ! I pardon thee in vain, for thy life is condemned.   At the tribunal of God, within a year, I await thee.' "

1313.   The fate of the persecutors of the Order is not unworthy of notice.   A year and one month after the above horrible execution, the Pope, Clement V., was attacked by a dysentery, and speedily hurried to his grave.   His dead body was transported to Carpentras, where the court of Rome then resided.   It was placed at night in a church which caught fire, and the mortal remains of the holy Pontiff were almost entirely consumed.   His relations quarreled over the immense treasures he left behind him, and a vast sum of money, which had been deposited for safety in a church at Lucca, was stolen by a daring band of German and Italian freebooters.   Before the close of the same year, King Philip IV. died of a lingering disease which had baffled all the art of his medical attendants, and the condemned criminal, upon the strength of whose information the Templars were originally arrested, was hanged for fresh crimes. "History attests," says Raynouard, " that all those who were foremost in the persecution of the Templars came to an untimely and miserable death. The last days of Philip IV. were imbittered by misfortune. His nobles and clergy leagued against him to resist his exactions. The wives of his three sons were accused of adultery, and two of them were publicly convicted of that crime.

" The chief cause of the ruin of the Templars," justly remarks Fuller, " was their extraordinary wealth. As Naboth's vineyard was the chiefest ground of his blasphemy, and as in England Sir John Cornwall, Lord Fanhope, said merrily, not he, but his stately house at Ampthill, in Bedfordshire, was guilty of high treason, so certainly their wealth was the principal cause of their overthrow. We may believe that Philip IV. would never have taken away their lives if he might have taken their lands without putting them to death, but the mischief was, he could not get the honey unless he burnt the bees." King Philip IV., the Pope, and the European sovereigns, appear to have disposed of all the personalty of the Templars, the ornaments, jewels, and treasures of their churches and chapels, and during the period of five years, over which the proceedings against the Order extended, they remained in the actual receipt of the vast rents and revenues of the Fraternity. King Philip IV. put forward a claim upon their lands in France to the extent of a million dollars for the expenses of the prosecution, and Louis, his son, claimed a further sum of $300,000. " I do not know," says the celebrated Voltaire, " how much went to the Pope, but evidently, the share of the Cardinals, the Inquisitors delegated to make the process good, amounted to immense sums." The Pope, according to his own account, received only a *small portion* of the personalty of the Order, but others make him a large participator in the good things of the Fraternity.

BEAUTIFUL AND FERTILE PLAINS IN THE VALLEY OF THE JORDAN.

CHAPTER II.

PERSECUTIONS IN ENGLAND.

O SUFFERING Saviour, let me be
   Patient when heaviest cares invade!
Resigned when earthly blessings flee,
   And grateful while enjoyments fade!
Thou wast rejected, Son of God!
   Near to the Highest is thy seat;
'Tis mine to meet the stormy flood,—
   Give me a place beneath thy feet!

THE violent proceedings described in the last chapter excited the astonishment of Europe. On the 20th of November, 1307, the King of England, Edward II., summoned the Seneschal of Agen to his presence, and examined him concerning the truth of the horrible charges preferred against the Templars. On the 4th of December, he wrote letters to the Kings of Portugal, Castile, Aragon, and Sicily, to the following effect: "To the magnificent Prince the Lord Dionysius, by the Grace of God the illustrious King of Portugal, his very dear friend, Edward, by the same grace King of England, etc. Health and prosperity. It is fit and proper, inasmuch as it conduceth to the honor of God and the exaltation of the faith, that we should prosecute with benevolence those who come recommended to us by strenuous labors and incessant exertions in defense of the Catholic faith, and for the destruction of the enemies of the Cross of Christ. Verily, a certain clerk (Bernard Peletin), drawing nigh unto our presence, applied himself, with all his might, to the destruction of the Order of the brethren of the Temple of Jerusalem.

27

He dared to publish before us and our council certain horrible and detestable enormities repugnant to the Catholic faith, to the prejudice of the aforesaid brothers, endeavoring to persuade us, through his own allegations, as well as through certain letters which he had caused to be addressed to us for that purpose, that by reason of the premises, and without a due examination of the matter, we ought to imprison all the brethren of the aforesaid Order abiding in our dominions.   But considering that the Order, which *hath been renowned for its religion and its honor*, and in times long since passed away was instituted, as we have learned, by the Catholic Fathers, exhibits, and hath from the period of its first foundation exhibited, a becoming devotion to God and His holy Church, and also, up to this time, hath afforded succor and protection to the Catholic faith in parts beyond sea, it appeared to us that a ready belief in an accusation of this kind, hitherto altogether unheard of against the Fraternity, was scarcely to be expected.   We affectionately ask, and require of your royal Majesty, that ye, with due diligence, consider of the premises, and turn a deaf ear to the slanders of ill-natured men, who are animated, as we believe, not with a zeal of rectitude, but with a spirit of *cupidity and envy*, permitting no injury unadvisedly to be done to the persons or property of the brethren of the aforesaid Order, dwelling within your kingdom, until they have been legally convicted of the crimes laid to their charge, or it shall happen to be otherwise ordered concerning them in these parts."   This noble letter from the young King has a melancholy comment in the later proceedings and in his own judicial murder, September 21, 1327 (twenty years after).

1307. A few days after the transmission of this letter, King Edward wrote to the Pope, expressing his disbelief of the horrible and detestable rumors spread abroad concerning the Templars. He represents them to his holiness as universally respected by all men in his dominions for the purity of their faith and morals. He expresses great sympathy for the affliction and distress suffered by the Master and Brethren, by reason of the scandal circulated concerning them; and he strongly urges the Pope to clear, by some fair course of inquiry, the character of the Order from the unjust

The Pope's Letter condemning the Templars, and ordering their Arrest.

and infamous aspersions cast against it. On the 22d of November, 1307, however, a fortnight previously, the Pope had issued the following bull to King Edward: " Clement V., Bishop, servant of the servants of God, to his very dear son in Christ, Edward, the illustrious King of England, health and apostolical blessing. Presiding, though unworthy, on the throne of pastoral preëminence, by the disposition of Him who disposeth all things, we fervently seek after this one thing above all others; we with ardent wishes aspire to this, that shaking off the sleep of negligence, whilst watching over the Lord's flock, by removing that which is hurtful, and taking care of such things as are profitable, we may be able, by the divine assistance, to bring souls to God. In truth, a long time ago, about the period of our first promotion to the summit of the apostolical dignity, there came to our ears a light rumor to the effect that the Templars, though fighting ostensibly under the guise of religion, have hitherto been secretly living in perfidious apostasy, and in detestable heretical depravity. But, considering that their Order, in times long since past away, shone forth with the grace of much nobility and honor, and that they were for a length of time held in vast reverence by the faithful, and that we had then heard of no suspicion concerning the premises, or of evil report against them ; and also that, from the beginning of their religion, they have publicly borne the cross of Christ, exposing their bodies and goods against the enemies of the faith, for the acquisition, retention, and defense of the Holy Land, consecrated by the precious blood of our Lord and Saviour Jesus Christ, we were unwilling to yield a ready belief to the accusation."

The Pope then states, that afterwards, however, the same dreadful intelligence was conveyed to the King of France, who, animated by a lively zeal in the cause of religion, took immediate steps to ascertain its truth. He describes the various confessions of the guilt of idolatry and heresy made by the Templars in France, and requires the King forthwith to cause all the Templars in his dominions to be taken into custody on the same day. He directs him to hold them, in the name of the Pope, at the disposition of the Holy See, and to commit all their real and personal property to the hands of certain trustworthy persons, to be faithfully preserved until the Pope shall give further directions concerning it. King Edward II. received this bull immediately after he had dispatched his letter to the Pope, exhorting the Pope not to give ear to the accusations against the Order. The King was now either convinced of the guilt of the Templars on the high authority of the Pope, or more likely hoped to turn the proceedings against them to a profitable account, as he yielded a ready and prompt compliance with the pontifical commands. An order in Council was made for the arrest of the Templars, and the seizure of their property. Inventories were directed to be taken of their goods and chattels, and provision was made for the sowing and tilling of their lands during the period of their imprisonment.

On the 26th of December, 1307, the King wrote to the Pope, informing him that he would carry his commands into execution in the best and speediest way that he could; and on the 8th of January, 1308, the Templars were suddenly arrested in all parts of England, and their property was seized into the King's hands. Sir Knight William de la More was at this period Master of the Temple, or Preceptor of England. He succeeded the Master Brian le Jay, who was slain, as before mentioned, in the battle of Falkirk, July 22, 1298, and was taken prisoner, together with all his brethren of the Temple at London, and committed to close custody at Canterbury Castle. He was afterwards liberated on bail at the instance of the Bishop of Durham.

1308. On the 12th of August, the Pope addressed the bull *Faciens Misericordiam* ("Using Mercy") to the English Bishops as follows:—" Clement V., Bishop, servant of the servants of God, to the venerable brethren the Archbishop of Canterbury, and his suffragans, health and apostolical benediction. The Son of God, the Lord Jesus Christ, using mercy with his servant, would have us taken up into the eminent mirror of the apostleship, to this end, that being, though unworthy, his Vicar upon earth, we may, as far as human frailty will permit in all our actions and proceedings, follow his footsteps." He describes the rumors which had been spread abroad in France against the Templars, and his unwillingness to believe them, " because it was not likely, nor did seem credible, that such religious men, who continually shed their blood

The King's Seizure of Property of the Order, and Disaffection of the Pope.

for the name of Christ, and were thought to expose their persons to danger of death for his sake ; and who often showed many and great signs of devotion, as well in the divine offices as in fasting and other observances, should be so unmindful of their salvation as to perpetrate such things ; we were unwilling to give ear to the insinuations and impeachments against them, being taught so to do by the example of the same Lord of ours, and the writings of canonical doctrine. But afterwards, our most dear son in Christ, Philip IV., the illustrious King of the French, to whom the same crimes had been made known, *not from motives of avarice* (since he does not design to apply or to appropriate to himself any portion of the estates of the Templars, nay, has washed his hands of them!), but inflamed with zeal for the orthodox faith, following the renowned footsteps of his ancestors, getting what information he properly could upon the premises, gave us much instruction in the matter by his messengers and letters."

1308. The Pope then gives a long account of the various confessions made in France, and of the absolution granted to such of the Templars as were truly contrite and penitent. He expresses his conviction of the guilt of the Order, and makes provision for the trial of the Fraternity in England. King Edward in the meantime had begun to make a thievish disposition of their property, and the Pope, on the 4th of October, 1308, wrote him to the following effect: " Your conduct begins again to afford us no slight cause of affliction, inasmuch as it hath been brought to our knowledge from the report of several Barons, that in contempt of the Holy See, and without fear of offending the divine Majesty, you have, of your own sole authority, distributed to different persons the property which belonged formerly to the Order of the Temple in your dominions, which you had got into your hands at our command, and which ought to have remained at our disposition. We have therefore ordained that certain fit and proper persons shall be sent into your kingdom, and to all parts of the world where the Templars are known to have had property, to take possession of the same conjointly with certain Prelates specially deputed to that end, and to make an inquisition concerning the execrable excesses which the members of the Order are said to have committed."

To this letter of Pope Clement V., King Edward II. sent the following reply as short and pithy as it was false:—" As to the *goods* of the Templars, we have done nothing with them up to the present time, nor do we intend to do with them aught but what we have a right to do, and what we know will be acceptable to the Most High."

1309. On the 13th of September, the King granted letters of safe conduct "to those discreet men, the Abbot of Lagny, in the diocese of Paris, and Master Sicard de Vaur, Canon of Narbonne," the Inquisitors appointed by the Pope to examine the Grand Preceptor, William de la More, and brethren of the Temple in England. The same day he wrote to the Archbishop of Canterbury, and the Bishops of London and Lincoln, enjoining them to be personally present with the Papal Inquisitors, at their respective sees, as often as such Inquisitors, or any one of them, should proceed with their inquiries against the Templars.

1309. Among the prisoners confined in the Tower were William de la More, Knight, Grand Preceptor of England, otherwise Master of the Temple ; Himbert Blanke, Knight, Grand Preceptor of Auvergne, one of the veteran warriors who had fought to the last in defense of Palestine, had escaped the slaughter at Acre, and had accompanied the Grand Master from Cyprus to France, whence he crossed over to England, and was rewarded for his meritorious and memorable services, in defense of the Christian faith, with *a dungeon in the Tower*. Radulph de Barton, Priest of the Order of the Temple, Custos or Guardian of the Temple Church, and prior of London ; Michael de Baskeville, Knight, Preceptor of London ; John de Stoke, Knight, Treasurer of the Temple at London ; together with many other Knights and serving brethren of the same house. There were also in custody in the Tower, the Knights Preceptors of the Preceptories of Ewell in Kent, of Daney and Dokesworth in Cambridgeshire, of Getinges in Gloucestershire, of Cumbe in Somersetshire, of Schepeley in Surrey, of Samford and Bistelsham in Oxfordshire, of Garwy in Herefordshire, of Cressing in Essex, of Pafflet, Huppleden, and other Preceptories, together with several Priests and Chaplains of the Order. A general scramble took place for possession of the goods and chattels of the imprisoned Templars; and the King, to check the robberies that were committed, appointed Alau de Goldyngham and John de Medefeld to inquire into the value of the property that had been carried off, and to inform him of the names of the parties who had obtained possession of it. The sheriffs of the different counties were also directed to summon juries, through whom the truth might be better obtained.

On the 22d of September, the Archbishop of Canterbury, acting in obedience to the Papal commands, before a single witness had been examined in England, caused to be published in all churches and chapels a Papal bull, wherein the Pope declares himself perfectly convinced of the guilt of the Order, and solemnly denounces the penalty of excommunication against all persons, of whatever rank, station, or condition in life, whether clergy or laity, who should knowingly afford, either publicly or privately, assistance, counsel, or kindness to the Templars, or should dare to shelter them, or give them countenance or protection, and also laying under interdict all cities, castles, lands, and places, which should harbor any of the members of the proscribed Order! At the commencement of the month of October, 1309, the Inquisitors arrived in England, and immediately published the bull appointing the commission, enjoining the citation of criminals and of witnesses, and denouncing the heaviest ecclesiastical censures against the disobedient, and against every person who should dare to impede the Inquisitors in the exercise of their functions. Citations were made in St. Paul's Cathedral, and in all churches of the ecclesiastical Province of Canterbury, at the end of High Mass, requiring the Templars to appear before the Inquisitors at a certain time and place, and the articles of accusation were transmitted to the constable of the Tower, in Latin, French, and English, to be read to all the Templars imprisoned in that fortress.

On Monday, the 20th of October, after the Templars had been languishing in the English prisons for *more than a year and eight months*, the tribunal constituted by the Pope to take the Inquisition in the Province of Canterbury, assembled in the Episcopal Hall of London. It was composed of the Bishop of London; Dieudonné, Abbot of the Monastery of Lagny, in the Diocese of Paris;

and Sicard de Vaur, Canon of Narbonne, the Pope's chaplain, and hearer of causes in the Pontifical Palace. These were assisted by several foreign notaries.

1309. After the reading of the Papal bulls, and some preliminary proceedings, the articles of accusation—a monument of human folly, superstition, and credulity—were solemnly exhibited. It was urged against the Templars: "1. That at their first reception into the Order, or at some time afterwards, or as soon as an opportunity occurred, they were induced or admonished by those who had received them within the bosom of the fraternity, to deny Christ or Jesus, or the Crucifixion; or at one time God, and at another time the blessed Virgin, and sometimes all the saints. 5. That the receivers told and instructed those that were received, that Christ was not the true God, or sometimes Jesus, or sometimes the person crucified. 7. That they said He had not suffered for the redemption of mankind, nor been crucified but for his own sins. 9. That they made those they received into the Order spit upon the Cross, or upon the sign or figure of the Cross, or the image of Christ. 10. That they caused the Cross itself to be trampled under foot. 11. That the brethren themselves did sometimes trample on the same Cross. 14. That they worshiped *a cat*, which was placed in the midst of the congregation. 16. That they did not believe the sacrament of the altar nor the other sacraments of the Church. 24. That they believed, and so it was told them, that the Grand Master of the Order could absolve them from their sins. 25. That the Visitor could do so. 26. That the Preceptors, of whom many were laymen, could do it. 36. That the receptions of the brethren were made clandestinely. 37. That none were present but the Brothers of the said Order. 38. That for this reason there has for a long time been a vehement suspicion against them. 46. That the brothers themselves had idols in every province, viz., heads; some of which had three faces, and some one, and some a man's skull. 47. That they adored that idol, or those idols, especially in their great chapters and assembles. 48. That they worshiped them. 49. As their God. 50. As their Saviour. 51. That some of them did so. 52. That the greater part did. 53. They said that those heads could save them.

Accusations against the Fraternity. Devotedness of the Order.

54. That they could produce riches. 55. That they had given to the Order all its wealth. 56. That they caused the earth to bring forth seed. 57. That they made the trees to flourish. 58. That they bound or touched the heads of the said idols with cords, wherewith they bound themselves about their shirts, or next their skins. 59. That at their reception the aforesaid little cords, or others of the same length, were delivered to each of the Brothers. 60. That they did this in worship of their idols. 61. That it was enjoined them to gird themselves with the said little cords, as before-mentioned, and continually to wear them. 62. That the brethren of the Order were generally received in that manner. 63. That they did these things out of devotion. 64. That they did them everywhere. 65. That the greater part did. 66. That those who refused the things above-mentioned at their reception, or to observe them afterwards, were killed or cast into prison." *

The remaining articles, twenty-one in number, are directed principally to the mode of confession practised amongst the Fraternity, and to matters of heretical depravity.—Such an accusation as this, justly remarks Voltaire, *destroys itself.* Might we not have thought that their amazing self-devotedness, during the last dying-struggle of Acre alone—death-rattle of Syria—might have spared them such palpable inventions, even had they fallen into material misdemeanors, which is not proved in law?

Eminent Sir Knight William de la More, the Grand Preceptor

---

* The original draft of these articles of accusation, with the corrections and alterations, is preserved in the Tresor des Chartres. *Raynouard,* Monumens Historiques, pp. 50, 51. The proceedings against the Templars in England are preserved in MS. in the British Museum, Harl. No. 252, 62, f. p. 113 ; No. 247, 68, f. p. 144. Bib. Cotton. Julius, b. xii. p. 70 ; and in the Bodleian Library and Ashmolean Museum. The principal part of them has been published by *Wilkins* in the Concilia Magnæ Britanniæ, tom. ii. p. 329–401, and by *Dugdale,* in the Monast. Angl. vol. vi. part ii. p. 844–848. Many of the charges are of the same filthy, indecent, and smutty nature as the questions propounded to penitents in European confessionals to the present day. They exhibit a familiarity, on the part of the priests who framed them, with the vilest thoughts. Sodomy—the crime against nature—masturbation, everything charged by St. Paul against the Gentiles in the first chapter of Romans, and crimes that the Gentiles themselves never imagined, were put on paper and openly read by these filthy monks, as charges against the Knights Templars.

of England, and thirty more of his brethren, being interrogated before the Inquisitors, positively denied the guilt of the Order, and affirmed that the Templars who had made the confession alluded to in France *had lied*. They were ordered to be brought up separately to be examined.   On the 23d of October, Sir Knight William Raven, being interrogated as to the mode of his reception into the Order, states that he was admitted by Eminent Sir Knight William de la More, the Master of the Temple at Temple Coumbe, in the diocese of Bath, that he petitioned the Brethren of the Temple that they would be pleased to receive him into the Order to serve God and the blessed Virgin Mary, and to end his life in their service; that he was asked if he had a firm wish so to do; and replied that he had; that two brothers then expounded to him the strictness and severity of the Order, and told him that he would not be allowed to act after his own will, but must follow the will of the Preceptor; that if he wished to do one thing, he would be ordered to do another; and that if he wished to be at one place, he would be sent to another; that having promised so to act, he swore upon the holy Gospels of God to obey the Master, to hold no property, to preserve chastity, never to consent that any man should be unjustly despoiled of his heritage, and never to lay violent hands on any man, except in self-defense, or upon the Saracens.   He states that the oath was administered to him in the chapel of the preceptory of Temple Coumbe, in the presence only of the Brethren of the Order; that the rule was read over to him by one of the Brothers, and that a learned serving brother, named John de Walpole, instructed him, for the space of one month, upon the matters contained in it.   The prisoner was then taken back to the Tower, and was directed to be strictly separated from his brethren, and not to be suffered to speak to any one of them.

1309.   The next two days (October 24th and 25th) were taken up with a similar examination of Sir Knight Hugh de Tadecastre and Thomas le Chamberleyn, who gave precisely the same account of their reception as the previous witness.   Sir Knight Hugh de Tadecastre added, that he swore to succor the Holy Land with all his might, and defend it against the enemies of the Christian faith; and that after he had taken the customary oaths and the three

KNIGHTS TEMPLARS.   431

Mode of Reception in England.   Use of Girdles of Chastity.

vows of CHASTITY, POVERTY, and OBEDIENCE, the mantle of the Order with the Cross and the Coif were delivered to him in the church, in the presence of the Master, the Knights, and the Brothers, all seculars being excluded. Sir Knight Thomas le Chamberleyn added, that there was the same mode of reception in England as beyond the sea, and the same mode of taking the vows; that all seculars were excluded, and that when he himself entered the Temple Church to be professed, the door by which he entered was closed after him; that there was another door looking into the cemetery, but that no stranger could enter that way. On being asked why none but the brethren of the Order were permitted to be present at the reception and profession of brothers, he said he knew of no reason, but that it was so written in their Book of Rules.

1309. Between the 25th of October and the 17th of November, thirty-three Knights, Chaplains, and serving Brothers, were examined, all of whom positively denied every article imputing crime or infidelity to their Order. When Sir Knight Himbert Blanke was asked why they had made the reception and profession of brethren secret, he replied, " through our own unaccountable folly." They avowed that they wore little cords round their shirts, but for no bad end. They declared that they never touched idols with them, but that they were worn by way of penance, or according to a Knight of forty-three years' standing, by the instruction of the holy father St. Bernard. Sir Knight Richard de Goldyngham says that he knows nothing further about them than that they were called Girdles of Chastity. They state that the receivers and the party received kissed one another on the face, but everything else regarding the kissing was false, abominable, and had never been done.

1309. Radulph de Barton, priest of the Order of the Temple, and Custos or Guardian of the Temple Church at London, stated, with regard to Article 24, that the Grand Master in Chapter could absolve the brothers from offenses committed against the rules and observances of the Order, but not from private sin, as he was not a priest. That it was perfectly true that those who were received into the Order swore not to reveal the secrets of the Chapter, and that when any one was punished in the Chapter, those who were present at it durst not reveal it to such as were absent; but if any Brother revealed the mode of his reception, he would be deprived of his chamber, or else stripped of his habit.   He declares that the Brethren were not prohibited from confessing to priests not belonging to the Order of the Temple; and that he had never heard of the crimes and iniquities mentioned in the articles of inquiry previous to his arrest, except as regarded the charges made against the Order by Bernard Peletin, when he came to England from King Philip of France.   He states that he had been Custos of the Temple Church at London for ten years, and for the last two years had enjoyed the dignity of Preceptor at the same place.   He was asked about the death of Sir Knight Walter le Bachelor, formerly Preceptor of Ireland, who died in the Temple at London, but he declares that he knows nothing about it, except that the said Walter was fettered and placed in prison, and there died; that he certainly had heard that great severity had been practised towards him, but that he had not meddled with the affair on account of the danger of so doing; he admitted also that the aforesaid Walter was not buried in the cemetery of the Temple, as he was considered excommunicated on account of his disobedience of his superior, and of the Rule of the Order.

Many of the Brethren thus examined had been from twenty to thirty, forty, forty-two, and forty-three years in the Order, and some were veteran warriors who had fought for many a long year upon the thirsty plains of Palestine.   Eminent Sir Knight Himbert Blanke, Grand Preceptor of Auvergne, had been in the Order *thirty-eight years*.   He was received at the city of Tyre, had been engaged in constant warfare against the infidels, and had fought to the last in defense of Acre.   Sir Knight Robert le Scott, a Brother of twenty years' standing, had been received at the Pilgrim's Castle, at Athlit, the famous fortress of the Knights Templars in Palestine, by the Grand Master, William de Beaujeu, the hero who died so gloriously at the head of his Knights at the last siege and storming of Acre, A. D. 1291.   He states that from levity of disposition he quitted the Order after it had been driven out of Palestine, and absented himself for two years, during which period he came to Rome, and confessed to the Pope's Penitentiary, who imposed on him a heavy penance, and enjoined him to return to his brethren in the East, and that he went back and resumed his habit at Nicosia in the island of Cyprus, and was readmitted to the Order by command of the present Grand Master, James de Molay. He adds, also, that Himbert Blanke (the previous witness) was present at his first reception at the Pilgrim's Castle.

1309. On the 22d day of the inquiry, the following entry was made on the record of the proceedings:—" Memorandum. Brothers Philip de Mewes, Thomas de Burton, and Thomas de Staundon, were advised and earnestly exhorted to abandon their religious profession, who severally replied that *they would rather die than do so.*" On the 19th and 20th of November, seven lay witnesses, unconnected with the Order, were examined before the Inquisitors in the chapel of the monastery of the Holy Trinity. William le Dorturer, notary public, declared that the Templars rose at midnight, and held their Chapters before dawn, and he *thought* that the mystery and secrecy of the receptions were owing to a bad rather than a good motive, but declared that he had never observed that they had acquired, or had attempted to acquire, anything unjustly. Gilbert de Bruere, clerk, said that he had never suspected them of anything worse than *an excessive correction of the Brethren.* William Lambert, formerly a " Messenger of the Temple," knew nothing bad of the Templars, and thought them perfectly innocent of all the matters alluded to. And Richard de Barton, priest, and Radulph de Rayndon, an old man, both declared that they knew nothing of the Order, or of the members of it, but what was *good* and *honorable.*

1309. On the 25th of November, a provincial council of the Church, composed of the bishops, abbots, priors, heads of colleges, and all the principal clergy, assembled in St. Paul's Cathedral, and a papal bull was read, in which the infamous Pope Clement V. dwells most pathetically upon the awful sins of the Templars, and their great and tremendous fall from their previous high estate. Hitherto, says he, they have been renowned throughout the world as the special champions of the Faith, and the chief defenders of the Holy Land, whose affairs have been mainly regulated by those brothers.　The Church, following them and their Order with the plenitude of its especial favor and regard, armed them with the emblem of the Cross against the enemies of Christ, exalted them with much honor, enriched them with wealth, and fortified them with various liberties and privileges.　The Pope displays the sad report of their sins and iniquities which reached his ears, filled him with bitterness and grief, disturbed his repose, smote him with horror, injured his health, and caused his body to waste away! He gives a long account of the crimes imputed to the Order, of the confessions and depositions that had been made in France, and then bursts out into a paroxysm of grief, declares that the melancholy affair deeply moved all the faithful, that all Christianity was shedding bitter tears, was overwhelmed with grief, and clothed with mourning.　He concludes by decreeing the assembly of a general Council of the Church at Vienne to pronounce the abolition of the Order, and to determine on the disposal of its property, to which Council the English clergy are required to send representatives.

1309.　In Scotland, in the meantime, similar proceedings had been instituted against the Order.　On the 17th of November, Sir Knight Walter de Clifton being examined in the parish church of the Holy Cross at Edinburgh, before the Bishop of St. Andrews and John de Solerio, the Pope's chaplain, states that the Brethren of the Order of the Temple in the kingdom of Scotland received their orders, rules and observances from the Master of the Temple in England, and that the Master in England received the rules and observances of the Order from the Grand Master and the chief convent in the East.　That the Grand Master or his deputy was in the habit of visiting the Order in England and elsewhere; of summoning Chapters and making regulations for the conduct of the Brethren, and the administration of their property.　Being asked as to the mode of his reception, he states that when William de la More, the Master, held his Chapter at the Preceptory of Temple Bruere in the county of Lincoln, he sought of the assembled Brethren the habit and the fellowship of the Order; that they told him that he little knew what it was he asked, in seeking to be admitted to their fellowship; that it would be a very hard matter for him, who was then his own master, to become the servant of another, and to have no will of his own; but notwithstanding their representations of the rigor of their rules and observances, he still continued earnestly to seek their habit and fellowship. He states that they then led him to the chamber of the Master, where they held their Chapter, and that there, on his bended knees, and with his hands clasped, he again prayed for the habit and the fellowship of the Temple. That the Master and the Brethren then required him to answer questions to the following effect:—Whether he had a dispute with any man, or owed any debts? whether he was betrothed to any woman? and whether he had any secret infirmity of body? or knew of anything to prevent him from remaining within the bosom of the Fraternity? And having answered all these questions satisfactorily, the Master then asked of the surrounding Brethren, "Do ye give your consent to the reception of Brother Walter?" who unanimously answered that they did; and the Master and the Brethren then standing up, received him the said Walter in this manner. On his bended knees, and with his hands joined, he solemnly promised that he would be the perpetual servant of the Master, and of the Order, and of the Brethren, for the purpose of defending the Holy Land. Having done this, the Master took out of the hands of a Brother Chaplain of the Order the Book of the Holy Gospels, upon which was depicted a Cross, and laying his hand upon the book, and upon the Cross, he swore to God and the Blessed Virgin Mary to be for ever thereafter chaste, obedient, and to live without property. And then the Master gave to him the white mantle, and placed the coif on his head and admitted him to the kiss on the mouth, after which he made him sit down on the ground, and admonished him to the following effect: that from thenceforth he was to sleep in his shirt, drawers, and stockings, girded with a small cord over his shirt; that he was never to tarry in a house where there was a woman in the family way; never to be present at a marriage or at the purification of women; and likewise instructed and informed him upon several other particulars. Being asked where he had passed his time since his reception, he replied that he had dwelt three years at the preceptory of Blancradok in Scotland; three years at Temple Newsom in England;

one year at the Temple at London, and three years at Aslakeby. Being asked concerning the other Brothers in Scotland, he stated that John de Hueflete was Preceptor of Blancradok, the chief house of the Order in that country, and that he and the other Brethren, having heard of the arrest of the Templars, threw off their habits and fled, and that he had not since heard aught concerning them.

Forty-one witnesses, chiefly abbots, priors, monks, priests, and serving men, and retainers of the Order in Scotland, were examined upon various interrogatories, but nothing of a criminatory nature was elicited. The monks observed that the receptions of other orders were public, and were celebrated as great religious solemnities, and the friends, parents, and neighbors of the party about to take the vows were invited to attend ; while the Templars, on the other hand, shrouded their proceedings in mystery and secrecy, and therefore they *suspected the worst.* The priests thought them guilty, because they were always against the Church ! Others condemned them because (as they say) the Templars closed their doors against the poor and the humble, and extended hospitality only to the rich and the powerful. The Abbot of the Monastery of the Holy Cross at Edinburgh declared that they appropriated to themselves the property of their neighbors, right or wrong. The Abbot of Dumferlyn knew nothing of his own knowledge against them, but had *heard* much, and *suspected* more. The serving men and the tillers of the lands of the Order stated that the Chapters were held sometimes by night and sometimes by day, with extraordinary secrecy. Some of the witnesses had heard old men say that the Templars would never have lost the Holy Land if they had been good Christians.

1310. On the 9th of January, A.D. 1310, the examination of witnesses was resumed at London, in the parish church of St. Dunstan's West, near the Temple. The rector of the Church of St. Mary de la Strode declared that he had strong *suspicions* of the guilt of the Templars ; he had, however, often been at the Temple Church, and had observed that the priests performed divine service there just the same as elsewhere. William de Cumbrook, of St. Clement's Church, near the Temple, the Vicar of St. Martin's-in-the-Fields, and many other priests and clergymen of different churches in London, all declared that they had nothing to allege against the Order.

1310.   On the 27th of January John de Stoke, a serving brother of the Order of the Temple of seventeen years' standing, being examined by the Inquisitors in the Chapel of the Blessed Mary of Berkyngecherche at London, states amongst other things, that secular persons were allowed to be present *at the burial of Templars;* that the brethren of the Order all received the sacraments of the church at their last hour, and were attended to the grave by a chaplain of the Temple.   Being interrogated concerning the burial of the Knight Templar Walter le Bachelor, Grand Preceptor of Ireland, who had been confined in the penitential cell in the Temple, for disobedience to his superiors, and was reported to have been there starved to death, he deposes that the said Knight was buried like any other Christian, except that he was not buried in the burying-ground, but in the court of the house of the Temple at London; that he confessed to Richard de Grafton, a priest of the Order, then in the island of Cyprus, and partook, as he believed, of the sacrament.   He states that he himself and Radulph de Barton carried him to his grave at the dawn of day, and that the deceased Knight was in prison, as he believes, for the space of eight weeks.   That he was not buried in the habit of his Order, and was interred without the Cemetery of the Brethren, because he was considered to be excommunicated, in pursuance, as he believed, of a rule or statute among the Templars, to the effect that every one who privily made away with the property of the Order, and did not acknowledge his fault, was deemed excommunicated.

1310.   On the 30th of March, the Papal Inquisitors opened their commission at Lincoln, and numerous Templars were examined in the Chapter-house of the Cathedral, amongst whom were some of the veteran warriors of Palestine, who had moistened with their blood the distant plains of the far East.   Sir Knight William de Winchester, a member of twenty-six years' standing, stated that he had been received into the Order at the Castle *de la Roca Guille,* in the province of Armenia, bordering on Syria, by the valiant Grand Master William de Beaujeu.   He states that the same mode of reception existed there as in England, and every-

28

where throughout the Order. Sir Knight Robert de Hamilton declares that the girdles said to be worn by the brethren were called *Girdles of Nazareth,* because they had been pressed against the column of the Virgin at that place, and were worn in remembrance of the blessed Mary.

1310. At York, the examination commenced on the 28th of April, and lasted until the 4th of May, during which period twenty-three Templars, prisoners in York Castle, were examined in the Chapter-house of the Cathedral, and followed the example of their brethren in maintaining their innocence. Sir Knight Thomas de Stanford, a member of thirty years' standing, had been received in the East by the Grand Master William de Beaujeu, and Radulph de Rostona, a priest of the Order, of twenty-three years' standing, had been received at the Preceptory of Lentini in Sicily, by Eminent Sir Knight William de Canello, the Grand Preceptor of Sicily. Sir Knight Stephen de Radenhall refused to reveal the mode of reception, because it formed part of the secrets of the Chapter, and if he discovered them he would lose his chamber, be stripped of his mantle, or be committed to prison.

Passing from these trials, in which only imprisonment and threats had been brought to bear, we must now open the dark page in the history of the Order in England. All the Templars in custody there had been examined separately, and had, notwithstanding, deposed in substance to the same effect, and given the same account of their reception into the Order, and of the oaths that they took. Any reasonable and impartial mind would consequently have been satisfied of the truth of their statements; but it was not the object of the Inquisitors to obtain evidence of the *innocence,* but proof of the *guilt* of the Order. At first, King Edward II., to his honor, forbade the infliction of torture upon the illustrious members of the Temple in his dominions—men who had fought and bled for Christendom, and of whose piety and morals he had a short time before given such ample testimony to the principal sovereigns of Europe. But the virtuous resolution of the weak King was speedily overcome by the all-powerful influence of the blood-thirsty Pope, who wrote to him in the month of June, 1310, upbraiding him for preventing the Inquisitors from submitting the Templars to the discipline of the rack. Influenced by the admonitions of the Pope, and the solicitations of the clergy, the King sent orders to the constable of the Tower, to deliver up the Templars to certain jailers appointed by the Inquisitors, in order that the Inquisitors might do with the bodies of the Templars whatever should seem fitting, in accordance with ecclesiastical law. The ecclesiastical council then assembled, and ordered that the Templars should be again confined in separate cells; that fresh interrogatories should be prepared, to see if by such means the *truth* could be extracted, and if by straitenings and confinement they would *confess nothing further*, then the torture was to be applied ; but it was provided that the examination by torture should be conducted without the *perpetual mutilation or disabling of any limb, and without a violent effusion of blood!* and the Inquisitors and the Bishops of London and Chichester were to notify the result to the Archbishop of Canterbury, that he might again convene the assembly for the purpose of passing sentence, either of absolution or of condemnation.

1310. Fresh instructions were then sent by the King to the constable of the Tower and the sheriffs of London, informing them that the King, on account of his respect for the holy apostolic see, had conceded to the Inquisitors the power of examining the Templars by *torture ;* and strictly enjoining them to deliver up the Templars to the Inquisitors, and receive them back when required so to do. The King then acquainted the mayor, aldermen, and commonalty of his faithful city of London, that out of reverence to the Pope he had authorized the Inquisitors, sent over by him, to question the Templars by *torture ;* and he commands them, in case it should be notified to them by the Inquisitors that the prisons provided by the sheriffs were insufficient for their purposes, to procure without fail fit and convenient houses in the city, or near thereto, for carrying into effect the contemplated measures. Shortly afterwards, he again wrote to the mayor, aldermen, and commonalty of London, acquainting them that the sheriffs had made a return to his writ, to the effect that the four gates (prisons) of the city were not under their charge, and that they could not therefore obtain them for the purposes required ;

and he commands the mayor, aldermen, and commonalty, to place those four gates at the disposal of the sheriffs. Shortly afterwards orders were given for all the Templars in custody in London to be loaded with chains and fetters. The myrmidons of the Inquisitors were to be allowed to make periodical visits to see that the imprisonment was properly carried into effect, and were to be allowed to *torture* the bodies of the Templars in any way that they might think fit.

1311. On the 30th of March, the examination was renewed before the Inquisitors and the Bishops of London and Chichester, at the several churches of St. Martin's Ludgate, and St. Botolph's Bishopsgate. The Templars had now been in prison in England for the space of *three years and some months*. During the whole of the previous winter they had been confined *in chains* in the dungeons of the city of London, compelled to receive their scanty supply of food from the officers of the Inquisition, and to suffer from cold and hunger. They had been made to endure all the horrors of solitary confinement, and had none to solace or to cheer them during the long hours of their melancholy captivity. They had been already condemned collectively by the unfeeling Pope, as members of an heretical and idolatrous society, and as long as they continued to persist in the truth of their first confessions, and in the avowal of their innocence, they were treated as obstinate, unreconciled heretics, living in a state of excommunication, and doomed, when dead, to everlasting punishment in hell. They had heard of the miserable fate of their brethren in France, and they knew that those who had confessed crimes of which they had never been guilty, had been immediately declared reconciled to the Church, had been absolved and set at liberty, and they knew that freedom, pardon, and peace could be immediately purchased by a confession of guilt. Notwithstanding all this, every Templar, at this last examination, *persisted* in the maintenance of his innocence, and in the denial of all knowledge of, or participation in, the crimes and heresies imputed to the Order. They were therefore again sent back to their dungeons, and loaded with chains; and the Inquisitors, disappointed of the desired confession, addressed themselves to the enemies of the Order for the necessary proofs of guilt.

1311. During the month of April, seventy-two witnesses were examined in the chapter-house of the Holy Trinity. They were nearly all monks, Carmelites, Augustinians, Dominicans, and Minorites. Their evidence is all hearsay, and the nature of it will be seen from the following choice specimens:—Henry Thanet, an Irishman, had *heard* that a certain Preceptor of the Pilgrim's Castle was in the habit of making all the brethren he received into the Order to deny Christ. He had *heard* also that a certain Templar had in his custody a brazen head with two faces, which would answer all questions put to it. Master John de Nassington had *heard* that the Templars celebrated a solemn festival once a year, at which they worshiped a *calf*. John de Eure, Knight, Sheriff of the county of York, deposed, that he had once invited William de la Fenne, Preceptor of Wesdall, to dine with him, and that after dinner the Preceptor drew a book out of his bosom, and delivered it to the Knight's lady to read, who found a piece of paper fastened into the book, on which were written abominable heretical doctrines, to the effect that Christ was not the Son of God, nor born of a virgin, but conceived of the seed of Joseph, the husband of Mary, after the manner of other men, and that Christ was not a true but a false prophet, and was not crucified for the redemption of mankind, but for his own sins; and many other things contrary to the Christian faith. On the production of this evidence Sir Knight William de la Fenne was called in and interrogated; he admitted that he had dined with the Sheriff of York, and had lent his lady a book to read, but he swore that he was ignorant of the piece of paper fastened into the book, and of its contents. It appears that the Sheriff of York had kept this discovery to himself for the space of six years.

William de la Forde, a priest, rector of the parish of Crofton, in the diocese of York, had *heard* William de Reynbur, priest of the Order of St. Augustine, who was then dead, say, that the Templar, Patrick of Rippon, son of William of Gloucester, had confessed to him, that at his entrance into the Order he was led, clothed only in his shirt and trowsers, through a long passage to a secret chamber, and was there made to deny his God and his Saviour; that he was then shown a representation of the crucifixion, and was told that since he had previously honored that emblem he must now dishonor it and spit upon it, and that he did so.   After this they brought an image, as it were, of a calf, placed upon an altar, and they told him he must kiss that image, and worship it, and he did so.   And after all this they covered up his eyes and led him about, kissing and being kissed by all the brethren, but he could not recollect in what part.   The worthy priest was asked when he had *first heard* all these things, and he replied, *after* the arrest of the brethren by the King's orders.

1311.   Robert of Oteringham, senior of the Order of Minorites, stated that on one occasion he was partaking of the hospitality of the Templars at the preceptory of Ribstane in Yorkshire, and that when grace had been said after supper, the chaplain of the Order reprimanded the brethren, saying, " The devil will burn you ; " and hearing a bustle, he got up, and, as far as he recollects, saw one of the brothers of the Temple standing, his arms being laid aside, having his face to the west and his back towards the altar.   He then states, that about twenty years before that time, he was the guest of the Templars, at the preceptory of Wetherby in Yorkshire, and when evening came, he heard that the Preceptor was not coming to supper, as he was arranging some relics that he had brought with him from the Holy Land ; and afterwards at midnight he heard a confused noise in the chapel, and getting up he looked through the keyhole, and saw a great light therein, either from a fire or from candles, and on the morrow he asked one of the brethren of the Temple the name of the saint in whose honor they had celebrated so grand a festival during the night, and that brother, aghast and turning pale, thinking he had seen what had been done amongst them, said to him, " Go thy way, and if you love me, or have any regard for your own life, never speak of this matter ! "   John de Wederel, another Minorite, stated that he had lately *heard* in the country, that a Templar, named Robert de Baysat, was once seen running about a meadow uttering, " Alas ! alas ! that ever I was born, seeing that I have denied God and sold myself to the devil ! "   N. de Chinon, another Minorite, had *heard* that a certain Templar had a son who peeped through a chink in the wall of the chapter-room and saw a person, who was about to be professed, slain because he would not deny Christ, and afterwards the boy was asked by his father to become a Templar, but refused, and he immediately shared the same fate. Twenty other witnesses, who were examined in each other's presence, related similar absurdities.

At this stage of the proceedings, the Papal Inquisitor, Sicard de Vaur, exhibited two rack-extorted confessions of Templars which had been obtained in France. The first was from Robert de St. Just, who had been received into the Order by Eminent Sir Knight Himbert, Grand Preceptor of England, but had been arrested in France, and there tortured. In this confession Robert de St. Just states that, on his admission to the vows of the Temple, he denied Christ, and spat *beside* the Cross. The second confession had been extorted from Geoffrey de Gonville, Knight of the Order of the Temple, Preceptor of Aquitaine and Poitou. In this confession (which had been revoked, but of which revocation no notice was taken by the Inquisitors), Geoffrey de Gonville states that he was received into the Order in England in the house of the Temple at London, by Robert de Torvile, Knight, the Master of all England, about twenty-eight years before that time; that the Master showed him on a missal the image of Jesus Christ on the Cross, and commanded him to deny him who was crucified; that, terribly alarmed, he exclaimed, "Alas! my lord, why should I do this? I will on no account do it." But the Master said to him, "Do it boldly; I swear to thee that the act shall never harm either thy soul or thy conscience;" and then proceeded to inform him that the custom had been introduced into the Order by a certain bad Grand Master, who was imprisoned by a certain sultan, and could escape from prison only on condition that he would establish that form of reception in his Order, and compel all who were received to deny Jesus Christ. But the deponent remained inflexible. He refused to deny his Saviour, and asked where were his uncle and the other good people who had brought him there, and was told that they were all gone. And at last a compromise took place between him and the Master, who made him take his oath that he would tell all his brethren that he had gone through the customary form, and never reveal that it had been dispensed with. He states also that the ceremony was instituted in memory of St. Peter, who three times denied Christ. This Knight had been tortured in the Temple at Paris, by the brothers of St. Dominic, in the presence of the Grand Inquisitor, and he made his confession when suffering on the rack. He afterwards revoked it, and was then tortured into a withdrawal of his revocation.

1311. Ferinsius le Mareschal, a secular knight, being examined, declared that his grandfather entered into the Order of the Temple, active, healthy, and blithesome as the birds and the dogs, but on the third day from his taking the vows he was dead, and, as he *now suspects*, was killed because he refused to participate in the iniquities practiced by the brethren. An Augustine monk declared that he had heard a Templar say that a man after death had no more soul than a dog. John de Gertia, a Minorite, had *heard* from a certain woman called Cotacota, who had it from Exvalettus, Preceptor of London, that one of the servants of the Templars entered the Temple hall where the Chapter was held, and secreted himself, and after the door had been shut and locked by the last Templar who entered, and the key had been brought by him to the superior, the assembled Templars jumped up and went into another room, and opened a closet, and drew therefrom a certain black figure with shining eyes, and a cross, and they placed the cross before the Master, and this figure they placed upon the cross, and carried to the Master, who kissed the said image upon the back side, and all the others did the same after him. And when they had finished kissing, they all spat three times upon the cross, except one, who refused, saying, " I was a bad man in the world, and placed myself in this Order for the salvation of my soul ; what could I do worse ? I will not do it ; " and then the brethren said to him, " Take heed, and do as you see the Order do ; " but he answered that he would not do so, and then they placed him in a well which stood in the midst of the house, and covered the well up, and left him to perish. Being asked as to the time when the woman heard this, the deponent stated that she told it to him about fourteen years back at London, where she kept a shop for her husband, Robert Cotacota.

KNIGHTS TEMPLARS. 445

Absurd Testimony. Rack-extorted Confessions. Firmness of the Sufferers.

1311. John Walby de Bust, another Minorite, had *heard* John de Dingeston say that *he had heard* that there was in a secret place of the house of the Templars at London a gilded head, and that when one of the Masters was on his death-bed, he summoned to his presence several Preceptors, and told them that if they wished for power, and dominion, and honor, they must worship that head. Gaspar de Nafferton, Chaplain of the parish of Ryde, deposed that he was in the employ of the Templars when William de Pokelington was received into the Order. That he well recollected that the said William made his appearance at the Temple on Sunday evening, with the equipage and habit of a member of Order, accompanied by William de la More, the Master of the Temple, William de Grafton, Preceptor of Ribbestane and Fontebriggs, and other brethren. That the same night, during the first watch, they assembled in the church, and caused the deponent to be awakened to say mass. That, after the celebration of the mass, they made the deponent with his clerk go out into the hall beyond the cloister, and then sent for the person who was to be received; and on his entry into the church, one of the brethren immediately closed all the doors opening into the cloister, so that no one within the chambers could get out, and thus they remained till daylight; but what was done in the church the deponent knew not. The next day, however, he saw the said William clothed in the habit of a Templar, looking very sorrowful. The deponent also declared that he had threatened to peep through a secret door to see what was going on, but was warned that *it was inevitable death* so to do. He states that the next morning he went into the church, and found the books and crosses all removed from the places in which he had previously left them.

The evidence given before this Papal tribunal affords melancholy proof of the immorality, the credulity, and the profligacy of the age. *Abandoned women* were brought before the Inquisitors, and were induced unblushingly to relate, in the presence of the Archbishop of Canterbury and the English Bishops, the most disgusting and ridiculous enormities; and evidence was taken down by notaries, and quietly listened to by the most learned and distinguished characters of the age, which in these days would be scouted with scorn and contempt from almost every court in Christendom. On the 22d of April, all the Templars in custody in the Tower and in the prisons of the city were assembled before the Inquisitors and the Bishops of London and Chichester, in the Church of the Holy Trinity, to hear the depositions of the witnesses publicly read.   The Templars required copies of these depositions, which were granted them, and they were allowed eight days from that period to bring forward any defenses or privileges they wished to make use of.   Subsequently, before the expiration of the eight days, the officer of the Bishop of London was sent to the Tower with scriveners, and witnesses, to know if they would then set up any matters of defense, to whom the Templars replied that they were unlettered men, ignorant of the law, and that all means of defense were denied them, since they were not permitted to employ those who could afford them fit counsel and advice.   They observed, however, that they were desirous of publicly proclaiming the faith, and the religion of themselves and of the Order to which they belonged, of showing the privileges conceded to them by the Chief Pontiffs, and their own depositions taken before the Inquisitors, all which they said they wished to make use of in their defense.

1311.   On the eighth day, being Thursday the 29th of April, they appeared before the Papal Inquisitors and the Bishops of London and Chichester, in the Church of All Saints of Berkyngecherche, and presented to them the following declaration, which they had drawn up amongst themselves, as the only defense they had to offer against the injustice, the tyranny, and the persecution of their powerful oppressors; adding, that if they had in any way done wrong, they were ready to submit themselves to the orders of the Church.   This declaration is written in the Norman-French of that day as follows, viz. :

" Be it known to our honorable father, the Archbishop of Canterbury, primate of all England, and to all the Prelates of Holy Church, and to all Christians, that all we Brethren of the Temple here assembled, and every one of us are Christians, and believe in our Saviour Jesus Christ, in God the Father Omnipotent, etc., etc. . . . . . And we believe all that the Holy Church believes and teaches us.   We declare that our religion is founded on vows of obedience, chastity, and poverty, and of aiding in the conquest of the Holy Land of Jerusalem, with all the power and might that God affordeth us.   And we firmly deny and contradict, one and all of us, all manner of heresy and evil doings, contrary to the faith of Holy Church.   And for the love of God, and for charity, we beseech you, who represent our holy father the Pope, that we may be treated like true children of the Church, for we have well guarded and preserved the faith, and the law of the Church, and of our own religion, that which is good, honest, and just, according to the ordinances and the privileges of the court of Rome, granted, confirmed, and canonized by Common Council; the which privileges, together with the rule of our Order, are en- registered in the said court.   And we would bring forward all Christians (save our enemies and slanderers), with whom we are conversant, and among whom we have resided, to say how and in what manner we have spent our lives.   And if, in our examina- tions, we have said or done anything wrong through ignorance of a word, since we are unlettered men, we are ready to suffer for Holy Church like him who died for us on the Blessed Cross.   And we believe all the sacraments of the Church.   And we beseech you, for the love of God, and as you hope to be saved, that you judge us as you will have to answer for yourselves and for us be- fore God.   And we pray that our examination may be read and heard before ourselves and all the people, in the very language and words in which it was given before you, and written down on paper."

1311.   The above declaration was presented by Eminent Sir William de la More, the Master of the Temple; the Knights Templars Philip de Mewes, Preceptor of Garwy; William de Burton, Preceptor of Cumbe; Radulph de Maison, Preceptor of Ewell; Michael de Baskevile, Preceptor of London; Thomas de Wothrope, Preceptor of Bistelesham; William de Warwick, Priest; and Thomas de Burton, Chaplain of the Order; together with twenty serving brothers.   The same day the Inquisitors and the two Bishops pro- ceeded to the different prisons of the city to demand if the prison- ers confined therein wished to bring forward anything in defense of the Order, who severally answered that they would adopt and abide by the declaration made by their brethren in the Tower. In the prison of Aldgate there were confined William de Sautre, Knight, Preceptor of Samford; William de la Ford, Preceptor of Daney; John de Coningeston, Preceptor of Getinges; Roger de Norreis, Preceptor of Cressing; Radolph de Barton, priest, Prior of the New Temple; and several serving brethren of the Order. In the prison of Crepelgate were detained William de Egendon, Knight, Preceptor of Shepeley; John de Moun, Knight, Preceptor of Dokesworth; and four serving brethren. In the prison of Ludgate were five serving brethren; and in Newgate was confined Himbert Blanke, Knight, Grand Preceptor of Auvergne.

1311. The above declaration of faith and innocence was far from agreeable to the Papal Inquisitors, who required a confession of *guilt*, and the torture was once more directed to be applied. The King sent fresh orders to the Mayor and the Sheriffs of the city of London, commanding them to place the Templars in separate dungeons; to load them with chains and fetters; to permit the myrmidons of the Inquisitors to pay periodical visits to see that the wishes and intentions of the Inquisitors, with regard to the severity of the confinement, were properly carried into effect; and, lastly, to inflict torture upon the bodies of the Templars, and generally to do whatever should be thought fitting and expedient in the premises, according to the ecclesiastical law. In conformity with these orders, we learn from the record of the proceedings, that the Templars were placed in solitary confinement in loathsome dungeons; that they were put on a short allowance of bread and water, and periodically visited by the agents of the Inquisition; that they were moved from prison to prison, and from dungeon to dungeon; were now treated with rigor, and anon with indulgence; and were then visited by learned prelates, and acute doctors in theology, who, by exhortation, persuasion, and by menace, attempted in every possible mode to wring from them the required avowals. We learn that all the engines of terror wielded by the Church were put in force, and that torture was unsparingly applied, "*usque ad judicium sanguinis!*" (even to the judgment of death.) The places in which these atrocious scenes were enacted were the Tower, the prisons of Aldgate, Ludgate, Newgate, Bishopsgate, and Crepelgate, the house formerly belonging to John de Banguel, and the tenements once the property of the Brethren of Penitence.   It appears that some French monks were sent over to administer the torture to the unhappy captives, and that they were questioned and examined in the presence of notaries whilst suffering under the torments of the rack.   The relentless perseverance and the incessant exertions of the foreign Inquisitors were at last rewarded by a splendid triumph over the powers of endurance of two poor serving brethren, and one Chaplain of the Order, who were at last induced to make the long-desired avowals.

1311.   On the 23d of June, Sir Knight Stephen de Stapelbrugge, described as an apostate and fugitive of the Order of the Temple, captured by the King's officers in the city of Salisbury, deposed in the house of the head jailer of Newgate, in the presence of the Bishops of London and Chichester, the Chancellor of the Archbishop of Canterbury, Hugh de Walkeneby, Doctor of Theology, and other clerical witnesses, that there were two modes of profession in the Order of the Temple, the one good and lawful, and the other contrary to the Christian faith.   That he himself was received into the Order by Brian le Jay, Grand Preceptor of England, at Dynneslee, and was led into the chapel, the door of which was closed as soon as he had entered ; that a crucifix was placed before the Master, and that a Brother of the Temple, with a drawn sword, stood on either side of him ; that the Master said to him, " Do you see this image of the crucifixion ? " to which he replied, "I see it, my Lord ; " that the Master then said to him, " You must deny that Christ Jesus was God and man, and that Mary was his mother ; and you must spit upon this cross ; " which the deponent, through immediate fear of death, did with his mouth, but not with his heart, and he spat *beside* the cross, and not on it ; and then falling down upon his knees, with eyes uplifted, with his hands clasped, with bitter tears and sighs, and devout ejaculations, he besought the mercy and the favor of Holy Church, declaring that he cared not for the death of the body, or for any amount of penance, but only for the salvation of his soul !

1311. On Saturday, the 25th of June, Thomas Tocci de Thoroldeby, serving Brother of the Order of the Temple, described as an apostate who had escaped from Lincoln after his examination at that place by the Papal Inquisitors, but had afterwards surrendered himself to the King's officers, was brought before the Bishops of London and Chichester, the Archdeacon of Salisbury, and others of the clergy, in St. Martin's Church, in Vinetriâ; and being again examined, he repeated the statement made in his first deposition, but added some particulars with regard to penances imposed and absolutions pronounced in the Chapter, showing the difference between sins and defaults, the Priest having to deal with the one, and the Master with the other.   He declared that the little cords were worn from honorable motives, and relates a story of his being engaged in a battle against the Saracens, in which he lost his cord, and was punished by the Grand Master for a default in coming home without it.   He gives the same account of the secrecy of the Chapters as all the other brethren, states that the members of the Order were forbidden to confess to the Friars Mendicants, and were enjoined to confess to their own chaplains.   That they did nothing contrary to the Christian faith, and as to their endeavoring to promote the advancement of the Order by any means, right or wrong, that exactly the contrary was the case, as there was a statute in the Order to the effect, that if any one should be found to have acquired anything unjustly, he should be deprived of his habit, and be expelled the Order.   Being asked what induced him to become an apostate, and to fly from his Order, he replied that it was through fear of death, because the Abbot of Lagny (the Papal Inquisitor), when he examined him at Lincoln, asked him if he would not confess anything further, and he answered that he knew of nothing further to confess, unless he was to say things that were not true; and that *the abbot, laying his hand upon his breast, swore by the Word of God that he would make him confess before he had done with him!* and that being terribly frightened, he afterwards bribed the jailer of the castle of Lincoln, giving him forty florins to let him make his escape.

1311. The Abbot of Lagny, indeed, was as good as his word, for on the 29th of June, four days after this imprudent avowal, Thomas Tocci de Thoroldeby was brought back to St. Martin's Church, and there, in the presence of the same parties, he made a third confession, in which he declares that, coerced by two Templars with drawn swords in their hands, he denied Christ with his mouth, but not with his heart; and spat *beside* the cross, but not on it; that he was required to spit upon the image of the Virgin Mary, but contrived, instead of doing so, to give her a kiss on the foot. He declares that he had heard Brian le Jay, the Master of the Temple at London, say a hundred times over, that Jesus Christ was not the true God, but a man : and that the smallest hair out of the beard of one Saracen, was of more worth than the whole body of any Christian. He declares that he was once standing in the presence of Brother Brian; when some poor people besought charity of him for the love of God and our lady the blessed Virgin Mary ; and he answered, " *Que dame, allez vous pendre à votre dame*" ("What Lady, go and be hanged to your Lady,") and violently casting a half-penny into the mud, he made the poor people hunt for it, although it was in the depth of a severe winter. He also relates that at the Chapters, the priest stood like a beast, and had nothing to do but to repeat the psalm, "God be merciful unto us, and bless us," which was read at the closing of the Chapter. This witness further states, that the priest had no power to impose a heavier penance than a day's fast on bread and water, and could not even do that without the permission of the brethren. He is made also to relate that the Templars always favored the Saracens in the holy wars in Palestine, and oppressed the Christians, and he declares, speaking of himself, that for three years before he had never seen the body of Christ without thinking of the devil, nor could he remove that evil thought from his heart by prayer, or in any other way that he knew of ; but that very morning he had heard mass with great devotion, and since then had thought only of Christ, and thinks there is no one in the Order of the Temple whose soul will be saved, unless a reformation takes place.

1311. Previous to this period, the ecclesiastical Council had again assembled, and these last depositions of Stephen de Stapelbrugge

and Thomas Tocci de Thoroldeby having been produced before
them, the solemn farce of their confession and abjuration was immediately publicly enacted.   It is thus described in the record of
the proceedings:—" To the praise and glory of the name of the
Most High Father, and of the Son, and of the Holy Ghost, to the
confusion of heretics, and the strengthening of all faithful Christians, begins the public record of the reconciliation of the penitent
heretics, returning to the orthodox faith published in the Council,
celebrated at London in the year 1311.   In the name of God,
Amen.   In the year of the incarnation of our Lord, 1311, on the
twenty-seventh day of the month of June, in the hall of the palace
of the Bishop of London, before the venerable fathers the Lord
Robert by the grace of God Archbishop of Canterbury, Primate of
all England, and his suffragans in provincial council assembled, appeared Stephen de Stapelbrugge, of the Order of the Chivalry of
the Temple; and the denying of Christ and the blessed Virgin
Mary his mother, the spitting upon the Cross, and the heresies and
errors acknowledged and confessed by him in his deposition, being displayed, the same Stephen asserted in full council, before the
people of the city of London, introduced for the occasion, that all
those things so deposed by him were true, and that to that confession he would wholly adhere; humbly confessing his error on his
bended knees, with his hands clasped, with much lamentation and
many tears, he again and again besought the mercy and pity of
holy mother Church, offering to abjure all heresies and errors, and
praying them to impose on him a fitting penance, and then the
book of the Holy Gospels being placed in his hands, he abjured the
aforesaid heresies in this form:—'I, Stephen de Stapelbrugge, of
the Order of the Chivalry of the Temple, do solemnly confess,'
etc., etc., (he repeats his confession, makes his abjuration, and then
proceeds:) 'and if at any time hereafter I shall happen to relapse
into the same errors, or deviate from any of the articles of the
faith, I will account myself *ipso facto* excommunicated; I will
stand condemned as a manifest perjured heretic, and the punishment inflicted on perjured relapsed heretics, shall be forthwith imposed upon me without further trial or judgment.' "

He was then sworn upon the Holy Gospels to stand to the sen-

The Apostates absolved and reconciled to the Church.

tence of the Church in the matter, after which Thomas Tocci de Thoroldeby was brought forward to go through the same ceremony, which being concluded, these two poor serving brothers of the Order of the Temple, who were so ignorant that they could not write, were made to place their mark on the record of their abjuration. " And then our lord, the Archbishop of Canterbury, for the purpose of absolving and reconciling to the unity of the Church the aforesaid Thomas and Stephen, conceded his authority and that of the whole Council to the Bishop of London, in the presence of me the notary, specially summoned for the occasion, in these words : ' We grant to you the authority of God, of the blessed Mary, of the blessed Thomas the Martyr our patron, and of all the saints of God (*sanctorum* atque *sanctarum* Dei, " the male and female saints), to us conceded, and also the authority of the present Council to us transferred, to the end that thou mayest reconcile to the unity of the Church these miserables, separated from her by their repudiation of the faith, and now brought back again to her bosom, reserving to ourselves and the Council the right of imposing a fit penance for their transgressions.' And as there were two penitents, the Bishop of Chichester was joined to the Bishop of London for the purpose of pronouncing the absolution, which two Bishops, putting on their mitres and pontificals, and being assisted by twelve priests in sacerdotal vestments, placed themselves in seats at the western entrance of the Cathedral Church of St. Paul, and the penitents, with bended knees, humbly prostrating themselves in prayer upon the steps before the door of the Church, the members of the Council and the people of the city standing around ; and the psalm, *Have mercy upon me, O God, after thy great goodness*, having been chanted from the beginning to the end, and the subjoined prayers and sermon having been gone through, they absolved the said penitents, and received them back to the unity of the Church in the following form :—' In the name of God, Amen. Since by your confession we find that you, Brother Stephen de Stapelbrugge, have denied Christ Jesus and the blessed Virgin Mary, and have spat *beside* the Cross, and now taking better advice wishest to return to the unity of the holy Church with a true heart and sincere faith, as you assert, and all heretical depravity having for that purpose been previously abjured by you according to the form of the Church, we, by the authority of the Council, absolve you from the bond of excommunication wherewith you were held fast, and we reconcile you to the unity of the Church, if you shall have returned to her in sincerity of heart, and shall have obeyed her injunctions imposed upon you.' " Thomas Tocci de Thoroldeby was then absolved and reconciled to the Church in the usual manner, after which various psalms (Gloria Patri, Kyrie Eleyson, Christe Eleyson, etc., etc.) were sung, and prayers were offered up, and then the ceremony was concluded.

1311. On the 1st of July, an avowal of guilt was wrung by the Inquisitors from John de Stoke, Chaplain of the Order, who, being brought before the Bishops of London and Chichester, in St. Martin's Church, deposed that he was received in the mode mentioned by him on his first examination; but a year and fifteen days after that reception, being at the Preceptory of Garwy in the diocese of Hereford, he was called into the chamber of James de Molay, the Grand Master of the Order, who, in the presence of two other Templars of foreign extraction, informed him that he wished to make proof of his obedience, and commanded him to take a seat at the foot of the bed, and the deponent did so. The Grand Master then sent into the Church for the crucifix, and two serving brothers, with naked swords in their hands, stationed themselves on either side of the doorway. As soon as the crucifix made its appearance, the Grand Master, pointing to the figure of our Saviour nailed thereon, asked the deponent whose image it was, and he answered, "The image of Jesus Christ, who suffered on the Cross for the redemption of mankind;" but the Grand Master exclaimed, "Thou sayest wrong, and art much mistaken, for he was the son of a certain woman, and was crucified because he called himself the Son of God; and I myself have been in the place where he was born and crucified, and thou must now deny him whom this image represents." The deponent exclaimed, " Far be it from me to deny my Saviour;" but the Grand Master told him he must do it, or he would be put into a sack and be carried to a place which he would find by no means agreeable, and there were swords in the room, and brothers ready to use them, etc., etc. ; and the deponent asked if such was the custom of the Order, and if all the brethren did the same ; and being answered in the affirmative, he, through fear of immediate death, denied Christ with his *tongue*, but not with his *heart*. Being asked in whom he was told to put his faith after he had denied Christ Jesus, he replies, " In that great Omnipotent God who created the heaven and the earth ! "

1311. On Monday, July 5th, at the request of the Ecclesiastical Council, the Bishop of Chichester had an interview with Eminent Sir William de la More, the Master of the Temple, taking with him certain learned lawyers, theologians, and scriveners. He exhorted and earnestly pressed him to abjure the heresies of which he stood convicted, by his own confessions and those of his brethren, respecting the absolutions pronounced by him in the Chapters, and submit himself to the disposition of the Church. But the Master declared that he had never been guilty of the heresies mentioned, and that he would not abjure crimes which he had never committed ; so he was sent back to his dungeon. The next day, the Bishops of London, Winchester, and Chichester, had an interview in Southwark with the Knight Templar Philip de Mewes, Preceptor of Garwy, and some serving brethren of the New Temple at London, and told them that they were manifestly guilty of heresy, as appeared from the Pope's bulls, and the depositions taken against the Order both in England and France, and also from their own confessions regarding the absolutions pronounced in their Chapters, explaining to them that they had grievously erred in believing that the Master of the Temple, who was a mere layman, had power to absolve them from their sins by pronouncing absolution, and they warned them that if they persisted in that error they would be condemned as heretics, and that, as they could not clear themselves therefrom, it behooved them to abjure all the heresies of which they were accused. The Templars replied that they were ready to abjure the error they had fallen into respecting the absolution and all heresies of every kind, before the Archbishop of Canterbury, and the Prelates of the Council, whenever they should be required so to do, and they humbly

A Number of Templars absolved and reconciled to the Church.

and reverently submitted themselves to the orders of the Church, beseeching pardon and grace. A sort of compromise was then made with most of the Templars in custody in London. They were required publicly to repeat a form of confession and abjuration drawn up by the Bishops of London and Chichester, and were then solemnly absolved and reconciled to the Church.

1311. On the 9th of July, Michael de Baskevile, Knight, Preceptor of London, and seventeen other Templars, were absolved and reconciled in full Council, in the Episcopal Hall of the see of London, in the presence of a vast concourse of the citizens. On the 10th of the same month, the Preceptors of Dokesworth, Getinges, and Samford, the Guardian of the Temple Church at London, Radulph de Evesham, Chaplain, with other Priests, Knights, and serving brethren of the Order, were absolved by the Bishops of London, Exeter, Winchester, and Chichester, in the presence of the Archbishop of Canterbury, and the whole Ecclesiastical Council. The next day many more members of the Fraternity were publicly reconciled to the Church on the steps before the south door of Saint Paul's Cathedral, and were afterwards present at the celebration of High Mass in the interior of the sacred edifice, when they advanced in a body towards the high altar bathed in tears, and falling down on their knees, they devoutly kissed the sacred emblems of Christianity. The day after (July 12), nineteen other Templars were publicly absolved and reconciled to the Church in the same place, in the presence of the Earls of Leicester, Pembroke, and Warwick, and afterwards assisted in like manner at the celebration of High Mass. The Priests of the Order made their confessions and abjurations in Latin; the Knights pronounced them in Norman-French, and the serving brethren for the most part repeated them in English. The vast concourse of people collected together could have comprehended but very little of what was uttered, whilst the appearance of the penitent brethren, and the public spectacle of their recantation, answered the views of the Papal Inquisitors, and doubtless impressed the commonalty with a conviction of the guilt of the Order. Many of the Templars were too *sick* (from the effect of torture) to be brought down to Saint Paul's, and were therefore absolved and reconciled to the

Church by the Bishops of London, Winchester, and Chichester, at Saint Mary's Chapel near the Tower. Among these last were many veteran warriors in the last stage of decrepitude and decay. " They were so old and so infirm," says the public notary who recorded the proceedings, " that they were unable to stand ;" their confessions were consequently made before two masters in theology ; they were then led before the west door of the Chapel, and were publicly reconciled to the Church by the Bishop of Chichester ; after which they were brought into the sacred building, and were placed on their knees before the high altar, which they devoutly kissed, whilst the tears trickled down their furrowed cheeks. All these penitent Templars were now released from prison, and directed to do penance in different monasteries. Precisely the same form of proceeding was followed at York ; the reconciliation and absolution being there carried into effect before the south door of the Cathedral.

A few months after the close of these proceedings, William de la More, known in our history as " The Martyr," the Master of the Temple in England, *died of a broken heart in his solitary dungeon in the Tower, persisting with his last breath in the maintenance of the innocence of his Order.* King Edward II., in pity for his misfortunes, directed the Constable of the Tower to hand over his goods and chattels, valued at the sum of about $24.00, to his executors, to be employed in the liquidation of his debts, and he commanded Geoffrey de la Lee, guardian of the lands of the Templars, to pay the arrears of his prison pay (fifty cents per diem) to the executor, Roger Hunsingon. Did the memory of this mean and contemptible act occur to him on his own miserable death twenty years later?

We here give a full list of the Masters of the Temple, otherwise Grand Priors or Grand Preceptors of England. Magister R. de Pointon. Rocelinus de Fossa. Richard de Hastings (A. D. 1160). Richard Mallebeench. Geoffrey, son of Stephen (A. D. 1180). Thomas Berard (A. D. 1200). Amaric de St. Maur (A. D. 1203). Allan Marcel (A. D. 1224). Amberaldus (A. D. 1229). Robert Mountforde (A. D. 1234). Robert Sanford (A. D. 1241). Amadeus de Morestello (A. D. 1254). Himbert Peraut (A. D. 1270).

Robert Turville (A. D. 1290). Guido de Foresta (A. D. 1292). James de Molay (A. D. 1293). Brian le Jay (A. D. 1295). WILLIAM DE LA MORE THE MARTYR.

The only other Templar in England whose fate merits particular attention is Himbert Blanke, the Grand Preceptor of Auvergne. He appears to have been a knight of high honor and of stern unbending pride. From first to last he had boldly protested against the violent proceedings of the Inquisitors, and had fearlessly maintained, amid all his trials, his own innocence and that of his Order. This illustrious Templar had fought under *four successive Grand Masters* in defense of the Christian faith in Palestine, and after the fall of Acre, had led in person several daring expeditions against the infidels. For these meritorious services he was rewarded in the following manner: After having been tortured and half-starved in the English prisons for the space of five years, he was condemned, as he would make no confession of guilt, to be shut up in a loathsome dungeon, to be loaded with double chains, and to be occasionally visited by the agents of the Inquisition, to see if he would confess *nothing further*. In this miserable situation he remained until death at last put an end to his sufferings.

On the imprisonment of the Templars in England, the Temple at London, and all the preceptories dependent upon it, with the manors, farms, houses, lands, and revenues of the Order, were placed under the survey of the Court of Exchequer, and extents were directed to be taken of the same, after which they were confided to the care of certain trustworthy persons, styled "Guardians of the lands of the Templars," who were to account for the rents and profits to the King's exchequer. These guardians were directed to pay various pensions to the old servants and retainers of the Templars dwelling in the different preceptories, also the expenses of the prosecution against the Order; and they were at different times required to victual the King's castles and strongholds. **1312.** In the month of February, the King gave the Temple manors of Etton and Cave to David, Earl of Athol, directing the guardians of the lands and tenements of the Templars in the county of York to hand over to the said Earl all the corn in those manors, the oxen, calves, ploughs, and all the goods and chattels of the Templars existing therein, together with the ornaments and utensils of the chapel of the Temple. But on the 16th of the following May, the Pope addressed bulls to the King, and to all the Earls and Barons of the kingdom, setting forth the proceedings of the Council of Vienne, France, and the publication of a Papal decree, vesting the property late belonging to the Templars in the Brethren of the Hospital of St. John, and he commands them forthwith to place the members of that Order in possession thereof. Bulls were also addressed to the Archbishops of Canterbury and York and their suffragans, commanding them to enforce by ecclesiastical censures the execution of the Papal commands. King Edward and his nobles very properly resisted this decree, and on the 21st of August, 1312, the King wrote to the Prior of the Hospital of St. John at Clerkenwell, telling him that the pretensions of the Pope to dispose of property within the realm of England, without the consent of Parliament, were derogatory to the dignity of the crown and the royal authority. The following year the King granted the Temple at London, with the church and all the buildings therein, to Aymer de Valence, Earl of Pembroke; and on the 5th of May of the same year, he caused several merchants, from whom he had borrowed money, to be placed in possession of many of the manors of the Templars.

1313. Yielding, however, at last to the exhortations and menaces of the Pope, the King, on the 21st of November, granted the property to the Hospitalers, and sent orders to the guardians of the lands of the Templars, and to various powerful Barons who were in possession of the estates, commanding them to deliver them up to certain parties deputed by the Grand Master and Chapter of the Hospital of St. John to receive them. At this period many of the heirs of the donors, whose title had been recognized by the law, were in possession of the lands, and the judges held that the King had no power of his own sole authority to transfer them to the Order of the Hospital. The thunders of the Vatican were consequently vigorously made use of, and all the detainers of the property were doomed by the Roman Pontiff to ever-

1322. lasting damnation. Pope John XXII., in one of his bulls, bitterly complains of the disregard by all the King's subjects of the

Papal commands. He laments that they had hardened their hearts and despised the sentence of excommunication fulminated against them, and declares that his heart was riven with grief to find that even the ecclesiastics, who ought to have been as a wall of defense to the Hospitalers, had themselves been heinously guilty in the premises.

1324. At last the Pope, the Bishops, and the Hospitalers, by their united exertions, succeeded in obtaining an act of parliament, vesting all the property late belonging to the Templars in the brethren of the Hospital of St. John, in order that the intentions of the donors might be carried into effect by the appropriation of it to the defense of the Holy Land and the succor of the Christian cause in the East. This statute gave rise to the greatest discontent. The heirs of the donors petitioned parliament for its repeal, alleging that it had been made against law, and against reason, and contrary to the opinion of the judges; and many of the great Barons who held the property by a title recognized by the common law, successfully resisted the claims of the Order of the Hospital, maintaining that the parliament had no right to interfere with the tenure of private property, and to dispose of their possessions without their consent. This struggle between the heirs of the donors on the one hand, and the Hospitalers on the other, **1334.** continued for a lengthened period; and in 1334 it was found necessary to pass another act of parliament, confirming the previous statute in their favor, and writs were sent to the sheriffs commanding them to enforce the execution of the acts of the legislature, and to take possession, in the king's name, of all the property unjustly detained from the brethren of the Hospital of St. John.

Whilst the vast possessions, late belonging to the Templars, thus continued to be the subject of contention, the surviving brethren of that dissolved Order continued to be treated with the utmost inhumanity and neglect. The Ecclesiastical Council had assigned to each of them a pension of *eight cents a day* for subsistence; but this small pittance was not paid, and they were consequently in great danger of dying of hunger. King Edward II., pitying their miserable situation, wrote to the Prior of the Hospital of St. John, at Clerkenwell, earnestly requesting him to take their hard lot into his serious consideration, and not suffer them to come to beggary in the streets. The Archbishop of Canterbury also exerted himself in their behalf, and sent letters to the possessors of the property, reproving them for the non-payment of the allotted stipends. This inhumanity, says he, awakens our compassion, and penetrates us with the most lively grief. We pray and conjure you in kindness to furnish them, for the love of God and for charity, with the means of subsistence. The Archbishop of York caused many of them to be supported in the different monasteries of his diocese.

We have already seen that the Temple at London, the chief house of the English province of the Order, had been granted (A.D. 1313) by King Edward II., to Aymer de Valence, Earl of Pembroke. As Thomas Earl of Lancaster, the King's cousin and first prince of the blood, however, claimed the Temple by escheat, as the immediate lord of the fee, the Earl of Pembroke, on the 3d **1315.** of October, at the request of the King, and in consideration of the grant to him by his Sovereign of other land, gave up the property to the Earl of Lancaster. This Earl of Lancaster was President of the Council, and the most powerful and opulent subject of the kingdom; and we are told that the students and professors of the common law made interest with him for a lodging in the Temple, and first gained a footing therein as his *lessees*. They took possession of the old Hall and the gloomy cells of the military monks, and converted them into the great and most ancient Common Law University in England. From that period to the present time, the retreats of the religious warriors have been devoted to "the studious and eloquent pleaders of causes," a new kind of TEMPLARS, who, as Fuller quaintly observes, now "defend one Christian from another, as the old ones did Christians from Pagans."

Subsequently to this event the fee simple or inheritance of the place passed successively through various hands. On the memorable attainder and ignominious execution before his own castle of the Earl of Lancaster, it reverted to the Crown, and was again granted to Aymer de Valence, Earl of Pembroke, who was shortly

afterwards murdered at Paris. He died without issue, and the Temple accordingly once more vested in the Crown. It was then granted to the royal favorite, Hugh le Despenser, the younger; and on his attainder and execution by the Lancasterian faction, it came into the hands of King Edward III., who had just then ascended the throne (January 25, A.D. 1327), and was committed by him to the keeping of the Mayor of London, his escheator in the city. The Mayor closed the gate leading to the waterside, which stood at the bottom of the present Middle Temple Lane, whereby the lawyers were much incommoded in their progress backwards and forwards from the Temple to Westminster. Complaints were made to the King on the subject, who, on the 2d day **1330.** of November wrote as follows to the Mayor: "The King to the Mayor of London, his escheator in the same city. Since we have been given to understand that there ought to be a free passage through the court of the New Temple at London to the River Thames, for our justices, clerks, and others, who may wish to pass by water to Westminster to transact their business, and that you keep the gate of the Temple shut by day, and so prevent those same justices, clerks of ours, and other persons, from passing through the midst of the said court to the waterside, whereby as well our own affairs as those of our people in general are oftentimes greatly delayed, we command you that you keep the gates of the said Temple *open by day*, so that our justices and clerks, and other persons who wish to go by water to Westminster may be able so to do by the way to which they have hitherto been accustomed."
1331. The following year, the King wrote the Mayor, his escheator in the city of London, informing him that he had been given to understand that the pier in the said court of the Temple, leading to the river, was so broken and decayed, that his clerks and law officers, and others, could no longer get across it, and were consequently prevented from passing by water to Westminster. "We, therefore," he proceeds, "being desirous of providing such a remedy as we ought for this evil, command you to do whatever *repairs* are necessary to the said pier, and to defray the cost thereof out of the proceeds of the lands and rents appertaining to the said Temple now in your custody; and when we shall have been informed

of the things done in the matter, the expense shall be allowed you in your account of the same proceeds."

1333. Two years afterwards the King committed the custody of the Temple to William de Langford, and farmed out the rents and proceeds thereof to him for the term of ten years, at a rent of $120.00 per annum, the said William undertaking to keep all the houses and tenements in good order and repair, and so deliver them up at the end of the term. In the meantime, however, the Pope and the Bishops had been vigorously exerting themselves to obtain a transfer of the property to the Order of the Knights Hospitalers of Saint John. The Hospitalers petitioned the King, setting forth that the church, the cloisters, and other places within the Temple, were consecrated and dedicated to the service of God, that they had been unjustly occupied and detained from them by Hugh le Despenser the younger, and, through his attainder, had lately come into the King's hands, and they besought the King to deliver up to them possession thereof. King Edward accordingly commanded the Mayor of London, his escheator in that city, to take inquisition concerning the premises.

From this inquisition, and the return thereof, it appears that many of the founders of the Temple Church, and many of the brethren of the Order of Knights Templars, then lay buried in the Church and Cemetery of the Temple; that the Bishop of Ely had his lodging in the Temple, known by the name of the Bishop of Ely's Chamber; that there was a chapel dedicated to St. Thomas à Becket, which extended from the door of the TEMPLE HALL as far as the ancient gate of the Temple; also a cloister which began at the Bishop of Ely's Chamber, and ran in an easterly direction; and that there was a wall which ran in a northerly direction as far as the said King's highway; that in the front part of the cemetery towards the north, bordering on the King's highway, were thirteen houses formerly erected, with the assent and permission of the Master and brethren of the Temple, by Roger Blom, a messenger of the Temple, for the purpose of holding the lights and ornaments of the church; that the land whereon these houses were built, the cemetery, the church, and all the space enclosed between St. Thomas's Chapel, the church, the cloisters, and the wall running in a northerly direction, and all the buildings erected thereon, together with the hall, cloisters, and St. Thomas's Chapel, were sanctified places dedicated to God; that Hugh le Despenser occupied and detained them unjustly, and that through his attainder and forfeiture, and not otherwise, they came into the King's hands.

1337. After the return of this inquisition, the said sanctified places were assigned to the prior and brethren of the Hospital of Saint John; and the King, on the 11th of January, directed his writ to the Barons of the Exchequer, commanding them to take inquisition of the value of the said sanctified places, so given up to the Hospitalers, and of the residue of the Temple, and certify the same under their seals to the King, in order that a reasonable abatement might be made in William de Langford's rent. From the inquiry made in pursuance of this writ before John de Shoreditch, a Baron of the Exchequer, it further appears that on the said residue of the Temple upon the land then remaining in the custody of William de Langford, and withinside the great gate of the Temple, were another HALL and four chambers connected therewith, a kitchen, a garden, a stable, and a chamber beyond the great gate; also eight shops, seven of which stood in Fleet street, and the eighth in the suburb of London, without the bar of the New Temple; that the annual value of these shops varied from $2.50, $3.25, $3.75, and $4.00; that the fruit out of the garden of the Temple sold for $15.00 per annum in the gross, that seven out of the thirteen houses erected by Roger Blom were each of the annual value of $2.75; and that the eighth, situated beyond the gate of entrance to the church, was worth four marks per annum. It appears, moreover, that the total annual revenue of the Temple then amounted to about $365.00, equal to about $5,000 of our present money, and that William de Langford was abated $64.00 of the said rent.

1340. Three years after the taking of this inquisition, King Edward III., in consideration of the sum of $500.00, which the prior of the Knights Hospitalers promised to pay him towards the expense of his expedition into France, granted to the said prior all the residue of the Temple then remaining in the King's hands, to hold, together with the cemetery, cloisters, and the other sanctified places, to the said prior and his brethren, and their successors, of the King and his heirs, for charitable purposes, for ever. From this grant it appears that the porter of the Temple received $12.25 per annum, and four cents a day wages, which were paid him by the Hospitalers. At this period Philip Thane was prior of the Hospital; and he exerted himself to impart to the celebration of divine service in the Temple Church, the dignity and splendor it possessed in the time of the Templars. He, with the unanimous consent and approbation of the whole Chapter of the Hospital, granted to Hugh de Lichefield, priest, and to his successors, guardians of the Temple Church, towards the improvement of the lights and the celebration of divine service therein, all the land called Ficketzfeld, and the garden called Cotterell Garden; and two years afterwards he made a further grant, to the said Hugh and his successors, of a thousand fagots a year to be cut out of the wood of Lilleston, and carried to the New Temple to keep up the fire in the said church.

1362. King Edward III., notwithstanding the grant of the Temple to the Hospitalers, exercised the right of appointing to the porter's office, and by his letter patent he promoted Roger Small to that post for the term of his life, in return for the good service rendered him by the said Roger Small.

1312. At the period of the dissolution of the Order of the Templars many of the retainers of the ancient Knights were residing in the Temple, supported by pensions from the crown. These were of the class of free servants of office, they held their posts for life, and not having been members of the Order, they were not included in the general proscription of the Fraternity. On the seizure by the sheriffs and royal officers of the property of their ancient masters, they had been reduced to great distress, and had petitioned the King to be allowed their customary stipends. Edward II. had accordingly granted to Robert Styfford, clerk, Chaplain of the Temple Church, two deniers a day for his maintenance in the house of the Temple at London, and $1.25 a year for necessaries, provided he did service in the Temple Church; and when unable to do so, he was to receive only his food and lodging. Geoffrey Talaver Geoffrey de Cave, clerk, and John de Shelton, were also, each of them, to receive for their good services, annual pensions for the term of their lives. Some of these retainers, in addition to their various stipends, were to have a gown of the class of free-serving brethren of the Order of the Temple each year; one old garment out of the stock of old garments belonging to the brethren; one mark a year for their shoes, etc.; their sons also received so much *per diem*, on condition that they did the daily work of the house. These domestics and retainers of the ancient brotherhood of the Knights Templars, appear to have transferred their services to the learned society of lawyers established in the Temple, and to have continued and kept alive amongst them many of the ancient customs and observances of the old Knights. The Chaplain of the Temple Church took his meals in the hall with the lawyers, as he had been wont to do with the Knights Templars; and the rule of their Order requiring "two and two to eat together," and "all the fragments to be given in brotherly charity to the domestics," continued to be observed, and *prevails to this day;* whilst the attendants at table continued to be, and are still called *paniers*, as in the days of the Knights Templars.

1333. A few years after the lawyers had established themselves in the convent of the Temple, the Judges of the Court of Common Pleas were made KNIGHTS, being the earliest instance on record of the grant of the honor of Knighthood for services purely civil, and the professors of the common law, who had the exclusive privilege of practicing in that court, assumed the title or degree of FRÈRES SERJENS, or FRATRES SERVIENTES (Serving Brothers), so that an order of Knights and Serving Brethren was most curiously revived in the Temple, and introduced into the profession of the law. It is true that the word *Serviens, Serjen,* or Sergeant, was applied to the professors of the law long before the reign of Edward III., but not to denote a *privileged Brotherhood.* It was applied to lawyers in common with all persons who did any description of work for another, from the Sergeant-at-Law, who prosecuted the pleas of the crown in the County Court, to the *Serviens* or *Serjen* who walked before the Patriarch Heraclius in the

Judges and others admitted into the Order of the Temple.

streets of Jerusalem. The priest who worked for the Lord was called Sergeant of the Lord, and the lover who served the lady of his affections Sergeant of Love. It was in the Order of the Temple that the word *Frères Serjens,* or *Fratres Servientes,* first signified an honorary title or degree, and denoted a powerful privileged class of brethren. The *Fratres Servientes armigeri,* or *Frères Serjens des Armes,* of the chivalry of the Temple, were of the rank of gentlemen. They united in their own persons the monastic and the military character, they were allotted one horse each, they wore the Cross of the Order of the Temple on their breasts, they participated in all the privileges of the brotherhood, and were eligible to the dignity of Preceptor. Large sums of money were frequently given by seculars who had not been advanced to the honor of Knighthood, to be admitted amongst this highly esteemed order of men. These *Frères Serjens* of the Temple wore linen *coifs,* and red caps close over them. At the ceremony of their admission into the Fraternity the Master of the Temple placed the coif upon their heads, and threw over their shoulders the white mantle of the Temple. He then caused them to sit down on the ground, and gave them a solemn admonition concerning the duties and responsibilities of their profession. The Knights and Sergeants of the Common Law, on the other hand, have ever constituted a privileged *fraternity,* and always address one another by the endearing term *Brother.* The religious character of the ancient ceremony of admission into this legal brotherhood, which took place in the Temple Church, and its strong similarity to the ancient mode of reception into the Fraternity of the Temple, are curious and remarkable. The Chief-Justice, says an ancient MS. account of the creation of Sergeants-at-Law, points out to them many bright examples of their predecessors, and then places the *coifs* upon their heads, and indues them one by one with red caps, and so they are created Sergeants-at-Law. In his admonitory exhortation the Chief-Justice displays to them the moral and religious duties of their profession. "Walk in the vocation in which you are called. . . . . Learn the worship of reverence to authority, and pity to the poor." He tells them the coif is *sicut vestis candida et immaculata,* "the emblem of purity and virtue," and he commences a portion of his discourse in the Scriptural language used by the Popes in the famous bull conceding to the Templars their vast spiritual and temporal privileges. It has been supposed that the coif was first introduced by the clerical practitioners of the common law to hide the *tonsure* of those priests who practiced in the Court of Common Pleas, notwithstanding the ecclesiastical prohibition. This was not the case. The early portraits of our Judges exhibit them with a coif of very much larger dimensions than the coifs now worn by the Sergeants-at-Law, very much larger than would be necessary to hide the *mere clerical tonsure.* A covering for that purpose indeed would be absurd.

1337. From the inquisition into the state of the Temple, it appears, as we have already seen, that in the time of the Knights Templars there were TWO HALLS in the Temple, the one being the hall of the Knights, and the other the hall of the *Frères Serjens*, or serving-brethren of the Order. One of these halls, the present Inner Temple Hall, had been assigned, the year previous to the taking of that inquisition, to the prior and brethren of the Hospital of St. John, together with the church, cloisters, etc., as before mentioned, whilst the other hall remained in the hands of the crown, and was not granted to the Hospitalers. It was probably **1340.** soon after this period that the Hospitalers conceded the use of *both halls* to the professors of the law, and these last, from dining apart and being attached to different halls, at last separated into two societies. When the lawyers originally came into the Temple as lessees of the Earl of Lancaster, they found engraved upon the ancient buildings the armorial bearings of the Order of the Temple, which were, on a shield argent, a plain cross gules, and (*brochant sur le tout*) the Holy Lamb bearing the banner of the Order, surmounted by a red cross. These arms remained the emblem of the Temple until the fifth year of the reign of Queen Elizabeth, when unfortunately the Society of the Inner Temple, yielding to the advice and persuasion of Master Gerard Leigh, a member of the College of Heralds, abandoned the ancient and honorable device of the Knights Templars, and assumed in its place a galloping winged horse called a Pegasus, or, as it has been explained to us, " a horse striking the earth with its hoof, or *Pegasus luna on a field argent!* " Master Gerard Leigh, we are told, " emblazoned them with precious stones and planets, and by these strange arms he intended to signify that the knowledge acquired at the learned seminary of the Inner Temple would raise the professors of the law to the highest honors, adding, by way of motto, *volat ad æthera virtus*, and he intended to allude to what are esteemed the more liberal sciences, by giving them Pegasus forming the fountain of Hippocrene, by striking his hoof against the rock, as a proper emblem of lawyers becoming poets, as Chaucer and Gower, who were both of the Temple!"

The Society of the Middle Temple, with better taste, still preserves, in that part of the Temple over which its sway extends, the widely-renowned and time-honored badge of the ancient Order of the Temple.

On the dissolution of the Order of the Hospital of St. John (A.D. 1540), the Temple once more reverted to the crown, and the lawyers again became the immediate lessees of the sovereign. In the reign of James I., 1603–1625, however, some Scotchman attempted to obtain from his majesty a grant of the fee simple or inheritance of the Temple, which being brought to the knowledge of the two law societies, they forthwith made " humble suit " to the king, and obtained a grant of the property to themselves. By **1609.** letters patent, bearing date the 13th of August, King James granted the Temple to the Benchers of the two societies, their heirs and assigns forever, for the lodging, reception, and education of the professors and students of the laws of England, the said Benchers yielding and paying to the said king, his heirs and successors, fifty dollars yearly for the mansion called the Inner Temple, and fifty dollars yearly for the Middle Temple.

There are but few remains of the ancient Knights Templars now existing in the Temple beyond the CHURCH. The present Inner Temple Hall was the ancient HALL OF THE KNIGHTS, but it has at different periods been so altered and repaired as to have lost almost every trace and vestige of antiquity. In the year 1816 it was nearly rebuilt, and the following extract from " The Report and Observations of the Treasurer on the late Repairs of the Inner

Temple Hall," may prove interesting, as showing the state of the edifice previous to that period. " From the proportions, the state of decay, the materials of the eastern and southern walls, the buttresses of the southern front, the pointed form of the roof and arches, and the rude sculpture on the two doors of public entrance, the hall is evidently of very great antiquity. . . . . . The northern wall appears to have been rebuilt, except at its two extremities, in modern times, but on the old foundations. . . . . The roof was found to be in a very decayed and precarious state. It appeared to have undergone reparation at three separate periods of time, at each of which timber had been unnecessarily added, so as finally to accumulate a weight which had protruded the northern and southern walls. It became, therefore, indispensable to remove all the timber of the roof, and to replace it in a lighter form. On removing the old wainscoting of the western wall, a perpendicular crack of considerable height and width was discovered, which threatened at any moment the fall of that extremity of the building with its superincumbent roof. . . . . The turret of the clock and the southern front of the hall are only cased with stone ; this was done in the year 1741, and very ill executed. The structure of the turret, composed of chalk, ragstone, and rubble (the same material as the walls of the church), seems to be very ancient. . . . . The wooden cupola of the bell was so decayed as to let in the rain, and was obliged to be renewed in a form to agree with the other parts of the southern front.

" Notwithstanding the Gothic character of the building, in the year 1680, during the treasurership of Sir Thomas Robinson, prothonotary of C. B., a Grecian screen of the Doric order was erected, surmounted by lions' heads, cones, and other incongruous devices. In the year 1741, during the treasurership of John Blencowe, Esq., low windows of Roman architecture were formed in the southern front. The dates of such innovations appear from inscriptions with the respective treasurers' names."

This ancient hall formed the far-famed refectory of the Knights Templars, and was the scene of their proud and sumptuous hospitality. Within its venerable walls they at different periods entertained King John, King Henry III., the haughty legates of the Roman Pontiffs, and the embassadors of foreign powers. The old custom, alluded to by Matthew Paris, of hanging around the walls the shields and armorial devices of the ancient Knights, is still preserved, and each succeeding treasurer of the Temple still continues to hoist his coat of arms on the wall, as in the high and palmy days of the warlike monks of old. Here, in the time of the Knights Templars, the discipline was administered to disobedient brethren, who were scourged upon their bare backs with leathern thongs. Here also was kept, according to the depositions of the witnesses who brought such dark and terrible accusations against the Templars before the ecclesiastical tribunal assembled in London, the famous black idol with shining eyes, and the gilded head, which the Templars worshiped! and from hence was taken the refractory knight, who having refused to spit upon the Cross, was plunged into the well which stood in the middle of the Temple court! The general chapters of the Templars were frequently held in the Temple Hall, and the Vicar of the church of St. Clements, at Sandwich, swore before the Papal Inquisitors assembled at London, that he had heard that a boy had been murdered by the Templars in the Temple, because he had crept by stealth into the Hall to witness the proceedings of the assembled brethren.

At the west end of the hall are considerable remains of the ancient convent of the Knights. A groined Gothic arch of the same style of architecture as the oldest part of the Temple Church forms the roof of the present buttery, and in the apartment beyond is a groined vaulted ceiling of great beauty. The ribs of the arches in both rooms are elegantly molded, but are sadly disfigured with a thick coating of plaster and barbarous whitewash. In the cellars underneath these rooms are some old walls of immense thickness, the remains of an ancient window, a curious fireplace, and some elegant pointed Gothic arches corresponding with the ceilings above ; but they are now, alas! shrouded in darkness, choked with modern brick partitions and staircases, and soiled with the damp and dust of many centuries. These interesting remains form an upper and an under story, the floor of the upper story being on a level with the floor of the hall, and the floor of the under story on a level with the terrace on the south side thereof. They were formerly connected with the church by means of a covered way or cloister, which ran at right angles with them over the site of the present cloister-chambers, and communicated with the upper and under story of the chapel of St. Anne, which formerly stood on the south side of the church. By means of this corridor and chapel the brethren of the Temple had private access to the church for the performance of their strict religious duties, and of their secret ceremonies of admitting novices to the vows of the order. In A. D. 1612, some brick buildings three stories high were erected over this ancient cloister by Francis Tate, Esq., and being burnt down a few years afterwards, the interesting covered way which connected the church with the ancient convent was involved in the general destruction, as appears from the following inscription upon the present buildings:—VETUSTISSIMA TEMPLARIORUM PORTICU IGNE CONSUMPTA, ANNO 1678, NOVA HÆC, SUMPTIBUS MEDII TEMPLI EXTRUCTA, ANNO 1681, GULIELMO WHITELOCKE ARMIGERO, THESAURARIO. (" The very ancient portico of the Templars being consumed by fire in the year 1678, these new buildings were erected at the expense of the Middle Temple in the year 1681, during the treasurership of William Whitelocke, Esq.")

The cloisters of the Templars formed the means of communication between the halls of the church and the cells of the serving brethren of the order. During the formation of the present new entrance into the Temple, by the church, at the bottom of the Inner Temple lane, a considerable portion of the brickwork of the old houses was pulled down, and an ancient wall of great thickness was disclosed. It was composed of chalk, ragstone, and rubble, exactly resembling the walls of the church. It ran in a direction east and west, and appeared to have formed the extreme northern boundary of the old convent. The exact site of the remaining buildings of the ancient Temple cannot now be determined with certainty.

Among the many interesting objects to be seen in the ancient church of the Knights Templars which still exists in a wonderful state of preservation, is the PENITENTIAL CELL, a dreary place of solitary confinement formed within the thick wall of the building, only four feet six inches long and two feet six inches wide, so

Penitential Cell.   The dreary Chamber for disobedient Brethren.

narrow and small that a grown person cannot lie down within it. In this narrow prison the disobedient brethren of the ancient Templars were temporarily confined in chains and fetters, " in order that their souls might be saved from the eternal prison of hell." The hinges and catch of a door firmly attached to the door-way of this dreary chamber still remain, and at the bottom of the staircase is a stone recess or cupboard, where bread and water were placed for the prisoner. In this cell Walter le Bachelor, Knight, Grand Preceptor of Ireland, *is said* to have been starved to death.

BASTINET, WITH CAMAIL AND VENTAIL—A.D. 1360.

VIEW OF THE JORDAN VALLEY FROM THE KHAN OF THE GOOD SAMARITAN, JERUSALEM, JERICHO ROAD.

CHAPTER III.

THE POSSESSIONS OF THE KNIGHTS TEMPLARS AT THE PERIOD OF
THEIR VIOLENT DISSOLUTION A. D. 1312.

Erect anew your beauteous gate,
   Your Temple sacred to the Name Divine;
Let purest gold His altar decorate
   On all its pinnacles the mountain marbles shine:
Oh, Lebanon, thine ancient Cedars bring;
   Prepare, ye priestly choirs, Jehovah's praise to sing:
Descend, great God, return and dwell with thine!
   Tremble, oh earth! with reverent, glad surprise,
      Before His awful Holiness
         And Majesty Divine:
      Abase yourselves in subject lowliness,
         Ye lords of earth and skies.

IN addition to the statements in the last chapter concerning their London property, we add that the Knights Templars had first established the chief house of their Order in England, without Holborn Bars, on the south side of the street, where Southampton House formerly stood, adjoining to which Southampton Buildings were afterwards erected; and it is stated, that about a century and a half ago, part of the ancient chapel annexed to this establishment, of a circular form, and built of Caen stone, was discovered on pulling down some old houses near Southampton Buildings in Chancery Lane. This first house of the Temple, established by Hugh de Payens himself, before his departure from England, A. D. 1130, on his return to

Palestine, was adapted to the wants and necessities of the Order in its infant state, when the Knights, instead of lingering in the Preceptories of Europe, proceeded at once to Palestine, and when all the resources of the society were strictly and faithfully forwarded to Jerusalem, to be expended in defense of the faith.   But when the Order had greatly increased in numbers, power, and wealth, and had somewhat departed from its original purity and simplicity, we find that the Superior and the Knights resident in London began to look abroad for a more extensive and commodious place of habitation.   They purchased a large space of ground, extending from the White Friars westward to Essex House without Temple Bar, and commenced the erection of a convent on a scale of grandeur commensurate with the dignity and importance of the chief house of the great religio-military society of the Temple in Britain. It was called the *New* Temple, to distinguish it from the original establishment at Holborn, which came thenceforth to be known by the name of the *Old* Temple.   This New Temple was adapted for the residence of numerous military monks and novices, serving brothers, retainers, and domestics.   It contained the residence of the Superior and of the Knights, the cells and apartments of the chaplains and serving brethren, the council chamber where the Chapters were held, and the refectory or dining-hall, which was connected by a range of handsome cloisters with the magnificent Church, consecrated by the Patriarch.   Alongside the river extended a spacious pleasure-ground for the recreation of the brethren, who were not permitted to go into the town without the leave of the Master.   It was used also for military exercises and the training of horses.

1185.   The year of the consecration of the Temple Church, Geoffrey, the Superior of the Order in England, caused an inquisition to be made of the lands of the Templars in this country, and the names of the donors thereof, from which it appears, that the larger territorial divisions of the Order were then called bailiwicks, the principal of which were London, Warwic, Couele, Meritune, Gutinge, Westune, Licolnscire, Lindeseie, Widine, and Eboracisire (Yorkshire).   The number of manors, farms, churches, advowsons, demense lands, villages, hamlets, windmills, and water-

✠ ANNO · AB · INCARNA
TIONE · DOMINI · M̄ · C · LXXXV ·
DEDICATA · hEC · ECCLESIA · IN · hONO
RE · BEATE · MARIE · AD · N̄O · ERACLIO · DEI · GR̄A ·
SC̄E · RESVRECTIONIS · ECCLESIE · PATRI
ARChA · IIII · IDVS · FEBRVARII · Q̄ · ET̄A · ANNALI̅ ·
PET̄CTIB · DE · IVNIA · SP̄NITET̄IA̅ · X̄ · DIES · INDVLSIT ·

THE ANCIENT INSCRIPTION ON THE TEMPLE CHURCH AS IT STOOD OVER THE DOOR LEADING INTO THE CLOISTER.

Translation of the Inscription on the Temple Church,

AS IT STOOD OVER THE DOORWAY LEADING INTO THE CLOISTER.

———•◦•———

ON THE 10TH OF FEBRUARY,

IN

THE YEAR FROM THE INCARNATION OF OUR LORD, 1185,

THIS CHURCH WAS CONSECRATED IN HONOR OF THE BLESSED MARY

BY THE LORD HERACLIUS,

BY

THE GRACE OF GOD PATRIARCH OF THE CHURCH OF THE RESURRECTION

WHO HATH GRANTED AN INDULGENCE OF SIXTY DAYS

TO THOSE YEARLY VISITING IT.

KNIGHTS TEMPLARS. 479

Establishments belonging to the Temple.   Possessions of the Order.

mills, rents of assize, rights of common and free warren, and the amount of all kinds of property possessed by the Templars in England at the period of the taking of this inquisition, are astonishing. Upon the great estates belonging to the Order, prioral houses had been erected, wherein dwelt the procurators or stewards charged with the management of the manors and farms in their neighborhood, and with the collection of the rents. These prioral houses became regular monastic establishments, inhabited chiefly by sick and aged Templars, who retired to them to spend the remainder of their days, after a long period of honorable service against the infidels in Palestine. They were cells to the principal house at London. There were also under them certain smaller administrations established for the management of the farms, consisting of a Knight Templar, to whom were associated some serving brothers of the Order, and a Priest who acted as almoner. The commissions or mandates directed by the Master of the Temple to the officers at the head of these establishments were called precepts, from the commencement of them, " *Præcipimus tibi*," we enjoin or direct you, etc., etc. The Knights to whom they were addressed were styled *Præceptores Templi*, or Preceptors of the Temple, and the districts administered by them *Præceptoria*, or Preceptories.

1185. It will be proper here to take a more general survey of the possessions and organizations of the Order both in Europe and Asia. " Their circumstances," says William of Tyre, writing from Jerusalem about the period of the consecration at London of the Temple Church, " are in so flourishing a state, that at this day they have in their convent (the Temple on Mount Moriah) more than three hundred Knights robed in the white habit, besides serving brothers innumerable. Their possessions indeed beyond the sea, as well as in these parts, are said to be so vast, that there cannot now be a province in Christendom which does not contribute to the support of the aforesaid brethren, whose wealth is said to equal that of sovereign princes."

The eastern provinces of the Order were, 1. Palestine, the ruling province. 2. The principality of Antioch. 3. The principality of Tripoli. In Palestine the Templars possessed, in addition to the Temple at Jerusalém, the chief house of the Order, and the residence of the Master, the fortified city of Gaza, the key of the kingdom of Jerusalem on the side next Egypt, which was granted to them in perpetual sovereignty, by Baldwin, King of Jerusalem; also the Castle of Safed, in the territory of the ancient tribe of Naphtali; the Castle of the Pilgrims, in the neighborhood of Mount Carmel; the Castle of Assur near Joppa, and the house of the Temple at Joppa; the fortress of Faba, or La Feue, the ancient Aphek, not far from Tyre, in the territory of the ancient tribe of Asher; the hill-fort Dok, between Bethel and Jericho; the castles of La Cave, Marle, Citern Rouge, Castel Blanc, Trapesach, Sommelleria of the Temple, in the neighborhood of Acre, Castrum Planorum, and a place called Gerinum Parvum. The Templars, moreover, purchased the Castle of Beaufort and the city of Sidon; they also got into their hands a great part of the town of Acre, where they erected a famous TEMPLE, and almost all the sea-coast of Palestine was in the end divided between them and the Hospitalers of St. John. The principal houses of the Temple in the PROVINCE OF ANTIOCH were at Antioch itself, at Aleppo, and Haram; and in the PRINCIPALITY OF TRIPOLI, at Tripoli, Tortosa, the ancient Antaradus; Castel Blanc in the same neighborhood; Laodicea and Beyrout.

In the western province of APULIA AND SICILY, the Templars possessed numerous houses, viz., at Palermo, Syracuse, Lentini, Butera, and Trapani. The house of the Temple at this last place has been appropriated to the use of some monks of the Order of St. Augustin. In a church of the city is still to be seen the celebrated statue of the Virgin, which Brother Guerrege and three other Knights Templars brought from the East, with a view of placing it in the Temple Church on the Aventine hill in Rome, but which they were obliged to deposit in the island of Sicily. This statue is of the most beautiful white marble, and represents the Virgin with the infant Jesus reclining on her left arm; is of about the natural height, and, from an inscription on the foot of the figure, it appears to have been executed by a native of the island of Cyprus, A. D. 733. The Templars possessed valuable estates in Sicily, around the base of Mount Etna, and large tracts of land between Piazza and Calatagirone, in the suburbs of which last place there was a Temple house, the church whereof, dedicated to the Virgin Mary, still remains. They possessed also many churches in the island, windmills, rights of fishery, of pasturage, of cutting wood in the forests, and many important privileges and immunities. The chief house was at Messina, where the Grand Prior resided.

UPPER AND CENTRAL ITALY also contained numerous preceptories of the Order of the Temple, all under the immediate superintendence of the Grand Prior or Preceptor of Rome. There were large establishments at Lucca, Milan, and Perugia, at which last place the arms of the Temple are still to be seen on the tower of the Holy Cross. At Placentia there was a magnificent and extensive convent, called Santa Maria del Tempio, ornamented with a very lofty tower. At Bologna there was also a large Temple house, and on a clock in the city is the following inscription. "*Magister Tosseolus de Miolâ me fecit . . . Fr. Petrus de Bon, Procur. Militiæ Templi in curiâ Romanâ,* MCCCIII." In the church of St. Mary in the same place, which formerly belonged to the Knights Templars, is the interesting marble monument of Peter de Rotis, a priest of the Order.

In the PROVINCE OF PORTUGAL, the military power and resources of the Order were exercised in almost constant warfare against the Moors, and Europe derived essential advantage from the enthusiastic exertions of the warlike monks in that quarter against the infidels. In every battle, indeed, fought in the south of Europe, after the year 1130, against the enemies of the Cross, the Knights Templars are to be found taking an active and distinguished part. They were extremely popular with all the princes and sovereigns of the great Spanish peninsula, and were endowed with cities, villages, lordships, and splendid domains. The Grand Prior or Preceptor of Portugal resided at the Castle of Tomar. It is seated on the River Narboan, in Estremadura, and is still to be seen towering in gloomy magnificence on the hill above the town. The castle at present belongs to the Order of Christ, and was lately one of the grandest and richest establishments in Portugal. It possessed a splendid library, and a handsome cloister, the archi-

An Oratory dedicated to the Martyrs Marin and Pentaleon.

tecture of which was much admired.   The houses or preceptories
of the Temple in the province of Castile and Leon were those of
Cuenca, and Guadalfagiara; Tine and Aviles in the diocese of
Oviedo, and Pontevreda in Galicia.   In Castile alone the Order
is said to have possessed twenty-four bailiwicks.

In ARAGON the Templars possessed the castles of Dumbel, Ca-
banos, Azuda, Granena, Chalonere, Remolins, Corbins, Lo Mas de
Barbaran, Moncon, and Montgausi, with their territories and dependencies.   They were lords of the cities of Borgia and Tortosa;
they had a tenth part of the revenues of the kingdom, the taxes
of the towns of Huesca and Saragossa, and houses, possessions,
privileges, and immunities in all parts.   They possessed likewise
lands and estates in the Balearic Isles, which were under the
management of the Prior or Preceptor of the Island of Majorca,
who was subject to the Grand Preceptor of Aragon.

In GERMANY AND HUNGARY the houses and preceptories most
known were at Homburg, Assenheim, Rotgen in the Rhingau,
Mongberg in the Marché of Brandenbourg, Nuitz on the Rhine,
Tissia Altmunmunster near Ratisbon in Bavaria, Bamberg, Mid-
dleburgh, Hall, and Brunswick.   The Templars possessed the fiefs
of Rorich, Pausin, and Wildenheuh in Pomerania, an establishment at Bach in Hungary, several lordships in Bohemia and Mo-
ravia, and lands, tithes, and large revenues, the gifts of pious
German crusaders.   In GREECE the Templars also possessed lands
and establishments.   Their chief house was at Constantinople, in
the quarter called Ὁμόνοια, where they had an oratory dedicated
to the holy martyrs Marin and Pentaleon.   In FRANCE the principal preceptories were at Besançon, Dole, Salins, à la Romagne,
à la ville Dieu, Arbois in Franche Comté; Dorlesheim near Mols-
heim, where there still remains a chapel called Templehoff; Fau-
verney, where a chapel dedicated to the Virgin still preserves the
name of the Temple; Des Feuilles, situate in the parish of Vil-
lett, near the Chateau de Vernay, and Rouen, where there were
two houses of the Temple; one of them occupied the site of the
present *maison consulaire*, and the other stood in the street now
called La Rue des Hermites.   The preceptories and houses of the
Temple in France, indeed, were so numerous, that it would be a

TOWER OF THE PRECEPTORY OF TEMPLE BRUERE, LINCOLNSHIRE.

wearisome and endless task to repeat the names of them. Between Joinville and St. Dizier may still be seen the remains of Temple Ruet, and old chateau surrounded by a moat; and in the diocese of Meaux are the ruins of the great manorial house of Choisy le Temple. Many interesting tombs are there visible, together with the refectory of the Knights, which has been converted into a sheepfold. The chief house of the Order for France, and also for Holland and the Netherlands, was the Temple at Paris, an extensive and magnificent structure, surrounded by a wall and a ditch. It extended over all that large space of ground, now covered with streets and buildings, which lies between the Rue du Temple, the Rue St. Croix, and the environs de la Verrerie, as far as the walls and the fossés of the Port du Temple. It was ornamented with a great tower, flanked by four smaller towers, erected by the Knight Templar Brother Herbert, almoner to the King of France, and was one of the strongest edifices in the kingdom. Many of the modern streets of Paris which now traverse the site of this interesting structure preserve in the names given to them some memorial of the ancient Temple. For instance, *La rue* (street) *du Temple, La rue des fossés du Temple, Boulevard du Temple, Faubourg du Temple, rue de Faubourg du Temple, Vieille rue du Temple*, etc., etc.

All the houses of the Temple in Holland and the Netherlands were under the immediate jurisdiction of the Master of the Temple at Paris. The preceptories in these kingdoms were very numerous, and the property dependent upon them was of great value.

In ENGLAND there were in bygone times the preceptories of Aslakeby, Temple Bruere, Egle, Malteby, Mere, Wilketon, and Witham, in Lincolnshire. North Feriby, Temple Hurst, Temple Newsom, Pafflete, Flaxflete, and Ribstane, in Yorkshire. Temple Cumbe, in Somersetshire. Ewell, Strode and Swingfield, near Dover, in Kent. Hadescoe, in Norfolk. Balsall and Warwick, to Warwickshire. Temple Rothley, in Leicestershire. Wilburgham Magna, Daney, and Dokesworth, in Cambridgeshire. Halston, in Shropshire. Temple Dynnesley, in Hertfordshire. Temple Cressing and Sutton, in Essex. Saddlescomb and Chapelay, in Sussex. Schepeley, in Surrey. Temple Cowley, Sandford, Bistelesham, and Chalesey, in Oxfordshire. Temple Rockley, in Wiltshire. Upleden and Garwy, in Herefordshire. South Badeisley, in Hampshire. Getinges, in Worcestershire. Giselingham and Dunwich, in Suffolk.

There were also several smaller administrations established, as before mentioned, for the management of the farms and lands, and the collection of rent and tithes. Among these were Liddele and Quiely in the diocese of Chichester; Eken in the diocese of Lincoln; Adingdon, Wesdall, Aupledina, Cotona, etc. The different preceptors of the Temple in England had under their management lands and property in every county of the realm.

In Leicestershire the Templars possessed the town and the soke of Rotheley; the manors of Rolle, Babbegrave, Gaddesby, Stonesby, and Melton; Rotheley wood, near Leicester; the villages of Beaumont, Baresby, Dalby, North and South Mardefeld, Saxby, Stonesby, and Waldon, with land in above *eighty* others! They had also the Churches of Rotheley, Babbegrave, and Rolle; and the Chapels of Gaddesby, Grimston, Wartnaby, Cawdwell, and Wykeham.

In Hertfordshire they possessed the town and forest of Broxbourne, the manor of Chelsin Templars, and the manors of Laugenok, Broxbourne, Letchworth, and Temple Dynnesley; demesne lands at Stanho, Preston, Charlton, Walden, Hiche, Chelles, Levecamp, and Benigho; the Church of Broxbourne, two watermills, and a lock on the River Lea; also property at Hichen, Pyrton, Ickilford, Offeley Magna, Offeley Parva, Walken Regis, Furnivale, Ipolitz, Wandsmyll, Watton, Therleton, Weston, Gravele, Wilien, Leccheworth, Baldock, Datheworth, Russenden, Codpeth, Sumershale, Buntynford, etc., etc., and the Church of Weston. In the county of Essex they had the manors of Temple Cressynge, Temple Roydon, Temple Sutton, Odewell, Chingelford, Lideleye, Quarsing, Berwick, and Witham; the Church of Roydon, and houses, lands, and farms, both at Roydon, at Rivenhall, and in the parishes of Prittlewall and Great and Little Sutton; an old mansion-house and chapel at Sutton, and an estate called Finchinfelde in the hundred of Hinckford. In Lincolnshire the

Templars possessed the manors of La Bruere, Roston, Kirkeby, Brauncewell, Carleton, Akele, with the soke of Lynderby, Aslakeby, and the Churches of Bruere, Asheby, Akele, Aslakeby, Donington, Ele, Swinderby, Skarle, etc. There were upwards of thirty churches in the county which made annual payments to the Order of the Temple, and about forty windmills. The Order likewise received rents in respect of lands at Bracebrig, Brancestone, Scapwic, Timberland, Weleburne, Diringhton, and a hundred other places ; and some of the land in the county was charged with the annual payment of sums of money towards the keeping of lights eternally burning on the altars of the Temple Church. William Lord of Asheby gave to the Templars the perpetual advowson of the Church of Asheby in Lincolnshire, and they in return agreed to find him a priest to sing for ever twice a week in his Chapel of St. Margaret.

In Yorkshire the Templars possessed the manors of Temple Werreby, Flaxflete, Etton, South Cave, etc. ; the Churches of Whitcherche Keluntune, etc. ; numerous windmills and lands and rents at Nehus, Skelture, Pennel, and more than sixty other places besides. In Warwickshire they possessed the manors of Barston, Shirburne, Balshale, Wolfhey, Cherlecote, Herbebure, Stodleye, Fechehampstead, Cobington, Tysho and Warwick ; lands at Chelverscoton, Herdwicke, Morton, Warwick, Hetherburn, Chesterton, Aven, Derset, Stodley, Napton, and more than thirty other places, the several donors whereof are specified in Dugdale's History of Warwickshire (p. 694) ; also the Churches of Sireburne, Cardington, etc., and more than thirteen windmills. In 12 Hen. II., William Earl of Warwick built a new Church for them at Warwick. In Kent they had the manors of Lilleston, Hechewayton, Saunford, Sutton, Dartford, Halgel, Ewell, Cocklescomb, Strode, Swinkfield Mennes, West Greenwich, and the manor of Lydden, which now belongs to the Archbishop of Canterbury ; the advowsons of the Churches of West Greenwich and Kingeswode juxta Waltham ; extensive tracts of land in Romney marsh, and farms and assize rents in all parts of the county. In Sussex they had the manors of Saddlecomb and Shipley ; lands and tenements at Compton and other places ; and the advowsons of the Churches of Shipley, Wodmancote, and Luschwyke.

In Surrey they had the manor farm of Temple Elfand or El-fant, and an estate at Merrow in the hundred of Woking. In Gloucestershire, the manors of Lower Dowdeswell, Pegsworth, Amford, Nishange, and five others which belonged to them wholly or in part, the Church of Down Ammey, and lands in Frampton, Temple Guting, and Little Rissington. In Worcestershire, the manor of Templars Lawern, and lands in Flavel, Temple Brough-ton, and Hanbury. In Northamptonshire, the manors of Asheby, Thorp, Watervill, etc., etc.; they had the advowson of the Church of the manor of Hardwicke in Orlington hundred, and we find that "Robert Saunford, Master of the soldiery of the Temple in Eng-land," presented to it in the year 1238. In Nottinghamshire, the Templars possessed the Church of Marnham, lands and rents at Gretton and North Carleton; in Westmoreland, the manor of Temple Sowerby; in the Isle of Wight, the manor of Uggeton, and lands in Kerne. But it would be tedious further to continue with a dry detail of ancient names and places; sufficient has been said to give an idea of the enormous wealth of the Order in this country, where it is known to have possessed some hundreds of manors, the advowson or right of presentation to Churches innu-merable, and thousands of acres of arable land, pasture, and wood-land, besides villages, farm-houses, mills, tithes, rights of common, of fishing, of cutting wood in forests, etc., etc. There were also several preceptories in Scotland and Ireland, which were depend-ent on the Temple at London.

The annual income of the Order in Europe has been roughly estimated at $30,000,000! According to Matthew Paris, the Tem-plars possessed *nine thousand* manors or lordships in Christendom, besides a large revenue and immense riches arising from the con-stant charitable bequests and donations of sums of money from pious persons. The Templars, in imitation of the other monastic establishments, obtained from pious and charitable people all the advowsons within their reach, and frequently retained the tithe and the glebe in their own hands, deputing a priest of the Order to perform divine service and administer the sacraments. The manors of the Templars produced them rent either in money, corn, or cattle, and the usual produce of the soil. By the custom

CHAPEL OF THE PRECEPTORY OF TEMPLE SWINGFIELD, DOVER.

in some of these manors, the tenants were annually to mow three days in harvest, one at the charge of the house, and to plow three days, whereof one at the like charge; to reap one day, at which time they should have a ram from the house, sixteen cents, twenty-four loaves, and a cheese of the best in the house, together with a pailful of drink. The tenants were not to sell their horse-colts if they were foaled upon the land belonging to the Templars, without the consent of the Fraternity; nor marry their daughters without their license. There were also various regulations concerning the cocks and hens and young chickens.

King Henry II., for the good of his soul and the welfare of his kingdom, granted the Templars a place situate on the river Fleet, near Bainard's Castle, with the whole current of that river at London, for erecting a mill; also a messuage near Fleet street; the Church of St. Clement, and the Churches of Elle, Swinderby, and Skarle in Lincolnshire, Kingeswode juxta Waltham in Kent, the Manor of Stroder in the hundred of Skamele, the vill of Kele in Staffordshire, the hermitage of Flikeamstede, and all his lands at Lange Cureway, a house in Brosal, and the market at Witham; lands at Berghotte, a mill at the bridge of Pembroke Castle, the vill of Finchinfelde, the Manor of Rotheley, with its appurtenances, and the advowson of the church and its several chapels, the Manor of Blalcolvesley, the Park of Halshall, and three *fat bucks* annually, either from Essex or Windsor Forest. He likewise granted them an annual fair at Temple Bruere, and superadded many rich benefactions in Ireland.

The Templars, in addition to their amazing wealth, enjoyed vast privileges and immunities within this realm. They were freed from all amerciaments in the Exchequer, and obtained the privilege of not being compelled to plead except before the King or his Chief Justice. By special grant from the Kings of England, they enjoyed free warren in all their demesne lands, also the power of holding courts to judge their villains and vassals, and to try thieves and malefactors; they were relieved from all the customary feudal suits and services, from the works of parks, castles, bridges, the building of royal houses, and all other works; and also from waste regard and view of foresters, and from toll in all markets and fairs, and at all bridges, and upon all highways throughout the kingdom.   They had also the chattels of felons and fugitives, and all waifs within their fee.   In addition to the particular privileges conceded to them by the Kings of England, the Templars enjoyed, under the authority of divers Papal bulls, various immunities and advantages, which gave great umbrage to the clergy.   They were freed, as before mentioned, from the obligation of paying tithes, and might, with the consent of the Bishop, receive them.   No brother of the Temple could be excommunicated by any bishop or priest, nor could any of the churches of the Order be laid under interdict except by virtue of a special mandate from the Holy See.   When any Brother of the Temple, appointed to make charitable collections for the succor of the Holy Land, should arrive at a city, castle, or village, which had been laid under interdict, the churches, on their welcome coming, were to be thrown open (once within the year), and divine service was to be performed in honor of the Temple, and in reverence for the holy soldiers thereof.   The privilege of sanctuary was thrown around their dwellings; and by various Papal bulls it is solemnly enjoined that no person shall lay violent hands either upon the persons or the property of those flying for refuge to the Temple houses.

Sir Edward Coke, in the second part of the " Institute of the Laws of England," observes, that the Templars did so overspread throughout Christendom, and so exceedingly increased in possessions, revenues, and wealth, and specially in England, as you will wonder to read in approved histories, and withal obtained so great and large privileges, liberties, and immunities for themselves, their tenants, and farmers, etc., as no other Order had the like." He further observes, that the Knights Templars were *cruce signati*, " designated by the Cross," and as the Cross was the ensign of their profession, and their tenants enjoyed great privileges, they did erect crosses upon their houses, to the end that those inhabiting them might be known to be the tenants of the Order, and thereby be freed from many duties and services which other tenants were subject unto.   " And many tenants of other lords," he says, " perceiving the state and greatness of the Knights of the

The Templars and Hospitalers Conservators of their own Privileges.

said Order, and withal seeing the great privileges their tenants enjoyed, did set up crosses upon their houses, as their very tenants used to do, to the prejudice of their lords."

This abuse led to the passing of the statute of Westminster, the second, chap. 33, which recites, that many tenants did set up crosses, or cause them to be set up on their lands in prejudice of their lords, that the tenants might defend themselves against the chief lord of the fee by the privileges of TEMPLARS, and enacts that such lands shall be forfeited to the chief lords or to the King. Sir Edward Coke observes, that the Templars were freed from tenths and fifteenths to be paid to the King; that they were discharged of purveyance; that they could not be sued for any ecclesiastical cause before the ordinary, *sed coram conservatoribus suorum privilegiorum;* and that of ancient time they claimed that a felon might take to their houses, having their crosses for his safety, as well as to any church. And concerning these conservers or keepers of their privileges, he remarks, that the Templars and Hospitalers "held an ecclesiastical court before a canonist, whom they termed 'the Conservator of their privileges,' which judge had indeed more authority than was convenient, and did daily, in respect to the height of these two orders, and at their instance and direction, encroach upon and hold plea of matters determinable by the common law, for 'when more is given to a person than is right, he derives more than is lawful;' and this was one great mischief. Another mischief was, that this judge likewise at their instance, in cases wherein he had jurisdiction, would make general citations as 'for the Salvation of the Soul,' and the like, without expressing the matter whereupon the citation was made, which also was against law, and tended to the grievous vexation of the subject." To remedy these evils another act of parliament was passed, prohibiting the Templars from bringing any man in plea before the keepers of their privileges, for any matter the knowledge whereof belonged to the King's court, and commanding such keepers of their privileges thenceforth to grant no citation at the instance of the Templars, before it be expressed upon what matter the citation ought to be made.

The Grand Master of the Temple, at this period, ranked in

494　　　　　　　　　KNIGHTS TEMPLARS.

Council of Knights of the East and West.　Grand Master.　General Titles.

Europe as a Sovereign Prince, and had precedence of all embassadors and peers in the general councils of the Church. He was elected to his high office by the Chapter of the Kingdom of Jerusalem, which was composed of all the Knights of the East and of the West who could manage to attend. The western nations or provinces of the Order were presided over by the Provincial Masters, otherwise Grand Priors or Grand Preceptors, who were originally appointed by the Grand Master at Jerusalem, and were in theory mere trustees or bare administrators of the revenues of the Fraternity, accountable to the treasurer-general at Jerusalem, and removable at the pleasure of the Grand Master. The Superior of the Temple at London is always styled " Master of the Temple," and holds his chapters and has his officers corresponding to those of the Grand Master in Palestine. The latter, consequently, came to be denominated *Magnus Magister*, or GRAND MASTER. The titles given indeed to the superiors of the different nations or provinces into which the Order of the Temple was divided, are numerous and somewhat perplexing. In the East, these officers were known only, in the first instance, by the title of Prior, as Prior of England, Prior of France, Prior of Portugal, etc., and afterwards Preceptor of England, Preceptor of France, etc. ; but in Europe they were called Grand Priors, and Grand Preceptors, to distinguish them from the Sub-priors and Sub-preceptors, and also Masters of the Temple. The Prior and Preceptor of England, therefore, and the Grand Prior, Grand Preceptor, and Master of the Temple in England, were one and the same person. There were also at the New Temple at London, in imitation of the establishment at the chief house in Palestine, in addition to the Master, the Preceptor of the Temple, the Prior of London, the Treasurer, and the Guardian of the Church, who had three chap-.ains under him called Readers.

The Master at London had his general and particular, or his ordinary and extraordinary Chapters. The first was composed of the Grand Preceptors of Scotland and Ireland, and all the provincial Priors and Preceptors of the three kingdoms, who were summoned once a year to deliberate on the state of the Holy Land, to forward succor, to give an account of their stewardship, and to

KNIGHTS TEMPLARS. 495

Meetings of Chapters in the Preceptories. Seal of the Knights of the Temple.

frame new rules and regulations for the management of the temporalities. The ordinary Chapters were held at the different Preceptories, which the Master of the Temple visited in succession. In these Chapters new members were admitted into the Order; lands were bought, sold, and exchanged; and presentations were made by the Master to vacant benefices. Many of the grants and other deeds of these Chapters, with the seal of the Order of the Temple annexed to them, are to be met with in the public and private collections of manuscripts throughout England. One of the most interesting and best preserved, is the Harleian charter (83, c. 39), in the British Museum, which is a grant of land made by William de la More THE MARTYR, the last Master of the Temple in England, to the Lord Milo de Stapleton. It is expressed to be made by him, with the common consent and advice of his Chapter, held at the Preceptory of Dynneslee, on the feast of Saint Barnabas the Apostle, and concludes, " In witness whereof, we have to this present indenture placed the seal of our Chapter." A fac-simile of this seal is given at the head of the present chapter. On the reverse of it is a man's head, decorated with a long beard, and surmounted by a small cap, and around it are the letters TESTIS SVM AGNI. The same seal is to be met with on various other indentures made by the Master and Chapter of the Temple. The more early seals are surrounded with the words, Sigillum *Militis* Templi, "Seal of the *Knight* of the Temple;" as in the case of the deed of exchange of lands at Normanton in the parish of Botisford, in Leicestershire, entered into between Amadeus de Morestello, Master of the Chivalry of the Temple in England, and his Chapter, of the one part, and the Lord Henry de Coleville, Knight, of the other part. The seal annexed to this deed has the addition of the word *Militis*, but in other respects it is similar to the one above delineated.

The Master of the Temple in England sat in Parliament as first baron of the realm, but that is to be understood among priors only. To the parliament holden in the twenty-ninth year of King Henry III., there were summoned sixty-five Abbots, thirty-five Priors, and the Master of the Temple. The oath taken by the Grand Priors, Grand Preceptors, or Provincial Masters in Europe, on their assumption of the duties of their high administrative office, was drawn up in the following terms:—" I, *A. B.*, Knight of the Order of the Temple, just now appointed Master of the Knights who are in ———, promise to Jesus Christ my Saviour, and to his Vicar the Sovereign Pontiff and his successors, perpetual obedience and fidelity. I swear that I will defend, not only with my lips, but by force of arms and with all my strength, the mysteries of the faith; the seven sacraments, the fourteen articles of the faith, the creed of the Apostles, and that of Saint Athanasius; the books of the Old and the New Testament, with the commentaries of the holy fathers, as received by the Church; the unity of God, the plurality of the persons of the holy Trinity; and the doctrine that Mary, the daughter of Joachim and Anna, of the tribe of Judah, and of the race of David, remained always a virgin before her delivery, during and after her delivery. I promise likewise to be submissive and obedient to the Master-general of the Order, in conformity with the statutes prescribed by our father Saint Bernard; that I will at all times in case of need pass the seas to go and fight; that I will always afford succor against the infidel kings and princes; that in the presence of three enemies I will fly not, but cope with them, if they are infidels; that I will not sell the property of the Order, nor consent that it be sold or alienated; that I will always preserve chastity; that I will be faithful to the king of ———; that I will never surrender to the enemy the towns and places belonging to the Order; and that I will never refuse to the religious any succor that I am able to afford them; that I will aid and defend them by words, by arms, and by all sorts of good offices; and in sincerity and of my own free will, I swear that I will observe all these things."

1154. Among the earliest of the Masters, or Grand Priors, or Grand Preceptors of England, whose names figure in history, is Richard de Hastings, who was at the head of the Order in that country on the accession of King Henry II. to the throne, and was employed by that monarch in various important negotiations. He was the friend and confidant of Thomas à Becket, and vainly endeavored to terminate the disputes between that haughty Prelate

Minister of the Soldiery of the Temple. Rich Treasures deposited in the Temple.

and the King. Richard de Hastings was succeeded by Richard Mallebeench, who confirmed a treaty of peace and concord which had been entered into between his predecessor and the Abbot of Kirkested. The next Master of the Temple appears to have been Geoffrey, son of Stephen, who received the Patriarch Heraclius as his guest at the new Temple on the occasion of the consecration of the Temple Church. He styles himself "*Minister* of the Soldiery of the Temple in England."

In consequence of the high estimation in which the Templars were held, and the privilege of sanctuary enjoyed by them, the Temple at London came to be made "a storehouse of treasure." The wealth of the King, the Nobles, the Bishops, and of the rich Burghers of London, was generally deposited therein, under the safeguard and protection of the Military Friars. The money collected in the churches and chapels for the succor of the Holy Land was also paid to the Treasurer of the Temple, to be forwarded to its destination; and the Treasurer was at different times authorized to receive the taxes imposed upon the movables of the ecclesiastics, also the large sums of money extorted by the rapacious Popes from the English clergy, and the annuities granted by the King to the Nobles of the kingdom. The money and jewels of Hugh de Burgh, Earl of Kent, the Chief Justiciary, and at one time governor of the King and kingdom of England, were deposited in the Temple, and when that nobleman was disgraced and committed to the Tower, the King attempted to lay hold of the treasure. Matthew Paris gives the following curious account of the affair: "It was suggested," says he, "to the King, that Hubert had no small amount of treasure deposited in the New Temple, under the custody of the Templars. The King, accordingly, summoning to his presence the Master of the Temple, briefly demanded of him if it was so. He, indeed, not daring to deny the truth to the King, confessed that he had money of the said Hubert, which had been confidentially committed to the keeping of himself and his brethren, but of the quantity and amount thereof he was altogether ignorant. Then the King endeavored with threats to obtain from the brethren the surrender to him of the aforesaid money, asserting that it had been fraudulently subtracted from his treasury. But they

498 KNIGHTS TEMPLARS.

The King seizes the Treasures of Hugh de Burgh.   Extortions of the Pope.

answered to the King, that money confided to them in trust they would deliver to no man without the permission of him who had intrusted it to be kept in the Temple. And the King, since the above-mentioned money had been placed under their protection, ventured not to take it by force. He sent, therefore, the Treasurer of his court, with his Justices of the Exchequer, to Hubert, who had already been placed in fetters in the Tower of London, that they might exact from him an assignment of the entire sum to the King. But when these messengers had explained to Hubert the object of their coming, he immediately answered that he would submit himself and all belonging to him to the good pleasure of his Sovereign. He therefore petitioned the brethren of the Chivalry of the Temple that they would, in his behalf, present all his keys to his lord the King, that he might do what he pleased with the things deposited in the Temple. This being done, the King ordered all that money, faithfully counted, to be placed in his treasury, and the amount of all the things found to be reduced into writing, and exhibited before him."

The Kings of England frequently resided in the Temple, and so also did the haughty legates of the Roman Pontiffs, who there made contributions in the name of the Pope upon the English bishoprics. Matthew Paris gives a lively account of the exactions of the Nuncio Martin, who resided for many years at the Temple, and came there armed by the Pope with powers such as no legate had ever before possessed. "He made," says he, "whilst residing at London in the New Temple, unheard of extortions of money and valuables. He imperiously intimated to the Abbots and Priors that they must send him rich presents, desirable palfreys, sumptuous services for the table, and rich clothing; which being done, that same Martin sent back word that the things sent were insufficient, and he commanded the givers thereof to forward him better things, on pain of suspension and excommunication."

The convocations of the clergy and the great ecclesiastical councils were frequently held at the Temple, and laws were there made by the Bishops and Abbots for the government of the Church and monasteries in England.

Part Fifth.

FROM THE MARTYRDOM OF JAMES DE MOLAY, A. D. 1313, TO THE PRESENT PERIOD, A. D. 1874.

VIEW OF MOUNT OLIVET.

CHAPTER I.

THE KNIGHTS OF ST. JOHN, A. D. 1291 TO 1873.

> CHEER up, ye blessed warrior band,
> With Him in danger, heart and hand,
>   You have maintained your post:
> The warfare ended, think ye now
> When majesty adorns His brow
>   He will forget His host?
> Ah no,—a shameful captain he,
> Who after strife and victory
>   His people should disown!
> But follow ye your faithful Lord,
> And ye shall share His great reward,
>   His kingdom and His throne.

THE record of the Knights Hospitalers, or St. John (afterwards of Cyprus and Rhodes, finally of Malta), is one of the most brilliant chapters in human history. There is so much to be said that is honorable to their bravery, perseverance, and self-sacrifice, that the difficulty of *condensation* in narrating their gallant exploits for five hundred years is greater than that of writing out an ordinary history. In our sketch we chiefly follow Taaffe ("History of the Knights of Malta"), but have drawn considerably upon De Vertot. In page 161 we give a list of the Grand Masters of this Brotherhood from 1289 to 1799.

With grief Europe heard of the fall of Acre. Quickly was it followed by that of Tyre and all the towns along the Syrian coast, from which the Latin inhabitants who could, fled by sea. Beyrout

502 KNIGHTS HOSPITALERS.

The Influence throughout the Holy Land of the Actions of the two Orders.

was the last Christian town to fall, though some say that Nicopolis, near Jerusalem, held out two years after. Glory to the Hospitalers, for of these was the little garrison whose valor rendered it inexpugnable so long under reiterated assaults; nor did it ever yield to human arms, but was thrown down by an earthquake, which buried the whole—soldiers, citadel, city. This Nicopolis was the ancient Emmaus, named in *Luke* xxiv. 13. The present may be in the immediate vicinity of the same spot; but otherwise no vestige of its predecessor.

Besides the Pilgrim Castle near Tripoli, the Knights Templars had built another of nearly that name between Caifa and Cæsarea at Athlit, of which the ruins still exist, as we have shown in a previous chapter. This fell after Acre. Its foundations were an old tower that had long belonged to the Order of the Temple, and was on the seaside. In the new erection they were assisted by various pilgrims and the German Hospitalers. Many antiquities and ancient coins and treasures are still found in digging in the mountain there. The Templars built also a castle in Acre, the chief there.

The miserable outcasts of the two Military Orders filled Christendom with their doleful tales, and increased the poverty of every country; and from the fall of Acre, Villani dates the beginning of the decline of the commercial towns in maritime Italy; since from that day out they lost half the advantages that Eastern traffic brought. For Acre had been a universal resort, and in the middle of Syria, nay, in the middle of the civilized world, as at equal distances between the East and West, and almost on European frontier and transit for commerce from all those distant lands, and had interpreters of every language and people of every class and inhabitants of every climate. Therefore, in losing Acre, the world lost one of its elements. And the Holy Land, with its thickly-populous districts and its innumerable clusters of villages, quantities of strong castles, and eighty cities inhabited by Franks for the most part, and owing their defense to the Latins, was all reduced to a devastated wilderness-state, "in which it shall remain, please God, until the day of Judgment," is the aspiration of a Moslem writer.

What other circular was necessary than what Villiers had written already? And it had sufficed to call the Knights of his Order of every age and rank, who, instantly renouncing everything else, hurried down into the various ports of Christendom with most laudable ardor, young or old, in health or not; no delay, no excuse, but each one striving to be first, and embarking in any ship to be found, and all these put into Cyprus; so that not a day passed but some Hospitalers arrived from Europe. All of them might be bound for Acre, but Cyprus was on their road, and there, alas! they learned *they had to go no farther*.

The nearly-exterminated Order reduced to half a dozen wounded men, without money, and in proportion, to perfect beggary; this European flow made it revive. The same may be said of the Templars. Nor is this island within forty leagues of Palestine, had they not both some property in it already. Henry II., descended from Guy de Lusignan, who deceased a century before, was then its King, and so of Norman blood. He showed his friendship by the cordiality with which he received the rest of the Templars and Hospitalers after their irreparable loss, and placed them in Limisso, one of his chief towns. Perhaps it was from pure compassion, or that it was the advice of some evil-wisher; for Pope Nicholas IV. (1288–1292) had the repute of loving those peerless Knights. But he appears to have taken a most undue advantage of their miserable state, when he proposed to unite the Hospitalers and Templars *into one order*, whose common Grand Master, to prevent jealousy, should be elected by neither of them but *by himself*, and likewise always for the future *by the Holy See.* But that project was promptly rejected. The same Pope, A. D. 1292, showed his liberality, by applying to the schismatic Greek Church to join him in renouncing for a time all religious differences, for defense of universal Christianity against the Saracens; and also had recourse to the Pagan Tartars. But of the whole powers of Christendom, not one, except the Templars and Hospitalers alone, took any real part in the attempt. Yet before it there was a general Chapter held at Limisso in Cyprus, so faithfully responded to that scarcely ever before, since the foundation of the Order, such a number of the Hospitalers of all nations had appeared.   There (it is tradition) the Grand Master John de Villiers, hardly recovered from his wounds, entered with a sorrowful countenance, yet that magnanimity which usually is seen in virtue, and in a calm and slow tone said: "Of the ancient rule of our Order, my being present may possibly appear an infraction, and therefore, not to scandalize you, my cherished Brethren, I have some documents to prove that I had sworn to the population that, useless as I had become from my wounds, I should endeavor to survive for the purpose of leading away as many as I could from the Acre-slaughter, as was likewise my duty as Sovereign of that unfortunate city.   And I plead it as an exception, no way derogatory to what continues as our standing statute, that none shall recede without command, and that a Knight of ours made prisoner is *a Knight dead*.   With regard to the few of our Knights who came with me, they have no excuse to make, since *they had my orders*, for which the entire responsibility is mine, in consideration of their wounded condition, and that it would be an idle sacrifice of lives.   Read these affidavits then; and I am ready either to be deposed, or even suffer death, or obtain your entire approval of my conduct, according to what you may determine; for which I retire."

After some minutes, the whole Chapter followed Villiers and declared him *completely vindicated*, and humbly besought him not to abandon them.   "Then, abandon you I will not; but persevere in being your Grand Master and loving father; and allow me to begin by thanking you," as re-entering the hall he sat down, "for the promptitude with which you have obeyed my orders.   And far better than had Divine Providence allowed you to be in time for Acre, since there you could only have increased superfluous deaths, but here you show that Holy Land has not lost all its defenders.   But by the courage that animates you, I see we have still men worthy of the name of Hospitalers and capable of remedying all our losses.   Acre is indeed ours as the sepulcher of so many of our gallant brethren.   It is for you to replace them and liberate Jerusalem from the barbarians' iron despotism."

Observing Limisso to be an open town with only a well-fortified citadel in the center, too small for the Order's residence, some proposed removing to one of the Italian ports. This was instantly quashed with indignation, by the Grand Master and chief Knights, as contrary to the spirit of their institution, which did not permit them *to go far from Palestine*, but be always at hand, and ready to profit by any opportunity. This sentiment met universal applause, and was immediately drawn up as a sort of perpetual statute. And the Chapter ended by determining to fortify Limisso and erect it into a regular establishment of Hospitality. Nor is there any earlier approximation to the naval, than when it was resolved that the ship which had conveyed them from Acre should be used in clearing the coasts from the continual attacks of Saracen pirates. Nor did this prevent cavalry from being the Order's principal care still; as we find (even five years later) certain lands set apart for forage for their horses, whereas there is little or nothing about *galleys* in these documents as yet. Such was the commencement of the navy of the Order of Malta. No auspicious one certainly, to commence in a period of abeyance (which some called decline, or extinction) after having lived a trifle above two hundred years, far from promising future maritime glory. Fortunately their young efforts were not crushed by the Sultan, Othman (Osman) I., 1299–1326, who enraged that the two bodies (Templars and Hospitalers) whom he had thought to have put an end to were reviving. The fleet he sent against them was lost, and he himself died shortly after. A new Pope, Celestine V., chosen A.D. 1294, soon abdicating, one perhaps too unworldly for this world, even during his short reign, found time to praise the Hospitalers. His learned and wily successor, Boniface VIII., A. D. 1294, letting himself go to the audacious temptation of what was partly offered to him by the unjust kings of Europe themselves, and the unhappy circumstances of the times, tried to erect a despotism, both spiritual and temporal; but whatever he was to others, he imitated his predecessors in being kind to the Order. "Claret devotione conspicua Ordo St. Johannis Hierosolumitani" (this eminent Order of St. John of Jerusalem is bright with devotion), are the words in his brief to the King of Portugal, and in another to the English King Edward I., not dissimilar. And now Villiers died.

That donations from private persons were still coming to the

Hospitalers, and that though the Knights Teutonics had relinquished their name of German Hospitalers they bore no ill will to those they had left, is clear from a reliable German record in which a father, retired from the world as dead to it from the moment he had joined the Teutonics, witnesses his son's confirmation of his own gift to the Hospital. Later it might be otherwise, but now they had known them too well and recently not to esteem and love all three of the military orders. The successor of Villiers was Sir Otho de Pins in 1298, who died on his voyage to seek protection from Rome, and so the election took place of Sir William Villaret.

In 1299 the head of the Tartars sent to Pope Boniface VIII. to proclaim Jerusalem *free*, and that the Tartar had liberated it from the Mohammedan yoke, and so that the Christians might come back to repeople their lands. He sent letters of the same tenor to the Grand Masters of the Hospitalers and Templars, inviting them to return and enter into peaceful enjoyment of their former possessions. Villaret was at the time of his election Prior of St. Gilles, nor did he come instantly to Cyprus on his election, but first visited various houses of the Order in France, including that of the Hospitaleresses under his own sister. And if it be interesting we may learn that the dress of these ladies consisted in a robe of scarlet cloth, and a cross of white linen with eight points. Ever since the Palos had been at Acre, years before its destruction, even further back than St. Louis' Crusade, Cyprus had heard of Tartary and of Christian propensities in the Tartars, or at least their finest horde; so now a body of Hospitalers' horse, was sent, A.D. 1301, in furtherance of the league that had been proposed by Pope Nicholas IV., A.D. 1288; these, with the Tartars, advanced all over Palestine, and had even the comfort to enter Jerusalem, but found it, like all the other towns in those parts, lying quite open, the Saracens having razed everything like a fortification after taking Acre.

If the Khan of Tartary was, as is said, a person of extraordinary intelligence, and an assiduous reader of the *Cyropedia* and the life of Alexander, and that those princes were his models, no wonder he preferred Christianity to Mohammedanism, for he could not but observe that what is against nature must be false. All beneficent natural changes are slow and gradual as the corn, the tree, the human creature. With what invisible slowness does the flower produce the fruit and this enlarge and ripen!

But unnatural things are for the most part sudden and violent, and nearly always wicked or disastrous, like earthquakes or hurricanes. But he and his were soon forced to return to their own country in consequence of a civil war, and so the Hospitalers had to retreat from evident inability to withstand the Sultan of Cairo, who was coming.

In the meantime, Sir Theobald Gaudin, who had been made Grand Master of the Templars after De Beaujeu was killed at Acre, went with the King of Cyprus to make a diversion on the Syrian coast, and took Tortosa; but in 1302 it was won back by the Saracens with the loss of one hundred and twenty of the Templars, which being considered a great number, prepares us to disbelieve the exaggerations of the times. Not that the fusion of Hospitalers and Templars was in itself bad, but the design of depriving them of their independence for the benefit of a third, reminds you of the lawyer and two clients. And towards the end of 1304, when the two Grand Masters, of whom one was the glorious but unfortunate James De Molay, who had now succeeded to Gaudin, spoke to each other for the last time, the greatest difficulty was got over it is said by their mutual generosity. They were ready, each, to abdicate for the whole mixed body to elect their chief, who, as long as any of the existing Templars lived, was to be of their Order, and after them things were to be as before. But though the two generous chiefs were agreed thus, not so their Knights, whose ratification was quite necessary, and therefore the whole plan miscarried, and the substance of their argument was sent in his own name by De Molay afterwards, in his answer to the Pope, whether De Molay dictated it or availed himself of that prepared, already, by his immediate predecessor Gaudin, who had been elected by *the only ten Templars* who got alive from Acre and was succeeded by one of them, De Molay. "But my answer shall be simply that I cannot go till after I have settled respecting an island," replied the Hospitaler on their second interview that same day, " and many islands being in these seas, no one knows which I mean, none even of my own Knights, except my brother, perhaps, in case I should die. But as to you, I will make no secret of it, but present you another offer, since it is no fault of yours if you do not accept my former one. It is now two hundred years and more that our Orders have uniformly been together, or if ever at all separated, not for long, and often have we shared the greatest dangers and fought and bled side by side. Even our rivalry, as some choose to call it, cannot but bind us close. I would rather have said emulation, for we have always had the same cause. If there be any difference in our rule it is very little. For me I love to think we form *but one* and derive from the same stem, and believe you are of similar sentiments. So I regret to see you no more. Wishing well to the Teutonics in Germany, their branching off was long before my time. But you and I have always been together and have both spilled a little of our blood at Acre, and known noble Beaujeau and Claremont. I will tell you, therefore, the island in my mind's eye is *Rhodes*, so famous in ancient ages, and that shall become famous and opulent, and in every way a desirable residence in ours also. Now with your assistance we shall take that beautiful spot and strong, and we shall both reside there as at Acre. Besides, our rule is, as I have said, essentially the same, and it is your duty as well as mine to fix ourselves as near Jerusalem as we can. Whereas, if you decide for Europe I have dark forebodings. Your Order, as well as mine, has many enemies, but yours worse, and gives greater food for envy. In Rhodes we shall be, as it were, our own masters, and have our own good swords to protect us. But in Europe are malicious tongues, stronger than the brightest courage, there called pride and pretension. There your fawning courtier is the hero, and nocturnal falsehood invests what triumphs over the best and bravest. Better in our island of roses (the name Rhodes signifies a *Rose*), than in Paris with whatever splendor. Think on it well before giving me a refusal. You will reap honor wherever you go. If *riches*, these will bring you flattery and ruin. Remember I told you so."

" We have both our duties," answered De Molay, with pensive

sadness, "and you must cleave to your Knights and I to mine. The Morea and the glories of Greece and Constantinople are the dreams of mine. Yet all you say afflicts me. No doubt of wealth and honors ; but what are they to produce ? Farewell."

The generous pair never met again. He and his Templars embarked for the Piærus that very evening, and shortly after he of the Hospital went reconnoitering several of the neighboring islands. During which came other letters from the new Pope Benedict IX., and to the Grand Master of the Templars may have been a sort of duplicate of this. And if he of the Hospital was called only to hide the monstrous enormity, his disobedience was easily pardoned on De Molay's being forwarded to Greece, and reaping full success ; for the luckless nobleman obeyed and went into the trap *via* Poitiers to Paris and was lost. " Quickness and great secrecy " were the Pope's injunctions ; and writing in the earlier part of June, he says he would expect to hear their opinion on grave matters relative to the Holy Land, on the 15th of next November. But upon his return from the islands, Sir William Villaret finding his Knights in ill-humor as ill-treated by the court of Cyprus, and wishing to be in a house of their own, where they might attend to their duties and have to render an account to none but their own superior and Grand Master alone, he thought it best to avail himself of the Pontifical orders and go to Europe to try to organize a body to aid him in his projected invasion ; more especially seeing he was not to have the Templars, and that Rhodes, which had once been Genoese and was now Greek, nominally belonged in reality to Saracen pirates, a bold, fierce and lawless race, resembling the Malays of this day. Their resistance was sure to be desperate. He kept his secret, and pretended it was a Crusade which, however small, would suffice for his views. But he died previous to his voyage towards the end of 1306. Early in the next year the Order chose another Villaret, who, whether his brother or not, was at all events his near relation, and known to be acquainted with his secret.

Sir Fulk de Villaret, the moment he was elected, sailed for France. The letter of Pope Clement V. was directed to Sir William, though it was Sir Fulk who came to answer it in person, as required. Another brief to Sir Fulk himself after his return from France at Rhodes (against which he had advanced, but not conquered, except in some little part), is dated August, 1307, and from expressions in it we cannot but perceive the Pope had recently spoken with the unconscious Fulk, who, however, heard nothing to make him suspect the frightful truth, though abundant ill-will certainly met his ears. But having never had a personal interview with the hapless De Molay, he might exert his prudence in the elevated dignity he was now clothed with, to avoid one, and be desirous of removing from that dangerous position as fast as he could, well aware that his own Order was exposed to envy as well as that of the guiltless Templars. Things were already running high, not perhaps publicly, but in the minds of the Pontifical and French courts, for they captured De Molay a few weeks afterwards, of a Friday, on the 13th of October, 1307. Although the Pope did not declare it till a year after, yet it was equivalent to the capture in 1307. In France he soon got what he wanted. A great Crusade was impossible; but to gather a body of resolute individuals was easy. He might be in the greater hurry to return, but the Courts had a gloomy aspect, though he knew that while the Hospitalers kept at a distance, and clear of inordinate show, their merit to Christendom and the Holy Land would be avowed, but that to be near was dangerous. Gratitude was a reed not to be much relied on, happy if not converted into crime.

Nor had he even a personal acquaintance with De Molay. So Fulk ought not to be suspected; but it was better *heave off*, and he did so. The financial means were chiefly by *a subscription of ladies*, particularly those of Genoa, who sold their jewels for that purpose. Some of these Genoese Amazons took the Cross themselves, whose cuirasses, made small and with bulges to receive their breasts, were shown in the arsenal long after. He had only to select the number of warriors he desired from several. Many of the most illustrious houses in Germany took the white Cross on that occasion. But he was so reserved and perhaps severe a man, that not one of them dared to inquire where he was going to.

So passing Rhodes to lull away suspicions of the Saracens, he sailed to Cyprus, and there, taking all his Knights and their effects, sailed again, to the astonishment of the King of Cyprus and every one else. But when out of sight of Cyprus Sir Fulk veered northeast and keeping Syria on his right, instead of landing, went into port on the coast of Asia Minor and anchored. Immense was the surprise of his whole fleet, and even none of his own choice Knights but wondered where he could be bound for. Thence, however, he appears to have sent to the Emperor of Constantinople, asking him for the investiture of Rhodes, which pride and anti-Latin hate refused, though leave would only have been *titular*, for the expulsion of the Saracen pirates would not have been a whit the easier.

Pirates seem to have been indeed at that time the only real inhabitants of the island, the Venetians having all decamped long before, and most of the Greeks still earlier. Nor did this refusal produce much effect on Sir Fulk, whose spies had already made their reports concerning the island and capital, so that he had determined where he would disembark. Only it made him declare his project to his followers, unanimous in their approbation. So he let his allies think, and call themselves *Crusaders*, and such he called them, to gratify their vanity and give them the pomp and circumstance of a crusade.

His invasion succeeded. All the lesser islands and part of Rhodes itself yielded nearly without a struggle, but by little and little the difficulties grew. The pirates who were at sea came back and the war became long and bloody. In consequence, the Crusaders went away one after another, and Sir Fulk had scarcely any one more than his own Hospitalers to support him. Yet so strenuous were his exertions that he engaged the Florentine bankers to advance him a loan of money, a difficult matter in those times, and he had the ability to infuse his own spirit into his little army, resolution to conquer or die. Sanguinary in the highest degree were several attempts to take the city into which the pirates had at last retreated after a terrible resistance of four years. But take it he did in the end. What remained of the outlaws escaped by sea, being the first to proclaim their defeat throughout the islands of the Archipelago and along the coast of Lycia, still at expense of a great number of his bravest Hospitalers, and one shout of admiration resounded through all Christendom of " Knights of Rhodes," a title that was to endure, illustrious far above two centuries.

A letter from one of the English Kings in 1309, shows what has been already observed, that the Order was still considered rather equestrian than naval. Thus, that glorious body of the select of all Christians on the edge of its orbit, or not far from it, wheeled its second course of more than another hundred years under seventeen Grand Masters.

Had it depended upon Philip IV. of France, the Hospitalers had fared like the Templars. The Teutonics were safe in their native Germany, but the snare was evidently set for both the others. That ultimate conversation in Cyprus had been their crisis. So the Templars deciding for Southern Europe sealed their destiny, and Rhodes saved the Hospitalers.

It is clear that the Pope was far from inclined against the warriors he eulogized as they deserved, at the very moment he was inviting them into his clutches. From which we are far from deducing any malignity of intention in him, but a weak and ineffectual dislike of what he had promised the King of France, and therefore he hesitated for a whole year from when King Philip had all the Templars through his dominions thrown into prison as malefactors in one day in 1307. The Pope had weighty displeasure at what the King had done, in seizing on the Templars to burn them, and confiscate their property in 1307, and only in 1308 did he consent to condemn their entire Order. Bsovius, Gurlter, and all the annalists of that unhappy body, are of one accord on this point. The miserable Pontiff made several attempts to free himself from his horrible promises, but they had been the price of his tiara, and his abject nature was too eaten up by ambition to descry any way but executing it. It seemed to him necessary, as if crime and injustice can *ever* be necessary. Not that Clement wished worse to the Templars or better to the Hospitalers; but, as he condemned one he would have condemned both; abandoned both to the flames if required. It might be partly age's feebleness; and piety leaveth to a dotard that not-warrantable excuse, but unenviable palliation. At such fearful and extravagant iniquities, imputed to his venerated Order, well might the unfortunate De Molay, as full of wonder, make a great sign of the Cross, and exclaim, that "such enormous inventors merited what is inflicted on liars and coiners, among Saracens and Tartars!" What punishment is that? To have their paunches ripped open, and their heads cut off! They had read what purported to be his avowal and was not.

While such were the nefarious transactions in Europe, Sir Fulk Villaret, the Grand Master of Hospitalers, had been accomplishing the conquest of Rhodes—rather, we should say, the liberation of its native Christian population from their lawless tyrants, those Mohammedan pirates. The next thing was to reduce, or rather visit (for that was enough) its dependencies—the islets, of which there are several, the principal being the Ancient Coos, country of Hippocrates and Apelles, since Lango (at present Stanchis), erected into a fief in favor of persons who had distinguished themselves in the last Rhodian war, not without commensurate obligations and charges regarding galleys and troops.

Calamo, renowned for its honey, had two excellent ports, and abounded in fresh-water springs; and, to Villaret's surprise, showed a tolerable commercial town close to the ruins of a fine city. Calchi was fertile, with a strong castle to keep off corsairs. Lero (1314) gloried in its quarries of marble. The soil of several of those islets was rich. One was splendidly wooded; another famous for wine; another drove a good trade in sponges, brought from the bottom of the sea by divers—nor could any youth be married until he was able to remain a certain number of minutes deep under water. But chiefly one was prized for its ship-carpenters, who had the art of building light craft renowned for swiftness all over the Levant—sail, oar, or both ways.

One of the smallest islets, though designated as magisterial, because considered more peculiarly assigned to the Grand Master, as forming part of his private domain, St. Nicholas del Cardo, is by Basio called Palena, and in another place Palmosa; and that is Patmos (Patmos, now Palmosa), where St. John wrote his Revelation. And if it be so, however sterile, it is interesting to a Christian.

After reviewing these in the company of Anthony De Beck, Villaret returned to Rhodes, eager to indulge in a life of luxury and repose from his devoirs.   But that was not yet to be ; and the pirates who had escaped had roused their Mohammedan brethren of Asia Minor—among whom a thriving Tartar horde, and it is possible with some Comnenian blood.   Yet the celebrated Ottoman had to retreat, although the Knights were not given time to erect walls.   New proof that valiant hearts and hands are the best of fortifications, and need none.   But, although Ottoman was driven from Rhodes, he attacked the other adjoining islets and ravaged them ; and an obstinate and fierce war ensued, during which the Knights are said to have received much assistance from Amadeo V., of Savoy ; and that to perpetuate the memory, his descendants have ever since worn the white Cross and as a device the word *Fert*, meaning *Fortitudo ejus Rhodum tenuit* (" his Fortitude held Rhodes ").

Villaret and some Knights went to Avignon, and Villaret was sentenced to accept a priory, but totally independent of any future Grand Master and only responsible to the Holy See, which to the guiltless Order was a double sacrifice, losing the rent of a Priory and paying a Prior in no way obedient to it ; and having a Grand Master either directly named by the Pope, or indirectly chosen under his influence.   His station was conferred, A.D. 1319, on Sir Helion de Villanova by a few Knights summoned to elect him in the Papal Palace itself ; which, if an honor, was such a one as induced the belief in many people that he was not merely favored by the Pontiff, as he was publicly, but that he altogether received the dignity from him and not from the Order.   If so, he testified his gratitude in kind by selling one of the Order's estates to the Pope near his native Cahors.   The pecuniary embarrassments of the Order were real in proportion to its flushed expectations when promised the exaggerated property of the Templars, but in point of fact only just so great as a usurer might wish, or perhaps cause, in order to lend it ready-money at an enormous interest, or purchase its lands cheap.

When Villanova embarked in 1332, it was with some difficulty on the score of his health, which was not yet strong enough to support so long a voyage, in the Pontifical opinion. There had been transactions as to adding to the fortifications of the city of Rhodes, and the other chief towns of the Islands, as well as various strong towers and castles round all its coasts, not omitting several fortresses in the environing islets. The shipping, too, had considerably increased, and now merited the name of a fleet. Just previous to the arrival of Villanova, the king of Castile had attempted to create a new Order, and endow it with the spoils of the Templars, but the Pope refused his consent, which did not make any essential change, since they went to Calatrava just the same, which could not but occasion discontent in the Spanish language at Rhodes.

. One of the first things which Villanova and his Senate had to decide, was whether to enter into a league with France and Venice against the Turk, which that the Order assented to, is not curious, nor that the Venetians soon left them in the lurch.

A violent Turkish campaign rendered the year 1346 more full of fierce conflicts and dissensions than usual, in which the Hospitalers took a prominent part; when in the midst of such scenes Villanova died, to the great grief of the Pope, and was succeeded by Sir Deodate de Gozou, who during his short reign did much, both as to the Turkish war and domestic policy; and sent a circular to the Priors of Denmark, Sweden and Norway, lamenting that they had never paid any *responsions* since the loss of Acre, yet could not but have learned the Order was seated at Rhodes. So he cited them formally to send them yearly to the receiver at Flanders. Responsions were only a very easy quit-rent on Commanderies, leaving abundant sufficiency to the holders, a priory being the aggregate of several Commanderies.

Sir Deodate won a sea fight against the Turks, near Lemnos, taking a hundred and twenty of their small vessels, and put to flight the thirty-two largest, and while he kept the Order neutral between Genoese and Venetians, when these latter aver the former won a victory celebrated through all that century, he protesting he could not prevent individual Knights from siding with either, and that individuals could not do much harm on either side, since they counterbalanced each other.

The Order was in great esteem then, both in Europe and the Levant, most of the chief Captains in Spain and Italy being Knights of Rhodes, and as for the Pontifical States (at that time a principal Italian power), nearly all its governors of celebrity, including even the Duke of Spoleto, were of the same.

Sir Deodate finding many of his commanders so protected by the Pope and the Kings of France and Castile, Aragon, Portugal, England and others, that he was unable to reduce them to obedience, abdicated his power, and while consent was coming he employed his hours in the useful toil of adding to the fortifications of the city of Rhodes, when in December, 1353, he had a stroke of apoplexy, that at his great age was instant death.

His successor was Sir Peter de Cornillan, or Cormelian, a Provençal gentleman, Prior of St. Gilles, and remarkable for the regularity of his life and austere and ancient manners; as the new Pontiff well observes in his brief to the Knights, approving highly of their choice. "Sweet as the perfumes of myrrh."

The *twenty-ninth* Grand Master was Roger de Pins, 1355. He held a Chapter at Rhodes, in which many excellent statutes were made for the administration of the Knights. He governed for ten years, and had the revised laws sent to each Priory.

The *thirtieth* Grand Master, Raymond de Berenger, came in in 1365. He captured Alexandria, Egypt, and burnt a piratical fleet there. Preparing for impending war, he addressed orders to all the Knights, and wrote letters to the European powers, imploring their aid to Christendom. A Chapter-General was held at Rhodes in 1366.

The *thirty-first* Grand Master, Robert de Julliac, assumed the reins in 1374.

The *thirty-second* Grand Master, Heredia Castellan d' Emposta, followed in 1377. He is cited as one of the best and most worthy of the potentates of the Order. In an incursion into the Morea, he was taken prisoner by the Turks, and underwent the harshest slavery. In the great Papal quarrels of the day he undertook to act as arbiter, and abdicated about 1383.

The *thirty-third* Grand Master, Richard Caracciolo, installed 1383, was never at Rhodes, and is scarcely recognized in history.

A *locum-tenens* held in the person of Bartlo Caraffa, for a few months. During this period occurred a tremendous defeat of the Christian armies at Nicopolis, by Bajazet, in which the Knights of Rhodes suffered severely.

The *thirty-fourth* Grand Master, A.D. 1396, was Philip de Naillac. His conciliatory manners did much good among his people. The destruction of Smyrna by Timour the Tartar, A.D. 1399, which alarmed the Christian world, set the Knights on preparing against a threatened invasion from that monster who had devastated Hungary. The wise policy of Naillac prevented a civil war in Cyprus. He visited the Great Council at Pisa, Italy, in 1409, and extended his journey to England. After an absence of eleven years he returned to Rhodes, convened a Chapter-General there in 1420, and died June, 1421. Two regulations were adopted in this Chapter, which we cite, viz. :

"1. No Knight, under any pretext whatsoever, can cite a companion before any other tribunals, ecclesiastical or civil, than those of his Order alone."

"2. None but a member can be present at a Chapter-General."

The *thirty-fifth* Grand Master of the Knights of Rhodes was Anthony Fluvian (de la Riviere), who was installed A.D. 1421, and died Oct. 26, 1437. The Sultan was threatening an invasion from Cairo, and the Order mortgaged its possessions to build a fleet. Amongst the naval equipments, cannon were included. A Chapter-General was held at Rhodes 1428, and statutes were passed pronouncing all idle duels and illegal homicides both opprobrious and criminal, and repressing corruption in officers, and systematic debauchery, with severity. Fluvian at his death left to the Order property to the value of 200,000 gold crowns. At this period the number of Knights at Rhodes was about 1000.

The *thirty-sixth* Grand Master was John de Lastic, 1437–1454. In September, 1440, an Egyptian fleet attacked Rhodes, but was easily repulsed. Cannon and musketry were used on both sides. This defeat of the Saracenic invasion was complete. Chapters-General were held at Rhodes, 1445 and 1449, at which many excellent laws were passed.

The capture of Constantinople, 1451, by Mahomet II., alarmed

Europe and Rhodes, and every preparation was made for defense, when De Lastic died, May 19, 1454.

The *thirty-seventh* Grand Master, James de Milly, 1454–1461. The Turkish fleet destroyed a town in Rhodes, in 1457, but proceeded no further. Chapters-General were held, 1454 and 1459, in which it was ordered that the statutes regarding hospitality should be hung up *where the Knights could not avoid seeing them every day,* to have that fundamental duty well impressed on their minds. Milly died August 17, 1461.

The *thirty-eighth* Grand Master was Peter Raymond Zacosta, 1461–1467. A Chapter-General was called in 1462. March 23, 1463, he summoned all the Knights of the Order to hasten to Rhodes, and the Pope threatened every recusant with excommunication. The island, in 1464, was greatly afflicted by the plague, and by its miserable sequel, *famine.* Zacosta defended Lesbro personally, and with gallantry, against the Turks. He died on a visit to Rome, February, 1467, and was buried, by the Pope's command, in St. Peter's Church, where his statue yet presents the appearance of an old man whose long beard reached to his girdle.

The *thirty-ninth* Grand Master, John Orsini, held 1467–1476. He repeated the summons of his predecessor, in order to present a sufficient front to the menaces of Mahomet II. The fortifications of the island were greatly strengthened and enlarged. Orsini entered into alliance with Persia, and furnished one hundred of his expertest gunners to discipline the Persian army. He called Chapters-General, 1471 and 1475, in which it was ordered that no dignity can be conferred on a Knight who has not paid his debts to the last farthing. He died June 8, 1476, as his monument still testifies in St. John's Church, at Rhodes.

The *fortieth* Grand Master, and one of the most brilliant in Rhodian annals, was Peter D'Aubusson, 1476–1503. All dread of Mahomet II. ceased when the news of his election went forth. He had been a soldier from childhood. In 1478 he called a Chapter-General, in which it was declared that any Knight seeking place in the Order, who should obtain a letter of recommendation from a foreign sovereign, should forfeit ten years of rank ! Absolute power was given the Grand Master in view of the long-expected attack from the Turks. The siege began May 23, 1480, and lasted ninety-nine days; a fleet of more than one hundred and sixty sail bringing the army of invasion. Three thousand seven hundred siege-guns, of largest caliber, were set in position, and played upon the walls. Among the Christians there was a sort of friendly rivalry in quickness of obedience, contrivance, industry, and valor during this whole siege. Nine of the towers were overthrown. At the explosion of the enormous cannon and mortars the whole island trembled, the noise being heard at Castel Rossa, one hundred miles distant. No such guns, no such terrific effects, had ever before been seen. Three hundred balls of flint, nine palms in diameter, were thrown against the Tower of St. Anthony, by which it was literally battered to pieces. Every military appliance was exhausted in the attack and defense; scaling-ladders, hand-grenades, fire-ships, Greek-fire, mining, and counter-mining. The full loss of the enemy was not less than one hundred thousand men. Repulsed, Mahomet II. died May 3, 1481, crying out in his last breath, " Rhodes! Rhodes! Rhodes! " Five Chapters-General were held under D'Aubusson, in which laws of great importance were enacted. He died June 30, 1503, aged above eighty, crowned with the plaudits of the Christian world.

The *forty-first* Grand Master was Almeric Amboise, 1503–1512. In 1510 he summoned all his Knights by circular, but no invasion came in his time. A Turkish ship was captured by his navy, armed with one hundred heavy cannon, her mainmast so large that six men could scarce encircle it with their arms, and with seven decks. Her loading was of immense value, silks, spices, money, etc., etc. Almeric died November 8, 1512.

The *forty-second* Grand Master was Guido de Blanchefort, 1512, who died on his way from France to Rhodes.

The *forty-third* Grand Master was Fabricius Caretto, 1512–1521. The number of Knights casting votes in this election was five hundred and fifty, every one competent and ready to take any command assigned him, great or small, without demur. As Rhodes was in daily danger of a Turkish siege he early called a Chapter-General, at which, among other proceedings, money was voted to buy artillery in France.   Carretto was a rare linguist, a remarkably kind, mild, courteous man.   He died January, 1521, leaving Rhodes in an excellent state of defense.

The *forty-fourth* Grand Master was Philip Villers de L'Isle Adam, 1521–1534, signal for genius and experience, renowned for every worthy gift, and strength of mind and body.   On his way from France to assume the reins of government, he passed safely through a pirate fleet awaiting him.   From the day of his arrival he devoted himself to the fortification of the island and preparations for defense.   The Sultan Solyman sent a message of war. He set the example to the people by destroying his own garden and summer-house, followed by a general waste of every tree outside the walls.   The country wells were filled up.   The peasants were summoned into the city, with all their movables.   The siege began June 26, 1522, and resulted, December 20, in the surrender of the island, under a most honorable capitulation, to the Turks, who had sustained the most tremendous losses.   During this long and horrible siege the Grand Master never once lost his quiet, placid look.   He was always gracious and kind to every one.   Eating with the common soldiers, he always took a personal and most active part in the most ferocious combats.   Three great banners were attendant upon his person : The Grand Standard of the Order, one sent from the Pope in D'Aubusson's time, and one in which the White Cross of the Order was quartered with his own arms. The number of the enemy exceeded two hundred and fifty thousand.   On the 1st of January, 1523, the Grand Master and his remaining forces sailed, by virtue of the capitulation, in fifty vessels, leaving the island, after a possession of two hundred and thirteen years, in the hands of the Turks.   Charles V. of Spain (Emperor of Germany) said to his soldiers : "Nothing was ever so well lost as Rhodes."

Few were the Knights that outlived that dreadful siege.   In sailing for Candia, many of the vessels were lost.   On landing the impassible, white-haired Grand Master, burst into a flood of weeping.   There he summoned a Chapter-General.   Sailing farther west, he landed at Messina early in May, after a tempestuous voyage.   Thence they removed to Italy, where L'Isle Adam had an interview with Pope Adrian VI. (who died a few days afterwards), and remained in the Eternal City until January 25, 1524. A Chapter-General was called at Viterbo, Italy, in 1526–27, and the island of Malta, tendered by Charles V., King of Spain, was accepted as the final home of the Order. This island is about sixty miles in circuit. It was an arid rock covered in many places with sand. The soil had been brought from the nearer countries, with which the small tillage was done. It had neither river, rivulet, nor spring. In summer it was intolerably hot, with not one forest tree to relieve the eye. But the necessity of the times over-rode all this. L'Isle Adam, after a tour through Europe and England, sailed July 18, 1529, for Malta, where he died August 22, 1534.

The *forty-fifth* Grand Master was A. Del Ponte, 1534–35, recommended by L'Isle Adam, on his death-bed. He was a literary and eloquent man. He died aged seventy, in November, 1535.

The *forty-sixth* Grand Master was Desiderio di S. Galla, 1536; but expired in France September 26 of the same year, and so never reached his government. He had displayed signal bravery and ability at the last siege of Rhodes.

The *forty-seventh* Grand Master was Homedez, 1536–1553. Three hundred and sixty Knights being present at the election. He, too, was honorably distinguished at Rhodes, having lost an eye in the siege. He summoned a Chapter-General in 1539, and received dictatorial powers in view of the coming invasion by Sultan Solyman. In 1551, the island was defended against a corsair, Dragut, who was driven away with loss. Homedez died September 6, 1553, at the age of ninety, decrepit in mind and body.

The *forty-eighth* Grand Master was Claudius de la Sengle, 1553–1557.

The *forty-ninth* Grand Master was Parisot, 1557–1568. He is better known as Valetta. His name is honorably associated with the great siege that followed. He laid the foundation of a new city to be called after his own name. He summoned the Knights from all quarters by circular, dated February 26, 1558, in preparation for the Turkish invasion. Of Knights and Servants-at-arms that obeyed, there were but little over five hundred, making the whole garrison eight thousand one hundred and fifty-five. On Friday, May 18, the great armament came in sight. This siege ended, September 7th, in the total defeat of the Turks, with the loss of thirty thousand men. The defenders of the island lost nine thousand. The island was rendered waste; everything had to be rebuilt. Valetta died of apoplexy, August 21, 1568.

The *fiftieth* Grand Master was Peter del Monte, 1568–1572. He ordered the body of his predecessor to be conveyed into the new city of Valetta, and a noble tomb raised over him. He set himself so busily to the erection of the city, that on March 18, 1571, it was occupied. In the great naval fight of Lepanto, October 7, 1571, the supreme leader, Don John, was a Knight of Malta, and was much aided by his brethren of the Order. Del Monte died January 20, 1572.

The *fifty-first* to the *seventieth* Grand Masters, inclusive, governed in comparatively quiet times, and need not to be particularized here. In the Catalogue of Grand Masters, page 161, their names and dates will be found. In 1609, the Order proposed to the Shah of Persia to assist him in his war with the Turks. In the loss of Candia to the Turks, 1669, the Order suffered heavily. The Maltese fortifications were greatly strengthened, 1670, in expectation of a new invasion. In 1675 great losses were experienced from the plague. In 1742 a long truce was made with the Sultan of Turkey. The European revolutions of 1789 deprived the Order of nearly all its revenues. In 1797, at the election of Hompesch, the last Grand Master, the Cross of the noble Valetta was sent to Paul, Emperor of Russia, by which he was installed and saluted PROTECTOR of the Order. Napoleon, on his expedition to Egypt, 1798, visited Malta, found the powder spoiled in the magazines, the provisions worthless, and treason everywhere. The common people had been corrupted, Knights in high station were agreed upon surrendering to France instead of Russia, and the island, with all its traditions, suddenly became French. One of the best-fortified towns in existence was taken, June 10, without a shot; and when

the conqueror entered, he remarked, pithily, " Well for us that we had friends inside to open the gate."

The only history of this affair that we have is so thoroughly English that we hesitate to use it. Taaffe says, in this anti-Gallican spirit that runs through all his work, " The Turks never destroyed so much as the French during their first days at Malta, pulling down all the statues of renowned heroes, and chiseling out the coat-of-arms everywhere ; a barbarous profanation!" Grand Master Hompesch sailed for Europe June 19, 1798, and abdicated his office in effect, and this closed the history of the island in its connection with this celebrated Order. Dividing its career into three parts, we have—

First Period—The Order of St. John while in Palestine, 1113 to 1291, 178 years.

Second Period—While in Rhodes, 1309 to 1523, 214 years.

Third Period—While in Malta, 1530 to 1798, 268 years. The remainder of the period of their existence (25 years) was given to the wanderings of the Order, after the losses of Acre and of Rhodes, respectively. The English General, Pigot, captured the island of Malta from the French September 5, 1800. At the peace of Amiens, March 27, 1802, the English engaged to surrender the island to the Knights, but violated this pledge, and it remains an English possession to this day. A few Knights of the Order in St. Petersburg, October 29, 1798, elected the Emperor Paul as Grand Master ; but upon the murder of that crowned fool, March 21, 1801, the Russian farce was ended. In Catania and various places, the Order was privately maintained in the hope of a better day, the Grand Master being only acknowledged as *locum tenens*, and sovereign of the second or third class. At Vienna the Order has an embassador, many of the Austrian officers being Knights of Malta, as was the Arch-duke Charles, whose sudden death overthrew all plans for the restoration of the Order that were based upon him.

Having followed Mr. Taaffe as the most exact writer at our command, we close the chapter by inserting his plan of Restoration of this long-glorious Order, not as presenting anything feasible, but as a most thoughtful summary of the ancient merits of

526   KNIGHTS HOSPITALERS.

Plan for Reorganizing the Order.   Terms of Association.

the Order and an expression of affectionate regret, in which every reader will join, at its destruction.*

ASSOCIATION.

Seeing it undertakes to merit its restoration by doing that which none can do half so well (nor at all), modifying itself to the time (again in advance of its age, as almost always), practically useful to manhood and civilization, in the words of its princely Norman founder, *pro utilitate hominum*, true and primitive scope of its institution, the Order of St. John of Jerusalem is restored thus:

1. That it be divided into two distinct classes, *Knights professed* and *Knights free ;* equally honorable, since of two brothers the elder will frequently be of the second, the younger of the first, as often happens actually, though by favor and not by law. Let only all favor then be annihilated, and law take its place.

2. *Knights professed* to remain as of yore, with this difference: necessary result of exempting it from all favor, rendering the few still fewer (as they ought), recognizing the Pope only in his spiritual capacity strictly, like other Roman Catholics, and not in the least otherwise more than any other temporal sovereign. This class will then subside into a kind of senate, or select chapter-general, from whom are to be elected, and they alone elect, the Grand Master, and to them belong the six highest posts of the Order after the Grand Master. Indeed, it is chiefly from the luster of the past, like a fine monument of antiquity, that this class is preserved pretty much *in statu quo*, though never to be permitted to take their vows until forty years old, as who should be dispassionate to discuss, decide, govern; of whom the six eldest necessarily, and six more at the Grand Master's choice, shall form his privy council.

3. The Commander-in-Chief of the troops in the Order's pay is to obey the Grand Master alone.

4. Pardon, and nominations, and graces of every description, are to come from the Grand Master in council or chapter-general, except that he can in no way facilitate the profession, which must preserve its ancient rigid form— the protecting powers neither intermeddling with it themselves, nor allowing it in others.

5. *Knights free* form the substantial, powerful, and active—the real and superior, though in name the second class—and their exemption from celib-

---

* The *Almanach de Gotha* for 1873 says, "The Order of St. John was called *Rhodes* in 1309, and Malta in 1530. Since the death of the last Grand Master, Brother Thomas de Contara, in 1805, the Order has been governed by a Lieutenant of the Grand Master, and by the Sacred College at Rome."

Plan for Reorganizing the Order.   Terms of Association.

acy and strict genealogical proofs is no more than a change of words, since such exemptions are in full use already, but by favor, and nearly the same as to religion—at least every form of Christianity.

6. Here, too, let all such favors not be abrogated, but simply become law. And let the Grand Master (now at Rome) be authorized to issue a proclamation that this class is open to all Christians and Mohammedans (since the Order has no longer Mohammedans to make war with, but to be their cordial friends), on their producing three short documents.   1. That the candidate is of no disreputable parentage.   2. Himself of honest conduct.   3. That he has the means and the will to submit to the Order's pecuniary regulations.   Whoever has had its cross from any royal hands already, is recognized as already a member of this class; but after the date of such proclamation similar distinctions can be conferred by none but the Grand Master, or his deputy, with the legal formalities.*

7. This class, with the representatives of the land, is to form a sort of House of Commons.   But the Order, never having been nor caring to degenerate into a speaking society, they are neither to speak, vote, or even meet; but to be merely and individually consultive, and each of them separately, when, where, and if they like, transmit their written opinions to the senate.†

8. Every power can become protecting by simply permitting its subjects to enter the Order and found commanderies, or those called *jus patronatus*, and paying now sixteen per cent., and devolving entirely to the Order, when the line for whom the foundation was made falls extinct.   What is to merit restoration, and which only the Order by its permanent and military residence can do, and is to undertake, is to render the passage by the Euphrates to India and toward Mecca safe and excellent for the subjects of all the protecting powers, quite *gratis* as to protection and escort.   There shall be no more the division of languages, and there shall be only two tables, quite equal, and each presided by one of the six, or his *locum tenens*, who must always be a Knight professed.   Equally among this second class, and the rest of the Knights professed; all the other posts, military and civil (except the six first), shall be in common.‡

9. The Turks are besought to reflect, and that vast changes have visited

---

* This is no windy crotchet, but the matured proposal of a dignitary of the Order itself, and quite conformable to the actual state of things, and the unsettled condition of a crowd of youths in every country.

† If this be a poor House of Commons, is it not better than none?   Look at Syria, and would it not better its condition?

‡ The Russian and Prussian Knights would be thus amalgamated with us. Nor that King or Emperor, with so many Orders of their own already, will probably object to this.   Said knights would be at no expense, for they will be held to have entered long ago.

Plan for Reorganizing the Order.   Terms of Association.

both them and us; and that our Order offers them as warm a friendship as its former enmity; and therefore the Sultan is requested not only to become one of the protecting powers, but likewise, seeing that to him belongs the only country which supplies a short passage from the Mediterranean to the Euphrates—not indeed to decrease his territories, but rather increase them—is besought to confer on himself a new dignity, perfectly imperial, by occupying the glorious post of the Emperor Charles V., and as he erected Malta into an independent sovereign fief in favor of the Order, so the Sultan also as to a part of Syria. We covet neither Damascus nor Jerusalem, but only a slip of sufficient width to form a small monarchy from the sea a little south of St. Jean d'Acre, in a slanting line over the hills on the east of the Lake of Galilee to Zebdeni, and thence to Anab on the Euphrates, and northward directly from Scanderoon through Aleppo to Bir. It would be certainly a new glory to the Porte to have an independent Christian sovereign for one of its dignitaries, reigning over a distinguished collection from all Europe, with the guarantee of every European nation. None of the knights can take any part in the traffic which they protect.

10. So the investiture and an annual falcon should be established as under Charles V.; nor is it more than of a piece with all the Order's history that it, who mostly went before its age, should now too be the first to invite Mohammedans to their intimacy and partnership.

11. Within that restricted domain the Order should reign, with all its ancient liberties more developed. A judicature apart for the inhabitants, with their own laws, and a jury of their own language and religion, *judicium parium.* The mouth of the Orontes cleansed, steamers and shipping might ascend to Antioch, and thence boats to within fifty miles of El-Bir, across which plain a road, railroad, or canal would easily be constructed, thence by Euphrates, or by the ancient (if re-opened) canal round by Bagdad to Bassora, escorted by the Order's steamers of war, both in going and coming, once a month or oftener.

12. From the Mediterranean to El-Bir there shall be a continuous line of cottages, like the walk in a garden, small proprietors, all European. No duties whatever, the Order's whole territory shall be a free port, religious liberty on the most complete scale, as in the best parts of America, a place of universal refuge.* No taxes whatever, direct or indirect, on the poorer people; and on the rich a single one only, the income tax, on a plan to be

---

* Nothing of the magnificent scenery and historical recollections. Nor to oppose by the Nile, but assist it. Why not both? Any disasters or eventualities, the Red Sea closed, here is another passage. Not either, but both. Why should commerce and the world rely upon one alone? Commerce and civilization are now the same under different names. How necessary is a place of refuge for all unhappy men of all opinions, our own times fully prove. America is too far off; England too dear!

Plan for Reorganizing the Order. Terms of Association.

determined, from five to twenty per cent. or more, on every kind of income. The Order's history enables one to promise that there shall not be a beggar, no more than there is in parts of Turkey, to whose honor be it observed. Not to nourish war, but to prevent it—which that universality of arming is more likely to produce than vain projects of disarming—the entire little state shall form one little military school, to furnish all the protecting powers with excellent young officers; not precisely a college, but something between that and the army, from cadets up to captains, and every expense shall be incurred to secure it at once; the name of affording the best and most illustrious military education in the world, without one single exception, and worthy of the Order's ancient fame, as if it had been asleep until now, being a difficult acquisition, but to be acquired at any price. With its characteristic simultaneousness, all the Order's outlays must be simultaneous, and, as it were, extravagant. The time for economy may come, but hereafter.*

13. To prevent the least fear of its becoming a nest of pirates, smugglers, and conspirators, strangers are to be turned out on the slightest suspicion, without why or wherefore. And a stern trial in case of natives; nor shall these be tried for any minor offense, but for high treason, by putting their country in danger of losing its charter, which is this.

14. To face the immense expenses of such a restoration there are: 1st. The actual possessions of the Order, which, however small, are far greater than at the downfalls of Jerusalem, Acre, Rhodes, Malta. As we rose from the three first, why not as well from the last? Harder then than now! 2d. The passage money of £300 each new knight, which may be calculated at a great sum, and the sixteen per cent. on the *jus patronatus*, commanderies, presents, and sundry other items. But if all these be insufficient at the beginning, when so many houses are to be erected, the huge cost of steamers and of an army, however small, when paid so generously and splendidly to have choice soldiers, and the military educated on a magnificent scale, and roads and conveyances of all sorts, and so many other unforeseen expenses, then a little loan must be contracted, and guaranteed to be paid off in a given number of years, as it will certainly soon be, by the increase of the country's revenue. The Knights were always capital financiers, as even Malta proves, which they received a poor, naked rock, and left it an island of palaces.†

---

* The attention of all men must be turned to our glorious past, and then they will not attend to some present defects. This, at whatever cost, from the very beginning, and the laughers will be put down for ever. We must render it the fashion for all the distinguished military and naval men in Europe to speak well of us. Our repute once settled, and praise will be universal.

† And it were bare justice; for this restoration, as much for the future as the present, why should not generations to come pay their part as well as ourselves?

Plan for Reorganizing the Order.   Terms of Association.

15. As the Order never was dependent on the Emperor, notwithstanding the investiture and falcons, so neither will it be on the Sultan, although he will be its supreme lord, and the Knights will hold it as a part of his dominions.   For the Order would be another Order if it lost any one of its three essential epithets.   Sovereign as the sole Order that has its Grand Master within itself, independent from the day of its creation to this hour, neutral between Christians, without exception, through all its long annals; for never did it take any part in the sanguinary religious wars of Christians against Christians in any of the by-gone centuries; which long past is the best security man can give, that as they were neutral all that long and most difficult time between Christians, so they will be for the future between Mussulmans too.   It ever was sovereign, independent, and neutral, and is again recognized as such.

16. All the protecting powers bind themselves to receive into their armies those of their born subjects who return with favorable testimonials of their having served the Order in Syria, that is, receive them in the same rank as high as captain, inclusive.*

17. The hired troops shall be paid with the utmost generosity, to have them all picked men; and as to the commander-in-chief, and generals, and admirals, if recommended warmly by France, England, Austria, Prussia, and Russia, they shall have *carte blanche* for their pay and outfit.

18. The free Knights, even when embodied in the above corps, shall never receive pay or more than forage, board, and lodging, but must find their own horses, tents, dress, equipments.

19. This offer (though this paper, by a Knight Commander of that very second class, to wit, without profession, is undoubtedly a *prima facie* evidence that it will be accepted) must be made to the whole Order, and ratified by it or refused.   The honor of the idea of this reform, and now proposing it on his own individual responsibility, appears to the writer quite too dear and unique a distinction not to appropriate it entirely to himself, as he does in the most total sense, by signing it with his name, John Taaffe.†

---

* It is to be expected that all the protecting powers will keep up diplomatic relations with the Order, and take part in its restoration; and certainly such favors will be more than compensated by the obligations to which it will have subjected itself.   It would be still more useful to the Turkish pilgrims and the commercial caravans of Turkey than to Christendom.   This, and the evident utility to the Sultan's Rajah populations, might perhaps be sufficient, even if he did not choose to avail himself of the invitation for Mohammedans to enter the Order.   At all events, it becomes the charity and highmindedness of the Knights of Malta to make the offer.

† In every other sense he cannot but lose by it, as he is fully aware; for what he now shares with a few of the most select in Europe would be rendered less rare and exclusive—almost quite common.

20. Italian, as most universally known in the Levant, is to be its diplomatic language.

21. If Normandy be a part of France now, yet it was being held in fief by England when the Norman on the English throne was a near relation of the Order's founder; so perhaps France and England should take the lead in this restoration with a brotherly feeling.

The claims of the half-insane Emperor of Russia to be styled Grand Master of St. John may be examined in the following paper:

Proclamation appointing the Emperor Paul as Grand Master of the Order of St. John:

"We, the Bailiffs, Grand Crosses, Commanders, Knights of the Grand Priory of Russia, and all other Members of the Order of St. John of Jerusalem, present in this Imperial City of St. Petersburg, reflecting on the disastrous situation of our Order, its total want of resources, the loss of its sovereignty and chief place of residence, the dispersion of its members, wandering through the world without a chief or any fixed spot of rendezvous, the increasing dangers by which it is threatened, and the plans formed by usurpers to invade its property and ruin it entirely, being desirous and in duty bound to employ all possible methods to prevent the destruction of an Order equally ancient and illustrious, which has ever been composed of the most select nobility, and which has rendered such important service to the Christian world; whose institutions were founded on such excellent principles as must not only be the firmest support to all legitimate authority, but tend to its sure preservation and future existence; animated by gratitude toward his Imperial Majesty, the Emperor of all the Russias, for the favors bestowed on our Order; penetrated with veneration for his virtues, and confidently relying on his sacred word, 'that he will not only support us in our institutions, privileges, and honors, but that he will employ every possible means to re-establish our Order in its original independent situation, where it contributed to the advantage of Christendom in general, and of every different state in particular;' knowing the impossibility in our present circumstances—the members of our Order being generally dispersed—of preserving all the forms and customs prescribed in our constitution and statutes; but being, nevertheless, desirous to secure the dignity and the power inherent to the sovereignty of our Order, by making a proper choice of a successor to D'Aubusson L'Isle Adam, and La Valette: We, the Bailiffs and Grand Crosses, the Commanders, and Knights of the Grand Priory of Russia, and all other Members of the Order of St. John of Jerusalem, assembled at St. Petersburg, the chief place of residence of our Order, not only in our names, but in those of the other languages, Grand Priories in general, and all their members in particular, who shall unite themselves to us by a firm adhesion

---

Appointing the Emperor Paul of Russia Grand Master of the Order.

---

to our principles, proclaim His Imperial Majesty, the Emperor and Autocrat of all the Russias, Paul I., as GRAND MASTER OF THE ORDER OF ST. JOHN OF JERUSALEM. In virtue of the present proclamation, we promise, according to our laws and statutes, and that by a sacred and solemn engagement, obedience, submission, and fidelity to His Imperial Majesty, the Most Eminent Grand Master.

"Given at St. Petersburg, the residence of our Order, this present Wednesday, the 27th October, 1798."

Acceptation of the Emperor Paul of the post of Grand Master, in answer to the above proclamation.

"We, by the grace of God, Paul I., Emperor and Autocrat of all the Russias, etc.

"In consideration of the wish expressed to us by the Bailiffs, Grand Crosses, Commanders, Knights of the Illustrious Order of St. John of Jerusalem, of the Grand Priory of Russia, and other members assembled together in our capital, in the name of all the well-disposed part of their fraternity, we accept the title of Grand Master of this Order, and renew on this occasion the solemn promises we have already made in quality of Protector, not only to preserve all the institutions and privileges of this Illustrious Order forever unchanged in regard to the free exercise of its religion with everything relating to the Knights of the Roman Catholic faith, and the jurisdiction of the Order, the seat of which we have fixed in this our imperial residence; but also we declare that we will unceasingly employ for the future, all our care and attention for the augmentation of the Order, for its re-establishment in the independent position which is requisite for the salutary end of its institution, for assuring its solidity, and confirming its utility. We likewise declare, that in taking thus upon us the Supreme Government of the Order of St. John of Jerusalem, and considering it our duty to make use of every possible means to obtain the restoration of the property of which it has been so unjustly deprived, we do not intend in any degree, as Emperor of all the Russias, to the smallest right or advantage which may strike at, or prejudice any of the powers of, our allies; on the contrary, we shall always have a peculiar satisfaction in contributing at all times, everything in our power toward strengthening our alliance with the said powers. Our grace and imperial favor toward the Order of St. John of Jerusalem in general, and each of its members in particular, shall ever remain invariably the same.

"Given at St. Petersburg, the 13th November, in the year 1798, in the third year of our reign.

"(Signed)   PAUL.
"(Countersigned)   PRINCE BESHOROELKO."

NOTE.—It is averred by a recent traveler, but with what truth we are unable to affirm, that upon one of the royal palaces in St. Petersburg the Banner of the Order of Malta is raised every morning!

CHAPTER II.

THE KNIGHTS TEMPLARS FROM A.D. 1312 TO A.D. 1874.

SAY what hast thou brought from the distant shore,
　For thy wasted youth to pay?
Hast thou treasure to win thee joys once more?
　Hath thou vassals to smooth thy way?

" I have brought but the palm-branch in my hand,
　Yet I call not my bright youth lost;
I have won but high thought in the Holy Land,
　Yet I count not too dear the cost!

" I look on the leaves of the deathless tree,
　These records of my track;
And better than youth in its flush of glee,
　Are the memories they give me back!

" They speak of toil, and of high emprise,
　As in words of solemn cheer,
They speak of lonely victories
　O'er pain, and doubt, and fear.

" They speak of scenes which have now become
　Bright pictures in my breast;
Where my spirit finds a glorious home,
　And the love of my heart can rest.

" The colors pass not from these away,
　Like tints of shower or sun;

> Oh! beyond all treasures that know decay,
> Is the wealth my soul hath won!
>
> " A rich light theme o'er my life's decline,
> An inborn light is cast;
> For the sake of the palm from the holy shrine,
> I bewail not my bright days past!"

E have now brought our story from the region of history into the arena of tradition, into the field of debate, fierce and furious. There are three theories concerning the modern history of the Templars, and the debate is fierce and furious. One denies all merger of the Knights Templars into any organization whatsoever, affirming, in gross, that their light was extinguished, their oil exhausted, their lamps utterly broken, and the shreds cast aside in the death of De Molay.

The second finds in the Order of Freemasonry the succession of Knight Templary.

The third recognizes the merger of the gallant Brotherhood of the Temple into the Order of Christ, a Portuguese Order, of which Sir Edmund Burke, Ulster King of Arms, expatiates in his " Book of Orders of Knighthood " (London, 1858, 8vo, pp. 409) in these terms:

THE ORDER OF CHRIST.

The Order of the Templars having been abolished in France by King Philip IV., its property confiscated, and its members persecuted and expelled with the sanction and authority of Pope Clement V.; it was revived in Portugal, where it flourished under the name of *the " Knighthood of Our Lord Jesus Christ."* The extreme persecutions which the Templars were subjected to in France, apparently for the mere sake of seizing hold of their property, under the pretext of their conspiring against the state, roused universal sympathy with the sufferers, while the Portuguese government needing, in addition, their support and valor, as a bulwark against the Spanish Moors at Algravia, King Dionysius, otherwise called Denis (A. D. 1279–1325), devised a means of giving

The Order of Christ, Successor of the Knights Templars.

an Asylum to the Knights and their Order in Portugal, without openly violating the decision of the Pope. He transferred (A. D. 1317) the castles and vassals, as also the Statutes of the Order of the Templars, to a new Order which he founded under a different name, and for which he received, after two years' negotiations, the sanction of Pope John XXII. (A. D. 1316–1334).

Nor was Dionysius deceived in his expectations. With grateful feelings, *the Knights of the Order of Christ* joined the Portuguese kings in their Crusades against the infidels, and accompanied them in their adventurous campaigns of Africa and India, while the kings, on their part, acknowledged the important services of the Knights, by increasing their possessions with the increase of their own conquest, and procured for the Grand Prior of the Order, from Pope Calixtus III. (A. D. 1455–58), an investment of power equal to that of a Bishop. As an encouragement to further conquests and discoveries, they were finally promised, also, the independent possession (under, however, Portuguese protection), of all the countries which they might happen to discover.

Under such favorable circumstances, the new Order grew in power and wealth to such an extent as to raise the fears of the subsequent kings of Portugal, who began to endeavor to limit and curtail the concessions made by their predecessors, especially as regarded the eventual discoveries made by the Order, which instead of, as originally stipulated, being its own independent property, were now to be marked *Crown domains;* leaving to the Knights only the civil jurisdiction, and a certain military preponderance in them. Nor was the limitation confined to the future conquests of the Order alone ; even the territories which were already in their possession, the Pope thought fit to include in the new contract, when laid before him for sanction. Subsequently, King John III. (A. D. 1521–1557) even procured from Pope Adrian VI. (A. D. 1522), an Edict by which the functions of Administrator and Grand Master of the Order were exclusively transferred to the Portuguese Crown.

The principal seat of the Order was originally Castro Marino, in the Diocese of Faro ; but in 1366, it was transferred to Tomer (seven leagues from Santaran), where a fine cloister is still to be seen.

The Order of Christ, Successor of the Knights Templars.

No one could present himself as candidate in this Order who was not able to prove his noble descent, and a three years' military noviceship in the wars against the infidels. The members were originally bound to make the three vows of Chastity, Poverty, and Obedience; but Pope Alexander VI. (A. D. 1492–1503) released them from the two first, on condition that they should apply the third part of their revenues to the building and support of the Tomar Cloister, the priests of which he bound to the whole of the three vows. It serves now, together with the seminary at Coimbra, as a theological institution for the priests of the Order, as an immediate fief of the Crown. The Order now possesses twenty-six

JEWELS WORN BY GRAND CROSS KNIGHTS.   KNIGHTS.

villages and farms, and four hundred and thirty-four prebends. Since 1789, the members consist (besides the Grand Master and Great Commander) of six Knights of the Grand Cross, four hundred and fifty Commanders, and an unlimited number of Knights.

Foreigners are exempt from the rules, but, at the same time, are excluded from participation in the revenues of the Order. Catholics, only, of noble descent can be admitted to the Order. The Knights Grand Cross wear the decoration across the right

The Order of Christ, Successor of the Knights Templars.

shoulder towards the left side, by a broad red ribbon, while the left side of the breast is adorned with the star. The Commanders wear the same cross and star around the neck, and the Knights have the cross suspended at the button hole, though when in uniform, they wear it now also round the neck. Members are allowed to adorn the badge with precious stones.

Mr. Woof in his "Sketch of the Knights Templars," etc. (London, 1865, 8vo, 75 pp.), says during this Order: "In the Papal States it still exists publicly, the jewel or badge being a Passion Cross of red enamel, charged with a similar Cross of white enamel, the Pontifical branch differing in being composed of one class only, not subjected to nobiliary proofs, and superadding a crown to their badge." In the *Almanach de Gotha*, 1873 (an authority of eminence), we find this: " ORDER OF CHRIST.—King Denis of Portugal, in 1317, now under (*Saint Siege*) the Holy See. It was confirmed by Pope John XXII. in 1132, for persons of high birth only. The origin of the Order was in that of the ancient Order of the Temple."

As a summary of this subject in general in accordance with the statements of Burke, we append a note from our usually exact American historian, Dr. A. G. Mackey:

The Order of Christ.—After the overthrow of the Order of Knights Templars throughout Europe, Denis I., King of Portugal, in 1317, solicited of Pope John XXII. permission to re-establish the Order of the Temple in his dominions, under the name of the Order of Christ, and to restore to it the possessions which had been wrested from the Templars. The Pope consented, approved the statutes which had been submitted to him, and in 1319 confirmed the Institution, reserving to himself and to his successors the right of creating Knights, which has given rise to the Pontifical branch of the Order which exists at Rome. The Knights follow the rule of St. Benedict, and conform in all points to the statutes of the Order of the Temple. The Grand Mastership is vested in the King of Portugal; and the Order having been secularized in 1789, the members were divided into the three classes of six Grand Crosses, four hundred and fifty Commanders, and an unlimited number of Knights. It was designated the

Order of Christ, Successor of the Knights Templars.   Other Knightly Orders.

Most Noble Order, and none but those *nobly descended*, of unsul
lied character, could be admitted.   Grandfathers having been me-
chanics was an impediment to the exaltation even of Knights of
the third class.   The Grand Cross and Commanders had generally
valuable grants and great privileges ; the latter were also enjoyed
by the Knights, with pensions, with reversion to their wives.

Much has also been said in this connection of the Spanish Order
of Calatrava in conjunction with the Knights Templars.   But
there seems to be no analogy between the two Orders save that
both (as numerous other organizations of Knighthood) were devoted to the defense of the Christian faith.   The history of the
Knights of Calatrava, abridged from Burke, is as follows: " It was
for a long time known as the *Order of Salvatierra.*   A. D. 711
the Moors acquired possession of a great part of Spain.   An uninterrupted warfare of three hundred years ensued, in which the
Christian powers gradually recovered the country.   Assisted by
the Knights Templars, King Alphonso VII. (Raimond) A. D.
1147, captured the city of Calatrava and confided it to their custody.   Ten years later the Templars withdrew and the King created a new Order of Knights for its defense, with the same vows
of Poverty, Obedience, and Chastity.   This was subsequently confirmed by Pope Alexander III.   The Order received its Statutes
from the Chapter-General of the Cistercian monks.   A. D. 1163
they elected an independent Grand Master.   In the anarchy in
Spain which occurred at the close of the Twelfth Century, the
war of religion was almost exclusively carried on by the *Knights
of Calatrava.*   At the great battle near Fort Alarcos the Span-
iards were totally defeated, Calatrava lost, and the Order nearly
annihilated.   They then removed to Salvatierra.   They gained a
decisive victory, July 16, 1212, over the Moors, and returned to
Calatrava, where they became very powerful and influential.   In
1489 Pope Innocent VIII. transferred the government of the Order to the King of Spain, and destroyed its independence."

Two other Spanish Orders, which in 1523 were transferred with
that of Calatrava to the Crown, deserve a moment's attention
here, viz., the Military Order of St. James of Compostella and
the Order of Alcantara.   That of Compostella originated in the

necessity of guarding from the robbers that infested the mountains of Spain, the pilgrims to the shrine of St. James the elder at Compostella. About the year A. D. 1174, thirteen noblemen, in imitation of the movement at Jerusalem, seventy years before, united their strength and wealth for this purpose. They received a bull from the Pope dated July 5, 1175, granting Statutes and ample powers. Hospitals were erected and all that was praiseworthy in the Knights Templars and Hospitalers imitated. The Knights made vows of Poverty, Obedience, and Celibacy. They promised not to listen, in their combats with the Saracens, to the voice of ambition, glory, covetousness, or bloodshed, but to have only these objects in view, the protection of Christians and the conversion of infidels. Candidates for this Order must be descended from a purely Christian race. The Order was very successful. Its red cross shone by the side of the royal standard in many great battles against the Moslem. They became extremely wealthy and, as we have seen, lost their independence in 1523.

The Order of Alcantara was greatly favored and patronized by Ferdinand III. (A. D. 1217–1252) King of Leon. It had been formed by the brothers Barriento, about A. D. 1170. In 1177 Pope Alexander raised it to Knightly Order, and in 1183 Pope Lucius III. confirmed the Papal decree. The vow included Poverty, Chastity, and Obedience. The crest of the Order, a pear-tree, refers to the town of Pereiro (a pear-tree) in which it was first established. The ribbon is green. The duties were the defense of the Christian religion and continued war against the Moors. They fought bravely for the cause of religion and the father-land, and acquired such wealth, authority, and power as eventually to lose their independence as already remarked.

The similarity of these four Portuguese and Spanish Orders of Knighthood with those of the Templars and Hospitalers will now appear. The same analogy justifies the introduction of a brief sketch, from Burke, of

THE ORDER OF THE HOLY SEPULCHER.

The Order may justly rival in antiquity that of St. Lazarus, credible authors dating its origin as early as the year A.D. 69, when St. James, the first Bishop of Jerusalem, intrusted the guardianship of the Holy Sepulcher

Order of the Holy Sepulcher.   Rules and Regulations thereof.

to a number of men distinguished for piety and high birth. Some writers, however, consider that it originated with the Canons Regular, whom St. Helena, mother of Constantine the Great, introduced into her new church of Calvary; while others again assert that the Knights of the Holy Sepulcher arose in the time of Godfrey de Bouillon, or his successor Baldwin, and that by the latter the Patriarch of Jerusalem was nominated first Grand Master. But the most probable date may, with some historical truth, be fixed at a much later period, in the year 1496, during the papacy of Alexandria VI. His Holiness sought, in fact, to be considered as the founder of the Order, by means of which he intended to stimulate zeal for religion and for pilgrimages.

The Grand Mastership, and the right of nominating Knights, were originally vested in the Holy See, though the Pope ceded subsequently those rights to the Guardian Father of the Sacred Tomb. Noble descent was one of the conditions of the reception. The duties of the Knights were to hear mass daily; combat, live, and die for the Christian religion; to procure substitutes in the war with the infidels, in case their own presence should be prevented by unavoidable circumstances; to grant constant protection to the servants of the Church; to prevent all sorts of unjust feuds, quarrels, disputes, and usury; to favor peace amongst Christians; protect widows and orphans; to abstain from swearing and cursing; and to guard carefully against intemperance, lewdness, etc., etc. These heavy and severe duties were amply compensated for by the extraordinary privileges granted to the Knights by the Pope or the Guardian; so extraordinary, indeed, that we can hardly conceive how or by what means they could be secured or guaranteed by the Knights. Among those privileges was the right conceded to members of the Order to legitimatize bastards, change their names, grant escutcheons, possess church property though married, to be exempt from taxes on salt, wine, beer, etc., and to cut down and bury the bodies of those who were executed on the gallows.

This Order, formerly spread throughout France and the rest of Europe, was reconstructed by Louis XVIII., on the 19th of August, 1814, as a royal institution, and also in Poland. In the latter country, it expired at the revolution of 1830, but it is still extant within a very small circle of Knights, elected by the Guardian from the most respectable pilgrims who come to Jerusalem.

The badge is worn around the neck, or at the button-hole, by a black watered ribbon, while the star is only allowed to those Knights who have visited Jerusalem. The collar consists of small red enameled crosses joined together by gold rings. When, in 1847, a Latin Patriarch was once more established at Jerusalem, the Roman Propaganda transferred to him the right of conferring the Order of the Holy Sepulcher.

We now take up what is called the " French theory," that the

List of Grand Masters, from the Death of Jacques de Molay.

Order was not annihilated either by the bull of Clement V. or the despotism of Philip IV., or the treachery and meanness of Edward II., but is due to the action of De Molay himself, who in anticipation of his fate, A. D. 1313, appointed John Mark Larmenius as his successor in office. From that time to the present a regular and uninterrupted succession of Grand Masters has been maintained, as follows:

LIST OF GRAND MASTERS OF KNIGHTS TEMPLARS, 1313 to 1873.

(From Mackey's *Lexicon of Freemasonry*.)

John Mark Larmenius.....................	1313
Thomas Theobald Alexandrinus; otherwise	
Francis Thomas Theobald.................	1324
Arnold de Braqué..........................	1340
John de Claremont........................	1349
Bertrand du Guesclin......................	1357
John Arminiacus...........................	1381
Bernard Arminiacus........................	1392
John Arminiacus...........................	1419
John de Croy	1451
Bernard Imbault...........................	1472
Robert Lenoncourt........................	1478
Galeatius de Salazar.......................	1497
Philip Chabot	1516
Gaspard de Galtiaco Tavanensis..............	1544
Henry de Montmorency.....................	1574
Charles de Valois.........................	1615
James Ruxellius de Granceio	1651
James Henry, Duc de Duras.................	1681
Philip, Duke of Orleans....................	1705
Louis Augustus Bourbon....................	1724
Louis Henry Bourbon Condè	1737
Louis Francis Bourbon Conty................	1741
Louis Hercules Timoleon, Duc de Cossé Brissac.	1776
Claude M. R. Chevillon	1792
Bernard Raymund Fabrè Palaprat	1804
Sir William Sidney Smith..................	1838
Died..............	1840

The documents containing these facts are numerous, but their genuineness has been controverted. The following letter of transfer from John Mark Larmenius, successor of De Molay, to Francis Thomas Theobald, is one of the most important of these :

I, Brother John Mark Larmenius, of Jerusalem, by the grace of God, and by the most secret decree of the venerable and most holy martyr, Grand Master of the Militia of the Temple (to whom be honor and glory), confirmed by the Common Council of the Brethren, invested with the Supreme and Grand Mastership over the universal Order of the Temple, to all who shall see these decretory letters, *thrice greeting :*

" Be it known to all, both present and future, that with declining strength, owing to extreme age, and having duly considered the perplexity of affairs, and the weight of government, for the greater glory of God, the protection and safety of the Order, of the brethren, and of the statutes, I, the aforesaid, humble Master of the Militia of the Temple, having resolved to deposit the Grand Mastership in more able hands;

" Therefore, by the help of God, and with the unanimous consent of the Knights of the Grand Convent, I have conferred, and by this present decree do confer for life the Grand Mastership, authority, and privileges of the Order of the Temple upon the eminent Commander, and my very dear brother, Francis Thomas Theobald, of Alexandria, with power, according to the laws of the time and affairs, to confer the Supreme and Grand Mastership and supreme authority of the Order of the Temple on another brother, eminently endowed with nobility of the institution and of quality, and with probity of manners. Wherefore, for the perpetuity of the Mastership, that the line of successors may be uninterrupted, and for upholding the integrity of the statutes, I also decree that the Mastership be not transferred without the consent of the General Convent of Fellow-Soldiers of the Temple, as often as it shall be necessary to assemble this Grand Convent, and matters being thus arranged amongst them, a successor may be elected at the will of the Knights.

" And lest the duties of the supreme office languish, let there be now and perpetually four Deputy Grand Masters, having supreme power, eminence, and authority over the universal Order, saving the rights of the Grand Master; which Deputy Masters are to be elected from among the seniors according to the rank of profession. Which statute I commend to the brethren of our aforesaid sacred, worshipful, and most happy Master, the Martyr (to whom be honor and glory). Amen.

" Lastly, with the decree of the Grand Convent of the Brethren, by my supreme delegated authority, I will, declare, and decree the Scotch Templars *deserters of the Order*, cast off with an anathema, they and their brethren of St. John of Jerusalem, despoilers of the dominions of the Militia (to whom may God show mercy), without the pale of the Temple, now and for ever.

Introduction of the Knights of the Temple into Scotland by King David I.

"Therefore I have appointed signs, unknown to and out of the reach of the false brethren, to be orally delivered by Fellow-Soldiers, and in the manner that in the Grand Convent it has already been pleased to deliver them.

"But which signs are only communicated after due profession and consecration as a Knight, according to the statutes, rites, and usages of Fellow-Soldiers of the Temple, transmitted by me to the aforesaid eminent Commander, as I have had them delivered into my hands from the Worshipful Master and most holy Martyr (to whom be honor and glory). Let it be done as I have said. Let it be done. Amen.

"Given by me, John Mark Larmenius, the 13th day of February, 1324."

The Fraters of this Order in Scotland, who are numerous and influential, spurn the imputation in this "Paper of Transfer" of Larmenius, and pronounce the whole document a forgery.

Lawrie in his History of Fremasonry in Scotland, assures us that the Knights of the Temple were introduced into Scotland before 1153, by King David I., who established them at the Temple on the Southesk, and who was so attached to the brotherhood, that we are told by an old historian, "*Sanctus David de præclara Militia Templi optimos fratres secum retinens, eos diebus et noctibus morum suorum fecit ipse custodes.* Malcolm, the grandson of David, conferred on the Brethren *in liberam et puram eleemosynam unum plenarium toftum in quolibet burgo totius terræ,*" which foundation was enlarged by his successors, William the Lion and Alexander II. The charter of the latter is still in the possession of Lord Torphichen, whereby he grants and confirms *Deo et fratribus Templi Salomonis de Jerusalem omnes illas rectitudines libertatis et consuetudines quas Rex David et Rex Malcolm et decessus pater meus Rex Willielmus eis dederunt et concesserunt, sicut scripta eorum authentica attestant.*" This curious document, after enumerating certain of these rights and liberties, viz.: the king's sure peace; the privilege of buying, selling, and trading with all his subjects; freedom from all tribute and toll, etc., proceeds at much length to enumerate the privileges granted. These general privileges, throughout Europe, were very extensive. The Templars were freed from all tithes to the Church, and their priests were entitled to celebrate mass, and to absolve from sins to the same extent as bishops—a privilege which was strongly objected to by the latter. Their houses possessed the right of sanctuary or asylum for criminals. They could be witnesses in their own cause, and were exempted from giving testimony in the cause of others. They were relieved by the Papal bulls from all taxes, and from subjection and obedience to any secular power. By these great immunities the Order was rendered in a manner independent, but it would appear nevertheless, that both the Templars and Hospitalers considered themselves subjects of the countries to which they belonged, and took part in the national wars, for we find by the Ragman Roll, *Frère Johan de Sautre, Mestre de la Cheualerie del Temple en Escoce,* and another brother swearing fealty to Edward I. in 1296; and the author of the " Annals of Scotland," noticing the Battle of Falkirk, 12th July, 1298, informs us that the only persons of note who fell were Brian le Jay, Master of the English Templars, and the Prior of Torphichen in Scotland, a Knight of another Order of religious soldiery. The former of these Chevaliers met his death by the hand of the redoubted Sir William Wallace, who advanced alone from the midst of his little band, and slew him with a single blow, albeit he was a knight of high military renown.

Little is known of the further history of the Knights Templars in Scotland from the time of Alexander II. to the beginning of the Fourteenth Century, except that their privileges were continued to them by succeeding kings, whose bounty and piety were in those ages continually directed towards the religious Orders. By their endowments and the bequests of the nobles, the possessions of the Fraternity came to be so extensive, that their lands were scattered *per totum regnum Scotiæ, a limitibus versus Angliam, et sic discendo per totum regnum usque ad Orchades.*

The date of the spoliation of the Templars in Scotland corresponds of course with that of the persecution of the Order in other countries, but it is to the credit of our forefathers, that we can obtain no account of any member having been subjected to personal torture or suffering amongst them; their estates however appear to have been duly transferred to the possession of their rivals the Knights Hospitalers, into which Order, like their brethren in England, it is not improbable that a number of the Templars entered.

The Knights of St. John had also been introduced into Scotland by David I. and had a charter granted to them by Alexander II., some years after that to the Templars. The Preceptory of Torphichen, in West Lothian, was their first, and continued to be their chief residence, and by the accession of the Temple lands and other additions, their property at the time of the Reformation came to be immense.

About the commencement of the reign of James IV. a union was effected between the Knights of the Temple and of Saint John, and the lands belonging to either body were consolidated. No documentary evidence has been discovered to point out the precise period of this junction; and if such evidence does exist, it will probably be found among the records of the Hospital. But the fact of the union is established beyond all doubt and cavil by the Charter of King James, of date 19th October, 1488, confirming the grants of lands made by his predecessors to the Knights of the Temple and St. John.—*Deo et Sancto Hospitali de Jerusalem et fratribus ejusdem Militiæ Templi Salomonis.* From that Charter we learn that both Orders were then united and placed under the superintendence of the Preceptor of Saint John, and there can be no doubt that such an arrangement was both natural and political. In Scotland alone the Knights of the Temple possessed independent property, and the ban against them being still in force throughout Europe, their sphere of action was necessarily contracted, whilst on the other hand the Knights of the Hospital were possessed of great influence and wealth, and high in the favor of the Continental Sovereigns. Both Orders were therefore represented in the Scottish Parliament by the Preceptor of Saint John; and down to the period of the Reformation the union remained unbroken.

From the era of the Reformation the combined Order of the Temple and Hospital appears in Scotland only as a Masonic body; but the late Mr. Deuchar averred that so early as 1590 a few of the Brethren had become mingled with the Architectural Fraternities, and that a Lodge at Stirling, patronized by King James, had a Chapter of Templars attached to it, who were termed cross-legged Masons, and whose initiatory ceremonies were performed, not in a room, but in the Old Abbey, the ruins of which are still to be seen in the neighborhood. The first authentic notice we can find on the subject is in M. Thory's excellent "Chronology of Masonry," wherein it is recorded that about 1728 Sir John Mitchell Ramsay, the well-known author of "Cyrus," appeared in London with a system of Scottish Masonry, up to that date perfectly unknown in the metropolis, tracing its origin from the Crusades, and consisting of three degrees, the Ecossais, the Novice, and the Knight Templar. The English Grand Lodge rejected the system of Ramsay, but if credit is to be given to a letter from the Duke of Perth to Lord Ogilvie in 1745, recently published, it shone forth for a moment at Holyrood at that date. During his short stay at that palace, Charles Stuart is stated to have taken his profession as a Templar, and to have "looked most gallantly in the white robe of the Order," which is not improbable, as the works of Thory, Clavel and others have since proved that to obtain their objects the Stuart family made unceasing use of Freemasonry in all its forms, endeavoring to apply its ancient legends to the modern history of Charles I., and to the cruelty of Cromwell and his confederates. After the Battle of Culloden, Ramsay, as is well known, along with the other adherents of the Stuart family, transferred his system to the Continent, where it became the corner-stone of the *hauts-grades*, and the foundation of those innumerable ramifications into which an excellent and naturally simple institution has been extended in France, Germany and other countries abroad.

In pursuing the very curious subject of the *hauts-grades*, we may observe however that they never obtained much consideration during the lifetime of Ramsay, although they were invariably traced to him and to Scotland, the fairy-land of foreign Masonry, but gathered their chief impulse from the dissensions in the Masonic Lodges at Paris about the middle of last century, which induced the Chevalier de Bonneville and other distinguished persons at the Court of France, to form themselves into a separate institution named the *Chapitre de Clermont*, in honor of one of the Princes of the Blood, Louis de Bourbon, Prince de Clermont, then presiding over the Masonic Fraternities. In this chapter they established, amongst other degrees, the Ramsay system of the Masonic Templars, which along with other high grades was soon conveyed into the northern kingdoms of Europe by the officers of the French army, but especially by the Marquis de Bernez and the Baron de Hund, the latter of whom amplified it into his *Templar Régime de la Stricte Observance*, which occupied for several years so prominent a place in the secret societies of Germany.   This adventurer appeared in that country with a patent under the sign-manual of Prince Charles Stuart, appointing him Grand Master of the seventh province, which he affirmed had been made over to him by the Earl Marischal on his death-bed, and with a plausible tale of the antiquity of his Order, which he derived, of course, from Scotland, where the chief seat of the Templars was Aberdeen, and the delusions on the subject took such a hold in Germany that they were not altogether dispelled until a deputation had *actually visited Aberdeen*, and found amongst the worthy and astonished Brethren there no trace either of very ancient Templars or Freemasonry.   From some of the Continental States it is conjectured that Masonic Templary was transplanted into England and Ireland, in both of which countries it has continued to draw a languid existence.

During the whole of the Eighteenth Century, the Scottish Order can be but faintly traced ; though Mr. Deuchar had in 1836 the assurance of well-informed Masons that thirty or forty years previous, they knew old men who had been members of it for sixty years, and it had sunk so low at the time of the French Revolution, that the sentence which the Grand Lodge of Scotland fulminated in 1792 against all degrees of Masonry except those of St. John, was expected to put a period to its existence.   Soon after this, however, some active individuals revived it, and with the view to obtaining documentary authority for their Chapters, as well as of avoiding any infringement of the Statutes then recently enacted against secret societies, adopted the precaution of accepting Charters of Constitution from a body of Masonic Templars, named the Early Grand Encampment, in Dublin, of whose origin we can find no account, and whose legitimacy, to say the least, was quite as questionable as their own.   Several Charters of this description were granted to different Encampments of Templars in Scotland about the beginning of the present century; but these bodies maintained little concert or intercourse with each other, and were certainly not much esteemed in the country. Affairs were in this state, when about 1808, Mr. Alexander Deuchar was elected Commander or Chief of the Edinburgh Encampment of Templars; and his brother Major David Deuchar, along with other officers of the Royal Regiment, was initiated into the Order. This infusion of persons of higher rank and better information gave an immediate impulse to the Institution; and a General Convocation of all the Templars of Scotland, by representatives, having taken place in Edinburgh, they unanimously resolved to discard the Irish Charters, and to rest their claims, as the representatives of the Ancient Knights, on the general belief and traditions of the country. They further determined to entreat the Duke of Kent, the Chief of the Masonic Templars in England, to become the Patron Protector of the Order in North Britain, offering to submit themselves to His Royal Highness in that capacity, and to accept from him a formal Charter of Constitution. The Duke of Kent lost no time in complying with their request, and his Charter erecting them into a Conclave of "Knights of the Holy Temple and Sepulcher, and of St. John of Jerusalem, H. R. D. M. ✠ K. D. S. H.," bears date the 19th of June, 1811. By a provision in it Mr. Deuchar, who had been nominated by the Brethren, was appointed Grand Master for life.

These new and vigorous measures rescued the Order from obscurity; and in its improved condition we find that it continued rapidly to flourish, numbering in the course of a few years no less than forty Encampments or Lodges, holding its Conclave in different parts of the British Dominions. In 1828, the Order seemed to have received a fresh impulse, and assumed a novel and interesting aspect by the judicious introduction of the Ancient Chivalric costume and forms. Dissensions, nevertheless, unfortunately occurred from 1830 to 1835, tending to impede its progress, and for a while it may be said to have again almost fallen into abeyance. In the end of the latter year, however, a body of gentlemen undertook the trouble and expense of resuscitating it, with the

The R. A. Degrees become a Prerequisite to Admission into the Temple Order.

view of establishing in Edinburgh Masonic reunions somewhat resembling those of the Prince of Wales's Lodge in London, where humbler Brethren are not subjected to heavy pecuniary payments. At their suggestion, Mr. Deuchar resigned the Grand Mastership, and the statute was strictly enforced by which it was imperative that all candidates for admission should be Royal Arch Masons; while new regulations were also established. In January, 1836, Admiral Sir David Milne, G. C. B., was unanimously elected Grand Master; and at a general election the same month, Lord Ramsay (afterwards Marquis of Dalhousie), was appointed his Deputy; the various other offices in the Order being filled by gentlemen generally well known, and of an honorable station in society. In the course of three months after the election, not fewer than a hundred persons, chiefly men of fortune, officers, and members of the learned professions had been received into the Edinburgh Canongate Kilwinning Priory or Encampment alone.

On the demise of Admiral Sir David Milne, the Knights in Chapter-general unanimously chose His Grace George Augustus Frederick John, sixth Duke of Athol, K. T., to be Grand Master, who was installed with great pomp on the 11th of March, 1846, in the Music Hall, Edinburgh, which was gorgeously decorated for the occasion with the banners of the Knights, etc. Under his judicious sway various Priories were established and dormant ones revived, and the Order has assumed an importance and dignity worthy of the highest class of gentlemen connected with the Masonic Institutions of Scotland.

This sketch of the Templars would probably be incomplete without alluding more particularly to the *Ordre du Temple* in France. Mills, Sutherland, de Magny, Dumas, Burnes, Gregoire, and other authorities, all show that the Order although suppressed has never been dissolved in that country.

The persecution of the Templars in the Fourteenth Century does not close the history of the Order; for though the Knights were spoliated the Order was not annihilated. In truth, the cavaliers were not guilty—the brotherhood was not suppressed—and, startling as is the assertion, there has been a succession of Knights Templars from the Twelfth Century even down to these days;

35

the chain of transmission is perfect in all its links. James de Molay, the Grand Master at the time of the persecution, anticipating his own martyrdom, appointed as his successor in power and dignity Johannes Marcus Larmenius of Jerusalem, and from that time to the present there has been a regular and uninterrupted line of Grand Masters. The Charter by which the supreme authority has been transmitted is judicial and conclusive evidence of the Order's continued existence. This Charter of transmission, with the signatures of the various Chiefs of the Temple, is preserved at Paris, with the ancient statutes of the Order, the rituals, the records, the seals, the standards, and other memorials of the early Templars.

The brotherhood has been headed by the bravest cavaliers in France; by men who, jealous of the dignities of knighthood, would admit no corruption, no base copies of the Orders of Chivalry, and who thought that the shield of their nobility was enriched by the impress of the Templars' red cross. Bertrand du Guesclin was the Grand Master from 1357 till his death in 1380, and he was the only French commander who prevailed over the chivalry of our Edward III. From 1478 to 1497, we may mark Robert Lenoncourt, a cavalier of one of the most ancient and valiant families of Lorraine. Philippe Chabot, a renowned captain in the reign of Francis I., wielded the staff of power from 1516 to 1543. The illustrious family of Montmorency appear as Knights Templars, and Henry, the first Duke, was the chief of the Order from the year 1574 to 1614. At the close of the Seventeenth Century, the Grand Master was James Henry de Duras, a Marshal of France, the nephew of Turenne, and one of the most skillful soldiers of Louis XIV. The Grand Masters from 1724 to 1776 were three princes of the royal Bourbon family. The names and years of power of these royal personages who acknowledged the dignity of the Order of the Temple were Louis Augustus Bourbon, Duke of Maine, 1724–1737; Louis Henry Bourbon Condè, 1737–1741; and Louis Francis Bourbon Conty, 1741–1746. The successor of these princes in the Grand Mastership of the Temple was Louis Hercules Timoleon, Duke de Cosse Brissac, the descendant of an ancient family, long celebrated in French history for its loyalty and gallant bearing. He accepted the office in 1776, and sustained it till he died in the cause of royalty at the beginning of the French Revolution. It had then its Grand Master, Bernardus Fabre Palaprat; and there are Colleges in England and in many of the chief cities in Europe.

Thus the very ancient sovereign Order of the Temple is now in full and chivalric existence, like those Orders of Knighthood which were either formed in imitation of it, or had their origin in the same noble principles of chivalry. It has mourned as well as flourished, but there is in its nature and constitution a principle of vitality which has carried it through all the storms of fate; its continuance by representatives as well as by title, is as indisputable a fact as the existence of any other chivalric fraternity. The Templars of these days claim no titular rank, yet their station is so far identified with that of the other Orders of Knighthood, that they assert equal purity of descent from the same bright source of chivalry: nor is it possible to impugn the legitimate claims to honorable estimation, which the modern Brethren of the Temple derive from the antiquity and pristine luster of their Order, without at the same time shaking to its center the whole venerable fabric of knightly honor.

To this we have only to add that on the demise of the Grand Master Bernard Raymund, in 1838, he was succeeded in the regency of the Order by Admiral Sir Wm. Sidney Smith, who held sway till his death in 1840; and that at that date it numbered amongst the British subjects enrolled as its office-bearers the names of the Duke of Sussex, Grand Prior of England; the Duke of Leinster, Grand Prior of Ireland; the Earl of Durham, Grand Prior of Scotland; the Chevalier Burnes (Grand Master of Scottish Freemasons in India), Grand Preceptor of Southern Asia; the Chevalier Tennyson D'Eyncourt, Grand Prior of Italy; General George Wright, Grand Prior of India, etc., etc., while amongst its functionaries in France we find the Prince Alexander de Wirtemberg, the Dukes de Choiseul and Montmorency, and the Counts Le Peletier D'Aunay, de Lanjuinais, de Brack, de Chabrillan, de Magny, de Dienne, and others equally distinguished. Latterly, in consequence of political changes in France, an institu-

tion so much identified with ancient nobility and tradition has
naturally fallen into abeyance, but it still numbers about thirty
British members, most of whom are officers in the Public Service
in India, received by the Grand Preceptor of Southern Asia, under
legatine powers from the Grand Master, Bernard Raymund, sanctioned by the Duke of Sussex, without whose approval no British
subject was admissible.

We have expressed our belief that the Knights Templars of
Scotland, on the persecution of the Order in the Fourteenth Century, took refuge with Robert Bruce, and this opinion is confirmed
by a French authority, which states that, having deserted the
Temple, they ranged themselves under the banners of that Prince,
by whom they were formed into a new Order, the observances of
which were based on those of the Templars, and became, according to him, the source of Scottish Freemasonry. This statement
corresponds with the celebrated Charter of Larmenius, already
referred to, in which the Scottish Templars are excommunicated
as *Templi desertores anathemate percussos ;* and, along with the
Knights of St. John, *dominiorum Militiæ spoliatores,* placed for
ever beyond the pale of the Temple, *extra gyrum Templi nunc,
et in futurum ;* and it is likewise supported in some measure by
the authority of the eminent annalist of Freemasonry, M. Thory,
who, in his *Acta Latomorum,* states, that Robert Bruce founded
the Masonic Order of Heredum de Kilwinning after the Battle of
Bannockburn, reserving to himself and his successors on the
throne of Scotland, the office and title of Grand Master. And
that the last of the Stuarts believed that he possessed this hereditary right and distinction, and in virtue of it granted Charters of
Constitution to Lodges abroad, is beyond all question ; nay, there
is the strongest reason to conclude that the whole system of Templary advanced by Ramsay and other partisans of the exiled House
was based on the conviction that the Chevalier de St. George was
the hereditary head of the " Royal Order " of Bruce, and that
that Order was formed from the relics of the Scottish Templars.
It is in favor of this belief, moreover, that the Ancient Mother
Kilwinning Lodge certainly possessed in former times other
degrees of Masonry than those of St. John, and that we have still

amongst us—apparently deriving their right from her—Brethren who claim to be representatives of Bruce's Royal Order, which although not very prominent in this country, enjoys the highest celebrity in France, where it was established by Charter from Scotland, and even by the Pretender himself in the course of last century, and is now conferred as the highest and most distinguished degree sanctioned by the Grand Orient, under the title of the Rose Croix Heredum de Kilwinning.   It may be interesting to mention, that the introduction on the Continent of this ancient branch of our national Masonry has been commemorated by a splendid medal struck at Paris, bearing, amongst other devices, the Royal Arms and Motto of Scotland ; and that the Brethren of the Lodge of Constancy at Arras still preserve with reverence an original Charter of the Order, granted to their Chapter in 1747, by Charles Edward Stuart, and signed by that unfortunate prince himself, as the representative of the Scottish kings.   Nor can anything indicate more strongly the high estimation in which the chivalry of the Rosy Cross of Kilwinning is held in France, than the fact that the Prince Cambaceres, Arch-chancellor of the Empire, presided over it as Provincial Grand Master (the office of supreme head being, as already noticed, inherent in the Crown of Scotland) for many years, and that he was succeeded in his dignity by the head of the illustrious family of Choiseul.

The history of Sir W. Sidney Smith's connection with the Order of Knights Templars is so well substantiated, and is brought so near to our own period, that we copy copiously from John Barrow's "Life and Correspondence of Admiral Sir William Sidney Smith."   (London, 1848, 2 vols.)

From the end of 1815, Sir Sidney mostly made his residence in Paris, France.   It was here, in fact, that he carried on the vast correspondence with the Knights Liberators, and also with another Order of Knighthood, of which he became a member, invested at the fountain head, in a curious and romantic manner, the history of which is as follows:

The first introduction of Sir Wm. Sidney Smith into the Order of Knights Templars appears to have been occasioned by an official visit to Cyprus, and an accidental piece of service he had an opportunity of performing in that island, by putting down an insurrection of Janissaries and others, in the year 1799, the same year in which the siege of Acre was raised.   For this

The Cross of St. John worn by Richard I. bestowed upon Sir Sidney Smith.

service the Archbishop of the island bestowed upon him the Cross of St. John of Jerusalem, the same which had been worn by King Richard I. of England in the days of the Crusaders; and which Sir Sidney, by his last will, "gave and bequeathed unto the Order of the Templars to be kept in deposit in the treasury thereof, from whence it originally came into King Richard's hands, and to be worn by the Grand Master and his successors in perpetuity."

The following is Sir Sidney's own account of his obtaining this Cross, which he wore during his life, and which is now in possession of the convent of the Order of St. John of Jerusalem, at Paris. The paper is in Sir Sidney's own writing, but has no address, though judging by the appeal made on a point of conscience and religion, it was probably meant for the English bishop resident in Paris at that time, viz., Dr. Luscomb.

"In the exercise of my duty (says Sir Sidney), representing the king in his dignity, as his Minister Plenipotentiary at the Ottoman Porte, and being decorated by Sultan Selim with his imperial aigrette, and with a commission to command his forces by sea and land, on the coast of Syria and Egypt, consequently representing that sovereign in his authority, in the absence of the Grand Vizier (his highness being the one to exert it, when present), and as the Captain Pasha was expressly put personally under my orders, I thought it my duty to land at Cyprus, for the purpose of restoring subordination, and the hierarchy of authority, on a sudden emergency, which arose from the bursting out of an insurrection of Janissaries, Arnants and Albanians, in the year 1799, after the raising of the siege of Acre.

"On visiting the venerable Greek Archbishop afterwards, at the capital (Nicosia), to prevent him from disgracing himself by a visit to me, which I understood was his intention, his grace met me outside the city gates. I, of course, dismounted to receive his welcome and animated harangue, at the termination of which he embraced me paternally, and at the same moment adroitly threw the Templar's Cross, which he wore as an episcopal decoration on his breast, *around the neck of his English guest*, saying, 'This belonged to an Englishman formerly, and I now restore it. It belonged to St. Richard (Agio Ricardo), surnamed "Cœur-de-Lion," who left it in this church at his departure, and it has been preserved in our treasury ever since. Eighteen archbishops, my predecessors, have signed to the receipt thereof, in succession. I now make it over to you, in token of our gratitude for saving all our lives, the archbishops, ecclesiastics, laymen, citizens, and peasantry.'

"You are aware that the Grand Master of the Knights Templars was at Cyprus when he received the mandate of the King of France, Philip IV. and Clement V. to go to Paris and justify himself and the Order against the foul charges of two apostate knights, suborned by those who speculated on their spoils from confiscation. The Grand Master never returned, but was

The Order established without Papal Authority. Sir Sidney ordained a Templar.

burnt, A.D. 1313, near the Pont Neuf, with other knights, then falsely accused and unjustly dealt by. You may not be aware that the surviving knights, justly despising the impotent Bull that pretended to abolish an Order, not created by, and totally independent of the papal authority, the forced terms of which Bull (*suspendo in perpetuo*) admitted the impossibility of abolition and extinction, and forthwith that a new Grand Master was elected in secret and has continued to maintain the Order in due form and consistence ever since.

"Thus *it has not ceased to exist*. And the Grand Master and his council recognizing me as a new Knight Templar elect, duly received me, and voting me to be qualified by the above antecedents, recorded me as Grand Prior of England, an authority which Richard I. exercised after he had become the purchaser of the land of the Order in Cyprus.

"I have ceded this dignity to a most illustrious and a more worthy personage (the Duke of Sussex, Grand Master of England). Nevertheless, I do not thereby cease to belong to the Order, having received a higher dignity therein. It is unquestionably a holy Order, considering its origin and attributes among the primitive Christians; and considering that I did not understand the whole of the Greek Archbishop's speech, at the moment of the investiture, I may have been ordained without being quite aware of it, and if so, or under the doubt in my mind, which suddenly arises by learning that the Grand Prior of Portugal is a candidate for church preferment, which proves him to be an Ecclesiastic, I hesitate to take the oath as tendered to me, to enable me to receive my half pay in its precise form, requiring me to assert that I am not in holy orders. My appeal to your Lordship is to have my mind satisfied on the historically recorded quality of the Knights Templars in England, previous (probably) to my taking the said required oath."

Sir Sidney having thus legitimately, it may be said, become a Templar, was ever after a most zealous member of the "Order of the Temple." The white cloak, marked on the left breast with a red cross, always hung in his bedroom. The rank which he held in the Order was high, as well in England as in France.

In a letter addressed to a friend, dated 28th October, 1839, from Paris, he says:

"I am most anxious to leave Paris before another insurrection; though as Regent of the 'Order of the Orient,' and of the '*Milice du Temple*,' denominated the Order of the Temple, I must always have a *pied à terre* (foot of ground) here, a *residence magistral*."

Sir Sidney being at Paris when he was made Grand Cross of the Bath, received this address:

"La Loge Chapitrale de l'Amité de Paris, a'l Amiral Sir Sidney Smith. Illustrious Brother: It is with most sincere satisfaction we are informed that the Queen of England, on her coronation, has raised you to the rank of Grand Cross of the Order of the Bath, and that by this mark of high favor, her Majesty has acknowledged your eminent services, too long forgotten.

"Every circumstance which relates to you becomes personally interesting to each member of our society, of which you are so deservedly considered *Le venerable d'honneur* (Honorary Master). Accept then, Most Illustrious Brother, our sincere congratulations on this distinguished testimony of esteem, which has been bestowed upon you by a young sovereign. Nothing can add to our feelings of admiration for your talents, the usefulness of which is not confined alone to your own country, nor increase our veneration for your noble character, or our gratitude for your philanthropic devotion to the progress of general civilization."

Here follow the signatures, amongst which is the name of the French *avocat* who defended Marshal Ney, and this address was considered by both French and English as a great compliment to be paid by that party unto an Englishman !

The following letter of M. Raoul to Mr. Spencer Smith, proves the great respect in which his memory was held by the Fraternity of the Knights Templars at Paris.

"ORDER OF THE TEMPLE, PARIS, August 24, 1841.

"SIR: No one can be more flattered than I am at the demand which you have made of me, and I now respond by forwarding to you a copy of my address pronounced in the name of the Order of the Temple over the tomb of our illustrious and venerable regent, William Sidney Smith. Permit me in turn to repeat a request here which I made to Mr. Arabin. It is to obtain a bust in plaster of our dignified confrere to place in our *convent magistral*, opposite to that of our Grand Master James de Molay. To this request I join this: to give us a copy, certified by the testamentary executor, or by yourself, of that part of the Admiral's will which names the Order of Knights Templars, of which he was one of the most ardent subjects. This testimony of his affection will be deposited in our archives.

"J. M. RAOUL."

Sir Sidney Smith, to His Royal Highness, the Duke of Sussex, a Brother Knight Templar :

PARIS, RUE D'ANJOU, ST. HONORÉ, No. 6,
8 February, 1830.

DEAR AND MOST ILLUSTRIOUS SIR AND BROTHER:

As I cannot obtain any satisfactory account of your Royal Highness's health in answer to my indirect inquiries, I have determined to ask it direct. The

Religion of the Templars resembles that of the Greek Church.

weather is against invalids, but as a thaw has come, after a third hard frost, which has frozen the Seine for a second time this winter, it is to be supposed the same may have happened in England, as the wind is from the N. E., and I will hope for its good effect on our illustrious Grand Prior.

I am induced to entertain and encourage this hope, not only on account of so highly valued a friend, but because your Royal Highness's full energies are called for in these times, which, though not so critical as they have been, are wanted to consolidate the good to be achieved in a state of peace.

The speech from the throne alludes to the final settlement of Greece, as well as the pacification, and that my brother Knights here, as well as myself, consider as concerning our Order essentially, and affording an opening for its resurrection and consolidation under the auspices of a liberal nation. Greece can never be a monarchy without a wealthy and respectable aristocracy. The population of that country, long in slavery, and now rising from its ashes, does not afford the materials for its formation. The religion of the Templars is the nearest to that of the Greek primitive church, being such as Christianity was when the four first Popes resided in Antioch, before the Bishop of Rome—who sat second in rank in the Council held at Chalcedon—before that prelate attributed supremacy to himself. The present Greek Church is sadly deficient in education and knowledge, even of its own history. Its military chiefs are turbulent, lawless, insubordinate freebooters, such as the Cimbri were, and cannot of themselves form an enlightened senate. Enlightened men of other countries, without excluding any, can alone introduce arts and sciences, and prevent any one European nation from such a degree of preponderance as to excite the jealousy of others. The Emperor of Russia, in withdrawing his objection to a prince of one of the contracting parties to the treaty of the 6th of July, does not consent to the removal of his agent, the present president. This, we are given to understand here, makes Prince Leopold hesitate to accept a crown where he would find a permanent foreign influence in possible opposition, with great local following in the same line; but the Grand Prior Anglicanus, with the followers he would have, might establish a counterpoise that would prevent the effect of an exclusive foreign influence. Capo d'Istria, with considerable talent, allowed patriotism, and much personal ambition, might be content with the Grand Prior of all Turkey, and *swarm* Greek subjects from every part of that empire, and many there are in Asiatic Ionia, and other parts of Asia, to repeople the depopulated country, not to be erected in a kingdom without a sufficient number of subjects in its present state to give it any weight in the scale of nations and maintain its independence. It is a mistake to suppose that the Porte cares for the personal subjection of any class not of the Mohammedan religion, beyond the revenue arising from the capitation tax; that is, a given sum, and that and more would be secured to it by a treaty with a crowned *Grand Maitre*. The islands alone, under an

The Order a Christian Military Power in the Levant.

intelligent and just government, would be able to furnish the sum. This is the last and reserved part of the plan. The first is, in case Prince Leopold should decline on account of the permanent presence of the present president, that your Royal Highness should procure the offer, and accept it as a preliminary step. In this hope I subscribe myself your Royal Highness's affectionate and obedient GULIELMUS BARBARICUS.

6th February, 1830.

P. S.—A circumstance not to be lost sight of in contemplating the consequences of the resurrection of the Order in the Levant, is, that its existence as a Christian military power is not now to be established in the Sultan's mind, but is necessarily in the knowledge of the historian and men of suitable education in all the public offices of the Porte by oral tradition, and official documents in their archives. Much as the Turks object to novelties and innovations, such as the new "Kingdom of Greece," they are attached to precedent, and a letter from the Grand Master of the Order of the Temple would find a suitable reception, and be met by an answer in due form, according to precedent, if not in the Ottoman Turkish records, in those of Sultan Selim, the first brought from Cairo. Saladin's royal residence, when he absorbed Egypt by a nominal conquest, very glad to perform a few acts of sovereignty, such as hanging the former government at the town gate, and withdrawing, with a dwindled army, from an overwhelming population, similar only in religion, but with another language and other interests, leaving a single Turk Pasha, as nominal government during the good pleasure of the Divan, composed of native lawyers or imported slaves (Mamelukes), the real governors of the country, as possessing the villages and fiefs, the real sources of revenue. This, in fact, was the state of things till very recent times, Murad and Ibrahim Beys sharing the supreme power when the French army landed in 1798. The Ottoman Porte, on the recovery of the territory by the effect of the combined operation, appointed a Pasha as formerly. The person selected was the Kahaia of my officially subordinate colleague, the then Captain Pasha. He was dispossessed by the present Viceroy, Mehemed Ali, who afterwards got rid of the Mamelukes, his instruments in that rebellion, as they were on the point of dispossessing them. This deposed Pasha is now the Seraskier commanding-in-chief the moving army under the Grand Vizier, who commands everything as first minister holding the Sultan's seal. He is now my volunteer correspondent, recalling to my recollection our cordial co-operation and intimacy at Aboukir as the ground of it. He would do anything I might be able to convince him was for the good of the State, and it would not be difficult to demonstrate to him that a certain revenue, without their resorting to their vexatious and ruinous way of collecting it, would go far to silence the clamor for pay around him, or allow that which is devoted to an expensive navy to go to the army; a Greek subsidiary navy supplying the place of the former by treaty with the

G. M. O. T., King of Greece, an ally as much interested that Don Cossacks and Mogay Crim Tartars should not establish autocracy in place of a limited constitutional monarchy.

History tells us that the destruction of the ancient Templars resulted from the combined craftiness of Philip IV. of France, and Pope Clement IV., in 1305. Two degraded Templars, whose names are unworthy of record, being thrown into prison, concerted a scheme to be laid before the King, containing charges against the Order of every species of vice and immorality, and accusing them of heresy. On such loose grounds, and from two such villains, royal letters under seal were issued to all governors and officers of the crown, with orders to arm themselves and all under their command, on that day month after the date of the orders, and then to open them in the night, and to act according to the directions they contained. The result was that almost every Templar in France, with their Grand Master Jacques de Molay, was taken into custody, their property of every description being seized and confiscated.

The Temple of Paris, the chief sanctuary of the Order in France, was broken open, and entered by the king in person. An act of accusation immediately issued. The king wrote to the Pope, to announce to him the proceedings, and requiring his co-operation. He wrote also to the King of England, Edward II., who was not inclined to believe the slanderous accounts against the Knights Templars; but letters from the Pope convinced him of his error, and he joined the confederacy. After this the English Templars were all seized and thrown into prison. Examinations were conducted, and confessions were extorted by torture. For three years the French King, the Pope, the Cardinals, the Bishops, and relentless Priests carried on their infamous proceedings.

Of many hundreds, who boldly stood forward as defenders of the Knights, between fifty and sixty were brought into a field behind the Abbey of St. Antoine, and there committed to the flames, all asserting their innocence and that of the Order. To crown the whole, the savage Clement, so unworthy of his name and of his calling, ordered a Council with the view of abolishing

Sir Sidney Smith created Regent of the Templars.

the Order; but discussions having produced disagreements, induced the Pope to put an end to the session; and assisted by a few Cardinals and Prelates, on whom he could depend in a secret consistory, he abolished the Order by his own authority. Two years after this, Philip being seated on Clement's right hand, attended by an imposing force of soldiers, the Pope read the Bull of abolition in deep silence, which was published in the following month.

To consummate their iniquitous proceedings, Molay, the Grand Master, and Guy, Grand Prior of Normandy, who had all this time remained in prison at Paris, were brought before an Archbishop, condemned to death, and burned on one of the small islands on the Seine, about the spot where the statue of Henri IV. is now erected on the Pont Neuf.

Voltaire calls the Templars an institution of armed monks, who make a vow of living at the same time in the character of anchorites and soldiers, and were accused of uniting the reproach of these two professions—the debauchery and the cruelty of the warrior with the insatiable passion of avarice. It was their wealth and their growing power that caused their destruction.

The paper that follows was kindly sent to the editor by a friend, to whom he is indebted for many other documents of value.

Notwithstanding the many British and foreign decorations which were conferred upon Sir Sidney Smith, there was no honor he prized so highly as the office of *Regent of the Templars*, to which he was unanimously elected upon the death of Fabre de Palaprat, the last Grand Master of that Order. Shortly after that event, a deputation of the knights waited upon Sir Sidney and expressed a wish that he should be their new Master, an honor which he unhesitatingly declined, from a conviction of his unworthiness; but he consented to preside over their councils as Regent, according to the statutes, until some person better fitted by his talents and lofty qualities to undertake so great a charge, should be put in nomination, an event that never occurred during his life.

It is generally supposed that the Order of the Temple was abolished, and history has taken great pains to mislead the people with regard to the licentiousness and wicked lives of the Templars. These statements are altogether false. That the Order was suppressed by all the sovereigns of Europe cannot be denied; but as none of them created it, they could not abolish it. That irregularities and luxuries crept into their community, may be con-

Causes that led to the Destruction of the Templars.   The Order not abolished.

ceded; no institution as yet has ever reached perfection; but that the enormous wealth and property they possessed was the ostensible cause of their downfall, is now generally admitted.   Avarice and the desire of spoliation, however, were not the only causes for the persecution unto death of these valiant knights; the laity were not alone to blame, for their ignorant prejudices were inflamed by the Church of Rome; and although tardy justice has lately (six hundred years after the cruel butchery of so many good and gallant Christians) opened the eyes of the world to the infamy of the charges brought against the Templars, and sought to be established by perjury and torture, no historian has yet revealed the secret cause of the rancorous enmity of the Church of Rome towards them.

Sir Sidney Smith was of opinion that it was a battle between the followers of St. Peter and St. John, a war between the churches of the West and the East, Rome and Jerusalem.   The Templars approached nearer to the primitive Christians than any sect then in existence; they were decidedly *antipapists;* the gospel of St. John was the groundwork of their faith, the Patriarch of Jerusalem their spiritual chief.   In those days of Papal ascendency throughout Europe, how offensive must have been the position of these gallant Christian dissenters from the Church of Rome, alike formidable by their wealth and their numbers in every kingdom, dangerous from their learning, their natural courage, increased by religious fervor, the fame of their high military prowess and warlike renown rendering such a body of valiant nobles and chivalrous knights the terror of any kingdom, while their dissent from the Romish dogmas almost paralyzed the councils of the Vatican!   But working with that unison for which the Church of Rome has ever been so remarkable, its priests, in the most distant lands, received their secret orders, and acting upon the superstitions of an ignorant and bigoted people, one universal cry for *Justice upon the Templars,* which polluted its very name and achieved the downfall of that body, which had devoted itself, life and limb, to the cause of virtue and the protection of innocence.

Thus, in one general move, fell all the renowned Knights of the Temple. Their property was sacked and pillaged, their revenues and estates confiscated to the sovereigns of Europe, or granted to other Military Orders; but the Order itself was not abolished, for there is indisputable evidence of a successor having been appointed to Jacques de Molay, immediately after his execution, and continued down to these times, so that the most celebrated Knights of Christendom enrolled themselves secretly under the banner of the Temple, thus evincing their attachment to the virtuous principles of the Order, even though shorn of the splendor which its worldly riches displayed in the olden time.

Extract of a letter addressed to Captain Arabin:

CAEN, June 29, 1841.

A recent work, entitled "Regle et Statuts Secrets des Templiers, par Maillard de Cambuse, Paris, 1840," gives a list of all the successive Grand Masters of the Order of the Temple. The last and forty-sixth Grand Master is stated to be "Sir Guillaume Sidney Smith, born in 1764, elected in 1838, died May 26, 1840." His election took place in the latter half of 1838—the precise month and day are not given—so he was Grand Master only about one year and eight months. The Order had been left in a very agitated and disordered state by the previous Grand Master, Fabre Palaprat, who died 18th February, 1838. Then an *interregnum* ensued till the close of that year, when Sir Sidney Smith succeeded him. In page 544, the author says: "Sir Sidney Smith, elected Grand Master in 1838, found the Order in this situation. The projected reforms could only be executed in part during the short period of his government, which terminated at his death, May 26, 1840." It appears Sir Sidney was at the head of forty English Knights of the Order, which was one reason of his election. With their assistance he had already successfully resisted certain injurious measures of the preceding Grand Master, Fabre Palaprat.

This work would furnish materials for a curious and interesting chapter on the history and nature of the Order which the admiral presided over at the end of his life. It is really a curious volume, furnishing much new information about the Templars. Among other things, it seems to render it probable that the earliest Freemasons' lodge in England was founded by some recreant and seceding Templars, and it is generally understood that all the lodges in the world at present are offshoots from that early British one.

During Sir Sidney Smith's regency of the Temple, Don Pedro, of Portugal, the late Emperor of the Brazils was desirous to be elected Grand Master of the Order. In the conscientious discharge of his high functions, Sir Sidney, although he had known that prince from his infancy, having taken him and all his family, as we have seen, to the Brazils, when Napoleon invaded Portugal in the year 1806, and notwithstanding Don Pedro's magnificent offer to reëstablish the Order in Portugal, in all its former splendor, with lands and houses as the seat of a Grand Prior and some hundreds of Knights, yet fully impressed with the solemnity of the oath which is enjoined by the rules of the Order, and of the democratic nature of its institutions, he refused his sanction to the desire expressed by many of the Council to put his Royal Highness in nomination, averring, that he could not regard rank as having any claim *per se*, in an Order where promotion should be based solely upon the merits of the candidate; and he observed,

Sir Sidney Smith protecting the Principles of the Order.

that he was more proud to serve under their late excellent Grand Master, Fabre de Palaprat (a doctor in medicine), than to hold the high office of Regent, not only because of his real merits, although a persecuted man, but because of the profession to which he belonged; as he had many opportunities in the course of his life of witnessing the conduct of both officers and men in times of peril and danger, and he was bound to declare that he had never seen displayed such acts of Christian heroism, of both mental and physical courage, and self-devotion, as he had seen on the part of *the medical staff* of both army and navy !

In the course which the gallant Admiral pursued relative to Don Pedro, there is no doubt that Sir Sidney was actuated by a desire to maintain the principles of the Order within their proper sphere, under those modifications which the changes of society had rendered necessary; and that charity, the love of our fellow-creatures, and raising the voice in the cause of the oppressed should abound, instead of that literal *drawing of the sword*, in the use of which Don Pedro had fondly hoped he might apply his influence as

Grand Master of the Temple, in maintaining the stability of his daughter's throne.

The passage in the will of Sir Sidney Smith already referred to, is this : " I give and bequeath my JERUSALEM CROSS, worn by King Richard the First of England and Cyprus in the Crusades, to the Order of the Temple, to be kept in deposit in the treasury thereof, from whence it originally came into King Richard's hands, and to be worn by the Grand Master and his successors in perpetuity."

We add an engraving of the Coat of Arms of Grand Master Smith, particularly as showing the augmentation of King Richard's Cross at the bottom, with the addition of the name.

The tomb of this heroic and exemplary man, whose deeds of daring through a long life of active military and naval service, rival those of the Sir Knights to which our volume is devoted, is in Père la Chaise, Paris, and that the last Grand Master, successor of James de Molay, lies by the side of a beloved wife. It was erected by a subscription of the English inhabitants of Paris. It is simple, of white marble, divided into two compartments. The profile of Sir Sidney, seen in the engraving, was executed by Danton after David. In the lower compartment are some verses, of which it is difficult to decide which is in poorest taste, the poetry or the sentiment. On the right of the bust is this inscription :

Sir William Sidney Smith, G. C. B.,
Admiral of the Red,
Grand Cross of the Order of the Bath,
Grand Cross of several Foreign Orders, etc
Born 21 July, 1764.
Died 26 May, 1840.

From Sir Richard Woofe's very excellent work we quote a few passages to close this chapter.

An order called the "Masonic Knights Templars, Hospitalers of St. John of Jerusalem, Palestine, Rhodes, and Malta," has existed in this country for an uncertain period. Members, being Freemasons of a certain degree, were received into it as of the combined Orders of the Temple and St. John, and their distinguishing badge, with other regalia, was a white enameled cross of eight points charged with a cross pattee of red enamel, and surmounted by the Grand Master's Crown, worn from a red and white ribbon. The writer is informed that this was not the original jewel of the Masonic Templars, but that it was usurped from the Ordre du Temple of France, some years since, by which considerable offense was occasioned at the time, and protests elicited from members of the latter Order. In 1853 a remodeling of the statutes of this Order occurred, and the incorporated portion of St. John was dismissed, the Order becoming in the new statutes "Masonic Knights Templars " only, and a red enameled cross pattee, worn from a white ribbon, was adopted as the jewel of a Companion, with a patriarchal cross of red enamel, worn from a similar ribbon, for a Commander. A few Encampments clung to old traditions, and, as the change had been never wholly approved, a desire to return to ancient costume gained strength and found favor. In 1862 the Grand Conclave of England, the governing body, again revived the

KNIGHTS TEMPLARS. 565

History of the Order.   Number of Encampments.   Grand Masters.

title of the Order, and restored the jewel to Commanders only, but in other respects the revival is incomplete.   Such is the position of the "Masonic Templars," etc., at this time.

The number of Encampments owning allegiance to the Grand Conclave of England, according to the report of May, 1864, is ninety-six ; they are distributed as follows : London 6, the Provinces 64, the 21st Regiment 1, Australia 3, Canada 7, China 2, Corfu 1, Demarara 1, East Indies 8, Gibraltar 1, Halifax, Nova Scotia, 1, Malta 1.   Four of these, Hull, Bristol, and two in London, are said to have existence from time immemorial, and an Encampment at Bath, not now meeting, and one other, now dormant or extinct, have claimed similar antiquity.   The charters of seven others bear date from 1791 to 1796.

Let us here proceed to inquire, without reference to secret and mysterious sources, of which the foundation is so speculative as to be of little worth, what are the claims of the Order to a descent from the early Templars, and their brethren of the Hospital ?   The fact is, or is not, and in either case needs no concealment.

It is difficult to obtain knowledge of the proceedings of the Masonic Templars in England, they were necessarily of a secret description, and the Order probably kept but scant records.   One writer states positively that it was introduced into this country on the 19th November, 1779.   This is evidently too modern a date, as a record did, and may still exist, of a meeting of the then called Grand Encampment of England, at Carisbrook, Isle of Wight, in 1780, and of a subsequent meeting at Winchester.   It is obvious that no such organization as a "Grand Encampment" would have been perfected in so short a period.   The earliest Encampments on record appear to have been London, York, Bristol, Bath, and Salisbury.   H. R. H. Edward Duke of Kent was Patron of the Order, Sir Thomas Dunckerly being Grand Master.   The latter is described in the "Freemason's Magazine" of October, 1793, as "Most Eminent and Supreme Grand Master of Knights of Rosa Crucis, Templars, Kadosh, etc., of England, under his Royal Highness Prince Edward, Patron of the Order."   Sir Thomas was followed by General Walter Rodwell Wright, who resigned in 1812, and was succeeded by H. R. H. the Duke of Sussex, who was installed as Grand Master on the 6th of August, in that year.   The Duke of Sussex was succeeded in 1846 by the late Colonel Charles Kemeys Kemeys Tynte, F. S. A., who died in 1860, and was followed by the present much respected Grand Master, the Most Eminent Brother William Stuart, of Aldenham Abbey, Herts.

It has been stated that the Duke of Sussex called in most of the old Charters and Books of the Encampments under his rule, and granted new Charters, the Books and old Charters being retained ; but there does not appear to be any foundation for this.

The records of the Baldwyn Encampment, Bristol, in 1780, have reference to a long previous existence, evidenced by a vellum document, wherein the Encampment is styled as of the "Order of Knights Templar of St. John of Jerusalem, Knights Hospitalers, and Knights of Malta, etc." This document refers to other than existing Encampments. That the early Templars had considerable property in Bristol is well known, the importance of their possession in that City being attested by the Parish of Temple and the Temple Church. A tradition exists that the Baldwyn Encampment is the lineal successor of an institution founded in Bristol by the warrior monks whose Order there dwells in name though its glory has passed away.

It has been frequently asserted that the early Templars were all members of the Masonic Fraternity, and that 27,000 of the latter went out to the Holy Land. Whether this be true or not, the architectural remains of the Templars appear a remarkable evidence of greater assistance and skill than could be expected from their martial followers.

Preston states : "During the reign Hy. 2. the Grand Masters of the Knights Templars superintended the Masons, and employed them in building their Temple in Fleet Street, A. D. 1155. Masonry continued under the patronage of this Order till the year 1199."

The Knights of St. John also befriended the Masonic Order, and it may be here observed that the emblems of the Freemasons are plentifully found in the architectural ornaments of Malta. Preston again says: "During the short reigns of Edward V. and Richard III., Masonry was on the decline; but on the accession of Henry VII., A.D. 1485, it rose again into esteem under the patronage of the Master and fellows of the Order of St. John at Rhodes (now Malta), who assembled their Grand Lodge in 1500, and chose Henry their protector." Dr. Burnes says: " From the era of the Reformation the combined Order appears in Scotland only as a Masonic body, but there are some records to indicate that, so early as 1590, a few of the brethren had become mingled with the architectural fraternities, and that a Lodge at Stirling, patronized by King James, had a Chapter of Templars attached to it, who were termed cross-legged Masons, and whose initiatory ceremonies were performed, not in a room, but in the Old Abbey, the ruins of which are still to be seen in the neighborhood." This quotation is only introduced in an English consideration of the subject, as implying, from the peculiar nature of the Masonic institution, that an early connection with the latter could hardly exist in one country without obtaining in another. As far as can be collected, the tradition of the Order (and tradition must not be entirely ignored) appears to be, that when upon their persecution and suppression, the early Templars were compelled to cast off the garb of their Order and mingle with the world, large numbers entered the commanderies of the Hospitalers, some struggled secretly to preserve their Order, and others sought refuge and held their conclaves in the society of Freemasons, and that the meetings of the latter section are to this day represented in our encampments.

Further History of the Order in England. The Temple Order as a Masonic Body.

In How's "Freemason's Manual" (1862), we find: "The rites observed in receiving and affiliating members approached in a remarkable degree to the practice of Freemasonry. One writer indeed, Rosetti, distinctly asserts that the Templars were a branch of the masonic constitution." Referring to the clerical brethren of the Order, who devoted themselves to its civil and religious affairs, How says: "From the best information we are possessed of regarding the Order, we believe there can be little doubt that these learned clerks introduced the whole fabric of craft masonry into the body of the Templars, and that not only was the speculative branch of the science by them incorporated with the laws and organization of the Knights, but to their operative skill were the Templars indebted for their triumphs in architecture and fortification. In our opinion the practice of masonry soon became a prominent feature of the Order, and that masonic secrets alone were the far-famed mysteries of the Templars."—"The Templars, we believe there is no doubt, amalgamated their body with that of their ancient brothers-in-arms, the Knights of St. John. In the preceptories of the Order which remained in England, the secrets imparted to the newly-installed brother of the Temple included, for many years, the degrees known as Knight of St. John and Knight of Malta." In giving consideration to the present institution of English Masonic Templars, How says: "When the late Duke of Sussex was in the zenith of his power as Grand Master of Masons in England, he wished also to obtain the supreme authority in the higher degrees, as well in craft as in Royal Arch Masonry; and to this end, carrying out the wishes of the majority of the brethren in this country, he applied to the Emperor Alexander of Russia, as the nominal head of the Knights of Malta. At the Duke's death, the supreme authority in England was conferred upon that worthy and highly esteemed mason, the late Colonel Kemeys Tynte, who was styled Grand Master of the Knights Templars, an innovation which caused considerable discontent at the time, and in some measure tended to results to be regretted."

There appears no authority for the supposition that the late Duke of Sussex was ever appointed Grand Prior of the Hospitaler Order in England, and the known succession of Grand Priors appears to preclude the possibility of his having been so; consequently the masonic claims must stand without this assistance. How, after making observation as to the legality of the Duke's supposed appointment by the Emperor Alexander, says: "Having shown that the title of the Duke of Sussex, as derived from the Emperor of Russia, was, to say the least, unsatisfactory, are we not justified in taking another and a very different view of the subject? The Order having in the course of time fallen into decay, and infirmity having been displayed in its government and management, the English Knights, whose encampments had been in healthy condition for many years, were fully entitled to take the steps necessary for their own good government; and this course we fully believe would have been followed by the ancient brethren of the Order, and indecision or weakness manifested themselves at the fountain-head.   Viewed from this point, the rule of the Duke of Sussex, accepted, though not elected by the Knights in England, seems perfectly satisfactory; nor can we see that any real important objection can be made to the assumption of the title of Grand Master, if the Order think fit to confer it upon their head."

In Laurie's excellent "History of Freemasonry and the Grand Lodge of Scotland," occurs: "To prove that the Order of Knights Templars was a branch of Freemasonry, would be a useless labor, as the fact has been invariably acknowledged by Freemasons themselves, and none have been more zealous to establish it than the enemies of their Order; the former have admitted the fact, not because it was creditable to themselves, but because it was true ; and the latter have supported it, because by the aid of a little sophistry, it might be employed to disgrace their opponents.   We know the Knights Templars not only possessed the mysteries, but performed the ceremonies and inculcated the duties of Freemasons."   Brother Laurie attributes the calamities of the Templars, to some extent, to their being Freemasons, and assembling in secret to practice the rites of that Order.

In a French ritual of about 1780, in the degree of "Black and White Eagle " (30°), the transmission of Freemasonry by the Templars is most positively asserted.

The general statements and assertions as to the claims of the Scotch Order of Masonic Templars are calculated without inquiry to induce a belief that there is an existing proof of its descent from the veritable Knights of old.   The writer was much influenced by these statements, but failing to procure information which he could offer as from an official source, he can present only the result of his inquiries, and he is bound to say that in this result he finds no stronger claim than is possessed by those institutions of the Order from time immemorial existing in England.

In the Scotch Statutes of 1856 (Supplement, Chap. II.), occurs the following startling announcement: "There is but one Chapter-General, and one Grand Master for the whole world; and from the Order having been suppressed in 1309 in all countries except Scotland, it shall always be held in that Langue."   But by a note to the preface of the same statutes, it appears that "The present body in Scotland merely claims to be the legitimate descendants, by adoption, of the original Knights of the Order.   The ' Royal Order' of Scotland has never claimed, as alleged by some writers, to be ' derived from the ancient Order of the Knights Templars.' "

There is no doubt that the ancient Order was not suppressed in Scotland as in other countries, and it is generally admitted that many of the Templars joined Robert Bruce, and fought in his cause, until the issue of the battle of Bannockburn secured his throne.   It is very generally believed that Robert

The Royal Order of Scotland. Severe Attack upon the Order by Prof. Robinson.

Bruce founded a Masonic Order called the "Royal Order," and in which it is said, all the Templars who had aided his fortunes were enrolled. It is beyond doubt that in consequence of the general persecution of the Order, the Scotch Knights amalgamated with the Order of St. John, taking much of their wealth with them, and their identity was so far maintained as to leave satisfactory proof of the fact, for by a charter of King James IV., recorded entire in the Registry of the Great Seal of Scotland, dated two centuries after the amalgamation of the Orders, they are referred to as brethren of the Hospital of Jerusalem and Temple of Solomon. Upon the loss of their possessions, the Knights are said to have drawn off in a body with the Grand Prior, David Seaton, at their head. It would be difficult to trace the Order with accuracy through succeeding troublous years. Lord Dundee appears to have held the office of Grand Master at the time of the battle of Killiecrankie, and to have been followed by John, Earl of Mar, and the Duke of Athol.

The learned Roman Catholic Professor, James Burton Robinson, who has unnecessarily (May, 1862) committed himself by an attack upon the Freemasons, in "A lecture delivered before the Historical Society connected with the Catholic University," says: "The Knights, say the recent German Protestant historian of Masonry, who were lucky enough to escape from France, assembled in one of the Scotch Hebrides, the Isle of Mull. In this island, on the feast of St. John, 1307, the members of the Order reorganized their old institution, with its ancient mysteries and aims. To these were added the desire of restoring the Order to its ancient splendor and power, as well as the passion of vengeance. By their entrance into the Masonic Corporation they concerted the perpetuation of their Order; hence the origin of the Scotch degrees of Masonry."

The Professor also observes, that it was "the remnant of the French Templars only who entered into the Masonic Order, the German Knights, for example, were incorporated with the Knights Hospitalers of St. John." As compared with the bitter attack on Freemasons which the Professor's lecture contains, the words of one of the ancient Masonic charges have a great significance. "Extend your pity to those who in ignorance condemn that which they have never had the opportunity to comprehend."

It has been supposed that the Masonic Order of Templars was carried from this country and Scotland into Ireland, but the information on the subject is very meager. In the book of "Service" of the Irish Templars, we find: "In Ireland, where the possessors of the Templars were never numerous or large, they appear, on the persecution of the Order, to have been partially incorporated with the Knights of St. John, and, when the Houses of the Order were dissolved in the Sixteenth Century, to have sought refuge with them in the body of Freemasons, among whom their ceremonies have been preserved, until the revival of the Grand Encampment of Ireland under the able Presidency of the Duke of Leinster." This statement is of too general a description to be historically useful, and must of course be taken *cum grano salis.*

In France, Germany, and Sweden, are institutions of Templars more or less closely connected with Freemasons; little information of these is possessed in this country, and no doubt inquiry would be amply repaid. It is not improbable that their origin would be found in the Scotch system.

In a sketch of the Order of Templars read before an Encampment at Charleston, South Carolina, in 1855, by Commander T. S. Gourdin, the author says: "The South Carolina Encampment, No. 1, of Knights Templars, and the Appendant Orders, was established in 1780, as is evident from the old seal in our archives. But it does not appear from what source our ancestors derived their first Charter, all our records previous to November 7th, 1823, having been lost or consumed by fire."

There does not appear to be any accurate information of the establishment of the Masonic Templars in America. But during the latter part of the past century and commencement of the present unsuccessful attempts were made to form a General Grand Encampment for the United States, and the present General Grand Encampment was not formed until the 21st June, 1816, at New York, when DeWitt Clinton was elected Grand Master.

One of the Appendant Orders in America is that of Knights of Malta, though Commander Gourdin says : " The Knights of St. John of Jerusalem, sometimes called the Knights Hospitalers, and the Knights of Malta, were not Freemasons. On the contrary they seem to have been inimical to Freemasonry, for in 1840, the Grand Master of the Order of Malta caused the Bull of Clement XII. to be published in that island, and forbade the meetings of the Freemasons. On this occasion several Knights and many citizens left the island; and, in 1741, the Inquisition pursued the Freemasons at Malta. The Grand Master proscribed their assemblies under severe penalties, and six Knights were banished from the island, in perpetuity, for having assisted at a meeting. In fact, unlike the Templars, they had not even a secret form of reception. Reghellini says that he was unable to procure a copy of the secret ritual of the Knights of Malta. The reason is obvious—there is none."

From the tone of Commander Gourdin's " Sketch," it would appear that the belief is in favor of the American Order having been derived from the early Encampments to this country.

No opinions have been offered in the foregoing pages, and those who read must draw their own inference and conclusion. Very many well-informed persons entertain no doubt that a connection between the Masonic Order and the ancient Templars existed (and is illustrated in the present Encampments), though not in the sense of the former being entitled to be considered Knights by succession from the early Order. These persons are perhaps

Encampment at Charleston, S. C.   Appendant Orders in America.

nearest the truth, and it is probably in this view of the subject that we must search for an explanation of the problem, rather than by an endeavor to prove that the Masonic Order is the representative of the warrior monks in their chivalric capacity. Others are found to assert the claims of the Scottish Order, whilst they deny those of the English and other countries; this ground is, however, hardly tenable when we consider the early Encampments of this country, the acceptance of an English charter by the Scotch Templars, and, notwithstanding this, the published statement of the latter in their statutes that the Order was planted in this country from their own.

The few foregoing facts and statements, collected from a wide and by no means thoroughly explored field, are diffidently offered as a slight contribution to the knowledge of an interesting subject, in the hope that other and more competent laborers may be induced to give their efforts to the discovery of new information, and thus aid in dissipating that mystery which has so long surrounded the Masonic Templars.

But whatever difference of opinion may exist on rival claims of descent, let us hope that all will unite to perpetuate in its full integrity that grand principle which has ever been, and we trust may ever continue, the shining light and watch-word of the time-honored Orders: the great virtue of CHARITY.

CÆSAREA, AN IMPORTANT MILITARY STATION DURING THE CRUSADES.

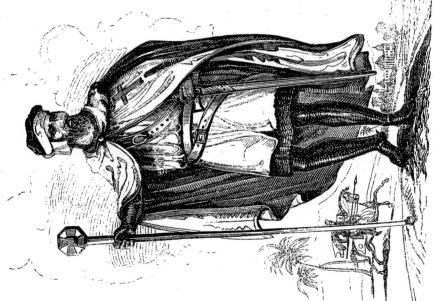

ANCIENT AND MODERN COSTUMES OF THE KNIGHTS TEMPLARS.

CHAPTER III.

THE GRAND ENCAMPMENT OF THE UNITED STATES.

IT would be a waste of effort to trace up the introduction of Knight Templary into the United States. It is no question of legitimate Masonic history. That the system came within the term "Unorganized Masonry" until the present century is too evident for argument. A few Sir Knights having received the Orders in Scotland, Ireland, or elsewhere, meeting together by appointment in Philadelphia, Boston, New York, etc., in a retired place, and first testing each other by diploma and unwritten evidence, would make no scruple of organizing themselves for the nonce into an "Encampment" or "Conclave," and assume control of "territorial jurisdiction," confer the Orders, elect officers, issue certificates, etc., etc. If this is not the history of the introduction of Knight Templary upon this Continent, there is no better, we regret to be compelled to say, at our command.

Nor is it derogatory to the legitimacy of the succession, or the merits of the system of Templary, to admit these conclusions. For in this manner only could *Freemasonry itself* have been extended from the date of its origin to the organization of the Grand Lodge of England, A. D. 1717. Prior to that period, there was no Grand Lodge or central authority whatever that possessed power to issue warrants—there was no such thing extant as a Lodge Charter (warrant) hailing from such central organization. A proper number of Masons had an inherent right to assemble in a secure place, apply the essential tests to each other, open a Lodge and initiate, pass and raise worthy applicants. This is all that can be said of Knight Templary up to a very recent period. It

574   KNIGHTS TEMPLARS.

Knight Templary in the United States.   The General Grand Encampment.

is all that can be said of the spread of *any* branch of Masonry, however important or consequential it may *now* be esteemed by its votaries.

Much labor has been expended by the Eminent Frater Alfred Creigh, LL. D. to establish the fact that an Encampment of Knights Templars was worked in Philadelphia prior to 1790. This is very probable. Emt. J. S. Gourdin proved that an Encampment was worked in South Carolina as early as 1780. This is equally probable. These facts, however, are of no importance in point of history. There was no Templar Organization in the world at that period, authorized to grant warrants for Encampments. Sir Knights, anywhere in the United States, could meet, and probably *did* meet, as we have said, and increase their numbers by inherent right, keeping no records and granting no certificates.

If these views are correct, our History as a system of pure Knightly Orders must begin in June, 1816, at which time "Delegates, or Knights Companions from eight Councils and Encampments of Knights Templars and Appendant Orders" assembled in the City of New York, and "formed, adopted, and ratified" a Constitution. Quoting from a recent republication of the proceedings of the General Grand Encampment from 1816 to 1856, we find the names of these organizations, but without a glimpse as to their origin, history, or the authority under which they were formed. They were entitled as follows:

Boston Encampment..............Boston, Mass.
St. John's Encampment ....Providence, R. I.
Ancient Encampment............New York City.
Temple Encampment............Albany, N. Y.
Montgomery Encampment........Stillwater, "
St. Paul's Encampment..........Newburyport, Mass.
Newport Encampment...........Newport, R. I.
Darius Council ....Portland, Me.

It will be seen that the Philadelphia Encampments, and those of South Carolina, Connecticut, etc., were not represented in this convention. The moving spirit of the whole affair was the learned and zealous THOMAS SMITH WEBB (deceased 1819), to whom Freemasonry in all its grades is greatly indebted. His lectures, monitors, correspondence and personal appeals in extended travels, added to his remarkable tact in selecting lieutenants to extend his works, point him out as the most remarkable Mason this country has ever produced. The peculiar rituals wrought in the Knightly Orders in the United States give evidences of his talent. If he found Freemasonry built in " brick " he left it in " marble."

The new organization, 1816, styled itself " The General Grand Encampment of the United States," which title was retained until 1856, when the superfluous word " General " was stricken out. The first officers elected were:

DeWitt Clinton..........General Grand Master.
Thomas Smith Webb.....Deputy General Grand Master.
Henry Fowle...........General Grand Generalissimo.
Ezra Ames............General Grand Captain General.
Rev. Paul Dean.........General Grand Prelate.
Martin Hoffman........General Grand Senior Warden.
John Carlisle..........General Grand Junior Warden.
Peter Grinnell.........General Grand Treasurer.
John J. Loring.........General Grand Recorder.
Thomas Lowndes.......General Grand Warder.
John Snow.............General Grand Standard Bearer.
Jona. Schieffelin........General Grand Sword Bearer.

Several of these were men of first rank in social as well as fraternal importance. DeWitt Clinton was one of the marked men of the nation.

The Second Convocation was also held in New York. It was opened September 16, 1819. The death of the Deputy General Grand Master, Webb, was announced. Officers were now elected for *seven* years, viz. :

DeWitt Clinton..........General Grand Master.
Henry Fowle...........Deputy General Grand Master.
John Snow.............General Grand Generalissimo.
Ezra Ames............General Grand Captain General.
Paul Dean.............General Grand Prelate.
Martin Hoffman........General Grand Senior Warden.

John Carlisle.............General Grand Junior Warden.
Peter Grinnell..........General Grand Treasurer.
John J. Loring..........General Grand Recorder.
Thomas Lowndes........General Grand Warder.
Jona. Schieffelin ....General Grand Standard Bearer.
Eben. Wadsworth........General Grand Sword Bearer.

The attendance was small, and but slight growth of the Knightly Orders under the new organization was reported. Charters had been granted for Encampments at Colchester, Conn., Worthington, Ohio, and perhaps other places. Grand Encampments had been organized in Massachusetts (including Rhode Island) and New York. The record of the three years' doings, however, is scanty.

The Third Convocation was held likewise in New York, September 18, 1826, and "opened with the customary solemnities." During the intervening seven years, considerable activity had been manifested. Grand Encampments had been formed in New Hampshire, Vermont, Georgia, North Carolina, South Carolina and Virginia, so that delegates were present from six State Grand Encampments. Committees upon Finance, Constitutional Amendments, Charters, and the doings of the Grand Officers were appointed. The United States Minister to Mexico, Joel R. Poinsett, announced that under his advice a Grand Encampment of Mexico had been formed, which event was hailed with exultation.

Officers were now elected for *three* years, viz.:

DeWitt Clinton..........General Grand Master.
Jonathan Nye...........Deputy General Grand Master.
John J. Loring..........General Grand Generalissimo.
William G. Hunt........General Grand Captain General.
Rev. Gregory T. Bedell...General Grand Prelate.
Joseph W. White........General Grand Senior Warden.
John H. Cotton........General Grand Junior Warden.
Peter Grinnell.........General Grand Treasurer.
Oliver M. Lowndes.......General Grand Recorder.
Isaac W. Hubbard........General Grand Warder.
James Eyland..........General Grand Standard Bearer.
Thomas Hubbard........General Grand Sword Bearer.

The Fourth Convocation was held in New York Sept. 14, 1829. The lamented death of DeWitt Clinton was announced. Delegates from five Grand Encampments were present. Officers were elected as follows, viz. :

Jonathan Nye...........General Grand Master.
Ezra S. Cozier...........Deputy General Grand Master.
Josiah Whittaker........General Grand Generalissimo.
James Eyland...........General Grand Captain General.
Rev. Ezekiel L. Bascom...General Grand Prelate.
Thomas Hubbard........General Grand Senior Warden.
Isaac W. Hubbard.......General Grand Junior Warden.
Peter Grinnell..........General Grand Treasurer.
James Herring...... ...General Grand Recorder.
George W. Haller........General Grand Warder.
Alex. E. McConnell......General Grand Standard Bearer.
Ezra Griswold..........General Grand Sword Bearer.

The Fifth Convocation was held in Baltimore, Md., November 29, 1832. The flood of anti-masonry which was then deluging the land, had affected the growth and threatened indeed the very existence of the Knightly Orders. Four Grand Encampments were represented. Several Past Grand Officers, to whom the keeping of the funds of the General Grand Encampment had been intrusted, had proved delinquent. The following officers were elected, viz. :

Jonathan Nye...........General Grand Master.
James M. Allen..........Deputy General Grand Master.
James Herring..........General Grand Recorder.
etc., etc.

Resolutions were adopted " highly approving the firm and dignified manner in which the several Encampments had conducted their affairs relative to the persecuting and violent spirit with which they had been assailed by a political party, which, in assailing the Orders of Masonry, aim a blow at all the free institutions of the country."

The Sixth Convocation was held in Washington, D. C., December 7, 1835. Delegates from five Grand Encampments were in attendance. Two of the delinquents named at the last Convention had proved defaulters, and are held up to public severity.

578 KNIGHTS TEMPLARS.

Knight Templary in the United States. The General Grand Encampment.

The following officers were elected, viz.:

James M. Allen..........General Grand Master.
Joseph K. Stapleton......Deputy General Grand Master.
Charles Gilman..........General Grand Recorder.
etc., etc.

A copy of the Constitution of the General Grand Encampment was published in the proceedings. Under this no Encampment was allowed to confer the Orders for a less sum than twenty dollars. Seven intermediate Degrees were recognized, including the four constituting the American system of the Royal Arch. Three Knightly Orders were recognized, viz.: Knights of the Red Cross, Knights Templars, Knights of Malta.

The Seventh Convocation was opened at Boston, Mass., September 12, 1838. The business was mostly of a routine nature, and of little interest. Delegates from four Grand Encampments were in attendance. The following officers were elected:

James M. Allen..........General Grand Master.
Joseph K. Stapleton......Deputy General Grand Master.
Charles Gilman..........General Grand Recorder.
etc., etc.

The committee on " the General State of Masonry " report that there was every reason for thanksgiving and rejoicing in the prospects of the institution, and they trust " the time is not far distant when the Order will again stand forth to the world in all its ancient splendor." The presence of Joel R. Poinsett at the Convocation is courteously acknowledged.

The Eighth Convocation was opened at New York, September 14, 1841. Delegates from four Grand Encampments were in attendance. The proceedings are devoid of special interest, and it is evident that the system of American Templary had, as yet, taken but little root. A lengthy report from the General Grand Master, James M. Allen, appears in the record, the model of all subsequent reports of this nature. Since the era of Thomas Smith Webb, Allen appears to have been the only officer in that position who had given personal effort by travel and correspondence to the duties of his post.

The following officers were elected, viz. :

James M. Allen ....General Grand Master.
Joseph K. Stapleton ....Deputy General Grand Master.
Charles Gilman ....General Grand Recorder.
etc., etc.

The proceedings were singularly uninteresting, and it is difficult to discover in the record what inducement called gentlemen of business habits and talent together to work such dry details.

The Ninth Convocation was opened at New Haven, Conn., September 10, 1844. Delegates from five Grand Encampments were in attendance. The presence of William B. Hubbard among them marks "the better day" in the history of the Knightly Orders. The Constitution, with revisions, was again published in the proceedings. The following officers were elected, viz. :

Archibald Bull.............General Grand Master.
Joseph K. Stapleton........Deputy General Grand Master.
Charles Gilman.......... ...General Grand Recorder.
etc., etc.

A seal for the General Grand Encampment was now adopted, the same which has been continued to the present time. Another case of money default by a Past Grand Officer was announced, proving that extreme looseness in the financial system of the Organization was the rule. The proceedings of the body as usual were dull and void of those interesting incidents that should enter into the transactions of so important a body.

The Tenth Convocation was opened at Columbus, Ohio, September 14, 1847. Delegates from the Grand Encampments of New York, Massachusetts and Rhode Island, Connecticut and Ohio were in attendance, but the representatives from *Subordinate* Encampments were numerous, including bodies in Illinois, Kentucky, Tennessee, Maine, Virginia, and Georgia. The latter was worthily represented by the Hon. William T. Gould. Money to the amount of $1,283 had been placed in the Treasury of the General Grand Encampment during the three years, and other signs of prosperity were visible. Reports upon subjects prescribed by the Constitution begin to be more elaborate and historical.

The following officers were elected, viz.:

William B. Hubbard.......General Grand Master.
Joseph K. Stapleton........Deputy General Grand Master.
Charles Gilman ....General Grand Recorder.
etc., etc.

Suitable regalia for the officers of the General Grand Encampment had been procured at an expense of $144.

A Register of the Subordinate Encampments appears in the proceedings, as follows:

Maine ....2 Encampments.
New Hampshire...........1   "
Pennsylvania..............1   "
District of Columbia.......1   "
Virginia 1   "
South Carolina...........1   "
Georgia...................1   "
Alabama 1   "
Mississippi...............1   "
Louisiana.................1   "
Kentucky 5   "
Tennessee................1   "
Illinois 1   "
Missouri.................1   "
———
19

These are the results of thirty-one years of Knightly effort. But from this time forward the growth was rapid. A MASTER was now in command!

The Eleventh Convocation opened at Boston, Mass., September 10, 1850. Delegates from five Grand Encampments were in attendance, strengthened by representatives from eight Subordinate Encampments. Among prominent Masonic names the record of this Convocation contains those of B. B. French, Morgan Nelson, John L. Lewis, Kent Jarvis, John R. Bradford, and others not heretofore present. The Report of William B. Hubbard is elaborate and full; in itself a historical document of interest. The question of Masonic intercourse with Sir Knights made in clandestine organizations, was ably discussed by John L. Lewis and others. The following officers were elected, viz.:

William B. Hubbard........General Grand Master.
William H. Ellis ....Deputy General Grand Master.
Benj. B. French............General Grand Recorder.
     etc., etc.

This election placed the records and proceedings in the hands of a most competent Recorder, to whom the subsequent history of the Knightly Orders in the United States is largely indebted for its accuracy and fullness.

The institution entitled "The Grand Encampment of Pennsylvania," was pronounced illegal, and intercourse with the same forbidden. The General Grand Encampment declined to warrant the establishment of an Encampment in Canada.

In the Register of Grand and Subordinate Encampments, appended to the proceedings, appear the names of twenty-seven Encampments. The date is now given, "Year of the Order, 732," which establishes the origin of Knight Templary, A. D. 1118; an erroneous conclusion.

The Twelfth Convocation was opened at Lexington, Kentucky, September 13, 1853. Delegates from six Grand Encampments were in attendance, backed up by the representatives of nine Subordinates. Among the eminent men of the Knightly Fraternity in attendance, were Albert G. Mackey, Philip C. Tucker, William S. Rockwell, Philip Swigert, and others. The address of William B. Hubbard, like his former one, was extended and luminous. He assured his Fraters that "the cause of Templar Masonry was never so prosperous as at the present time," and that "as a society it occupies the front rank amongst the societies of the world, for intelligence, chivalric honor and moral worth."

The officers elected were as follows, viz.:

William B. Hubbard........General Grand Master.
William Tracy Gould ....Deputy General Grand Master.
Benj. B. French...........General Grand Recorder.
     etc., etc.

A committee was appointed, of whom William B. Hubbard was chairman, to amend the Constitution of the body.

The Register of Grand and Subordinate Encampments, shows the following Grand Encampments in existence, viz.:

Maine, Vermont, Massachusetts and Rhode Island, Connecticut, New York, Virginia, Kentucky, Ohio; in all eight. The number of Subordinate Encampments was thirty-nine.

The Thirteenth Convocation was opened at Hartford, Conn., September 9, 1856. The General Grand Master's address was almost a volume in itself. A man of wealth and elegant leisure, a scholar by sympathy and taste, aged, and bearing the burden of large experience, he had given the greater part of his time during the intervening term, to the duties of his office, made onerous by his originality and self-devotedness. The conclusion of this paper is extremely affecting: "With the brightest reminiscences, then, of social scenes with you, and such as you whom I am soon to meet above—with the most unswerving confidence in Him whose emblem it is our honor to bear—with sanguine hope in the perpetuity of our Order, whose increasing prosperity it has been my joy to witness, commending you, each and all, to God and to your own pious thoughts, to the work to which you are called, and in which you are devotedly engaged, and to the glorious reward which assuredly awaits the valiant Templar who holds out faithful to the end, I beg leave to bid you, officially, but most affectionately, farewell."

Delegates from ten Grand Encampments were in attendance, and representatives from fifteen Subordinate Encampments.

Among the noted men of the Order met for the first time, in Grand Encampment, were Philip T. Schley, T. S. Gourdin, Henry Buist, Henry C. Lawrence, William Hacker, William C. Munger, John W. Simons, Robert Macoy, Robert Morris, Philip C. Tucker, Jr., Henry C. Deming, J. Q. A. Fellows, John Christie, Wm. B. Thrall, Jas. Sorley, A. O'Sullivan, and others.

The Committee to draft amendments to the Constitution reported that they had been greatly aided by Robert Morris, and at their request his name was added to their number. As a matter of history it is proper to state that the present Constitution of the Knightly Order was drafted by Sir Knight Morris during the week preceding the Convocation of 1856, he working under the immediate instructions of William B. Hubbard.

This document, which was adopted with unanimity, established numerous and radical changes in the government of this branch of Masonry. The name of the organization itself was changed to that of " THE GRAND ENCAMPMENT OF THE UNITED STATES."

The title of Subordinates was changed from "Encampments" to "Commanderies." Titles of officers were altered to correspond. The powers heretofore intrusted to Grand officers (below that of Grand Master) were curtailed. Financial matters were settled upon a more responsible basis.

The following officers were elected, viz.:

William B. Hubbard...........Grand Master.
Henry C. Deming ....Deputy Grand Master.
Benj. B. French..............Grand Recorder.
etc., etc.

Forms for the transaction of Templar business were inserted in the proceedings.

In the Table of Grand Encampments it is seen that those organizations have now been perfected, severally, in

Maine ....Formed 1852
Massachusetts and Rhode Island........   "   1805
Vermont...............................   "   1825
Connecticut...........................   "   1827
New York ....   "   1814
Ohio ....   "   1843
Kentucky ....   "   1847
Virginia ....   "   1823
Pennsylvania ....   "   1854
Indiana...............................   "   1854
Texas ....   "   1855

With 95 Commanderies and 2,744 members.

The Fourteenth Convocation was opened September 13, 1859, at Chicago, Illinois. Delegates from fourteen Grand Commanderies and seventeen Subordinate Commanderies were in attendance. Among prominent Masonic names that appeared for the first time in this Convocation may be instanced, Thomas R. Austin, Winslow Lewis, Thomas A. Doyle, Giles M. Hillyer, Alfred

584 KNIGHTS TEMPLARS.

Grand Encampment of the United States.   Grand Commanderies.

Creigh, Theodore S. Parvin, Luke E. Barber, Albert Pike, Samuel G. Risk, James R. Hartsock, Henry L. Palmer, and others.

The address of the Grand Master is again lengthy and detailed. A fraternal correspondence had been opened with the Grand Conclave of Knights Templars of England and Wales.   He had made many official visitations and held large correspondence upon Templar proceedings all through his extended jurisdiction.   A splendid Honorarium had been bestowed upon him by order of the Grand Encampment.

The following officers were elected, viz. :

> Benjamin B. French ....Grand Master.
> David S. Goodloe .... Deputy Grand Master.
> Samuel G. Risk................Grand Recorder.
>   etc., etc.

A form of Templar's Uniform was adopted corresponding as nearly as practicable with the surcoat and mantle of the original Order.   But this was abrogated at the next Convocation.

The Grand Encampment gracefully refers to the fact that "after fifteen years' labor for the benefit of the Grand Encampment, twelve of which have been given with unexampled talent and zeal to the onerous post of Grand Master, the M. E. William Blackstone Hubbard this day retires from the position to which he has given a world-wide renown."

In the Table of Grand Commanderies are named the following :—

> Maine 1852
> Massachusetts and Rhode Island...............1805
> Vermont 1824
> Connecticut 1827
> New York ....:...........1814
> Ohio 1843
> Kentucky.................................1847
> Virginia.................................1823
> Pennsylvania 1854
> Indiana 1854
> Texas.................................1855
> Michigan 1857

Grand Encampment. Fifteenth and Sixteenth Convocations.

Illinois 1857
Mississippi 1857
California 1858
Tennessee 1859
        No. of Commanderies 137
        No. of Members.............5,743

The Fifteenth Convocation was opened September 1, 1862, in the city of New York, in pursuance of a call from the Grand Master. Delegates from nine Grand Commanderies and three Subordinate Commanderies were in attendance.

The Grand Master announced that owing to the Civil War then raging, it was impracticable to hold this Triennial Convocation at *Memphis, Tennessee*, pursuant to adjournment; therefore he had issued a summons for the present session to be known as a *Special Convocation*. The adjourning order was then changed, and on the 7th of September the regular Convocation was opened in the same place.

The Grand Master in his opening address referred with singular felicity to the strife then shaking the land, and gave in detail a report of his official labors, which had been extremely arduous. The death of the Grand Recorder, Samuel G. Risk, was feelingly announced; through the personal efforts of J. Q. A. Fellows the papers and records of the Grand Encampment had been preserved and forwarded through the lines.

A new form of Templars' Costume was adopted, that of the Convocation of 1859 being found "poorly adapted to the requirements of modern Templars, expensive and liable to injury."

The following officers were elected, viz.:

Benjamin B. French............Grand Master.
David S. Goodloe ....Deputy Grand Master.
John D. Caldwell ....Grand Recorder.
            etc., etc.

The Sixteenth Convocation opened September 5, 1865, at Columbus, Ohio. Delegates from thirteen Grand Commanderies and five Subordinate Commanderies were in attendance. Among the distinguished Fraters here first in attendance upon the Grand Encampment, the names of Robert D. Holmes, H. G. Reynolds,

William S. Gardner, G. F. Gouley, H. Clay Preston, and others.
The Grand Master in a full address, says with exultation, " You
can hardly conceive of the pleasure and the satisfaction that it gives
me, who have been so long and so highly honored by my brethren,
to look upon faces so familiar, and yet which have been so long
estranged ; to clasp hands, between which the troubles of the times
have so long prevented a friendly and a brotherly grasp ; and to
interchange words of cordial greeting with those noble hearts
which, amid the whirlwind of treachery, beat firmly, and truly in
patriotic cadence to the music of the Union !

" My fellow-soldiers of the Cross, I give to you a cordial welcome,
and I implore upon you a heavenly blessing.   To all who are here
assembled, I tender, in behalf of the Grand Encampment of the
United States, our thanks for the countenance here given us, and
for the general and cordial welcome we have here received."

The following officers were elected, viz. :

Henry L. Palmer.............Grand Master.
William S. Gardner...........Deputy Grand Master.
John D. Caldwell.............Grand Recorder.
etc., etc.

An elaborate Appendix is given with the proceedings containing
much valuable historical matter relative to Knights Templars.

The Seventeenth Convocation opened September 15, 1868, at
St. Louis, Missouri.   Delegates from twenty-five Grand Commanderies and six Subordinate Commanderies were in attendance.
The Grand Master delivered a well-worded address, in which he
summed up an active three years' term of official duty.

The Deputy Grand Master reported a " Consecration Service,"
which was spread out upon the records. This had been used in con-
secrating Knightly banners by the Boston Fraters. He also communicated much valuable matter from the manuscripts of Thomas
Smith Webb.

The following officers were elected, viz. :

William S. Gardner...........Grand Master.
J. Q. A. Fellows.............Deputy Grand Master.
John D. Caldwell.............Grand Recorder.
etc., etc.

The death of William B. Hubbard, January 5, 1866, and others was feelingly announced.

The Eighteenth and last Convocation opened at Baltimore, Maryland, September 19, 1871, with delegates from twenty-seven Grand Commanderies and twenty-four Subordinate Commanderies. The contrast presented in the condition of the organization in 1856 and 1871, is well put in the Grand Recorder's preface to this book of proceedings:

The Grand Encampment of Knights Templars for the United States is no longer a child in swaddling clothes. To the "*General Grand Encampment*" of 1856, when the present Constitution was adopted by its ten constituent Grand Encampments, has succeeded the Grand Encampment of 1871, with its twenty-seven constituent Grand Commanderies. Then there were thirty-four representatives in Council; now, one hundred and forty-four. The ninety Subordinate Commanderies, with the three thousand members of that day, have been succeeded by five hundred and fifty Subordinate Commanderies, enrolling a membership of twenty-nine thousand at the last meeting. At Hartford, no escort accompanied the Grand Body to its Asylum, while the delegates who came up to our feasts at Baltimore were escorted by twenty Grand, and seventy-six Subordinate Commanderies, with their five thousand brave Knights, fully uniformed, with banners and music.

From the farthest borders of our common and united country, did these pilgrims come to do homage at the shrine of Templarism. And to do justice to all these, to the occasion, and to themselves, did the Grand Commandery of Maryland and her Subordinates of Baltimore successfully exert themselves, aided by the generous citizens of the Monumental City.

Great honor was indeed paid to the Grand Encampment in its reception by the citizens and craft of Baltimore. The Grand Master of Craft Masonry (John H. B. Latrobe), in an address of welcome, said: "The manufactories of New England—the furnaces of Pennsylvania—the cotton fields of the South—the industry of the West—the mines of California—are here in conclave. With no political purpose to advance, the thousands on thousands—though they meddle not with tariffs or imposts, or deal with other duties than those that man owes to his God, to his fellow-beings, and to himself—will exert an influence for good extending far beyond the limits of Lodges or Commanderies, and co-extensive with the Union.

"If the asperities of warfare have not yet all been removed, this meeting will aid in effacing them. If, ignorant of each other in the past, we have ever failed in that forbearance which even the most intimate intercourse demands, we learn now a lesson in this first of virtues. If prejudice has heretofore localized and limited our friendships, it will disappear upon the better acquaintance that this gathering will promote; and I am sure, Most Eminent, that, before we shall have separated, the North, the South, the East, and the West, will have joined hands here on the soil of Maryland, in the bonds of a fellowship as warm as it will be enduring and patriotic. Whether, then, Most Eminent, as Templars, as Masons, or as fellow-citizens, the Grand Master of Masons in Maryland takes especial pride in saying, 'Welcome, thrice welcome, Knights Templars of the Union.'"

The Grand Master's address is given in great detail in 82 pages. It is almost exhaustive, embracing every question, and presenting information upon almost every topic that has ever agitated the Knightly Fraternity. The death of Benj. B. French is fitly noticed; also that of Edward H. Gill, of Virginia, William Field, of Rhode Island, E. G. Storer, of Connecticut, Giles M. Hillyer, of Mississippi, and others.

This official address is followed by another almost equally elaborate and from the same pen, which had been delivered some years before in Massachusetts, and which is remarkable as bringing to light the true motives and views of the founders of this Organization. The silence preserved by this elegant writer, relative to the "manner of introduction of Templary into the United States," is very expressive; there *is no information* to be had under that head.

The income of the Grand Encampment for the preceding term, was $4,386.64.

A delegation of seven officers from the "Grand Priory of the United Orders of Knights Templars and Knights Hospitalers of

St. John of Jerusalem, etc., under the jurisdiction of the Supreme Grand Conclave of England and Wales, and dependencies of the British Crown and Dominion of Canada " was received, under the escort of a Guard of Honor, and with the Grand Honors appropriate to the occasion.   These distinguished guests wore the full costume of English Knights Templars, and attracted great attention.   The Grand Master made them an address of welcome which was duly responded to.

Among the propositions discussed at this Convocation, was a petition from the Grand Commandery of Virginia, for permission to *withdraw* from all connection with the body !   In the memorial which is presented with force and directness, this curious suggestion is made : Knighthood is in its infancy in our country, and the Grand Encampment is in the cradle.   And when she shall grow up to manhood, it will be the most mighty engine for good or evil that will then exist on this continent.   And some ambitious spirit, with will and wisdom to hold the reins and guide the power, gain a seat on the Grand Master's throne, and we know such men will, by some means, gain that elevation, he will be able, and probably will use his position to shake the stablity of this republic, should it then exist, even to its center ; and, perhaps, bury liberty in death. When such are our views, may we not ask to be allowed to withdraw from the Grand Encampment, and would she not be wise to grant our request.

The action of the Grand Encampment upon this request was decided :

Resolved, That the Grand Encampment, entertaining for the Grand Commandery of Virginia the most courteous and Knightly feeling of Fraternal Brotherhood, and being anxious to preserve intact the Knightly array of its constituent Grand Commanderies, and to " continue to preserve the good, well-being, and perpetuation of the principles of Templar Masonry," does decline and refuse " to allow the Grand Commandery of Virginia, in peace, in honor, and in recognition, to withdraw from the jurisdiction of the Grand Encampment," as prayed for in its memorial.

On the third day of the Convocation a Grand Parade and Review were held, in which seventy-six Commanderies participated.   These represented thirty States and Territories. More than five thousand Sir Knights in prescribed costume joined in this unparalleled demonstration of Knightly vigor. Thirty bands made music for the occasion. The Fraters were arranged in Twelve Divisions, led by a troop of mounted Red Cross Knights with caparisoned steeds and lances. The spectators are computed to have exceeded two hundred thousand persons.

The following officers were elected, viz.:

John Quincy Adams Fellows........Grand Master.
James Herron Hopkins..........Deputy Grand Master.
Vincent Lumbard Hurlbut ....Grand Generalissimo.
Benjamin Dean ....Grand Captain-General.
Irving Marvin Smith............Grand Senior Warden.
William Samuel Patton ....Grand Junior Warden.
John W. Simons ....Grand Treasurer.
Theodore S. Parvin ....Grand Recorder.
William Wallace Goodwin ... .Grand Standard-Bearer.
Charles Rankin Woodruff ....Grand Sword-Bearer.
Russell Smith Taft..............Grand Warder.

The adjournment was to New Orleans, La., the first Tuesday in December, 1874.

Biographical sketches of four Past Grand Masters are appended to the proceedings: William B. Hubbard, Benjamin B. French, Henry L. Palmer, William S. Gardner. These are embellished with good steel-plate portraits.

No statistical tables are given in this bulky and comprehensive volume, but from scattered data we may compute the present status of Knight Templary in the United States at

FIVE HUNDRED COMMANDERIES,

AND

THIRTY THOUSAND FRATERS.

This volume may be fitly closed with an original poem recently composed for an assemblage of Commanderies in Philadelphia, Penn., by Sir ROBERT MORRIS, LL. D., designed to express the *moral* or purpose of the Knightly Orders in the present time. There is no Holy Sepulcher to redeem. The Holy Land is no longer in the region of religious but political controversy. The cross-hilted sword has given its point and edge "to round a moral and adorn a tale." The military work of the Order is escort duty upon Masonic occasions. The real purpose (if the teaching of its Rituals can be relied upon) is Charity and Brotherly Kindness.

The Master is Come, and Calleth for Thee.

"The MASTER is come, and calleth for thee."—*John* xi. 28.

" All these blessings shall come on thee, and overtake thee, *if thou shalt hearken unto the voice of the LORD thy God:* the LORD shall set thee on high: He shall command the blessing upon thee: He shall establish thee an holy people: He shall make thee plenteous in goods: He shall open unto thee HIS good treasure."—*Deuteronomy* xxviii.

OH gallant KNIGHTS, in fitting garb arrayed,
With *helmet* high, and *cross*, and glittering *blade,*—
Met to do honor to a Stranger Knight,
Worn in life's strife, and *weary* of the fight,—
Brave WARRIORS in a warfare not to cease,
Till all mankind shall find CELESTIAL peace,—
    While in this noble Chamber met,
        Where zeal, and light, and love abound,
    Let's sit around the MASTER'S feet,
        And listen to His gracious SOUND;
    The MASTER,—PRINCE IMMANUEL,
        The SOUND, that WORD we love so well!

If in this matchless Fane, our LORD *would* come,—
If now and here, JESUS *would* make His home,—

If face to face, 'twere ours to see that *head*,
Once scarred with thorns, once buried with the dead,—
If in our hands, that *hand* were laid, so torn
With cruel spikes, alas! on cross-tree borne,—
What startling questions! gallant Templars, might
Our GRAND COMMANDER ask of us, to-night.

(I.)

"Servant of Jesus, bold and free,
"What hast *thou* done, SIR KNIGHT, for me?"

I saw a widow's tears,—I heard the cry,—
Her little ones in rags and misery,—
Her household lamp gone out, her firelight dead,
In loneliness and lack of needed bread.
Then, MASTER, *in Thy place* I stood! my hand
Was opened wide to that unhappy band:
I fed them, clothed them, heard the widow's prayer
Praising his name who saved them from despair.
This, oh Lord, I did for Thee,
Thou hadst done *so much* for me!

(II.)

"Servant of Jesus, bold and free,
"What hast *thou* done, SIR KNIGHT, for me?"

I found a brave man compassed round with foes;
On every side reproaches, threats and blows;
In innocence he bravely strove and well,
And many a foe beneath his good sword fell:
But nature fainting, soon his arm were numb,
Had not my cross-hilt sword relieving, come.
Then, MASTER, *in Thy place* I stood! my blade
Flew swiftly from its scabbard to his aid:
I shielded him, I smote till close of day,
And drove them wounded and ashamed away.
This, oh Lord, I did for Thee,
Thou hadst done *so much* for me!

(III.)

"Servant of Jesus, bold and free,
"What hast *thou* done, SIR KNIGHT, for me?"

I saw a drooping heart:—his youth had fled,
Friends of his manhood all had joined the dead;
He stood beside a monumental stone,
A mourner, broken-hearted and alone:
Hopes, once as bright and flowery as the spring,
All withered, flown upon returnless wing.
    Then, MASTER, *in Thy place* I stood! I showed
    From Thine own speech, the promises of God,—
    Pointed Thy form upon the radiant Throne,
    And bade him make those promises his own.
        This, oh Lord, I did for Thee,
        Thou hadst done *so much* for me!

(IV.)

"Servant of Jesus, bold and free,
"What hast *thou* done, SIR KNIGHT, for me?"

MASTER DIVINE, in all life's weary round,
None so unhappy as *myself* I found:
Blind, naked, sin-polluted, wholly lost,
A wreck upon the ocean tempest-tossed;
Nought could *I do* to gain Thy loving smile,
For all my doings, like myself, were vile.
    Then, MASTER, to THYSELF I flew! I plead
    Thy righteousness who conquered o'er the dead!
    Placed all my hopes and trust within Thy hand,
    And now, obedient, wait Thy full command!
        This, oh Lord, I did for Thee,
        Thou hadst done *so much* for me!

Sir Knights, well done! the high award is given;
  His open WORD assures us of His praise;
It is not far from faithful heart to Heaven;
  Almost we see Him by faith's earnest gaze:
Sir Knights, well done! 'tis written bold and free,—
"Ye did it *unto them* and *unto me!*"

It is but little any man can do,
  So brief is life, so trifling human power;
But as, on earthly pilgrimage, we go,
  There are occasions every day and hour,
Wherein His hand is seen, and be our care
To act as JESUS would were JESUS there!

The widow's tears are His,—for " Jesus wept!"
  The imperiled Knight is *His*,—leap forth ye blade!
The broken heart is His,—while others slept
  Christ in Gethsemane so wept and prayed!
HE left this sin-struck world, Sir Knights, to us,
To teach its comfort and remove its curse!

Leap forth, good swords! stand, warriors, on your feet!
  In serried ranks bear one another up!
BY THIS SIGN CONQUER! it is full, complete,
  Ye need no other sign, no other hope!
And when from nerveless hands the sword shall fall,
The MASTER will reward and comfort all!

AD MAJOREM GLORIAM DEI!

AIN LIFTA, NEAR JERUSALEM.

INDEX.

LIST OF SUBSCRIBERS

TO

ADDISON'S KNIGHTS TEMPLARS.

LIST OF SUBSCRIBERS.

ALABAMA.

NAME.	WHEN KNIGHTED.	COMMANDERY.		KNIGHTLY RANK.
Bacon, John Philip.....	May 28, 1868.	Mobile.............	No. 2	Sir Knight.
Baker, Adam R...	Sept. 10, 1863.	Montgomery........	" 4	Grand Warder.
Barnard, Francis J.....	Mar. 14, 1860.	Mobile.............	" 2	Em. Commander.
Blair, A. J.............	——, 1861.	Selma.	" 5	Grand Captain-General.
Brown, Peleg..........	April 26, 1854.	Alabama............	" 6	Grand Commander.
Browder, John N.......	Sept. 4, 1863.	Montgomery........	" 4	Grand Captain-General.
Caldwell, Oliver........	Jan. 12, 1871.	Mobile.............	" 2	Sir Knight.
Calhoun, Jos. Carroll...	June 7, 1849.	Mobile.............	" 2	Sir Knight.
Conboy, Thomas.......	July 6, 1871.	Mobile...	" 2	Sword Bearer.
Davidson, Henry C.....	Jan. 31, 1873.	Montgomery........	" 4	Sir Knight.
Foote, Moses Scott....	Mar. 14, 1872.	Mobile.............	" 2	Sir Knight.
Foster, Wm. Story.....	July 13, 1871.	Mobile.............	" 2	Grand Junior Warden.
Fulmer, Hiram C......	April 1, 1870.	Selma...	" 5	Warder.
Hampshire, Jos. Henry	June 17, 1869.	Mobile.............	" 2	Recorder.
Harris, Dan...........	Dec. 27, 1862.	Mobile.............	" 2	Senior Warden.
Hazard, James B......	Jan. 14. 1865.	Mobile.............	" 2	Treasurer.
Hellen, Enoch F	Mar. 18, 1863.	Mobile.............	" 2	Sir Knight.
Jacob, Bernhard.......	Mar. 14, 1871.	Selma.	" 5	Sword Bearer.
Krause, G. F. Wm......	Nov. 28, 1872.	Mobile.............	" 2	Sir Knight.
Luckie, James B... ...	Nov. —, 1864.	Montgomery.......	" 4	Sir Knight.
Martin. John W	Mar. 15, 1873.	Montgomery.......	" 4	Sir Knight.
McCarty, Lewis B......	April 19, 1869.	Cœur-de-Lion......	" 8	Generalissimo.
McMillan, Isaac A......	Feb. —, 1870.	Selma.............	" 5	Recorder.
Nelson, Andrew B......	Mar. 21, 1872.	Mobile.............	" 2	Sir Knight.
Nettles, John M......	April 2, 1856.	Mobile	" 2	Sir Knight.
Norris, Geo. Dashiell..	May —, 1848.	Huntsville..........	" 7	Grand Generalissimo.
Peters, Carsten........	Mar. 6, 1868.	Alabama	" 6	Warder.
Prout, William D	June 1, 1864.	Mobile.............	" 2	Sir Knight.
Primo, Manuel..........	Mar. 12, 1869.	Mobile.............	" 2	Junior Warden.
Reid, Geo. P. L........	Nov. —, 1860.	Washington	" 1	Deputy Grand Commander.
Sayre, Daniel..........	Nov. 17, 1866.	Montgomery	" 4	Grand Recorder.
Smith, Daniel.........	Mar. 6, 1869.	Alabama......... ...	" 6	Captain-General.
Vestal, John Hamden..	June 27, 1872.	Selma	" 5	Senior Warden.
Wadsworth, Wm. D....	April 2, 1870.	Montgomery.......	" 4	Sir Knight.
Ware, James M........	Mar. —, 1872.	Montgomery.......	" 4	Sir Knight.
Wilkins, John Douglas.	June 21, 1872.	Selma	" 5	Captain of the Guard.
Winter, John Gano....	Jan. 24, 1872.	Montgomery.......	" 4	Prelate.
Winter, John Gindrat..	June 12, 1871.	Montgomery	" 4	Junior Warden.
Young, Jas. Rattray....	Jan. 10, 1863.	Mobile	" 2	Sir Knight.

ARKANSAS.

NAME.	WHEN KNIGHTED.	COMMANDERY.		KNIGHTLY RANK.
Barber, Luke E........	Nov. 14, 1853.	Hugh de Payens.....	No. 1	Grand Commander.
Brodie, John..........	....	Hugh de Payens	" 1	Recorder.
Sallé, Robert E........	May 23, 1871.	Bertrand du Guesclin	" 2	Grand Standard Bearer.
Thornburgh, George...	....	Hugh de Payens....	" 1	Grand Warder.

CALIFORNIA.

NAME.	WHEN KNIGHTED.	COMMANDERY.		KNIGHTLY RANK.
Abell, Alex. Gurdon....	June 16, 1852.	California...........	No. 1	Grand Commander.
Akerly, Benjamin......	—— —, 1870.	California...........	" 1	Grand Prelate.
Angus, John A.........	Dec. —, 1867.	California...........	" 1	Sir Knight.
Barss, Fred'k F........	Oct. 27, 1858.	El Dorado	" 4	Grand Commander.
Becker, Fred. J	Mar. 11, 1868.	Oroville	" 5	Sword Bearer.
Bond, Morris H........	Mar. 5, 1868.	Stockton............	" 8	Sir Knight.
Bourne, Elisha W......	Feb. 26, 1858.	California...........	" 1	Grand Treasurer.
Brady, Alex. B........	Oct. 2, 1859.	Nevada.............	" 6	Generalissimo.
Brown, Philip T.......	Aug. 6, 1873.	Stockton............	" 8	Sir Knight.
Brett, Richard W......	Feb. 6, 1863.	California...........	" 1	Sir Knight.
Bruning, Henry N......	July 21, 1870.	Cœur-de-Lion.......	" 9	Captain-General.
Callow, Thomas........	Nov. 21, 1858.	Oroville.............	" 5	Grand Generalissimo.

NAME.	WHEN KNIGHTED.	COMMANDERY.	KNIGHTLY RANK.
Caswell, Thos. H......	April —, 1855.	Nevada............. No. 6	Grand Commander.
Cavis, Jos. Mills	Nov. 23, 1869.	Stockton .... " 8	Sir Knight.
Celio, Carlo Jos......	May 31, 1870.	El Dorado........... " 4	Sentinel.
Coleman, John C......	Feb. 28, 1858.	Nevada............. " 6	Sir Knight.
Colby, Gilbert W......	April 16, 1873.	Oroville............. " 5	Sir Knight.
Conner, John Wm.....	July 2, 1869.	California. .... " 1	Sir Knight.
Cutler, Benoni B......	Aug. 28, 1873.	Sacramento .... " 2	Sir Knight.
Churchill, Clark... ...	July —, 1866.	California .... " 1	Sir Knight.
Donald, Alfred.........	Oct. 3, 1872.	Nevada............. " 6	Sir Knight.
Driver, Thomas.......	June 8, 1867.	Stockton .... " 8	Sir Knight.
Duncan, Jas. Wesley...	May 9, 1873.	.... " –	Sir Knight.
Earl, John Ogden.....	April 23, 1863.	California .... " 1	Generalissimo.
Edwards, Henry......	Feb. 14, 1873.	California .... " 1	Sir Knight.
Ellis, John S..........	Dec. 24, 1858.	California .... " 1	Captain General.
English, Jas. Lawrence	Oct. 25, 1854.	Sacramento .... " 2	Grand Commander.
Evans, Geo. Spafford...	Sept. 22, 1871.	Stockton .... " 8	Sir Knight.
Farran, Chas. James..	Sept. 20, 1872.	California .... " 1	Sir Knight.
Farrell, Jas. Alexander.	Feb. 17, 1866.	Nevada............. " 6	Sir Knight.
Fletcher, William.....	Nov. 8, 1869.	Maryville........... " 7	Captain General.
Fox, John G..........	June —, 1864.	California .... " 1	Sir Knight.
Gardner, Melvin S.....	May 18, 1871.	Nevada............. " 6	Sir Knight.
Gilbert, Geo. H.......	Jan. 2, 1868.	El Dorado .... " 4	Senior Warden.
Gluyas, James........	Nov. 25, 1869.	Nevada............. " 6	Standard Bearer.
Graves, Samuel.......	Dec. —, 1825.	California .... " 1	Gr. Standard Bearer, N. Y.
Graves, Hiram T.......	Nov. —, 1859.	California .... " 1	Grand Senior Warden.
Glass, Louis..........	May 21, 1873.	Oroville .... " 5	Sir Knight,
Hathaway, Francis.. ..	Nov. 9, 1872.	Nevada............. " 6	Sir Knight.
Hedges, Edward R.....	April 27, 1867.	Stockton............ " 8	Em. Commander.
Helm, James H........	Nov. 9, 1859.	Nevada............. " 6	Em. Commander.
Hosmer, Dan'l M.......	April 26, 1872.	California .... " 1	Sir Knight.
Hook, Thomas Kent...	July 10, 1869.	Stockton...... ... " 8	Junior Warden.
Irwin Chas. F.........	June 18, 1868.	El Dorado .... " 4	Generalissimo.
Jackson, St. John.....	Mar. 26, 1872.	Oroville............. " 5	Sir Knight.
Johnson, J. Monroe...	——— —, 1866.	California .. .. " 1	Sir Knight.
Kendig, Daniel..... ...	Sept. 1, 1870.	Nevada............. " 6	Sir Knight.
Kent, Thos. Weston...	Nov. 22, 1869.	Marysville.......... " 7	Sir Knight.
Kernan, Thos. H.......	Nov. 2, 1861.	Marysville.......... " 7	Sir Knight.
Lawrence, Wm. Lee...	Oct. 21, 1859.	Marysville.......... " 7	Em. Commander.
Leech, Reuben.........	April 16, 1868.	Nevada............. " 6	Sword Bearer.
Lee, Benjamin B......	July 5, 1873.	Nevada....... ..... " 6	Sir Knight.
Litchfield, Jos. M......	Sept. 6, 1872.	California .... " 1	Sir Knight.
Lothrop, Isaac...	Dec. 10, 1873.	Stockton............ " 8	Sir Knight.
Lott, Charles Fayette.	Mar. 15, 1868.	Oroville.... .... " 5	Em. Commander.
Mack, Geo. Franklin..	May 19, 1873.	El Dorado .... " 4	Sir Knight.
McKenzie, Geo. A.....	Jan. 16, 1874.	Stockton .... " 8	Sir Knight.
Marsh, Charles.........	April —, 1855.	Nevada .... " 6	Grand Commander.
Maurice, Jr. Amasa...	——— —, 1849.	Oroville............. " 5	Em. Commander.
Morse, E. Eaton......	Oct. 23, 1857.	California.......... " 1	Captain-General.
Murphy, R. W., M. D...	Nov. 28, 1868.	Sacramento......... " 2	Captain-General.
Neff, Jacob Hart......	Nov. 15, 1866.	Nevada............. " 6	Sir Knight.
Norcross, Daniel.......	Nov. 12, 1858.	.... " –	Sir Knight.
Orme, Henry Sayre....	——— —, 1863.	Cœur-de-Lion ...... " 9	Grand Captain-General.
Pryor, Athanasius.....	May 1, 1873.	Nevada............. " 6	Sir Knight.
Rock, John Wm........	——— —, 1855.	Sacramento......... " 2	Em. Commander.
Rolfe, Ianthis J......	April 3, 1873.	Nevada............. " 6	Sir Knight.
Reece, Thos. White.. .	Oct. 6, 1873.	Marysville.......... " 7	Sir Knight.
Richardson, Jerome B..	Jan. 17, 1873.	California........... " 1	Sir Knight.
Titus, Isaac Sutven....	Oct. 24, 1858.	Stockton............ " 8	Grand Commander.
Temple, Francis P. F..	——— —, 1870.	Cœur-de-Lion...... " 9	Prelate.
Watson, John Andrew.	May 24, 1860.	Sacramento......... " 2	Sir Knight.
Watt, William.........	May 17, 1866.	Nevada............. " 6	Standard Bearer.
Wells, Michael Henry..	Mar. 13, 1861.	Oroville............. " 5	Sir Knight.
Wilkins, Edmund T...	April 12, 1866.	Marysville........ .. " 7	Generalissimo.

CONNECTICUT.

NAME.	WHEN KNIGHTED.	COMMANDERY.	KNIGHTLY RANK.
Ambler, Peter W.......	May 15, 1873.	Crusader.... ....No. 10	Sentinel.
Amsbury, Edgar.......	May 19, 1871.	Crusader........... " 10	Captain-General.
Anderson, Jr., Albert..	Mar. 14, 1872.	Crusader........... " 10	Warder.
Beckwith, Jason.......	July 17, 1857.	Palestine........... " 6	Deputy Grand Commander
Belden, John A........	Mar. 28, 1873.	Clark............ ... " 7	Sir Knight.
Billings, Charles E.....	Jan. 3, 1868.	Washington......... " 1	Em. Commander.
Boardman, Horace F...	Mar. 7, 1870.	Cyrene............. " 8	Sir Knight.
Blackburn, Fred	May 24, 1872.	Crusader........... " 10	Guard.

NAME.	WHEN KNIGHTED.	COMMANDERY.		KNIGHTLY RANK.
Brewer, Risdon A......	May 19, 1871.	Clinton.............	No. 3	Senior Warden.
Brooks, Benjamin F....	Mar. 14, 1872.	Crusader............	" 10	Recorder.
Bronson, Homer D.....	April 11, 1873.	Clark...............	" 7	Sir Knight.
Bryan, Burton G......	April 25, 1873.	Clark...............	" 7	Sir Knight.
Bullock, Israel M......	April 10, 1868.	Hamilton...........	" 5	Grand Sword Bearer.
Burdick, Gilbert R.....	Nov. 18, 1872.	Cyrene.............	" 8	Recorder.
Calkins, Daniel........	May —, 1856.	Palestine...........	" 6	Grand Commander.
Carroll, Thos. R.......	Jan. 29, 1864.	Palestine...........	" 6	Sir Knight.
Cobb, Jr., Charles H...	Sept. 10, 1869.	Columbian......... .	" 4	Recorder.
Crofut, Charles H....	Feb. 2, 1866.	Crusader...........	" 10	Prelate.
Curtiss Charles I......	Dec. 9, 1870.	Clark...............	" 7	Warder.
Cholwell, George R....	Mar. 28, 1865.	Clinton	" 3	Sir Knight.
Davis, E. S...........	Nov. 2, 1866.	Crusader...........	" 10	Treasurer.
Dolbeare, Christ R.....	July 22, 1870.	Columbian.........	" 4	Sir Knight.
Drummond, Chauncey.	Mar. 7, 1873.	Clinton.............	" 3	Sir Knight.
Fuller, George W.....	Sept. 27, 1865.	Palestine...........	" 6	Sir Knight.
Golding, Augustus C...	Sept. 13, 1867.	Clinton.............	" 3	Em. Commander.
Gruman, Cholwell J....	Mar. 10, 1865.	Clinton.............	" 3	Sir Knight.
Hatch, Chauncey M....	—, —.	Hamilton...........	" 5	Prelate.
Hovey, Philo B.........	Nov. 17, 1858.	Palestine...........	" 6	Senior Warden.
Hoyt, Edwin.........	Sept. 3, 1825.	Clinton·...........	" 3	Generalissimo.
Johnson, Daniel S.....	Jan. 31, 1870.	Cyrene.............	" 8	Sir Knight.
Lines, H. Wales.......	Nov. 30, 1866.	St. Elmo...........	" 9	Grand Senior Warden.
Lockwood, Sylvester B.	Mar. 1, 1872.	Clinton.............	" 3	Sir Knight.
Miles, George Y.......	July 2, 1869.	Clinton.............	" 3	Sir Knight.
Miller, David H........	Jan. 1, 1869.	Crusader...........	" 10	Guard.
Neal, B. F.............	Sept. —, 1860.	Clark...............	" 7	Recorder.
Olmstead, Fred. S.....	June 6, 1871.	Crusader...........	" 10	Standard Bearer.
Parmelee, Fred. A.....	May 4, 1863.	Palestine...........	" 6	Grand Junior Warden.
Peck, Samuel F.......	Sept. 5, 1870.	Clinton.............	" 3	Sir Knight.
Phelps, Dwight.......	June —, 1870.	Clark...............	" 7	Sir Knight.
Raymond, Joseph R....	Mar. 15, 1865.	Clinton.............	" 3	Sir Knight.
Scott, Hiram Keeler....	Dec. 9, 1864.	Crusader...........	" 10	Sir Knight.
Sickman, James M.....	June 9, 1871.	Clark	" 7	Sir Knight.
Smith, Asa...........	May 31, 1853.	Clinton.............	" 3	Grand Captain-General.
Stevens, George C.....	April 23, 1866.	Clinton.............	" 3	Sir Knight.
Storey, William W....	May 31, 1853.	Clinton.............	" 3	Grand Commander.
Storey, Jas. W........	July 3, 1863.	Clinton.............	" 3	Em. Commander.
Stratton, Charles S., } Gen. Tom Thumb }	July 30, 1863.	Hamilton...........	" 5	Sir Knight.
Strong, George........	May 5, 1865.	Palestine...........	" 6	Sir Knight.
Swift, Orville H.......	May 29, 1868.	Crusader...........	" 10	Sir Knight.
Vodwarka, Jos. F......	Mar. 24, 1864.	Palestine...........	" 6	Generalissimo.
Walker, Aaron T.......	June 12, 1868.	Columbian..........	" 4	Sir Knight.
Welton, Nelson J......	Oct. 13, 1865.	Clark	" 7	Em. Commander.
West, Albert H.......	Jan. 30, 1871.	Cyrene.............	" 8	Sir Knight.
Williams, Henry H.....	May 12, 1871.	Clinton.............	" 3	Sentinel.

DELAWARE.

Hodgman, Stillman A..	Dec. 30, 1857.	St. John's..........	No. 1	Em. Commander.
McIntire, Henry B.....	Feb. 25, 1869.	St. John's.........	" 1	Generalissimo.
Yates, George R.......	April 10. 1868.	St. John's......... .	" 1	Sir Knight.

DISTRICT COLUMBIA.

James, Charles H......	June 22, 1872.	Columbia...........	No. 2	Sir Knight.
Mackey, Albert G., M.D.	Mar. 15, 1845.	Washington........	" 1	Grand Warder, Gr. En. U. S.
Shaw, John T.........	Dec. 8, 1871.	Potomac	" 3	Sir Knight.
Stansbury, Charles F. .	July 22, 1860.	Washington	" 1	Em. Commander.

FLORIDA.

Ferguson, George F....	—— —, 1872.	Baron	No. 3	Capt. Guard.
Johnson, Fred'k. W....	Nov. 21, 1873.	Baron	" 3	Sir Knight.
McClintock Wm......	Nov. 8, 1872.	Baron	" 3	Sir Knight.
Murray, Robt. D., M.D.	June 20, 1873.	Baron	" 3	Sir Knight.
Otto, Joseph..........	....	Baron	" 3	Capt. General.
Porter, Jos. Y., M.D....	Nov. 11, 1873.	Baron	" 3	Sir Knight.

NAME.	WHEN KNIGHTED.	COMMANDERY.		KNIGHTLY RANK.

GEORGIA.

NAME.	WHEN KNIGHTED.	COMMANDERY.		KNIGHTLY RANK.
Adam, George.........	April 16, 1872.	Georgia.............	No. 1	Sir Knight.
Anderson, Geo. Thomas	Oct. 14, 1866.	Cœur-de-Lion.......	" 4	Grand Generalissimo.
Ballantyne. Thomas....	Nov. 6, 1869.	Palestine..........	" 7	Generalissimo.
Barker, Geo. Rogers....	April 25, 1863.	St. Omer..........	" 2	Warder.
Brodie, Alexander M...	April 4, 1859.	Georgia.............	" 1	Warder.
Brown, Finley D.... ...	Oct. —, 1868.	Chicago	" 19	Sir Knight.
Chandler, Thomas W...	April —, 1863.	Cœur-de-Lion.......	" 4	Grand Commander.
Cook, J. S.............	Oct. 29, 1867.	Georgia.............	" 1	Sir Knight.
Conway, George W....	Mar. 10, 1873.	Georgia	" 1	Sir Knight.
Dawkins, De Witt C....	Oct. —, 1854.	St. Omer............	" 2	Sir Knight.
Denning, David H......	Jan. 29, 1865.	Georgia.............	" 1	Sir Knight.
Dunham, Samuel.......	April 3, 1862.	Georgia.............	" 1	Sir Knight.
Estill, John Holbrook..	Jan. 5, 1868.	Palestine..........	" 7	Recorder.
Epps, G. Wilson	April —, 1858.	St. Aldemar	" 3	Sir Knight.
Hackett. Elisha L......	July 5, 1866.	Palestine..........	" 7	Treasurer.
Hamilton, Sam'l Pugh.	Dec. 21, 1867.	Palestine..........	" 7	Dep. Grand Commander.
Hardeman, 'Wm..... ..	Feb. 23, 1848.	Georgia.............	" 1	Sir Knight.
Hunter, Richard J.....	—— —, 1862.	St. Aldemar	" 3	Treasurer.
Hawkins, William S....	Dec. 16, 1873.	Palestine..........	" 7	Sir Knight.
Kellam, D. S...........	April 21, 1871.	Cœur-de-Lion.......	" 4	Recorder.
Marsh. John G........	April 1, 1865.	Georgia.............	" 1	Sir Knight.
McCabe, Francis	April 10, 1864.	Georgia.............	" 1	Sir Knight.
McLin, Jas. G.........	June 1, 1859.	Cœur-de-Lion.......	" 4	Sentinel.
Moore, Montague M....	Mar. 10, 1861.	St. Aldemar........	" 3	Recorder.
Navy, John E...	April 26, 1856.	Georgia.............	" 1	Sentinel.
Obear, George S.......	July 4, 1850.	St. Omer	" 2	Grand Commander.
Oliver, John..........	April 9, 1873.	Palestine....	" 7	Sir Knight.
Pollard. Wm. J.......	Jan. 24, 1864.	Georgia.............	" 1	Em. Commander.
Nunn, Richard J......	—— —, —.	Palestine..........	" 7	Grand Sword Bearer.
Rich, William H.	Oct. 26, 1864.	Georgia.............	" 1	Prelate.
Ryan, Daniel John.....	Mar. 30, 1869.	Palestine....	" 7	Recorder.
Rockwell, Wm. Samuel	Nov. 11, 1870.	Palestine..........	" 7	Captain-General.
Stulb, John...........	May 10, 1864.	Georgia.............	" 1	Sir Knight.
Tuller, Wm. Henry....	April —, 1863.	Cœur-de-Lion.......	" 4	Grand Commander.
Watson, Chas. Thos....	Jan. 17, 1872.	Cœur-de-Lion.......	" 4	Sir Knight.
Whitman, Samuel P.. .	Jan. 24, 1864.	Georgia	" 1	Sir Knight.
Wayne, Jr., T. Smythe	Mar. 16, 1872.	Palestine..........	" 7	Junior Warden.

ILLINOIS.

NAME.	WHEN KNIGHTED.	COMMANDERY.		KNIGHTLY RANK.
Allen, James Vanloon..	Feb. —, 1871.	Cyrene.............	No.23	Standard Bearer.
Andrus, Wm. David Eli.	Aug. 23, 1865.	Crusader..........	" 17	Grand Sword Bearer.
Armitstead, Thos. E...	June 19, 1873.	Galena.....	" 40	Prelate.
Barry, George........	Feb. 14, 1870.	Belvidere..........	" 2	Em. Commander.
Blakesley, Asa W......	Feb. 8, 1861.	Beauseant..........	" 11	Grand Junior Warden.
Brewster, Daniel.......	Mar. 12, 1864.	Waukegan..........	" 12	Em. Commander.
Blackshaw, Edw., M.D.	Oct. 17, 1865.	Urbana...........	" 16	Prelate.
Bayle, Hugh Echlin....	Sep. 28, 1872.	Belvidere..........	" 2	Junior Warden.
Bullard, Jairus Thayer.	Dec. 20, 1869.	St. Paul...	" 34	Sir Knight.
Cornelius, Jesse Wm...	Oct. 18, 1873.	Bethany..........	" 28	Sir Knight.
Calderwood, John C....	Sept. 29, 1871.	Galena.............	" 40	Warder.
Chambers, Leonard W.	Jan. 29, 1869.	Hospitaler.........	" 31	Em. Commander.
Clarke, Haswell Cordis.	Oct. 23, 1869.	Ivanhoe	" 33	Em. Commander.
Colburn, Walter N.....	Nov. —, 1869.	Beauseant..........	" 11	Prelate.
Coleman, Mahlon	Sept. 29, 1871.	Galena	" 40	Senior Warden.
Cross, Wm. Tyler......	July 15, 1872.	Temple.............	" 20	Sir Knight.
Cunningham. Hugh T...	Nov. 12, 1870.	Cyrene.............	" 23	Warder.
Corwith, David Nash...	Dec. 12, 1873.	Galena.............	" 40	Guard.
Denker, Richard P.....	Nov. —, 1854.	Joliet............	" 4	Em. Commander.
Dunning, Chas. W.....	Dec. 23, 1868.	Cairo...	" 13	Generalissimo.
Duffy, Thos. Walker...	Mar. 18, 1867.	St. Paul	" 34	Prelate.
Dunlap, James M......	—— —, —.	Hospitaler	" 31	Recorder.
Douglas, James.......	—— —, 1843.	Cyrene.............	" 23	Sir Knight.
Enslow, James H......	Nov. 20, 1868.	St. Paul...........	" 34	Sir Knight.
Elliott, Demas.........	Sept. 30, 1872.	St. Paul...........	" 34	Sir Knight.
Fiddick, Richard H....	Jan. 13, 1872.	Galena.............	" 40	Treasurer.
Fox, Osmond..........	Dec. 28, 1870.	Joliet............	" 4	Generalissimo.
Gear, Hezekiah H......	Mar. 8, 1872.	Galena.............	" 40	Sir Knight.
Gideon, Alfred L.......	Jan. —, 1871.	Mt. Pulaski........	" 39	Captain-General.
Greene, Wm. Laban...	May —, 1865.	Hugh de Payens....	" 29	Treasurer.
Hammond, Jacob B....	May —, 1865.	Elwood............	" 6	Generalissimo.
Hattenhauer, R. C.....	Oct. 13, 1867.	St John............	" 26	Em. Commander.

NAME.	WHEN KNIGHTED.	COMMANDERY.	KNIGHTLY RANK.
Hayden, Geo. Dwight..	Mar. 18, 1867.	Belvidere........... No. 2	Em. Commander.
Hill, H. Harrison.......	April 18, 1870.	St. Paul.... ...... " 34	Sir Knight.
Hubbard, Hiram W....	Nov. 12, 1852.	Cyrene.... .... " 23	Grand Generalissimo.
Hurlbut, Vincent L....	May 24, 1859.	Apollo............. " 1	{ Grand Generalissimo. { Grand Encampment U. S.
Hutchins, Azro D......	Oct. 19, 1861.	Waukegan.......... " 12	Em. Commander.
Jorgenson, Louis H....	May 24, 1864.	Cairo.............. " 13	Grand Captain-General.
King, Wm. Wallace....	June 14, 1871.	Apollo............. " 1	Sir Knight.
Kingsley, Thos. Henry.	April 8, 1868.	Belvidere.......... " 2	Sir Knight.
Lee, Caleb E...........	July 1, 1870.	Cairo .... " 13	Sir Knight.
Ladd, Chas. Knox.....	Aug. 28, 1871.	Temple............ " 20	Sir Knight.
Morgan, Wm. Jasper..	Oct. 27, 1866.	Cyrene.... .... " 23	Generalissimo.
Marshall, Jas. Edwin...	Nov. 5, 1870.	Cyrene............ " 23	Recorder.
Martin, Wm. Henry....	May 14, 1872.	Galena............ " 40	Sir Knight.
McGuire, Robert Louis	June 20, 1864.	Elwood............ " 6	Em. Commander.
McKinlay, Robert Lang	Dec. 10, 1869.	Palestine.......... " 27	Grand Warder.
McLain, Calvin W. ...	— —, —.	Hospitaler......... " 31	Em. Commander.
Morrison, Geo. Bissell.	Dec. 10, 1872	Cyrene............ " 23	Sir Knight.
Moffitt, John Blair.....	Feb. 10, 1873.	Temple............ " 20	Sir Knight.
Mesigh, Joseph........	— —, 1866.	Temple............ " 20	Em. Commander.
Moore, Wm. Irvin.....	April 10, 1866.	Temple............ " 20	Treasurer.
Mateer, Sam'l Alex'r...	May 21, 1873.	Joliet............. " 4	Recorder.
Nash, John Fisk.......	Nov. —, 1860.	Ottawa.... .... " 10	Grand Sword Bearer.
Olney, Smith..........	Feb. 6, 1871.	St. Paul.......... " 34	Recorder.
Orr, Wm. Lindsay.....	May 11, 1868.	Hugh de Payens... " 29	Em. Commander.
Parkinson, Thos. L....	Jan. 2, 1867.	Cyrene............ " 23	Treasurer.
Phelps, Elijah Palmer..	April 13, 1867.	Cyrene............ " 23	Warder.
Pumpelly, Jonathan N.	Dec. —, 1869.	Mt. Pulaski........ " 39	Em. Commander.
Price, William........	May 28, 1873.	Joliet............. " 4	Captain of the Guard.
Robertson, N.T.P., M.D.	— —, 1867.	St. Paul.......... " 34	Em. Commander.
Robinson, Benj. Edgar.	Feb. —, 1867.	St. Paul.......... " 34	Em. Commander.
Ronch, Samuel........	June 9, 1868.	De Molay.......... " 24	Captain of the Guard.
Sanford, Edward.......	....	Blaney............ " 5	Generalissimo.
Smith, Robt. Bingham.	Oct. 16, 1862.	Belvidere.......... " 2	Em. Commander
Smith, John Corson....	April 26, 1871.	Galena............ " 40	Grand Warder.
Staley, Geo. William...	Sept. 10, 1872.	Cyrene............ " 23	Sir Knight.
Toole, John H.........	Feb. 3, 1871.	Mt. Pulaski........ " 39	Generalissimo.
Torgerson, Ole.......	Dec. 11, 1869.	Cyrene............ " 23	Captain of the Guard.
Trewatha, Peter.......	Jan. 31, 1873.	Galena............ " 40	Sir Knight.
Wann, Daniel........	Mar. 22, 1872.	Galena............ " 40	Sir Knight.
Wardner, Horace, M.D.	April 29, 1865.	Cairo.............. " 13	Prelate.
Wheeler, Geo. Sullivan.	July 25, 1865.	Waukegan.......... " 12	Sir Knight.
Whitehead, Thos. Jas..	April 1, 1873.	Cyrene............ " 23	Sir Knight.
Zeigler, Philo Hamlin..	April 10, 1866.	Temple............ " 20	Em. Commander.
Zuck, Francis M.......	Mar. --, 1866.	Palestine.......... " 27	Sir Knight.

INDIANA.

NAME.	WHEN KNIGHTED.	COMMANDERY.	KNIGHTLY RANK.
Abbott, John.	....	Terre Haute....... No. 16	Treasurer.
Ader, Henry, M.D.....	Aug. 8, 1871.	Marion............ " 21	Sir Knight.
Allen, William.	Feb. 4, 1856.	Aurora............ " 17	Em. Commander.
Albert, Stephen.......	Nov. 24, 1866.	New Albany...,.... " 5	Recorder.
Armstrong, Samuel E..	Aug. —, 1871.	Terre Haute....... " 16	Sir Knight.
Austin, William W....	Mar. 21, 1865.	Richmond......... " 8	Em. Commander.
Arvine, John S.....	....	Thos. H. Lynch.... " 14	Treasurer.
Adkinson, Lewis G....	Feb. 1, 1870.	Thos. H. Lynch.... " 14	Prelate.
Abbott, John W..	Jan. 6, 1870.	Thos. H. Lynch.... " 14	Sir Knight.
Bacon, Orison H......	April 8, 1873.	St. John's......... " 24	Sir Knight.
Beale, Henry L.......	Nov. 20, 1865.	Baldwin........... " 2	Em. Commander.
Bennett, Jas. Clark....	Jan. 31, 1868.	Baldwin........... " 2	Sir Knight.
Bishop, Erville B......	Nov. 10, 1868.	Muncie............ " 18	Grand Captain-General.
Brackenridge, Chas. S..	Dec. 7, 1867.	Fort Wayne........ " 4	Grand Warder.
Burk, Robt. W........	May 11, 1868.	Cambridge......... " 6	Sir Knight.
Barrett, Stinson J.....	May 27, 1870.	Thos. H. Lynch.... " 14	Guard.
Bondurant, Evermont G.	June 2, 1871.	Thos. H. Lynch.... " 14	Sir Knight.
Carson, Robert R.....	June 27, 1872.	St. John's......... " 24	Sir Knight.
Carver, Thos. G., D.D..	— —, 1872.	La Fayette........ " 3	Prelate.
Charlesworth, Sam'l O.	Feb. 7, 1873.	Madison........... " 22	Sir Knight.
Chute, Charles F......	Aug. —, 1871.	Terre Haute....... " 16	Sir Knight.
Cockburn, George T....	July 1, 1872.	St. John's......... " 24	Sir Knight.
Crooks, James.........	July —, 1872.	Terre Haute....... " 16	Sir Knight.
Croasdale, Jonathan....	Feb. 19, 1869.	Terre Haute....... " 16	Sir Knight.
Cruft, Charles........	May 15, 1867.	Terre Haute....... " 16	Grand Commander.
Cooper, Moses O......	Mar. 26, 1868.	Thos. H. Lynch.... " 14	Sir Knight.
Crose, John A.........	Mar. 16, 1867.	Greencastle........ " 11	Prelate.

NAME.	WHEN KNIGHTED:	COMMANDERY.		KNIGHTLY RANK.
Culley, Eugene	July 15. 1869.	Thos. H. Lynch	No. 14	Standard Bearer.
Catherwood, Samuel	Nov. 27, 1866.	Greencastle	" 11	Treasurer.
Daniells, Almond	June 20, 1871.	Madison	" 22	Recorder.
Day, Henry Albert	Jan. 5, 1867.	Greencastle	" 11	Em. Commander.
Dodge. Joseph B.	Sept. —, 1858.	Warsaw	" 42	Warder.
Durff, John R.	July 15, 1872.	New Albany	" 5	Junior Warden.
Dukes, Rowland Jas.	May 30, 1873.	New Albany	" 5	Sir Knight.
Davis, William T.	Feb. 19, 1872.	Thos. H. Lynch	" 14	Captain of the Guard.
Elvin, Robert F.	Dec. 23, 1869.	Thos. H. Lynch	" 14	Sir Knight.
Fetta, Christian	Mar. 20, 1865.	Richmond	" 8	Em. Commander.
Gilgour, William	Feb. 24, 1870.	Thos. H. Lynch	" 14	Junior Warden.
Gierlow, John	—— —, 1859.	South Bend	" 13	Em. Commander.
Gibson, Daniel	May 16. 1872.	Fort Wayne	" 4	Warder.
Goodwin, John	Nov. 19, 1872.	Baldwin	" 2	Sir Knight.
Gorgas, Albert J.	May 16, 1870.	Baldwin	" 2	Recorder.
Greenlee. E. A.	June —, 1868.	La Fayette	" 3	Recorder.
Grove, John B.	Feb. 7, 1868.	Thos. H. Lynch	" 14	Em. Commander.
Gent, Joseph F.	May 27, 1870.	Thos. H. Lynch	" 14	Generalissimo.
Hacker, William	May 3, 1848.	Baldwin	" 2	Grand Commander.
Haigh, Sidney E	June 21, 1871.	Madison	" 22	Recorder.
Hamilton, Andrew H.	April 30, 1867.	Fort Wayne	" 4	Deputy Grand Commander.
Hamilton, De Witt C.	Dec. 19, 1867.	Thos. H. Lynch	" 14	Recorder.
Hamilton, Elbridge G.	Sept. 7, 1866.	Laporte	" 12	Grand Commander.
Hamilton. Charles.	Jan. 5, 1869.	Thos. H. Lynch	" 14	Em. Commander.
Harper,J.E.C.Franklin.	June 20, 1871.	Madison	" 22	Prelate.
Hayes, Joseph R	Mar. 17, 1873.	St. John's	" 24	Sir Knight.
Hazelrigg, Harvey G.	Feb. 8, 1853.	La Fayette	" 3	Grand Commander.
Hess. John H		Thos. H. Lynch	" 14	Em. Commander.
Hurd, Orrin D	Mar. 9, 1869	Fort Wayne	" 4	Em. Commander.
Hussey. Edward S	Sept. 14, 1868	Terre Haute	" 16	Sir Knight.
Hays, Jas. McDannold.	Mar. 16, 1867.	Greencastle	" 11	Treasurer.
Hays, Mahlon	Nov. 10, 1871.	Thos. H. Lynch	" 14	Sir Knight.
Jackson, Robert M.	Dec. 19, 1867.	Thos. H. Lynch	" 14	Warder.
Johnson, Richard M.	July 2, 1872.	Thos. H. Lynch	" 14	Sir Knight.
Johnson, Simeon S.	Aug. 2, 1867.	New Albany	" 5	Em. Commander.
Kirk, George W. F.	Jan. 30, 1868.	Baldwin	" 2	Em. Commander.
Kitchen, Sylvester J.	Nov. 12, 1872.	La Fayette	" 3	Sir Knight.
Keith, Isham	Dec. 21, 1870.	Thos. H. Lynch	" 14	Guard.
Locke, Erie	Nov. 25, 1857.	Raper	" 1	Captain-General.
Long, Thomas B.	Jan. 28, 1871.	Terre Haute	" 16	Standard Bearer.
Long, Henry, M.D.	Feb. 12, 1869.	Baldwin	" 2	Recorder.
Lozier, Rev. John H.	Oct. 3, 1871.	Franklin	" 23	Prelate.
Lynch, Augustus D	Dec. 18, 1865.	Baldwin	" 2	Em. Commander.
Lynch, Daniel	Jan. 6, 1871.	Thos. H. Lynch	" 14	Sword Bearer.
Lyle, John D.		Thos. H. Lynch	" 14	Recorder.
McQueen, Joshua D.	Mar. 6, 1868.	Thos. H. Lynch	" 14	Guard.
McGary, Ennis N.,M.D.	Nov. 26, 1872.	Madison	" 22	Sir Knight.
McGrew, Gifford H. G.	Sept. 4, 1873.	Cambridge	" 6	Sir Knight.
Miles, Lorenzo C.	Jan. 25, 1872.	St. John's	" 24	Senior Warden.
Moore, Thomas	June 9, 1873.	Baldwin	" 2	Sir Knight.
Morton, John E				
Munson, Wm. L.	Nov. 27, 1867.	Raper	" 1	Sir Knight.
McEwen, Archie	Dec. 21, 1870.	Thos. H. Lynch	" 14	Sir Knight.
McCormack, Patrick H.	Feb. 4, 1873.	Thos. H. Lynch	" 14	Sir Knight.
Mothershead, F. M.	Jan. 17, 1873.	Thos. H. Lynch	" 14	Sir Knight.
Mounts, Henry		Raper	" 1	Sir Knight.
Newsom, David	Dec. 18, 1873.	Thos. H. Lynch	" 14	Sir Knight.
Palmer, Edwin D	Oct. —, 1856.	Richmond	" 8	Grand Commander.
Patrick, Ephraim W.	—— —, 1856.	Lavalette	" 15	Sir Knight.
Phelps, Ithamar D	Jan. 8, 1869.	La Porte	" 12	Sword Bearer.
Prather, Thos. B.	Jan. 2. 1872.	Thos. H. Lynch	" 14	Junior Warden
Pence, George	June 9, 1873.	Thos. H. Lynch	" 14	Warder.
Redmond, John E.	Nov. 10, 1871.	Thos. H. Lynch	" 14	Generalissimo.
Reiter, George		Fort Wayne	" 4	Generalissimo.
Schenck, B. F.	Nov. 12, 1872.	Madison	" 22	Sir Knight.
Schrier, Williard B.	June 29, 1872.	St. John's	" 24	Sir Knight.
Schwingronber, Fred.	May 15, 1867.	Terre Haute	" 16	Recorder.
Schmidlap, John D.	Oct. 11, 1870	Madison	" 22	Grand Standard Bearer.
Shewmaker, Uriah	Dec. 5, 1868.	Terre Haute	" 16	Sir Knight.
Shields, James G	Nov. 29, 1860.	New Albany	" 5	Em. Commander.
Shaw, Robt. James	Mar. 29, 1869.	New Albany	" 5	Grand Senior Warden.
Sloan, George W.	Jan. 11, 1865.	Raper	" 1	Sir Knight.
Souders, C.		South Bend	" 13	Sir Knight.
Smick, Manford M.	May 23, 1872.	Fort Wayne	" 4	Recorder.
Smith, C. H.	—— —, 1866.	Madison	" 22	Sir Knight.

NAME.	WHEN KNIGHTED.	COMMANDERY.	KNIGHTLY RANK.
Smythe, Gonzalva C...	Sept. —, 1871.	Greencastle........No. 11	Captain-General.
Stanley, James Joseph.	May —, 1867.	Terre Haute........ " 16	Sir Knight.
Stellwagon, Jos. A.....	Jan. 13, 1859.	Fort Wayne........ " 4	Em. Commander.
Stevens, Stanley L.....	Jan. —, 1868.	Raper .... " 1	Junior Warden.
Snipes, William R	Jan. 2, 1872.	Thos. H. Lynch .... " 14	Standard Bearer.
Shultz, Gideon S.......	June 9, 1873.	Thos. H. Lynch .... " 14	Sword Bearer.
Stevens, John T........	Feb. 2, 1870.	Thos. H. Lynch .... " 14	Captain-General.
Sayre, Thomas C.......	May 27, 1870.	Thos. H. Lynch .... " 14	Sir Knight.
Sweeney, Zachery T....	Feb. 3, 1873.	Thos. H. Lynch .... " 14	Sir Knight.
Stateler, Frank	Feb. 19, 1872.	Thos. H. Lynch .... " 14	Sir Knight,
Summers, Wm. D......	Jan. 22, 1873.	Thos. H. Lynch .... " 14	Sir Knight.
Terry, John..........	June 19, 1866.	Warsaw........... " 10	Treasurer.
Thomas, Henry M......	Mar. 16, 1872.	Greencastle....... " 11	Sword Bearer.
Thomas, Richard......		Thos. H. Lynch ... " 14	Em. Commander
Trotter, J. Albert......	Feb. 19, 1868.	Thos. H. Lynch .... " 14	Captain-General.
Wheatley, Wm. M.....		Raper .... " 1	Sir Knight.
Whelan, Kosciusko....	Feb. 4, 1868.	Cambridge........ " 6	Recorder.
White, Henry C........	Feb. 7, 1873.	Madison .... " 22	Sentinel.
Wesner, Allen	Aug. 8, 1871.	Marion............ " 21	Sir Knight.
Whitney, William B...	Mar. 31, 1871.	Thos. H. Lynch .... " 14	Sir Knight.

IOWA.

NAME.	WHEN KNIGHTED.	COMMANDERY.	KNIGHTLY RANK.
Ainsworth, Edward E..	Feb. 1, 1869.	Temple ....No. 4	Grand Warder.
Alexander, Wm. M.....	Nov. 28, 1870.	Pilgrim............ " 20	Generalissimo.
Baugh, Downing......	Jan. —, 1865.	Honorius.......... " 8	Grand Prelate.
Bishop, Stephen A.....	June 11, 1859.	Baldwin.......... " 11	Generalissimo.
Bower, Robt. Farmer...	April 18, 1851.	Damascus .... " 5	Grand Commander.
Butler, Milo A.........	Sept. 29, 1870.	Excalibur .... " 13	Em. Commander.
Brobst, Sam. McLain..	Dec. 15, 1872.	Palestine .... " 2	Sir Knight.
Bean, Sylvester S......	Sept. 7, 1870.	Pilgrim............ " 20	Senior Warden.
Butler, Jacob	Feb. —, 1870.	Pilgrim............ " 20	Em. Commander.
Beam, John............	April 13, 1872.	Pilgrim............ " 20	Sir Knight.
Cate, Lester..........	Jan. 24, 1873.	Temple .... " 4	Standard Bearer.
Calder, William	July 11, 1865.	De Molay.......... " 1	Captain-General.
Cheek, Jesse W	Feb. 23, 1872.	Temple .... " 4	Recorder.
Clarke, Robt. Lee.....	May 26, 1873.	St. John's........ " 21	Sir Knight.
Clark. John Norwood..	Jan. 15, 1857.	Palestine.......... " 2	Recorder.
Comegys, Cornelius P..	Jan. 24, 1873.	Damascus.......... " 5	Junior Warden.
Chamberlain, Dewitt C.	Mar. 20, 1872.	Pilgrim .... " 20	Sword Bearer.
Collins, Allen	Dec. 29, 1870.	Pilgrim............ " 20	Sir Knight.
Dougherty, John B....	April 11, 1855.	De Molay.......... " 1	Treasurer.
Duckworth, Wm. Albert	Mar. 9, 1871.	St. John's........ " 21	Sir Knight.
Evans, Thomas	Oct. 6, 1870.	Pilgrim........... " 20	Recorder.
Fleschman, J. E........	Feb. 7, 1866.	Temple............ " 4	Sir Knight.
Graham, Seth	Dec. 21, 1872.	Temple .... " 4	Treasurer.
Gregg, Eli H	Dec. 21, 1871.	Baldwin............ " 11	Standard Bearer.
Goodykoonts, Dan. F..	May 26, 1869.	Excalibur .... " 13	Sir Knight.
Getchell, Fred'k.......	Feb. 1, 1869.	Temple............ " 4	Generalissimo.
Guilbert, Edward A....		Siloam............. " 3	Grand Commander.
Hammond, J. R........	Jan. 24, 1873.	Temple............ " 4	Senior Warden.
Hanson, Asa P........	April 2, 1872.	Oriental........... " 22	Sword Bearer.
Harris, H. C..........	April 9, 1869.	Temple............ " 4	Senior Warden.
Hartsock. James Rush..	Oct. —, 1846.	Palestine.......... " 2	Grand Commander.
Hatch, W. H..........	June 1, 1869.	Temple............ " 4	Junior Warden.
Hills, Fred'k Clark....	Dec. 20, 1869.	Columbian........ " 18	Em. Commander.
Howard, Henry	Dec. —, 1865.	De Payens........ " 6	Treasurer.
Hobbs, John W........	Jan. 24, 1873.	Damascus.......... " 5	Sir Knight.
Kennedy, J. H	Oct. 22, 1873.	Temple............ " 4	Sir Knight.
Knight, John M...... .	Feb. 4, 1873.	Temple..... ...... " 4	Sir Knight.
Kimball, Orane A......	Feb. —, 1870.	Pilgrim .... " 20	Junior Warden.
Lamb, Caleb..........	Jan. —, 1857.	Oriental........... " 22	Em. Commander.
Langridge, Wm. Baker.	....	De Molay.......... " 1	Grand Recorder.
Law, Wm. James	Dec. 20, 1870.	St. John's......... " 21	Em. Commander.
Lininger, G. Wash'gton	—— —, 1861.	Ivanhoe........... " 17	Deputy Grand Commander.
Leighton, Henry C....	July, —, 1872.	De Payens........ " 6	Em. Commander.
Leffingwell, William...	Jan. 11, 1855.	De Molay.......... " 1	Grand Commander.
Long, Jas. H	Jan. 3, 1873.	Temple......... ... " 4	Sir Knight.
Loy, Jacob............	Dec. 15, 1873.	Pilgrim .... " 20	Sir Knight.
Luke, Zephaniah C....	Mar. 20. 1863.	Palestine........... " 2	Grand Treasurer.
McIntyre, James S... .	Sept. 8, 1870.	Pilgrim............ " 20	Sir Knight.
Macy, J. C............	Sept. 5, 1873.	Temple............ " 4	Warder.
McDoel, Wm. Henry...	Jan. 10, 1868.	Damascus.......... " 5	Recorder.
McClary, B. J.........	Feb. 10, 1871.	Temple.... .... " 4	Standard Bearer.

NAME.	WHEN KNIGHTED.	COMMANDERY.		KNIGHTLY RANK.
McWorkman, Daniel...	Feb. 27, 1856.	Damascus	No. 5	Junior Warden.
Martin, Ancil E.......	May 9, 1871.	Trinity	" 16	Sir Knight.
Moulton, Moses M....	Feb. 17, 1869.	Trinity	" 16	Recorder.
Nims, Leslie S........	Mar. 21, 1873.	Baldwin	" 11	Sir Knight.
Overton, Fernando C...	Oct. 4, 1871.	St. John's	" 21	Captain-General.
Parvin, Theo. Sutton..	....	Palestine	" 2	Grand Recorder.
Parish, John C........	April 18, 1867.	Temple	" 4	Deputy Grand Commander.
Patterson, W. A......	Jan. 27, 1869.	Temple	" 4	Sword Bearer.
Pickton, Peter	April 3, 1867.	Baldwin	" 11	Grand Sword Bearer.
Peterson, Andrew.....	Dec. 23, 1870.	Pilgrim	" 20	Sir Knight.
Powers, Jacob H......	Feb. —, 1870.	Pilgrim	" 20	Treasurer.
Robinson, Hiram	April 26, 1872.	Temple	" 4	Captain-General.
Rogers, Alexander B...	Aug. —, 1870.	Excalibur	" 13	Sir Knight.
Stillans. Wm. Clark ...	April 13, 1872.	Pilgrim	" 20	Guard.
Sayre, David Edward..	Dec. 28, 1871.	Constantine	" 23	Warder.
Scholtz, L.............	Jan. 27, 1873.	Temple	" 4	Sir Knight.
Sehorn, Jacob Good....	May 18, 1870.	Palestine	" 2	Captain-General.
Shepard, C. D........	Jan. 11, 1867.	Temple	" 4	Sir Knight.
Stearns, Esbeeck......	Nov. 20, 1867.	Baldwin	" 11	Sword Bearer.
Stilson, Arthur Clark...	Feb. 9, 1867.	Damascus	" 5	Prelate,
Smart, J. J...........	April 4, 1873.	Temple	" 4	Sir Knight.
Smith, W. A...........	July 1, 1857.	Temple	" 4	Standard Bearer.
Sneer, George.........	Mar. 1, 1873.	Temple	" 4	Prelate.
Taylor, John W., Jr....	Jan. 27, 1871.	Siloam	" 3	Sir Knight.
Tucker, Howard......	May 20, 1866.	Damascus	" 5	Warder.
Van Saun, Geo. B.....	June —, 1860.	Baldwin	" 11	Grand Generalissimo.
Wells, Guy.	July 20, 1865.	Damascus	" 5	Generalissimo.
West, Harry..........	May 3, 1872.	Temple	" 4	Sword Bearer.
Wicks, G. B..........	Jan. 27, 1873.	Temple	" 4	Standard Bearer.
Wilson, J. W.........	Oct. 12, 1872.	Oriental	" 22	Captain-General.
Whitmarsh, John G...	May 11, 1871.	Excalibur	" 13	Warder.
Woodward, W. Elijah.	June 7, 1864.	St. Omer	" 15	Grand Generalissimo.

KANSAS.

NAME.	WHEN KNIGHTED.	COMMANDERY.		KNIGHTLY RANK.
Bassett, Owen A... ...	....	De Molay	No. 4	Grand Generalissimo.
Brown, John Henry....	—- 1858.	Leavenworth	" 1	Grand Commander.
Byington, Dwight... ..	June 21, 1865.	Leavenworth	" 1	Generalissimo.
Carr, Erasmus Theo....	Aug. —, 1864.	Leavenworth	" 1	Grand Recorder.
Gilmore, George T....	Feb. 6, 1873.	Topeka	" 5	Recorder.
Gould, William O......	Mar. 29, 1860.	Leavenworth.	" 1	Grand Commander.
Lakin, Samuel K.......	Jan. 31, 1871.	Topeka	" 5	Senior Warden.
Philbrick, John L......	June 28, 1854.	Washington	" 5	Dep. Grand Commander.
Reid, Aquila J........	April 14, 1863.	De Molay	" 4	Treasurer.
Sheldon, Silas E......	Dec. 28, 1869.	Topeka	" 5	Em. Commander.
Utley, Jordan N......	Dec. 26, 1867.	Washington	" 2	Sir Knight.

KENTUCKY.

NAME.	WHEN KNIGHTED.	COMMANDERY.		KNIGHTLY RANK.
Abert, Wm. Stone.....	May 30, 1870.	Newport	No. 13	Sir Knight.
Adams, D. A.........	June 10, 1873.	Bradford	" 9	Sir Knight.
Apperson, Lewis......	June 8, 1871.	Montgomery	" 5	Generalissimo.
Ashurst, Josiah T......	— , 1867.	Bradford	" 9	Captain-General.
Beeler, Jos. Louis....	Mar. 29, 1872.	Louisville	" 1	Sir Knight.
Bentley, Matthew H...	Jan. 27, 1873.	Covington	" 7	Sir Knight.
Billingsley, Chas. F....	Jan. 13, 1868.	Louisville	" 1	Grand Standard Bearer.
Bostwick, Henry......	June 7, 1864.	Covington	" 7	Grand Commander.
Brown, George.......	Nov. 28, 1872.	Owensboro	" 15	Sir Knight.
Buckner, Edmund G...	Nov. 26, 1872.	Owensboro	" 15	Warder.
Barlow, John H.......	Feb. —, 1851.	Newport	" 13	Em. Commander.
Caldwell, Richard B...	Jan. 21, 1869.	De Molay	" 12	Generalissimo.
Casseday, Sam'l, Jr.....	May 30, 1871.	Louisville	" 1	Senior Warden.
Chambers, J. D.......	June 10, 1873.	Bradford	" 9	Sir Knight.
Chew, Samuel H......	Nov. 2, 1867.	Webb	" 2	Em. Commander.
Clarke, John.........	— , 1855.	Bradford	" 9	Dep. Grand Commander.
Cloyd, Stephen W....	May 17, 1870.	Louisville	" 1	Standard Bearer.
Croninger, Lorenzo D..	Dec. —, 1853.	Covington	" 7	Junior Warden.
Cofer, Martin H......	June 20, 1873.	Owensboro	" 15	Sir Knight.
Davis, Edward C......	April 23, 1872.	Owensboro	" 15	Junior Warden.
Davies, John B.......	— , 1854.	De Molay	" 12	Sir Knight.
Davis, Theodore C.....	June 28, 1872.	Covington	" 7	Sir Knight.
Duncan, Wm. J.......	Mar. 11, 1868.	De Molay	" 12	Captain-General.
Duvall, L. E....	Mar. —, 1871.	Louisville	" 1	Sir Knight

NAME.	WHEN KNIGHTED.	COMMANDERY.		KNIGHTLY RANK.
Elliott, John W........	Feb. —, 1873	Bradford...........	No. 9	Junior Warden.
Fish, L. B.............	May 20, 1869.	Louisville.........	" 1	Sir Knight.
Fulton, Hiram Ward. .	April —, 1864.	Henderson.........	" 14	Em. Commander.
Fuqua, Joseph A.......	May 9, 1873.	Owensboro'........	" 15	Standard Bearer.
Hall, Edwin G........	— —, 1870.	De Molay.........	" 12	Sir Knight.
Hatchitt, Clay H.......	Feb. 19, 1873.	Frankfort....	" 4	Sir Knight.
Hathaway, R. M........	Aug. —, 1845.	Owensboro'........	" 15	Grand Prelate.
Hillsman, Wm. H., M.D.	— —, 1872.	Owensboro'........	" 15	Sir Knight.
Hinch, Leonard........	— —, 1865.	Bradford...........	" 9	Senior Warden.
Hensley, Edward.......	Oct. 31, 1871.	Frankfort.........	" 4	Sir Knight.
Jackson, A. R.........	April 23, 1852.	Paducah	" 11	Em. Commander.
Johnson, Campbell H...	Dec. 26, 1871.	Henderson........	" 14	Prelate.
Kenney, Charles O.....	June 1, 1866.	Bradford..........	" 9	Recorder.
Lampkin, Geo. F......	— —, 1866.	Bradford....	" 9	Captain-General.
Lell, John Wm.........	Mar. —, 1871.	Webb.............	" 2	Standard Bearer.
Lovely, Jesse.........	May 6, 1871.	Cynthiana	" 16	Sir Knight.
Lyon, Geo. Wm........	April 1, 1869.	Covington	" 7	Senior Warden.
McClintock, I. L......	May —, 1872.	Louisville.........	" 1	Sword Bearer.
Meffert, Fred'k Jacob..	May 1, 1872.	De Molay.........	" 12	Sir Knight.
Miller, Emory K......	May 27, 1869.	Louisville.........	" 1	Captain-General.
Mitchell, Mantine L....	— —, 1872.	De Molay.........	" 12	Sir Knight.
Megill, Henry, M. D....	— —, 1852.	Owensboro'........	" 15	Standard Bearer.
Montgomery, J. Greg'y.	May 16, 1872.	Cynthiana	" 16	Captain-General.
Milne, Colin R	June 19, 1873.	Owensboro'........	" 15	Sir Knight.
Moore, James H.......	— —, 1862.	Bradford.........	" 9	Generalissimo.
Moss, Thos. E........		Paducah	" 11	Em. Commander.
Munger, Wm. Coleman.	— —, 1852.	Louisville.........	" 1	G. J. Warden, Gr. En. U. S.
Morris, LL.D., Robert..	....	....	" —	Em. Commander.
Marble, Levi W.......	Nov. 23, 1872.	Owensboro'.	" 15	Sir Knight.
Mason, William N.....	April 29, 1872.	Owensboro'........	" 15	Capt. Guard.
Neale, William J.......	— —, 1867.	Bradford.........	" 9	Standard Bearer.
Neal, H. H............	— —, 1863.	Louisville.........	" 1	Grand Junior Warden.
Netherland, Geo. Edgar.	June 2, 1873.	Louisville.........	" 1	Sir Knight.
Ogden, J. Daviess, M.D.	April 29, 1872.	Owensboro'.... ...	" 15	Treasurer.
Osborne, John R......	Aug. 27, 1872.	Owensboro'.	" 15	Sir Knight.
Parker, Samuel S......	Mar. 23, 1866.	Louisville.........	" 1	Grand Generalissimo.
Payne, Edward Henry..	June 14, 1873.	Louisville.........	" 1	Guard.
Poyntz, J. M., M.D....	June —, 1867.	Cynthiana	" 16	Grand Sword Bearer.
Ramsay, Richard H....	Sept. 16, 1869.	Covington	" 7	Recorder.
Russell, Milton C.....	Nov. 10, 1868.	Maysville.........	" 10	Em. Commander.
Ryan, William........	Jan. 31, 1867.	De Molay.........	" 12	Grand Standard Bearer.
Sangston, James A.....	July 21, 1868.	Louisville.........	" 1	Recorder.
Sewell, John F........	July 27, 1859.	Louisville.........	" 1	Grand Junior Warden.
Shafer, Louis A........	Mar. 7, 1872.	De Molay.........	" 12	Sir Knight.
Sneed, Stephen K......	Dec. 28, 1871.	Henderson.........	" 14	Generalissimo.
Stewart, J. Q. A., M.D.	April 15, 1872.	Owensboro'........	" 15	Senior Warden.
Thornton, T. E.......	— —, 1867.	Bradford	" 9	Sir Knight.
Van Meter, John S.....	May 14, 1872.	Webb.............	" 2	Generalissimo.
Woodruff, Chas. Rankin	Oct. 5, 1854.	Louisville.........	" 1	{ Grand Sword Bearer, Gr. Encpt. U. S.
Walsh, Anthony R.....	— —, 1873.	Louisville.........	" 1	Sir Knight.
Warren, Wm. H......	— —, 1864.	Webb.............	" 2	Grand Commander.
Warner, Wm. Alva....	Sept. —, 1863.	Louisville.........	" 1	Grand Commander.
Wigal, James P........	Jan. 16, 1872.	Henderson........	" 14	Captain of the Guard.
Woodward, James.....	July 6, 1871.	De Molay.........	" 12	Sir Knight.
Wandling, John........	April 15, 1872.	Owensboro'........	" 15	Captain-General.
Woodford, Wm. H.....	May —, 1872.	Owensboro'........	" 15	Warder.

LOUISIANA.

NAME.	WHEN KNIGHTED.	COMMANDERY.		KNIGHTLY RANK.
Adams, E. E..........	April 12, 1871.	Orleans............	No. 3	Recorder.
Brown, Sam. H	— —, 1873.	....	" —	
Cree, Harvey.........	Feb. 11, 1872.	....	" —	
Clarke, John Hawley..	— —, 1861.	Orleans...........	" 3	Grand Generalissimo.
Carnahan, H. S........	April 26, 1872.	Jacques De Molay.	" 2	Sir Knight.
Fellows, John Q. A....	Aug. 8, 1856.	Orleans...........	" 3	Gr. Master Gr. Encpt. U. S.
Francis, M. W.........	Aug. 8, 1871.	Jacques De Molay.	" 2	Sir Knight.
Girard, Michel Eloi....	— —, 1861.	Girard	" 4	Em. Commander.
Hughes, David........	Mar. 7, 1873.	Jacques De Molay.	" 2	Sir Knight.
Ittmann, George B.....	Feb. 2, 1872.	Jacques De Molay.	" 2	Sir Knight.
Lambert, Richard......	— —, 1861.	....	" —	Grand Commander.
Murphy, Wm. E		Orleans...........	" 3	Sir Knight.
Pike, Zebulon M.......	Jan. 20, 1865.	Jacques De Molay.	" 2	Grand Sword Bearer.
Sontag, Gustav	Nov. 10, 1863.	Jacques De Molay.	" 2	Grand Recorder.

NAME.	WHEN KNIGHTED.	COMMANDERY.		KNIGHTLY RANK.
Stevenson, John A.....	— —, 1863.	Jacques De Molay.	No. 2	Grand Commander.
Stewart, William H....	Jan. 7, 1861.	Jacques De Molay.	" 2	Prelate.
Sypher, Abram J......	....	Orleans...........	" 3	Sir Knight.
Todd, Sam'l Manning..	— —, 1858.	Jacques De Molay.	" 2	Grand Commander.
Todd, James..........	Dec. 12, 1869.	Jacques De Molay.	" 2	Sir Knight.
Wright, S. B....:......	Dec. 1, 1869.	Orleans...........	" 3	Sir Knight.

MAINE.

NAME.	WHEN KNIGHTED.	COMMANDERY.		KNIGHTLY RANK.
Alden, Silas...........	April 19, 1850.	St. John's	No. 3	Grand Captain-General.
Alden, Warren L.......	Jan. 13, 1851.	St. John's	" 3	Sir Knight.
Bailey, M. E. D.......	June 21, 1864.	Lewiston	" 6	Generalissimo.
Belknap, Charles W....	May 28, 1866.	Portland..........	" 2	Sir Knight.
Bowen, George........	Mar. 15, 1869.	St. John's........	" 3	Treasurer.
Drummond, Josiah H..	Mar. —, 1860.	St. Alban.........	" 8	Dep. Grand Commander.
Farnham, Augustus B..	May 20, 1867.	St. John's.........	" 3	Em. Commander.
Hayes, Joseph M......	Nov. 15, 1865.	Dunlap	" 5	Generalissimo.
King, Marquis F......	....	St. Alban.........	" 8	Sir Knight.
Knowles, Freeman.....	May 2, 1853.	St. John's.........	" 3	Sir Knight.
Lynde, John Horr......	Mar. 2, 1863.	St. John's.........	" 3	Grand Generalissimo.
Marston, Arlington B..	June 2, 1862.	St. John's.........	" 3	Generalissimo.
Sanborn, John L.......	Oct. 22, 1867.	Claremont........	" 9	Sir Knight.
Seymour, Denison E...	April 24, 1865.	St. Bernard	" 11	Grand Sword Bearer.
Thompson, W. L., M.D.	— —, 1868.	Trinity...........	" 7	Senior Warden.

MARYLAND.

NAME.	WHEN KNIGHTED.	COMMANDERY.		KNIGHTLY RANK.
Kelsey, Wm. Augustus.	— —, 1873.	Crusade...........	No. 5	Sir Knight.

MASS. and R. I.

NAME.	WHEN KNIGHTED.	COMMANDERY.		KNIGHTLY RANK.
Almy, Samuel Holder..	July 19, 1866.	Berkshire..........		Captain-General.
Bullock, James W.....	May 7, 1869.	Calvary.	No. 13	Treasurer.
Chapin, Edward Pliny..	June 8, 1868.	Springfield........		Treasurer.
Cheever, Tracy P	— —, 1857.	Palestine..........		Grand Senior Warden.
Chickering, Henry.....	Feb. 22, 1864.	Berkshire		Grand Captain-General.
Choate, Humphrey.....	Jan. 1, 1872.	St. Omer		Sir Knight.
Conner, S. S..........	May 30, 1873.	Springfield........		Sir Knight.
Crowson, Ernest... ...	June 30, 1871.	Springfield........		Sir Knight.
Cushman, Alb't Homer.	Nov. 20, 1866.	St. John's.........	" 1	Em. Commander.
Davis, Chas. Aaron ...	April 1, 1859.	Natick............		Generalissimo.
Davis, Robert Lewis...	Jan. —, 1858.	Gethsemana.......		Generalissimo.
Dean, Benjamin	— —, 1855.	St. Omer..........		Gr. Capt.-Gen. Gr. En. U. S.
Fairfield, R. M........	....	....		Sir Knight.
Fenner, William H....	April 15, 1862.	Calvary..........	" 13	Sword Bearer.
Gibbs, Howard A......	May —, 1871.	Springfield........		Sir Knight.
Grecian Lodge.........	Chart'd 1825.	....		
Hersey, Francis C. ...	June 10, 1867.	St. Omer		Junior Warden.
Hackett, Elisha L......	July 5, 1866.	Palestine..........	" 7	Treasurer.
Haigh, John..	Feb. 24, 1865.	Bethany		Em. Commander.
Hall, Clark Ford, M. D..	Sept. 29, 1870.	Berkshire..........		Recorder.
Hooper, Wallace Dupee.	April 7, 1873.	St. Omer		Sir Knight.
Hosea, Geo. Francis ...	June 2, 1869.	Wm. Parkman.....		Sword Bearer.
Kingman, Geo. Warren.	Feb. 15, 1869.	St. Omer		Captain-General.
Lewis, Winslow, M. D..	— —, 1833.	Boston		{ Grand Generalissimo } Grand Encp't U. S.
Longee, Stephen Noble.	Jan. 13, 1871.	Holy Sepulcher....		Sir Knight.
Longee, Jos. Merrill...	May 14, 1872.	Woonsocket.......		Captain-Guard.
Luther, John Pierce....	June 11, 1867.	Calvary..........	" 13	Em. Commander.
Magoon, Samuel A.....	June 4, 1872.	Haverhill.........		Sir Knight.
McLellan Chas. W.....	June 30, 1868.	St. Omer..........		Senior Warden.
Miller, Geo. Henry....	Aug. 13, 1872.	Woonsocket.......		Recorder.
Parker, Walter Ed.....	Aug. 12, 1869.	Woonsocket.......		Em. Commander.
Pierce, Chas. A	June 22, 1868.	Springfield		Sir Knight.
Pierce, Frederick A...	Mar. —, 1858.	De Molay..........		Recorder.
Phillips, Thomas.... ..	Oct. 3, 1865.	Calvary..........	" 13	Em. Commander.
Porter, James M......	Jan. 22, 1866.	Springfield........		Junior Warden.
Pease, Theodore D.....	Oct. 27, 1873.	Springfield........		Sir Knight.
Rawson, Henry M.....	Sept. 3, 1861.	Calvary..........	" 13	Recorder.
Robinson, Silas F.....	Jan. 27, 1869.	De Molay..........		Sir Knight.
Rockwood, W. De Luce.	Nov. 18, 1865.	St. Omer		Sentinel.
Rollins, Geo. D........	April 2, 1863.	Springfield..... ...		Sentinel.

NAME.	WHEN KNIGHTED.	COMMANDERY.	KNIGHTLY RANK.
Salmon, Wm. Francis..	Dec. 26, 1855.	Pilgrim............	Em. Commander.
Sanborn, Wm. H.......	Nov. 4, 1872.	St. Omer	Sir Knight.
Sanford, Jr., Baalis....	July 30, 1866.	Old Colony.......	Captain-General.
Saunders, Caleb.......	Oct. 13, 1864.	Bethany	Em. Commander.
Scoboria, Peter G......	May 17, 1871.	St. Omer..........	Sir Knight.
Seagrave, Daniel... ...	June 21, 1860.	Worcester Co......	Sir Knight.
Spuik, Joseph E.......	June —, 1870.	Calvary........... No.13	Captain-General.
Stevens,Francis,J.,M.D	—— —, 1858.	Haverhill..........	Senior Warden.
Stedman, Samuel M....	Aug. 26, 1867.	Bethany...........	Sir Knight.
Stoddard, Granville M..	Feb. 24, 1865.	Bethany...........	Generalissimo.
Thomas,Jr.,Zephania H	Mar. 21, 1860.	Boston............	Senior Warden.
Thompson, Alex. Y....	June —, 1861.	Worcester.........	Prelate.
Townsend, Geo. James.	June 10, 1871.	Natick............	Prelate.
Van Slyck, Nicholas...	....	Calvary...........	Grand Commander.
Waterhouse, Mark A...	June 3, 1872.	St. Omer	Sir Knight.
White, Wm. Roland....	Dec. 4, 1871.	Springfield........	Sir Knight.
Williams, Sylvester....	Mar. 16, 1868.	Springfield........	Sir Knight.
Weil, Louis............	July 28, 1868.	Bethany	Sir Knight.

MICHIGAN.

NAME.	WHEN KNIGHTED.	COMMANDERY.	KNIGHTLY RANK.
Allison, Henry E......	Nov. 24, 1868.	Pontiac........... No. 2	Treasurer.
Benedict, Edward D...	Feb. 27, 1857.	De Molai.......... " 5	Grand Commander.
Benedict, Chas. B.....	Sept. 23, 1864.	....	Sir Knight.
Chandler, Geo. W.....	Jan. —, 1869.	Lansing.......... " 25	Captain-General.
Chipman, Hobart H....	Mar. 26, 1872.	De Molai.......... " 5	Junior Warden.
Coe, Charles W.......	July —, 1869.	Fenton........... " 14	Warder.
Edwards, Wm. S......	Dec. 10, 1864.	Eureka........... " 3	Em. Commander.
Eimer, Frank.........	May 13, 1872.	Muskegon .... " 22	Recorder.
Fitzgerald, Jerome B..	Mar. 16, 1866.	Niles............. " 12	Generalissimo.
Fox, Perrin V.........	Mar. 11, 1870.	De Molai.......... " 5	Sir Knight.
Gaw, James...........	Aug. 12, 1873.	Muskegon. .... " 22	Sir Knight.
Gay, Charlie.........	Jan. —, 1867.	Pilgrim.......... " 23	Em. Commander.
Grant, Lewis.........	Jan. 19, 1871.	Monroe .... " 19	Recorder.
Green, Algernon M....	Aug. 25, 1871.	Pilgrim........... " 23	Captain-General.
Grisson, Chas. E......	Feb. 6, 1869.	St. John's........ " 24	Grand Junior Warden.
Haight, William F....	Feb. 13, 1873.	Monroe........... " 19	Warder.
Harvey, James, M. D..	Oct. —, 1869.	Romeo........... " 6	Em. Commander.
Hazeltine, Charles S...	April 16, 1868.	De Molai .... " 5	Sir Knight.
Henry. D. Farrand....	Dec. 21, 1866.	Detroit........... " 1	Sir Knight.
Hills, Charles T.......		Muskegon .... " 22	Em. Commander.
Hurd, George R.......	Feb. 20, 1868.	Monroe .... " 19	Em. Commander.
Innes, William P......	Jan. 5, 1855.	De Molai.......... " 5	Grand Commander.
La Bour, George W....	Sept. 7, 1872.	De Molai.......... " 5	Sir Knight.
Lane, John	Jan. 20. 1866.	Monroe .... " 19	Senior Warden.
Latimer, W. Irving....	Feb. 3, 1865.	Pilgrim.......... " 23	Em. Commander.
Lawrence, William S..	June 27, 1869.	Peninsular........ " 8	Generalissimo.
Look, Henry M.......	Aug. 29, 1866.	Pontiac........... " 2	Em. Commander.
Kellie, James C.......	Jan. 19, 1871.	Monroe........... " 19	Junior Warden.
King, Ephraim.......	June 10, 1872.	Muskegon .... " 22	Sir Knight.
Kitton, John C........	Oct. 3, 1869.	John Clark........ " 20	Recorder.
Kruger, Charles J.....	Mar. 29, 1862.	De Molai.......... " 5	Grand Captain-General.
McConnell, John......	Nov. 11, 1856.	De Molai.......... " 5	Recorder.
Mosser, John G.......	June —, 1873.	Pilgrim .... " 23	Sir Knight.
Munro, George C......	Jan. —, 1852	Eureka........... " 3	Em. Commander.
Mussey, George D.....	Jan. 7, 1873.	Romeo........... " 6	Recorder.
Nelson, Frederick E...	June 12, 1868.	Pilgrim........... " 23	Sentinel.
Noble, Garra B.......	Mar. 11, 1853.	Detroit........... " 1	Grand Commander.
Noble, Francis W.....	Mar. 11, 1853.	Detroit. .... " 1	Sir Knight.
Noble, H. Shaw......	—— —, 1867.	Monroe........... " 19	Em. Commander.
Nottingham, Calvin W.	Sept. 26, 1873.	Pilgrim .... " 23	Sir Knight.
O'Brien, Thomas J.....	....	De Molai.......... " 5	Sir Knight.
Papst, Rudolph.......	April 25, 1870.	Livingston........ " 27	Recorder.
Parker, Edward F.....	May 21, 1872.	Muskegon........ " 22	Sir Knight.
Perry, John..........	Mar. 25, 1872.	De Molai.......... " 5	Sir Knight.
Randall, Leonard H....	Feb. 10, 1865.	De Molai.......... " 5	Deputy Grand Commander.
Reed, Geo...........	July 15, 1873.	Muskegon......... " 22	Sir Knight.
Reiter, David H.......	Sept. —, 1873.	Niles............. " 12	Sir Knight.
Reynolds, Richard W..	June 3, 1873.	De Molai.......... " 5	Sir Knight.
Sheldon, Charles L....	Aug. —, 1869.	Fenton........... " 14	Sir Knight.
Saunders, Edwin......	Jan. 10, 1871.	St. Bernard....... " 16	Em. Commander.
Silver, Thomas M.....	Oct. 29, 1864.	Eureka............ " 3	Senior Warden.
Smith, Irving M........	Dec. 21, 1866.	St. Bernard........ " 16	{ Grand Senior Warden, Grand Encampment, U.S.

NAME.	WHEN KNIGHTED.	COMMANDERY.		KNIGHTLY RANK.
Smith, George	Feb. —, 1867.	Lexington	No. 27	Em. Commander.
Smith, Martin S	—, 1865.	Detroit	" 1	Grand Treasurer.
Spaulding, Oliver L	—, 1864.	St. John's	" 24	Grand Commander.
Spencer, Alva G	June 14, 1871.	Muskegon	" 22	Sir Knight.
Stearns, George F	June 12, 1868.	Pilgrim	" 23	Treasurer.
Sterling, Chas. Jewett	Mar. 27, 1868.	Niles	" 12	Recorder.
St. Clair, Eugene G	June —, 1873.	Marquette	" 30	Sir Knight.
Teal, W. E		Baldwin	" 2	Sir Knight.
Trump, Edwin	—, 1862.	Fenton	" 14	Recorder.
Voorhis, George	Dec. 7, 1861.	De Molai	" 5	Em. Commander.
Waters, Thomas J	June 22, 1869.	Muskegon	" 22	Captain-General.
Wagener, Samuel H	Jan. —, 1862.	Muskegon	" 22	Senior Warden.
Waltman, Joseph	Jan. 10, 1865.	Monroe	" 19	Generalissimo.
Warner, Jerome B	May 1, 1856.	Marshall	" 17	Sir Knight.
Whitney, George	April 29, 1873.	Muskegon	" 22	Sir Knight.
Wilson, Herman	July —, 1873.	Muskegon	" 22	Sir Knight.

MINNESOTA.

NAME.	WHEN KNIGHTED.	COMMANDERY.		KNIGHTLY RANK.
Ames, A. Elisha, M. D.	Jan. 9, 1855.	Zion	No. 2	Grand Commander.
Allen, Andrew	Sept. 13, 1873.	Lake City	" 6	Sir Knight.
Baldwin, Dwight M	Mar. 4, 1871.	Lake City	" 6	Grand Sword Bearer.
Brink, C. R	Mar. 6, 1872.	Lake City	" 6	Sir Knight.
Bronson, William G	Aug. 15, 1871.	Damascus	" 1	Sir Knight.
Carver, Henry L	—, 1864.	Damascus	" 1	Grand Commander.
Chapman, Charles A	—, 1864.	Mankato	" 4	Em. Commander.
Cooley, Geo. W	Aug. 5, 1871.	Zion	" 2	Junior Warden.
Durkee, William C	—, 1867.	Mankato	" 4	Em. Commander.
Eisenhand, William	Oct. 1, 1873.	Lake City	" 6	Sir Knight.
Friedrich, John M	Sept. 13, 1873.	Lake City	" 6	Sir Knight.
Hawkins, William E	Oct. 9, 1871.	Lake City	" 6	Sir Knight.
Herschler, Morris	Mar. 18, 1871.	Lake City	" 6	Sir Knight.
Hotchkiss, E. A	Dec. 2, 1872.	Mankato	" 4	Sir Knight.
Joss, Frederick	Sept. 19, 1866.	Damascus	" 1	Sir Knight.
Kreiger, Robert	Mar. —, 1870.	Lake City	" 6	Warder.
Mahler, Charles F	Jan. 3, 1865.	Damascus	" 1	Senior Warden.
McBride, John	April 21, 1870.	Lake City	" 6	Sir Knight.
Nash, Allen F	May 19, 1873.	Cœur-de-Lion	" 3	Sir Knight.
Richter, John M	Mar. 4, 1871.	Lake City	" 6	Guard.
Smith, Louis C	Mar. 18, 1871.	Lake City	" 6	Sir Knight.
Wiser, P. K	—, 1870.	Mankato	" 4	Sir Knight.
Williams, Wm. B	Mar. 6, 1872.	Lake City	" 6	Sir Knight.
Walker, William	Aug. 18, 1873.	Mankato	" 4	Sir Knight.

MISSISSIPPI.

NAME.	WHEN KNIGHTED.	COMMANDERY.		KNIGHTLY RANK.
Bahin, G. J	Aug. —, 1865.	Rosalie	No. 5	Grand Captain-General.
Becton, John E	July —, 1873.	St. Cyr	" 6	Sir Knight.
Brown, Jr., Wm. J	Aug. 1, 1871.	Mississippi	" 1	Treasurer.
Buck, John Thomas	April 1, 1870.	Mississippi	" 1	Deputy Grand Commander.
Blackmore, Thos. J	Feb. 3, 1871.	Winona	" 7	Recorder.
Carr, David	—, 1872.	Koscinsko	" 11	Senior Warden.
Clarke, Henry	—, 1857.	Rosalie	" 5	Em. Commander.
Coe, Marion N	April 22, 1869.	St. Cyr	" 6	Prelate.
Cornwell, L. S	—, 1856	"	" —	Sir Knight.
Comfort, Jas. Samuel	—, 1872.	Koscinsko	" 11	Warder.
De Lap, Enoch Geo	—, 1867.	Rosalie	" 5	Grand Commander.
Davis, John Bradford	—, 1872.	Koscinsko	" 11	Sir Knight.
Dicks, George I	—, 1870.	Rosalie	" 5	Sir Knight.
Dixon, Robert S	June —, 1869.	Rosalie	" 5	Generalissimo.
Duncan, Henry L	—, 1868.	St. Cyr	" 6	Recorder.
Fairchild, William A	June 25, 1866.	Magnolia	" 2	Em. Commander.
Fulson, John K	—, 1865.	St. Cyr	" 6	Grand Commander.
Guice, E. J	July —, 1873.	Rosalie	" 5	Sir Knight.
Henry, Edmund T	Jan. 16, 1868.	Magnolia	" 2	Grand Commander.
Hendricks, J. O	May 10, 1871.	St. Cyr	" 6	Recorder.
Holt, John S	—, 1859.	Rosalie	" 5	Generalissimo.
Hudspeth, John B	Mar. 22, 1873.	St. Cyr	" 6	Sir Knight.
Hussey, G. St. Clair, M.D.	Feb. 3, 1852.	Rosalie	" 5	Captain-General.
Jones, David W	Nov. 27, 1866.	Mississippi	" 1	Grand Prelate.
Keim, Charles Hy	Aug. —, 1871.	Rosalie	" 5	Junior Warden.
Kendrick, Ansel H	—, 1858.	Rosalie	" 5	Generalissimo.
King, J. Stebbins, M.D.	June —, 1869.	Rosalie	" 5	Recorder.

NAME.	WHEN KNIGHTED.	COMMANDERY.	KNIGHTLY RANK.
Lewis, J. McAdory, M.D.	—— —, 1872.	Kosciusko..........No. 11	Grand Warder.
Lucas, John Copeland..	—— —, 1872.	Kosciusko.......... " 11	Sir Knight.
Lord, Rev. William W.	—— —, 1854.	Magnolia .... " 2	Grand Prelate.
McConnico, Sam. B....	—— —, 1869.	St. Cyr............. " 6	Em. Commander.
McIlwaine, Chas. H....	June 19, 1872.	Rosalie............. " 5	Sir Knight.
Newman, William......	—— —, 1865.	Rosalie............. " 5	Grand Generalissimo.
O'Reilly, Hamilton E...	....	Magnolia.......... " 2	Senior Warden.
Patton, William S......	—— —, 1855.	Cyrene............. " 9	{ Grand Junior Warden, } Grand Encampment, U. S.
Palmore, W. F.........	Mch. —, 1873.		Sentinel.
Powell, John W........	July 25, 1866.	Magnolia........... " 2	Em. Commander.
Speed, Frederic.......	April —, 1873	Magnolia.......... " 2	Sir Knight.
Savory, Phineas M....	Jan. —, 1870.	Ivanhoe .... " 10	Deputy Grand Commander.
Smythe, Daniel L.. .	May 1, 1872.	Kosciusko.......... " 11	Grand Senior Warden.
Taylor, Jas. Nickson...	—— —, 1872.	Kosciusko.......... " 11	Sentinel.
Ure, John...........	Dec. 28, 1865.	Excalibar.......... " 5	Grand Commander.
Van Davis, Wm......	June —, 1872.	Kosciusko.......... " 11	Generalissimo.
Whitsey, Thos. Wm....	....	St. Cyr........... " 6	Em. Commander.
Walker, Nelson S... ..	April 24, 1873.	Cœur-de-Lion..... " 13	Treasurer.

MISSOURI.

NAME.	WHEN KNIGHTED.	COMMANDERY.	KNIGHTLY RANK.
Anderson, William W..	Oct. 13, 1869.	Cyrene............ No. 13	Grand Junior Warden.
Allen, James X	May 19, 1870.	Ivanhoe............ " 8	Sentinel.
Aldrich, H. L..........	Mar. 23, 1871.	Ivanhoe............ " 8	Sir Knight.
Brown, J. H..........	Aug. 21, 1871.	St. Louis.......... " 1	Standard Bearer.
Bockee, Jacob S......	Dec. 31, 1869.	Excalibar.......... " 5	Captain-General.
Callender, Wm. H.....	July 25, 1871.	St. Aldemar....... " 18	Recorder.
Chevalier, Edward Y...	April 22, 1869.	Excalibar.......... " 5	Standard Bearer.
Collins, George A	Aug. 30, 1868.	Excalibar.......... " 5	Sir Knight.
Dale, Wm. H.	Mar. 27, 1871.	St. Louis.......... " 1	Senior Warden.
Dougherty, W.W., M.D.	Nov. 27, 1865.	Liberty .... " 6	Em. Commander.
Fitz, John W..........	Nov. 29, 1869.	St. Louis.... ...... " 1	Guard.
Foote, Charles H......	—— —, 1868.	Excalibar.......... " 5	Sir Knight.
Fowler, Edwin........	Oct. 29, 1872.	St. Louis.......... " 1	Sir Knight.
Fetherston, Edward R..	Mar. 20, 1872.	Cœur-de-Lion..... " 14	Sir Knight.
Gouley, Geo. Frank....	—— —, 1857.	St. Louis.......... " 1	Grand Commander.
Gould, J. F	Aug. 28, 1871.	St. Louis.......... " 1	Sir Knight.
Grant, Peter B	Nov. 27, 1865.	Liberty .... " 6	Grand Standard Bearer.
Gutbrod, Otto J.......	Sept. 12, 1871.	St. Louis.......... " 1	Sir Knight.
Gould, George G......	Feb. 17, 18 6.	Excalibar.......... " 5	Recorder.
Hart, James M........	Nov. 9. 1871.	Ivanhoe............ " 8	Sir Knight.
Hunter, Dewitt C......	May 9, 1868.	O'Sullivan .... " 15	Em. Commander.
Hymers, Edward H. ...	Aug. 29, 1871.	St. Aldemar....... " 18	Recorder.
Kennedy, Peter........	Nov. 29, 1865.	St. Louis.... ..... " 1	Sir Knight.
Kerr, S. N	April 1, 1864.	St. Louis.......... " 1	Em. Commander.
Kline, Lewis E........	Aug. 16, 1873.	St. Aldemar....... " 18	Sir Knight.
Kidd, William R......	Mar. 20, 1865.	Excalibar .... " 5	Guard.
Kimlin, Thomas	May 9, 1872.	Cœur-de-Lion...... " 14	Sir Knight.
Lightburne, Alvan	Nov. 27, 1865.	Liberty .... " 6	Em. Commander.
Lee, William	May 5, 1870.	St. Louis.......... " 1	Sir Knight.
Loker, William N.....	May 7, 1856.	St. Louis.......... " 1	Grand Treasurer.
Morris, James M.....	April 12, 1868.	Excalibar .... " 5	Sir Knight.
McDonald, Donald M.. .	June 17, 1870.	Hugh de Payens ... " 4	Junior Warden.
Mullins, Alphonse D...	June —, 1873.	Cœur-de-Lion...... " 14	Sir Knight.
Nixon, Geo. H........	Oct. 3, 1870.	St. Louis.......... " 1	Recorder.
O'Connor, Daniel......	Nov. —, 1870.	Ascalon.......... .. " 16	Standard Bearer.
Pitts, William R.......	May 20, 1869.	Excalibar.......... " 5	Sword Bearer.
Payne, Walter S.......	Sept. 12, 1867.	St. Aldemar....... " 18	Em. Commander.
Powell, Hugo	Oct. 23, 1873.	Excalibar.......... " 5	Sir Knight.
Root, Jr., Oren.......	—— —, 1864.	St. Graal.......... " 12	Grand Commander.
Randolph, Chas. B.....	Feb. 11, 1869.	Ivanhoe............ " 8	Generalissimo.
Ready, Thomas C......	Mar. 29, 1873.	St. Louis .... " 1	Sir Knight.
Rhodus, Henry M.....	Jan. 20, 1868.	St. Louis .... " 1	Generalissimo.
Reister, Charles J......	Nov. 4, 1872.	St. Louis.......... " 1	Sir Knight.
Ro Bards, John L.....	Sept. 10, 1869.	Excalibar.......... " 5	Sir Knight.
Stone, William H......	June 16, 1856.	St. Louis.......... " 1	Grand Generalissimo.
Shepherd, John........	....	Emmanuel......... " 7	Em. Commander.
Silvester, Henry......	Oct. 22, 1866.	St. Aldemar....... " 18	Generalissimo.
Thomas, Dan'l Warren.	Mar. —, 1873.	Ivanhoe............ " 8	Sir Knight.
Throckmorton, Wm ...	April 29, 1872.	St. Louis.......... " 1	Sir Knight.
Tolman, James H......	Feb. 6, 1866.	Ascalon............ " 16	Senior Warden.
Ure, John............	Dec. 28, 1865.	Excalibar .... " 5	Em. Commander.
Wintle, Geo. B.........	Sept. 14, 1871.	Ivanhoe............ " 8	Guard.
Young, Nathaniel H....	Dec. —, 1871.	St. Louis........... " 1	Sir Knight.

NAME.	WHEN KNIGHTED.	COMMANDERY.	KNIGHTLY RANK.
NEBRASKA.			
Blake, John............	May 28, 1870.	Mount Carmel...... No. 3	Em. Commander.
Crist, Henry L.........	May 28, 1870	Mount Carmel...... " 3	Generalissimo.
Hill, William E.... ...	Jan. 3, 1867.	Mount Olivet ...... " 2	Deputy Grand Commander.
Hart, Henry Moore.....	May 28, 1870.	Mount Carmel...... " 3	Captain-General.
Long, Eben Knapp....	Mar. —, 1868.	Mount Calvary..... " 1	Em. Commander.
Moore, James W......	April 10, 1868.	Mount Olivet ...... " 2	Grand Junior Warden.
McFall, Andrew J.....	May 28, 1870.	Mount Carmel...... " 3	Senior Warden.
Oakley, Rolland H.....	Sept. 23, 1869.	Mount Moriah .... " 4	Grand Captain-General.
Rogers, Wm. Taylor....	June 16, 1873.	Mount Carmel...... " 3	Sir Knight.
Tuxbury, Albert.......	—— —, 1868.	Mount Olivet ...... " 2	Captain-General.
Wheeler, Daniel H.....	Feb. —, 1867.	Zion................ U. D.	Grand Captain-General.
NEVADA.			
Henley, M. James......	Dec. 13, 1872.	De Witt Clinton.... No. 1	Sir Knight.
NEW HAMPSHIRE.			
Baker, Royal F........	Feb. 19, 1873	Sullivan .... No. 6	Sir Knight.
Black, Charles S.... ...	Jan. —, 1868.	Hugh de Payens ... " 7	Sir Knight.
Brown, Edmund	Dec. 16. 1869.	North Star......... " 4	Sword Bearer.
Dudley, Charles E.....	Feb. 19, 1873.	Sullivan .... " 6	Sir Knight.
Edes, George C........	Feb. 19, 1873.	Sullivan .... " 6	Sir Knight.
Fellows, Joseph W....	Feb. 1, 1868.	Trinity............ " 1	Grand Commander.
Greene, Chauncey H....	Nov. 12, 1867.	St. Gerard .... " 9	Grand Senior Warden
Haskins, Wm. Arthur..	Aug. 8, 1870	St. Gerard .... " 9	Em. Commander.
Harris, John A.........	Dec. 10, 1860.	Mount Horeb...... " 3	Grand Recorder.
Hatch, Albert R........	—— —, 1843.	De Witt Clinton.... " 2	Grand Commander.
Howard, Alonzo D.....	Dec. 10, 1872.	Sullivan .... " 6	Sir Knight.
Kent, Edward B........	Sept. 6, 1866.	North Star......... " 4	Generalissimo.
Page, Samuel B........	July 26, 1869.	St. Gerard .... " 9	Grand Standard Bearer.
Rounsevel, Ashton W..	Feb. 19, 1873.	Sullivan........... " 6	Sir Knight.
Wait, Albert S.........	July 24, 1866.	Sullivan........... " 6	Generalissimo.
NEW JERSEY.			
Agens, Thomas........	....	Damascus.......... No. 5	Sir Knight.
Anderson, Abraham....	April 16, 1868.	Cyrene............. " 7	Sir Knight.
Battey, David S........	Sept. 7, 1864.	Damascus.......... " 5	Grand Generalissimo.
Bechtel, Charles	—— —, 1860.	Palestine .... " 4	Grand Commander.
Bensen, John W.......	June 26, 1871.	St. Omer.......... " 13	Warder.
Borden, Jerome B.....	—— —, 1853.	Cœur-de-Lion ...... " 8	Grand Commander.
Boylan, Lawrence......	Feb. 25, 1869.	Damascus.......... " 5	Sir Knight.
Buzby, Edwin S	April 2, 1869.	Ivanhoe........... " 11	Warder.
Burrows, Rev. Lansing.	Dec. —, 1869.	Ivanhoe........... " 11	Prelate.
Cutter, George E......	Aug. 20, 1867.	Hugh de Payens ... " 1	Recorder.
Camfield, Marcus J.....	May 13, 1869.	Damascus.......... " 5	Recorder.
Campbell, Edward A...	Nov. 22, 1866.	Damascus.......... " 5	Captain-General.
Cœur-de-Lion, No. 8..	April 2, 1868.		
Congdon, Jos. William.	—— —, 1866.	St. Omer.......... " 13	Grand Sword Bearer.
Corson, Thos. Johnson.	Oct. 12, 1859.	Palestine .... " 4	Grand Commander.
Chandler, Marcus	June 16, 1870.	Damascus...... .. " 5	Sword Bearer.
Clark, Jacob M........	Dec. 13, 1870.	St. John's .... " 9	Captain-General.
Clift, Edward	May 29, 1869.	Mt. Moriah........ " 11	Em. Commander.
Crosby, Geo. E........	May 26, 1870.	Damascus.......... " 5	Sir Knight.
Davis, Levi	Mar. 29, 1869.	Ivanhoe........... " 11	Em. Commander.
Denniston, Geo. Frank.	July 13, 1869.	St. John's......... " 9	Recorder.
Drohan, Martin M	June 1, 1869.	Hugh de Payens ... " 1	Em. Commander.
Goodwin, Wm. Wallace	April 25, 1856	Cyrene............. " 7	{ Grand Standard Bearer, Grand Encpt. U. S.
Grear, Leonard L......	May 13, 1872.	St. Omer.......... " 13	Standard Bearer.
Hutt, Jacob L..........	—— —, 1865.	Odo de St. Amand . " 12	Generalissimo.
Inslee, Ayers D........	... .	Cœur-de-Lion...... " 8	Sir Knight.
Lyford, Chas. H.......	July 18, 1871.	Olivet............. " 10	Sir Knight.
Newlin, John Williams.	Nov. 21, 1866.	Olivet............. " 10	Em. Commander.
Norwood, James F.. ..	Nov. 11, 1872.	St. Omer.......... " 13	Sir Knight.
Pruyn, Augustus.......	June —, 1868.	Damascus.... .... " 5	Em. Commander.
Parkinson, George H...	June 16, 1870.	Damascus......... " 5	Sir Knight.
Peck, James..........	May 27, 1869.	Damascus......... " 5	Sir Knight.
Prince, William V.....	April 30, 1872.	Olivet.. .... " 10	Sir Knight.

NAME.	WHEN KNIGHTED.	COMMANDERY.	KNIGHTLY RANK.
Royle, Vernon.........	Oct. 23, 1871.	St. Omer...........No. 13	Recorder.
Runyon, Albert L.....	Aug. 30, 1871.	Cœur-de-Lion...... " 8	Sir Knight.
Secor, Ambrose T.....	....	.... " —	Sir Knight.
Shawda, John A.......	Aug. 1, 1871.	Hugh de Payens... " 1	Sir Knight.
Shull, John G.........	Aug. 23, 1871.	Palestine........... " 4	Sir Knight
Smith, Rev. Marshall B.	Nov. 24, 1854.	St. Omer... ...... " 13	Prelate.
Smith, Joseph M......	Jan. —, 1866.	Damascus........... " 5	Sir Knight.
Snowden, Edward P...	April 25, 1872.	Damascus.......... " 5	Sir Knight.
Snow, Geo. W.........	Dec. 20, 1870.	Hugh de Payens ... " 1	Captain-General.
Storer, David A........	May 13, 1868.	Cœur-de-Lion..... " 8	Sword Bearer.
Vandervoort, R. W....	Dec. 6, 1866.	Damascus.......... " 5	Sir Knight.
Ward, Henry M.......	Sept. —, 1868.	Damascus.......... " 5	Sir Knight.
Wiese, Frederick G....	May 29, 1866.	Ivanhoe........... " 11	Grand Senior Warden.
Wilson, James L.......	July —, 1868.	Olivet.............. " 10	Sir Knight.

NEW YORK.

NAME.	WHEN KNIGHTED.	COMMANDERY.	KNIGHTLY RANK.
Aikman, Chas..........	Sept. 21, 1866.	De Witt Clinton...No. 27	Em. Commander.
Anthony, Jesse B......	Sept. 2, 1863.	Apollo .... " 15	Generalissimo.
Amos, Wm. Henry.....	Nov. 23, 1869.	Cyrene............ " 39	Sir Knight.
Anderson, William T..	——, 1866.	Ivanhoe.......... " 36	Sir Knight.
Babcock, George.......	April 17, 1857.	Apollo .... " 15	Grand Commander.
Babcock, Charles B....	Oct. 26, 1858.	Cœur-de-Lion...... " 23	Sword Bearer.
Bagley, Willis L........	July 22, 1872.	Delaware........... " 44	Sir Knight.
Baker, William H......	July 1, 1867.	Lake Erie.......... " 20	Junior Warden.
Baker, Jeremiah S.....	....	Morton .... " 4	Sir Knight.
Baker, George O.......	Oct. 31, 1867.	.... " —	Sir Knight.
Barnard, Harvey.......	May 29, 1857.	Utica............. " 3	Em. Commander.
Barnard, Charles E.....	Oct. 4, 1861.	Utica.............. " 3	Treasurer.
Bartlett, John S.......	—— —, 1865.	St. Omer.......... " 19	Generalissimo.
Beatty, Claudius F.....	Sept. 21, 1869.	Clinton .... " 14	Em. Commander.
Black, Robert.........	Dec. 19, 1865.	Clinton .... " 14	Grand Captain-General
Belloni, Jr., Louis J ..	—— —, 1870.	Cœur-de-Lion...... " 23	Sir Knight.
Bell, Walter T........	June 3, 1873.	Bethlehem. ...... " 53	Recorder.
Bernhard, W. H.......	Dec. 27, 1858.	Clinton .... " 14	Generalissimo.
Bilger, James M.......	Jan. —, 1865.	Cœur-de-Lion..... " 23	Generalissimo.
Bowen, Goodrich J...	Mar. 29, 1869.	Lake Erie.......... " 20	Recorder.
Button, Thomas.......	Feb. 25, 1868.	Cyrene........... " 39	Guard.
Branch, Charles T.....	July 19, 1869.	Delaware .... " 44	Recorder.
Briggs, John.........	May 18, 1863.	Lake Erie.......... " 20	Prelate.
Bunnell, Bellostee....	Jan. 7, 1853.	Genesee .... " 10	Senior Warden.
Case, Jr., Franklin B..	June 12, 1872.	Manhattan......... " 31	Em. Commander.
Case, Whitney A.......	Nov. 26, 1864.	Lake Erie.......... " 20	Sir Knight.
Casler, Richard W....	Mar. 14, 1873.	Little Falls........ " 26	Sir Knight.
Chatman, James W....	Sept. —, 1867.	Hugh de Payens... " 30	Recorder.
Chittenden, Thomas C.	June 29, 1966.	Watertown........ " 11	Grand Sword Bearer.
Coburn, John W......	July —, 1872.	Bethlehem........ " 53	Sir Knight.
Cobb, Jr., Lyman......	May 20, 1867.	Yonkers .... " 47	Em. Commander.
Colton, Aaron.........	—— —, 1864.	Lafayette .... " 7	Em. Commander.
Conover, John T......	—— —, 1865.	Cœur-de-Lion..... " 23	Em. Commander.
Cook, George E........	June 24, 1872.	Delaware.......... " 44	Sir Knight.
Cowles, Daniel F......	Jan. 27, 1871.	Holy Cross... ..... " 51	Generalissimo.
Cowan, Stafford H	Sept. —, 1873.	Bethlehem......... " 53	Sir Knight.
Craig, Charles.	Sept. 23, 1853.	Genesee............ " 10	Em. Commander.
Crawford, George R...	June —, 1870.	Bethlehem......... " 53	Generalissimo.
Crandall, Merritt.......	May 6, 1859.	Genesee........... " 10	Sir Knight.
Crosier, George W	Feb. 1, 1869.	Lake Erie.......... " 20	Sir Knight.
Curtis, George D......	Oct. 18, 1870.	Clinton .... " 14	Generalissimo.
Cushing, M. D........	June —, 1867.	Dunkirk .... " 40	Recorder.
Davison, Chas. L......	Nov. 29, 1872.	St. Omer. .. .. " 19	Recorder.
Deal, John M.........	Mar. 12, 1859.	Apollo........ ... " 15	Sir Knight.
De Land, Levi Justus..	May 7, 1873.	Zenobia........... " 41	Sir Knight.
Douglas, Van Ness.....	Feb. 7, 1873.	Genesee........ .. ... " 10	Warder.
Donaldson, Frank J....	Dec. —, 1873.	Clinton .... " 14	Sir Knight.
Edgar, William Bell....	May 24, 1869.	Yonkers .... " 47	Treasurer.
Evry, Stephen M......	Jan. 30, 1865.	Lake Erie.......... " 20	Recorder.
Fondey, Townsend	Mar. 20, 1857.	Temple............ " 2	Grand Senior Warden.
Flagler, Benjamin	....	Genesee............ " 10	Senior Warden.
Field, William P......	Sept. 18, 1866.	Genesee.......... " 10	Standard Bearer.
Fox, Christopher G....	Oct. 19, 1857.	Hugh de Payens.... " 30	Grand Senior Warden.
Gardner, Geo. Judd....	Jan. 21, 1857.	Central City...... " 25	Recorder.
Gardner, Rowland W..	—— —, 1867.	Dunkirk .... " 40	Sir Knight.
Gardner, Robert P.....	Dec. 26, 1865.	Hugh de Payens ... " 30	Junior Warden.
Gray, Charles B........	....	Delaware .... " 44	Em. Commander.

NAME.	WHEN KNIGHTED.	COMMANDERY.		KNIGHTLY RANK.
Griswold, Frank H.....	Sept. 7, 1866.	Salem Town ......No. 16		Em. Commander.
Gugel, Jr., Frederick...	May 3, 1867.	Ivanhoe............ " 36		Em. Commander.
Graham, James M.....	Feb. 18, 1867.	Lake Erie.......... " 20		Sir Knight.
Goodall, Alb. Gallatin.	Dec. 19, 1856.	Morton .... " 4		Em. Commander.
Hamlin, John........	May 16, 1841.	Poughkeepsie...... " 43		Em. Commander.
Hanour, Peter J.......	April 3, 1871.	Lake Erie .... " 20		Guard.
Harrington, Geo. S....	Mar. 15, 1872.	Genesee .... " 10		Guard.
Hare, Noah W........	Mar. —, 1863.	Zenobia............ " 41		Sir Knight.
Harvey, Henry B.....	April 28, 1863.	Apollo............. " 15		Em. Commander.
Harris, Thos. Bird.....	April 4, 1854.	Genesee............ " 10		Dep. Grand Commander.
Henion, James Z......	Mar. 11, 1873.	Genesee............ " 10		Sir Knight.
Heineman, John C....	Oct. 28, 1867.	Clinton ... . " 14		Captain-General.
Hill, John T.........	June 20, 1873.	St. Omer.......... " 19		Sir Knight.
Hill, Frederick C.....	Aug. 1, 1859.	Lake Erie.......... " 20		Warder.
Hine, Omar A........	Jan. 10, 1868.	St. Lawrence...... " 28		Em. Commander.
Hodge, John.........	June 18, 1869.	Genesee............ " 10		Sir Knight.
Holley, Byron.......	July 16, 1872.	Cyrene............. " 39		Generalissimo.
Hooper, Rev. Mont. R.	Nov. 14, 1870.	Yonkers............ " 47		Sir Knight.
Hoole, John.........	....	York.............. " 54		Em. Commander.
Howell, Sidney O......	May 6, 1873.	Delaware .... " 44		Sir Knight.
Hoyer, F. F........	Nov. 2, 1857.	Lake Erie.......... " 20		Sir Knight.
Hungerford, Thos. A..	June 21, 1870.	Cyrene............. " 39		Sir Knight.
Helliwell, T. B.......	Dec. 27, 1872.	Apollo............. " 15		Sir Knight.
Inglis, James........	Feb. —, 1853.	Hugh de Payens ... " 30		Recorder.
Ives, Rev. Angus M...	Nov. 14, 1870.	Yonkers............ " 47		Prelate.
Johnson, John Z......	Nov. 15, 1870.	De Witt Clinton... " 27		Junior Warden.
Jones, E. Darwin	Feb. 19, 1869.	Temple .... " 2		Sir Knight.
Knight, James........	Dec. 19, 1870.	Lake Erie.......... " 20		Sir Knight.
Klein, Hawley.......	May 30, 1864.	Lake Erie.......... " 20		Em. Commander.
Latimore, Thomas C...	Dec. 1, 1865.	Utica .... " 3		Recorder.
Little, John M. H.....	July 10, 1871.	Delaware .... " 44		Sir Knight.
Lytle, A. Eugene......	Oct. 24, 1862.	Salem Town ...... " 16		Dep. Grand Commander.
Lounsberry, Allen O...	....	.... " —		Sir Knight.
La Roche, C. P. T.....	Dec. 20, 1867.	Genesee .... " 10		Em. Commander.
Macoy, Robert......	Mar. —, 1850.	Morton .... " 4		Grand Recorder.
McNall, Thos. J	Mar. 17, 1871.	Genesee .. .. " 10		Sir Knight.
McCue, John	July 10, 1868.	Genesee .... " 10		Sir Knight.
Murray, Jacob H......	May 11, 1868.	Ivanhoe............ " 36		Sentinel.
Magill, James W......	May 21, 1869.	Little Falls........ " 26		Recorder.
McCredie, James......	Jan. 12, 1854.	Lake Erie.......... " 20		Grand Junior Warden.
McDowell, Simon V...	Feb. 26, 1869.	Monroe .... " 12		Generalissimo.
McNish, David B.....	July 7, 1873.	Lake Erie.......... " 20		Sir Knight.
McWilliams, John J...	....	Hugh de Payens ... " 30		Sir Knight.
Meech, Henry L.......	Aug. 13, 1866.	Lake Erie.......... " 20		Sir Knight.
Mimne, Marshall A....	Nov. 22, 1869.	.... " —		Sir Knight.
Moller, Wm. Francis...	....	Cœur-de-Lion...... " 23		Captain-General.
Mooney, Philetus De...	Feb. 20, 1872.	Zenobia............ " 41		Sir Knight.
Mott, Abraham C.....	Sept. 17, 1869.	Yonkers .... " 47		Recorder.
Morgan, Darwin E....	Sept. 9, 1859.	Hugh de Payens ... " 30		Generalissimo.
Moriarty, Albert P....	April —, 1851.	Morton............. " 4		Recorder.
Moses, William.......	Jan. 21, 1867.	Lake Erie.......... " 20		Standard Bearer.
Nelson, Charles H.....	Jan. 17, 1873.	Rome .... " 45		Sir Knight.
Newcomb, John G.....	Nov. 15, 1870.	Clinton ... . " 14		Guard.
Newell, Myron S......	Dec. 19, 1873.	Genesee............ " 10		Sir Knight.
Nolan, John D.......	July 2, 1872.	Clinton .... " 14		Sir Knight.
Oakley, George W.....	— —, 1865.	Hugh de Payens ... " 30		Sir Knight.
Penfield, Hiram L......	....	Genesee .... " 10		Sir Knight.
Penfield, George W....	June 20, 1873.	Genesee .... " 10		Sir Knight.
Parker, James B.......	Sept. 26, 1873.	Genesee .... " 10		Sir Knight.
Rassiga, August......	Sept. 19, 1873.	Ivanhoe............ " 36		Sir Knight.
Ratcliff, F...........	Dec. 9, 1864.	Apollo.......... ... " 15		Sir Knight.
Rockwood, Ebenezer A.	— —, 1868.	Hugh de Payens ... " 30		Sword Bearer.
Reilly, John M........	April —, 1854.	Clinton .... " 14		Sir Knight.
Roome, Charles.......	Nov. 23, 1866.	Cœur-de-Lion .... " 23		Grand Generalissimo.
Runcie, John T.......	Feb. 1, 1870.	DeWitt Clinton... " 27		Sir Knight.
Rouse, H. R..........	Mar. 24, 1871.	Cortland........... " 50		Recorder.
Rakes, Charles.......	May 3, 1864.	Genesee............ " 10		Sword Bearer.
Raymond, W. C., M.D.	Sept. 1, 1865.	Genesee............ " 10		Generalissimo.
Rankins, Richard M....	Dec. 24, 1873.	Little Falls. .... " 26		Sir Knight.
Sage, W. Lincoln.....	— —, 1870.	Monroe .... " 12		Junior Warden.
Sease, Samuel A......	— —, 1870.	Delaware.......... " 44		Sir Knight.
Seacord, Edward M....	June 13, 1870.	Cortland........... " 50		Generalissimo.
Seymour, T. J........	July 8, 1873.	Delaware .... " 44		Sir Knight.
Shaler, M. F..........	Jan. 6, 1853.	Lake Erie.......... " 20		Guard.
Shacklady, Christ. Wm.	May 25, 1866.	Apollo............. " 15		Sir Knight.

NAME.	WHEN KNIGHTED.	COMMANDERY.	KNIGHTLY RANK.
Shelley, Wm. W........	Oct. 23, 1865.	Hugh de Payens...No. 30	Sir Knight.
Shoemaker, Charles H.	Mar. 4, 1873.	Little Falls .... " 26	Sir Knight.
Sickels, Daniel........	— —, 1849.	Palestine .... " 18	Em. Commander.
Simons, John W.......	— —, 1849.	Clinton .... " 14	} Grand Master Gr. Encpt. New York.
Stephens, Robert.....	— —, 1865.	Manhattan......... " 31	Em. Commander.
Stewart, Cyrus........	Jan. 27, 1871.	Holy Cross......... " 51	Em. Commander.
Stebbins, Asa D......	Feb. 7, 1873.	Genesee .... " 10	Sir Knight.
Stone, Rev. Ward., M.D.	Aug. 25, 1873.	Hugh de Payens ... " 30	Sir Knight.
Stone, Elonzo N.......	Jan. 8, 1866.	Batavia .... " 34	Generalissimo.
Sy, Charles W........	May 10, 1861.	Cœur-de-Lion...... " 23	Recorder.
Smart, Joseph W.....	Sept. 27, 1872.	Apollo............. " 15	Sir Knight.
Spencer, Burral, Jr....	Nov. 5, 1866.	Lake Erie......... " 20	Guard.
Southwick, Geo. Wm..	May —, 1867.	Manhattan......... " 31	Grand Standard Bearer.
Seymour, Joseph.......	— —, 1853.	Central City ...... " 25	Sir Knight.
Tanner, John R.........	Jan. 24, 1873.	Rome............. " 45	Sir Knight.
Teson, Charles........	April 22, 1864.	Apollo............. " 15	Sentinel.
Thielen, Mathew.......	Aug. 21, 1871.	Lake Erie......... " 20	Warder.
Thom, William........	Jan. 24, 1873.	Little Falls .... " 26	Junior Warden.
Thomas, R. H.........	for Kane	Lodge Library......	
Torrance, George A....	Jan. 1, 1869.	Genesee .... " 10	Captain-General.
Underhill, Jno. Torboss	Nov. 25, 1872.	Bethlehem......... " 53	Sword Bearer.
Van Orden, Edwin S...	June 16, 1868.	Clinton .... " 14	Recorder.
Voke, Edmund........	July 10, 1868.	Genesee........... " 10	Sword Bearer.
Wade, Franklin A......	April 29, 1868.	Lake Erie......... " 20	Sir Knight.
Wadhams, Boyd A.....	Oct. 19, 1869.	Clinton .... " 14	Sir Knight.
Warren, George L ...	— —, 1867.	Cortland .... " 50	Em. Commander.
Webster, Rev. John G..	— —, 1860.	Zenobia........... " 41	Grand Prelate.
Welch, Orrin........	Aug. 9, 1855.	Central City...... " 25	Grand Commander.
Wells, Frank.........	— —, 1873.	Crusader.......... " 56	Sir Knight.
Williams, John D.....	Feb. 26, 1868.	St. Omer.......... " 19	Em. Commander.
Williams, Rees G	May 3, 1861.	Utica............. " 3	Sir Knight.
Wiltsie, G. Fred......	Jan. —, 1862.	Hudson River...... " 35	Grand Warder.
Wheeler, Avery G.....	July 20, 1866.	Salem Town....... " 16	Recorder.
Whitmore, George.....	Jan. 3, 1868.	St. Omer.......... " 19	Standard Bearer.
Wood, Richard........	Sept. 26, 1872.	Apollo .... " 15	Sir Knight.
Worthington, Chas. G..	Dec. 23, 1872.	Hugh de Payens... " 30	Sir Knight.
Walter, Peter D	May 6, 1868.	Genesee .... " 10	Treasurer.

OHIO.

NAME.	WHEN KNIGHTED.	COMMANDERY.	KNIGHTLY RANK.
Ammel, Charles S......	Sept. —, 1871.	Mt. Vernon........ No. 1	Senior Warden.
Arrick, Charles H.....	July 10, 1871.	Hope.............. " 26	Treasurer.
Bailey, Francis D.....	July 7, 1867.	Hope.............. " 26	Captain-General.
Baxter, Jr., Sam. A ...	Dec. 13, 1871.	Shawnee.......... " 14	Junior Warden.
Bolon, William L......	July 10, 1871.	Hope.............. " 26	Sword Bearer.
Bumgarner, Harvey R..	July 6, 1867.	Hope.............. " 26	Sir Knight.
Burdick, Leander	Feb. 1, 1861.	Toledo............ " 7	Grand Junior Warden.
Buzick, Ira	Mar. 9, 1871.	Mt. Vernon........ " 1	Sir Knight.
Carson, E. T	Sept. —, 1847.	Cincinnati......... " 3	Grand Commander.
Carroll, Chandler W....	June 12, 1871.	Hope .... " 26	Captain-General.
Coleman, Horace, M. D.	Nov. 26, 1847.	Coleman........... " 17	Generalissimo,
Corzilius, Philip W ...	May 23, 1872.	Mt. Vernon........ " 1	Junior Warden.
Dungan, Le Roy S.....	Aug. 29, 1873.	Mt. Vernon........ " 1	Sir Knight.
Foerster, George.......	Jan. 10, 1871.	Cyrus .... " 10	Warder.
Glasgow, D. E........	Nov. 13, 1871.	Hope .... " 26	Sword Bearer.
Haynes, Harry........	Mar. 31, 1871.	Toledo............ " 7	Sword Bearer.
Hardin, Hugh.........	Dec. 13, 1859.	Shawnee.......... " 14	Sir Knight.
Jarvis, Kent...........	Dec. 25, 1845.	Massillon........... " 4	} Grand Generalissimo. Grand Encp't U. S.
Johns, Elias H........	Nov. 10, 1868.	Shawnee.......... " 14	Captain-General.
Jones, Edward J.......	Oct. —, 1869.	Mt. Vernon........ " 1	Sword Bearer.
Jones, Nathan........	May 20, 1871.	Crestline.......... " 21	Recorder.
Kauffelt, N. J. D.......	Feb. 3, 1870.	Mt. Vernon........ " 1	Sir Knight.
Kile, Samuel E........	Sept. —, 1869.	Mt. Vernon........ " 1	Warder.
Lamprecht, Wm. H....	May 7, 1873.	Crestline........... " 21	Sir Knight.
Levering, Allen.......	Oct. 19, 1870.	Crestline.......... " 21	Standard Bearer.
McKinney, Arthur L...	Feb. 22, 1867.	Coleman .... " 17	Captain-General.
Nesbitt, James........	Jan. 19, 1853.	Coleman .... " 17	Grand Recorder.
Prugh, Augustus A.....	Nov. 16, 1865.	Mt. Vernon........ " 1	Sir Knight.
Romejs, Jacob..... ...	April 21, 1871.	Toledo............ " 7	Sir Knight.
Rowland, George H....	Oct. 12, 1865.	Mt. Vernon........ " 1	Standard Bearer.
Ryan, James B........	July 10, 1871.	Hope.... .... " 26	Senior Warden.
Schabet, John A.......	— —, 1864.	Crestline.......... " 21	Sir Knight.

NAME.	WHEN KNIGHTED.	COMMANDERY.	KNIGHTLY RANK.
Schnetzler, H. Marcus.	May 28, 1869.	Toledo............ No. 7	Sir Knight.
Schimpff, Charles......	Nov. 29, 1870.	Shawnee........... " 14	Sir Knight.
Senter, Orestes A. B...	April 19, 1866.	Mt. Vernon........ " 1	Recorder.
Smith, John E.........	Aug. —, 1870.	Crestline........... " 21	Generalissimo.
Snyder, Daniel.........	Dec. 13, 1859.	Shawnee........... " 14	Standard Bearer.
Sutor, J. Hope.........	Oct. 22, 1872.	Cyrus .... " 10	Recorder.
Sharp, John Henry....	June 28, 1866.	Mt. Vernon........ " 1	Standard Bearer.
Toortillott, G. R......	Jan. 14, 1867.	Toledo............. " 7	Standard Bearer.
Vail, John Davis......	June 9, 1873.	Hope .... " 26	Sir Knight.
Van Cleve, La Fayette.	Nov. —, 1862.	Reed .... " 6	Grand Prelate.
Williams, Henry H....	Jan. 17, 1870.	Coleman........... " 17	Recorder.
Walker, Wm. Thomas.	Feb. 9, 1872.	Toledo............. " 7	Sir Knight.
Watson, Algeraus C.. .	Aug. 29, 1873.	Mt. Vernon .... " 1	Sir Knight.

PENNSYLVANIA.

NAME.	WHEN KNIGHTED.	COMMANDERY.	KNIGHTLY RANK.
Allen, William H	—— —, 1853.	St. John's.......... No. 4	Grand Commander.
Allen, William W.....	April 28, 1868.	St. Alban........... " 47	Em. Commander.
Anthony, William H...	Mar. 16, 1871.	Freck............. " 39	Captain-General.
Auble, Hampton.......	Jan. 4, 1872.	St. John's.......... " 4	Sir Knight.
Burns, Chas. Carroll.,..	Mar. 31, 1869.	St. John's.......... " 4	Recorder.
Bunn, Horace F.......	Dec. 14, 1869.	St. Alban.......... " 47	Captain-General.
Burbank, Andrew J...	Nov. 23, 1871.	Franklin........... " 44	Treasurer.
Borhek, John G.......	Mar. 30, 1873.	St. John's.......... " 4	Guard.
Boner, Henry Smith ...	Feb. 22, 1870.	Freck............. " 39	Em. Commander.
Church, Henry........	Jan. 25, 1870.	North Western.... " 25	Sir Knight.
Curtis, John W........	June —, 1873.	St. Alban.......... " 47	Junior Warden.
Darling. Horace M.....	—— —, 1869.	Ivanhoe........... " 31	Sir Knight.
Derby, Charles F......	Oct. 4, 1872.	Dieu Le Veut...... " 45	Sir Knight.
Dick, John............	May 11, 1871.	North Western...... " 25	Sir Knight.
Egle, William H.......	Dec. 28, 1855.	Pilgrim............. " 11	Grand Junior Warden.
Elton, Joseph H.......	Nov. 12, 1869.	Alleghany .... " 35	Captain-General.
Ellis, Warale.........	Sept. —, 1872.	St. John's.......... " 4	Sir Knight.
Estep, David P........	Dec. 11, 1866.	Pittsburg .... " 1	Em. Commander.
Fisher, John Jacob....	Sept. 12, 1867.	Talbot.... .... " 43	Em. Commander.
Foster, Francis H.....	May 31, 1866.	North Western...... " 25	Generalissimo.
Freck. Jos. Mathias....	Sept. 12, 1867.	Freck............. " 39	Treasurer.
Gahlenbeck, August...	Mar. 24, 1871.	St. John's.......... " 4	Sir Knight.
Gilbough, James M..:.	May 24, 1867.	St. Alban.......... " 47	Sir Knight.
Griffing, Geo. H.......	June 4, 1869.	St. John's.......... " 4	Sir Knight.
Grant, David Denison..	Feb. 25, 1873.	Franklin........... " 44	Recorder.
Gulick, Henry	—— —.1871.	Freck............. " 39	Sir Knight.
Grand Lodge Library...	Pennsylvania		
Hanold, John.........	Feb. 1, 1856.	Kadosh............ " 29	Em. Commander.
Helfrich, Geo. Henry..	Jan. 26, 1866.	Freck............. " 39	Recorder.
Harkness, Thos. C.....	—— —, 1867.	Dieu Le Veut...... " 45	Generalissimo.
Harper, Samuel.......	Dec. 22, 1871.	Tancred........... " 48	Captain-General.
Hawkins, Warren E...	Jan. 24, 1872.	Franklin........... " 44	Sir Knight.
Hipple, Torrence C....	....	Hospitaler.......... " 46	Em. Commander.
Hoffman, Theodore F..	May 23, 1872.	Freck............. " 39	Warder.
Hollinshead, Forman P.	Mar. 28, 1860.	St. John's.......... " 4	Sir Knight.
Hoyt, Franklin	Mar. 24, 1871.	St. John's... ...... " 4	Sir Knight.
Kauffman, Andrew J...	Jan. 29, 1864.	Cyrene........... " 34	Grand Captain-General.
King, Jr., Robert P....	Mar. 31, 1867.	St. John's....... .. " 4	Sir Knight.
Kirkendall, Ira M.....	Jan. 19, 1872.	Dieu Le Veut...... " 45	Sir Knight.
Kline, James N........	May 21, 1872.	Baldwin........... " 22	Sir Knight.
Knight, Richard.......	Aug. 28, 1873.	Freck............. " 39	Sir Knight.
Knipe, Frank C.......	May 31, 1866.	St. John's.......... " 4	Sir Knight.
Kramer, Elisha........	April 28, 1873.	Freck............. " 39	Sir Knight.
Kreamer, George W....	May 27, 1870.	St. John's.......... " 4	Sir Knight.
Lee, R. Lloyd.........	Jan. 26, 1869.	St. Alban.......... " 47	Em. Commander.
Macferran, William K..	Sept. 30, 1870.	St. John's.......... " 4	Sir Knight.
Master, William.......	May 23, 1873.	Dieu Le Veut...... " 45	Sir Knight.
Mann, Jos. Farron.....	July 3, 1867.	Lewistown........ " 26	Em. Commander.
Miller, George H......	May 23, 1872.	Freck............. " 39	Sword Bearer.
Millant, Dr. Warren R.	May 27, 1873.	St. Alban.......... " 47	Sir Knight.
Mitchell, Jas. S........	Aug. 26, 1873.	St. Alban.......... " 47	Sir Knight.
McNaughton, Wm. J..	Feb. 26, 1869.	St. John's......... . " 4	Sir Knight.
Meyer, Chas. Eugene..	....	Mary............. " 36	Grand Recorder.
Needham, Warren......	Mar. —, 1873.	North Western.... " 25	Sir Knight.
Nisley, Joseph H.......	May 6, 1869.	Pilgrim........... " 11	Captain-General.
Oellers, Richard G.....	June 5, 1871.	St. Alban.......... " 47	Sir Knight.
Pratt, Joseph T.......	June 6, 1870.	St. Alban.......... " 47	Generalissimo.
Prindle, Franklin C....	April 22, 1873.	St. Alban.......... " 47	Sir Knight.

NAME.	WHEN KNIGHTED.	COMMANDERY.		KNIGHTLY RANK.
Read, Chas. Tallman...	Oct. 24, 1856.	St. John's..........	No. 4	Sir Knight.
Read, Wm. Pratt, M.D.	June 27, 1873.	St. John's.........	" 4	Sir Knight.
Reichard, Henry C.....	May 31, 1872.	Dieu Le Veut......	" 45	Sir Knight.
Rhodes, Jr., Chas. C...	Feb. 25, 1873.	St. Alban..........	" 47	Sir Knight.
Riebenack, Max........	Nov. 30, 1870.	St. John's.........	" 4	Sir Knight.;
Rinedollar, Durbin....	June 3, 1869.	St. John's.........	" 4	Sir Knight.
Ritter, Albert	May 10, 1870.	De Molay........	" 9	Generalissimo.
Rodgers, John S........	Mar. 31, 1869.	St. John's.........	" 4	Sir Knight.
Ross, P. Richard.......	Sept. 21, 1870.	Cœur-de-Lion......	" 17	Sir Knight.
Ryan, Simeon Powers..	May 23, 1872.	Freck............	" 39	Junior Warden.
Schenck, Rev. A. V. C..	—— —, 1855.	St. Alban..........	" 47	Prelate.
Shaw, Matthew T.....	Mar. 28, 1872.	Freck	" 39	Sir Knight.
Shidle, Geter Crosby...	May 13, 1862.	Pittsburgh.........	" 1	Grand Commander.
Shiffert, Daniel A......	April 28, 1873.	Freck............	" 39	Sir Knight.
Shive, M.D., Peter C...	July 18, 1873.	Dieu Le Veut......	" 45	Sir Knight.
Simonds, Joseph H....	Oct. 24, 1871.	Franklin..........	" 44	Sir Knight.
Smart, Thomas H......	Oct. 23, 1870.	St. John's.........	" 4	Sir Knight.
Smull, John Augustus.	May 13, 1864.	Pilgrim............	" 11	Grand Standard Bearer.
Stewart, David W. S...	Mar. 31, 1869.	St. John's.........	" 4	Sir Knight.
Stowell, Calvin L.....	May 25, 1869.	Crusade..........	" 12	Em. Commander.
Thickins, William.....	May 23, 1872.	Freck............	" 39	Standard Bearer.
Thompson, Francis W..	April 22, 1873.	Franklin..........	" 44	Sir Knight.
Turner, Edmund H ...	June 10, 1857.	Mountain	" 10	Grand Commander.
Uberroth, A. Geo......	April 29, 1871.	St. John's.........	" 4	Sir Knight.
Vaughan, Robert H....	Mar. 31, 1869.	St. John's.........	" 4	Em. Commander.
Von-Olhausen, J. H...	May 23, 1872.	Freck............	" 39	Sir Knight.
Wadsworth, Jno. J.....	Oct. 30, 1867.	Mt. Olivet.........	" 30	Em. Commander.
Wells, Richard D......	Jan. 28, 1869.	St. Alban..........	" 47	Sir Knight.
Wells, Charles L.......	May 28, 1868.	St. Alban..........	" 47	Senior Warden.
Welsh, Stacy..	May 28, 1872.	St. Alban..........	" 47	Sir Knight.
Whitman, Edward G...	Nov. —, 1869.	St. John's.........	" 4	Sir Knight.;
Wightman, Thos. T ...	Mar. 17, 1873.	Tancred..........	" 48	Sir Knight.
Wöltjen, Charles H.....	Charter Mem.	Constantine.......	" 41	Generalissimo.
Wooley, James........	Aug. 28, 1873.	Freck	" 39	Sir Knight.
Wyckoff, Edward S....	Nov. 15, 1867.	St. John's.........	" 4	Sir Knight.
Young, John L........	Nov. 25, 1859.	Mary..............	" 36	Grand Warder.

TENNESSEE.

NAME.	WHEN KNIGHTED.	COMMANDERY.		KNIGHTLY RANK.
Anderson, Joseph R....	Sept. —, 1862.	Johnson Encampment....		Generalissimo.
Bell, George H........	Nov. —, 1867.	Cyrene.............No. 4		Junior Warden.
Pope, Gustavus A......	—— —, 1867.	Pulaski	" 12	Em. Commander.
Porter, George Camp...	July —, 1867.	Brownsville........	" 5	Em. Commander.
Spurgin, Bruce D......	Aug. 31, 1873.	Johnson Encampment....		Senior Warden.
Towler, Joseph M......	—— —, 1853.	De Molay.........No. 3		Grand Commander.
Warren, Eli A..........	May 3, 1873.	Johnson Encampment....		Junior Warden.

TEXAS.

NAME.	WHEN KNIGHTED.	COMMANDERY.		KNIGHTLY RANK.
Austin, Francis.......	—— —, 1868.	Dallas..............	No. 6	Generalissimo.
Allen, Charles C.......	—— —, 1871.	Colorado.	" 4	Sir Knight.
Brewster, Robert	June 11, 1848.	Ruthven...........	" 2	Em. Commander.
Bramlette, William ...	Sept. —, 1855.	Paris.............	" 9	Em. Commander.
Bingham, Chas. Ogden.	....	San Felippe de Austin	1	Warder.
Bower, Ed. G	....	Dallas..............	" 6	Grand Captain-General.
Bunger, W. G........	Oct. 12, 1869.	Ivanhoe...........	" 8	Junior Warden.
Burnham, R. E........	July 9. 1873.	Waco	" 10	Sir Knight.
Bird, Frank R........	Aug. 7, 1872.	Waco	" 10	Senior Warden.
Cheatham, James H...	July 20, 1871.	Paris..............	" 9	Guard.
Clement, Henry A.....	July 20, 1871.	Paris..............	" 9	Sir Knight.
Crist, Jacob...........	....	Palestine..........	" 3	Sword Bearer.
Drew, O. C...........	Nov. 21, 1869.	Ruthven...........	" 2	Captain-General.
Eley, Charles Norman..	Feb. 11, 1869.	San Felippe de Austin	1	Sir Knight.
Elgin, John E.........	Aug. 8, 1872.	Waco	" 10	Prelate.
Fulton, J. W..........	Aug. 28, 1871.	Paris..	" 9	Sir Knight.
Gooch, Gideon J.......	Feb. 20, 1870.	Palestine..........	" 3	Grand Junior Warden.
Good, John J.........	—— —, 1861.	Dallas.............	" 6	Em. Commander.
Gurley, Davis R.......	Aug. 8, 1872.	Waco	" 10	Grand Junior Warden.
Hooks, Hilliary C.....	July 19, 1871.	Paris	" 9	Guard.
Hunter, S. M..........	Nov. 17, 1871.	Ivanhoe...........	" 8	Senior Warden.
Hunter, Henry J......	April 18, 1870.	Palestine..........	" 3	Generalissimo.
Hunter, N. W.........	Feb. 21, 1870.	Palestine..........	" 3	Recorder.
Hutchenrider, H.......	Aug. 20, 1872.	Waco..............	" 10	Sword Bearer.

NAME.	WHEN KNIGHTED.	COMMANDERY.		KNIGHTLY RANK.
Haynie, James A......	Aug. 9, 1873.	Waco.............	" 10	Captain-General.
Jones, John B.........	Feb. —, 1861.	Ruthven...........	" 2	Grand Prelate.
Kennedy, William H...	July 4, 1872.	San Felippe de Austin	1	Sir Knight.
Likens, Jas. Bradford..	— —, 1858.	Ruthven...........	" 2	Grand Prelate.
McClure, Robert.......	— —, 1866.	Palestine	" 3	Em. Commander.
Massey, Ephraim P....	Mar. 24, 1866.	Waco	" 10	Recorder.
Mohl, Frederick.......	Nov. 15, 1857.	Ruthven...........	" 2	Sir Knight.
Openheimer, L. M.....	— —, 1866.	Ivanhoe...........	" 8	Grand Senior Warden.
Ozmeat, James W.....	Feb. 6, 1871.	Palestine	" 3	Em. Commander.
Owens, S. A..........	Aug. 9, 1873.	Waco	" 10	Generalissimo.
Page, Frederick H.....	April 25, —.	Waco	" 10	Sir Knight.
Penland, Sam. M......	July 31, 1873.	San Felippe de Austin	1	Sir Knight.
Preston, Calvin W.....	July 17, 1873.	San Felippe de Austin	1	Sir Knight.
Price, Rufus..........	June —, 1869.	Ruthven...........	" 2	Sir Knight.
Richey, Thos. C.......	Aug. 7, 1872.	Waco	" 10	Junior Warden.
Ramsay, James P.....	....	Ruthven...........	" 2	Senior Warden.
Richey, Benj. F........	Aug. 8, 1872.	Waco	" 10	Treasurer.
Riveire, John M.......	Dec. 9, 1873.	Waco	" 10	Sir Knight.
Robason, Seth	Nov. 7, 1872.	Waco	" 10	Sir Knight.
Scherffins, Henry	July 29, 1869.	Ruthven...........	" 2	Captain-General.
Simpson, B. C....	July 4, 1872.	Ruthven...........	" 2	Sir Knight.
Smith, D. C	June 27, 1872.	Ruthven...........	" 2	Sir Knight.
Smith, Charles........	Jan. 14, 1874.	Waco	" 10	Sentinel.
Sorley, James.........	Feb. —, 1849.	San Felippe de Austin	1	G. Capt.Gen.,G. Encpt.,U.S.
Sears, James E........	Aug. 16, 1872.	Waco	" 10	Standard Bearer.
Speight, Jos. Warren ..	Dec. —, 1871.	Waco	" 10	Em. Commander.
Taylor, Edward W.....	April 11, 1849.	Ruthven...........	" 2	Grand Commander.
Tucker, Philip C......	Feb. 13, 1849.	San Felippe de Austin	1	Grand Commander.
Wakelee, David	Dec. 3, 1858.	San Felippe de Austin	1	Recorder.
Wiggin, C. C.........	Mar. 12, 1872.	Ruthven...........	" 2	Guard.
Willis, Joe S..........	Dec. 9, 1873.	Waco	" 10	Sir Knight.
Wright, Samuel P.....	— —, 1868.	Waco	" 10	Sir Knight.

VERMONT.

Bailey, Myron W......	— —, 1859.	Lafayette	No. 3	Captain-General.
Brinsmaid, Wm.......	April 5, 1864.	Burlington........	" 2	Deputy Grand Commander.
Chapman, Thad. M.....	Aug. —, 1866.	Mt. Calvary.......	" 1	Em. Commander.
Farnsworth, Jos. S....	Jan. —, 1855.	Vermont...........	" 4	Grand Junior Warden.
Hollenbeck, John B....	Feb. 28, 1850.	Burlington........	" 2	Grand Recorder.
Houghton, Edmund C..	Jan. 6, 1872.	Taft..............	" 8	Grand Standard Bearer.
Marshall, A. S.........	Jan. 5, 1873.	Killington.........	" 6	Junior Warden.
Marvin, Rigney D.....	May 3, 1870.	Lafayette	" 3	Sir Knight.
Perkins, Jos. L., M.D..	Oct. 10, 1865.	Palestine	" 5	Grand Commander.
Ross, Oliver E.........	Aug. —, 1863.	Mt. Calvary.......	" 1	Sir Knight.
Sabin, Simeon Boynton	Dec. 20, 1870.	Killington.........	" 6	Sir Knight.
Taft, Russell S........	— —, 1864.	Burlington........	" 2	Gr. Warder Gr. Encpt. U.S.
Tyler, George O.......	Jan. 17, 1866.	Burlington........	" 2	Captain-General.
Whitcomb, Wm. H. S..	Dec. 29, 1865.	Burlington........	" 2	Grand Recorder.
Whitney, Pardon K....	Mar. 28, 1856.	Vermont...........	" 4	Senior Warden.
Willard, Daniel L......	June —, 1873.	Vermont....... ...	" 4	Sir Knight.

VIRGINIA.

Allen, William W......	Aug. 25, 1871.	De Molay..........	No. 4	Sir Knight.
Allen, William T......	— —, 1856.	Richmond	" 2	Prelate.
Arnall, Chas. S........	June 5, 1871.	Stevenson	" 8	Treasurer.
Athey, Thomas B.....	Nov. —, 1872.	Old Dominion	" 11	Sir Knight.
Bailey, Samuel A......	Jan. 17, 1845.	De Molay..........	" 4	Em. Commander.
Benedict, Isbon.......	— —, 1857.	Richmond	" 2	Sir Knight.
Berkeley, Dr. Carter...	June 5, 1871.	Stevenson	" 8	Guard.
Bodeker, Henry.......	— —, 1863.	Richmond	" 2	Guard.
Brown, J. Thompson ..	April —, 1870.	Richmond	" 2	Guard.
Buff, August..........	Feb. 11, 1865.	Portsmouth........	" 5	Sir Knight.
Bumgardner, Wm. L...	June 5, 1871.	Stevenson	" 8	Captain-General.
Burrows, J. L.........	— —, 1848.	Richmond	" 2	Sir Knight.
Craighill, Ed. A.......	Feb. 20, 1864.	De Molay	" 4	Sir Knight.
Cook, Henry..........	Nov. —, 1872.	Old Dominion	" 11	Sir Knight.
Danforth, C. F........	Mar. 19, 1872.	Richmond	" 2	Sir Knight.
DeWitt, Thos. H......	— —, 1851.	Richmond	" 2	Captain-General.
Dillard, Jas. S........	Oct. 21, 1871.	De Molay	" 4	Prelate.
Dove, John, M. D.....	Jan. —, 1820.	Richmond	" 2	Grand Recorder.
Dunn, Andrew S.......	Mar. 22, 1872.	Old Dominion......	" 11	Sir Knight.

NAME.	WHEN KNIGHTED.	COMMANDERY.	KNIGHTLY RANK.
Field, John A.	Nov. —, 1872.	Old Dominion......No. 11	Sir Knight.
Grigg, Joseph L.	Nov. —, 1872.	Old Dominion...... " 11	Sir Knight.
Harris, Benj. M.	June 23, 1856.	Richmond .... " 2	Senior Warden.
Johnson, LaFayette ...	——, 1862	Johnson .... " 14	Grand Generalissimo.
Jordan, Henry	May 16, 1866.	Grice.............. " 16	Treasurer.
Kersey, Matthew	Jan. —, 1870.	Old Dominion..... " 11	Senior Warden.
Lundin, Charles	Nov. 25, 1862.	Richmond .... " 2	Standard Bearer.
McDaniel, Jno. Robin.	Jan. 8, 1843.	De Molay .... " 4	Grand Commander.
McLean, Donald	Mar. 7, 1873.	Old Dominion .... " 11	Sir Knight.
Padgett, John W.	Nov. —, 1872.	Old Dominion..... " 11	Sir Knight.
Page, William L.	Mar. 17, 1849.	De Molay.......... " 4	Treasurer.
Perry, John	Feb. 9, 1858.	Richmond.......... " 2	Sir Knight.
Phillips, Chas. C.	June 5, 1871.	Stevenson.......... " 8	Warder.
Price, Isaac Newton	Aug. 25, 1871.	De Molay .... " 4	Sir Knight.
Reed, Francis A.	Dec. 18, 1868.	Old Dominion .... " 11	Em. Commander.
Riddick, Wm. J.	May 26, 1857.	Richmond........ " 2	Recorder.
Rogers, T. F.	Mar. 13, 1871.	Grice ... . " 16	Captain-General.
Scoville, L. W.	Sept. 6, 1872.	De Molay .... " 4	Sir Knight.
Shinn, George R.	Sept. 6, 1868.	Old Dominion..... " 11	Captain-General.
Sizer, John T.	June 14, 1858.	Richmond . ... " 2	Standard Bearer.
Taylor, Albert G.	June 20, 1864.	Dove .... " 7	Recorder.
Trowbridge, W. H.	....	Dove .... " 7	Sir Knight.
Terrell, John Jay	June 20, 1863.	De Molay .... " 4	Sir Knight.
Walton, Joseph A.	Aug. —, 1871.	Portsmouth........ " 5	Captain-General.
Whitehead, H. C.	Sept. 12, 1871.	Grice .... " 16	Senior Warden.
Winship, Frank Clark.	Feb. 28, 1870.	Wheeling .... " 1	Junior Warden.

WISCONSIN.

NAME.	WHEN KNIGHTED.	COMMANDERY.	KNIGHTLY RANK.
Campbell, Stephen N.	Sept. 23, 1871.	Berlin ....No. 10	Sir Knight.
Carpenter, Alb't Von H.	Nov. —, 1860.	Wisconsin .... " 1	Grand Commander.
Chapman, Chandler P.	Mar. 22, 1873.	Robert Macoy...... " 3	Sir Knight.
Goss, Homer Smith	June 26, 1866.	Fort Winnebago... " 4	Em. Commander.
Latimer, Levi E.	Sept. —, 1868.	Chippewa.......... " 8	Senior Warden.
Sackett, Hobart S.	Feb. 3, 1873.	Berlin.............. " 10	Sir Knight.
Toms, J. W.	May 20, 1871.	La Crosse.......... " 9	Sir Knight.
Watts, Jeremiah	Jan. 28, 1868.	Racine............. " 7	Grand Captain-General.
Woodhull, John W.	Sept. 20, 1862.	Berlin............. " 10	Em. Commander.
Wright, David H... ...	May 31, 1859.	Robert Macoy...... " 3	Dep. Grand Commander.

ENGLAND and IRELAND.

NAME.	WHEN KNIGHTED.	COMMANDERY.	KNIGHTLY RANK.
Griffiths, C. C. Whitney	Dec. 19, 1861.	{ Preceptory of St. Ar- naud, Worcester..... }	Grand Expert of England.
Hughan, Wm. James	....	Truro, England...... ...	Sir Knight.
McGuffick, Wm.	May —, 1847.	Union Command'ry, No. 4	Sir Knight.

Printed in the United States
54458LVS00002B

9 780766 100190